CARLING

FOOTBALL
FACT & QUIZ BOOK

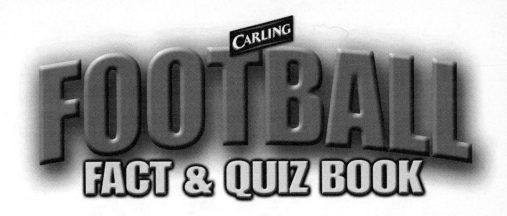

CARLING FOOTBALL FACT & QUIZ BOOK

CHRIS MATTHEWS

ILLUSTRATIONS BY PETER COUPE

STOPWATCH

Stopwatch Publishing Limited
1–7 Shand Street, London SE1 2ES

for
Bookmart Limited
Registered Number 2372865
Desford Road
Enderby
Leicester LE9 5AD

This edition published 2001

Printed and bound by Omnia Books Limited

ISBN 1-84193-076-8

The views and opinions of the writer are not necessarily
those of the Bass Brewers Limited.

Cover design by Communiquè

FOREWORD

In no other country is the game of football loved as much as it is in the UK. So we welcome all lovers of the "Beautiful Game" to this latest edition of The Carling Football Fact and Quiz Book. Inside you will find challenging quizzes on all aspects of the game of football, be it the clubs, the players, the rules or even the grounds where the game is played, as well as a wealth of facts that stretch from the beginnings of football to the modern day.

No matter how great or how small your knowledge of the game there is something in this book for everyone. If you want the latest facts and figures they are all here, or if you are feeling nostalgic, then you can look back at the past records of all the league and cup competitions. What's more this compendium is not confined to the English Football League, but includes questions and facts about the European game and and indeed football from all over the world.

You will find the questions lively and entertaining, and the facts interesting and enlightening. And as we all know, football can supply some very humorous moments and we have captured these in the final chapter. So after you have pulled your hair out trying to answer all the questions; once you have stretched your mind with the wealth of knowledge contained in the facts section; be prepared to hold onto your rattle as you laugh your way through the verbal howlers by some of football's leading figures.

The best of luck to you. You are going to need it!

CONTENTS

THE QUIZZES

QUIZ CONTENTS

MIX AND MATCH

A Selection of Questions

about Football

THE FOOTBALL FACT AND QUIZ BOOK

1. Where did Derby County play before they moved to Pride Park?
2. Which European country did John Charles play for?
3. Who was the top scorer in the 1998 World Cup finals?
4. Which football knight was nicknamed 'The Wizard of Dribble'?
5. At which of his former clubs did Francis Lee become chairman?
6. What is the surname of brothers David and Dean, the former a defender and the latter a striker?
7. Which country did Liverpool's Ron Yeats come from?
8. Who succeeded Mike Walker as manager of Everton?
9. Which ex-Wolves player has served as chairman of the PFA?
10. Which Dundee Utd player was voted Scottish Footballer of the Year in 1991?
11. Who did Joe Fagan succeed as manager of Liverpool?
12. Which club has been managed both by Mike Walker and Martin O'Neill?
13. 'The Spireites' is the nickname of which English club?
14. How many hat-tricks did Alan Shearer score for Blackburn in 1995/96?
15. What is the home ground of Macclesfield?

1. In which year did Bobby and Jackie Charlton win their last caps for England?

2. Where do Wycombe Wanderers play?

3. Where did the first World Cup take place?

4. Who did former England cricket captain Ian Botham play football for?

5. Which footballer inspired pop group The Wedding Present to name an album after him?

6. Who was succeeded as manager at Middlesborough by Bryan Robson?

7. Who was voted South American Player of the Year in 1987 and 1994?

8. When did the first League Cup take place?

9. Who was the first black player to captain the England side?

10. In which year were the last Home International Championships played?

11. What is the NASL?

12. Who was substituted after only 10 minutes of the 1999 F.A. Cup final?

13. Who was voted PFA Player of the Year in 1991?

14. What were Aberdeen the first club to have in Scotland?

15. When did Sweden host the World Cup?

1. 1970 2. Adams Park 3. Uruguay 4. Scunthorpe Utd 5. George Best 6. Lennie Lawrence 7. Carlos Valderrama 8. 1961 9. Paul Ince 10. 1984 11. North American Soccer League 12. Roy Keane 13. Mark Hughes 14. An all-seater stadium 15. 1958.

1. Which club was Paul Goddard playing for when he made his international debut?

2. Where did Ray Clemence start his league career?

3. What nationality is Leeds Utd player Harry Kewell?

4. Which player was captain of the Euro '96 Scotland squad?

5. What colour shirts do Norway play in?

6. Which player earned the nickname 'Bite yer legs'?

7. In which country do Metz play their football?

8. Who was appointed England coach after similar spells at Swindon and Chelsea?

9. Who was reportedly the world's highest-paid player in 2000?

10. At which Premier club is Bill Kenwright the chairman ?

11. Whic was the first British side to win the European Cup-winners' Cup?

12. Which hymn is traditionally sung before the F.A. Cup final?

13. On which island was Matt Le Tissier born?

14. Which club has conceded the fastest ever F.A. Cup final goal?

15. Why was David Platt banned from the bench at Sampdoria?

THE FOOTBALL FACT AND QUIZ BOOK

1. against which country did Gary Lineker make his last international appearance?

2. Which club did Peter Schmeichel join after leaving Old Trafford?

3. Who won the first Scottish final to go to a penalty shoot-out?

4. When scoring against Sweden in 1958, who became England's leading scorer?

5. Who produced the 1980s report, 'The State of Football'?

6. Which two English clubs have won the European Cup playing at Wembley?

7. Which club did French goalkeeper Bernard Lama play for in 1998?

8. How old was Duncan Edwards when he made his league debut?

9. Where did Stuart Pearce start his league career?

10. Which goalkeeper has made 583 league appearances for Charlton Athletic?

11. Who was Bob Paisley's first signing as manager of Liverpool?

12. Who was manager of Wimbledon before Egil Olsen?

13. Where was the 1970 F.A. Cup replay held?

14. Who left Baldock Town to sign for Watford?

15. In 1997/98, who was the only Spaniard playing in the Premier League?

1. Sweden 2. Sporting Lisbon 3. Aberdeen 4. Bobby Charlton 5. Sir Norman Chester 6. Liverpool and Manchester Utd 7. West Ham Utd 8. 16 9. Coventry City 10. Sam Bartram 11. Phil Neal 12. Joe Kinnear 13. Old Trafford 14. Kevin Phillips 15. Albert Ferrer.

THE FOOTBALL FACT AND QUIZ BOOK

1. What is Manchester Utd full-back Denis Irwin's first name?
2. Who are the only team to go through an entire league season without losing?
3. At which club did Peter Withe make his league debut?
4. Which club did Rory Delap play for before Derby County?
5. Who won the first game between Celtic and Rangers in 1888?
6. Which AC Milan player was voted European Footballer of the Year in 1996?
7. Who was known as 'The Clown Prince'?
8. Who was Blackburn Rovers' main benefactor in the nineties?
9. What colour shirts do Brighton and Hove Albion play in?
10. Which club did Alf Ramsay manage when winning the championship?
11. Which former England player had 'I love the lads' written on a T-shirt under his team-shirt?
12. Where did Liverpool sign John Barnes from?
13. What country does Tottenham's Sergei Rebrov play his international football for?
14. How many other clubs has Arsenal's Tony Adams played for?
15. Which presenter left the BBC for ITV in 1999?

1. Joseph 2. Preston North End 3. Southport 4. Norwich City 5. Celtic 6. George Weah 7. Len Shackleton 8. Jack Walker 9. Blue and white stripes 10. Ipswich Town 11. Ian Wright 12. Watford 13. Ukraine 14. None 15. Des Lynham.

THE FOOTBALL FACT AND QUIZ BOOK

1. Which England player took Shakespeare's 'Henry V' to read at Euro 2000 for inspiration?

2. What was the name of the dog that discovered the World Cup trophy in 1966?

3. For which country does Manchester City forward Paulo Wanchope play international football?

4. Where did Stoke City play before moving to the Britannia Stadium?

5. Which team's mascot is Cyril the Swan?

6. Who played Newcastle in the 1999 F.A. Cup semi-final?

7. Which striker signed for Leeds Utd in 1980 from Rangers?

8. What came into official use in the 1950s?

9. Which club have won the European Cup the most times?

10. Which London ground featured the Shelf?

11. Which Northern Ireland goalkeeper plays for Wigan?

12. Who won the all-Merseyside F.A. Cup final in 1986?

13. Which veteran Cameroon player appeared in the 1990 World Cup?

14. Which double-barrelled striker played for Nottingham Forest in the 60s?

15. Which city hosted the opening game of Euro 2000?

THE FOOTBALL FACT AND QUIZ BOOK

1. What is the present name of the European Nations Cup?
2. Where did Sunderland play before moving to the Stadium of Light?
3. Arthur Drewry, F.I.F.A. president from 1956-61, was chairman of which club?
4. How many times did Bobby Moore captain England in full internationals?
5. Which former English league club used to play at Peel Park?
6. Which current league team were the first winners of the F.A. Challenge Trophy?
7. What nationality is former F.I.F.A. president Joao Havelange?
8. Which trophy did French sculptor Albert Lafleur design?
9. In which South American Country do Liverpool F.C. play?
10. Which team have won the most domestic league titles in the world?
11. Which team won the first Football League Championship?
12. Who lost to Denmark in the semi-finals of the 1992 European Championship?
13. Where did Sir Alex Ferguson start his managerial career?
14. The headquarters of U.E.F.A. are in which country?
15. Who was the youngest player to captain a side in a F.A. Cup final?

1. European Championship 2. Roker Park 3. Grimsby Town 4. 90 5. Accrington Stanley 6. Macclesfield Town 7. Brazilian 8. The Jules Rimet Trophy 9. Uruguay 10. Rangers 11. Preston North End 12. Holland 13. St. Mirren 14. Switzerland 15. David Nish for Leicester City.

THE FOOTBALL FACT AND QUIZ BOOK

1. Which club have won more English League titles than anyone else?

2. Who beat Manchester Utd 3-1 in the 2000 World Club Championship?

3. Which English team did Athletico Madrid model their home strip on?

4. What did the League Cup change its name to in 1982?

5. Which French Stadium was opened for the 1998 World Cup finals?

6. How many times has Steve Coppell been manager at Crystal Palace?

7. Which goalkeeper scored in the 1967 Charity Shield?

8. Who did Arsenal sign from Internazionale in January 1999?

9. Who are Ipswich Town's sponsors?

10. What, in Italian football, is catenaccio?

11. Which Premier League manager was knighted in 1999?

12. Which manager received a knighthood in 1967?

13. Which club has had the longest unbroken run in the top division in Engand?

14. Where did Bobby Robson begin his playing career?

15. Which country did Mike England play for?

1. Liverpool 2. Vasco da Gama, Brazil 3. Sunderland 4. The Coca-Cola Cup 5. Stade de France 6. Four 7. Pat Jennings 8. Kanu 9. Brewers Greene King 10. The defensive tactical system perfected by Italy in the 60s 11. Sir Alex Ferguson 12. Sir Alf Ramsay 13. Arsenal 14. Fulham 15. Wales.

THE FOOTBALL FACT AND QUIZ BOOK

1.   Which country did Thomas Brolin play for?
2.   Who replaced Joao Havelange as president of F.I.F.A.?
3.   At which stadium was the Euro 2000 final played?
4.   Which Spurs player in 1994/95 was in the team which won the 1990 World Cup?
5.   At which club did brothers Ray, Rodney and Danny Wallace play together?
6.   Who was Alan Harris assistant to at Barcelona?
7.   Which two island teams contest the Upton Park Cup?
8.   Where do club F'91 Dudelange play?
9.   What did Japan form in 1991?
10. Which Manchester City manager made the fedora hat popular?
11. What did Manchester Utd first broadcast in 1998?
12. What appeared in a F.A. Cup final for the first time in 1891?
13. Who did the Soviet Union play its last international against in November 1991?
14. In which city is the World Club Cup always held?
15. Where would you watch Fluminense play their home games?

THE FOOTBALL FACT AND QUIZ BOOK

1. What idea was tried in an Italian cup match between Bologna and Sampdoria in 1999?
2. When was the idea of two referees at a match first proposed by William Cuff, a member of the Football League management committee?
3. Which French club have George Weah and David Ginola both played for?
4. Which two players are Scotland's joint top scorers?
5. Which was the first country to retain the World Cup?
6. Where was Birmingham manager Trevor Francis born?
7. In a Euro 2000 qualifier against Poland, what feat did midfielder Paul Scholes achieve?
8. What city do Real Betis play in?
9. Who was Andy Cole playing for when he made his international debut?
10. Who did Steve Archibald appear for in a F.A. Cup final?
11. Which Geordie did Ipswich reject after a trial in 1982?
12. Who was captain of Italy for the 1994 World Cup final?
13. What has Dion Dublin broken at Aston Villa and Manchester Utd?
14. What are the names of the Hamilton brothers, who have both played for Northern Ireland?
15. Which former Southampton player is now a successful racehorse trainer?

1. Having two referees 2. 1935 3. Paris St. Germain 4. Kenny Dalglish and Denis Law 5. Italy 6. Plymouth 7. He scored a hat-trick 8. Seville 9. Manchester Utd 10. Spurs 11. Paul Gascoigne 12. Franco Baresi 13. His neck and his leg 14. Bryan and Billy 15. Mick Channon.

THE FOOTBALL FACT AND QUIZ BOOK

1. Which footballer's nickname is 'Psycho'?
2. Which captain took his side to victory in the World Cup at the age of 40?
3. What is the 'Golden Boot' awarded for each season?
4. Why was Eric Cantona given 120 hours community service in 1995?
5. Which Italian club have won the 'scudetto' the most times?
6. What job was Nevill Southall in before taking up professional football?
7. With which club did Brian Kidd begin his league career?
8. Which comedian once had a trial for Hearts?
9. Which Dutch club did Liverpool sign Sander Westerveld from?
10. In the England versus Holland friendly in 1988, who scored for both sides?
11. Which St. Blazey old-boy has gone on to play for England?
12. Where was Norwegian goalkeeper Espen Baardsen transferred to from Spurs in 2000?
13. At which Spanish club would you find Russian internationals Karpin and Mostovoi playing?
14. What colour shirts do Hamburg SV play in?
15. Which three Italian clubs has David Platt played for?

1. Stuart Pearce 2. Dino Zoff 3. The player that has scored the most goals 4. For attacking a fan 5. Juventus 6. Dustman 7. Manchester Utd 8. Ronnie Corbett 9. Vitesse Arnhem 10. Tony Adams 11. Nigel Martyn 12. Watford 13. Celta Vigo 14. White shirts with red and black flashing 15. Bari, Juventus and Sampdoria.

THE FOOTBALL FACT AND QUIZ BOOK

1. Which club is the subject of Gary Nelson's book 'Left Foot in the Grave'?
2. Appointed in June 2000, how long was Bruce Rioch manager of Wigan Athletic?
3. What was the nickname of Russian keeper Lev Yashin, who would dress from head to toe in black?
4. What colours did Leeds Utd play in before changing to all white?
5. Which two brothers played in the 1975 European Cup final?
6. Which important match did Jack Taylor referee in 1974?
7. On the last day of the 1999/00 season, which Premiership side was relegated?
8. Who are the only Scottish side to have had an artificial pitch installed?
9. What colours do the New Zealand football team play in?
10. Which veteran Yugoslavian captain plays in the the Japanese J-League?
11. What is Tottenham star Sol Campbell's middle name?
12. Which Everton full-back made his last England appearance in the 1970 World Cup against Germany?
13. Who were the first foreign team England lost to in 1929?
14. When Scotland played Ireland in 1929, who scored five goals for Scotand in their 7-3 win?
15. Who were runners-up to Kidderminster Harriers when they won the 1999/00 Conference title?

1. Torquay Utd 2. Nine months 3. 'The Black Octopus' 4. Yellow and blue 5. Eddie and Frank Gray 6. The World Cup Final 7. Wimbledon 8. Stirling Albion 9. All white 10. Dragan Stojkovic 11. Jeremiah 12. Keith Newton 13. Spain 14. Hughie Gallacher 15. Rushden and Diamonds.

THE FOOTBALL FACT AND QUIZ BOOK

1. Who did Chelsea beat in the 1998 European Super-Cup?
2. What trophy was stolen in Brazil and never recovered?
3. Which manager was in charge of two teams that were relegated in the 2000/01 season
4. Who were the first English club to win the F.A. Cup without an Englishman?
5. Where does Sir Alex Ferguson's son play club football?
6. Which league tried 'kick-ins' instead of 'throw-ins' in 1993/94?
7. Who are the only side to have beaten Germany in a penalty shoot-out in a major competition?
8. Who has won the PFA Fair Play trophy seven times from 1994 to 2000?
9. Who said 'If Everton were playing at the bottom of my garden, I'd draw the curtains'?
10. Who is Wales's most capped player?
11. Which Arsenal player needed treatment after hitting himself in the face, during a goal celebration, with the corner flag?
12. Which Manchester City manager signed his own son, Kevin?
13. For which club did Gary McAllister make his English debut?
14. Which Manchester Utd player's red card cost him a 1999 F.A. Cup final place?
15. Which club were once called West Herts?

THE FOOTBALL FACT AND QUIZ BOOK

1. When England beat Germany in Euro 2000, how many years was it since the last victory (apart from friendlies)?
2. Which comedian was a director at Luton Town?
3. Which team does Liverpool goalkeeper Sander Westerveld play international matches for?
4. Who won the Champions' League in 2000?
5. Who is Glasgow Rangers' record scorer?
6. When did Sunderland move into the Stadium of Light?
7. Which team play at Highfield Road?
8. Which seaside town reached the F.A. Cup final in 1983?
9. Which city was David Beckham born in?
10. Which Scottish club are sponsored by pop group Wet, Wet, Wet?
11. Which ex-Wimbledon player presented 'Gladiators'?
12. Who did Arsenal beat in the first home game of the 2000/01 season?
13. How many goals did Alan Shearer score for Newcastle in the 1999 F.A. Cup semi-final?
14. Which is the only team in the Scottish League that has its ground in England?
15. Who is the author of 'Fever Pitch'?

THE FOOTBALL FACT AND QUIZ BOOK

1. Which English club do Dietmar Hamann and Markus Babbel play for?
2. How much did Real Madrid spend in transfer fees during the summer of 2000?
3. Which Brazilian won the 1999 European and World Footballer of the Year awards?
4. Which English team has scored the record amount of goals in a match?
5. Who has scored the record amount of goals in a Scottish match?
6. Who scored on his debut for Celtic, after a £7 million transfer in summer 2000?
7. In the 1998 Cup-Winners' Cup final, who scored three goals for Chelsea?
8. What is the biggest margin of victory in an F.A. Cup final?
9. Which African country did England beat to reach the 1990 World Cup semi-finals?
10. How many years did Charlton share a ground with Crystal Palace?
11. Which two countries played in the last international to be played at Wembley?
12. Who did England play in their opening game in Euro '96?
13. Who is 'Emmerdale' barmaid Sheree Murphy engaged to?
14. Who was the first-ever English 'derby game' between in 1892?
15. Who is Edson Arantes do Nascimento better known as?

THE FOOTBALL FACT AND QUIZ BOOK

1. Which Scottish team were runners-up in both the Scottish F.A. Cup and League Cup finals in 2000?
2. What happened to Andres Escobar after scoring an own goal for Colombia in the 1994 World Cup?
3. Who was England manager for Euro '96?
4. When was the first World Cup held?
5. Who do Wesley Brown and Quinton Fortune play for?
6. What was the first match from the Premier League to be televised?
7. What did the Accrington Stanley team advertise in the eighties?
8. What is the most common score in a professional football match?
9. Which former Manchester Utd star appeared drunk on Terry Wogan's chat show?
10. Which club did 'Razor' Ruddock make his debut for?
11. Which club has been managed by George Graham and Harold Wilkinson?
12. Who played cricket for Leicestershire in the day and football for Doncaster later that evening?
13. Who did Danish referee Kim Milton Nielsen send off in the 1998 World Cup?
14. How many goals did Peter Osgood score for England?
15. Why was Robbie Fowler fined after one of his goal celebrations?

1. Aberdeen 2. He was murdered 3. Terry Venables 4. 1930 5. Manchester Utd 6. Nottingham Forest v Liverpool 7. Milk 8. 2-1 9. George Best 10. Spurs 11. Leeds Utd 12. Chris Balderstone 13. David Beckham 14. None 15. It was alleged he was mimicking sniffing drugs.

THE FOOTBALL FACT AND QUIZ BOOK

1. Which Welsh international starred in the film 'Lock, stock and two smoking barrels'?

2. Which TV presenter has scored 48 goals for England?

3. Which England player was born on Jersey?

4. Which Wimbledon player scored Jamaica's first-ever goal in the World Cup finals in 1998?

5. What is the professional nickname of David Beckham's wife?

6. Which midfielder has played for Liverpool and Sampdoria?

7. How many teams are relegated from the Premier League each season?

8. Which team did not take part in the 1999/00 F.A. Cup?

9. Which Swedish side have won the UEFA Cup twice?

10. Which English club was managed by Sir Stanley Matthews?

11. Who were the first team to lose an F.A. Cup Final?

12. What is the nickname of Forfar?

13. Which Scottish club's shirts are black and white stripes, stippled with red dots?

14. Who succeeded Alan Ball as manager of Portsmouth?

15. Which English team appeared in the first World Club Championship?

1. Vinnie Jones 2. Gary Lineker 3. Graham Le Saux 4. Robbie Earle 5. Posh Spice 6. Graeme Souness 7. Three 8. Manchester Utd 9. IFK Gothenburg 10. Port Vale 11. Royal Engineers 12. The Loons 13. Dunfermline Athletic 14. Tony Pulis 15. Manchester Utd.

THE FOOTBALL FACT AND QUIZ BOOK

1. Who did Rangers buy from Fiorentina for £5.5 million in July 1998?
2. Which Liverpool player was known as 'Barney'?
3. Why was the 1901 match between Newcastle and Sunderland abandoned?
4. In which city is the Italian transfer market, or 'mercato', held?
5. Which two teams appeared in both the 1908 and 1912 Olympic football finals?
6. How many clubs are promoted to Serie A in Italy each season?
7. Where were F.A. Cup finals played before WWI?
8. Which country do Apolonia play in?
9. Which country was threatened with expulsion from Euro 2000 because of the behaviour of their fans?
10. Which Scotland star has played for both Manchester Utd and Manchester City?
11. Who was appointed the first England manager?
12. Which Argentinian scored the 'hand of god' goal?
13. Which club was Steffan Iversen leading scorer for in 1999/00?
14. Where does keeper Pegguy Arphexad play his football in England?
15. Who did England play when celebrating the centenary of the Football Association?

1. Andrei Kanchelskis 2. Alan Kennedy 3. Because of crowd trouble 4. Milan 5. England and Denmark 6. Four 7. Crystal Palace 8. Albania 9. England 10. Denis Law 11. Walter Winterbottom 12. Diego Maradona 13. Tottenham Hotspur 14. Leicester City 15. Rest of the World XI.

THE FOOTBALL FACT AND QUIZ BOOK

1. What is the nickname of Aberdeen?
2. Who became the youngest league manager when he joined QPR at the age of 29?
3. What was unusual about the 1998 World Cup match between South Africa and Denmark?
4. Which club used to play at 'The Old Showground'?
5. What was introduced into English football in 1976?
6. Who did Scarborough play in their first league match in 1987?
7. Which businessman became Middlesborough chairman in 1994?
8. Which league do Don Pernil play in?
9. Which Yorkshire club has won the league title in three successive years?
10. Which Italian club did Ian Rush spend one season with?
11. Which Everton player was nicknamed 'The Golden Vision'?
12. Which Nigerian played at Ajax and Internazionale before moving to Highbury?
13. Who is Real Madrid's young goalkeeping star?
14. Where do Newell's Old Boys play?
15. Where did QPR have to play their home games in the 1984/85 UEFA Cup because their own artificial pitch was banned?

1. The Dons 2. Frank Sibley 3. Three substitutes were sent off 4. Scunthorpe Utd 5. Red cards 6. Wolves 7. Steve Gibson 8. Andorran league 9. Huddersfield Town 10. Juventus 11. Alex Young 12. Kanu 13. Casillas 14. Argentina 15. Highbury.

THE FOOTBALL FACT AND QUIZ BOOK

1. Which club does Estonian Mark Poom keep goal for?

2. Who was England manager for the 1982 World Cup finals?

3. If a team is knocked out of the first round of the Champions' League, which cup do they enter?

4. Which country does Georgi Kinkladze play for?

5. How many times have Lithuania played international games against England?

6. In which country do Young Africans FC play?

7. Who left Arsenal for Real Madrid in 1999?

8. Which Liverpool player won the Footballer of the Year award in 1988 and 1990?

9. Which league do Odense play in?

10. Who won the Premier League in 1994/95?

11. Who scored a penalty for England against Argentina in the 1998 World Cup?

12. What was Franz Beckenbauer's nickname?

13. What colours do West Ham and Aston Villa play in?

14. Which London stadium used to house a Shed End?

15. What was player's agent Rachel Anderson barred from in 1998?

1. Derby County 2. Ron Greenwood 3. UEFA Cup 4. Georgia 5. None 6. Tanzania 7. Nicolas Anelka 8. John Barnes 9. Danish league 10. Blackburn Rovers 11. Alan Shearer 12. 'The Kaiser' 13. Claret shirts with blue sleeves 14. Stamford Bridge 15. The annual PFA dinner.

THE FOOTBALL FACT AND QUIZ BOOK

1. Which two clubs play at Selhurst Park?
2. When did England take part in their first World Cup tournament?
3. Which club did manager Joe Mercer win the League Championship with?
4. Which player is Brazil's leading goalscorer?
5. Who were the last English team to win the Champions' League?
6. Where did Bristol Rovers have to play five home games in 1990/91?
7. Who was the first British player to make 1000 first class appearances?
8. How many teams play in the Spanish Premier Division?
9. Which team have won the Premiership title the most times?
10. What was the predecessor of the Worthington Cup called?
11. Who did Arsenal transfer midfielder Stephen Hughes to?
12. What nationality is Fulham's chairman?
13. What inflatable creatures would you see being waved at Grimsby Town?
14. Which former Rangers and Scotland international player went to Newcastle and Everton?
15. Who was the first black player to captain England?

1. Crystal Palace and Wimbledon 2. 1950 3. Manchester Utd 6. Ashton Gate 7. Pat Jennings 8. Twenty 9. Manchester City 4. Pele 5. Manchester Cola Cup 11. Everton 12. Egyptian 13. Fish 14. Duncan Ferguson 15. Paul Ince. Utd 10. The Coca-

THE FOOTBALL FACT AND QUIZ BOOK

1. How much did Crockenhurst FC receive from Gillingham for Tony Cascarino?
2. Which is the red half of Bristol?
3. In which Asian league do Selangor FA play?
4. Which sixties Tottenham player scored 44 goals for England?
5. Which Italian club plays in Udine?
6. Which Argentinian was sent off when Trevor Cherry was sent off for England?
7. Who won the League of Wales title in 1999/00?
8. Which team does American Joe Max-Moore play for?
9. Which two Leeds players have been charged with alleged violent conduct?
10. Who did Paul Jewell join after keeping Bradford City in the Premier League?
11. Mexican club Necaxa is the result of a merger between which two teams?
12. Who was the manager of Scotland for their Euro 2000 qualifying games?
13. Which team knocked holders Manchester Utd out of the 1999/00 Champions' League?
14. Which Nationwide team plays in red and blue vertical stripes?
15. What was introduced at Anfield in 1957?

1. £250 plus a set of tracksuits 2. Bristol City 3. Malaysian 4. Jimmy Greaves 5. Udinese 6. Daniel Bertoni 7. Total Network Solutions 8. Everton 9. Bowyer and Woodgate 10. Sheffield Wednesday 11. El Tranvias and Luz y Fuerza 12. Craig Brown 13. Real Madrid 14. Crystal Palace 15. Floodlights.

THE FOOTBALL FACT AND QUIZ BOOK

1. What is the name of Leicester City's mascot?

2. Which Scottish club are known as 'The Diamonds'?

3. What were Nationwide League referees paid per match in 1998/99?

4. Which club does Bobby Robson manage?

5. How many times have Wales beaten Holland in international games?

6. Who does John Gregory manage?

7. Which diminutive Brazilian played for Middlesborough in the nineties?

8. How many teams play in the Togo First Division?

9. Which country won the women's World Cup in 1996?

10. At which club did Paul Gascoigne make his league debut?

11. In how many English cities could you find a derby match?

12. Which Chelsea player was nicknamed 'Chopper'?

13. Who do Moroccans Kachloul and El Khalej play for?

14. Which league do Troyes play in?

15. What was the result of a match-fixing charge against AC Milan in 1979/80?

1. Filbert the Fox 2. Airdrieonians 3. £195 4. Newcastle Utd 5. None 6. Aston Villa 7. Juninho 8. 10 9. USA 10. Newcastle Utd 11. 7. - London, Manchester, Liverpool, Bristol, Nottingham, Sheffield, Birmingham 12. Ron Harris 13. Southampton 14. French league 15. They were relegated to Serie B.

THE FOOTBALL FACT AND QUIZ BOOK

1. Which film featured a football team in a WWII prisoner of war camp?
2. What league do Proodeftiki play in?
3. Which club did German Christian Ziege join in 1999/00?
4. What is the nickname of Atletico Madrid?
5. Which two countries each had three teams in the 2000/01 Champions' League quarter-finals?
6. Which football federation does not allow players to leave their home league?
7. For how many consecutive games did Batistuta score in Serie A games?
8. What did the B & Q Cup become in 1995?
9. Which player was the top scorer in the Premier League in 1999/00?
10. Who did Fijian coach Billy Sing nominate as FIFA Player of the Year in 1995?
11. How many times have Morocco qualified for the World Cup finals?
12. What is the literal translation of Faustino Asprilla's surname?
13. Which German team was nicknamed 'Der Club' between the two World Wars?
14. Who does George Boateng play international football for?
15. What is the nickname of goalkeeper Rene Higuita?

1. Escape to Victory 2. The Greek league 3. Middlesborough 4. The mattress makers' 5. England and Spain 6. Saudi Arabia 7. Eleven 8. The Scottish League Challenge Cup 9. Kevin Phillips 10. Daniel Amokachi 11. Four 12. Aspirin 13. Nuremburg 14. Ghana 15. 'El Loco'.

THE FOOTBALL FACT AND QUIZ BOOK

1. What colour shirts do Heart of Midlothian wear?
2. Where do the club Kosova Albanians play their football?
3. Who were the first English club to play 3000 league games?
4. From which club did Leeds Utd sign Darren Huckerby?
5. Which club sold Gabriel Batistuta to Roma in 2000?
6. Where do Newcastle Utd play their home games?
7. What is the name of David Beckham's son?
8. What were Nigeria the first African team to win?
9. How many clubs play in the Vietnam First Division?
10. Which team did Peter Mellor first play for in an F.A. Cup Final?
11. Who scored England's disallowed 'goal' in France '98 against Argentina?
12. What national side are predictably nicknamed 'The Pharaohs'?
13. 'The Cranes' is the nickname of which African national team?
14. How many goals did Hernan Crespo score in 62 appearances for River Plate?
15. Who was Real Madrid's youngest ever first-team debutant aged 17 years and 4 months?

1. Maroon 2. Canada 3. Notts County 4. Coventry City 5. Fiorentina 6. St. James' Park 7. Brooklyn 8. The Olympic Games football gold medal 9. 12 10. Fulham 11. Sol Campbell 12. Egypt 13. Uganda 14. 24 15. Raul.

THE FOOTBALL FACT AND QUIZ BOOK

1. Which league would you watch Maccabi Netanya play in?
2. Where did Arsenal play their home games in the Champions' League in 1999/00
3. What country did former Wimbledon manager Joe Kinnear play for?
4. Which Austrian was told he would never play for his country again after missing a friendly, but was recalled seven months later?
5. How old was Patrick Kluivert when he started playing in the Ajax youth system?
6. Which Spanish player won a gold medal at the Barcelona Olympics in 1992?
7. Which French national plays his football for Cameroon?
8. Which German won his 100th international cap in France '98?
9. Which league club has Graham Taylor had most success with?
10. How many goals did Kanu score in his 54 league games with Ajax?
11. Whose first club was made up of his brothers, cousins and uncles?
12. For how many consecutive games in the Dutch league did Dennis Bergkamp score?
13. Which South African team was known as Cape Town Spurs in 1994?
14. Which club did Jack Hayward buy into in 1991?
15. Who was club captain at Spurs for the 2000/01 season?

1. Israeli League 2. Wembley 3. Republic of Ireland 4. Andreas Herzog 5. Seven 6. Luis Enrique 7. Patrick Mboma 8. Jurgen Klinsmann 9. Watford 10. 25 11. Iran's Ali Daei 12. Ten 13. Ajax Cape Town 14. Wolverhampton 15. Sol Campbell.

THE FOOTBALL FACT AND QUIZ BOOK

1. Who did Newcastle sign from Ipswich in 1999?
2. What is significant about the date 20 January 1974?
3. Which national team are nicknamed the 'Socceroos'?
4. Which country was Dunga the captain of?
5. Where would you be if you were watching Zimbru Chisinau play a home game?
6. What is the 'Eredivisie'?
7. Which Real Madrid coach said that he wouldn't swap Mijatovic for Ronaldo?
8. How much was Miklos Molnar's get-out clause from his contract at Seville set at?
9. Which Italian scored a hat-trick against Liverpool on his home debut for Middlesborough?
10. What is Brazilian Romario's favourite pastime?
11. How many successive league titles did Enzo Schifo win in his first spell at Anderlecht?
12. Which defender does Alan Shearer fear the most?
13. In what sport is Ole Gunnar Solskjaer's father a champion?
14. Who is Croatia's top goalscorer?
15. Which club did Kevin Richardson and Cyrille Regis both play for?

THE FOOTBALL FACT AND QUIZ BOOK

1. What is case C-415/93 in the European Community Court of Justice better known as?

2. Which English club has won the Welsh Cup twice?

3. Who scored the 'Premier League Goal of the Season' in 2000?

4. Which Scottish team took their nickname from a Robert Burns poem?

5. What have the inhabitants of the village near Plovdiv voted to change the name of their town to?

6. Why does Frenchman Ibrahim Ba bleach his hair blond?

7. Which Scotsman helped Monaco win their first title for nine years in 1997?

8. If Denilson stays at Real Betis for the duration of his 11 year contract, how much will he have eventually cost them?

9. Which Conference side are known as 'The Glovers'?

10. Where would you see Nexxar Lions playing Rabat Ajax?

11. Which Champions' League club does Albertz play for?

12. How many goals did Gianluca Vialli score in his 20 games at U-21 level?

13. What was Napoli's nickname for Gianfranco Zola, after the former occupant of the club's 'number 10' shirt?

14. Where do Thai Farmers Bank play their football?

15. What nickname did Liverpool striker David Fairclough acquire?

THE FOOTBALL FACT AND QUIZ BOOK

1. How much did Newcastle pay Wimbledon for Carl Cort?
2. What does David Ginola help the UN campaign against?
3. Which two Premier clubs were fined £50,000 each in 1990 after their players were involved in a fight on the pitch?
4. How many teams play in the Primera Division in Mexico?
5. What did David Beckham win in his first season at Manchester Utd?
6. An unknown, who scarcely qualified as a professional, how much did Francois Biyick cost Laval in 1985?
7. How many goals did Kevin Phillips score for Sunderland in 1999/00?
8. How many times has Mexican Garcia Aspe been sent off when playing for his country?
9. How old was Croatian Zvonimir Boban when he was made captain of Dinamo Zagreb?
10. Which two clubs has Didier Deschamps won the European Cup with?
11. Which Nigerian attacked two reporters who tried to photograph him with his girlfriend?
12. Who does Spanish coach Javier Clemente consider the best player in the world?
13. Who is Jose Roberto Gama de Oliveira better known as?
14. In which league would you see Bodo-Glimt play Odd?
15. How many penalties did Eric Cantona score in the 1994 F.A. Cup final?

1. £7 million 2. Land mines 3. Manchester Utd and Arsenal 4. 18 5. The F.A. Youth Cup 6. £75,000 7. Thirty 8. Three times 9. 18 10. Marseille and Juventus 11. Jay Jay' Okocha 12. Fernando 'Hierro' Ruiz 13. Bebeto 14. Norwegian 15. Two.

THE FOOTBALL FACT AND QUIZ BOOK

1. Who purchased Birmingham City in 1993?

2. What league do Ruzomberok play in?

3. Which African team are nicknamed 'The Leopards'?

4. Who threatened to quit the Dutch team after being substituted after 25 minutes of the Euro '96 game with Switzerland?

5. How many times has Carlos Valderrama been voted South American Player of the Year?

6. Which player almost turned down a move to Juventus, as 'the thought of playing in Italy was scary'?

7. Apart from Arsenal, how many clubs has Tony Adams played for?

8. Who was Everton's top scorer in 1999/00?

9. Who was voted Norwegian Player of the Year in 1995?

10. Why did Frank de Boer stay behind after Ajax training sessions?

11. Which Japan and Yokohama Marinos player has played in the J-League since its formation?

12. Which team does Alexei Lalas play for?

13. Which Italian left-back's father won 14 caps for Italy?

14. How many goals did American Eric Wynalda score in his first ten games in the Bundesliga?

15. Where do the Santiago Wanderers play?

1. David Sullivan 2. Slovakian 3. The Congo Democratic Republic 4. Clarence Seedorf 5. Three times 6. Zinedine Zidane 7. None 8. Kevin Campbell 9. Henning Berg 10. To practise his dead-ball skills 11. Masami Ihara 12. USA 13. Paolo Maldini 14. Nine 15. Chile.

THE FOOTBALL FACT AND QUIZ BOOK

1. What toy was modelled on U.S. women's striker, Mia Hamm?
2. Which East Anglian rivals contested the 1972/73 Texaco Cup?
3. Which national team are nicknamed 'The Stallions'?
4. What did hooligans steal from Argentinian Diego Simeone's bag as he took a press conference?
5. In which decade was the first live match commentary on the radio?
6. What team does disc jockey John Peel support?
7. Which team plays at The Valley?
8. Which club did Dan Petrescu make his debut for?
9. Which current player had never heard of Leeds Utd until he signed for them?
10. Which German was voted European Footballer of the Year in 1997?
11. What did Nigerian Okechukwu Uche receive when he scored Fenerbahce's 2,000th league goal?
12. What relation is Jason Roberts of West Bromwich Albion to former England player Cyrille Regis?
13. Where do the Go Ahead Eagles club play?
14. When German international Christian Ziege signed for AC Milan, how much was the fee?
15. Which Paraguayan goalkeeper received a six-match suspension in 1997, for assaulting Faustino Asprilla in a World Cup qualifying game?

1. Women's World Cup Barbie 2. Norwich and Ipswich 3. Burkina Faso 4. His football boots 5. The twenties 6. Liverpool 7. Charlton Athletic 8. Steaua Bucharest 9. Lucas Radebe 10. Matthias Sammer 11. A cheque for $10,000 12. Nephew 13. Holland 14. Nothing, it was a free transfer 15. Jose Chilavert.

THE FOOTBALL FACT AND QUIZ BOOK

1. Which England player broke his leg twice in the 1999/00 season?

2. Which Spurs captain lifted the 1980 and 1981 F.A. Cup?

3. Who was captain of England for Euro '96?

4. Who scored 50 goals for Tottenham in 1986/87?

5. What TV programme did Dickie Davis present?

6. Where would you watch UTA Arad play their football?

7. Which club did Peter Schmeichel win the Danish League five times with?

8. What counntry does Manchester Utd captain Roy Keane play for?

9. Which German keeper saved Gareth Southgate's penalty in the Euro '96 semi-final shoot-out?

10. What tactical guide did Andy Gray write in 1998?

11. Who did Real Madrid consider too short to make a top full-back?

12. Which Conference side are known as 'The Robins'?

13. Who was Scotland manager for the 1978 World Cup in Argentina?

14. Which Scottish club are known as 'The Wasps'?

15. Which cup do Guernsey and Jersey teams compete for?

1. Stuart Pearce 2. Steve Perryman 3. David Platt 4. Clive Allen 5. World of Sport 6. Romania 7. Brondby 8. Republic of Ireland 9. Andreas Kopke 10. Flat Back Four 11. Roberto Carlos 12. Altrincham 13. Ally Macleod 14. Alloa Athletic 15. The Upton Park Cup.

THE FOOTBALL FACT AND QUIZ BOOK

1. How long was the Italian ban on signing foreign players?
2. When is the Turkish Cup final played?
3. Where would you be if you were watching Grasshoppers play Servette?
4. What national team has Roy Hodgson managed?
5. Which Scottish keeper joined Manchester Utd in 1998?
6. How many times have Honduras qualified for the World Cup finals?
7. Which English team did Dynamo Moscow model their shirt colours after?
8. With which club did Johan Cruyff end his playing career?
9. Who was manager of Celtic when they won the European Cup?
10. Who played in grey shirts for the first half of the 1996 season?
11. In which South American country do Velez Sarrsfield play?
12. Which club did Dennis Wise sign as an apprentice with?
13. Who was the only player to score for Germany in Euro 2000?
14. How long were Accrington Stanley in the Football League?
15. Who is Brazilian Waldir Pereira better known as?

1. 16 years 2. April 3. Switzerland 4. Switzerland 5. Jim Leighton 6. Once 7. Blackburn Rovers 8. Feyenoord 9. Jock Stein 10. Manchester Utd 11. Venezuela 12. Southampton 13. Mehmet Scholl 14. 41 years 15. Didi.

THE FOOTBALL FACT AND QUIZ BOOK

1. Where would you see Jokerit play Jazz Pori?
2. What name is given to the top goalscorer in Spain?
3. Who was given odds of 25/1 to score against Everton in the 1994 F.A.Cup final?
4. Who did Bert Konterman leave to join Rangers in summer 2000?
5. Where did John Gregory start his managerial career?
6. Which Wigan striker moved to Tranmere Rovers in 2000/01?
7. Which Manchester City winger plays for the Republic of Ireland?
8. Who does Brazilian Mario Jardel play his club football for?
9. Who did Arsenal sign from Real Mallorca for £7.2 million in summer 2000?
10. Which Manchester Utd player was made captain for the game in March 2001 that marked his 500th appearance for the club?
11. Which of the Lancashire clubs has spent the longest in the top division?
12. Which goalkeeper captained England during several wartime internationals?
13. What colour stripes do Fenerbahce have on their shirts?
14. Which national team is nicknamed 'The Desert Warriors'?
15. Which two brothers played in the first World Cup match for Mexico in 1930?

1. Finland 2. 'El Pichichi' 3. Peter Schmeichel 4. Feyenoord 5. Portsmouth 6. Stuart Barlow 7. Mark Kennedy 8. Galatasaray 9. Lauren Bison-Flame Mayer 10. Dennis Irwin 11. Everton 12. Frank Swift 13. Yellow and blue 14. Algeria 15. Manuel and Fernando Rosas.

1. What Welsh Cup was first played for in 1878?
2. What was unique about the World Cup match between Canada and the USA in 1976?
3. Which Belgian club provided all 11 players for an international against Holland in 1964?
4. Where will you find teams called K1, B36, HB and Sumba?
5. What was the Caribbean Nations Cup called before 1999?
6. What bird is above the shield on the Bradford City club badge?
7. For which country did striker Billy Meredith play?
8. Which English team influenced Juventus in their choice of shirt colours?
9. What was the name of the book written by Arsenal's Tony Adams after his drink problem?
10. Who sponsors Arsenal's home shirts?
11. Who sponsors Arsenal's away shirts?
12. Which African side are nicknamed 'The Red Devils'?
13. Who did George Graham start his managerial career with in 1982?
14. Who did Jesper Blomquist leave to join Manchester Utd?
15. Where do Pohang Steelers play their football?

1. The Welsh F.A. Cup 2. First World Cup match played on an artificial pitch 3. Anderlecht 4. Faroe Islands 5. The Shell Caribbean Cup 6. A Bantam 7. Wales 8. Notts County 9. Addicted 10. Dreamcast 11. Sega 12. Congo 13. Millwall 14. Parma 15. South Korea.

THE FOOTBALL FACT AND QUIZ BOOK

1. Which England manager died in April 1999?
2. When did the Fairs Cup become the UEFA Cup?
3. What ground did Baron Craven give his name to?
4. What team do youngsters Joe Cole and Michael Carrick play for?
5. Who started the 2000/01 season as manager of Bradford City?
6. Where did Everton sign Alex Nyarko from?
7. What nationality is Middlesborough goalkeeper Mark Schwarzer?
8. What pop group is named after Crewe Alexandra's manager, Dario Grady?
9. Which German player is nicknamed 'Iron Foot'?
10. How many clubs play in the Swiss National First Division?
11. Which Derby County player signed in 2000, has played for Ajax, Saarbrucken and Dynamo Tbilisi?
12. Where did George Burley begin his managerial career?
13. Which ground has the shortest and narrowest pitch in the Premiership?
14. What is the title of George Graham's autobiography?
15. Which Brazilian side's shirts have red and black hoops?

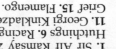

THE FOOTBALL FACT AND QUIZ BOOK

1. Which German has won the most international caps for his country?

2. Which Arsenal player has also played for FC Metz and Stade Reims?

3. Whose nickname was 'Crazy Horse'?

4. Who is the most capped player in Australia?

5. How many times was Scottish winger Willie Johnston sent off?

6. Who earned a suspension in 1999 for pushing the referee over during a match?

7. Which team does retired TV commentator Brian Moore support?

8. Who were the only four European teams to take part in the 1930 World Cup?

9. Where did Aston Villa sign Alpay Ozalan from in summer 2000?

10. What colour shirts do the Republic of Ireland play in?

11. Which national team is nicknamed 'The Zebras'?

12. How much did Leeds pay Lens for Oliver Dacourt in 2000?

13. Where did Liverpool manager Gerard Houillier begin his managerial career in 1973?

14. Who did Coventry sell Robbie Keane to?

15. Who is manager of Charlton Athletic?

1. Lothar Matthaus 2. Robert Pires 3. Emlyn Hughes 4. Alex Tobin 5. 15 times 6. Paulo di Canio 7. Gillingham 8. Yugoslavia, Belgium, France and Romania 9. Fenerbahce 10. Green 11. Botswana 12. £7.2 million 13. Le Touquet 14. Internazionale 15. Alan Curbishley.

THE FOOTBALL FACT AND QUIZ BOOK

1. Which vegetable was Graham Taylor unkindly associated with?

2. What is the Christian name of Arsenal's Kanu?

3. What important goal did Luc Nilis score in 1998?

4. Which Leicester player has played at Bristol City, Gillingham and Norwich City?

5. When was Harry Redknapp appointed manager of West Ham?

6. Who was the youngest player to score a Premiership goal for Spurs, aged 17?

7. Where did Sunderland sign Julio Arca from in 2000?

8. What is the capacity of St. James' Park?

9. Which former Manchester Utd and Aston Villa defender has won the most international caps for the Republic of Ireland?

10. For how many seconds are goalkeepers allowed to hold the ball?

11. When did Manchester Utd win their first League title?

12. Who did Leeds sign striker Mark Viduka from?

13. What animal is on Chelsea's club badge?

14. Who changed Crystal Palace's shirt colours to resemble Barcelona's?

15. Which Conference side is nicknamed 'The Wings'?

1. A turnip 2. Nwankwu 3. Belgium's 200th goal 4. Ade Akinbiyi 5. October 1994 6. Andy Turner 7. Argentinos Juniors 8. Approx 52,300 9. Paul McGrath 10. Six 11. 1907/08 12. Celtic 13. A lion 14. Malcolm Allison 15. Welling Utd.

THE FOOTBALL FACT AND QUIZ BOOK

1. What happened in Derby County's first game at Pride Park?

2. Where did Don Revie go after resigning as England manager in 1977?

3. Which country do Etar Veliko Tamovo play their football?

4. What colour shirts do Dutch team Go Ahead Eagles wear?

5. Who sponsors Aston Villa's shirts?

6. Which former English league club lost the 1924 Welsh Cup?

7. What did Brazilian team Santos FC win in 1962 and 1963?

8. What is the capacity of Highbury?

9. What is Charlton Athletic's nickname?

10. Where does that nickname come from?

11. How much did Internazionale pay Coventry for Robbie Keane?

12. Who sold Alessandro Pistone to Everton for £3 million in 2000?

13. How much did Derby pay Manchester Utd in 2000, for Danny Higginbotham?

14. When did Argentina host the World Cup finals?

15. What national team are nicknamed 'The Black Panthers'?

1. Floodlight failure 2. United Arab Emirates 3. Bulgaria 4. Red and yellow striped shirts 5. nil 6. Merthyr Town 7. The World Club Cup 8. 38,500 9. The Addicks 10. 'Addicks' is south London slang for Haddock, which is what the team always ate for post-match meals in pre-war days 11. £13 million 12. Newcastle Utd 13. £2 million 14. 1978 15. Angola.

THE FOOTBALL FACT AND QUIZ BOOK

1. Which club has won the European Cup the most times?
2. What club did Ken Bates become chairman of in 1982?
3. Who did Bobby Moore take over the England captaincy from in 1963?
4. Who were relegated from the Premier League in 1998/99?
5. Who was voted FIFA World Player of the Year for 2000?
6. Where will the 2002 World Cup final be played?
7. Who has won the League Championship a record 18 times?

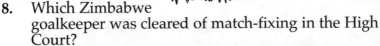

8. Which Zimbabwe goalkeeper was cleared of match-fixing in the High Court?
9. How much did Dwight Yorke cost Manchester Utd in 1998/99?
10. Where did West Ham Utd sign Frederic Kanoute from in 2000?
11. Which Liverpool player has previously played for Middlesborough, Tottenham and Everton?
12. How much did Claus Jensen cost Charlton in summer 2000?
13. Which three players signed for Bradford City in summer 2000, all having played for Sheffield Wednesday at one time in their career?
14. What colour shirts do Estonian side Lantana Tallin play in?
15. Which Republic of Ireland full-back plays for Spurs?

1. Real Madrid 2. Chelsea 3. Jimmy Armfield 4. Charlton, Blackburn and Nottingham Forest 5. Zinedine Zidane 6. International Stadium, Yokohama 7. Liverpool 8. Bruce Grobelaar 9. £12.6 million 10. Lyon 11. Nick Barmby 12. £4 million 13. Dan Petrescu, Ian Nolan and Peter Atherton 14. Black and white stripes 15. Stephen Carr.

1. Why were 19 points deducted from Peterborough Utd in the 1967/68 season?
2. Which London club took their name from a Woolwich armoury?
3. Which Peruvian scored a hat-trick against Iran in the 1978 World Cup finals?
4. Which club is the book 'Cherries in the Red' about?
5. Who did Coventry sell to Middlesborough in 2000?
6. Which former Ajax player joined Ipswich for £1 million from Vitesse Arnhem in 2000?
7. Which two players joined Ipswich from Ajax on free transfers in 2000?
8. Who did Lillian Thuram score two goals for in the 1998 World Cup semi-finals?
9. Which Hamburg player was transferred to Everton for £2.5 million in 2000?
10. What is Muzzy Izzet's real christian name?
11. How much did Fabian Barthez cost Manchester Utd when he signed from AS Monaco?
12. How much did Tottenham pay Dynamo Kiev for Sergei Rebrov?
13. How much did Sunderland pay KV Mechelen for Tom Peeters?
14. Who scored the winning goal in the 2001 F.A. Cup final?
15. Who did Bradford City sell Dean Windass to in March 2001?

1. For making illegal payments to players 2. Arsenal 3. Teofilio Cubillas 4. Bournemouth 5. Noel Whelan 6. Martijn Reuser 7. Nabil Abdiallah and Guillermo Graaven 8. France 9. Thomas Gravesen 10. Mustapha 11. £7.8 million 12. £11 million 13. £250,000 14. Michael Owen 15. Middlesborough.

THE FOOTBALL FACT AND QUIZ BOOK

1. Which manager transferred Gary McAllister to Liverpool?
2. Which two players hold the goal-scoring record for the Republic of Ireland?
3. Which club did Derby sign Finn Simo Valakari from on a free transfer?
4. At 6ft 6in, who is the tallest keeper in the Premier League?
5. What is the British transfer record, set by Leeds Utd in 2000/01?
6. Which player was involved in that trannsfer?
7. According to Roy Keane, what sort of sandwiches are eaten at Old Trafford?
8. Who sponsors Bradford City's shirts?
9. Which two clubs have won the Second Division title the most times?
10. Who did AS Monaco replace Fabien Barthez with, after selling him to Manchester Utd?
11. Who were the three candidates for the FIFA World Player of the Year for 2000?
12. Who was the leading goal-scorer in the 1966 World Cup?
13. How much did Middlesborough pay Coventry for Noel Whelan?
14. How much did Leicester City pay Birmingham City for Gary Rowett?
15. Where do Nagoya Grampus Eight play?

1. Gordon Strachan 2. Niall Quinn and Frank Stapleton 3. Motherwell 4. Ed de Goey 5. £18 million 6. Rio Ferdinand, from West Ham to Leeds Utd 7. Prawn sandwiches 8. JCT 600 9. Leicester City and Manchester City (6) 10. Their former keeper, who returned from Marseilles 11. Zidane, Figo and Rivaldo 12. Eusebio 13. £2 million 14. £3 million 15. Japan.

THE FOOTBALL FACT AND QUIZ BOOK

1. Who are known as 'The Red Lichties'?
2. Who did Newcastle sell in 1995 for a then British record of £7 million?
3. Where did Charlton Athletic sign Rodostin Kishishev from in 2000?
4. How much did Racing Lens receive from Everton for Alex Nyarko?
5. Which team have recorded the biggest home win in the Premiership?
6. Who did West Ham Utd sell to Lyon for £6.3 million in 2000?
7. Who were the last newly-promoted club to win the Championship?
8. Who did Sir Alf Ramsay label as 'animals' in 1966?
9. Which three Premier teams were relegated from the Premier League in 1999/00?
10. After the Premier League was formed in 1992, who were the two teams involved in the first top-of-the-table match?
11. Which Scottish team got shipwrecked in 1923 on a close-season tour to the Canary Islands?
12. How many players were in the Aston Villa squad that won the Championship in 1981?
13. What do Newcastle supporters sing as their unofficial club anthem?
14. Peter Beagrie has played for seven different clubs. Which is the furthest south?
15. Where did Chelsea sign Jesper Gronkjaer from in 2001?

1. Arbroath 2. Andy Cole 3. Lilets Lovech 4. £4.5 million 5. Manchester Utd (beat Ipswich 9-0 in 1995) 6. Marc Vivien-Foe 7. Notts Forest, 1977/78 8. Argentina 9. Wimbledon, Sheffield Wednesday and Watford 10. Norwich City and Coventry City 11. Raith Rovers 12. Fourteen 13. Blaydon Races 14. Stoke City 15. Ajax.

THE FOOTBALL FACT AND QUIZ BOOK

1. In 14 years as president of Atletico Madrid, how many managers has Jesus Gil sacked?

2. Who succeeded Alan Shearer as England captain?

3. Who scored on his debut for Celtic after moving from England in summer 2001?

4. At Highbury in 1996, who called the referee a 'muppet'?

5. Who did Aston Villa sell Stan Collymore to?

6. Which team is based in Birkenhead?

7. Who missed the first penalty against Brazil in the 1994 World Cup Final shoot-out?

8. Who wrote 'My Chelsea Dream'?

9. Who sponsors Barnsley's home shirts?

10. Who was World Player of the Year for 1999?

11. Who became the first English club to field a team of eleven foreigners?

12. How many home games did Manchester Utd lose in the Premier League in the 1999/00 season?

13. When was Gordon Strachan appointed manager of Coventry City?

14. What Conference side is nicknamed 'The Bluebirds'?

15. Which club did England cricketer Brian Close play football at during the fifties?

1. Thirty 2. Tony Adams 3. Chris Sutton 4. Ian Wright 5. Leicester City 6. Everton 7. Roberto Baggio 8. Ken Bates 9. Big Thing 10. Rivaldo 11. Chelsea 12. None 13. 1996 14. Barrow 15. Bradford City.

THE FOOTBALL FACT AND QUIZ BOOK

1. Which 1993 Premier match was watched by 3,039 spectators?
2. How much did Everton pay Aston Villa for Steve Watson?
3. What is Leicester City striker Trevor Benjamin's only previous club?
4. Where did Newcastle sign Christian Bassedas from?
5. Which club has won the Third Division (South) the most times?
6. Which three clubs have won the Third Division (North) the most times?
7. Which three clubs were relegated from the English Premier League in 1998?
8. What is unique about Karl-Heinz Rumenigge and Diego Maradona?
9. How much did Steve McManaman cost Real Madrid when he moved from Liverpool?
10. What happened when Sevilla FC tried to buy Robert Prosinecki from Barcelona in 1996?
11. Now retired, Steve Ogrizovic holds the appearance record for which club?
12. Which two Arsenal managers have also been managers of Tottenham?
13. Which Manchester Utd striker plays for Trinidad and Tobago?
14. Who did Arsenal sell Emmanuel Petit and Marc Overmars to?
15. Which Spanish side are nicknamed 'The Parakeets'?

THE FOOTBALL FACT AND QUIZ BOOK

1. Who was Carling Player of the Year for 1999/00?
2. Which Scottish team plays at Pittodrie Stadium?
3. Who scored four goals for Manchester Utd against his old club in August 1999?
4. Why was Ray Wilkins sent off in an England World Cup game in 1986?
5. When did the League Cup Final move to Wembley?
6. Who were the first Dutch side to win the European Cup?
7. Who are the two French managers in the Premier League?
8. Who was sent off in the 2000 Charity Shield?
9. How many times have West Ham Utd won the F.A. Cup at Wembley?
10. How many goals did Steve Bull score for Wolves in his 559 appearances?
11. Who did Spurs sell to Watford in 2000 for £1.25 million?
12. Which Scottish club are known as 'The Honest Men'?
13. Where did Spurs sign Sergei Rebrov from?
14. Which Ipswich keeper received his England call-up in 2000?
15. In 1995 who were banned indefinately from European competitions because of hooliganism?

1. Kevin Phillips 2. Aberdeen 3. Andy Cole 4. For throwing the ball at the referee 5. 1967 6. Feyenoord 7. Arsene Wenger and Gerard Houllier 8. Roy Keane 9. Three times 10. 306 11. Espen Baardsen 12. Ayr Utd 13. Dynamo Kiev 14. Richard Wright 15. England.

THE FOOTBALL FACT AND QUIZ BOOK

1. Where is Australia's national stadium?

2. Which team were the first to win three successive F.A. Cups?

3. What was the nickname of Brazilian player Garrincha?

4. Which two Premiership clubs has Jimmy Floyd Hasselbaink played for?

5. Which Newcastle player is nicknamed 'Lurker'?

6. Which two brothers were in the 1958 World Cup squad for Wales?

7. Who sponsors Charlton Athletic's shirts?

8. Which Scottish club has played in two English F.A. Cup finals?

9. How many times have Scotland played Morocco in international games?

10. What colour boots did Swansea City's Jamaican player, Walter Boyd, wear?

11. How many times was Bobby Charlton booked in his career?

12. Which Scottish team did John Jeffries manage before moving to Bradford City?

13. Which English team did Brazilian Mirandinha play for in 1987/88?

14. How many times have Liverpool won the F.A. Cup?

15. Who were the first African side to play in the World

THE FOOTBALL FACT AND QUIZ BOOK

1. Which England player was 'as daft as a brush' according to manager Bobby Robson?

2. Who was Chelsea's first £100,000 signing?

3. Which team do Michael Parkinson and Dickie Bird support?

4. Which English club won the European Cup in 1980?

5. Which former Leeds striker now plays at Hamburg?

6. Who has made the most consecutive appearances for Chelsea?

7. Who were the first English club to win the 'double'?

8. Who was the first reigning monarch to attend a Cup Final?

9. Which football show did Frank Skinner and David Baddiel present?

10. Which Scottish team play at the Shyberry Excelsior Stadium?

11. Which club did Michael Mols play for before joining Rangers?

12. Where do ASEC Mimosa Abidjan play their football?

13. Who scored the first 'Golden Goal' in World Cup history to knock Paraguay out of the tournament?

14. Where is Liverpool's academy based?

15. Who does Malcolm Christie play for?

1. **Paul Gascoigne** 2. Tony Hateley 3. Barnsley 4. Nottingham Forest 5. Tony Yeboah 6. John Hollins 7. Preston North End in 1888/89 8. George V, 1914 9. Fantasy Football League 10. Airdrieonians 11. Utrecht 12. Ivory Coast 13. Laurent Blanc 14. Kirkby 15. Derby County.

THE FOOTBALL FACT AND QUIZ BOOK

1. What was the title of the book written by football official Graham Kelly?

2. Who did Aston Villa sell to Everton in summer 2000?

3. Who was the first Leicester City player to finish as leading scorer in the top division?

4. Which club appointed Kevin Keegan as manager in 1998?

5. By what score did Iran beat the Maldives in a World Cup qualifying match?

6. Who did Liverpool beat 10-0 in 1986?

7. Which Mexican club took their previous name from a German U-Boat?

8. Which team has recorded the biggest away win in the Premiership?

9. Which two countries have reached the semi-finals of the World Cup in their first finals appearance?

10. Who was the first London team that beat Manchester Utd in the 2000/01 league season?

11. Fantasy Football League appeared first in which daily newspaper?

12. At which Scottish club was Alex Ferguson a teenage apprentice?

13. What is the nickname of Newcastle United?

14. Which American stadium hosted the 1994 World Cup Final?

15. Who scored five goals for Ipswich when they beat Southampton 5-3 in 1982?

1. 'Sweet F.A.' 2. Steve Watson 3. Gary Lineker, 1984/85 4. Fulham 5. 17-0 6. Fulham 7. Atlante, formerly known as U-53 8. Manchester Utd (8-1 v Nottingham Forest, 1999) 9. Portugal and Croatia 10. Arsenal 11. Daily Telegraph 12. Queen's Park 13. The Magpies 14. The Rose Bowl, Pasadena 15. Alan Brazil.

THE FOOTBALL FACT AND QUIZ BOOK

1. What do Bradford Park Avenue and Southport have in common?
2. Which player had the words 'Just done it' on a T-shirt when he became Arsenal's record goalscorer?
3. In which city did Manchester Utd win the Champions' League?
4. Which Conference side is nicknamed 'The Sandgrounders'?
5. Who did Liverpool sign midfielder Bernard Diomede from for £3 million?
6. Which three teams have won the Fourth Division the most times?
7. How much did Newcastle Utd pay Velez Sarsfield for Christian Bassedas?
8. Which Manchester Utd midfielder has played for Spurs and Atletico Madrid?
9. If David Seaman hadn't taken up football, what would he have done?
10. Which Everton signing has played for IFK Gothenburg and Halmstad?

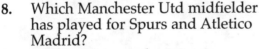

11. Which Coventry defender has won the Premiership title?
12. How many times did Bobby Charlton lead his country?
13. What hair product did David Beckham endorse until he got his head shaved?
14. When was the first time the Worthington Cup was played for?
15. Which Northern Ireland player joined Stockport in 1975?

1. They both once played league football 2. Ian Wright 3. Barcelona 4. Southport 5. Auxerre 6. Chesterfield, Doncaster Rovers and Peterborough Utd 7. £4 million 8. Quinton Fortune 9. A baker's apprentice 10. Niclas Alexandersson 11. Colin Hendry, with Blackburn Rovers 12. Three times 13. Brylcreem 14. 1999 15. George Best.

THE FOOTBALL FACT AND QUIZ BOOK

1. Which footballer started work as a hod carrier?
2. Which former Everton and Manchester City player is manager of Sunderland?
3. Who were the last winners of the Scottish Summer Cup?
4. Where do England train before home international matches?
5. How many goals did Savo Milosevic score in Euro 2000?
6. How many home league games did Crystal Palace win in 1997/98?
7. Which Brazilian cost Internazionale £18 million in 1997?
8. What was Hillsborough originally called?
9. What is the nickname of Moroccan league club FAR Rabat?
10. Who scored the first goal for France in the 1998 World Cup Final?
11. Who beat Italy 1-0 in the 1994 World Cup?
12. How many goals did Romanian Georghe Popescu score against Liechtenstein in a France '98 qualifying match?
13. What animal appears on the Leicester City club badge?
14. Who sponsors Chelsea's shirts?
15. Which team was originally called Newton Heath?

1. Vinnie Jones 2. Peter Reid 3. Partick Thistle 4. Bisham Abbey 5. 5 6. Two 7. Ronaldo 8. Owlerton 9. Les Militaires 10. Zinedine Zidane 11. Republic of Ireland 12. 4 13. A fox 14. Autoglass 15. Manchester Utd.

THE FOOTBALL FACT AND QUIZ BOOK

1. Which were the two teams in the European Cup Final at Heysel Stadium in 1985?

2. What nationality is Chelsea's Mario Stimac?

3. Which referee made a celebratory gesture in a Liverpool v Leeds game in February 2000?

4. Why were Leicester City's Tony Cottee and Andy Impey charged with misconduct in September 1999?

5. Which goalkeeper has made the most appearances for Sunderland?

6. Why were Darlington lucky in the 2000 F.A. Cup?

7. Which company sponsors Birmingham City's shirts?

8. Who was the fastest sending-off in the Premiership, after only 72 seconds?

9. Which country does Middlesborough's Hamilton Ricard play for?

10. Who does Gareth Barry play for?

11. Who is the Swiss president of FIFA?

12. Where do Aberdeen play their home football?

13. Which American goalkeeper moved from Columbus Crew to Liverpool?

14. Which team lost twice to the Faroe Islands in their 1998 World Cup qualifying group?

15. Which country won the 1984 European Championship?

1. Liverpool and Juventus 2. Croatian 3. Mike Reed 4. Their ticket distribution for the 1999 Worthington Cup Final 5. Jim Montgomery 6. They were put back in as 'lucky losers' 7. Auto glass 8. Tim Flowers, Blackburn Rovers 9. Colombia 10. Aston Villa 11. Sepp Blatter 12. Pittodrie 13. Brad Friedal 14. Malta 15. France.

THE FOOTBALL FACT AND QUIZ BOOK

1. Which club plays home games at the German Cup final venue?

2. What is the title of Frank Worthington's autobiography?

3. What colours do Bradford City play in?

4. What Liverpool player scored the first-ever goal shown on 'Match of the Day'?

5. Which club did Tahar El Khalej join Southampton from?

6. Which England winger plays for Real Madrid?

7. Where do Sunderland play?

8. Which English club has won the European Cup the most times?

9. How many times have they won it?

10. Which country has played in twelve successive Asian Cup of Nations finals?

11. Which team have their origins at Thames Ironworks?

12. Who scored for Bayern Munich against Manchester Utd in the 1999 Champions' League final?

13. What is the Italian word for football?

14. Which Scottish team plays at Cliftonhill Stadium?

15. Who became caretaker England manager after Glenn Hoddle resigned?

1. Hertha Berlin 2. 'One Hump or Two?' 3. Claret and amber shirts, claret shorts, claret and amber socks 4. Roger Hunt 5. Benfica 6. Steve McManaman 7. Stadium of Light 8. Liverpool 9. Four times 10. Saudi Arabia 11. Wes tHam United 12. Mario Basler 13. Calcio 14. Albion Rovers 15. Howard Wilkinson.

1. How many members does FIFA have?
2. How many of them have entered for the 2002 World Cup?
3. Who are the two countries co-hosting the 2002 World Cup?
4. What was the original name of Feyenoord?
5. Who apologised to the opposition after scoring his first goal for Arsenal in 1999?
6. At which ground do Brazil play most of their international games?
7. Which Italian international was known as 'Il Bambino D'Oro'?
8. Which midlands club is known as 'The Baggies'?
9. When is Gary McAllister's birthday?
10. Where did Middlesborough sign Christian Karembeu from in 2000?
11. Which Argentinian played for Birmingham City in 1978?
12. Who is Gerard Houllier's assistant at Liverpool?
13. What animal appears on the Middlesborough club badge?
14. Who beat Barcelona 3-0 in a European match in 2000?
15. Which team did Yorkshire wicketkeeper David

THE FOOTBALL FACT AND QUIZ BOOK

1. Who sponsors Coventry City's home shirts?

2. Who sponsors Coventry City's away shirts?

3. Who did Aldershot play their last league match against in 1992?

4. Who do Jamie Carragher and Steve Gerrard play for?

5. Which Scottish team play at the Recreation Park?

6. Which Premier league player scored the winning goal for Romania against England in the 1998 World Cup?

7. Which club is supported by Eddie Large and Bernard Manning?

8. Who did West Ham sell Eyal Berkovic to?

9. What nationality is former World Footballer of the Year, George Weah?

10. What animal made an appearance at the 1923 F.A. Cup Final?

11. Which country did Luis Hernandez play international football for?

12. How long were English clubs banned from Europe after the Heysel tragedy?

13. Which country's referees went on strike in 1997?

14. Who was English football's first £1000 player?

15. Which team did Chelsea beat 5-0 away, in a 1999 Champions' League match?

1. Subaru 2. Isuzu 3. Cardiff City 4. Liverpool 5. Alloa Athletic 6. Dan Petrescu 7. Manchester City 8. Celtic 9. Liberian 10. A white horse 11. Mexico 12. Five years 13. Spain 14. Alf Common 15. Galatasaray.

THE FOOTBALL FACT AND QUIZ BOOK

1. Who was Carling Manager of the Year for 1999/00?
2. Who were the only side Manchester Utd didn't beat in the 1999/00 season, but were still relegated?
3. Which three players were sent off in the Liverpool v Arsenal match in August 2000?
4. Which former Coventry City player, remembered for a horrific broken leg, took over as manager of Solihull Borough in January 2000?
5. To the beginning of the 2000/01 season, how many league clubs has Steve Claridge played for?
6. How old was Peter Lorimer when he made his league debut?
7. Which Irish striker did Internazionale sign in 2000?
8. Which country does Leeds Utd's Stephen McPhail play internationals for?
9. What number shirt does a centre-half traditionally wear?
10. Why was Oldham player Billy Cook banned for a year in 1915?
11. Which Frenchman scored a hat-trick on his debut in a 1953 World Cup qualifying game?
12. Which team plays at Mestalla?
13. Which north-west club is managed by Joe Royle?
14. In which country would you be, if you were watching a Bundesliga match?
15. In which competition can you name seven substitutes?

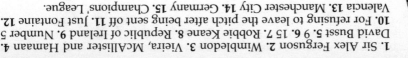

1. Sir Alex Ferguson 2. Wimbledon 3. Vieira, McAllister and Hamann 4. David Busst 5. 9 6. 15 7. Robbie Keane 8. Republic of Ireland 9. Number 5 10. For refusing to leave the pitch after being sent off 11. Just Fontaine 12. Valencia 13. Manchester City 14. Germany 15. Champions' League.

THE FOOTBALL FACT AND QUIZ BOOK

1. Who beat England in the quarter-finals of the 1954 World Cup?
2. Which two teams replayed an F.A. Cup tie in 1999, because one side had won with an 'unsporting' goal?
3. Which English centre-half joined Rangers in 1987?
4. Which goalkeeper has won over 100 caps for Sweden?
5. How much did Gary McAllister cost Liverpool in 2000?
6. Which company sponsors Blackburn Rovers' shirts?
7. Which Scottish team plays at Gayfield Park?
8. Which opera song from Turandot was the BBC's World Cup theme?
9. Which French team did Spurs loan Ossie Ardiles to during the 1982/83 season?
10. Which football club's name does actor Sean Bean have tattooed on his arm?
11. Which non-league club had a 'ground dispute' with Newcastle in the 1998/99 F.A. Cup?
12. Which French team plays at the Louis II stadium?
13. Which Welsh international has played for Liverpool, Wrexham, Chelsea and Huddersfield Town?
14. Who has been manager at Brighton and Celtic in the nineties?
15. When was Bryan Robson appointed as Middlesborough manager?

THE FOOTBALL FACT AND QUIZ BOOK

1. Which 2000/01 Chelsea duo were together at Atletico Madrid in 1999/00?
2. Which midfielder is player-coach at Gillingham?
3. Where was the 1983 F.A. Cup Final replayed?
4. Who is the only player to have scored a hat-trick in the F.A.Cup final?
5. How many spells did Gordon Cowans have with Aston Villa?
6. Which team were relegated to the Conference in 2000?
7. Which West Indian batsman has played football for Antigua and Barbuda?
8. Who sponsors Derby County's shirts?
9. Who won their ninth consecutive Scottish league title in 1974?
10. Which Chilean defender plays his football with West Ham United?
11. Which Liverpool player was nicknamed 'The Flying Pig'?
12. Where did Middlesborough sign Joseph Desire-Job from?
13. Which Scottish team plays at Somerset Park?
14. Who did Newcastle sell Silvio Maric to for £2 million in 2000?
15. How many times have Iceland qualified for the World Cup finals?

1. Claudio Ranieri and Jimmy Floyd Hasselbaink 2. Andy Hessenthaler 3. Wembley 4. Stan Mortenson in 1953 5. Three 6. Chester City 7. Viv Richards 8. EDS 9. Celtic 10. Javier Margas 11. Tommy Lawrence 12. Lens 13. Ayr Utd 14. FC Porto 15. None

THE FOOTBALL FACT AND QUIZ BOOK

1. How much did Internazionale pay Coventry City for Robbie Keane?

2. Which side missed winning the Italian title on the last day of the 1999/00 season?

3. How many goals did Darwen concede in Division Two in 1898/99?

4. Which two London clubs play in SW6?

5. Who scored the winning goal for Wimbledon in the 1988 F.A. Cup Final against Liverpool?

6. Which ex-England manager co-created 'Hazell' for the BBC?

7. What implements appear on the West Ham United club badge?

8. Which bearded Brazilian captained the team in the 1982 and 1986 World Cup Finals?

9. Which camera company sponsored the football league in the eighties?

10. Where did Paolo Di Canio start his playing career?

11. Who is Pierluigi Collina?

12. Who was sacked as Brazil's manager in October 2000?

13. How many times was Billy Bremner banned between 1964 and 1967?

14. Whic team does ex-Python Michael Palin support?

15. Which Conference side is nicknamed 'The Lilywhites'?

THE FOOTBALL FACT AND QUIZ BOOK

1. What happened to Roy Keane in the 2000 Charity Shield?
2. Who did Sudbury Town beat on penalties in the 1997 F.A. Cup?
3. Which Tottenham forward was found guilty of smoking cannabis?
4. Which Everton striker scored a hat-trick on his league debut in 1988?
5. When did Iraq play in the World Cup finals?
6. Which Brazilian was passed fit only 45 minutes before the 1998 World Cup Final?
7. When did the only all-English UEFA Cup final occur?
8. Which non-league player, now at Kingstonian, was known as 'The Lip' during Leatherhead's 1975 F.A. Cup run?
9. What number shirt did Eric Cantona wear for Machester Utd?
10. Who played in goal for Italy in Euro 2000?
11. What 'female' item of clothing was David Beckham photographed wearing during the 1998 World Cup?
12. How many times have Charlton Athletic qualified for Europe?
13. When did linesmen become 'assistant referees'?
14. What was Alan Brazil's nickname when he played for Ipswich?
15. Which chairman errected an electric fence at his club's home ground in 1985?

1. He was sent off 2. Brighton 3. Chris Armstrong 4. Tony Cottee (v Newcastle) 5. 1986 6. Ronaldo 7. 1972 8. Chris Kelly 9. Number 7 10. Toldo 11. A sarong 12. Never 13. 1996/97 14. Pele 15. Ken Bates.

1. Which two English coaches have managed Barcelona?
2. Which team's shirts have been sponsored by recording artist Fat Boy Slim?
3. Which postal district do Arsenal play in?
4. Which English club are nicknamed 'The Borderers'?
5. Where do Wolverhampton play their home games?
6. What are Bradford City player Lee Sharpe's two former clubs?
7. Which Italian team counts Luciano Pavarotti among its supporters?
8. What is the largest amount of teams to have contested the F.A. Cup?
9. Which country scored two goals in the last minute to win a Euro 2000 tie?
10. For which team did Dion Dublin make his league debut?
11. What was the nationality of the referee in the 1966 World Cup Final?
12. Who has written 'Left foot forward' and 'Left foot in the grave'?
13. Which Premier team does Jeremy Paxman support?
14. Who joined Sunderland in 1999, after 11 years at Arsenal?
15. What company sponsors Bolton Wanderers' shirts?

1. Terry Venables and Bobby Robson 2. Brighton 3. N5 4. Berwick Rangers 5. Molineux 6. Manchester Utd and Leeds Utd 7. Juventus 8. 674 9. Spain 10. Norwich City 11. Swiss 12. Gary Nelson 13. Leeds Utd 14. Steve Bould 15. Reebok.

THE FOOTBALL FACT AND QUIZ BOOK

1. Who won the Worthington Cup in 1999?

2. What was England's Bryan Robson nicknamed?

3. In which country would you find the Delle Alpi Stadium?

4. Who was left out of the 1998 Argentina World Cup squad for refusing to get his hair cut?

5. What is the title of Les Ferdinand's autobiography?

6. Which Liverpool player has played for Leeds Utd, Leicester City and Motherwell?

7. Who did Alan Shearer score his 300th goal in senior football against in 2000?

8. Who did Alan Shearer score his first goal in senior football against in 1988?

9. On their return to the Premier League in 2000/01, which team conceded four goals in their first match?

10. Which Nationwide league club plays in Lincolnshire?

11. Who is Spain's most capped player of all-time?

12. How many times have Charlton Athletic won the F.A. Cup?

13. Which Derby signing in 2000 has played for AIS, VIS, Bulleen and Kingston City?

14. Who took over as England captain when Bobby Moore was injured during 1973/74?

15. Which Dutchman is manager at Rangers?

1. Spurs 2. Captain Marvel 3. Italy 4. Redondo 5. Sir Les 6. Gary McAllister 7. Arsenal 8. Arsenal 9. Manchester City 10. Grimsby 11. Andoni Zubizarreta 12. Once, in 1947 13. Con Blastis 14. Martin Peters 15. Dick Advocaat.

THE FOOTBALL FACT AND QUIZ BOOK

1. Which women's football team was formed in 1969?

2. Who does Hassan Kachoul play for?

3. What is the title of the book written by Paul Merson?

4. Who does Spaniard Albert Ferrer play for?

5. What colour shirts do Middlesborough wear?

6. Which two teams played in the first match of the 1966 World Cup?

7. What bird appears on the Liverpool club badge?

8. How much did Leeds Utd receive from Manchester City for Alf-Inge Haaland?

9. Which manager retired in 1993 after 17 years in charge of the same club?

10. Which is England's most northerly League club?

11. Which Frenchman scored 26 goals for Arsenal in 1999/00?

12. Which Latvian, playing for Southampton, had his work permit refused twice by the Department of Employment?

13. Who is understudy goalkeeper to David Seaman at Arsenal?

14. Which Scottish league club plays at Shielfield Park?

15. Who sponsors Everton's shirts?

THE FOOTBALL FACT AND QUIZ BOOK

1. Which European country were in England's World Cup qualifying group in 1990, 1994 and 1998?

2. Which English club once played at Pink Bank Lane and Reddish Lane?

3. What was Kenari?

4. Which club used a hawk, a kestrel and an owl to scare away pigeons in 1998?

5. Who lost in the final of the 1978 European Cup?

6. Who scored all of Haiti's goals in the 1974 World Cup finals?

7. When was the last time Manchester City played in Europe?

8. Who was England's goalkeeper during the 1998 World Cup finals?

9. Who is Chelsea's current record goalscorer?

10. What is Barnsley manager Dave Bassett's nickname?

11. What did Just Fontaine win with OGC Nice and Stade de Reims?

12. Which Manchester Utd substitute scored 4 goals against Nottingham Forest in February 1999?

13. Why didn't Asa Hartford join Leeds Utd from West Bromwich Albion?

14. Which company sponsors Crewe's shirts?

15. What 'first' does Welshman Trevor Hockey hold?

1. Poland 2. Manchester City 3. An early form of Japanese football 4. Crewe Alexandra 5. FC Bruges 6. Sanon 7. 1978/79 UEFA Cup 8. David Seaman 9. Bobby Tambling 10. Harry 11. A Championship medal 12. Ole Gunnar Solskjaer 13. Because it was discovered that he had a 'hole in the heart' 14. L C Charles 15. First Welshman to be sent off in an international.

THE FOOTBALL FACT AND QUIZ BOOK

1. Who was the first Dutchman to be sent off in an international game?

2. Which former international joined Sporting Lisbon from Liverpool on a free transfer in 2000?

3. Which Scottish side plays at Glebe Park?

4. What is two-a-side football called?

5. Which English title-winning side were nicknamed 'Drake's Ducklings'?

6. At which club was Dixie Dean a goal-scoring legend?

7. How many clubs play in the National First Division in Slovakia?

8. How much did Celtic receive from Leeds Utd for Mark Viduka?

9. Which South African player was joint top scorer in the 1998 African Cup of Nations?

10. Which club did Celtic sign Ian Wright from?

11. What did Dutch international Niels Bohr win in 1922?

12. Where were Fire Brigade SC league champions of in 1993/94?

13. What award was given to Pele in December 1997?

14. What links Sunderland, West Ham United, West Bromwich Albion and Southampton?

15. Who was Scotland manager before Craig Brown?

1. Johan Cruyff 2. Phil Babb 3. Brechin City 4. Jorky-ball 5. Chelsea 6. Everton 7. 16 8. £6 million 9. Benedict McCarthy 10. West Ham United 11. A nobel prize 12. Mauritius 13. An honorary knighthood 14. They've all won the F.A. Cup while in Division Two 15. Andy Roxburgh.

THE FOOTBALL FACT AND QUIZ BOOK

1. How many goals did Luton's Joe Payne score in the 12-0 defeat of Bristol Rovers?
2. Which player appeared in nine of the first twelve F.A. Cup finals?
3. What is the nickname of Brechin City?
4. 'Confessions of a bad boy' was written by which former Welsh player?
5. Where did Chelsea sign Mario Stanic from in summer 2000?
6. What nationaity is Andrei Kanchelskis?
7. What was the UEFA Cup originally called?
8. Who scored an 87th minute equaliser in the 1984 F.A. Cup final for Brighton?
9. Which Manchester Utd goalkeeper was arrested on his stag night?
10. Which country do Oryx Douada play football in?
11. Which country has Billy Bingham been manager of?
12. Who scored Manchester Utd's fastest-ever goal in 1995?
13. Who started at Leeds Utd, moved to Blackburn and Newcastle, then returned to Leeds Utd?
14. Who did Pat Jennings win his last international cap against in the 1982 World Cup finals?
15. Which country do Leeds Utd full-backs Ian Harte and Gary Kelly play for?

THE FOOTBALL FACT AND QUIZ BOOK

1. What nickname is given to Celtic and Rangers?
2. What is the Italian F.A.'s national headquarters called?
3. Which former Leeds Utd manager has been manager at Spurs?
4. Which England midfield player joined Liverpool from Internazionale in 1997?
5. Which team's ground is nicknamed 'The Tub'?
6. What colour shirts do KR Reykjavik play in?
7. What country did Peter Nicholas play internationals for?
8. How long was Brazil's unbeaten run between 1993 and 1996?
9. How many different nationalities were in the Chelsea squad at the start of the 2000/01 season?
10. Which Scottish team plays at Broadwood Stadium?
11. Which company sponsors Crystal Palace's shirts?
12. Which north-east club did Brian Clough begin his managerial career with?
13. Who did England play in their opening match in Euro 2000?
14. Who was Glenn Hoddle's predecessor at Southampton?
15. For how much did Olympique Marseille sell Robert Pires to Arsenal?

1. 'The Old Firm'. 2. The Coverciano 3. George Graham 4. Paul Ince 5. Feyenoord 6. Black and white 7. Wales 8. 37 games 9. 14 10. Clyde 11. TDK 12. Hartlepool 13. Portugal 14. David Jones 15. £6 million.

THE FOOTBALL FACT AND QUIZ BOOK

1. What was Tom Finney's nickname?
2. Which Manchester City player has played for Derby and West Ham Utd?
3. Where do Jubilo Iwata play their football?
4. Which club did Mark Viduka leave to join Leeds Utd?
5. Which Belgian club plays in red and yellow stripes?
6. Which two Southampton players have devised their own internet-based fantasy football game called Big Money league.com?
7. Who was Carling Opta Man of the Year for the 1999/00 season?
8. Who won the European Cup in 1991?
9. Who was the first president of Barcelona?
10. Where do Eleven Men in Flight play their league football?
11. Which club transferred Luis Boa Morte to Southampton?
12. Who were Manchester Utd's opponents in Bobby Charlton's last home game?
13. What animal appears on the Coventry City club badge?
14. Who won the Golden Boot at the 1978 World Cup finals?
15. Who does film star Hugh Grant support?

1. 'The Preston Plumber' 2. Paulo Wanchope 3. J-League in Japan 4. Celtic 5. KV Mechelen 6. John Beresford and David Hughes 7. Paolo Di Canio 8. Red Star Belgrade 9. Walter Wild 10. Swaziland 11. Arsenal 12. Chelsea 13. An elephant 14. Mario Kempes 15. Fulham.

THE FOOTBALL FACT AND QUIZ BOOK

1. Where was Middlesborough's Christian Karembeu born?
2. What were Millwall the first to establish at their ground in 1985?
3. Who was Arsene Wenger's predecessor as Arsenal manger?
4. At whose ground do Clydebank play their home games?
5. Who did Hereford Utd, then of the Southern League, knock out of the F.A. Cup with a Ronnie Radford goal?
6. Where did Manchester Utd sign Fabian Barthez from in May 2000?
7. Who did Blackburn pay £400,000 to for Steve Harkness?
8. Who was sold by Motherwell in 1962 to finance the building of a new stand?
9. What, at West Bromwich Albion, was nicknamed 'Noah's Ark'?
10. Which national team does 'The Desert Pele', Majed Abdullah, play for?
11. What was the proposed club name of a merger between Fulham and Queen's Park Rangers in 1987?
12. Which Italian club were originally called Verdi F.C.?
13. Where do Try Again play their league football?
14. Which company sponsors Fulham's shirts?
15. What colours do Argentinian side Huracan play in?

THE FOOTBALL FACT AND QUIZ BOOK

1. Which Chelsea player allegedly said in March 2001 that the club had 'too many old players to do well'?

2. Which two players did George Graham sign from Wimbledon in 2000?

3. Which Conference side are nicknamed 'The Vics'?

4. What former footballer and presenter's name appeared in a West End theatre show?

5. Why did German Hans-Peter Briegel resign as coach of Besiktas in 1999/00?

6. Beside Van der Saar, who else appeared in goal for Holland in Euro 2000?

7. Which former Manchester Utd player is now assistant coach at Leeds Utd?

8. How long does the football season in Peru last?

9. Who are the 'Mackems'?

10. Where would you watch Libertad play football?

11. Who sponsors Ipswich Town's shirts?

12. Who did Manchester Utd beat 7-0 in October 1997?

13. Which Southampton player has appeared for Tennis Borussia Berlin, Kaiserslautern and FC Nuremburg?

14. Which city was the 1978 World Cup final played in?

15. Which manager has played with Aberdeen, Manchester Utd, Leeds Utd and Coventry City?

1. Which Scottish team are known as 'The Bhoys'?
2. How many of the four home nation's played in the European Championships in 1960?
3. What country do Urawa Red Diamonds play in?
4. Which country beat Yugoslavia 4-3 in Euro 2000 to knock Norway out of the competition?
5. Which Chelsea player has played for Leeds Utd, Boavista and Campomaio?
6. Which Leeds Utd player missed in the penalty shoot-out in England's 1998 World Cup match against Argentina?
7. From which club did Dennis Wise join Chelsea?
8. Which Celtic player was sent off in the CIS Cup final against Kilmarnock in March 2001?
9. Which country does Aston Villa defender Mark Delaney play for?
10. Which Charlton Athletic goalkeeper moved to Leicester City in summer 2000?
11. Who scored three goals for Bolton against Ipswich Town in the 2000 play-off semi-finals?
12. Why didn't Rangers enter the first Scottish F.A. Cup?
13. Which company sponsors Gillingham's shirts?
14. Where did Southampton sign Mark Draper from?
15. How much did Middlesborough pay Real Madrid for Christian Karembeu?

THE FOOTBALL FACT AND QUIZ BOOK

1. Which German scored in every World Cup finals tournament between 1958 and 1978?

2. Which club was Barry Fry manager of when they joined the league in 1981?

3. Why did Sultan Abdul Hamid ban all clubs playing 'British' football in Turkey?

4. Who scored for Chelsea in both the 1997 and 2000 F.A. Cup finals?

5. Which team does Ray Clemence's son play for?

6. Which two teams contested the Auto Windscreens Shield final in 2000?

7. Which Aberdeen player was Scottish Footballer of the Year in 1980?

8. What part of a reporter's body did Vinnie Jones allegedly bite in a Dublin bar?

9. Who won the Libertadores Cup in 2000?

10. Why was German Stefan Effenburg sent home from the 1994 World Cup?

11. What colour shirts do Bulgarian side Lokomotiv Sofia play in?

12. How much did Paul Gascoigne cost Everton when he signed for them in 2000?

13. Which country would you be in if you were watching Violet Kickers?

14. Which country does Newcastle Utd keeper Shay Given play for?

15. How many times did Manchester Utd win the league and cup double in the nineties?

1. Uwe Seeler 2. Barnet 3. He feared losing his empire and his power 4. Roberto Di Matteo 5. Spurs 6. Bristol City and Stoke City 7. Gordon Strachan 8. His nose 9. Boca Juniors 10. For making gestures to the crowd 11. Red and black stripes 12. Nothing, he was a free transfer 13. Jamaica 14. Republic of Ireland 15. Twice.

THE FOOTBALL FACT AND QUIZ BOOK

1. What was former English league club Gateshead originally known as?
2. How many times have Tunisia qualified for the World Cup finals?
3. Who was the youngest player to have appeared in the World Cup finals?
4. Where do Kuusysi Lahti play their football?
5. Where do Cowdenbeath play their home games?
6. Where does former Everton player Daniel Amokachi now play his football?
7. In 1995, which goalkeeper played in the Premier League at the age of 43?
8. Which Spanish club does Raul play for?
9. Who were Arsenal's previous sponsors before Dreamcast?
10. At which club is Karen Brady managing director?
11. Which Israeli joined Celtic from West Ham United?
12. Which two World Cup finals have Saudi Arabia appeared in?
13. Which team appeared in the 1993, 1994 and 1995 Champions' League final?
14. Which team appeared in the 1996, 1997 and 1998 Champions' League final?
15. Which country play their home games in Katowice, at the Stadion Slaski?

1. South Shields Adelaide 2. Twice 3. Norman Whiteside 4. Finland 5. Central Park 6. Besiktas in Turkey 7. John Burridge 8. Real Madrid 9. JVC 10. Birmingham City 11. Eyal Berkovic 12. 1994 and 1998 13. AC Milan 14. Juventus 15. Poland.

THE FOOTBALL FACT AND QUIZ BOOK

1. What are the two major monthly football awards?
2. Which club knocked down it's Trinity Road stand in summer 2000?
3. How old was Steve Coppell when he retired from the game as a player?
4. Which club did Kevin Campbell leave to play for Trabzonspor in Turkey?
5. What nationality was Arsenal winger Anders Limpar?
6. Which team played in the Charity Shield from 1984 to 1987?
7. What is the name of Phillip and Gary Neville's father?
8. Which national team are known as 'The Black Stars'?
9. What do Halifax Town and Lincoln City have in common?
10. Who used to wear the Number 6 shirt for West Ham United and England?
11. Which club did Chelsea sign Eidur Gudjohnsen from in summer 2000?
12. How much did Barcelona pay Arsenal for Overmars and Petit?
13. Who sponsors Leeds Utd's shirts?
14. Which 'Minder' provided the voice-over for the 'Match of the Seventies' TV series?
15. Who knocked Paraguay out of the 1986 World Cup?

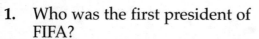

1. Who was the first president of FIFA?

2. Which Conference side are known as 'The Shrimps'?

3. What animal appears on the Derby County club badge?

4. Which company sponsors Grimsby Town's shirts?

5. Which three players made a 'home video' on their holidays at Ayia Napa?

6. Who won the League title at Anfield in 1989?

7. What scandal hit English football in 1963?

8. What country do teams play in the NASL?

9. What country does Nico Claesen play for?

10. What was the name of the first football club in Wales?

11. Who were the last London team to win the League Cup?

12. Which Blackburn team-mates had a fight on the pitch?

13. How did the Champions' League change in 1998?

14. Which two clubs play at the Luigi Ferraris Stadium in Italy?

15. What is the nickname of Turkish club Besiktas?

1. Robert Guerin 2. Morecambe 3. A ram 4. Dixon Motors plc 5. Rio Ferdinand, Frank Lampard and Kieron Dyer 6. Arsenal 7. Match-fixing 8. USA 9. Belgium 10. Druids 11. Spurs 12. David Batty and Graham Le Saux 13. Country's runners-up were allowed to play, as well as the champions 14. Sampdoria and Genoa 15. 'The Black Eagles'.

THE FOOTBALL FACT AND QUIZ BOOK

1. Where do F'91 Dudelange play their home games?
2. Which Premier referee's profession is a Chartered Surveyor?
3. Who scored a hat-trick for Celtic against Rangers in August 2000?
4. How much were Chelsea fined in 1991 for making illegal payments to their players?
5. When was the first England v Wales international at Wembley?
6. What was the profession of Stanley Matthews' father?
7. Which club did brothers Andy and David Linighan play for?
8. Who is Sven Goran Eriksson's assistant coach?
9. Which was striker Chris Armstrong's first club?
10. Who won the League Championship in 1968?
11. Where was the first F.A. Cup presented to the winning team in 1872?
12. In which national league do 'The Strongest' play?
13. Where do Celtic play their home games?
14. Who did Derby County sell to Lens for £4 million?
15. Which club does Japanese player Nakata play for?

1. Luxembourg 2. Barry Knight 3. Henrik Larsson 4. £105,000 5. 1952 6. Barber 7. Hartlepool Utd 8. Tord Grip 9. Wrexham 10. Manchester City 11. The Pall Mall Restaurant 12. Bolivia 13. Celtic Park 14. Esteban Fuertes 15. AS Roma.

THE FOOTBALL FACT AND QUIZ BOOK

1. When was the first penalty shoot-out in the World Cup finals?
2. Who were the two teams involved?
3. Where did Bradford City sign David Hopkin from in summer 2000?
4. Which Italian goalkeeper signed for Chelsea in summer 2000?
5. Who sponsors Huddersfield Town's shirts?
6. Which team would Chelsea goalkeeper Ed de Goey play international football for?
7. Who scored the only goal of the game when the Republic of Ireland beat Italy in the 1994 World Cup finals?
8. Which organisation elects the World Footballer of the Year?
9. Who made his club and international debut at the age of 17, in 1991?
10. Which team in the late seventies had a brown away kit?
11. Which league club did Peter Taylor manage before Gillingham?
12. With which club did Liam Brady finish his playing career?
13. Which South American country's stadium was used as a prison camp after a coup in 1973?
14. Who won the Watney Cup in 1970?
15. How much did Argentinos Juniors player Julio Arca cost Sunderland?

1. 1982 2. West Germany and France 3. Leeds Utd 4. Carlo Cudicini 5. Panasonic 6. Holland 7. Ray Houghton 8. FIFA 9. Ryan Giggs 10. Coventry City 11. Southend 12. West Ham United 13. Chile 14. Derby County 15. £3.5 million.

THE FOOTBALL FACT AND QUIZ BOOK

1. Which body was established in 1997?

2. Who won the F.A. Vase in 1998 and 1999?

3. What do Benfica and Sunderland have in common?

4. Which three Manchester City players scored hat-tricks in the 10-1 defeat of Huddersfield Town in 1987?

5. Which Welsh striker has advertised hair loss treatment?

6. Who was Italy's coach for Euro 2000?

7. Which Premiership manager is also a successful racehorse owner?

8. Who did Coventry City sell striker Peter Ndlovu to?

9. In which city did Arsenal play their 2000 UEFA Cup Final?

10. When West Ham United beat Sunderland 8-0 in 1968, who scored six of them?

11. Why was Arsenal's Sammy Nelson suspended in 1979?

12. Who do Dumbarton share the Cliftonhill Ground with?

13. Who sponsors Leicester City's shirts?

14. Which Conference team is known as 'The Blues'?

15. Who does Leeds Utd player Erik Bakke play international football for?

THE FOOTBALL FACT AND QUIZ BOOK

1. Which British monarch visited Goodison Park in 1913?
2. Where do Dandy Town Hornets play home games?
3. Which Brazilian is better known as Manuel Francisco dos Santos?
4. Where was the 1998 World Cup third-place match played?
5. Who were the two teams involved?
6. Which Middlesborough player has played for Fiorentina, Lazio and FC Bruges?
7. Who scored Scotland's goal in the 1-0 win over England in 1999?
8. When did Barclays sponsor the Football League?
9. How much were Derby County fined in 1983, for poaching manager Roy McFarland from Bradford City?
10. What team was Don Howe manager of in 1984?
11. Who was the first player-manager to win the Championship?
12. Which club did Ronnie Whelan make over 350 appearances for?
13. Which brothers played together at Leeds Utd, but not for Scotland?
14. Who scored a hat-trick against Luxembourg at Wembley in 1999?
15. Where did Manchester Utd win the 1999 European Cup?

1. George V 2. Bermuda 3. Garrincha 4. Parc des Princes, Paris 5. Croatia and Holland 6. Paul Okon 7. Don Hutchison 8. 1987 9. £10,000 10. Arsenal 11. Kenny Dalglish 12. Liverpool 13. Frank and Eddie Gray 14. Alan Shearer 15. Nou Camp, Barcelona.

THE FOOTBALL FACT AND QUIZ BOOK

1. Which club did Leeds Utd manager David O'Leary make his playing debut with?
2. Which club did former Prime Minister Harold Wilson support?
3. Who scored a hat-trick in the 1994 Manchester derby?
4. Which club lost to Feyenoord in the 1974 UEFA Cup Final?
5. Which player joined Manchester City from Wolves for £1 million in 1979?
6. Who were the only team to beat Egypt in the 1990 World Cup finals?
7. How many appearances did Dennis Wise make for Wimbledon?
8. Who scored a hat-trick in five minutes against Arsenal in 1994?
9. Which Sheffield Wednesday goalkeeper was sent off after only 12 seconds in a league match?
10. Why was Paul Gascoigne's move to Lazio delayed?
11. Who left Aston Villa to become England manager?
12. Which Nottingham Forest manager gave his son his debut?
13. Which rivals did Everton sell Nick Barmby to?
14. Who did Chelsea sell to Celtic for £6 million in 2000?
15. Which Romanian is remembered by French fans for spending more time on his love of cars than football?

1. Arsenal 2. Huddersfield Town 3. Andrei Kandelskis 4. Tottenham Hotspur 5. Steve Daley 6. England 7. 127 8. Robbie Fowler 9. Kevin Pressman 10. Because he was involved in a nightclub fracas 11. Graham Taylor 12. Brian Clough 13. Liverpool 14. Chris Sutton 15. Daniel Prodan.

THE FOOTBALL FACT AND QUIZ BOOK

1. Which former England striker was known as 'Sniffer'?

2. What was Lennart Johansson chairman of between 1984 and 1991?

3. Which Derby player was transferred to Lille for £500,000?

4. Where do Dundee play their home games?

5. Which London team beat Manchester Utd 5-0 in the 1999/00 season?

6. Which Scottish club are known as 'The Bully Wee'?

7. Where did Charlton sign Claus Jensen from in summer 2000?

8. Who became the first English club to win a European trophy in 1963?

9. At which club were David Seaman and Peter Reid in the same team?

10. In the 1960s, which club scored 100 goals for three successive seasons?

11. Who scored all the goals in Aston Villa's 2-2 draw with Leicester City in 1976?

12. At which club did Lee Chapman make his debut?

13. Which Middlesborough player was the first Bolivian to play league football?

14. Which French club knocked Celtic out of the 2000 UEFA Cup?

15. Who sponsors Norwich City's shirts?

1. Allan Clarke 2. The Swedish F.A. 3. Mikkel Beck 4. Dens Park Stadium 5. Chelsea 6. Clyde 7. Bolton Wanderers 8. Spurs 9. Queen's Park Rangers 10. Wolverhampton Wanderers 11. Chris Nicholl of Aston Villa 12. Stoke City 13. Jaime Moreno 14. Lyon 15. Colman's.

THE FOOTBALL FACT AND QUIZ BOOK

1. What did Crystal Palace win in 1977 and 1978?
2. Which team won the first Anglo-Italian Cup in 1970?
3. Which Scottish referee was in charge for two Euro 2000 games?
4. Who is the only Manchester Utd manager never to have lost against Manchester City?
5. Where did England play their first home games?
6. Who does Peruvian international Ysrael Zuniga play for?
7. At which club did Jimmy McIlroy win 51 of his 55 Northern Ireland caps?
8. Who scored Japan's only goal in the 1998 World Cup finals?
9. Where did Teddy Sheringham get involved in an incident with a dentist's chair?
10. Which boxing promoter took over Leyton Orient in 1995?
11. Who lost to IFK Gothenburg in the 1987 UEFA Cup final?
12. When did it become compulsory for all 92 league clubs to enter the League Cup?
13. Which club lost an F.A. Cup 5th round match 2-1, twice in 10 days?
14. Which German 'Number 9' scored 68 goals in 62 games for his country?
15. Which Scottish club plays at Tannadice?

1. The F.A. Youth Cup 2. Swindon Town 3. Hugh Dallas 4. Ron Atkinson 5. Kennington Oval 6. Coventry City 7. Burnley 8. Nakayamo 9. Hong Kong 10. Barry Hearn 11. Dundee Utd 12. 1967/68 13. Sheffield Utd 14. Gerd Muller 15. Dundee Utd.

THE FOOTBALL FACT AND QUIZ BOOK

1. What position does Billy the Fish play in the 'Viz' comic strip?

2. What was formed in 1991 in Japan?

3. What was the score in the first 'Old Firm' match of the 2000/01 season?

4. Which team do rock group Status Quo support?

5. In Don Revie's eight games in charge of England, who was the only ever-present player?

6. Who was Arsenal manager between 1986 and 1995?

7. Which side did Ryan Giggs score his first league goal against?

8. Who is Scotland's second most capped player?

9. Which Chelsea striker was nicknamed 'Mary'?

10. Which club, in 1984, did Dave Bassett manage for three days?

11. Which England keeper kept goal for Sheffield Wednesday in the 1966 F.A. Cup final?

12. Who did Elton John sell Watford to for £6 million in 1991?

13. Which Dutch side did Bobby Robson manage after leaving England?

14. Which home nation has no player with 100 international caps?

15. Who is Blackpool's most capped player?

1. Goalkeeper 2. The J-League 3. Celtic 6 Rangers 2 4. Spurs 5. Dave Watson 6. George Graham 7. Manchester City 8. Jim Leighton 9. Kerry Dixon 10. Crystal Palace 11. Ron Springett 12. Jack Petchey 13. PSV Eindhoven 14. Wales 15. Jimmy Armfield.

THE FOOTBALL FACT AND QUIZ BOOK

1. Who succeeded Bob Paisley as manager of Liverpool?
2. Which two clubs joined the Scottish League in the nineties?
3. Who was the first-ever foreign coach to lead the England team?
4. Where do Dunfermline Athletic play their home games?
5. Where does Ipswich Town manager George Burley's nephew Craig play his football?
6. Which former England player married a Beverley sister?
7. What South American team were the first winners of the Copa de Oro in 1993?
8. Which two Arsenal players both joined West Ham United on a free trannsfer in summer 2000?
9. What is above the shield on the Southampton club badge?
10. Whose fans are known as the 'Toon Army'?
11. When did the first foreign player sign for Chelsea?
12. Why was the 1915 F.A. Cup final known as 'The Khaki Cup'?
13. Which goalkeeper played for Chesterfield, Leicester City and Stoke City?
14. Which Conference side is known as 'The K's'?
15. Who won Player of the Year at Nottingham Forest for 1999/00?

THE FOOTBALL FACT AND QUIZ BOOK

1. What was the nickname of Hungarian Ferenc Puskas?
2. Which French centre-half was suspended for the 1998 World Cup Final?
3. Which Sunderland player missed a penalty in the shoot-out at the 1998 play-offs?
4. Which former Liverpool player has managed Newcastle, Fulham and England?
5. Which Internazionale manager was known as 'The Magician'?
6. Which team's shirts do Carling sponsor?
7. Which team lost three consecutive Division One play-off finals?
8. Who wore the 'Number 9' shirt at Chelsea after Chris Sutton was transferred to Celtic?
9. Who was the first professional player to appear for England against Scotland?
10. Which father and son both played for Nottingham Forest and Scotland?
11. Which Manchester Utd player put his christian name on his shirt instead of his surname?
12. Who did Brian Little leave to take over at Aston Villa in 1995?
13. Who bought 51% of Celtic in 1994?
14. Where did Chelsea sell Didier Deschamps to in 2000 for £2.3 million?
15. Which Rangers striker was transferred to Charlton in summer 2000?

THE FOOTBALL FACT AND QUIZ BOOK

1. Which country did Scotland beat in the 1990 World Cup tournament?

2. Who is the only Spanish-born player to have played for Chelsea?

3. Which London club play in red and white stripes?

4. Which team were third in the 1993 Premier League?

5. How were the winners of the Ford Sporting League decided?

6. In which cup final did Doncaster Belles meet Croydon in May 2000?

7. Which goalkeeper has gone from Leeds Utd to Arsenal to Leeds Utd and back to Arsenal?

8. Which club did Garth Crooks make his debut for?

9. In which country is the Santosh Trophy played for?

10. Which club were once known as St.Jude's?

11. Whose son, Shaun Wright-Williams, made his Premiership debut in 2000 for Manchester City?

12. Who do Dunn and Duff play for?

13. Which Scottish club play at Bayview Stadium?

14. What was Bradford City's only incursion into European football?

15. Which Manchester Utd player made his last league appearance at Stamford Bridge?

1. Sweden 2. Albert Ferrer 3. Brentford 4. Norwich City 5. On good behaviour and goals scored 6. Women's F.A. Cup Final 7. John Lukic 8. Stoke City 9. India 10. Queen's Park Rangers 11. Ian Wright's 12. Blackburn Rovers 13. East Fife 14. The Intertoto Cup, 2000 15. Bobby Charlton.

THE FOOTBALL FACT AND QUIZ BOOK

1. Which Engand player was sent off at Wembley in the 2000 qualifying game against Sweden?
2. Who was sent off in his only appearance as captain of Wales
3. What is the nickname of Daring Club Motema Pembe of the Congo Democratic Republic?
4. In Arsenal's squad for the 2000/01 season of 33 players, how many were English?
5. Which team's supporters formed a political party in the nineties, and pulled 14,838 votes?
6. Which Celtic manager was sacked after the cup humiliation against Inverness Caledonian Thistle?
7. Who was Tommy Docherty's first signing at Manchester Utd?
8. Who inflicted Brazil's first ever World Cup qualifying defeat in 1994?
9. Who made his twelfth visit to Wembley as a manager for the 1983 League Cup Final?
10. Which club left the Football League after only three seasons as members?
11. Which London club has had it's ground closed by the F.A. more times than any other in the league?
12. Who did Teddy Sheringham replace at Manchester Utd?
13. Which company sponsors Nottingham Forest's shirts?
14. Which Newcastle manager signed Alan Shearer?
15. What does E.S.F.A. stand for?

THE FOOTBALL FACT AND QUIZ BOOK

1. What did Jimmy Hill become the youngest chairman of in 1961?
2. What is the nickname given to the Jamaican national team?
3. After German reunification in 1990, which were the only two East German sides to be put in the Bundesliga First Division?
4. How many of Derby County's 2000/01 squad are English?
5. What Scottish club play at Firs Park?
6. What cup were Aberdeen the only winners of?
7. How is Duncan Edwards commemorated in the Parish Church of St. Francis, Dudley?
8. Who was manager of Leeds Utd when they won the 1992 League Title?
9. Which international player has appeared for Derby, Liverpool, Aston Villa and Nottingham Forest in the nineties?
10. In which year was the first Milk Cup Final played?
11. What was the former name of Arsenal Tube Station?
12. Who scored for England in his 100th international?
13. Why did Chelsea stop Babayaro celebrating his goals with a back-flip?
14. Who was the first European player to be sent off at Wembley?
15. Which two brothers signed for Barcelona together in 1999?

1. The PFA 2. 'The Reggae Boyz' 3. Dynamo Dresden and Hansa Rostock 4. 13 5. East Stirling 6. The Dryborough Cup 7. By a stained glass window 8. Howard Wilkinson 9. Dean Saunders 10. 1982 11. Gillespie Road 12. Bobby Charlton 13. After he broke his ankle doing it 14. Boris Stankovic 15. Ronald and Frank de Boer.

THE FOOTBALL FACT AND QUIZ BOOK

1. Where would you find the Maracana Stadium?
2. Which country hosted the 1984 European Championships?
3. Who did Ipswich Town sell Bobby Petta to?
4. Which Italian team won the 1974 Anglo-Italian Cup?
5. How much did West Ham United pay Lyon for Frederic Kanoute?
6. What else was Dennis Wise holding when he was presented with the F.A. Cup in 2000?
7. Who saved a penalty for West Ham United in the 1972 League Cup semi-final against Stoke City?
8. Who sponsors Manchester City's shirts?
9. What have Shamrock Rovers won more times than any other club?
10. Where did the Three Tenors sing before the 1998 World Cup Final in Paris?
11. What Chelsea goalkeeper was known as 'The Cat'?
12. Which country does is Charlton Athletic's captain, Mark Kinsella, play for?
13. Which club did Jurgen Klinsmann join after leaving Internazionale?

1. Brazil 2. France 3. Celtic 4. Fiorentina 5. £3.7 million 6. His baby son 7. Bobby Moore 8. EIDOS 9. The Football Association of Ireland Cup 10. Eiffel Tower 11. Peter Bonetti 12. Rebublic of Ireland 13. AS Monaco 14. Iwan Roberts 15. 'The Griffins'.

THE FOOTBALL FACT AND QUIZ BOOK

1. After a two-year unbeaten run, who defeated Hungary in 1956?

2. What did Hibernian and Celtic compete for in 1953?

3. Who, in the 1985 FA Cup final, was the first person to be sent off in a live TV match?

4. Which British manager was sacked by Real Madrid in 1990 and 1999?

5. Which Fourth Division team competed in the 1962 League Cup final?

6. Where were Iain Dowie and Alan Shearer in the same team?

7. What is the nickname of Dumbarton?

8. What colour shirts do Bradford City play in?

9. Who was the Tottenham manager who signed Teddy Sheringham?

10. What was the original name of West Ham United?

11. Which Liverpool player used to play at Ferencvaros?

12. Which Portugese player scored a hat-trick against Germany in Euro 2000?

13. What is the actual name of the trophy which was awarded to the winners of Euro 2000?

14. Where do Falkirk play their home games?

15. Where does Leeds Utd's Lucas Radebe come from?

1. Turkey 2. The Coronation Cup 3. Kevin Moran 4. John Toshack 5. Rochdale 6. Southampton 7. 'The Sons' 8. Claret and amber 9. Terry Venables 10. Thames Ironworks FC 11. Brad Friedel 12. Sergio Conceicao 13. The Henri Delaunay Cup 14. Brockwill Park 15. South Africa.

THE FOOTBALL FACT AND QUIZ BOOK

1. Which two clubs won the League Cup while playing in the Third Division?

2. Which club was Bob Lord chairman of ?

3. How many teams play in Malta's Premier League?

4. In Chelsea's squad of 36 players for the 2000/01 season, how many were English?

5. Who did England play in their first match after Euro 2000?

6. What was the result of that match?

7. Where did Celtic play their home games when their ground was being redeveloped?

8. How was the 1968 European Nations Cup semi-final between Italy and the USSR decided?

9. What were West Bromwich called before they added 'Albion'?

10. What is the nickname of Welsh League club Inter CableTel?

11. How many seasons have Leyton Orient played in the top division?

12. Which country does West Ham United's Frederic Kanoute play international football for?

13. Who did Gary Lineker play his last international match against?

14. Which two Fashanus played for Norwich and Wimbledon?

15. What company sponsors Portsmouth's shirts?

1. Queen's Park Rangers and Swindon Town 2. Burnley 3. Ten 4. Thirteen 5. France 6. 1-1 7. Hampden Park 8. On the toss of a coin 9. West Bromwich Strollers 10. 'The Seagulls' 11. One, (1962/63) 12. France 13. Sweden 14. Justin and John 15. Bishops Printers.

THE FOOTBALL FACT AND QUIZ BOOK

1. Who did England play in the first match of the 1998 World Cup?

2. At the beginning of the match, which TV presenter made the comment 'Shouldn't you lot all be at work'?

3. In L.S. Lowry's painting, 'Going to the Match', whose ground is featured?

4. Where was Terry Venables' last appearance as a player for Chelsea?

5. Who was the last goalkeeper to win the European Footballer of the Year?

6. Only played for once, which Spanish club won the Copa Iberoamericana in 1994?

7. Which Italian referee was in charge of the Euro 2000 final?

8. Which London club's chairman is Theo Paphitis?

9. Who replaced Johan Cruyff as manager of Barcelona?

10. Who did Bayern Munich beat in the 1974 European Cup final?

11. Which club are known as the 'Nerazzurri'?

12. Who tried to be owner, chairman and manager of Brentford all at the same time?

13. Where do Forfar Athletic play their home games?

14. How many goals did Cliff Bastin score for Arsenal in 42 league games in 1932/33?

15. Where is the Sir Norman Chester Centre for football research based?

1. Tunisia 2. Des Lynam 3. Bolton Wanderers 4. The Nou Camp 5. Lev Yashin 6. Real Madrid 7. Pierluigi Collina 8. Millwall 9. Bobby Robson 10. Atlético Madrid 11. Internazionale 12. Ron Noades 13. Station Park 14. 33 15. Leicester University.

1. Who won the Charity Shield in 2000?

2. What TV programme did Brian Moore present?

3. How much did Coventry City pay Arsenal for Jay Bothroyd in summer 2000?

4. Who did West Ham United play in the 1923 'White Horse' final?

5. In which Belgian city do Anderlecht play?

6. Which goalkeeper spent 20 seasons with Portsmouth?

7. Who was sent off in the 1998/99 F.A. Cup semi-final replay?

8. What Premier club does Stephane Henchoz play for?

9. Which ground is situated in Braemar Road?

10. Who were the first sponsors of the Premier League?

11. How many goals did Colin Bell score for England?

12. Who won the Dutch League in 1999/00?

13. Which African team are nicknamed 'The Eagles'?

14. Which former Celtic player is now a commentator with Channel 4 on Italian football?

15. Which Manchester Utd defender missed the entire 1999/00 season through injury?

THE FOOTBALL FACT AND QUIZ BOOK

1. Which three clubs did Viv Anderson play in League Cup finals for?
2. Which player's portrait hangs in the Scottish Portrait Gallery?
3. Who was the first Britain to be named World Manager of the Year?
4. Who sold Matt Jansen to Crystal Palace in 1997/98?
5. Where would you see Hearts of Oak play Obuasi Goldfields?
6. Where was West Ham United defender Steve Potts born?
7. What was Ryan Giggs' surname when he played for England Schoolboys?
8. Which player has made the most appearances for Holland?
9. Which German team play at the country's national stadium?
10. At which London club does former Arsenal player Luis Boa Morte now play?

11. Who sponsors Manchester Utd's shirts?
12. Where are Oneida Football club based?
13. Which Scottish team plays at Firhill Stadium?
14. Which Premiership club does Jody Morris play for?
15. Where was Sven Goran Eriksson's first coaching position?

1. Nottingham Forest, Arsenal and Sheffield Wednesday 2. Danny McGrain
3. Terry Venables, 1985 4. Carlisle Utd 5. Ghana 6. USA 7. Wilson 8. Aaron
Winter 9. Bayern Munich 10. Fulham 11. Sharp 12. Boston, USA 13. Hamilton
Academicals 14. Chelsea 15. Swedish Third Division side Degerfors.

THE FOOTBALL FACT AND QUIZ BOOK

1. Who are the Premier League's official statisticans?

2. Who rejoined Everton from Newcastle in August 2000?

3. When did Arsenal first win the 'Double'?

4. What is the nickname of Turkish side Fenerbahce?

5. Why couldn't the Brazilian Edu join Arsenal in summer 2000?

6. Which country would Peter Ndlovu play international football for?

7. Which country did Bruce Grobelaar play for?

8. Which Scottish club are known as 'The Dark Blues'?

9. Which Everton player moved to Espanol in the 1980s?

10. In which country do St. Catherine's Roma Wolves play?

11. Which London club was Attilio Lombardo player-manager of in 1998?

12. Who did Terry Venables impersonate in TV's 'Celebrity Stars in their Eyes'?

13. Which 'non-German' team has won the German League?

14. Which English striker's autobiography is called 'Strikingly Different'?

15. How many players were sent off in the 1998 World Cup finals?

1. Opta 2. Duncan Ferguson 3. 1970/71 4. 'The Canaries' 5. Because of an invalid passport 6. Zimbabwe 7. Zimbabwe 8. Dundee 9. Adrian Heath 10. Canada 11. Crystal Palace 12. Anthony Newley 13. Rapid Vienna, (1941) 14. Gary Lineker 15. 22.

THE FOOTBALL FACT AND QUIZ BOOK

1. Which ex-Chelsea player is manager at Swansea City?

2. Which Premier club does Titus Bramble play for?

3. Where was Brian Clough transferred from Middlesbrough to in 1961?

4. When was Peter Reid appointed manager at Sunderland?

5. Who was Tottenham's record signing before Rebrov?

6. How many goals did Francis Lee score for England?

7. Which former England player has appeared in TV commercials for McDonalds?

8. Where do Touch and Go play league football?

9. Which Leeds Utd player was sold to Juventus in 1957?

10. Which country does Sunderland keeper Thomas Sorenson play internationals for?

11. What was the original name of Uruguayian side, Penarol?

12. Who is Charlton Athletic's captain?

13. Which Scottish club play at Tynecastle Stadium?

14. Which two Midlands clubs have appeared in the most F.A. Cup finals?

15. Who was the only team Alan Shearer didn't score against in Euro '96?

1. Which is the largest ground in the Premier League?
2. When was a third-place play-off match introduced for the two losing F.A. Cup semi-finalists?
3. When was the last time the match was played?
4. How many goals did George Graham score in his Chelsea career?
5. Which Chelsea player has played for Benfica, FC Brugge and Croatia Zagreb?
6. Which company sponsors Preston North End's shirts?
7. Who was the first black referee on the Premier League list?
8. Who were the first Spanish Champions?
9. The Luzhniki Stadium is home to which Moscow club?
10. Who did John Collins join after leaving AS Monaco in 1998?
11. What did Brazil win outright after winning it three times?
12. Who did Arsenal buy for £10.5 million from Juventus in 1999?
13. Which Dutchman did Barcelona sell to Chelsea in August 2000?
14. Which club did Mick Harford make his debut for?
15. Which country won the 2000 African Cup of Nations?

THE FOOTBALL FACT AND QUIZ BOOK

1. For which country does Celestine Babayaro play his football?

2. Which Norwegian plays for Southampton?

3. Which year were numbered shirts first worn in league games?

4. Which Premier club is Peter Risdale the chairman of?

5. How many footballing brothers are there in the Flo family?

6. Where would you see Al Saad play Al Wakra?

7. Whose fans 'only sing when they're fishing'?

8. Which Bulgarian scored in each of his country's games in Euro '96?

9. What is the name of the Norwegian First Division?

10. Which Scottish club plays at Easter Road Stadium?

11. Which African country beat West Germany in the 1982 World Cup?

12. Which English club holds the record for the biggest victory in a European final?

13. In Euro '96, what was the result of Scotland's opening match against Holland?

14. Who sponsors Middlesbrough's shirts?

15. Which Watford player scored two hat-tricks in two days in April 1960?

1. Nigeria 2. Joe Tessen 3. 1939 4. Leeds Utd 5. Five 6. Qatar 7. Grimsby Town 8. Hristo Stoichkov 9. The Tippeliga 10. Hibernian 11. Algeria 12. Spurs (5–1 v Atletico Madrid, 1963) 13. 0–0 14. BT Cellnet 15. Cliff Holton.

THE FOOTBALL FACT AND QUIZ BOOK

1. With which club did Bobby Robson finish his playing career?
2. Who are known as 'The Addicks'?
3. Which is the oldest team in Scotland?
4. Which London club's eighth manager was Harry Redknapp?
5. In the Anglo-Scottish Cup, who were the only Scottish side to make the final?
6. When did Swansea Town become Swansea City?
7. Which Spanish team does keeper Iker Casillas play for?
8. Who did Terry Venables' Australian team lose to in the 1998 World Cup qualifying play-offs?
9. Who is Dave Hill's book 'Out of his Skin' about?
10. What happened to Cameroon's Kana Byik and Massing in their 1990 World Cup match against Argentina?
11. Where were the Pakistani team arrested for playing in shorts in 2000?
12. Who were the only team to win at Ibrox in the 1999/00 season?
13. Which English club is run by a Norwegian business consortium?
14. Who became Britain's most expensive teenager in 1999?
15. Which Edinburgh club play at Tynecastle?

1. Vancouver Royals of Canada 2. Charlton Athletic 3. Queen's Park 4. West Ham United 5. St.Mirren 6. 1970 7. Real Madrid 8. Iran 9. John Barnes 10. They were both sent off 11. Afghanistan 12. Dundee 13. Wimbledon 14. Robbie Keane 15. Heart of Midlothian.

THE FOOTBALL FACT AND QUIZ BOOK

1. Which Liverpool striker was disciplined for wearing a T-shirt supporting sacked Liverpool dockers?

2. Which Israeli side plays in green shirts and green shorts?

3. Which country's supporters won the 1997 FIFA Fair Play award?

4. Which Japanese team did Zico play for?

5. Who was Harry Redknapp's assistant manager at West Ham United?

6. Where was Arsenal's Paulo Vernazza born?

7. Which Nigerian striker plays for Birmingham City?

8. Which two teams play in the Rio 'derby'?

9. Whose catchphrase was 'Do I not like that'?

10. Which club's song is 'Carefree'?

11. What is referee David Elleray's profession?

12. Which Everton centre-half has been caretaker-manager for the club?

13. Whose last match for England was against Germany in the Euro '96 semi-final?

14. For what country does Derby's Branco Strupar play international football?

15. Which Conference side are known as 'The U's'?

1. Robbie Fowler 2. Maccabi Haifa 3. Republic of Ireland 4. Kashima Antlers 5. Frank Lampard Senior 6. London 7. Dele Adebola 8. Fluminense and Flamengo 9. Graham Taylor 10. Chelsea 11. A Housemaster at Harrow 12. Dave Watson 13. David Platt 14. Belgium 15. Sutton Utd.

THE FOOTBALL FACT AND QUIZ BOOK

1. Which popstar has a great affection for Watford?

2. Which three former Everton players have gone on to manage the club?

3. What was the previous name of the Intertoto Cup?

4. Which company sponsors Queen's Park Rangers shirts?

5. Which north-east side are nicknamed 'The Quakers'?

6. Which Scottish club plays at Caledonian Stadium?

7. Who joined Rangers in 1994 for a Scottish record fee?

8. Which African team had most of their players killed in a plane crash in 1993?

9. Which keeper completed his 23rd season at a Nationwide league club in 2000?

10. Which former England international scored twice for Hartlepool in 1998/99?

11. What was the title of the ITV documentary about Graham Taylor called?

12. What is the German equivalent of the F.A. Cup?

13. What did Pat Jennings do before he became a footballer?

14. Where did Ben Thatcher join Spurs from in 2000?

15. When was Peter Taylor appointed manager of Southend?

1. Elton John 2. Colin Harvey, Joe Royle and Howard Kendall 3. The Rappen Cup 4. Ericson 5. Darlington 6. Inverness Caledonian Thistle 7. Duncan Ferguson 8. Zambia 9. Alan Knight 10. Peter Beardsley 11. 'An impossible job' 12. DFB Pokal 13. Milkman 14. Wimbledon 15. December 1993.

THE FOOTBALL FACT AND QUIZ BOOK

1. What was the nickname of Russian goalkeeper Lev Yashin?

2. Who did Tim Sherwood join after winning a Championship medal at Blackburn?

3. What colour shirts do Polish side Legia Warsaw play in?

4. Which Romanian has played at Barcelona and Real Madrid?

5. What is West Ham United's ground called?

6. Who were Brazilian champions in 1999?

7. Which Newcastle Utd player plays for Zaire?

8. Which team won the last East German championship?

9. What number shirt does Sol Campbell wear at Tottenham?

10. What drinks company is advertised on Leeds Utd's shirts?

11. Who was the only English referee at the 1998 World Cup finals?

12. How much did Liverpool pay for Nick Barmby?

13. Which country does keeper Mark Bosnich play for?

14. Which famous Dutch club was formed in 1900?

15. For which Premiership team did Nolberto Salano play during the 2000-01 season?

1. 'The Black Panther' 2. Spurs 3. Green 4. Gheorghe Hagi 5. Boleyn Ground 6. Corinthians 7. Lomana Lua 8. Hansa Rostock 9. Number 5 10. Strongbow 11. Paul Durkin 12. £6 million 13. Australia 14. Ajax 15. Nolberto Solano.

THE FOOTBALL FACT AND QUIZ BOOK

1. Who is England's most capped international?
2. Which country does Liverpool's Vladimir Smicer play for?
3. Which Swedish club did Sven Goran Eriksson play his football at?
4. Which non-league player joined West Ham United for £40,000 for the 2000/01 season?
5. Which Scottish club plays at Rugby Park?
6. Which team are associated with the 'Inter-City Firm' of hooligans?
7. What was the first club that Tommy Docherty managed?
8. Who wrote an anthropological study of football supporters called 'The Soccer Tribe'?
9. Who did Helsingborg knock out of the 2000/01 Champions' League qualifying round?
10. Whose players were auctioned off when the team was expelled from the league in 1919?
11. Which English league team does St. Lucia international Ken Charlery play for?
12. Which West Ham United punk music-lover is nicknamed 'Psycho'?
13. What year did Arsenal win the Premier League?
14. Who sponsors Newcastle United's shirts?
15. Which player was top-scorer in Division One for three successive seasons between 1963 and 1965?

THE FOOTBALL FACT AND QUIZ BOOK

1. Where did Andy Sinton make his league debut?

2. Which country does Tottenham full-back Stephen Carr play for?

3. Who was Liverpool manager before Gerard Houllier?

4. What season did Celtic achieve Scotland's first 'double'?

5. Which club was portrayed in 'The Glory Game' by Hunter Davies?

6. Which country did George Weah play in after leaving Liberia?

7. Which country do Rotor Volvograd play in?

8. Whose fans used to stand in 'The Jungle'?

9. What is the longest-running international football competition?

10. Which Premier team does Norwegian Vegard Heggem play for?

11. What is the nickname of Dundee Utd?

12. Who were the first country to lose two World Cup finals?

13. Which player-manager of Rangers was sent off in his first match in 1986?

14. Which team won Le Tournoi de France in 1997?

15. What cup did a London Select XI contest in 1958?

1. Cambridge Utd 2. Republic of Ireland 3. Roy Evans 4. 1906/07 5. Spurs 6. Nigeria 7. Russia 8. Celtic's 9. The Copa America 10. Liverpool 11. The Terrors' 12. Hungary 13. Graeme Souness 14. England 15. The first Fairs Cup.

THE FOOTBALL FACT AND QUIZ BOOK

1. Which Midlands club finished in the highest position in the Nationwide league in 1999/00?
2. What are Scottish team Livingston also known as?
3. How many clubs play in the Singapore S-League?
4. Who were the opponents in Jackie Charlton's last game in charge of the Republic of Ireland side?
5. Which Derby County striker was stacking sheves at a supermarket before joining the club?
6. Which company sponsors Sheffield United's shirts?
7. How many goals did Andy Cole score against Ipswich in a 1995 League game?
8. Two of which club's directors resigned after making disparaging remarks about the local women?
9. Whose 'World Cup Diary' upset some of the England players in 1998?
10. Which other ground than Wembley also has twin towers?
11. Who joined the Los Angeles Aztecs after leaving Barcelona?
12. Which club used to play at Elm Park?
13. Who was arrested for drink-driving outside Buckingham Palace
14. Which two teams has the Sugar Puffs Honey Monster played for?
15. Which Scottish team plays at the West Lothian Courier Stadium?

1. Birmingham City 2. The Wee Jays' 3. 11 4. Holland 5. Malcolm Christie 6. Midas Games 7. Five 8. Newcastle Utd 9. Glenn Hoddle 10. Feethams (Darlington) 11. Johan Cruyff 12. Reading 13. George Best 14. Newcastle Utd and Manchester Utd 15. Livingston

THE FOOTBALL FACT AND QUIZ BOOK

1. Who was voted Young Player of the Year for 2000?

2. Where do Randers Freja play League football?

3. Which Lverpool player hosts a TV programme on soccer skills?

4. What was introduced to football in 1878 to help control the game?

5. Who was the first foreign player to win the Scottish Footballer of the Year?

6. Which country has the fourth best record in World Cup qualifying games, but has never reached the finals?

7. Which Nationwide team do the Nationwide sponsor?

8. Which four Italian clubs has Sven Goran Eriksson managed?

9. Who did Everton sell to Sunderland for £2.5 million in 2000?

10. What was Tony Adams jailed for in 1990?

11. Which Saint appears in the name of two English club's grounds?

12. Whose autobiography was called 'This One's On Me'?

13. Who took over as 'Match of the Day' presenter after Des Lynam's departure?

14. Which former Welsh player has coached Lebanon?

15. Which country does Middlesbrough's Joseph-Desire Job come from?

1. Harry Kewell 2. Denmark 3. Michael Owen 4. The referee's whistle 5. Brian Laudrup 6. China 7. Swindon Town 8. AS Roma, Fiorentina, Sampdoria and Lazio 9. Don Hutchison 10. Drink driving 11. James 12. Jimmy Greaves 13. Gary Lineker 14. Terry Yorath 15. Cameroon.

THE FOOTBALL FACT AND QUIZ BOOK

1. Who did Louis Van Gaal coach to win the 1995 European Cup?
2. What colour shirts do Uruguayan side Penarol wear?
3. Who has won the most international caps for Wales?
4. Who won the UEFA Cup in 1998?
5. Which Scottish side play their home games at Links Park?
6. What is the name given to groups of fans that organise choreographed displays of loyal support in Italy?
7. Which Yorkshire side used to play their home games at Leeds Road?
8. Who sponsors Southampton's shirts?
9. Who was the first substitute to come on in an F.A. Cup final?
10. Which former Charlton player coached the Faroe Islands in the Euro 2000 qualifiers?
11. Which England opponents substituted all eleven players in June 1990?
12. Where would you see the Black Aces play the Black Rhinos?
13. Which non-South American country played in the 1999 Copa America?
14. In which city do River Plate play?
15. Which three Italian teams has Swedish international Nils Liedholm coached?

1. Ajax 2. Black and yellow 3. Neville Southall 4. Internazionale 5. Montrose 6. Ultras 7. Huddersfield town 8. Friends Provident 9. Dennis Clarke, WBA, 1968 10. Allan Simonsen 11. Malta 12. Zimbabwe 13. Japan 14. Buenos Aires 15. Fiorentina, AS Roma and AC Milan.

THE FOOTBALL FACT AND QUIZ BOOK

1. Which Arsenal player was fined after an argument with a rickshaw driver on a tour of the Far East?

2. What is the Trippeligaen?

3. Where was Chelsea's Eidur Gudjohnsen born?

4. Which non-league team plays at Edgar Street?

5. Who was the first British player to be transferred under the Bosman ruling?

6. When was the only occasion New Zealand appeared in the World Cup finals?

7. Who has played for Liverpool, Hamburg, Southampton and Newcastle Utd?

8. Who is the all-time record goalscorer for Arsenal?

9. What colour shirts do Bolivian side Real Santa Cruz play in?

10. Which two former Bristol City strikers were both at Maine Road during the 2000-01 season, one as a manager, the other as a player?

11. Which side play St. Pauli in their 'derby' match?

12. Who was the first Division Three player in the seventies to be capped by England?

13. Whose fans sit at the Gladwys Street End?

14. Where do Morton play their home games?

15. Which Conference side are known as 'The Poppies'?

THE FOOTBALL FACT AND QUIZ BOOK

1. Which company sponsors Sheffield Wednesday's shirts?
2. In 1981, who scored the winning goal in the 100th F.A. Cup Final?
3. Where was Malcolm MacDonald appointed manager in 1980?
4. Where do Motagua play their football?
5. What country does Everton's Alex Nyarko play for?
6. Which Scottish team does GMTV presenter Lorraine Kelly support?
7. After spending five years in the Conference, which team regained their League status in 1998?
8. Which team did Cyrille Regis play for in an F.A. Cup Final?
9. Which English player received a two-match international ban in 1998?
10. For which country has Soh Chin Aun apparently played 250 internationals for?
11. What was the result of Bill Nicholson's first match as manager of Spurs?
12. Who tried to merge Queen's Park Rangers and Fulham in 1987?
13. Who received a six-month prison sentence in 1979 for running a brothel?
14. In which year did Canada reach the World Cup finals?
15. Which England forward's autobiography was called 'Clown Prince of Soccer'?

1. Chupa Chups 2. Ricky Villa 3. Fulham 4. Honduras 5. Ghana 6. Dundee Utd 7. Halifax Town 8. Coventry City 9. Paul Ince 10. Malaysia 11. Spurs 10 Everton 4 12. Marler Estates 13. Peter Storey 14. 1986 15. Len Shackleton.

THE FOOTBALL FACT AND QUIZ BOOK

1. What is the title of Chris Hulme's story about a prison football team?
2. Who played for Orient, West Bromwich Albion and Real Madrid?
3. How much did Newcastle pay Blackburn Rovers for Alan Shearer in 1996?
4. Who was the first British player to be transferred for £500,000?
5. Who scored seven goals in the first seven Premier matches of the 2000/01 season?
6. What nationality is Manchester Utd's Mikael Silvestre?
7. Who are the only Conference winners since 1986 not to have played League football?
8. Which Peruvian international striker played for Fort Lauderdale Strikers?
9. Where did Spurs sign the Portugese striker, Jose Dominguez from?
10. Which keeper won Championship medals with Blackburn Rovers and Everton?
11. What city do Vasco da Gama play in?
12. Which club used to play home games at Teignmouth Road?
13. Which club had more fans arrested than any other during 1999/00?
14. Which brothers played for Chelsea in the seventies?
15. Who scored a hat-trick for Charlton in the 1998 Division One play-off final?

1. Manslaughter Utd 2. Laurie Cunningham 3. £15m 4. David Mills 5. Michael Owen 6. French 7. Stevenage Borough 8. Teófilo Cubillas 9. Sporting Lisbon 10. Bobby Mimms 11. Rio de Janeiro 12. Torquay Utd 13. Leeds Utd 14. Ray and Graham Wilkins 15. Clive Mendonca.

THE FOOTBALL FACT AND QUIZ BOOK

1. Who did Terry Neill succeed as manager of Northern Ireland in 1971?

2. What colour shirts do River Plate play in?

3. Who sponsors Sunderland's shirts?

4. Who won the French title in 1999/00?

5. Which country does Newcastle's Shay Given play international football for?

6. Where do Motherwell play their home games?

7. What 'first' went to Lord Kinnaird in the 1877 F.A. Cup Final?

8. Whose first-ever penalty defeated Romania in a 1990 World Cup match?

9. Which member of Sunderland's 1973 F.A. Cup-winning team went into politics later?

10. Which club was Julio Iglesias reserve team goalkeeper at?

11. How many goals did John Barnes score for England?

12. Which League club did Mickey Cook set an appearance record for?

13. Which Dutch player was transferred from Real Madrid to Nottingham Forest?

14. Who spent 19 seasons with Celtic between 1978 and 1997?

15. Who is the longest serving club chaplain?

1. Billy Bingham 2. White with red sash 3. Reg Vardy 4. AS Monaco 5. Republic of Ireland 6. Fir Park Stadium 7. The first own-goal in a final 8. David O'Leary 9. Vic Hallom 10. Real Madrid 11. Eleven 12. Colchester Utd 13. Johnny Metgod 14. Pat Bonner 15. Rev. Michael Chantry at Oxford Utd.

THE FOOTBALL FACT AND QUIZ BOOK

1. How many consecutive League games did Phil Neal play for Liverpool from 1974?
2. What year were Football pools coupons first issued?
3. Which country did Terry Mancini play for?
4. How many international caps did Alan Ball win for England?
5. What was Sven Goran Erikson's nickname in Italy?
6. Which Manchester Utd player was known as 'The Black Prince'?
7. Which club did Chris Woods make his League debut with?
8. Which team represented England in the 1960/61 European Cup?
9. What trophy did Bristol City win in 1991?
10. What year was the penalty kick introduced?
11. With which club did Wilf Mannion end his playing career?
12. Which non-league club is Nigel Clough manager of?
13. Who were the first English club to play in the Cup-winners' Cup
14. Where do Partick Thistle play their home games?
15. What item of clothing is John Motson famous for wearing?

1. Which Bristol City manager was voted 1997 Manager of the Month by the League Manager's Association while he was at Barnsley?
2. Which club has not been out of the top division since 1919?
3. Who sponsors Stockport County's shirts?
4. Which club has a fanzine called 'Brian Moore's Head Looks Uncannily Like the London Planetarium'?
5. When did Andy Gray start as a TV presenter for Sky?
6. Who were the first English club to tour South America in 1914?
7. Who is the all-time leading goalscorer for Leeds United?
8. Which park lies between Goodison and Anfield?
9. Which league club's ground has hosted a cricket test match?
10. The Tottenham win over which team inspired Chas and Dave to write 'The Victory Song'?
11. Who is Scotland's most capped player?
12. Which European country was the first to host the World Cup?
13. Which player has played for Montpelier, Everton and Marseille?
14. At which ground did Paul Gascoigne play his last game for Spurs?
15. Which ex-Liverpool striker helped the development of the 'Predator' football boot?

THE FOOTBALL FACT AND QUIZ BOOK

1. Which three teams did the Futcher twins play together at?
2. Where does Sunderland striker Milton Nunez come from?
3. Which Republic of Ireland striker was transferred from Marseille to Nancy?
4. What colours do Nagoya Grampus Eight play in?
5. Which former Derby player became Middlesbrough manager in 1991?
6. When did Portsmouth last win the Championship?
7. How many goals did Mike Channon score for England?
8. Which club are nicknamed 'The Black Cats'?
9. Which manager was sacked following controversial remarks about disabled people?
10. What did Rochdale's Tony Ford receive in 1999?
11. Who did Southampton play in Glenn Hoddle's first game as manager?
12. Who scored the two goals for Vasco da Gama in the World Club Championships against Manchester Utd in January 2000?
13. Where did Spurs sign Dave McEwan from in 1999?
14. Where do Queen of the South play their home games?
15. Which Conference side are known as 'The Cardinals'?

1. Chester, Luton and Manchester City 2. Honduras 3. Tony Cascarino 4. Red 5. Colin Todd 6. 1950 7. 21 8. Sunderland 9. Glenn Hoddle 10. The PFA Merit Award 11. West Ham United 12. Romario 13. Dulwich Hamlet 14. Palmerston Park 15. Woking.

THE FOOTBALL FACT AND QUIZ BOOK

1. How much did Chelsea pay Ajax for Jesper Gronkjaer in 2001?
2. Which London club plays in Middlesex?
3. How many times did George Best play in the World Cup finals for Northern Ireland?
4. Who were the first team to appear in three consecutive Cup-Winners' Cup finals?
5. Whose fans can be heard at the end of Pink Floyd's 'Meddle' album?
6. Who sponsors Tottenham Hotspur's shirts?
7. Which club was Graeme Souness at for three years without playing a league match?
8. Who won the first penalty shoot-out in the F.A. Cup in 1991?
9. Which Scotland captain was banned 'for life' after an incident in a Danish nightclub?
10. What was the last year Newcastle won the F.A. Cup?
11. Which Englishman was coach of Australia during the 1998 World Cup qualifiers?
12. Which two clubs played in the first all-England tie in the European Cup in 1978/79?
13. What country did Stoke's John Mahoney play for?
14. What appeared on the Celtic home shirts in the 1990's?
15. Which player has appeared for CSKA Sofia, Barcelona and Parma?

THE FOOTBALL FACT AND QUIZ BOOK

1. Which European giants refuse to have a sponsorship name on their shirts?
2. Which two recent England strikers have played for both Everton and Liverpool?
3. Which Dutch player plays his football wearing glasses?
4. Which two teams did Sir Matt Busby play for in the 1930s?
5. Which player was, according to his song, 'Head over Heels in Love'?
6. Who did Manchester Utd beat 2-1 in an F.A. Cup semi-final replay in 1999?
7. Which non-league side forced Premier side Charlton Athletic to a replay in the 2000/01 F.A. Cup?
8. What was the nickname of Italian Franco Baresi?
9. What caused England's lowest Wembley crowd, against Chile in 1989?
10. Who started the magazine 'Football Monthly'?
11. Which Manchester Utd manager was sacked for breaking the 'moral code'?
12. Which goalkeeper left England for Brescia in summer 2000?
13. Which Scottish team plays it's home games at Hampden Park?
14. Which former South Korean international coached the team in the 1998 World Cup finals?
15. Who scored the winning goal in the 1999/00 F.A. Cup final?

1. Barcelona 2. Nick Barmby and Peter Beardsley 3. Edgar Davids 4. Manchester City and Liverpool 5. Kevin Keegan 6. Arsenal 7. Dagenham and Redbridge 8. 'The Emperor of Milan' 9. An Underground strike 10. Charles Buchan 11. Tommy Docherty 12. Pavel Srnicek 13. Queen's Park 14. Cha Bum Kun 15. Roberto Di Matteo.

THE FOOTBALL FACT AND QUIZ BOOK

1. From which Italian club did Chelsea sign Gabriele Ambrosetti?
2. Who plays their home games at The Hawthorns
3. Where did West Ham United sign Hayden Foxe from on a free transfer?
4. Who sponsors Tranmere's shirts?
5. How many championships did Dennis Bergkamp win at Ajax?
6. Who became the first black manager of an English club in 1993?
7. Where did Spurs sign keeper Neil Sullivan from in 2000?
8. Which league club did Sean O'Driscoll set a League appearance record at?
9. Who were the first brothers to win European Championship medals?
10. Which two English clubs have a horse on their club badge?
11. Which club did Efan Ekoku make his league debut with?
12. Who did David O'Leary succeed as manager of Leeds Utd?
13. Which manager has had the longest career since the war?
14. Who managed Rotherham, Queen's Park Rangers and Aston Villa in only six weeks?
15. Which team conceded 44 goals in eight qualifying games for Euro 2000?

1. Vicenza 2. West Bromwich Albion 3. Sanfrecce Hiroshima 4. Wirral Borough 5. One 6. Viv Anderson 7. Wimbledon 8. Bournemouth 9. The Koeman brothers 10. Ipswich Town and Gillingham 11. Bournemouth 12. George Graham 13. Brian Clough 14. Tommy Docherty 15. San Marino.

THE FOOTBALL FACT AND QUIZ BOOK

1. When was George Graham appointed manager of Spurs?
2. When was George Graham dismissed as manager of Spurs?
3. When did Maidstone Utd leave the Football League?
4. How much did Fulham pay for Louis Saha in summer 2000?
5. Which player's hairstyle caused chants of 'Pineapple-head'?
6. Who took over from Ron Greenwood as West Ham United manager in 1974?
7. Which Welsh winger played most of his career at Burnley?
8. Who scored England's first goal against Portugal in Euro 2000?
9. Which club does former Stevenage Borough striker Barry Hayles play for?
10. Which country's entire team wore red boots in the 1996 African Cup of Nations?
11. Which club was Craig Brown assistant manager with, from 1972 to 1977?
12. Who broke his neck in the 1956 F.A. Cup final?
13. At which Danish club did the Laudrup brothers begin their career?
14. Which former England international started his playing career at Alvechurch?
15. How did Graeme Souness cause a riot after his Galatasaray won the 1996 Turkish Cup final?

THE FOOTBALL FACT AND QUIZ BOOK

1. Which Argentinian midfielder plays for Middlesbrough?

2. Where do Omonia Nicosia play their football?

3. Which company sponsors Watford's shirts?

4. Which referee was 'grounded' by Paulo di Canio?

5. Where do Raith Rovers play their home games?

6. Who was the Minister of Sport who tried to introduce identity cards for football supporters?

7. Who was sacked as Arsenal manager for making illegal transfer payments?

8. Why did Sunderland have to change their nickname?

9. What were Sunderland's old nicknames?

10. Which airline's plane was damaged by members of the England team in 1996?

11. Which Brighton defender played in a white headband?

12. How many caps has Vinnie Jones won for Wales?

13. Who kept goal for Leeds Utd in the 1972 and 1973 F.A. Cup finals?

14. Which team has represented Northern Ireland the most times in the European Cup?

15. What caused Johnny Haynes to end his England career?

1. Carlos Marinelli 2. Cyprus 3. Phones 4U 4. Paul Alcock 5. Stark's Park 6. Colin Moynihan 7. George Graham 8. Because they moved from Roker Park to a new stadium 9. The Rokermen or The Rokerites 10. Cathay Pacific 11. Steve Foster 12. Nine 13. David Harvey 14. Linfield 15. A car crash.

THE FOOTBALL FACT AND QUIZ BOOK

1. How many games did John Toshack have as manager of Wales in 1994?
2. Who did Leeds Utd beat in the centenary cup final in 1972?
3. Who were the first club to knock Real Madrid out of the European Cup after five straight wins?
4. Who said that 'Italy was like a foreign country', in 1987?
5. Which country did 'Gigi' Riva play for in the sixties and seventies?
6. How many goals did Martin Chivers score for England
7. Where did Pat Nevin make his Scottish league debut?
8. Which Scottish team does singer Rod Stewart support?
9. Who did Steve McManaman make his England debut against in November 1994?
10. Which team did Roy Keane support as a boy?
11. Why did Barcelona revert to it's Catalan name in 1975?
12. Who became the first foreign manager to win the Bundesliga in 1996/97?
13. What colour shirts did Crystal Palace play in before Malcolm Allison changed them?
14. Which German non-league team beat Borussia Dortmund and Schalke 04 in the 1996 German Cup?
15. Who quit as manager of Barnet in March 2001?

1. One 2. Arsenal 3. Barcelona 4. Ian Rush 5. Italy 6. 13 7. Clyde 8. Celtic 9. Nigeria 10. Spurs 11. Because of the death of Franco 12. Giovanni Trapattoni 13. Claret and sky blue 14. Eintracht Trier 15. John Still.

1. Why was Mark Falco of Spurs fined £1500 in 1986?
2. Who was the last amateur to play in an F.A. Cup final?
3. Who finished bottom of the Premiership in 1998/99?
4. Which Scottish team are nicknamed 'The Pars'?
5. Which former Arsenal player went on to coach at Stamford Bridge?
6. Which club did David Seaman make his league debut for?
7. Which winger was killed in a car crash while playing for Real Madrid?
8. Which club did Alan Gilzean play for in the 1960s?
9. Who took over from Ossie Ardiles as manager of Japanese club Shimuzu S-Pulse?
10. What year was the F.A. Cup first sponsored by Littlewoods?
11. Which Tranmere Rovers player has the longest throw-in in Britain?
12. Which two city rivals have grounds on either side of the River Trent?
13. How many goals did Steve Coppell score for England?
14. What was the first club Ron Atkinson managed?
15. Who are the only Welsh club to win the F.A. Cup?

1. For making insulting gestures to Aston Villa supporters 2. Bill Slater, 1951 3. Nottingham Forest 4. Dunfermline Athletic 5. Graham Rix 6. Peterborough Utd 7. Laurie Cunningham 8. Spurs 9. Steve Perryman 10. 1995 11. Dave Challinor 12. Nottingham Forest and Notts County 13. 7 14. Cambridge Utd 15. Cardiff.

THE FOOTBALL FACT AND QUIZ BOOK

1. Which England player's portrait hangs in the National Portrait Gallery?
2. Who is West Ham United's most capped player?
3. Which Manchester Utd captain allegedly assaulted two women in a nightclub?
4. Which team did Nigel Winterburn leave Arsenal to join in summer 2000?
5. Who scored in all six of Brazil's games at the 1970 World Cup?
6. Who did Brian Clough spend 44 days as manager of in 1974?
7. Which Scottish club did George Best play for?
8. What is manager Jim Smith's nickname?
9. Who played his only England game against Malta in 1971?
10. Which country does Arsenal's Fredrik Ljungberg play for?
11. Where did Arsenal's Lee Dixon begin his career?
12. What top German club do Boris Becker and Steffi Graf support?
13. Which club did Rebrov score his first goal for Spurs against?
14. Who was Nigeria's top-scorer in the 1994 World Cup?
15. Which ex-England international started his career with Greenwich Borough?

1. Bobby Charlton 2. Bobby Moore 3. Roy Keane 4. West Ham United 5. Jairzinho 6. Leeds Utd 7. Hibernian 8. 'The Bald Eagle' 9. Colin Harvey 10. Sweden 11. Burnley 12. Bayern Munich 13. Everton 14. Daniel Amokachi 15. Ian Wright.

1. Which two Italian clubs are based in Torino?
2. What name is given to attacking full-backs in a five-man midfield?
3. Which two midlands club were relegated from the Nationwide Division One in 2000?
4. Who was Cameroon coach in the 2000 African Cup of Nations?
5. Which company sponsors West Bromwich Albion's shirts?
6. Where do Rangers play their home games?
7. Which club did brothers Jimmy and John Conway play together at in the 1970s?
8. Which England player has played in London, Manchester, Milan and Liverpool derbies?
9. Who dyes his hair green when playing for Nigeria?
10. Which Scottish club did Hansen and Johnston play for?
11. Who was the first person to miss a penalty in an F.A. Cup final?
12. Which Everton midfielder has won over 35 caps playing for Wales?
13. Which club did Guy Whittingham make his league debut for?
14. Who were the first Greek team to reach the European Cup final?
15. Which footballing figure started the 'Forza Italia' Party?

1. Torino and Juventus 2. Wing-backs 3. Port Vale and Walsall 4. Pierre Lechantre 5. West Bromwich Building Society 6. Ibrox 7. Fulham 8. Paul Ince 9. Taribo West 10. Partick Thistle 11. John Aldridge 12. Mark Pembridge 13. Portsmouth 14. Panathinaikos 15. Silvio Berlusconi.

THE FOOTBALL FACT AND QUIZ BOOK

1. Where does Belgium's Cedric Roussel play his football?
2. Which team does Formula One racing driver Johnny Herbert support?
3. Which non-league team was famous for its sloping pitch?
4. Which Norwegian international joined Munich 1860 in summer 2000?
5. Which Italian did Aston Villa transfer to Bradford City in 2000?
6. Which striker did Chelsea lose £4 million on when transferring him a year later?
7. What is the name of the restaurant in Leeds, run by Lee Chapman and his wife, Leslie Ash?
8. What is the nickname of East Fife?
9. Where do NK Osijek play their football?
10. Which Queen's Park Ranger's player of the seventies reportedly lost £500,000 on gambling?
11. Which West Ham United defender used to sport a skinhead cut?
12. Which Scottish team were formerly known as Ferranti Thistle?
13. Which club was once known as Abbey Utd?
14. Who moved to Bristol City from Leeds Utd in October 1976?
15. Which Japanese club did Ossie Ardiles manage in 1996?

1. Coventry City 2. West Ham United 3. Yeovil 4. Erik Mykland 5. Benito Carbone 6. Chris Sutton 7. Teatro 8. The Fifers 9. Croatia 10. Stan Bowles 11. Julian Dicks 12. Meadowbank Thistle 13. Cambridge Utd 14. Norman Hunter 15. Shimizu S-Pulse.

1. Which club did Graham Taylor win promotion from Division Four with in 1975/76?
2. Where do Ross County play their home games?
3. How many clubs has David Platt played for in his career?
4. Who were the first team to defeat Manchester Utd at Old Trafford in a European Cup tie?
5. Which manager was the subject of the BBC programme 'Premier Passions'?
6. Which assistant manager was imprisoned for having underage sex in 1999?
7. Who did Sheffield Utd sell Tony Currie to in 1976?
8. What international side do Wynalda, Dooley and Lalas play for?
9. Who took over as Celtic's manager in summer 2000?
10. Which Italian striker was transferred to Spain and back to Italy in deals amounting to over £50 million?
11. Which Nationwide team does Belgian international Gilles de Bilde play for?
12. Whose tackle ended Chelsea defender Paul Elliott's professional career?
13. Which Argentine did David Beckham kick when sent off in the 1998 World Cup?
14. Which Chelsea player allegedly assaulted a shopper in a supermarket?
15. Which Irish captain started his career at Welling and then

THE FOOTBALL FACT AND QUIZ BOOK

1. Which former footballer presented 'Friday Night's All Wright'?
2. How many times have Everton won the League Cup?
3. Who was Graham Taylor's successor at Watford in 1984?
4. Who scored the last minute goal for Italy that put Nigeria out of the 1994 World Cup?
5. Who did Mike Gatting's brother Steve play for in an F.A. Cup final?
6. In which league do Russian teams Spartak Moscow and Rostov play?
7. Which famous match did Gottfried Dienst referee?
8. Which Leeds Utd player scoored a hat-trick in his second game for the club in 1999?
9. Who won the F.A. Cup only 11 years after joining the Football League?
10. Which former Italian champions went into liquidation in 1993?
11. From which Dutch club did Manchester Utd sign Japp Stam?
12. Where did Derby manager Jim Smith begin his managerial career?
13. Who is the youngest player to have scored 100 goals?
14. Who were the first team to be automatically relegated from the league?
15. Who did Brazil beat in a penalty shoot-out in the 1994 World Cup Final?

1. Ian Wright 2. Never 3. Dave Bassett 4. Roberto Baggio 5. Brighton 6. The Vischaya 7. The 1966 World Cup Final 8. Michael Bridges 9. Wimbledon 10. Casale 11. PSV Eindhoven 12. Colchester 13. Jimmy Greaves 14. Lincoln City 15. Italy.

1. Which company sponsors Wimbledon's shirts?
2. Who wrecked the referee's changing-room after being sent off?
3. Which English 'Troublemaker' started his career with Stafford Rangers?
4. Who beat Liverpool 2-0 in 1988/89 to win the First Division title?
5. At which two south coast teams did John Gregory start his managerial career?
6. What was the name of the report that led to all-seater stadiums?
7. Which ground was built specifically for the 1998 World Cup?
8. Who scored Germany's winner from the penalty spot in the 1990 World Cup final?
9. How many Argentinians were sent off in that final?
10. How many points did Japan get in the 1998 World Cup finals?
11. Who was youth coach at Strasbourg in 1981?
12. How many times have West Ham United won the F.A. Cup?
13. Which team does comedian Frank Skinner support?
14. How many appearances did Bobby Charlton make for Manchester Utd?
15. Which manager was not happy when he was compared to Margaret Thatcher?

1. Tiny 2. Ian Wright 3. Stan Collymore 4. Arsenal 5. Portsmouth and Plymouth 6. Justice Taylor Report 7. Stade de France 8. Andreas Brehme 9. Two 10. None 11. Arsene Wenger 12. Three 13. West Bromwich Albion 14. 754 15. Alex Ferguson.

THE FOOTBALL FACT AND QUIZ BOOK

1. What did Uri Geller say were on Swansea City's pitch, which accounted for their poor league form?
2. When was the footballers' maximum wage law abolished?
3. What was Manchester City's original name?
4. Who is the only African to win the World Footballer of the Year award?
5. Where do Olimpik Tirane play their football?
6. What year was Trevor Francis appointed manager of Birmingham City?
7. Whose failure to get Wales into the 1994 World Cup cost him his job?
8. How many substitutes could be named for a Premiership match in 2000/01?
9. How many substitutes could be used in a Premiership match in 2000/01?
10. When was the last time Northern Ireland won the Home International Championship?
11. What does Scotland manager Craig Brown's brother Jock Brown do?
12. Who was the first footballer to move between British clubs for £20,000?
13. How old was Manchester Utd's Duncan Edwards when he died in the Munich air crash?
14. Who coached Brazil in the 1982 and 1986 World Cup finals?
15. Who has played for Crystal Palace, Queen's Park Rangers, Tottenham and Chelsea?

1. 'Black spirits' 2. January 1960 3. Ardwick FC 4. George Weah 5. Albania 6. 1996 7. Terry Yorath 8. Five 9. Three 10. 1984 11. Football commentator 12. Tommy Lawton 13. 21 14. Tele Santana 15. Terry Venables.

THE FOOTBALL FACT AND QUIZ BOOK

1. Where do St. Johnstone play their home games?
2. Which club is supported by politicians Michael Foot and David Owen?
3. From which club did Arsenal sign Dennis Bergkamp in 1995?
4. Who is the smallest striker to have played for England?
5. What colour shirts do Brazilian club Palmeiras wear?
6. Which team has scored the least amount of goals in a Premier League season?
7. Which international side did Steve Lomas captain during the 2002 World Cup qualifiers?
8. Who was Argentina's manager at the 1998 World Cup?
9. Which Brazilian's name means 'Little Man' in Portugese?
10. How many penalties does each side take before 'sudden death'?
11. When did Dennis Wise make his England debut?
12. Who sold his controlling stake in Tottenham in February 2001?
13. Which player went on strike at Nottingham Forest?
14. Which club has lost all of its last five appearances in the European Cup final?
15. Who was the youngest player in England's Euro 2000 squad?

1. McDiarmid Park 2. Plymouth Argyle 3. Inter Milan 4. Tottenham's Fanny Walden, 5ft 2ins 5. Green and white stripes 6. Leeds Utd, 28 goals, 1996/97 7. Northern Ireland 8. Daniel Passarella 9. Juninho 10. Five 11. 1991 12. Alan Sugar 13. Pierre van Hooijdonk 14. Benfica 15. Gareth Barry.

THE FOOTBALL FACT AND QUIZ BOOK

1. Who was the first woman to referee a professional league match?
2. Who is known as 'The Guv'nor'?
3. Where do Oriente Petrolero play their football?
4. What was the first European final to be settled on penalties?
5. Who won that match?
6. Whose autobiography was called 'The Good, the Bad and the Bubbly'?
7. Which former manager was allegedly involved in brown-paper-bag bungs?
8. Who is Life Vice-President at Chelsea?
9. Which referee sent off the first player in an F.A. Cup final?
10. How old was Michael Owen when he scored his first goal for England?
11. Who were the two teams in the 1960 European Cup final that finished 7-3?
12. Which Italian club is known as the 'Blucerchiati' (the 'blue-and-hoops')?
13. Which team does comedian Vic Reeves support?
14. Which two brothers scored their 200th league goal on the same day in the 1950s?
15. When did Brian Clough retire as a football manager?

1. Wendy Toms 2. Paul Ince 3. Bolivia 4. 1980 European Cup-winners' Cup 5. Valencia beat Arsenal 6. George Best 7. Brian Clough 8. Lord Attenborough 9. Peter Willis 10. 18 11. Real Madrid beat Eintracht Frankfurt 12. Sampdoria 13. Darlington 14. Arthur and Jack Rowley 15. 1993.

THE FOOTBALL FACT AND QUIZ BOOK

1. Which two teams contested the 2000 F.A. Cup final?

2. Which rock star brothers are passionate Manchester City fans?

3. What is the nickname of East Stirling?

4. What TV programme does James Richardson present?

5. Which company sponsors Wolverhampton Wanderer's shirts?

6. Which Arsenal player scored his first goal for the club in September 2000, aged 19?

7. Which is the most north-westerly team in the football league?

8. When were substitutes first introduced into English league football?

9. What was the first rule for substituting players?

10. Who was the first substitute in English football?

11. Who is the Republic of Ireland's record goalscorer?

12. Which Scotland manager died at the stadium shortly after seeing his team play Wales in 1985?

13. What was the score in the 1961 England v Scotland match?

14. Who has made the most appearances for Manchester City?

15. Why didn't Samassi Abou's transfer from West Ham United to Bradford City take place in 1998?

1. Chelsea and Aston Villa 2. Noel and Liam Gallagher 3. The Shire' 4. Football Italia 5. Goodyear 6. Ashley Cole 7. Carlisle Utd 8. 1965 9. They could only be substituted if the player going off the pitch was injured 10. Charlton's Keith Peacock 11. Frank Stapleton 12. Jock Stein 13. England won 9-3 14. Alan Oakes 15. Because he was diagnosed as having malaria.

THE FOOTBALL FACT AND QUIZ BOOK

1. In March 2001, which stadium hosted the first competitive English international game not to be played at Wembley for 39 years?

2. Who were the teams involved?

3. What was the score?

4. Who scored England's first goal?

5. Who scored England's second goal?

6. Who were the Champions of Division One in 1999/00?

7. Who did Newcastle beat 6-1 in a 1999 F.A. Cup replay?

8. When did Barrow lose their place in the Football League?

9. Which 6ft 8in Czech striker played for Anderlecht in the 2000/01 season?

10. Who did Manchester Utd beat in the semi-final to reach the 1968 European Cup final?

11. Which manager gave George Best his international debut?

12. Who took over from Lawrie McMenemy as manager of Northern Ireland in 2000?

13. Where was the original Spion Kop?

14. Who was Scotland's Young Player of the Year for 2000?

15. Which team did Sweden beat, which ensured England qualified for the Euro 2000 play-offs?

THE FOOTBALL FACT AND QUIZ BOOK

1. At 6ft 5in, who was the tallest striker in the Premier League in the 2000/01 season?
2. Which team does quiz host Nick Hancock support?
3. Which Bayern Munich player cost the world record fee for a 17-year old?
4. Which English player was runner-up for the 1998 World Footballer of the Year award?
5. Where do St. Mirren play their home games?
6. What is the nickname of Welsh league club Rhayader Town?
7. Who was the shortest striker in the Premiership in the 2000/01 season?
8. Who promised that Rangers would sign Catholics?
9. Who is former Everton and Norwich manager Mike Walker's goalkeeper son?
10. Which player had the shortest time on the pitch during Euro 2000?
11. In which year did Northern Ireland last beat the Republic of Ireland?
12. Who did Michael Owen make his league debut against?
13. How many caps did Glenn Hoddle win for England?
14. Who scored the winner for Scotland against Latvia in a World Cup qualifier in September 2000?
15. Where was Everton manager Walter Smith's first managerial position?

1. Arsenal's Kanu 2. Stoke City 3. Roque Santa Cruz 4. Michael Owen 5. St. Mirren Park 6. 'Thin Red Line' 7. Paul Dickov, (5ft 5in) 8. Graeme Souness 9. Ian Walker 10. Majeta Kezman of Yugoslavia, who came on as a substitute after 87 minutes, and was sent off 44 seconds later 11. 1999 12. Wimbledon 13. 53 14. Neil McCann 15. Rangers.

THE FOOTBALL FACT AND QUIZ BOOK

1. Which Scottish side are known as 'The Bairns'?

2. In which national league do Wankie play?

3. Which Tottenham goalkeeper is called 'Eric the Viking'?

4. Who does ex-Manchester Utd player Gary Pallister play his football with?

5. Who won the 1974 BBC 'Goal of the Season' with a 25-yard volley?

6. Who took Workington's place in the league in 1977?

7. When did England first lose to European opponents?

8. When did England first lose to European opponents at Wembley?

9. What is the Republic of Ireland's record victory?

10. What is the retirement age for referees in the Premier and Nationwide leagues?

11. When was the English Football Writers' Footballer of the Year title first awarded?

12. Which club does Finnish international goalkeeper Tuevo Moilanen play for?

13. Who was the first paid director in football in 1981?

14. Who did Teddy Sheringham replace when coming on as substitute in the 1999 Champions' League final?

15. Which Macclesfield Town player won an England cap in 1985?

1. Falkirk 2. Tanzania 3. Neil Sullivan 4. Middlesbrough 5. Alan Mullery 6. Wimbledon 7. 1929 8. 1953 9. 8-0 v Malta, 1983 10. 43 11. 1948 12. Preston North End 13. Malcolm MacDonald 14. Jesper Blomquist 15. Peter Davenport.

THE FOOTBALL FACT AND QUIZ BOOK

1. Which Englishman won the Scottish Footballer of the Year award in 1996?
2. Who was the oldest defender in Everton's 2000/01 squad?
3. Where would you be if you were watching Pamir Dushanbe play football?
4. Which English pop group are named after a French team?
5. Which team's supporters are credited with taking the first inflatables to matches in the 90s?
6. Which England player conceded the last-minute penalty against Romania in Euro 2000?
7. Who was fined £45,000 for spitting at Neil Ruddock?
8. Where did England play their first match of Euro 2000?
9. How tall was midfield dynamo Billy Bremner?
10. Which two top British club managers began their career at Wycombe Wanderers?
11. What did Cyril Knowles' brother become after leaving football?
12. Whose two goals against Malta sent the Republic of Ireland to the World Cup finals for the first time?
13. Who scored the winning goal when West Bromwich Albion won the F.A. Cup in 1968?
14. How many goals did Chris Sutton score in his one season at Chelsea?
15. Which former international became player-manager of Plymouth in 1992?

THE FOOTBALL FACT AND QUIZ BOOK

1. Who is the only person to have played for and managed both Bristol City and Bristol Rovers?
2. Which Chelsea board member died in a helicopter crash?
3. Which team does top chef Gary Rhodes support?
4. What was the first trophy Dennis Wise won as Chelsea captain?
5. Who was the first Republic of Ireland player to be sent off in an international?
6. Which African team are known as 'The Indomitable Lions'?
7. Where do San Lorenzo de Almagro play their football?
8. Which Rangers, West Bromwich Albion and Scotland player was sent off 21 times in his career?
9. Which club transferred Matthew Upson to Arsenal?
10. What did referee Rob Harris allow Tranmere to do in 1999, causing a cup match to be replayed?
11. Which Leeds United goalkeeper played in every Premier match in 1999/00?
12. Which Tottenham goalkeeper played in every Premier match in 1999/00?
13. What year was Jack Charlton appointed Republic of Ireland manager?
14. Which German player appeared in both the 1987 and 1999 European Cup finals?
15. Which Conference side are known as 'The Pitmen'?

THE FOOTBALL FACT AND QUIZ BOOK

1. Where do Stenhousemuir play their home games?
2. Who was appointed assistant manager at Bradford City in summer 2000?
3. Who resigned as Spurs manager after allegations of kerb-crawling?
4. What is the nickname of Paul Heath?
5. Which club does Icelandic defender Gudni Bergsson play for?
6. What other two sports does Michael Owen list as his hobbies?
7. Which two clubs originally shared Prenton Park?
8. Which country won the 1976 European Championship in a penalty shoot-out, Antonin Panenka scoring the winner?
9. What was the last trophy Kenny Dalglish won as manger of Liverpool?
10. On what condition did Wanderers hand back the F.A. Cup in 1878?
11. Why was the Brighton v York game abandoned in 1996?
12. In 1994, which Italian club was accused of obtaining prostitutes for match officials?
13. Which Welshman won the European Golden Boot award in 1984?
14. Of which Scottish club is David Murray the chairman?
15. What was Czech Karel Poborsky's nickname when he was at Manchester Utd?

THE FOOTBALL FACT AND QUIZ BOOK

1. Who retired from English international football in Euro 2000 after losing to Romania?

2. What did Ray Wilkins become the first England player to do?

3. How many times have Scotland reached the second round of an international tournament?

4. Which Swindon manager was fined £7,500 for betting on his own team's F.A. Cup match with Newcastle in 1990?

5. What did the Sherpa Van Trophy become in 1990?

6. What was Dennis Wise's nickname for Ruud Gullit?

7. Who were the first side from the First Division to lose an F.A. Cup tie on penalties?

8. What are the words that appear on the Liverpool club badge?

9. Which brothers temporarily saved Wolves from going bust in 1982?

10. How many games did Manchester Utd lose in the Premier Division during the 1999/00 season?

11. In 1997, which referee did Emmanuel Petit push to receive a suspension?

12. Which player was nicknamed 'The Gentle Giant'?

13. What is the nickname of Scottish side Peterhead?

14. Where do Rayos Del Nacaxa play their football?

15. Which Luton Town chairman found an unlit petrol bomb outside his house?

1. Alan Shearer 2. To get sent off in the World Cup finals 3. Never 4. Lou Macari 5. The Leyland Daf Trophy 6. 'The Yeti' 7. Manchester Utd in 1992 8. 'You'll never walk alone' 9. Bhatti Brothers 10. Three 11. Paul Durkin 12. John Charles 13. 'Blue Toon' 14. Mexico 15. David Kohler.

THE FOOTBALL FACT AND QUIZ BOOK

1. How many Bristol Rovers players were sent off in the league match with Wigan in December 1997?
2. How many League titles did Kenny Dalglish win as manager of Liverpool?
3. Which Italian club are nicknamed 'I Lupi' (The Wolves)?
4. Who scored a 'golden goal' penalty in the Euro 2000 semi-final between France and Portugal?
5. Who was the Argentinian sent off against England in 1966?
6. At which club would you hear 'Blue Moon' coming from the terraces?
7. Where do Ipswich Wanderers play?
8. Who won the European Player of the Year in 1966?
9. Which Brazilian plays at full-back for Arsenal?
10. Which Dutch team have a large red stripe on their shirts?
11. Who scored the winner for Liverpool in the 1978 European Cup final?
12. Which Premier club has Martin Edwards as chairman?
13. Which former player was nicknamed 'Chippy' after his love of chips?
14. Who was the first black player to play for the Republic of Ireland?
15. Who bought a 51% share in Portsmouth in 1996?

1. Four 2. Three 3. AS Roma 4. Zinedine Zidane 5. Antonio Rattin 6. Manchester City 7. Jewson Eastern Counties League 8. Bobby Charlton 9. Silvinho 10. Ajax 11. Kenny Dalglish 12. Manchester Utd 13. Liam Brady 14. Chris Hughton 15. Terry Venables.

THE FOOTBALL FACT AND QUIZ BOOK

1. Which year did Arsenal win the F.A. Cup and the Coca-Cola Cup?

2. Which Scottish side are known as 'The Accies'?

3. What league do Bray Wanderers play in?

4. Which goalkeeper was fined after giving a Nazi salute at White Hart Lane?

5. Which Manchester Utd player's nickname was 'Sparky'?

6. Who was sent off for the first time in 1993, in his 671st League game?

7. Which club has won the F.A. Cup the most times?

8. Which Latvian player appears for Southampton?

9. Who was France's manager at the 1998 World Cup?

10. At which ground would you find the Clock End?

11. Who was the Republic of Ireland's first player-manager, in 1973?

12. Which much-travelled striker's son made his international debut in goal in 1999?

13. Who was the first manager Dennis Wise played for?

14. Where do Stranraer play their home games?

15. When did Alan Mullery become the first player to be sent off while playing for England?

THE FOOTBALL FACT AND QUIZ BOOK

1. Which midlands club does recording star Robbie Williams support?

2. Which Tottenham player's nickname is 'Sicknote'?

3. Which West Ham United player is captain of England's U-21 team?

4. Who was the last team from the capital to win the Premier League?

5. Which England manager played at full-back for Tottenham?

6. Which Scottish club is nicknamed 'Jambo's'?

7. Which football family are Martin, Bradley, Les, Paul and Clive from?

8. Where do the Kaiser Chiefs play?

9. Which Aston Villa player scored at Coventry after only 13 seconds in September 1995?

10. Which two Dutch teams play in Rotterdam?

11. What is Swansea city's home ground called?

12. Which England player scored 44 goals in 57 appearances in the sixties?

13. What is the nickname of the Mozambique national side?

14. Which former Chelsea player was captain of France in the 1998 World Cup and Euro 2000?

15. Which three Rangers players were sent off against Celtic in an 'Old Firm' match in 1991?

1. Port Vale 2. Darren Anderton 3. Frank Lampard 4. Arsenal 5. Sir Alf Ramsay 6. Heart of Midlothian 7. The Allens 8. South Africa 9. Dwight Yorke 10. Sparta and Feyenoord 11. The Vetch field 12. Jimmy Greaves 13. 'The Mambas' 14. Didier Deschamps 15. Mark Walters, Terry Hurlock and Mark Hateley.

THE FOOTBALL FACT AND QUIZ BOOK

1. Who were the losing finalists in the 1998 and 1999 F.A. Cup?

2. How much did Aston Villa pay Fenerbahce for Alpay Ozalan in summer 2000?

3. Who is the chairman of Bradford City?

4. Which new Charlton signing has played for Lyngby and Naestued?

5. Which Scottish side plays at Borough Briggs?

6. Who was the manager of Ipswich Town's 1962 Championship winning side?

7. In autumn 1999, what did Galatasaray become the first Turkish side to do?

8. Which Spurs player was killed after being struck by lightning in 1964?

9. Who did Celtic beat when they won the European Cup in 1967?

10. Who is pop star Louise married to?

11. In the Euro '96 group matches, who did England beat 4-1?

12. Which Liverpool manager retired in 1974?

13. Which country does Jimmy Floyd Hasselbaink play for?

14. Who is England's youngest-ever goal scorer?

15. Which ex-sausage stuffer has played for Newcastle Utd, Spurs, Marseilles and Sheffield Wednesday?

1. Newcastle Utd 2. £5.6 million 3. Geoffrey Richmond 4. Claus Jensen 5. Elgin City 6. Alf Ramsay 7. To be floated on the Stock Exchange 8. John White 9. Internazionale 10. Jamie Redknapp 11. Holland 12. Bill Shankly 13. Holland 14. Michael Owen 15. Chris Waddle.

THE FOOTBALL FACT AND QUIZ BOOK

1. Who was sent off in the 2000 Worthington Cup Final?

2. Which country does Ole Gunnar Solskjaer play for?

3. How many teams are in the English Premier League?

4. How many times did former England manager Graham Taylor play for England?

5. Which Russian club were founded as Kor in 1923?

6. Which London club plays in E10?

7. Where would you see the series 'Dream Team'?

8. Which side has been managed by Brian Little, Martin O'Neill and Peter Taylor?

9. Who plays international matches at Windsor Park?

10. Who recorded 'Diamond Lights' in 1987?

11. Which Middlesbrough player has appeared for Sampdoria, Nantes and Real Madrid?

12. Which two London clubs are nicknamed 'The Bees'?

13. What is the nickname of Morocco?

14. Who beat Leeds Utd in the 1973 F.A. Cup final?

15. Whose nickname is the 'Baby-Faced Assassin'?

1. Clint Hill 2. Norway 3. Twenty 4. None 5. Lokomotiv Moscow 6. Leyton Orient 7. Sky TV 8. Leicester City 9. Northern Ireland 10. Glenn Hoddle and Chris Waddle 11. Christian Karembeu 12. Brentford and Barnet 13. The Atlas Lions' 14. Sunderland 15. Ole Gunnar Solskjaer.

THE FOOTBALL FACT AND QUIZ BOOK

1. What is the nickname of Clydebank?
2. Which country does Tottenham's Sergei Rebrov play for?
3. Which comedy programme does made-up Premier striker Julio Geordie appear on?
4. Who has scored the quickest goal in an F.A. Cup final?
5. Who won the Scottish 'treble' in 1969?
6. What is David Beckham's middle name?
7. Which Premier striker was sent off in the first two games of the 2000/01 season?
8. Who scored England's second goal at the Euro 2000 championships?
9. What was the original name of German league club Magdeburg?
10. Which country does Chelsea's Gustavo Poyet play for?
11. Who scored Arsenal's goals in the 1998 F.A. Cup final?
12. Where does a team called Robin Hood play league football?
13. What food have Stuart Pearce, Chris Waddle and Gareth Southgate all advertised?
14. Which London club's stadium is in Bermondsey?
15. Who are the only team to have conceded 100 goals in

THE FOOTBALL FACT AND QUIZ BOOK

1. Which Scottish club are nicknamed 'The Gable Enders'?
2. Which team won the Women's F.A. Cup in 2000?
3. Which African country are known as 'The Crocodiles'?
4. Which Aston Villa defender has played for Besiktas and Altay?
5. With which club did Brian Clough start his professional playing career?
6. Which former Tottenham player presents sports news and current affairs articles for the BBC?
7. Who is Arsenal's most capped player?
8. What is the name of Leicester City's American goalkeeper?
9. Which Everton manager won five titles with Rangers?
10. Who are the only Turkish side to have won a major European trophy?
11. Who won the Inter-Toto Cup in 1999?
12. Who appeared as Sacha Distel in a 1999 edition of 'Celebrity Stars in their Eyes'?
13. Which Argentinian played for Internazionale and Fiorentina?
14. Who are known as 'Bafana, Bafana' (The Boys, The Boys)?
15. Who did Bobby Moore make his last England appearance at Wembley against in November 1993?

1. Montrose 2. Arsenal 3. Lesotho 4. Alpay Ozalan 5. Middlesbrough 6. Garth Crooks 7. Kenny Sansom 8. Kasey Keller 9. Walter Smith 10. Galatasaray 11. West Ham United 12. David Ginola 13. Daniel Passarella 14. The South African national team 15. Italy.

THE FOOTBALL FACT AND QUIZ BOOK

1. Which Spanish club play at 'La Catedral' (The Cathedral)?

2. When was the first F.A. Cup final?

3. Which country do Coventry players Hadji and Chippo play for?

4. Who was Britain's first million pound footballer?

5. Who was the world's first million pound footballer?

6. Which two Scottish teams play in Edinburgh?

7. Which London club plays in SE16?

8. Where do Vasco Volcanoes play their home games?

9. Which London club did Bill Nicholson manage in 1961?

10. Whose training injury stopped a transfer to Old Trafford in 2000?

11. What year was the BBC's 'Match of the Day' first broadcast?

12. What essential protection was invented in 1874 by England forward Sam Weller Widdowson?

13. Which Michelin-starred chef once played football for Rangers?

14. What country does Liverpool's Patrick Berger play for?

15. Which Scottish club are known as 'The Doonhamers'?

1. Athletic Bilbao 2. 1872 3. Morocco 4. Trevor Francis 5. Johan Cruyff 6. Heart of Midlothian and Hibernian 7. Millwall 8. Bermuda 9. Spurs 10. Ruud van Nistelrooy 11. 1964 12. Shinguards 13. Gordon Ramsey 14. The Czech Republic 15. Queen of the South.

THE FOOTBALL FACT AND QUIZ BOOK

1. When was the first FA Cup final to go into extra time?

2. Which is Spain's oldest club?

3. What colour shirts do Kilmarnock play in?

4. Which Rovers finished bottom of Division One in 1992/93?

5. Which goalkeeper played for different clubs in all four divisions in 1986/87?

6. Who was booked after only 3 seconds of a match against Sheffield Utd in 1992?

7. When did the first floodlit matches take place?

8. How long was Andoni Goicoechea banned for after breaking Maradona's ankle?

9. Who were the two joint top-scorers in the First Division in 1984/85?

10. Which Bulgarian goalkeeper was renowned for wearing a toupee?

11. Who was the first black player to play for Rangers?

12. Which tiny football country beat Austria 1-0 in 1990?

13. What was the name of the media group that took over Leeds Utd in 1996?

14. Who was the first goalkeeper to save a penalty in an F.A. Cup final at Wembley?

15. Who succeeded Gerard Houllier as French coach in 1993?

1. Royal Engineers v Old Etonians, 1875 2. Athletic Bilbao 3. Blue and white stripes 4. Bristol Rovers 5. Eric Nixon 6. Vinnie Jones 7. 1878 8. 21 games 9. Gary Lineker and Kerry Dixon 10. Boris Mikhailov 11. Mark Walters 12. Faroe Islands 13. Caspian 14. Dave Beasant 15. Aime Jacquet.

THE FOOTBALL FACT AND QUIZ BOOK

1. Which two teams contested the first pay-for-view match in February 1999?
2. Which midlands club has won the First, Second, Third and Fourth Division Championships?
3. Who won the first Football League title in 1888/89?
4. Who scored a hat-trick after betting on his own team to beat Barnsley in 2000?
5. Why did the Italian Serie A not start until October 1 in 2000?
6. Which club has Gordon McQueen as first-team coach?
7. Which Scottish city has two teams whose grounds are 100 yards from each other?
8. Who did Leeds Utd beat in the 2000/01 Champions' League quarter-finals?
9. Which player scored the first goal of the 1998 World Cup finals in France?
10. Where does the Norwegian football season start and finish?
11. Who has played for Sampdoria, Juventus, Chelsea and Italy?
12. Who is the oldest player to have played in the Premiership?
13. Which British ground held a world record crowd of 149,547 for an international in 1937?
14. Which Italian full-back was sent-off in a Euro 2000 semi-final?
15. Which two teams play in Falkirk?

1. Oxford Utd and Sunderland 2. Wolverhampton Wanderers 3. Preston North End 4. Steve Claridge 5. Because several players were at the Olympic Games 6. Middlesbrough 7. Dundee 8. Deportivo La Coruna 9. Cesar Sampaio (Brazil) 10. April to November 11. Gianluca Vialli 12. John Burridge 13. Hampden Park 14. Gianluca Zambrotta 15. Falkirk and East Stirling.

THE FOOTBALL FACT AND QUIZ BOOK

1. Who did Liverpool beat in the 2000/01 F.A. Cup semi-finals?

2. Who is Aberdeen's most capped player?

3. What is Sol Campbell's proper Christian name?

4. Which car company have sponsored AC Milan, Bayern Munich, PSG and Eire?

5. Which player has appeared for West Ham, Spurs, Norwich, Sheffield Utd and England?

6. Who was the top-scorer in the first Premier League season?

7. Who stamped on Gareth Southgate in a 1994 F.A. Cup semi-final?

8. Who is the first Guinean footballer to play in the Premiership?

9. Which club released David Seaman before he had played a first-team match?

10. Which player has scored the most penalties in a season?

11. What is the nickname of St. Johnstone?

12. What did Ian Wright announce on a US chat show in June 2000?

13. Which Southampton striker, and PFA Young Player of the Year, never won an international cap?

14. Who did Cameroon striker Patrick Suffo sign for in summer 2000?

15. Who was Germany's caretaker manager after Euro 2000?

1. Wycombe Wanderers 2. Willie Miller 3. Sulzeer 4. Opel 5. Martin Peters 6. Teddy Sheringham 7. Roy Keane 8. Titi Camara 9. Leeds Utd 10. Francis Lee, 11. 'The Saints' 12. His retirement 13. Steve Moran 14. Sheffield Wednesday 15. Rudy Voller.

THE FOOTBALL FACT AND QUIZ BOOK

1. Who did Liverpool beat in the 2000/01 UEFA Cup semi-finals?

2. What is the nickname of Motherwell?

3. Which player has captained England, Liverpool and 'A Question of Sport' teams?

4. Where are Scottish Cup finals played?

5. When was the first World Cup final to go into extra time?

6. Which 'individual' former Chelsea and Coventry keeper appeared on 'Wogan'?

7. For what tactics were the Spurs team of Arthur Rowe renowned?

8. Which Spanish club plays at the Vicente Calderon Stadium?

9. Which team have conceded the fewest goals in any Premiership season?

10. Who were the first brothers to play in a World Cup-winning team?

11. Which club did Mario Kempes and Gabriel Batistuta play for?

12. Which manager signed Glenn Hoddle for Monaco?

13. Which Tranmere Rovers player cost Everton a record fee for a British goalkeeper in 1998?

14. Which Scandinavian club does Bent Skammelsrud play for?

15. Which town do Queen of the South play in?

THE FOOTBALL FACT AND QUIZ BOOK

1. Who were the first British team to be confirmed as champions in 2000/01?

2. Who were the first British team to ensure promotion in 2000/01?

3. Who were the first British team to be relegated in 2000/01?

4. When were 'Golden Goals' introduced?

5. Which manager led West Germany in four World Cup finals?

6. Which team lost their League status at the end of the 1969/70 season?

7. Who retired in 1993, after managing the same Scottish club for 21 years?

8. Who is Arsenal's most capped English player?

9. Which imaginary team do the 'Eastenders' characters support?

10. What is the nickname of Stenhousemuir?

11. Which Italian club play in the city of Bergamo?

12. Which two team's players were banned for match-fixing in 1914/15?

13. Which Lancashire team regularly used to start home games at 3.15 pm?

14. Who was head coach at Manchester City during the 2000/01 season?

15. Who won his only England cap against Egypt in 1986?

1. Celtic 2. Partick Thistle 3. Oxford Utd 4. 1996 5. Helmut Schon 6. Bradford Park Avenue 7. Jim McLean, Dundee Utd 8. Kenny Sansom 9. Walford 10. 'The Warriors' 11. Atalanta 12. Manchester Utd and Liverpool 13. Bury 14. Willie Donachie 15. Danny Wallace.

THE FOOTBALL FACT AND QUIZ BOOK

1. Which 'Ready, Steady, Cook' host supports Arsenal?
2. Where, in 1994, were five referees and four club directors arrested for match-fixing?
3. Who was the first Nigerian to play in the Premiership?
4. Who did Boca Juniors sell to Barcelona in 1982?
5. Who lost to the USA on penalties in the 1999 Women's World Cup Final?
6. Which player won a Scottish Cup winners' medal with both Celtic and Rangers?
7. From which club did Newcastle sign Nikos Dabizas?
8. Who scored Sunderland's winning goal in the 1973 F.A. Cup Final?
9. Who succeeded Bobby Robson as England manager?
10. Which Liverpool manager won six Championships and three European Cups between 1974 and 1983?
11. When did Italy re-allow foreign players in their league?
12. Which Scottish player and manager was known as the 'Chocolate Soldier'?
13. In which city was Paolo Di Canio born?
14. How many people watched the 1948 F.A. Cup Final on television?
15. What nationality is striker Hugo Sanchez?

1. Ainsley Harriot 2. Brazil 3. Efan Ekoku 4. Maradona 5. China 6. Alfie Conn 7. Olympiakos 8. Ian Porterfield 9. Graham Taylor 10. Bob Paisley 11. 1980 12. Graeme Souness 13. Rome 14. One million 15. Mexican.

THE FOOTBALL FACT AND QUIZ BOOK

1. Who was the first foreign manager to win the F.A. Cup?

2. Which South American club did Juninho and Denilsen play for?

3. Which brothers played for Belgium in Euro 2000?

4. What is a 'Semaine Anglaise' in France?

5. Where did Villa manager John Gregory begin his playing career?

6. Who was Chelsea's first Jamaican international?

7. When did Irish football divide into a north/south split?

8. What colours did Everton first play in?

9. Which player signed for Newcastle from Boca Juniors?

10. Which Colombian goalkeeper was jailed for his part in a kidnapping?

11. At £15 million, who is Chelsea's record signing?

12. Which former England player appeared for Ross County in 1999?

13. Who broke his toe when trying to break the fall of a bottle of salad cream with his foot in 1990?

14. Whose sister is an England international netball player?

15. Which Scottish captain was born in Scandinavia?

1. **Ruud Gullit** (1997) 2. Sao Paulo 3. Mpenza 4. A mid-week match 5. Northampton Town 6. Frank Sinclair 7. 1921 8. Black shirts with a scarlet sash 9. Nolberto Solano 10. Rene Higuita 11. Jimmy Floyd Hasselbaink 12. Mark Hateley 13. Dave Beasant 14. The Neville brothers 15. Richard Gough.

THE FOOTBALL FACT AND QUIZ BOOK

1. Which Premiership team had two of their manager's sons in their squad in the 2000/01 season?
2. Who was Liam Brady's assistant manager when he was at Celtic?
3. Who is credited with bringing football to Northern Ireland?
4. Which TV pundit has played for Dundee Utd, Aston Villa, Wolves and Everton?
5. Which former England player has won the League Championship with Aston Villa and Nottingham Forest?
6. Who does Dutchman Edgar Davids play for?
7. Which Scottish club are known as 'The Binos'?
8. Who inflicted England's first home World Cup defeat in 1997?
9. What nationality is Deportivo de La Coruna's Roy Makaay?
10. Which University runs a course in 'Football Industries'?
11. Which two teams played in the first-ever international match?
12. Where do Club Deportivo Los Millionarios and America de Cali play?

13. Which club did Bill Shankly make his managerial debut with Liverpool against?
14. Which team does former Prime Minister John Major support?
15. Which team has made the most appearances in F.A. Cup semi-finals?

THE FOOTBALL FACT AND QUIZ BOOK

1. Which England 'mascot' used to turn up to internationals in a top hat, red hunting jacket and Union Jack waistcoat?
2. What club did Former Tottenham player Steve Archibald buy in 2000?
3. When was the first time the F.A. Cup was played at Wembley?
4. What is the name of the family that ran Chelsea from 1903 to the 1970s?
5. Which three League clubs has Jackie Charlton managed?
6. What history did Graham and David Laws make in 1996/97?
7. Which club won the 2000 World Club Championship?
8. What were the Republic of Ireland originally called?
9. What is the subject of Stuart Cosgrove's book, 'Hampden Babylon'?
10. Which former Aston Villa player went on to become manager of Walsall?
11. What was the score when the USA beat Brazil in the 1998 Concacaf Gold Cup?
12. What is Liverpool's longest unbeaten league sequence?
13. Which Scottish club are known as 'The Spiders'?
14. Which Chilean striker signed for Lazio in 1998?
15. Who knocked Scotland out at the play-off stage to prevent them reaching the Euro 2000 championships?

1. Ken Bailey 2. East Fife 3. 1923 4. Mears 5. **Middlesbrough,** Newcastle Utd and Sheffield Wednesday 6. They were the first brothers on the referee's list 7. Corinthians 8. Irish Free State 9. Sex and scandel in Scottish football 10. Ray Graydon 11. 1-0 12. 31 games 13. Queen's Park 14. Marcelo Salas 15. England.

THE FOOTBALL FACT AND QUIZ BOOK

1. Who joined Liverpool from Leicester City in 1999/00 for £11 million?
2. In which country was Tony Dorigo born?
3. How many points did the F.A. decide to dock Chesterfield in April 2001?
4. Which country do Defensor Sporting and Bella Vista play in?
5. Which London club was founded as Glyn Cricket and Football Club in 1881?
6. What is the Republic of Ireland's record victory?
7. Which former Italian coach has been president of Lazio?
8. Which seaside town counts Des Lynham among their fans?
9. Which brothers played in the 1967 F.A. Cup final?
10. How many clubs are in the Italian Serie A?
11. What was the name of England's World Cup mascot in 1966?
12. Who was the first manager to be involved in 'bung' allegations in 1993?
13. Which England captain is the main subject of the book 'Football is my passport'?
14. Which brothers played for QPR and Tottenham in the seventies?
15. Which manager has appeared on television as a teenage pigeon fancier?

1. Emile Heskey 2. Australia 3. Nine 4. Uruguay 5. Leyton Orient 6. 8-0 (v Malta, 1983) 7. Dino Zoff 8. Brighton 9. Ron and Alan Harris 10. 18 11. World Cup Willie 12. Terry Venables 13. Billy Wright 14. The Morgan brothers 15. Gerry Francis.

1. Who did Manchester Utd beat in the 1999 Champions' League final?

2. Who was the first £1 million player to be transferred from Norwich City?

3. Which manager was fined after striking a fan in 1989?

4. How long is a normal period of extra time?

5. From which South American club did PSV Eindhoven sign Ronaldo?

6. Who were Leicester City's first opponents in the 2000/01 UEFA Cup?

7. How many times have Liverpool been relegated from the top division?

8. Which former owner of Everton has been chairman at Tranmere?

9. Who played for Wales and Bayern Munich on the same day in 1988?

10. What year did the Pools Panel first sit?

11. How many caps did Jackie Charlton win for England?

12. Which Tottenham international's father also played international football?

13. Which English club did Swede Martin Dahlin play for?

14. Which stadium hosted the 1970 World Cup final?

15. Which Scottish team are known as 'The Buddies'?

1. Bayern Munich 2. Kevin Reeves 3. Brian Clough 4. 30 minutes 5. Cruzeiro 6. Red Star Belgrade 7. Three times 8. Peter Johnson 9. Mark Hughes 10. 1963 11. 35 12. Steffen Iversen's 13. Blackburn Rovers 14. Azteca 15. St. Mirren.

THE FOOTBALL FACT AND QUIZ BOOK

1. Where did Robert Pires join Arsenal from?
2. For which club did Gary Lineker make his professional debut?
3. Which two England players were banned for life after match-fixing in 1965?
4. Which Italian team are nicknamed the 'Rossoneri'?
5. Which club was Steve Coppell in charge of for 32 days in 1996?
6. What is the name of the projected new stadium in Dublin, where the Republic of Ireland will play their home games?
7. Who used to play home games at the White City?
8. Which other Spanish team did Real Madrid play in the 2000 Champions' League final?
9. Which England player was sent off in a game against Sweden in 1998?
10. Which Italian coach was known as 'Il Mago' (The Magician)?
11. Which England manager introduced Bingo at England training camps?
12. Which midfielder scored the penalty for Liverpool which beat Barcelona in the UEFA Cup semi-final in April 2001?
13. Which Premier club vice-chairman died in 1996, after 57 years of service to one club?
14. Where has the World Club Cup been played since 1980?
15. What country does Celtic striker Henrik Larsson play for?

1. Marseille 2. Leicester City 3. Tony Kay and Peter Swan 4. AC Milan 5. Manchester City 6. The Arena 7. Queen's Park Rangers 8. Valencia 9. Paul Ince 10. Helenio Herrera 11. Don Revie 12. Gary McAllister 13. Bob Paisley, Liverpool 14. Tokyo 15. Sweden.

THE FOOTBALL FACT AND QUIZ BOOK

THE ENGLISH LEAGUE -

TEAM BY TEAM

ARSENAL

1. What name did Arsenal play under when formed in 1886?
2. Who sent the club a full set of red shirts in 1886?
3. Who did Bertie Mee make club captain when appointed manager in 1966?
4. Where did Arsenal play their home games in the Champions' League in 1998/99 and 1999/00?
5. Which French club was Robert Pires signed from?
6. Who scored the goal in the dying seconds of the 1979 F.A. Cup final against Manchester Utd?
7. Who were the opposition when a record 73,295 turned up for a league match at Highbury in 1935?
8. Who did Arsenal beat in the 1993/94 European Cup-Winner's Cup final?
9. Which club was Ian Wright signed from?
10. When did Royal Arsenal change their name to Woolwich Arsenal?
11. Which manager changed the team strip to red shirts with white sleeves in 1925?
12. Which brothers played for the club in the thirties?
13. Which architect designed the Art Deco style West Stand?
14. Who is the club's record league goalscorer?
15. What is the official name of Highbury?

1. Dial Square 2. Nottingham Forest 3. Frank McLintock 4. Wembley 5. Olympique Marseille 6. Alan Sunderland 7. Sunderland 8. Parma 9. Crystal Palace 10. 1891 11. Herbert Chapman 12. Les and Dennis Compton 13. Claude Ferrier 14. Cliff 'Boy' Bastin 15. Arsenal Stadium.

THE FOOTBALL FACT AND QUIZ BOOK

ARSENAL

1. Who has made the most league appearances for the club?
2. Who did Arsenal beat in the 1969/70 Fairs' Cup final?
3. Who did Arsenal beat in their first F.A. Cup final in 1930?
4. What was the former name of the 'Arsenal' tube station?
5. How much did Arsenal pay Juventus for Thierry Henry in August 1999?
6. Who is the last player to be capped for England at both football and cricket?
7. Who scored both goals in the 2-0 victory over Liverpool in the 1950 F.A. Cup final?
8. How many players did Arsenal use when winning the 1970/71 'double'?
9. When did Arsenal become the first club to print numbers on players' shirts?
10. Where was Dennis Bergkamp signed from?
11. What team was Arsene Wenger manager of before joining Arsenal in September 1996?
12. Who was signed in 1970 for £100,000 from Hibernian?
13. Who scored the goals that gave Arsenal a 2-0 victory at Anfield in 1989 and the League Championship?
14. Who did Arsenal sell Nicolas Anelka to in August 1999?
15. Who is the club's most capped player?

1. David O'Leary 2. Anderlecht 3. Huddersfield Town 4. Gillespie Road 5. £10 million 6. Arthur Milton 7. Reg Lewis 8. 16 9. 1933 10. Internazionale 11. Nagoya Grampus Eight 12. Peter Marinello 13. Alan Smith and Michael Thomas 14. Real Madrid 15. Kenny Sansom, England.

THE FOOTBALL FACT AND QUIZ BOOK

ASTON VILLA

1. Who formed the club in 1874?
2. When did Aston Villa win the League and Cup 'double', both on the same day?
3. Who signed for the club for £3.5 million after manager Brian Little had watched a video of goals he'd scored for Partizan Belgrade?
4. Who was the last Villa player to finish as top scorer in the top division?
5. Which club was Alpay Ozalan signed from for £5.6 million?
6. Which Colombian did Aston Villa sign from River Plate for £9.5 million in the 2000/01 season?
7. In which year did Aston Villa first win the F.A. Cup?
8. Which Italian club paid £5.5 million for David Platt?
9. How much did Doug Ellis pay for Dwight Yorke after a club tour of Trinidad and Tobago in 1990?
10. What went missing from a Birmingham sportswear shop in 1895?
11. Which brothers did Tommy Docherty sign for the club?
12. Who is the club's record league goalscorer?
13. Who was appointed manager in 1936, having returned from coaching in Austria?
14. Where do the club play their home games?
15. Why did Archie Hunter end up playing for Aston Villa in 1878?

ASTON VILLA

1. Who was sold to Manchester Utd in August 1998 for £12.6 million?

2. What were the club selling for 26 shillings each, before World War I?

3. Who did Villa beat in the 1982 European Cup final?

4. What is the club's nickname?

5. When did 'Deadly' Doug Ellis become chairman of the club?

6. Who was Frank Barson transferred to in 1922?

7. Who has made the most league appearances for the club?

8. Who did the Villa beat in the 1972 FA Youth Cup final?

9. Which manager succeeded Vic Crowe in 1974?

10. Which centre-forward did Villa sign for £4,700 from Tranmere Rovers in 1928?

11. What colour shirts do the team wear?

12. Which former Czechoslovakian coach was appointed manager after Graham Taylor in 1990?

13. Which club was David Ginola signed from in 2000?

14. Who did Villa beat 3-0 on the last day of the 1955/56 season to escape relegation?

15. Who is the club's most capped player?

1. Dwight Yorke 2. Replica shirts 3. Bayern Munich 4. 'The Villans' 5. December 1968 6. Manchester Utd 7. Charlie Aitken, 561 8. Liverpool 9. Ron Saunders 10. Tom 'Pongo' Waring 11. Claret shirts with sky-blue sleeves 12. Dr. Jozef Vengloš 13. Spurs 14. West Bromwich Albion 15. Paul McGrath, Republic of Ireland.

THE FOOTBALL FACT AND QUIZ BOOK

BARNET

1. What name did Barnet form under in 1912?
2. What year did Barnet turn professional?
3. Which former England player made a handful of appearances for the team in 1976?
4. What is the name of Barnet's ground?
5. Which Barnet chairman and self-confessed ticket tout took the team into league football?
6. Which sheepskin-clad TV football commentator is a fan of the club?
7. Which former England winger joined the side in the thirties?
8. What colours do the team play in?
9. When did Barnet win the Conference title and promotion to the League?
10. Who did they beat on the last day of the 1991 season to ensure promotion?
11. Which magazine has been the club's sponsors for the last three seasons?
12. What was the score in Barnet's first league match, at home to Crewe?
13. Who was striker Gary Bull's better-known relative?
14. What is the record attendance at Underhill?
15. What trophy did the club win in 1946?

1. Barnet and Alston 2. 1965 3. Jimmy Greaves 4. Underhill 5. Stan Flashman 6. John Motson 7. Lester Finch 8. Amber shirts with black trim, amber shorts and socks 9. 1991 10. Fisher Athletic 11. Loaded 12. Barnet lost 7-4 13. Steve Bull 14. 11,026 (v Wycombe in the F.A. Amateur Cup, 1951/52) 15. The F.A. Amateur Cup.

BARNET

1. Who succeeded Barry Fry as manager in 1993?

2. Who did Barnet lose to in the 1997/98 Third Division play-off semi-finals?

3. What is the record transfer fee received by Barnet?

4. Who is the club's most capped player?

5. Which ground had Barnet been trying to move to, a move finally rejected in 1999?

6. Which former England keeper was appointed manager in 1994?

7. Who has scored the most league goals for the club?

8. What year did the club reach the semi-final of the F.A. Trophy?

9. Which club was Sean Devine sold to in 1998/99?

10. Who is the club's record transfer signing?

11. Where were defenders Warren Goodhind and Mark Arber born?

12. Who was Dougie Freedman sold to in September 1995?

13. Who did Barnet lose to in the 1999/00 Third Division play-off semi-finals?

14. What is the club's nickname?

15. Who has made the most appearances for the club?

BARNSLEY

1. Under what name were Barnsley formed in 1887?

2. Despite finishing four points behind Barnsley, who were appointed to the First Division in 1914/15?

3. Who took over as manager from Mel Machin in 1993?

4. Who is the record league goalscorer for Barnsley?

5. Who was the youngest player to appear in a league match for the club?

6. Which Barnsley player took over as manager after Viv Anderson left to join Middlesbrough?

7. What is the record transfer fee received by the club?

8. What year did Barnsley win their only F.A. Cup?

9. How much did this cup-winning side cost?

10. What is the nickname of the club?

11. Which former Leeds Utd player was appointed player-manager in summer 1978?

12. Who is Barnsley's record transfer signing?

13. Who has made the most league appearances for the club?

14. What is Barnsley's record league victory?

15. Before the current red shirts, what were Barnsley's original colours?

1. Barnsley St. Peters 2. Arsenal 3. Viv Anderson 4. Ernest Hine, 123 5. Glyn Riley, (16 years 171 days) 6. John Hendrie 7. £4.25 million for Ashley Ward 8. 1912 9. £250 10. 'The Tykes' 11. Allan Clarke 12. Georgi Hristov, who was signed for £1.5 million 13. Barry Murphy, 514 14. 9-0 (v Loughborough Town) 15. Brown and white stripes.

BARNSLEY

1. Which international did manager Angus Seed sign in 1949?
2. Which manager took Barnsley into the top division for the first time?
3. Which club was skipper Neil Redfearn sold to?
4. Where was Georgi Hristov signed from?
5. When were the club relegated to the Fourth Division for the first time?
6. Which ex-Leeds Utd colleague took over from Allan Clarke as manager in 1980?
7. Which future national manager did Hunter play in his defence?
8. Where was Ashley Ward transferred to in December 1998?
9. Which club did Barnsley pay £6,500 to, for Danny Blanchflower?
10. Who was Danny Blanchflower transferred to in March 1951?
11. Which Slovenian captain joined the club in 1998?
12. Which former Nottingham Forest, Crystal Palace and Sheffield Utd boss took over as manager in June 1999?
13. Who beat the club in the Division One play-off final in May 2000?
14. Who was the only player to score a hat-trick in the 1999/00 season?
15. Who is Barnsley's most capped player?

BIRMINGHAM CITY

1. What name were the club founded as in 1875?
2. Which manager signed Archie Gemmill and Colin Todd?
3. When were Birmingham relegated to the Third Division for the first time in their history?
4. Who were the club's opponents in their first league game?
5. How old was Trevor Francis when he made his first team debut for Birmingham?
6. Who is the club's most capped player?
7. Which brothers bought out the board in the early nineties?
8. Where did Birmingham play host to Aston Villa in their first derby match?
9. Who was the goalkeeper who was instrumental in winning the 1921 Second Division title?
10. Who beat the club in the 1956 F.A. Cup final?
11. Against which team did Birmingham record their highest ever home attendance of 66,844, in a 1939 F.A. Cup match?

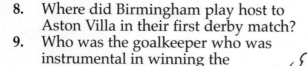

12. Who were Birmingham's opponents in the first Inter-Cities Fairs Cup semi-finals?
13. Who has made the most league appearances for the club?
14. Which manager succeeded Stan Cullis in 1970?
15. What is the club's nickname?

BIRMINGHAM CITY

1. Who did the club play in the 1931 F.A. Cup final?

2. Which full-back from the 1931 final was appointed manager in 1933?

3. How did striker Eddy Brown celebrate when he scored?

4. Which right-back died of polio in 1959?

5. When did the board add 'City' to the Birmingham name?

6. On what site was St. Andrew's built?

7. Which Argentinian defender was signed in 1978?

8. What are the club's colours?

9. Which midland rivals did Birmingham beat over two legs in winning the League Cup in 1963?

10. For which trophy did Terry Cooper manage the club to victory in 1991?

11. Who is the club's record league goalscorer?

12. Which newspaper and sex-line businessman took over the club in 1993?

13. When was Trevor Francis appointed manager?

14. Who beat Birmingham in the 1998/99 Division One play-off final?

15. Which former glamour model did David Sullivan appoint as managing director?

BLACKBURN ROVERS

1. Who formed the club in 1875?
2. What rival club was formed in 1878?
3. Which manager took the club into the Premiership at the end of the 2000/01 season?
4. What colour shirts do the team play in?
5. Where did the Blackburn shirt colours originate from?
6. Who did Blackburn buy from West Ham for £2,000 in 1913, doubling the British transfer record?
7. Who is the club's record league goalscorer?
8. Why did Blackburn win the Premiership title in the 1994/95 season, despite losing their last game at Liverpool?
9. Who did Jack Walker try to get as manger to replace Ray Harford in 1997?
10. Where do Blackburn play their home games?
11. Who beat Blackburn in the 1998/99 UEFA Cup?
12. What was the result of Blackburn's first game in the Football League?
13. Which club was Craig Hignett signed from for £2.5 million?
14. Who was captain when Blackburn won their first League Championship in 1912?
15. Who did Blackburn sign from Southampton for £7.5 million in June 1998?

1. A group of ex-public schoolboys 2. Blackburn Olympic 3. Graeme Souness 4. Blue and white halved shirts 5. The colours of Malvern School 6. Danny Shea 7. Simon Garner, 168 8. Because Manchester Utd failed to beat West Ham Utd 9. Sven Goran Eriksson 10. Ewood Park 11. Lyon 12. A 5-5 draw with Accrington 13. Barnsley 14. Bob Crompton 15. Kevin Davies.

BLACKBURN ROVERS

1. Which manager led the side to the Premiership title in 1995?
2. Who acquired a majority stake in the club in January 1991?
3. Who was Colin Hendry sold to in summer 1998?
4. How much did Blackburn pay Southampton for Alan Shearer?
5. Who did Blackburn beat when winning their first F.A. Cup in 1884?
6. Which player was sold back to Bolton for £1.6 million in 2000?
7. Who has made the most league appearances for the club?
8. Which textile magnate became club chairman in 1905?
9. When were Blackburn relegated to the Third Division for the first time?
10. Who was the first player to score a hat-trick in an F.A. Cup final?
11. How many goals did Tommy Briggs score in a league match against Bristol Rovers in 1953?
12. Who did Blackburn beat in the 1991/92 Division One play-off final?
13. Who did Blackburn sign from Norwich for £5 million?
14. Who was club captain of the Premiership-winning team?
15. Which player-manager won the Third Division title at the first attempt in 1979?

1. Kenny Dalglish 2. Jack Walker 3. Rangers 4. £3.3 million 5. Queen's Park 6. Per Frandsen 7. Derek Fazackerley 596 8. Laurence Cotton 9. 1971 10. William Townley 11. Seven 12. Leicester City 13. Chris Sutton 14. Tim Sherwood 15. Howard Kendall.

BLACKPOOL

1. What year did members of Victoria FC and Blackpool St. John's wind up, and form a new club called Blackpool?

2. How old was Stanley Matthews when he signed from Stoke in 1947?

3. Who is the club's most capped player?

4. Who did Blackpool appoint as manager in 1923?

5. Which cigar-toting manager took the club to the 1948 F.A. Cup final?

6. Where did the club play it's first home games?

7. Who scored 31 goals in his first season at the club, 40 the following year and 45 the year after that?

8. When did Blackpool finish runners-up to Manchester Utd in the League?

9. Who had a second spell as manager in 1978/79?

10. How much did QPR pay for Trevor Sinclair in 1993?

11. Who did the club merge with in 1899?

12. Who beat Blackpool in the 1951 F.A. Cup final?

13. What year was the 'Matthews Final'?

14. Who scored a hat-trick in the 'Matthews Final'?

15. In the nineties, where were Blackpool proposing to build a new ground?

THE FOOTBALL FACT AND QUIZ BOOK

BLACKPOOL

1. Which forward played a record 195 consecutive games for the club?
2. What is the club nickname?
3. Which manager dressed the side in tangerine?
4. Which World Cup-winning midfielder moved to Everton for a British record fee of £112,000 in 1966?
5. How much did Blackpool pay Millwall for Chris Malkin in 1996?
6. Where did Blackpool play their home games after merging with South Shore in 1899?
7. When was chairman Owen Oyston jailed after rape charges?
8. Which full-back went into a coma and subsequently died after heading the ball in the early twenties?
9. Where was centre-forward Jimmy Hampson signed from?
10. Who succeeded Gary Megson as manager in 1997?
11. What was the team's sole home win in the 1966/67 season?
12. Which full-back has made the most league appearances for the club?
13. Who did the team finish as runners-up to in winning promotion from the Fourth Division in 1984/85?
14. When did Stanley Matthews rejoin Stoke City?
15. Who beat Blackpool in the 1999/00 F.A. Cup 3rd round?

1. George Mee 2. 'The Seasiders' 3. Major Frank Buckley 4. Alan Ball 5. £275,000 6. Bloomfield Road (South Shore's ground) 7. 1996 8. Peter Fairhurst 9. Nelson 10. Nigel Worthington 11. 6-0 (v Newcastle) 12. Jimmy Armfield, 568 13. Chesterfield 14. 1961 15. Arsenal.

BOLTON WANDERERS

1. Which club do Bolton originate from, which formed in 1874?
2. What colours do the club play in?
3. As founder members of the Football League, who did they play their first league match against, at Pike's Lane, 8 September 1888?
4. Who was Bolton's long serving manager, holding office between 1919 and 1944?
5. Who defeated Bolton in the 1999/00 Worthington Cup semi-finals?
6. What is the name of Bolton's home ground?
7. Who did Bolton play in the first F.A. Cup final to be held at Wembley?
8. Who was forward David Jack sold to in October 1928, becoming the first British player to be transferred for over £10,000?
9. Who replaced Jimmy Armfield as manager in 1974?
10. Who is the club's record league goalscorer?
11. Which striker was sold to Manchester City in October 1967 to help balance the books?
12. Who did Bolton beat in the 1958 F.A. Cup final?
13. What did Peter Reid win with Bolton in 1978?
14. Who did the team lose to in the 1998/99 Division One play-offs semi-final?
15. Who has made the most league appearances for the club?

1. Christ Church Sunday School 2. White shirts, navy blue shorts, blue socks 3. Derby County (who won 6-3) 4. Charles Foweraker 5. Tranmere Rovers 6. The Reebok Stadium 7. West Ham United 8. Arsenal 9. Ian Greaves 10. Nat Lofthouse, 255 11. Francis Lee 12. Manchester Utd 13. The Second Division title 14. Watford 15. Eddie Hopkinson, 519.

BOLTON WANDERERS

1. How much did Liverpool pay for Jason McAteer in September 1995?
2. Which Bolton player scored the opening goal of the 1953 F.A. Cup final?
3. Where was Dutch international Per Frandsen transferred to in 1999?
4. Where was 1999/00 season's leading scorer transferred to in summer 2000?
5. Where did Bolton play their home games prior to 1997?
6. What is the club's nickname?
7. Who is the club's most capped player?
8. Who did Bolton beat 4-3 to win the 1994/95 Division One play-off final?
9. After winning promotion to Division One in 1978, where were the team playing ten years later?
10. How much did Bolton pay Wimbledon for Dean Holdsworth?
11. Which player-manager won promotion from Division Four?
12. Who was manager Bruce Rioch's assistant in 1992?
13. How many goals did the club score when returning to the Premiership by winning the Division One title in 1996/97
14. Who defeated Bolton in the 1999/00 F.A. Cup semi-final?
15. Which Notts County boss was appointed as Bolton Manager in October 1999?

BOURNEMOUTH

1. What name did the club form as in 1899?
2. In what year were Bournemouth Third Division champions?
3. Who beat Bournemouth in the 6th round of the 1956/57 F.A. Cup?
4. What did Bournemouth become the first winners of in 1984?
5. What is the name of Bournemouth's ground?
6. Which on-loan striker scored in ten successive games in the 2000/01 season?
7. Which club was forward Jon O'Neill signed from?
8. Who beat Bournemouth in the 1999/00 F.A. Cup 2nd round?
9. Who has scored the most goals in a season for the club?
10. Which club did manager John Bond leave for in 1973?
11. Which club poached manager Freddie Cox in 1958?
12. On the 1937 tour of Holland, what was the score when they played the Dutch national side?
13. Which club was Jamie Redknapp transferred to?
14. How many points did the team score when winning the Third Division title in 1987?
15. Which team knocked Bournemouth out of the 1974/75 F.A. Cup?

BOURNEMOUTH

1. After the 1997 rescue package, what is the team's full name?

2. From which club was Ted MacDougall signed?

3. Who took over as caretaker manager in 1983?

4. What year did the club sign its first professional player, from Southampton?

5. What colour shirts do the team wear?

6. Who were the opponents in the 1998 Auto Windscreens final?

7. Who is the club's most capped player?

8. What is the capacity of Dean Court?

9. Who set up a trust committee to co-ordinate the club's rescue in 1997?

10. Which club inspired Bournemouth's team shirts in 1971?

11. How much did Manchester Utd pay for Ted MacDougall?

12. Who is the club's all-time top scorer with 202 goals?

13. Which club was Mark Stein signed from?

14. From which club was loan striker Jermaine Defoe signed from?

15. How many goals did Ted MacDougall score against Margate in the 1971/72 F.A. Cup first round?

1. AFC Bournemouth Community Football Club 2. York City 3. Harry Redknapp 4. 1910 5. Red with black stripes 6. Grimsby Town 7. Gerry Peyton 8. 10,770 9. Trevor Watkins 10. A.C.Milan 11. £200,000 12. Ron Eyre 13. Chelsea 14. West Ham Utd 15. Nine.

THE FOOTBALL FACT AND QUIZ BOOK

BRADFORD CITY

1. What sporting contest led to Bradford's formation in 1903?
2. Who replaced Chris Hutchings as manager in 2000/01?
3. What is the name of Bradford's fanzine, the oldest in England, having been published continuously since 1984?
4. Which club did Bradford City refuse to join with in 1907?
5. Where do the club play their home games?
6. What happened on the last day of the 1984/85 promotion season?
7. Who has made the most league appearances for the club?
8. Which club was Peter Atherton signed from?
9. Who did Bradford sign David Wetherall from in July 1999?
10. Who is the club's record league goalscorer?
11. Where was Jim Jefferies manger before coming to Bradford?
12. Who scored the winning goal for Bradford in the 1911 F.A. Cup final against Newcastle Utd?
13. When did Bradford have to apply for re-election after finishing bottom of the Third Division (North)?
14. Who played for Bradford City and Bradford Park Avenue in two separate games on Christmas Day 1940?
15. Who did City beat 3-2 to guarantee promotion to the Premiership in May 1999?

1. An archery competition 2. Jim Jefferies 3. 'The City Gent' 4. Bradford Park Avenue 5. Valley Parade 6. The Valley Parade fire 7. Cec Podd, 502 8. Sheffield Wednesday 9. Leeds Utd 10. Bobby Campbell, 121 11. Hearts 12. James Speirs 13. 1949 14. Len Shackleton 15. Wolves.

BRADFORD CITY

1. When did Bradford City play Bradford Park Avenue for the first time in a competitive fixture?

2. Who replaced Chris Kamara as manager in 1998?

3. What name did City directors propose to call the club after the demise of Bradford Park Avenue?

4. Where did the club tour in the summer of 1914?

5. Which goalscoring trio helped the club win the Second Division title in 1908?

6. What colour shirts do the team play in?

7. Who is the club's most capped player?

8. Who did Newcastle Utd sign for £2 million in March 1997?

9. Who did Bradford sell goalkeeper George Swindin to in 1937?

10. What is the club's nickname?

11. Which management team were illegally poached by Derby County in 1982?

12. Which businessman took a controlling interest in the club in 1994?

13. Which team was Dan Petrescu signed from in 2000?

14. Which Ulster-born striker did manager George Mulhall sign in 1979?

15. Which midfielder's father had been a professional footballer with Blackpool?

1. 1911/12 2. Paul Jewell 3. Bradford Metro 4. Belgium, Switzerland and Germany 5. George Handley, James McDonald, Frank O'Rourke 6. Claret and amber stripes 7. Harry Hampton, Northern Ireland 8. Des Hamilton 9. Arsenal 10. 'The Bantams' 11. Roy McFarland and Mick Jones 12. Geoffrey Richardson 13. Chelsea 14. Bobby Campbell 15. Stuart McCall's.

BRENTFORD

1. Which former Crystal Palace chairman took control of the club in summer 1998?
2. How many times have Brentford reached the 6th round of the F.A. Cup?
3. What year was the club founded?
4. Who has made the most league appearances for the club?
5. Who is the club's most capped player?
6. Which sportsmen founded the club, when deciding on a winter activity?
7. What colours, those of the rowing club that fouded them, did the club originally wear?
8. What colours were they wearing in 1893, that gave the team their nickname?
9. What is the club's nickname?
10. Which two cups did Brentford win in 1898?
11. Who did the team lose 3-0 to in their first league match?
12. Who did Brentford lose to in 1995, in a play-off semi-final penalty shoot-out?
13. What season did the team win the Third Division (South) title?
14. What colours do the team play in?
15. Who did Brentford lose 2-1 to in the LDV Vans trophy final in April 2001?

BRENTFORD

1. Who did Brentford beat 1-0 to win the 1998/99 Division Three title?
2. When did the team join the Third Division (South)?
3. Who took five wickets for Middlesex against Surrey in the morning, and kept goal for Brentford in their first league home game in the afternoon?
4. Who replaced Frank McLintock as manager in 1987?
5. Where have Brentford played their home games since 1904?
6. Who did Ron Noades replace manager Mickey Adams with in July 1998?
7. When were Brentford promoted to Division One for the first time in their history?
8. Which manager took them to Division One by winning the Second Division title?
9. How many of their 21 home games did the team win in 1929/30?
10. Which chairman proposed that Brentford be merged with QPR in 1967?
11. Who was Dean Holdsworth sold to for £720,000?
12. When were the club relegated to Division Four for the first time?
13. Who is Brentford's record transfer signing?
14. Who is the club's record league goalscorer?
15. Who was the club's top goalscorer for the 1999/00 season?

1. Cambridge Utd 2. 1920 3. Jack Durston 4. Steve Perryman 5. Griffin Park 6. Himself 7. 1935 8. Harry Curtis 9. All of them 10. Jack Dunnett 11. Wimbledon 12. 1962 13. Hermann Hreidarsson, £850,000 from Crystal Palace 14. Jim Towers, 153 15. Lloyd Owusu.

BRIGHTON & HOVE ALBION

1. What were the team founded as in 1901?

2. Why did Brighton and Hove Utd have to change its name before they'd played a match?

3. What colour shirts do the team play in?

4. Appointed in 1919, how long was Charles Webb manager at the club?

5. Who is the club's record league goalscorer?

6. Where did Brighton play their home games, during a two-year enforced exile from the town?

7. What title did they win for the first time in 1910?

8. Who did they beat in the 1910 FA Charity Shield, as a result of winning the Southern League title?

9. What resistance movement against the board culminated in a protest from supporters of almost every league club in February 1997?

10. Who did Brighton play in the 1983 F.A. Cup final?

11. Who is the club's most capped player?

12. Which manager took the side to the top division for the first time in 1978/79?

13. How many goals did 20-year-old Adrian Thorne score in a 6-0 win over Watford in 1958?

14. How much did Liverpool pay Brighton for Mark Lawrenson?

15. Which Belarus player did Barry Lloyd sign in 1990/91?

1. Brighton and Hove Utd 2. Hove FC objected, because it sounded like they had been merged into the new club 3. Blue and white stripes 4. 28 years 5. Tommy Cook, 114 6. Gillingham's Priestfield Stadium 7. The Southern League title 8. Aston Villa 9. Fans United 10. Manchester Utd 11. Steve Penney, Northern Ireland 12. Alan Mullery 13. Five 14. £900,000 15. Igor Gurinovich.

BRIGHTON & HOVE ALBION

1. Which Brighton player scored the first Football League goal of the new millenium after 100 seconds against Exeter?
2. Which striker did manager Peter Taylor sign from Burton Albion?
3. Which former Liberal Democrat MP was appointed chief executive of the club?
4. What is the club's nickname?
5. Which manager won promotion to the Second Division in 1958?
6. Who scored five goals for Middlesbrough when they beat the club 9-0 in Brighton's first game in the Second Division?
7. Who succeeded Pat Saward as manager in 1973?
8. Which Romanian player did Barry Lloyd sign in 1990/91?
9. Why did the match against York on the last day of the 1995/96 season have to be abandoned?
10. A club record, how many goals did Peter Ward score in the 1976/77 promotion season?
11. Which music recording star has sponsored the club's shirts?
12. Where was Peter Ward transferred to in 1980?
13. Where did the club play home games prior to moving to Gillingham's ground?
14. Where did the team play when returning to Brighton in 1999/00?
15. How much did Brighton pay Manchester Utd for Andy Ritchie?

THE FOOTBALL FACT AND QUIZ BOOK

BRISTOL CITY

1. What name were City formed as in 1894?
2. Which Woolwich Arsenal boss did City install as their first manager in 1897?
3. Who did City play in the 1989 League Cup semi-finals?
4. Who did City finish runners-up to when winning promotion to Division One in 1997/98?
5. Who scored his 100th league goal playing with City in the 2000/01 season?
6. Who did City pay £1.2 million to in May 1998 for Ade Akinbiyi?
7. Which former Leeds Utd player was appointed manager in 1982?
8. Who did City finish runners-up to in Division One in 1906/07?
9. Whose winning goal, in an F.A. Cup tie against a Leeds Utd team with a months-old unbeaten home record, was the first goal photograph ever to appear on the front page of 'The Times'?
10. Which back-room trio took over the team when Tony Pulis left to join Portsmouth in 2001?
11. Who has made the most league appearances for the club?
12. How many successive wins did the team achieve in 1905/06?
13. Who did Alan Dicks succeed as manager in 1967?
14. Which future Swiss national coach was appointed caretaker manager in 1982?
15. Which former Leeds Utd team-mate did Terry Cooper sign for City in 1986?

1. Bristol South End 2. Sam Hollis 3. Nottingham Forest 4. Watford 5. Tony Thorpe 6. Gillingham 7. Terry Cooper 8. Newcastle Utd 9. Donnie Gillies' 10. Tony Fawthorp, Dave Burnside and Leroy Rosenior 11. John Atyeo, 597 12. Fourteen 13. Fred Ford 14. Roy Hodgson 15. Joe Jordan.

THE FOOTBALL FACT AND QUIZ BOOK

BRISTOL CITY

1. Who did City beat 3-0 in the 1986 Freight Rover Trophy final at Wembley?
2. Which former Sheffield Wednesday and Barnsley manager took over as City boss in June 2000?
3. When did City win promotion to the top flight of the Football League?
4. What is the club's nickname?
5. Who did City sell to Newcastle Utd for £1.75 million?
6. Who is the club's most capped player?
7. Who scored the winning goal against Portsmouth that clinched promotion in 1976?
8. Which Bristol City midfielder was the first Moldovan to ever play in English football?
9. Who did the team play in the 1909 F.A. Cup final?
10. Who is the club's record league goalscorer?
11. Who scored the winning goal for City against Arsenal at Highbury in their first match back in Division One in 1976?
12. Which club was midfielder Brian Tinnion signed from?
13. Where do City play their home games?
14. Which striker did Danny Wilson sign from Manchester City in 2000?
15. Who did City play in the 1999/00 Auto Windscreens Shield final at Wembley?

1. Bolton Wanderers 2. Danny Wilson 3. 1976 4. 'The Robins' 5. Andy Cole 6. Billy Wedlock, England 7. Clive Whitehead 8. Ivan Testimitanu 9. Manchester Utd 10. John Atyeo, 314 11. Paul Cheesley 12. Bradford City 13. Ashton Gate 14. Lee Peacock 15. Stoke City.

BRISTOL ROVERS

1. How many times have Rovers had to be re-elected to the Football League?
2. What name were they formed under in 1883?
3. What colour shirts did they first wear?
4. How much did Rovers pay QPR for Andy Tillson in November 1992?
5. Who did chairman Fred Ashmead sell the Eastville ground to in 1940 for £12,000?
6. Who replaced Brough Fletcher as manager in 1949?
7. Who beat Rovers in the 1989 Division Three play-off final?
8. Which centre-forward was sold to Preston North End in 1961?
9. What did Rovers have to wait over ten months for in 2000?
10. When did the club change it's name from Bristol Eastville Rovers to the current one?
11. What are the club's colours?
12. Which manager changed to the blue and white quartered shirts to 'make his players look larger than life'?
13. Which already relegated team beat Rovers on the last day of the 1999/00 season to deny them a play-off place?
14. Which manager left to take over as boss at QPR in 1991?
15. Who has scored the most league goals for the club?

BRISTOL ROVERS

1. Who beat Rovers in May 2001 to relegate them to the bottom division for the first time?
2. Who did Rovers sell to Fulham for £2 million in November 1998?
3. Who beat Rovers 12-0 in April 1936?
4. Why did Rovers have to play a handful of home games at Ashton Gate in 1980/81?
5. Which non-league ground did the team play at for ten years from 1986?
6. Who has made the most league appearances for the club?
7. Which manager won promotion to Division Two in 1973/74?
8. Where did Rovers start playing their home games in 1996?
9. With one cap, who is the only player to be capped by England while playing for Rovers?
10. Which two former players returned as manager and player-manager in 1996?
11. Who did Rovers sell Nigel Martyn to?
12. Who is the club's most capped player?
13. Who took over as caretaker manager in 2001?
14. Who did Rovers lose to in the 1990 Leyland Daf final at Wembley?
15. What is the club's nickname?

1. Wycombe Wanderers 2. Barry Hayles 3. Luton Town 4. After a fire at Eastville 5. Twerton Park 6. Stuart Taylor, 546 7. Don Megson 8. The Memorial Ground 9. Geoff Bradford 10. Ian Holloway and Gary Penrice 11. Crystal Palace 12. Neil Slatter, Wales 13. Garry Thompson 14. Tranmere Rovers 15. 'The Pirates'.

BURNLEY

1. What colours do the club play in?
2. What name did they play under when formed in 1881?
3. Where have Burnley been playing their home games since 1883?
4. Founder members of the League in 1888, what happened to the club in 1897?
5. When did Burnley make their sole appearance in the European Cup, being beaten by SV Hamburg?
6. Where did Burnley finish in the Second Division in 1999/00?
7. How many clean sheets did Burnley keep when winning promotion to the First Division in 1946/47?
8. How much did Burnley pay Luton for Steve Davis in December 1998?
9. When was the only time Burnley have won the F.A. Cup?
10. Which local sausage-maker joined the board in 1951, and became chairman four years later?
11. Who did Harry Potts replace as manager in 1977?
12. Which German side did Burnley beat in the 1966/67 European Fairs Cup?
13. What colour shirts did the club wear in 1910, prior to adapting the claret and blue of Aston Villa?
14. Who did Burnley play in the 1947 F.A. Cup final?
15. Who is the club's most capped player?

1. Claret with blue sleeves, white shorts and socks 2. Burnley Rovers 3. Turf Moor 4. They were relegated to the Second Division 5. 1960/61 6. Second 7. 25 8. £800,000 9. 1914 10. Bob Lord 11. Joe Brown 12. VfB Stuttgart 13. Green 14. Charlton Athletic 15. Jimmy McIlroy, Northern Ireland.

BURNLEY

1. When did Burnley win the League Championship for the first time?
2. Who is the club's record league goalscorer?
3. Where did Bob Lord set up one of the first football academies?
4. Which goalkeeper debuted for Burnley in 1907 and stayed at the club until 1928?
5. How much did Luton pay Burnley for Steve Davis in August 1995?
6. Who did Burnley beat by a point in winning the League title in 1960?
7. Which Irish side were Jimmy McIlroy and Alex Elder both signed from?
8. Still a league record, how many league games did Burnley go unbeaten in 1920/21?
9. Who did Burnley beat on the last day of the 1987 season to stay in the Football League?
10. How many goals did Andy Payton score as top-scorer in the 1999/00 season?
11. What was the Burnley side that included Ralph Coates, Dave Thomas, Martin Dobson and Leighton James nicknamed?
12. Who has made the most league appearances for the club?
13. What trophy did the club win in 1979?
14. Who scored both of Burnley's league hat-tricks in the 1999/00 season?
15. Who did Stan Ternent sign on a free transfer from Celtic in February 2000?

1. 1920/21 2. George Beel, 178 3. Gawthorpe Hall 4. Jerry Dawson 5. £750,000
6. Wolves 7. Glentoran 8. Thirty 9. Leyton Orient 10. Thirty 11. 'Team of the
Seventies' 12. Jerry Dawson, 522 13. The Anglo-Scottish Cup 14. Andy Payton
15. Ian Wright.

THE FOOTBALL FACT AND QUIZ BOOK

BURY

1. Which two clubs merged to form Bury in 1885?

2. Who was manager of the side that won the Third Division title in 1961?

3. What is the ground record attendance?

4. Who was the club's top scorer for the 1999/00 season?

5. Who was midfielder Colin Bell sold to?

6. Where was captain Chris Lucketti transferred to in 1999?

7. Who was the only ever-present player for the 1999/00 season?

8. Who has scored the most league goals for the club?

9. Still a record today, by what score did Bury win the 1903 F.A. Cup final?

10. How much did it cost Ipswich to buy David Johnson?

11. Who beat Bury in the 1st round of the 1999/00 Worthington Cup?

12. Which player made his international debut before his club debut?

13. What nationality is midfielder Kemajl Avdiu?

14. Who were the club sponsors in 1999/00?

15. Which famous pair of brothers have their mother and father working at the club?

BURY

1. What colour shirts do Bury play in?
2. Which club was goalkeeper Dean Kiely transferred to?
3. In 1992, what was the name of the supporters' bond launched by the club?
4. Where was Adrian Littlejohn transferred from?
5. Which Earl presented the Gigg Lane freehold to the club as a gift in 1922?
6. What position did the club finish when promoted from Division Three in 1995/96?
7. Which two players share the record transfer fee paid by Bury?
8. Which season were the club Second Division Champions for the second time?
9. What is the club's nickname?
10. How many goals did the side score in the 1999/00 league season?
11. Which Indian international got booked on his debut?
12. Where did Neil Warnock go after resigning as manager in 1999?
13. Which non-league club did Bury beat in the 1999/00 F.A. Cup first round?
14. Which two senior professionals were given the joint managership on a temporary basis after Warnock resigned?
15. Which former Burnley favourite became manager in 1984?

1. White 2. Charlton 3. The Shakers' Incentive Scheme 4. Oldham Athletic 5. Earl of Derby 6. Third 7. Chris Swailes and Darren Bullock 8. 1996/97 9. The Shakers 10. 61 11. Baichung Bhutia 12. Sheffield Utd 13. Tamworth 14. Andy Preece and Steve Redmond 15. Martin Dobson.

THE FOOTBALL FACT AND QUIZ BOOK

CAMBRIDGE UNITED

1. Under what name did the club form in 1919?
2. In which year did the team achieve the 'double' of Southern League Premier Division title and League Cup?
3. Who is the team's highest league scorer in a season?
4. What is the club nickname?
5. Who succeeded Bill Leviers as manager?
6. What nationality is goalkeeper Lionel Perez?
7. Who beat Cambridge in the 1990/91 F.A. Cup quarter-finals?
8. What are the club colours?
9. What was, in August 1992, the record transfer fee received by the club?
10. Who was the youngest player to appear for the club?
11. Who did they play on 2 May 1970 in a friendly?
12. Who did Cambridge beat in the Division Four 1989/90 play-off final?
13. Who did Cambridge replace in the league when elected in 1970?
14. What is Cambridge's home ground called?
15. Who did they finish runners-up to in the Southern League Premier Division in 1963?

1. Abbey United 2. 1969 3. David Crown, 24 4. The Us 5. Ron Atkinson 6. French 7. Arsenal 8. Amber shirts, black shorts, amber stockings 9. £1 million for Dion Dublin 10. Andy Sinton, 16 years 228 days v Wolves, 1982 11. Chelsea 12. Chesterfield 13. Bradford Park Avenue 14. The Abbey Stadium 15. Cambridge City.

CAMBRIDGE UNITED

1. When did the team change its name to Cambridge United?
2. What is the record transfer fee paid by Cambridge?
3. Which club had manager Bill Leviers played for as full-back?
4. Who beat Cambridge in the 1999/00 Worthington Cup 1st round?
5. Which former defender returned to the club as manager in 1985?
6. What was John Taylor's previous club?
7. Which two former Arsenal players did Ron Atkinson sign?
8. Who was Dion Dublin sold to in August 1992?
9. Who was the club's leading scorer in the 1999/00 season?
10. Where was striker George Riley transferred from?
11. For a record how many games did Cambridge go without a win from 8 October 1983?
12. Which club paid £350,000 for Alan Biley in 1980?
13. Who was striker Trevor Benjamin sold to in 2000?
14. Who took over from Tommy Taylor as manager in 1996?
15. Who has made most league appearances for the team?

CARDIFF CITY

1. What were the club formed as in 1899?

2. Who has scored the most league goals for the club?

3. Which former Ipswich player became manager in 1996?

4. Who was their top scorer in the league in 1999/00?

5. How many times have Cardiff won the Welsh Cup?

6. What year did Cardiff win the F.A. Cup, the only occasion the cup has been won by a club outside England?

7. Where was striker Robert Earnshaw born?

8. Who has made the most league appearances for the club?

9. What position did Cardiff finish in their first season in Division 2 in 1920/21?

10. Who were the holders of the European Cup-Winners Cup beaten by Cardiff in 1964/65?

11. Who beat Cardiff in the 3rd round of the 1999/00 F.A. Cup?

12. Which manager gave John Toshack his debut?

13. What year did the club win the Charity Shield?

14. Who bought 80% of the club in 2000?

15. What year did the club move to Ninian Park?

1. Riverside 2. Len Davies, 128 3. Russell Osman 4. Jason Bowen 5. 21 times 6. 1927 7. Zambia 8. Phil Dwyer, 471 9. Runners-up 10. Sporting Lisbon 11. Bolton Wanderers 12. Jimmy Scoular 13. 1927 14. Sam Hammam 15. 1910.

CARDIFF CITY

1. From which club did Cardiff sign Godfrey Ingram in September 1982?

2. Cardiff missed out on the 1924 league championship by 0.024 of a goal to which club?

3. When was the last time Cardiff played in the First Division?

4. What is the record transfer fee received by Cardiff?

5. Which club was Jorn Schwinkendorf signed from?

6. Who beat Cardiff in the 1999/00 Worthington Cup 1st round?

7. Who is the club's most capped player?

8. Who was John Toshack sold to in November 1970?

9. How much did Sheffield Utd pay for Nathan Blake?

10. Who was Simon Haworth transferred to in June 1997?

11. Who did Cardiff play in the quarter-finals of the 1970/71 European Cup-Winners Cup?

12. Which ex-Leeds player took over as manager in 1994?

13. Where was striker Kevin Nugent signed from?

14. What is the name of the Cardiff City fanzine?

15. Who beat Cardiff in the 1967/68 European Cup-Winners Cup semi-finals?

1. San Jose Earthquakes 2. Huddersfield Town 3. 1962 4. £500,000 for Simon Haworth 5. Waldhof Mannheim 6. Wimbledon 7. Alf Sherwood, Wales 8. Liverpool 9. £300,000 10. Coventry City 11. Real Madrid 12. Terry Yorath 13. Bristol City 14. 'Watch the Bluebirds fly' 15. SV Hamburg.

THE FOOTBALL FACT AND QUIZ BOOK

CARLISLE UNITED

1. Which two teams amalgamated in 1903 to form the club?
2. What year was Bill Shankly appointed manager?
3. Who has made most league appearances for the club?
4. Where was defender Peter Clark born?
5. Who is the club's all-time leading goalscorer?
6. How much did Carlisle receive from Crystal Palace for Matt Jansen in 1998?
7. Who did the team replace when elected to the Third Division (North) in 1928?
8. When did Michael Knighton become manager?
9. What colour are the club shirts?

10. Who were the opponents in Carlisle's first league game?
11. Who did Carlisle beat 3-2 in the 1972 Anglo-Italian Cup at the Olympic Stadium?
12. Who did Carlisle sell to Chester City in 1997/98?
13. Who is Carlisle's record signing?
14. Which non-league club beat Carlisle in the 1st round of the 1999/00 F.A. Cup?
15. Which goalkeeper scored an injury-time goal to save Carlisle from relegation to the Conference in 1998/99?

CARLISLE UNITED

1. What was manager Mervyn Day's former First Division club?
2. Why were Carlisle saved from relegation to the Conference in 1992?
3. Who, at 23, became the youngest player-manager in league history?
4. How long did Carlisle stay in the First Division after promotion in 1974?
5. Who became chairman in 1992?
6. What is Carlisle's home ground called?
7. Who did Carlisle lose to in the 1969/70 League Cup semi-finals?
8. Who did Carlisle beat in winning the 1997 Auto Windscreens Shield?
9. Who was top scorer for Carlisle in the 1999/00 season?
10. Who is the club's most capped player?
11. Which manager used to address fans over the tannoy before games with the words "This is your manager speaking"?
12. Who knocked the team out of the Worthington Cup 1st round in 1999/00?
13. In which year did Carlisle win the Northern League title for the only time?
14. Who returned for a third stint as manager in 1985?
15. How many goals did Hugh McIlmoyle score in the 1963/64 promotion season?

1. West Ham United 2. Because Aldershot had been expelled 3. Ivor Broadis
4. One season 5. Michael Knighton 6. Brunton Park 7. West Bromwich Albion
8. Colchester 9. Steve Soley 10. Eric Welsh, Northern Ireland 11. Bill Shankly
12. Grimsby Town 13. 1922 14. Bob Stokoe 15. 39.

CHARLTON ATHLETIC

1. What year were Charlton formed, by a group of boys playing football on the streets?

2. When did Charlton win promotion to Division One for the first time?

3. Who did they finish runners-up to in their first season in Division One?

4. When did Lennie Lawrence succeed Ken Craggs as manager?

5. Which Conference team took Charlton to a replay in the 2000/01 F.A. Cup?

6. Which club did Charlton sign Mark Kinsella from?

7. How much did Leeds Utd pay for Danny Mills in June 1999?

8. What was the record attendance at The Valley, for an F.A. Cup match against Aston Villa in 1938?

9. When were Charlton admitted to the Third Division (South)?

10. What is the club's nickname?

11. What year did Charlton win the F.A. Cup?

12. Who is the club's record league goalscorer?

13. Who was the club's manager between 1933 and 1956?

14. Which brothers arrived at the club in 1950?

15. When was Alan Curbishley appointed manager?

1. 1905 2. 1935/36 3. Manchester City 4. 1982 5. Dagenham & Redbridge 6. Colchester 7. £4.3 million 8. 75,031 9. 1921 10. 'The Addicks' 11. 1947 12. Stuart Leary, 153 13. Jimmy Seed 14. Eddie and Peter Firmani 15. June 1995.

CHARLTON ATHLETIC

1. Which two grounds did Charlton play at, between leaving The Valley in 1985 and returning to The Valley in 1992?
2. What are the club's colours?
3. Which former Footballer of the Year did Charlton sign from Barcelona?
4. Who has made the most league appearances for the club?
5. Who is the club's most capped player?
6. Who did Chalton lose to in the 1996 Division One play-off semi-final?
7. Which club did Charlton sign Neil Redfearn from in July 1998?
8. In what was thought to be Charlton's last match at The Valley in September 1985, which former turnstile operator scored for Charlton against Stoke?
9. Formed in protest against Greenwich Council, what group of supporters won 10% of the vote in the local elections in 1990?
10. What was the score at the end of full-time in the 1998/99 Division One play-off final against Sunderland?
11. Who was the Charlton goalkeeper for the penalty shoot-out in that play-off final?
12. Which club was Clive Mendonca signed from?
13. Who saved the club after the receivers had been called in due to debts of £1.5 million in 1984?
14. Which former Lyngby, Naestued and Bolton midfielder did Charlton pay £4 million for?
15. What position did the club finish in Division One in 1999/00?

CHELSEA

1. Who did Gus Mears try to persuade to move into Stamford Bridge in 1904?
2. Why did Chelsea become the only side to be elected to the Football League without kicking a ball?
3. What was the team's first strip, taken from Lord Chelsea's official colours?
4. Where was Jimmy Floyd Hasselbaink signed from for £15 million in summer 2000?
5. Apart from Chelsea, what is the only other club that keeper Carlo Cudicini has played for?
6. Which Scottish club was Tore Andre Flo transferred to in 2000/01?
7. Which Arsenal centre-forward replaced Billy Birrell as manager in 1952?
8. Which Bristol City striker was sold to Chelsea for £100,000 in 1972/73?
9. Which centre-forward was signed from Everton and sold to Notts County two years later?
10. Who did Chelsea beat 21-0 on aggregate in a 1971 European Cup-Winners' Cup tie?
11. When did Ken Bates take over as Chelsea chairman?
12. Who did Chelsea play their first League match against in September 1905?
13. Which Russian keeper was signed by Glenn Hoddle?
14. Which two pairs of brothers have played for Chelsea since the sixties?
15. Who has made the most league appearances for the club?

1. Fulham 2. Because the League wanted to expand by four clubs and also make inroads into London 3. Pale blue, white and black 4. Atletico Madrid 5. Castel di Sangro 6. Rangers 7. Ted Drake 8. Chris Garland 9. Tommy Lawton 10. Jeunesse Hautcharage of Luxembourg 11. 1982 12. Stockport County 13. Dimitri Kharine 14. Alan and Ron Harris and Graham and Ray Wilkins 15. Ron Harris, 655.

CHELSEA

1. When did Chelsea win their only League Championship?
2. What four trophies did Gianluca Vialli and the team win in 1998?
3. Which Croatian striker was signed from Parma for £5.6 million?
4. Which two Scottish internationals signed for the club in 1930?
5. When was the last greyhound meeting to be held at Stamford Bridge?
6. Who was sold to AC Milan in 1961, having scored 124 goals in 157 league games?
7. Where was Eddie McCreadie signed from for £5,000 in April 1962?
8. Who is the club's record league goalscorer?
9. When did Peter Houseman die in a car crash?
10. Which Chelsea keeper was nicknamed 'The Cat'?
11. Who beat Chelsea in the 1950 and 1952 F.A. Cup semi-finals?
12. Where was Dennis Wise signed from?
13. Who scored the winning goal against Real Madrid in the 1971 European Cup-Winners' Cup final?
14. At the start of the 2000/01 season, how many English players were in Chelsea's squad of 36?
15. Which long throw specialist was signed for £2,500 from Cambridge Utd in July 1968?

1. 1954/55 2. The League Cup, European Cup-Winners' Cup, European Super-Cup and Charity Shield 3. Mario Stanic 4. Hughie Gallacher and Alex Jackson 5. 1968 6. Jimmy Greaves 7. East Stirling 8. Bobby Tambling, 164 9. 1977 10. Peter Bonetti 11. Arsenal 12. Wimbledon 13. Peter Osgood 14. Thirteen 15. Ian Hutchinson.

CHELTENHAM TOWN

1. Who did Cheltenham beat 3-2 in April 1999 to secure the Conference title and promotion to the Football League?
2. When were the club formed?
3. What were the club's original coloured shirts, earning them the nickname of 'The Rubies'?
4. What colours did they change to two years later, still worn today?
5. What trophy did Cheltenham win in 1997/98?
6. Who did the team knock out of the F.A. Cup 2nd round in 1933/34?
7. Which former Aston Villa, Wolves and Everton striker played for the club in 1989/90?
8. What cup did Cheltenham win in 1958?
9. Who has been manager of Cheltenham since 1997?
10. Which 42-year-old former Chelsea winger left the club when they were elected to the League?
11. Who is the only ex-Cheltenham Town player to be capped by England?
12. How much did Derby County pay for Tim Ward?
13. How many games did Cheltenham go unbeaten in the Conference in 1997/98?
14. Who did Cheltenham beat in the 1997/98 F.A. Trophy?
15. Where do the club play their home games?

1. Yeovil Town 2. 1892 3. Deep red 4. Red and white stripes 5. The F.A. Trophy 6. Carlisle Utd 7. Andy Gray 8. The Southern League Cup 9. Steve Cotterill 10. Clive Walker 11. Tim Ward 12. £100 13. 17 14. Southport 15. Whaddon Road.

CHELTENHAM TOWN

1. What is the club nickname?

2. Where was centre-forward Peter Goring transferred to after World War II?

3. When were Cheltenham elected to the Conference?

4. Who is Cheltenham's record transfer signing?

5. Which former Southampton and England winger had a year as manager in 1979?

6. What is the record transfer fee received by the club?

7. Who did Cheltenham play in their first league match on 7 August, 1999?

8. Which Barbadian did Cheltenham sign on loan from Bristol City during the 2000/01 season?

9. How much did Kidderminster receive for Kim Casey in 1991?

10. Who has made the most appearances for the team?

11. Which three players were ever-present in the 1999/00 league season?

12. Who knocked Cheltenham out of the 1999/00 F.A. Cup in the 1st round?

13. Who did the club replace in the Football League?

14. Which club did Christer Warren join in 1995?

15. Who was the leading scorer for the club in the 1999/00 season?

1. 'The Robins' 2. Arsenal 3. 1985 4. Kim Casey, from Kidderminster Harriers 5. Terry Paine 6. £60,000 for Christer Warren 7. Rochdale 8. Greg Goodridge 9. £25,000 10. Roger Thorndale, 523 (702 in all competitions) 11. Steve Book, Jamie Victory and Mark Yates 12. Gillingham 13. Scarborough 14. Southampton 15. Neil Grayson.

CHESTERFIELD

1. How many league clubs are older than Chesterfield?

2. When were the club formed, as Chesterfield Town?

3. What colour shirts did manager Russell Timmeus adopt for the club in 1891?

4. Which previous club had keeper Charlie Bunyan played for, appearing in a 26-0 defeat by Preston N.E.?

5. When did the team join the Second Division?

6. When did the League replace Chesterfield with Lincoln City?

7. Before re-joining the League in 1921, who did members of the club have to buy the club back from?

8. What is the record transfer fee received by the club?

9. Who is Chesterfield's record league goalscorer?

10. Where do Chesterfield play their home games?

11. Which goalkeeper did they sell to Liverpool for £500 in 1905?

12. Who did Chesterfield beat 5-2 in the 1994/95 Third Division play-off semi-finals?

13. Who did the team beat 2-0 in that year's play-off final?

14. Who is Chesterfield's record transfer signing?

15. Which church's crooked spire gives the team its 'Spireites' nickname?

CHESTERFIELD

1. When did Chesterfield win their first Third Division (North) title?
2. Who succeeded Frank Barlow as manager in 1983?
3. Despite having a goal not given (although it had crossed the line), what was the result of the 1996/97 F.A. Cup semi-final against Middlesbrough?
4. Who was Kevin Davies transferred to in May 1997?
5. Which two players have won the most international caps?
6. Which former Sheffield coal-bagger debuted for the club in 1959?
7. Where are the club looking to build a new stadium?
8. Which year did Chesterfield win the Barnes Cup, the Derbyshire Minor Cup and the Sheffield Cup?
9. For which final did Gordon Banks play in with Chesterfield's junior side?
10. Who has made the most league appearances for the club?
11. Who was Gordon Banks sold to for £7,000 in 1959?
12. Who is the club president?
13. Who made the most league appearances for Chesterfield in the 1999/00 season?
14. What cup did Chesterfield win in 1981?
15. How many points did the F.A. decide would be deducted from Chesterfield in the 2000/01 season, for alleged financial irregularities?

1. 1931 2. John Duncan 3. 3-3 4. Southampton 5. Walter McMillen and Mark Williams, both Northern Ireland 6. Gordon Banks 7. Wheeldon Mill 8. 1892 9. The F.A. Youth Cup final in 1955/56 10. Dave Blakey, 613 11. Leicester City 12. His Grace the Duke of Devonshire 13. David Reeves 14. The Anglo-Scottish Cup 15. Nine.

COLCHESTER UNITED

1. The youngest side in the League, when were the club formed?
2. What is the team's nickname?
3. Why did Colchester Town, founded in 1874, play their first game against Braintree in October 1882, without their goalkeeper?
4. Why were the club grateful to the 4th Battalion King's Royal Rifle Corps in 1909?
5. Who scored 37 goals in Division Four in the 1961/62 season?
6. Who was transferred to Charlton Athletic in September 1996?
7. Who has made the most league appearances for the club?
8. What league were Colchester Town playing in before 1937?
9. Where do the club play their home games?
10. Which three League clubs did Colchester beat in the 1947/48 F.A. Cup?
11. Who beat the club in the 5th round, that same year?
12. Who did Colchester lose to in the 1997 Auto Windscreens final?
13. Who did the team beat in the 1997/98 Division Three play-off final?
14. Which Northern League club beat Colchester in the 1998/99 F.A. Cup?
15. When were Colchester relegated to the Conference?

1. 1937 2. 'The U's' 3. Because he had been 'accidentally' left behind' 4. For vacating the Layer Road site, thereby allowing the club to move in 5. Bobby Hunt 6. Mark Kinsella 7. Mickey Cook, 613 8. The Spartan League 9. Layer Road 10. Wrexham, Huddersfield Town and Bradford Park Avenue 11. Stanley Matthews' Blackpool 12. Carlisle 13. Torquay Utd 14. Bedlington Terriers 15. 1990.

COLCHESTER UNITED

1. What are the club's colours?
2. Who did Colchester beat 3-2 in the 5th round of the 1970/71 F.A. Cup?
3. Who scored two goals against Leeds Utd in that match?
4. Who did they play in the quarter-finals of the 1970/71 F.A. Cup?
5. Who succeeded Mick Mills as player-manager in 1990?
6. When did Colchester regain entry to the Football League after winning the Conference?
7. Who did the team beat in the 1991/92 F.A. Trophy final?
8. Which future Premiership manager was in charge of the club in 1994?
9. Where was Colchester's Zairean international, Lomana Tresor Lua- Lua transferred to in 2001?
10. Who is the club's record goalscorer?
11. Which two players both only missed one game in the 1999/00 season?
12. How much did Colchester pay Ipswich Town for Neil Gregory in 1998?
13. Who succeeded Mick Wadsworth as manager in August 1999?
14. What is the capacity of Layer Road?
15. Who was the club's top-scorer for the 1999/00 season?

1. Blue and white striped shirts, navy shorts, white socks 2. Leeds Utd 3. Ray Crawford 4. Everton 5. Ian Atkins 6. 1992 7. Witton Abbey 8. George Burley 9. Newcastle Utd 10. Martyn King, 130 11. Joey Keith and Neil Gregory 12. £50,000 13. Steve Whitton 14. 7,556 15. Steve McGavin.

COVENTRY CITY

1. Which cycle factory workers founded the club in 1883?
2. When did Coventry move to Highfield Road?
3. Who did Jimmy Hill replace as manager in 1961?
4. What are the club colours?
5. What did the club propose to call itself in the early eighties?
6. In which competition did Coventry make their only European appearance in 1970/71?
7. Who did Coventry beat in the 1987 F.A. Cup final?
8. How many consecutive league appearances did keeper Steve Ogrizovic make for the club between August 1984 and September 1989?
9. When were Coventry elected to the Second Division?
10. What was the result of their first Football League game, at home to Spurs, in August 1919?
11. Which chairman appointed Jimmy Hill as manager?
12. When did the team win the Third Division (South) title?
13. Who is the club's most capped player?
14. Who scored the winning goal in the 2-1 defeat of Sunderland in the 1963 F.A. Cup 5th round?
15. What were the team colours before manager Jimmy Hill replaced them with the sky-blue kit?

COVENTRY CITY

1. Who succeeded Ron Atkinson as manager in November 1996?
2. Who was goalkeeper when the club won the Second Division title in 1966/67?
3. How much did Aston Villa pay Coventry for Dion Dublin in November 1988?
4. What is the name of the proposed new stadium Coventry are hoping to build at the old Foleshill gasworks?
5. What is the club's nickname?
6. What was the club's old nickname, changed by Jimmy Hill?
7. Why were the last five minutes of the last game of 1977 against Bristol City played like a practice match, when both teams had to win to stay up?
8. Which managerial duo won the F.A. Cup in 1987?
9. Who defeated the club in the F.A. Cup the following year?
10. Who is the club's record league goalscorer?
11. Who took over the club as chairman in 1993?
12. Who did Coventry buy for £1 million from Arsenal in summer 2000?
13. What unwanted distinction did Coventry have in the 1999/00 season?
14. Who has made the most league appearances for the club?
15. How much did Coventry pay Wolves for Robbie Keane in August 1999?

1. Gordon Strachan 2. Alan Glazier 3. £5.75 million 4. Arena 2001 5. 'The Sky Blues' 6. 'The Glaziers' 7. The match had kicked off late, and Jimmy Hill flashed up scores of other finished games which meant both clubs were safe 8. John Sillett and George Curtis 9. Non-league Sutton Utd 10. Clarrie Bourton, 171 11. Bryan Richardson 12. Jay Boothroyd 13. The only one of the 92 League clubs not to win an away game 14. Steve Ogrizovic, 507 15. £6 million.

CREWE ALEXANDRA

1. What sport was originally played by the club's founders?

2. When was the football club formed, some ten years afterwards?

3. What is the favoured explanation for the suffix 'Alexandra'?

4. Why did Crewe replay their F.A. Cup match against Burton Swifts in 1888, having lost the first match?

5. After a second re-election application was turned down in 1896, who replaced Crewe in the league?

6. What cup did Crewe win in 1936 and 1937?

7. What is the club's nickname?

8. When was Dario Gradi appointed manager?

9. When did Crewe win their first promotion to the Third Division?

10. What is the record transfer fee received by the club?

11. Which two players were ever-present in the 1999/00 league season?

12. Where do Crewe play their home games?

13. Where was manager Dario Gradi born?

14. How many years did David Platt play with Crewe?

15. Which club was Dele Adebola sold to in 1997/98?

1. Cricket 2. 1877 3. From Princess Alexandra of Denmark, who married Queen Victoria's eldest son, later King Edward VII 4. Because Crewe complained that Burton's crossbars were too low 5. Gainsborough Trinity 6. The Welsh Cup 7. The Railwaymen' 8. June 1983 9. 1963 10. £3 million for Scott Johnson 11. Jason Kearton and Neil Sorvel 12. Gresty Road 13. Milan 14. Four 15. Birmingham City.

THE FOOTBALL FACT AND QUIZ BOOK

CREWE ALEXANDRA

1. How many games as manger did Dario Gradi celebrate on 14 December 1999?
2. Who did Crewe beat in the 1996/97 Division Two play-off final?
3. Which club paid £700,000 for Jermaine Wright in 1999?
4. Who is the club's most capped player?
5. How many goals did Tony Naylor score in a league match against Colchester in 1993?
6. What is the club's record transfer signing?
7. What colour shirts do the team wear?
8. Who has made the most league appearances for the club?
9. Which company, from an industry long associated with the town, sponsors the new stand?
10. At which Premier club did former Crewe players Neil Lennon and Rob Savage play together?
11. Which former Crewe player was appointed manager in 1960?
12. Which club did Seth Johnson join in May 1999?
13. Who is the club's record league goalscorer?
14. Which club did Crewe sign Rodney Jack from?
15. Who was the club's leading scorer for the 1999/00 season?

1. 900 2. Brentford 3. Ipswich Town 4. Bill Lewis, Wales 5. Five 6. £650,000 for Rodney Jack 7. Red 8. Tommy Lowry, 436 9. Railtrack 10. Leicester City 11. Jimmy McGugan 12. Derby County 13. Bert Swindells, 126 14. Torquay Utd 15. Mark Rivers.

CRYSTAL PALACE

1. When were the Crystal Palace team founded, formed by staff from the Crystal Palace building?
2. Disbanding soon after their formation, when were the next Palace team formed?
3. Despite playing in the Southern League, who did Palace play in the 1911 F.A. Cup 1st round?
4. Where did they play their home games after World War I?
5. What position did the team finish in the newly formed Third Division (S) in 1920/21?
6. Who succeeded Bert Head as manager in 1973?
7. Who did Crystal Palace play when inaugurating their new floodlights in the sixties?
8. What colour shirts did Palace play in prior to 1972?
9. Who is the club's most capped player?
10. When was Steve Coppell appointed manager for the first time?
11. When was Steve Coppell appointed manager for the fourth time?
12. Which keeper did Steve Coppell sign, thereby making him Britain's first million pound goalkeeper?
13. What is the record transfer fee received by Crystal Palace?
14. Where was sasa Curcic transferred to in June 1999?
15. When did the club start playing their home games at Selhurst Park?

1. 1861 2. 1905 3. Everton 4. 'The Nest' 5. First 6. Malcolm Allison 7. Real Madrid 8. Claret shirts with sky-blue pinstripes, with primrose collar and cuffs 9. Eric Young, Wales 10. 1984 11. January 1999 12. Nigel Martyn 13. £4.5 million for Chris Armstrong 14. NY/NJ Metro Stars 15. 1924.

CRYSTAL PALACE

1. Which businessman paid £23 million to take over Palace in 1988?

2. Which team did Palace finish Division Four runners-up to in 1961?

3. What was the club nickname prior to 1972?

4. Who did Steve Coppell sign in 1985 from non-league Greenwich Borough?

5. Who beat Palace in the 1990 F.A. Cup final?

6. When did the club have to seek re-election after finishing bottom of the Third Division (South)?

7. Who did Terry Venables swap with Arsenal for Kenny Sansom?

8. Who has made the most league appearances for the club?

9. Which club was Mark Bright signed from?

10. Why did Ian Wright vow never to play for Palace again in 1991?

11. Who is the club's record league goalscorer?

12. Why did the club change to red and blue striped shirts?

13. Who was the club's record transfer signing?

14. Where was midfielder Fan Zhiyi born, in 1970?

15. What new nickname did Malcolm Allison give the team in 1972?

1. Mark Goldberg 2. Peterborough Utd 3. 'The Glaziers' 4. Ian Wright 5. Manchester Utd 6. 1949 7. Clive Allen 8. Jim Cannon, 571 9. Leicester City 10. After chairman Ron Noades had criticised black players on television 11. Peter Simpson, 153 12. To 'make them look like Barcelona' 13. Valerian Ismael, £2.75 million from RC Strasbourg 14. Shanghai 15. 'The Eagles'.

DARLINGTON

1. What year were the present club founded?

2. What happened in the Durham Senior Cup replay in 1884?

3. What is the club's nickname?

4. Where do the club play their home games?

5. How did the club earn its nickname?

6. Who did Darlington beat to secure promotion back to the league in 1990?

7. Who was manager when they were promoted back to the league?

8. What did they win for the first time in their history in 1990/91?

9. Who poached manager Brian Little in 1991?

10. When did they win promotion to the Second Division?

11. When did Darlington beat Chelsea 4-1 in an F.A. Cup replay?

12. Who did the team beat in the 1999/00 Third Division play-off semi-final?

13. Who beat Darlington in the play-off final that year?

14. Who is the club's most capped player?

15. What two items from Darlington's past appear on the club badge?

1. 1883 2. They lost to Sunderland, after complaining that they'd been intimidated in the first game 3. 'The Quakers' 4. Feethams Ground 5. Because Feethams was rented from a prominent member of the local Quaker community 6. Welling Utd 7. Brian Little 8. The Fourth Division title 9. Leicester City 10. 1925/26 11. 1957/58 12. Hartlepool 13. Peterborough Utd 14. Jason Devos, Canada 15. A Quaker hat and Stephenson's Rocket, which ran on the Stockton-to-Darlington line.

DARLINGTON

1. What colour shirts do Darlington play in?
2. How much, in 1982, did Darlington need to prevent them being wound-up?
3. Which two clubs came to play friendlies, free of charge, to help the appeal?
4. Who was manager for the club's centenary in 1983?
5. Who did Darlington finish runners-up to, in gaining promotion from Division Four in 1965/66?
6. Which two former Middlesbrough team-mates formed a management team in 1995?
7. Who was the club's top scorer for 1999/00?
8. When the team were relegated to the Conference in 1988/89, how many games did they win in the season?
9. Who is the Darlington chairman, a former convicted safe-breaker?
10. Who is Darlington's record transfer signing?
11. Who is the club's top league goalscorer?
12. What is Darlington's record transfer fee received?
13. Who has made the most league appearances for the club?
14. Who was Jason Devos sold to in October 1998?
15. Which club was Nick Cusack signed from in January 1992?

1. Black and white shirts with red piping 2. £50,000 3. Sunderland and Southampton 4. Cyril Knowles 5. Doncaster Rovers 6. David Hodgson and Jim Platt 7. Marco Gabbiadini 8. 8 (out of 46) 9. George Reynolds 10. Nick Cusack, for £95,000 11. Alan Walsh, 90 12. £400,000 for Jason Devos 13. Ron Greener, 442 14. Dundee Utd 15. Motherwell.

DERBY COUNTY

1. Who founded the club in 1884?

2. Which country does Branko Strupar play for?

3. How much did Blackburn Rovers pay for Christian Dailly in August 1998?

4. When did Derby win the League Championship for the first time?

5. When did Derby move to Pride Park?

6. Who replaced Tim Ward as manager in 1967?

7. Who did manager Stuart McMillan break the country's transfer record for in 1947?

8. Who became chairman in September 1984?

9. Who did Derby play in the 1946 F.A. Cup final, the only time they won it?

10. What colours do Derby play in?

11. Which club was Croatian defender Igor Stimac bought from?

12. Opened by Her Majesty The Queen and Prince Phillip, who did Derby play their inaugural match at Pride Park against?

13. What record-winning margin did Bury beat Derby by in the 1903 F.A. Cup final?

14. Which Italian side did Derby lose to in the 1973 European Cup semi-final?

15. When did Derby win promotion to the Premiership?

1. Members of Derbyshire County Cricket Club 2. Belgium 3. £5.3 million 4. 1971/72 5. 1997 6. Brian Clough 7. Billy Steel 8. Robert Maxwell 9. Charlton Athletic 10. White shirts, black shorts, white socks 11. Hajduk Split 12. Sampdoria 13. 6-0 14. Juventus 15. 1995/96.

DERBY COUNTY

1. Where was striker Malcolm Christie signed from?
2. What is the club's nickname?
3. What colours did Derby play in before their present-day white shirts?
4. Where was Peter Doherty sold to, after scoring two goals in the 1946 F.A. Cup win?
5. Who has made the most league appearances for the club?
6. When did the club win their second league title?
7. Which club did Brian Clough buy Colin Todd from for £175,000?
8. Where did Derby play prior to Pride Park?
9. Which two players were sold to Liverpool in 1992?
10. Who was sold to Shrewsbury after scoring his 100th league goal for the club?
11. When did chairman Lionel Pickering appoint Jim Smith as manager?
12. Giving up on the idea of playing baseball in Derby, when did Francis Ley sell the Baseball Ground to the club for £10,000?
13. Which defender did Jim Smith break the club transfer record for in summer 1998, paying £2.75 million to Rosario Central?
14. Who has scored the most league goals for the club?
15. How many league goals did he score?

EVERTON

1. Who founded the club in 1878?
2. Which club was Portuguese midfielder Abel Xavier signed from?
3. When did Everton first go through the season unbeaten at home, winning the title the same year?
4. What is the club's nickname?
5. Which two players shared the pre-World War I record of 36 goals in a season?
6. Which Ghanaian international did Walter Smith pay Racing Lens £4.5 million for in 2000?
7. Which manager was sacked in the back of a London taxi by chairman John Moores?
8. When did St. Domingo's change their name to Everton?
9. Who was goalkeeper at the club during the sixties and early seventies?
10. Who did Everton pay £5.65 million to, when signing Nick Barmby in October 1996?
11. Who scored the winning goal in the 1906 F.A. Cup final win over Newcastle Utd?
12. Which Everton manager was nicknamed 'The Cat'?
13. Who was Everton's first black player, signed from Club Bruges for £3 million in 1994?
14. What is the club's motto - 'Nil satis nisi optimum'?
15. What was record league goalscorer 'Dixie' Dean's proper name?

EVERTON

1. One of the twelve founder members of the Football League, how many seasons have Everton spent outside the top division?
2. An all-time record, how many goals did 'Dixie' Dean score in the 1927/28 season?
3. Which 17-year-old was signed from Burnley in 1936 for £6,500?
4. Which former 'Coronation Street' actor is club chairman?
5. Who were runners-up to Everton in their 1984/85 Championship-winning season?
6. Which 16-year-old made his league debut at Blackpool in January 1966?
7. Why were the team known as 'The Black Watch' in their early days?
8. Who was signed on a free transfer from Middlesbrough in 2000?
9. Who was nicknamed 'The Golden Vision'?
10. Who was manager between Howard Kendall's first two spells in charge?
11. What was the original name of Goodison Park?
12. Who did Everton beat 3-1 in the 1984/85 European Cup-Winners' Cup final?
13. Who was signed from Blackpool for £110,000 in 1966 and sold to Arsenal in 1971?
14. Who scored two goals in the 1966 F.A. Cup final win over Sheffield Wednesday?
15. Who has made the most league appearances for the club?

1. Four 2. 60 3. Tommy Lawton 4. Bill Kenwright 5. Liverpool 6. Joe Royle 7. From wearing black shirts with a tartan sash 8. Paul Gascoigne 9. Alex Young 10. Colin Harvey 11. Mere Green 12. Rapid Vienna 13. Alan Ball 14. Mike Trebilcock 15. Neville Southall, 578.

EXETER CITY

1. Which Exeter reserve goalkeeper went on to become president of FIFA?
2. Which two clubs amalgamated to form Exeter City in 1904?
3. What was Exeter's original colour shirts?
4. Which manager took the club to the Fourth Division Championship in 1989/90?
5. What is the record transfer fee received by the club?
6. Who was the top league goalscorer in the 1999/00 season?
7. Which goalkeeper, making 186 consecutive appearances in a nine-year career with the club, was sold to Bolton Wanderers for £5,000?
8. When did the club win it's first-ever league promotion?
9. Where was Darren Rowbotham re-signed from in 1995?
10. What is the name of their home ground?
11. Which 17-year-old was sold to Arsenal for £2,000 in the 1928/29 season?
12. A club record, how many goals did Fred Whitlow score in the 1932/33 season?
13. Where was Tony Kellow signed from?
14. Who preceeded Noel Blake as manager in 1995?
15. Where did manager Arthur Chadwick take the team in 1914?

1. Stanley Rous 2. St. Sidwell's Utd and Exeter Utd 3. Green and white stripes
4. Terry Cooper 5. £500,000 for Martin Phillips 6. G. Alexander 7. Dick Pym 8.
1964 9. Shrewsbury Town 10. St. James' Park 11. Cliff 'Boy' Bastin 12. 33 13.
Falmouth Town 14. Peter Fox 15. On a tour of South America.

EXETER CITY

1. What is the club nickname?
2. What colour strip do Exeter play in?
3. Who did Exeter play in the 1931 F.A. Cup quarter-finals?
4. How many league games had 18-year-old Maurice Setters played for the club, before being sold to West Bromwich Albion in 1955?
5. Which Exeter player has won the most international caps?
6. On the 1914 tour of South America, which country did they draw 3-3 with, Exeter reputedly being their first international opposition?
7. Which club did Exeter finish runners-up to in Division Four in the 1976/77 promotion season?
8. Who did Exeter beat 4-0 in the 1980/81 F.A. Cup 5th round?
9. How many spells did Tony Kellow have with the club?
10. Who did Exeter beat 5-1 on a 1925 tour of Amsterdam?
11. Who did the club sell defender Chris Vinnicombe to in November 1989?
12. Why did Exeter survive in the Football League, despite finishing bottom of Division Three in 1995?
13. Which former England captain was appointed manager in 1983?
14. Who paid £500,000 for Martin Phillips in November 1995?
15. Who has made the most league appearances for the club?

1. 'The Grecians' 2. Red and white striped shirts, red shorts, red socks 3. Sunderland 4. Ten 5. Dermot Curtis, Eire 6. Brazil 7. Cambridge Utd 8. Newcastle Utd 9. Three 10. Ajax 11. Rangers 12. Because Conference winners Macclesfield Town's ground was not up to League standard 13. Gerry Francis 14. Manchester City 15. Arnold Mitchell, 495.

FULHAM

1. What was the team called when founded in 1879?
2. When did Fulham move to Craven Cottage?
3. When did Henry Norris turn down an approach from Gus Mears to move to Stamford Bridge?
4. Who scored a club record 43 goals in the 1931/32 season?
5. Which comedian was club chairman in the late fifties and early sixties?
6. Which Fulham player became Britain's first £100-a-week footballer in 1961?
7. What is the club nickname?
8. Which club was Chris Coleman signed from?
9. Which three future managers played together at Fulham?
10. Who did Fulham play in the 1958 F.A. Cup semi-finals?
11. Which manager took the club to Division One at the first attempt in 1959?
12. Who did manager Bobby Robson sell to Leicester for £150,000?
13. Which Fulham player has played for Lazio, Borussia Dortmund and Liverpool?
14. How much did Fulham pay Sunderland for Lee Clark in July 1999?
15. Who scored on his league debut for Fulham against Aston Villa in March 1963, having scored 40 goals for the club's junior team?

FULHAM

1. Who replaced Kevin Keegan as manager, after Keegan left to take charge of the England team?
2. Nicknamed the 'Galloping Hairpin', who was the first player to score 100 goals for the club?
3. What are the club's colours?
4. Which developers bought the club in 1986?
5. Who bought a majority shareholding in the club in 1997?
6. Who did Bobby Robson sign from Tonbridge for £1,000?
7. Which manager took Fulham to the Second Division title in 1948/49?
8. Who is the club's most capped player?
9. Which two England 'veterans' played for Fulham in the 1975 F.A. Cup final?
10. With which other club did chairman David Bulstrode try to form Fulham Park Rangers?
11. What was the club's record transfer fee received in February 1998?
12. Who did Kevin Keegan, as 'Chief Operating Officer', appoint as first team coach?
13. Which manager, who led the team out at the 1975 F.A. Cup final, died in April 2001?
14. Who is the club's record league goalscorer?
15. Which manager won the Division One Championship with Fulham in 2001?

GILLINGHAM

1. What name was the club founded as in 1891?
2. Who did they play their first league match against in 1920?
3. Who is the club chairman, a self-confessed Millwall fan?
4. Who scored six goals in a Third Division (South) game against Merthyr T, in 1930?
5. Who did Gillingham lose to in the 1998/99 Second Division play-off final?
6. What is the club's record league victory?
7. Who replaced Gillingham in the League when they finished bottom of the table in 1937/38?
8. What is the club nickname?
9. When were the club re-elected to the Football League?
10. Who was manager when they won the Fourth Division Championship in 1963/64?
11. How much did Manchester City pay for John Taylor in November 1999?
12. Who beat Gillingham in the 6th round of the 1999/00 F.A. Cup?
13. Who has made the most league appearances for the club?
14. Which club was striker Iffy Onuora signed from?
15. Who did Gillingham beat in the 1999/00 Second Division play-off final?

1. Excelsior F.C. 2. Southampton, 1-1 3. Paul Scally 4. Fred Cheesmur 5. Manchester City 6. 10-0 (v Chesterfield, 1997) 7. Ipswich Town 8. 'The Gills' 9. 1950 10. Freddie Cox 11. £1.5 million 12. Chelsea 13. John Simpson, 571 14. Swindon Town 15. Wigan Athletic.

GILLINGHAM

1. What colour shirts do the team play in?
2. Who did manager Peter Taylor leave to manage in 2000?
3. How many clean sheets did Jim Stannard keep in the 1995/96 season?
4. Which former Charlton player was appointed manager in 1981?
5. How much did Gillingham pay Reading for Carl Asaba in August 1998?
6. Which future Manchester Utd defender, and Huddersfield and Wigan manager did Keith Peacock sign?
7. Where do the club play their home games?
8. Which former ITV 'Big Match' commentator is among the team's supporters?
9. Who scored two hat-tricks in the 1999/00 season?
10. Who is the club's most capped player?
11. What is the name of Gillingham's well-known fanzine, which has been going for 10 years?
12. Which team shared Gillingham's ground for two years?
13. Who is the club's record league goalscorer?
14. Who became player-manager in June 2000?
15. Who beat Gillingham in the Third Division play-offs in 1987?

1. Blue and black stripes 2. Leicester City 3. 29 4. Keith Peacock 5. £600,000 6. Steve Bruce 7. Priestfield Stadium 8. Brian Moore 9. John Taylor 10. Tony Cascarino, Republic of Ireland 11. Brian Moore's Head Looks Uncannily Like The London Planetarium 12. Brighton 13. Brian Yeo, 135 14. Andy Hessenthaler 15. Swindon Town.

GRIMSBY TOWN

1. What were the club formed as in 1878?
2. How much were the receipts from their first game?
3. How many goals did Pat Glover score in the 1933/34 season?
4. How many times have Grimsby reached the F.A. Cup semi-finals?
5. When was Bill Shankly appointed manager at the club?
6. How many straight wins did the club achieve in 1952, still unbeaten to this day?
7. By what difference in goal average were Grimsby relegated in 1968?
8. Which manager won the Fourth Division title with Grimsby in his first season?
9. What inflatables were waved on the terraces in the early nineties?
10. Which manager took Grimsby from the Fourth Division to the Second Division in successive seasons?
11. Who is the club's record transfer signing?
12. What is the club's nickname?
13. Who is the club's most capped player?
14. Who did Bill Shankly reckon 'was the best header of a ball in the game'?
15. What colour shirts do the team wear?

THE FOOTBALL FACT AND QUIZ BOOK

GRIMSBY TOWN

1. Which Grimsby manager said of the side that they were 'the best football team I have seen in England since the war'?

2. Where do the club play their home games?

3. Who succeeded Alan Buckley as manager in 1994?

4. Which Italian player did Brian Laws have a punch-up with?

5. What trophy did the club win in 1998?

6. Which two teams did Grimsby beat in the 1998/99 play-offs to win promotion to Division One?

7. How many league goals did the team score in 1999/00?

8. When did Alan Buckley return for his second spell as manager?

9. Who is the club's record goalscorer?

10. Which Italian club was Ivano Bonetti signed from?

11. Who has made the most league appearances for the club?

12. Which club was Lee Ashcroft transferred from in August 1998?

13. What is the record transfer fee received by Grimsby?

14. What is the club's record league victory?

15. Where was John Oster transferred to in July 1997?

1. Bill Shankly 2. Blundell Park 3. Brian Laws 4. Ivano Bonetti 5. The Auto Windscreens Shield 6. Northampton and Fulham 7. 41 8. 1997 9. Pat Glover, 180 10. Sampdoria 11. Keith Jobling, 448 12. Preston North End 13. £1.5 million for John Oster 14. (v Darwen 1899) 9-2, 15. Everton.

HALIFAX TOWN

1. How did an 'Old Sport' found the club in 1911?
2. Which former Scottish international had a second spell as manager in 1996?
3. What is the name of Halifax's ground?
4. Which rugby league team do Halifax share their ground with?
5. What season were Halifax runners-up in Division Four?
6. Where did Halifax play for their first eight years after formation?
7. What is the club's record victory, achieved twice?
8. What colour shirts do Halifax Town wear?
9. Longer than any other league side since formal relegation began, for how long were Halifax in the Conference?
10. Who did Halifax lose to on the last day of the 1992/93 season, which condemned them to the Conference?
11. What is the record transfer fee received by Halifax?
12. What colour shirts did they wear in the early seventies?
13. Who did Halifax beat 2-0 to win the Conference title in 1998?
14. What position did Halifax finish in the 1999/00 season?
15. What did Halifax join in 1958?

1. Mr. A.E. Jones, using the nom de plume 'Old Sport', wrote to the Halifax Evening Chronicle suggesting a meeting to form a football club 2. George Mulhall 3. The Shay Stadium 4. Halifax Blue Sox 5. 1968/69 6. Sandhall 7. 6-0 8. Blue and white striped shirts 9. Five years 10. Hereford Utd 11. £300,000 for Geoff Horsfield 12. Tangarine shirts with blue numbers on the front 13. Kidderminster Harriers 14. 18th 15. The newly-formed Third Division.

THE FOOTBALL FACT AND QUIZ BOOK

HALIFAX TOWN

1. What is the club's nickname?
2. How many goals did Halifax concede when relegated from the Third Division in 1962/63?
3. Who is Halifax's record transfer signing?
4. Who did Halifax play, in front of a record crowd, in the 1953 F.A. Cup 5th round?
5. In which cup competition did Halifax beat Manchester Utd?
6. Who is the club's record league goalscorer?
7. How many goals did Halifax's William charles score in a 1934 match against Hartlepools Utd?
8. Which club did Geoff Horsfield join in October 1998?
9. Who scored the only hat-trick for Halifax in the 1999/00 season?
10. Who beat the club in the 1999/00 Worthington Cup 1st round?
11. Where did Chris Tate join the club from in July 1999?
12. Who has made the most league appearances for the club?
13. What is Halifax's record cup win?
14. Which player only missed one league match during 1999/00?
15. Who knocked the side out of the 1999/00 F.A. Cup in the 2nd round?

1. 'The Shaymen' 2. 106 3. Chris Tate, £150,000 4. Spurs 5. The Watney Cup 6. Ernest Dixon, 129 7. Six 8. Fulham 9. Jamie Paterson 10. West Bromwich Albion 11. Scarborough 12. John Pickering, 367 13. 7-0 (v Bishop Auckland, 1967) 14. Graham Mitchell 15. Reading.

HARTLEPOOL UNITED

1. What is the club nickname?
2. Who were the club's opponents in their first football league game in 1921?
3. Which former Tottenham player was appointed manager in 1989?
4. What is the furthest Hartlepool have reached in the F.A. Cup?
5. Which player has made the most appearances for the club?
6. What is the record transfer fee received by Hartlepool?
7. To which club was Don Hutchison sold in 1990/91?
8. What colour shirts do the team play in?
9. Who was appointed manager in March 1999?
10. What was the original name of the club founded in 1908?
11. Where was midfielder Gus Di Lella born?
12. To which team did Hartlepool finish runners-up in the 1956/57 Third Division (North)?
13. Which midfielder was an ever-present in the 1999/00 league campaign?
14. Who beat Hartlepool in the 2nd round of the 1999/00 F.A. Cup?
15. Who was manager of the club from 1965 to 1967?

1. The Pool 2. Wrexham 3. Cyril Knowles 4. 4th round 5. Wattie Moore 6. £300,000 from Chelsea for Joe Allon 7. Liverpool 8. Royal blue and white stripes 9. Chris Turner 10. Hartlepools Utd 11. Buenos Aires 12. Derby County 13. Paul Stephenson 14. Hereford Utd 15. Brian Clough.

HARTLEPOOL UNITED

1. What is the name of Hartlepool's ground?
2. From which club was Jan Ove Pedersen signed?
3. Who beat Hartlepool in the first round of the 1999/00 Worthington Cup?
4. Who did Hartlepool play in the 1999/00 Third Division play-off semi-final?
5. What is the highest transfer fee paid by Hartlepool?
6. What did manager Fred Westgate keep under the Clarence Road Stand?
7. When the twin boroughs of Old and West Hartlepool merged to form a single town, what did the club change its name to?
8. Who preceeded Cyril Knowles as manager?
9. From which club was Gary Strodder signed?
10. Who were the previous owners of Victoria Park?
11. What did the club change its name to in 1977?
12. Who was assistant manager to Brian Clough from 1965 to 1967?
13. What destroyed the Main Stand at the Victoria Ground in 1916?
14. Who beat Hartlepool 4-3 in the F.A. Cup 3rd round in 1957?
15. Which club was defender Chris Westwood signed from?

HUDDERSFIELD TOWN

1. What did the Alfred McAlpine stadium win in 1995?
2. Who was sold to Manchester City in 1960?
3. In which years did Town win a hat-trick of league titles?
4. Which millionaire acquired a 70% stake in the club in 1998/99?
5. Who was the benefactor that started the club with capital of £2,000?
6. What is the record transfer fee received by Huddersfield?
7. Who was manager of the team between 1956 and 1959?
8. Who scored the club's fastest ever league goal, ten seconds after the start against Sunderland in 1935?
9. Where was Ken Monkou signed from?
10. Who was manager of Huddersfield when they won the Second Division championship in 1970?
11. Who did Huddersfield lose to in the 1999/00 F.A. Cup?
12. What was the name of Huddersfield's ground, prior to the McAlpine Stadium?
13. Who did Town beat in the F.A. Cup final of 1921/22?
14. What was unusual about the 1-0 scoreline of the 1921/22 final?
15. Where did Clyde Wijnhard begin his playing career?

HUDDERSFIELD TOWN

1. Who did Steve Bruce succeed as manager?

2. What was the record attendance at Leeds Road?

3. What year did Town win the Fourth Division title?

4. Who were Huddersfield elected to replace in the Second Division in 1910?

5. Town scored their most league goals in a season in 1979/80. How many?

6. Who played in every league game during the 1999/00 campaign?

7. Who did Huddersfield beat in the 1995 play-off final?

8. Where did Herbert Chapman come from in 1921?

9. Who has made most league appearances for the club?

10. Who did Huddersfield sell Marcus Stewart to in February 2000?

11. How many times have Huddersfield been F.A. Cup runners-up?

12. Where was Lee Richardson transferred to in February 2000?

13. Where was Kenny Irons' only previous club?

14. What was the result of the first league game played at the McAlpine Stadium, in August 1994?

15. Who is Town's most capped player?

THE FOOTBALL FACT AND QUIZ BOOK

HULL CITY

1. What were Hull formed as in 1904?

2. Who has made most appearances for the club?

3. Which former Scottish international became manager in 1988?

4. What is the record transfer fee received by Hull?

5. Who beat the team in the 2nd round of the 1999/00 Worthington Cup?

6. Who was top league goalscorer for Hull in 1999/00?

7. How many international caps did 1997 manager Mark Hateley win for England?

8. What year were they runners-up in the Associate Members' Cup?

9. What is Hull's record transfer fee?

10. Which former Arsenal player became player-manager in 1970?

11. What is Hull's ground called?

12. Who beat Hull in the 1930 F.A. Cup semi-finals in a replay?

13. What is the club nickname?

14. What year did the team win the Third Division title?

15. What is unique about the floodlight pylons at Hull?

1. Hull Comets 2. Andy Davidson, 520 3. Eddie Gray 4. £750,000 for Andy Payton 5. Liverpool 6. John Eyre 7. 32 8. 1984 9. £200,000 for Peter Swan 10. Terry Neill 11. Boothferry Park 12. Arsenal 13. The Tigers 14. 1965/66 15. There are six of them.

HULL CITY

1. Which former British Davis Cup captain acquired the club in 1997?
2. Which club was Don Revie sold to in 1951?
3. Who is the club's all-time leading scorer?
4. What is the capacity of Boothferry Park?
5. What year did the team win the Third Division (North) for the first time?
6. What was Raich Carter a pioneer of in 1948?
7. What was 1946 Chairman Harold Needler's proposed capacity for the ground?
8. Who beat the team in the 3rd round of the 1999/00 F.A. Cup?
9. Which famous player returned as manager in 1978?
10. Which club was Andy Payton sold to in November 1991?
11. Who is the club's most capped player?
12. Where was Peter Swan signed from in March 1989?
13. What position did Hull finish in Division Three in 1999/00?
14. Who became manager in April 2000?
15. Who beat Hull in the 1949 F.A. Cup quarter-finals?

IPSWICH TOWN

1. What year were the club formed as the Ipswich Association FC?
2. Which family have had a presence on the board ever since the club's formation?
3. Who raised the money to build Portman Road?
4. Who became the first player to appear in a Football League match while wearing an electronic tag after being released from prison?
5. Who is the club's record league goalscorer?
6. How many managers has the club had in its history?
7. When did Ipswich win the League Championship?
8. Who did Ipswich beat in the 1980/81 UEFA Cup final?
9. How many goals did Ted Phillips score in the 1956/57 season?
10. When did the club join the Football League?
11. Where do the club play their home games, the same venue since 1884?
12. Which Scottish club was Dixie Moran bought from, breaking Ipswich's transfer record, for £12,000?
13. Soon after Ipswich Town turned professional in 1936, where did rival club Ipswich United start to play?
14. Who has made the most league appearances for the club?
15. Which two Ipswich managers left to manage England?

IPSWICH TOWN

1. What animal appears on the Ipswich Town badge?
2. Who got the club promoted in 1957, winning the Third Division (South) title?
3. Where was Marcus Stewart transferred from when joining the club in February 2000?
4. Which former Ipswich defender was appointed manager in December 1994?
5. Already nicknamed 'Town' or 'Blues', what other name are the team becoming known as?
6. How much did Newcastle pay for Kieron Dyer in July 1999?
7. When was Bobby Robson appointed manager at the club?
8. Which two Dutch internationals played for the club in the late seventies?
9. Which centre-forward did Alf Ramsay sign from Portsmouth for £6,000?
10. Who was the first Ipswich manager to be sacked, in 1990?
11. Which two central defenders did Bobby Robson sign in 1978?
12. Who did Ipswich beat in the 1999/00 Division One play-off final?
13. Who scored the winning goal in the 1978 F.A. Cup final win over Arsenal?
14. Which 18-year-old was signed on a free transfer from Ajax in 2000?
15. Who is the club's most capped player?

1. A white Suffolk Punch horse 2. Alf Ramsay 3. Huddersfield Town 4. George Burley 5. 'The Tractor Boys' 6. £6 million 7. 1969 8. Arnold Muhren and Frans Thijssen 9. Ray Crawford 10. John Duncan 11. Russell Osman and Terry Butcher 12. Barnsley 13. Roger Osborne 14. Guillermo Graaven 15. Allan Hunter, N.Ireland.

KIDDERMINSTER HARRIERS

1. What colour shirts do Kidderminster play in ?
2. What year did they win the F.A. Trophy?
3. Which team did Kidderminster replace in the Football League for 2000/01?
4. Where was Thomas Skovberg signed from?
5. Who was appointed manager at the end of the 1998/99 season?
6. What is the name of their ground?
7. Why are Kidderminster nicknamed the 'Harriers'?
8. What is the record transfer fee paid by Kidderminster?
9. Who was Andy Ducros transferred from?
10. Who was Kidderminster's first representative on the executive of the Birmingham County F.A. in 1897?
11. Which team did Kidderminster beat in their first Football League match?
12. How many goals did leading marksman Ian Foster score during the 1999/00 season?
13. Against which team did Kidderminster have their record attendance on 27 November 1948?
14. Who knocked Kidderminster out of the 1999/00 F.A. Cup?
15. Which two league clubs did Kidderminster beat in the 1993/94 F.A. Cup?

1. Red shirts with a white flash 2. 1986/87 3. Chester City 4. Esbjerg (Denmark) 5. Jan Molby 6. Aggborough Stadium 7. When they were formed, it was previously an athletics club 8. £100,000 for Andy Ducros 9. Nuneaton Borough 10. Arthur Millward 11. Torquay United 12. 17 13. Hereford Utd, 9,155 14. Welling Utd 15. Birmingham and Preston.

KIDDERMINSTER HARRIERS

1. What year were Kidderminster formed?
2. Why weren't Kidderminster promoted to the League when they won the Conference in 1994?
3. Who scored a hat-trick in the 5-0 victory over Southport in November 1999?
4. What is the record transfer fee received by Kidderminster?
5. Which club was Lee Hughes transferred to?
6. On how many occasions have Kidderminster won the West Midland League Cup?
7. Kidderminster were founder members of which league?
8. Who was club chairman when Kidderminster were refused league entry in 1994?
9. When were floodlights used for the first time in F.A. Cup history at Aggborough Stadium?
10. Where was Craig Hinton signed from in 1988?
11. Which country did Jan Molby play international games for?
12. Who was the only ever-present team member during the 1999/00 season?
13. What is the capacity of Aggborough Stadium?
14. Who scored the first goal for the team in August 1999?
15. Who was club manager before Jan Molby?

THE FOOTBALL FACT AND QUIZ BOOK

LEEDS UNITED

1. Why was the club formed in 1919?
2. Who was admitted to the Football League in place of Leeds City?
3. Which Frenchman was sold to Manchester Utd in 1993?
4. Who did Howard Wilkinson sign from Manchester Utd in 1989?
5. Which Leeds manager left to manage the Scottish national side?
6. Which three Scottish players were introduced during the 1973/74 Championship-winning season?
7. Who did Atletico Madrid pay £12 million for in July 1999?
8. What distinction does the Elland Road pitch hold?
9. Which club was Australian Mark Viduka signed from?
10. Who is the club's record league goalscorer?
11. Which manager helped the team win their first League Championship in 1968/69?
12. Why did Don Revie change the team's strip from blue and gold to all-white?
13. Who scored the winning goal in the 1968 League Cup final against Arsenal?
14. How long was the unbeaten run that helped Leeds win the 1968/69 Championship?
15. Who did Leeds play in the 2001 Champions' League semi-final?

1. Because Leeds City had been forcibly wound-up 2. Burslem Port Vale 3. Eric Cantona 4. Gordon Strachan 5. Jock Stein 6. David Harvey, Gordon McQueen and Joe Jordan 7. Jimmy Floyd Hasselbaink 8. It is the shortest and narrowest in the Premiership 9. Celtic 10. Peter Lorimer, 168 11. Don Revie 12. To be like Real Madrid 13. Terry Cooper 14. 28 games 15. Valencia.

LEEDS UNITED

1. How many goals did John Charles score in the 1953/54 season?
2. When the Leeds City players were auctioned off, who made the top price of £1,250?
3. Who refereed the controversial match between Leeds and West Bromwich Albion in 1971 which caused a pitch invasion?
4. Who spent 44 days as manager in 1974?
5. Who did Leeds buy from Sunderland in July 1999 for £5.6 million?
6. Who did Leeds play for permanent possession of the Fairs' Cup?
7. Who has made the most league appearances for the club?
8. Which Italian club was John Charles sold to in 1957 for £65,000?
9. Who did Leeds beat on the last day of the 1961/62 season to avoid being relegated to Division Three?
10. Who did David O'Leary sign from Lens for £7.2 million in 2000?
11. Who did Leeds beat in the 1967/68 Fairs' Cup final?
12. Which country did striker Tony Yeboah play for?
13. Which two players appeared in court in 2001 on charges of GBH?
14. Who beat Leeds in the 1969/70 European Cup final?
15. Who is the club's most capped player?

1. 42 2. Billy McLeod 3. Ray Tinkler 4. Brian Clough 5. Michael Bridges 6. Barcelona 7. Jack Charlton, 629 8. Juventus 9. Newcastle Utd 10. Olivier Dacourt 11. Ferencvaros 12. Ghana 13. Jonathan Woodgate and Lee Bowyer 14. Bayern Munich 15. Billy Bremner, Scotland.

LEICESTER CITY

1. What name were Leicester formed as in 1884?
2. Named after the Roman road where they were first formed, what was the team's nickname in their early years?
3. Which club did Leicester pay £5 million to when signing Ade Akinbiyi in 2000?
4. Who did Leicester beat in the 1997 League Cup replay?
5. Which club was Brian Little manager of before coming to Leicester in 1991?
6. Which manager signed Frank Worthington to the club in the seventies?
7. How much was Henry Webb, their first professional signed in 1888, paid per week?
8. Who was top scorer for City for four successive seasons from 1983?
9. When did Leicester Fosse reform as Leicester City?
10. How old was David Nish when he became the youngest captain in an F.A. Cup final in 1969?
11. Who has scored the most league goals for the club?
12. Who did Leicester beat 2-1 in winning the 1999/00 League Cup?
13. Where did Leicester sign Arthur Rowley from?
14. Who did Leicester play in the 1949 F.A. Cup semi-final?
15. Who replaced Mark McGhee as manager in 1995?

LEICESTER CITY

1. What is the club's nickname?

2. Who scored six goals for the club in a 10-0 demolition of Portsmouth in 1928?

3. Who got revenge with a 4-1 win over City in the 1934 F.A. Cup semi-final?

4. When did Leicester first win the second Division title?

5. Where have the team played home games since 1891?

6. What colours do the team play in?

7. Where was Darren Eadie signed from in December 1999?

8. Who scored a last-minute goal against Crystal Palace in the 1995/96 Division One play-off final?

9. Which manager signed Frank McLintock and David Nish for the club?

10. How many goals did Arthur Rowley score in the 1956/57 season?

11. Who has made the most league appearances for the club?

12. Who knocked City out of the 1997/98 UEFA Cup?

13. Where was Trevor Benjamin signed from for £1.5 million in 2000?

14. Why was Gordon Banks sold to Stoke City?

15. Who is the club's most capped player?

LEYTON ORIENT

1. What were Orient founded as in 1888?
2. Why did the club become known as Orient?
3. What name did they adopt after moving to Clapton in 1896?
4. How many London clubs had joined the Football League before Orient?
5. Who did Orient take over Brisbane Road from in 1937?
6. How long was Alec Stock manager at the club?
7. When did Orient win the Third Division (South) title?
8. Which former Newcastle and Nottingham Forest full-back was appointed manager in 1982?
9. Which boxing promoter took over the club in 1995?
10. Against which team, in two separate games, did the team predictably have both their best attendance and record receipts?
11. Who did the club play their first league match against in 1905?
12. Which speedway stadium did the club move to in 1929?
13. What colour shirts did the team wear during the 1998/99 season?
14. Who succeeded Frank Clark as manager in 1991?
15. What is the club nickname?

1. Glyn Cricket and Football Club 2. Because one of their players worked for the 'Orient Steam Navigation' Company 3. Clapton Orient 4. One 5. Leyton FC 6. Ten years 7. 1956 8. Frank Clark 9. Barry Hearn 10. West Ham Utd 11. Leicester Fosse 12. Lea Bridge 13. Croatia-style red and white chessboard shirts 14. Peter Eustace 15. 'The O's'.

LEYTON ORIENT

1. Who did Orient become a 'nursery club' for in the thirties?

2. Which two Nigerian internationals played for the side in the 1970s?

3. Who did Orient play in the 1978 F.A. Cup semi-final?

4. Why did the Rwanda Civil War nearly put the club out of business in 1994?

5. Who is Orient's record transfer signing?

6. Who is the club's record league goalscorer?

7. What is the record transfer fee received by the club?

8. Where was midfielder Ahmet Brkovic born?

9. Who did the club beat in the 1st round of the 1999/00 Worthington Cup?

10. Who was the only Orient player to score a hat-trick in the 1999/00 season?

11. Which forward was born in Senegal?

12. Where was John Chiedozie transferred to in August 1981?

13. How much did Orient pay Wigan for Paul Beesley in October 1989?

14. Which ex-West Ham player took over from Pat Holland in November 1996?

15. What colours do the team play in?

LINCOLN CITY

1. What 'disaster' happened to Lincoln in the 1986/87 season?
2. Although there was a Lincoln FC in 1861, when was the present club founded?
3. What did they become founder members of in 1889?
4. Where did they play their home games for the first nine years?
5. In 1902, they recorded their highest-ever league position, what was it?
6. Who was Lincoln's first full-time manager, a post he held for 19 years?
7. Which former Grimsby Town full-back was appointed manager in 1972?
8. What is the name of Lincoln's ground?
9. What happened at the last match Chris Murphy was manager, at an away game with Bradford City in 1985?
10. What is Lincoln's record league victory?
11. Which centre-forward helped the club win the Third Division (North) in 1931/32?
12. How long did Lincoln stay in the Conference after automatic relegation?
13. Who has made the most league appearances for the club?
14. What has been set up with the objective of buying back the ground's freehold from the council?
15. Which two players have been Lincoln's most capped?

1. They were the first team to be relegated automatically to the Conference 2. 1884
3. The Midland League 4. A field known as John O' Gaunts 5. Fifth in the Second
Division 6. Bill Anderson 7. Graham Taylor 8. Sincil Bank 9. The Valley Parade fire
10. 11-1 (v Crewe, 1951) 11. Allan Hall 12. One season 13. Tony Emery, 402 14. The
Sincil Bank Stakeholders' Association 15. David Pugh and George Moulson.

LINCOLN CITY

1. What is the current club nickname?

2. Who is the club's record league goalscorer?

3. Before the club were known as 'The Red Imps', what was its previous nickname?

4. What is the record transfer fee received by Lincoln?

5. Who did Lincoln sell striker Mick Harford to in 1979?

6. Which long-serving chairman took over as manager of the club for the 1998/99 season?

7. What are the club's home colours

8. What are the club's away colours?

9. Which of John Reames' assistant coaches is now manager of the club?

10. Which two players are the club's joint record signings?

11. Who has made the most appearances for the club?

12. Who was top scorer for Lincoln in 1999/00?

13. Which two Lincoln players have both had spells with Bristol City and Bristol Rovers?

14. Where was defender Steve Welsh born?

15. Which former Leeds Utd player succeeded Colin Murphy as manager in 1990?

1. 'The Red Imps', 2. Andy Graver, 144 3. 'The Citizens', 4. £500,000 for Gareth Ainsworth 5. Newcastle Utd 6. John Reames 7. Red and white striped shirts, black shorts and black socks 8. All violet 9. Phil Stant 10. Dean Walling and Tony Battersby, both £75,000 11. Tony Emery, 402 12. Lee Thorpe 13. Paul Miller and John Vaughan 14. Glasgow 15. Allan Clarke.

LIVERPOOL

1. How was the club formed in 1892?
2. Which manager replaced Phil Taylor in 1959?
3. When was the first league Merseyside derby game played?
4. How much did Markus Babbel cost Liverpool when signed from Bayern Munich in 2000?
5. Who was the last player before Nick Barmby to move directly across Stanley Park from Goodison to Anfield?
6. What name did a Liverpool Evening post journalist give to the Walton Breck Road end in the early 1900's?
7. Who is Liverpool's most expensive signing?
8. What record number of times have Liverpool won the League Championship?
9. Where was striker Ray Kennedy signed from?
10. Which manager led the club to a second 'double' of league title and UEFA Cup in 1976/77
11. Which two wingers helped Liverpool win the 1946/47 League Championship?
12. Who did Liverpool lose to in the 1964/65 European Cup semi-final?
13. Which Gerry and The Pacemakers song did the Kop adopt as their own?
14. How many consecutive League Cups did the team win after beating West Ham Utd in 1981?
15. Who is the club's most capped player?

1. Most of Everton had left Anfield after a row with the landlord, John Houlding, who formed a new team at the ground, Liverpool FC 2. Bill Shankly 3. 13 October, 1894 4. Nothing, he was a free transfer 5. Dave Hickson 6. Spion Kop 7. Emile Heskey, £11 million 8. 18 9. Arsenal 10. Bob Paisley 11. Billy Liddell and Bob Paisley 12. Internazionale 13. 'You'll never walk alone', 14. Three 15. Ian Rush, Wales.

LIVERPOOL

1. Who has made the most league appearances for the club?
2. Where did Bill Shankly sign Ian St. John from?
3. How much were Liverpool paid from Hamburg SV for Kevin Keegan?
4. How long were Liverpool banned from Europe after the Heysel tragedy in 1985?
5. Which two long-serving full-backs won back-to-back Championships in 1921/22 and 1922/23?
6. Which former winger is now Academy Director at Anfield?
7. Who was goalkeeper in the 1984 European Cup win over Roma?
8. Who took over as manager from Bob Paisley in 1983?
9. Who is the club's record league goalscorer?
10. Who scored the only goal in the 1981 European Cup final win over Real Madrid?
11. Who did Liverpool beat in the 1972/73 UEFA Cup final?
12. Who were Liverpool's opponents in the 1989 F.A. Cup semi-final that ended in tragedy at Hillsborough?
13. Who spent a year with Juventus in the late eighties?
14. Who did Liverpool play in the 2000/01 UEFA Cup final?
15. What notice did Bill Shankly erect above the players'

1. Ian Callaghan, 640 2. Motherwell 3. £500,000 4. Six years 5. Ephraim Longworth and Don McKinlay 6. Steve Heighway 7. Bruce Grobbelaar 8. Joe Fagan 9. Roger Hunt, 245 10. Alan Kennedy 11. Borussia Monchengladbach 12. Nottingham Forest 13. Ian Rush 14. Alaves 15. 'This is Anfield'.

LUTON TOWN

1. Which two teams merged in 1885 to form Luton Town FC?
2. What colours did Luton first play in?
3. When did the team become the first club in the south of England to turn professional?
4. Who has made the most league appearances for the club?
5. Who scored the goal that kept Luton in the First Division on the last day of the 1982/83 season, causing David Pleat to run dancing across the Maine Road pitch?
6. Where do Luton play their home games?
7. When did the team win the Third Division (South) title?
8. How many goals did centre-forward Joe Payne score in the 1936/37 season?
9. What organisation did Luton's supporters form when the club was put into administrative receivership?
10. What colour shirts did they wear in the First Division in 1974?
11. What is the club's nickname?
12. Who was sold to Arsenal for £2.5 million in January 1995?
13. How many games did Luton lose when winning the Second Division title in 1981/82?
14. Which future Northern Ireland manager played for the club in the late fifties?
15. Who scored four hat-tricks in the first half of the 1938/39 season?

1. The Wanderers and The Excelsiors 2. Cochineal pink shirts and navy-blue shorts 3. 1890 4. Bob Morton, 494 5. Raddy Antic 6. Kenilworth Road 7. 1936/37 8. 55 9. FLAG (Friends of Luton Action Group) 10. Fluorescent orange 11. 'The Hatters' 12. John Hartson 13. Four 14. Billy Bingham 15. Hugh Billington.

LUTON TOWN

1. How many goals did Joe Payne score in the 12-0 demolition of Bristol Rovers in April 1936?

2. Who did Luton play their first league game against in September 1897?

3. Whose goals helped manager Alec Stock win promotion from the Third Division in 1970?

4. Their only F.A. Cup final appearance, who did Luton lose to in the 1959 final?

5. Which Luton chairman had a firebomb pushed through his letterbox?

6. Who replaced Harry Haslam as manager in 1978?

7. Which club was Lars Elstrup signed from in August 1989?

8. Which well-known comedian was a director at Luton?

9. Who is the club's record goalscorer?

10. Which manager took the team to the top division for the first time in 1955?

11. Which two businessmen headed the management consortium that took over the club in 1999/00?

12. What year did Luton lay an artificial pitch?

13. Which chairman banned all away fans from the ground after a riot by Millwall fans?

14. Who did Luton beat in the 1988 League Cup final?

15. Who is the club's most capped player?

MACCLESFIELD TOWN

1. What year was the club formed?
2. What 'double' did the team achieve in 1911?
3. Who did Macclesfield beat in the first round of the 1968 F.A. Cup?
4. Which First Division side did they play in the third round, the same year?
5. Who did Macclesfield beat 2-0, in the first FA trophy final?
6. What colours do the team play in?
7. Who has made the most league appearances for the club?
8. Where do Macclesfield play their home games?
9. What league did they become founder members of in 1968?
10. Which former Manchester Utd and Northern Ireland player was appointed manager after Peter Wragg left for Halifax?
11. Why were the side not allowed entry to the Football League after winning the Conference title in 1995?
12. What trophy did Macclesfield win in 1996?
13. Whose hat-trick on the first day of the season helped win the Conference title in 1997?
14. How many Cheshire League titles have the team won?
15. When did trainer John Alcock impose strict diets, country walks, Turkish baths, and a smoking ban on the side?

1. 1874 2. The Manchester League and Cheshire Senior Cup 3. Stockport County 4. Fulham 5. Telford Utd 6. Royal blue shirts, white shorts, blue socks 7. Darren Tinson 8. Moss Rose 9. The Northern Premier League 10. Sammy McIlroy 11. Because the Moss Rose ground was deemed unsuitable 12. F.A. Trophy 13. Chris Byrne 14. Six 15. 1890.

MACCLESFIELD TOWN

1. What is the club's nickname?
2. Who were the club's first league victims in the F.A. Cup for twenty years in 1988?
3. Who did Macclesfield beat 4-0 in the second round, in the same year?
4. How did manager Peter Wragg calm his side's supporters during the Rotherham tie?
5. What position did the team finish in their first season in the Conference?
6. Who did Macclesfield replace in the Third Division in 1997?
7. What position did they finish in their first year in Division Three?
8. Why did manager Sammy McIlroy leave the club in 2000?
9. Which former Nottingham Forest and Manchester Utd player took over from McIlroy as manager?
10. Who is Macclesfield's record transfer signing?
11. Which Conference side did Sodje sign from?
12. Who has scored the most league goals for the club?
13. Who was the only ever-present for the 1999/00 league season?
14. What is the record transfer fee received by the club?
15. Who was the club's top-scorer for the 1999/00 season?

1. 'The Silkmen' 2. Carlisle Utd 3. Rotherham Utd 4. By climbing a football pylon 5. 11th 6. Hereford Utd 7. Second 8. To manage Northern Ireland 9. Peter Davenport 10. Efetobore Sodje, £30,000 11. Stevenage Borough 12. John Askey, 25 13. Darren Tinson 14. £40,000 for Mike Lake from Sheffield Utd 15. Richard Barker.

MANCHESTER CITY

1. What name did the club play under when formed in 1887?
2. Who did City beat in Vienna, in the 1969/70 European Cup-winners' Cup final?
3. Which Leeds Utd player did City pay £2.5 million for in 2000?
4. Which former 'World footballer of the Year' joined the club from AC Milan?
5. Who did City beat in the 1904 F.A. Cup final?
6. Where did Manchester City play before building the Maine Road Stadium in 1923?
7. Which wing-half did City sign in 1928?
8. What cup 'double' did the team achieve in 1969/70?
9. Which German keeper played in the 1956 F.A. Cup final with a broken neck?
10. Who did City beat on penalties in the 1999 Division Two play-off final?
11. Which leading Bolton goalscorer joined the club in October 1967?
12. Which Welsh international was sold to Manchester Utd in 1906 and returned to City in 1921?
13. Who was City's goalkeeper for the 1934 F.A. Cup victory against Portsmouth?
14. Who has made the most league appearances for the club?
15. Who did City beat in 1999/00 to ensure automatic promotion to the Premiership?

1. Ardwick FC 2. Gornik Zabrze 3. Alf-Inge Haaland 4. George Weah 5. Bolton Wanderers 6. Hyde Road 7. Matt Busby 8. The League Cup and European Cup-winners' Cup 9. Bert Trautmann 10. Gillingham 11. Francis Lee 12. Billy Meredith 13. Frank Swift 14. Alan Oakes, 565 15. Blackburn Rovers.

MANCHESTER CITY

1. Who is the club's most capped player?
2. How much did Ajax pay for Georgi Kinkladze in May 1998?
3. Which player was signed from Huddersfield Town in 1960 for £10,000 and sold to Torino in 1961 for £110,000?
4. What record attendance watched an F.A. Cup match against Stoke in March 1934?
5. What colours do the team play in?
6. Who was the manager when they won their first League Championship in 1936/37?
7. Which England full-back suffered a career-ending knee injury in the 1955 F.A. Cup final against Newcastle Utd?
8. Who is the club's record league goalscorer?
9. Who did Joe Mercer appoint as his assistant when made manager in 1965?
10. Which former favourite took over from Peter Swales as chairman in February 1994?
11. Which club was Shaun Goater transferred from?
12. Who did City beat on the last day of the 1967/68 season to win the League Championship?
13. Where was £3 million signing Lee Bradbury transferred from in July 1997?
14. Whose overhead kick won the 1976 League Cup Final against Newcastle Utd?
15. Where was midfielder Colin Bell signed from?

1. Colin Bell, England 2. £4.9 million 3. Denis Law 4. 84,569 5. Sky-blue shirts, white shorts 6. Wilf Wild 7. Jimmy Meadows 8. Tommy Johnson, 158 9. Malcolm Allison 10. Francis Lee 11. Bristol City 12. Newcastle Utd 13. Portsmouth 14. Dennis Tueart's 15. Bury.

MANCHESTER UNITED

1. Which club, formed in 1878, were the predecessors of Manchester Utd?
2. Which two names were rejected by the club before settling on 'United'?
3. Which two players made their debut at Anfield in November 1951?
4. How many league goals did David Beckham score in the 1999/00 season?
5. Which two Italian clubs did United beat in the 98/99 Champions' League?
6. Whose back-heeled goal for Manchester City relegated United to the Second Division in 1974?
7. When did the club achieve their first league and cup 'double'?
8. Who did United play when winning their first F.A. Cup final in 1909?
9. Where was captain Charlie Roberts sold, for £1,500 in 1913?
10. When was Matt Busby appointed manager?
11. Who has made the most league appearances for the club?
12. With an average age of 22, when did the Busby Babes win two successive Championships?
13. How many times have the team won the F.A. Cup?
14. Who scored the first goal at Old Trafford, when the club re-opened in 1949?
15. Which journalist coined the expression 'Busby Babes'?

MANCHESTER UNITED

1. What is the club's nickname?
2. What cup did United win five times in a row from 1953?
3. What time is on the stopped clock at Old Trafford, a memorial to the Munich air crash victims?
4. How many goals did George Best score in his 466 games for Manchester Utd?
5. Who did United beat in the 1967/68 European Cup final at Wembley?
6. Who beat United in the 1999/00 Champions' League quarter-finals?
7. Who is the club's record goalscorer?
8. How much did United pay Aston Villa for Dwight Yorke in August 1998?
9. Who scored the two goals for United in the 1999 Champions' League win over Bayern Munich?
10. Why did United have to play their 1956 European Cup match against Anderlecht at Maine Road?
11. Who replaced Ron Atkinson as manager in November 1986?
12. Which country did Andrei Kanchelskis play international football for?
13. Who scored the winning goal in the 1990 F.A. Cup final replay against Crystal Palace?
14. Where was Fabian Barthez signed from in 2000?
15. Who joined United in April 2001 for a new British record of £19.4 million?

1. 'Red Devils' 2. The FA Youth Cup 3. 3.40 4. 166 5. Benfica 6. Real Madrid 7. Bobby Charlton, 199 8. £12.6 million 9. Teddy Sheringham and Ole Gunnar Solskjaer 10. Because Old Trafford had no floodlights 11. Alex Ferguson 12. Russia 13. Lee Martin 14. AS Monaco 15. Ruud van Nistelrooy.

MANSFIELD TOWN

1. What was the club formed as in 1987?
2. What is the record transfer fee received by Mansfield?
3. Who has made the most league appearances for the club?
4. Which team beat Mansfield in the 1st round of the 1999/00 Worthington Cup?
5. What colour are the club shirts?
6. What is the name of Mansfield's ground, one of the oldest in the world?
7. What was the ground named after?
8. How many times did Mansfield apply to join the newly regionalised Third Division (North)?
9. Who did they replace in joining the Third Division (South) in 1931/32?
10. Who set a Third Division record of 55 goals in the 1936/37 season?
11. Where was striker Dudley Roberts transferred from in 1968?
12. Who did Mansfield beat in the 1987 Freight Rover Trophy, in the first penalty shoot-out at Wembley?
13. By what score did Mansfield beat Leeds at Elland Road in a 1994 League Cup match?
14. In the early sixties, where was outside-left Mike Stringfellow sold to?
15. Which two league sides did Mansfield beat in the 1928/29 F.A. Cup?

1. Mansfield Wesleyans 2. £650,000 for Colin Calderwood 3. Rod Arnold, 440 4. Nottingham Forest 5. Amber with royal blue trim 6. Field Mill Ground 7. A nearby cotton mill 8. 5 times 9. Newport County 10. Ted Hartson 11. Coventry City 12. Bristol City 13. 1-0 14. Leicester City 15. Barrow and Wolves.

MANSFIELD TOWN

1. What is the club's nickname?
2. What year did the club become Third Division Champions?
3. Which centre-forward helped the club score 108 goals and promotion in 1963?
4. Who became player-manager in 1996?
5. What is the highest transfer fee paid by Mansfield?
6. Who is the club's most capped player?
7. In 1965, who did Mansfield lose out on promotion to, because of an inferior goal average?
8. What was the only year that Mansfield had to apply for re-election to the league?
9. To which club was Colin Calderwood transferred in July 1993?
10. Which striker, signed in 1999, was a former professional tennis player and room-mate of Tim Henman?
11. What year did Mansfield get to the F.A. Cup quarter-finals?
12. Who did Mansfield beat 7-0 to secure the Fourth Division title in 1975?
13. Who was the only ever-present player in the 1999/00 league season?
14. Where was striker Lee Peacock transferred to?
15. How many seasons have Mansfield played in Division Two?

1. The Stags 2. 1977 3. Ken Wagstaff 4. Steve Parkin 5. £150,000 for Lee Peacock 6. John McClelland, N.I. 7. Bristol City 8. 1947 9. Spurs 10. Michael Boulding 11. 1968/69 12. Scunthorpe 13. Lee Williams 14. Manchester City 15. One year, 1977-78.

MIDDLESBROUGH

1. When did members of Middlesbrough Cricket Club form the club?
2. Where was Christian Karembeu signed from in 2000 for £2.1 million?
3. Which country does Hamilton Ricard play international football for?
4. Which rival side joined the Football League before Middlesbrough did?
5. Who was Gary Pallister transferred to for £2.3 million?
6. Which club did Herbert Bamlett sign George Camsell from in October 1925?
7. Why were the club docked three points in 1996/97?
8. Which manager took the team to their best-ever league finish in 1913/14?
9. Who did Middlesbrough sign as an amateur in 1951?
10. Which player made 356 appearances for the club without missing a game?
11. Who beat Middlesbrough in May 1986 on the last day of the season, which relegated them to the Third Division?
12. Where did the club play prior to the Riverside?
13. How many hat-tricks did George Camsell score when netting 59 league goals in the 1926/27 season?
14. How many matches did Middlesbrough host at Ayresome Park for the 1966 World Cup finals?
15. Which club was Juninho sold to in July 1997 for £12 million?

1. 1876 2. Real Madrid 3. Colombia 4. Middlesbrough Ironopolis 5. Manchester Utd 6. Durham City 7. For failing to play a game against Blackburn Rovers 8. Tom McIntosh 9. Brian Clough 10. David Armstrong 11. Shrewsbury Town 12. Ayresome Park 13. Nine 14. Three 15. Atletico Madrid.

THE FOOTBALL FACT AND QUIZ BOOK

MIDDLESBROUGH

1. Which goalkeeper has made the most league appearances for the club?
2. Why was Wilf Mannion suspended by the League in 1955?
3. Who was signed from Spurs for £42,000, after failing to make the first team at White Hart Lane?
4. What Cup did Middlesbrough win in 1976?
5. When did Middlesbrough become the first club to sign a player for £1,000?
6. Which millionaire businessman became chairman in 1994?
7. Despite replacing manager Raich Carter with Stan Anderson, where were the club relegated to in 1966?
8. Who is the club's most capped player?
9. Who did Jack Charlton sign on a free transfer from Celtic in 1973?
10. How many goals did Brian Clough score in the 9-0 win over Brighton in 1958?
11. Which club did Fabrizio Ravenelli play for before joining Middlesbrough?
12. How many goals did keeper Jim Platt concede in the 1973/74 promotion season?
13. Where did the club play their home games at the start of the 1986/87 season, due to legal battles over Ayresome Park?
14. What is the club's nickname?
15. When did Bryan Robson take over as manager from Lennie Lawrence?

1. Reg Williamson, 603 2. For making newspaper allegations about players receiving illegal payments 3. Graeme Souness 4. Anglo-Scottish Cup 5. 1905 (Alf Common) 6. Steve Gibson 7. The Third Division 8. Wilf Mannion, England 9. Bobby Murdoch 10. Five 11. Juventus 12. 30 13. Hartlepool 14. 'Boro' 15. May 1994.

MILLWALL

1. What name did the club begin playing under when formed?
2. Who was Millwall's top scorer in the 1999/00 season?
3. Who replaced Bruce Rioch as manager in 1992?
4. When did Millwall start to play at The Den, Cold Blow Lane?
5. What are the club's colours?
6. Who beat Millwall in the 1st round of the 1999/00 F.A. Cup?
7. Which factory's workers founded the club in 1885?
8. Who has made the most league appearances for the club?
9. When did Millwall become the first Third Division side to reach an F.A. Cup semi-final?
10. What is the club's nickname?
11. Which manager signed Tony Cascarino?
12. Who beat Millwall 3-1 at home in the 1993/94 Division One play-off semi-final?
13. Which manager introduced executive seats, PA music and a 'ladies' lounge before World War II?
14. What club was Teddy Sheringham sold to?
15. What trophy did the team win three times in a row in the late 19th century, thus keeping it permanently?

1. Millwall Rovers 2. Neil Harris, 25 3. Mick McCarthy 4. 1910 5. White with black trim 6. Hartlepool Utd 7. J.T. Morton's (Jam and marmalade factory) 8. Barry Kitchener, 523 9. 1900 10. 'The Lions' 11. John Docherty 12. Derby County 13. Charlie Hewitt 14. Nottingham Forest 15. The East End Cup.

THE FOOTBALL FACT AND QUIZ BOOK

MILLWALL

1. Why is the Scottish flag's rampant lion on the club's badge?
2. Where was Mark Kennedy sold to in March 1995 for £2.3 million?
3. Who replaced Peter Andersen as manager in 1982, and won promotion to the Second Division in 1985?
4. Who is the club's record league goalscorer?
5. Who beat the team in the 1999 Auto Windscreens Shield final?
6. What did the team become a founder member of in 1958?
7. Who did Millwall play in the inaugural match at the New Den?
8. Where was striker Paul Moody signed from?
9. When did the club play their first-ever season in the top division?
10. Who is the club's most capped player?
11. Who beat Millwall in the 1st round of the 1999/00 Worthington Cup?
12. Who did Millwall sign Paul Goddard from in December 1989?
13. Who captained Millwall to the Second Division Championship in 2000/01?
14. When did the team move to the New Den in Bermondsey?
15. Which club was Tony Cascarino sold to in March 1990?

NEWCASTLE UNITED

1. What were the team called before changing their name to Newcastle United in 1892?

2. Who appeared under the assumed name of 'Hamilton' to avoid detection by his college?

3. Which former Newcastle captain was appointed manager in 1962?

4. Where was Carl Cort transferred from in 2000 for £7 million?

5. How many goals did Hughie Gallacher score in the 1926/27 season?

6. What name were the team founded as in 1881?

7. Who is the club's record league goalscorer?

8. When did Newcastle win their first League title?

9. Who scored a last minute winner in Zagreb to put Newcastle into the group stage of the 1997/98 Champions' League?

10. Where was Bobby Robson manager before coming to St. James' Park?

11. Who replaced Kevin Keegan as manager in 1997?

12. Who was sold to Liverpool in July 1999 for £8 million?

13. Which Colombian forward was signed in 1996?

14. Who did Newcastle beat 6-2 on aggregate to win the 1968/69 Fairs Cup?

15. What nickname is given to Newcastle's supporters?

1. Newcastle East End 2. Colin Veitch 3. Joe Harvey 4. Wimbledon 5. 36 6. Stanley FC 7. Jackie Milburn, 177 8. 1905 9. Temuri Ketsbaia 10. PSV Eindhoven 11. Kenny Dalglish 12. Dietmar Hamann 13. Faustino Asprilla 14. Ujpesti Dozsa 15. 'The Toon Army'.

NEWCASTLE UNITED

1. What year did Newcastle start playing at St. James' Park?
2. Which club was Hughie Gallacher transferred from in 1925?
3. Which Chilean brothers were on the club's books in the early fifties?
4. What was Jackie Milburn's occupation before signing for Newcastle?
5. Who bought the club in December 1991?
6. What season did Kevin Keegan sign for Liverpool?
7. What is the club's nickname?
8. Which goalkeeper, with over 300 games for the club, succeeded Jack Charlton as manager in 1985?
9. Who scored the goals in the 1924 F.A. Cup final victory over Aston Villa?
10. Where was midfielder Christian Bassedas signed from for £4 million in 2000?
11. To which club did Jack Charlton sell Chris Waddle?
12. Who did Newcastle beat in the 1999/00 F.A. Cup semi-final?
13. Which club did Newcastle sign Andy Cole from?
14. Why was Hughie Gallacher suspended by the F.A. for 10 games in 1927/28?
15. Who did Alan Shearer score the 300th goal of his career against, on the last day of the 1999/00 season?

1. 1892 2. Airdrieonians 3. The Robledo brothers 4. A pit apprentice 5. Sir John Hall 6. 1982/83 7. 'The Magpies' 8. Willie McFaul 9. Stan Seymour and Neil Harris 10. Velez Sarsfield 11. Spurs 12. Chelsea 13. Bristol City 14. For pushing the referee into the post-match bath at Huddersfield 15. Arsenal.

NORTHAMPTON TOWN

1. Who founded the team in 1897?
2. Where did the club play home games prior to 1994?
3. What nickname did the team acquire, after the town's dominant industry when formed?
4. Who was appointed player-manager in 1907?
5. Who was the first black outfield player in the league, signed from Tottenham in 1912?
6. How many goals did Cliff Holton score in the 1961/62 season?
7. What is the club's record victory?
8. Where do the club play their home games?
9. Who did Northampton finish third behind in 1960/61 when winning promotion from Division Four?
10. Who did Town beat in the 1996/97 Third Division play-off final?
11. What colours do the team play in?
12. Which former Colchester and Cambridge Utd boss was appointed manager in 1995?
13. How many spells as manager has Bill Dodgin Jnr had with the club?
14. Which non-league club beat Northampton in the 1998/99 F.A. Cup?
15. Which Irish full-back was signed from Exeter to help win promotion in 1962/63?

1. School teachers from the Northampton and District Elementary Schools' Association 2. The County Ground 3. 'The Cobblers' 4. Herbert Chapman 5. Walter Tull 6. 36 7. 10-0 (v Walsall, 1927) 8. Sixfields Stadium 9. Peterborough and Crystal Palace 10. Swansea City 11. Claret shirts with white sleeves, white shorts and socks 12. Ian Atkins 13. Three 14. Yeovil Town 15. Theo Foley.

NORTHAMPTON TOWN

1. Which Northampton player went on to captain Arsenal, and then returned as manager in 1959?
2. When did the team win promotion to Division One for the first time in their history?
3. Who is Northampton's record transfer signing?
4. Why were Northampton not relegated from the Football League after finishing bottom of Division Three in 1994?
5. What is the record transfer fee received by the club?
6. What is the capacity of Sixfields Stadium?
7. Who beat Northampton in the 1997/98 Division 2 play-off final?
8. Which player appeared in every league game except the first, in the 1999/00 season?
9. Who has made the most league appearances for the club?
10. Which former Manchester Utd full-back was appointed manager in 1976?
11. Where did record signing Steve Howard join the club from in February 1999?
12. Who is the club's record league goalscorer?
13. Which Canadian striker joined Northampton from Plymouth Argyle in 1999/00?
14. Who paid £265,000 for Richard Hill in July 1987?
15. Who did the club beat on the last day of the 1999/00 season to win promotion to Division Two?

NORWICH CITY

1. When an amateur club called Norwich City was formed in 1868, what were the team's colours?
2. When was the modern-day Norwich City founded by two schoolmasters?
3. Where did the club play its first home games?
4. Why were the club nicknamed 'The Canaries'?
5. Who was manager when Norwich won the Second Division title in 1972?
6. Who paid £1 million for Kevin Reeves in 1980?
7. On the day of the Hillsborough disaster, who did Norwich play in the other F.A. Cup semi-final?
8. What position did Norwich finish in the first year of the Premiership?
9. What was the record transfer fee received by the club?
10. Who did Norwich beat in the 1993/94 UEFA Cup 1st round?
11. Which well-known cookery expert joined the Norwich board in 1997?
12. When did Norwich reach Division One for the first time in their history?
13. Who did Norwich play in the 1959 F.A. Cup semi-finals?
14. Who is the club's most capped player?
15. Who is the longest-serving manager in the club's history?

1. Violet and black shirts, white shorts, yellow and black tasselled caps 2. 1902 3. Newmarket Road 4. After the city's trade in breeding and exporting pet birds 5. Ron Saunders 6. Manchester City 7. Everton 8. Third 9. £5 million from Blackburn for Chris Sutton 10. Vitesse Arnhem 11. Delia Smith 12. 1972 13. Luton Town 14. Mark Bowen, Wales 15. John Bond, 1973-1980.

NORWICH CITY

1. What are the club colours?
2. Who did Norwich beat 4-3 in the first league match at Carrow Road in 1935?
3. What competition did the team win in 1962?
4. Which Bournemouth strike partnership did John Bond sign?
5. Which German team did Norwich beat in the 1993/94 UEFA Cup 2nd round?
6. Who suceeded Mike Walker as manager in 1998?
7. For how much was Darren Eadie transferred to Leicester City?
8. Who has made the most league appearances for the club?
9. With a combined age of 70, which two strikers helped win the League Cup in 1985?
10. Who is Norwich City's record league goalscorer?
11. Who were the opponents when the club had record receipts in November 1993?
12. Who is the club's record transfer signing?
13. Which country do Raymond De Waard and Fernando Derveld come from?
14. Who was top scorer for the club in the 1999/00 season?
15. Who beat Norwich in the second round of the 1999/00 Worthington Cup?

1. Yellow shirts, green shorts, yellow socks 2. West Ham United 3. The League Cup 4. Phil Boyer and Ted MacDougall 5. Bayern Munich 6. Bruce Rioch 7. £3 million 8. Ron Ashman, 592 9. Mick Channon and Asa Hartford 10. Johnny Gavin, 122 11. Internazionale 12. Jon Newsome, £1 million from Leeds Utd 13. Holland 14. Iwan Roberts 15. Fulham.

NOTTINGHAM FOREST

1. What four innovations were Forest the first team to introduce to the game?
2. When was Brian Clough appointed manager at the club?
3. When did Peter Taylor join the management team?
4. Who is the oldest player to appear for the club?
5. Which club was Canadian full-back Jim Brennan signed from?
6. What is Nottingham Forest's record victory in a competitive fixture?
7. When did the club win their first League Championship?
8. Who has scored the most league goals for the club?
9. Who did the club beat 1-0 in the 1980 European Cup final?
10. Which centre-forward scored 25 goals in his first season with the club, and a club record 36 in his second?
11. What is the club nickname?
12. When did the club win two successive European Cups?
13. Where did the team tour in the summer of 1905?
14. Which player, uncle of Sir Elton John, broke his leg in the 1959 F.A. Cup final against Luton Town?
15. What nickname did Forest adopt in 1882, which caused Notts County to drop them from their fixture list?

1. Referee's whistle, shinpads, goal-nets and crossbars 2. 1975 3. 1976 4. Dave Beasant 5. Bristol City 6. 14-0 v Clapton Orient, F.A. Cup 1st round, 1891 7. 1977/78 8. Grenville Morris, 199 9. Hamburg 10. Wally Ardron 11. 'Reds' 12. 1978/79 and 1979/80 13. South America 14. Roy Dwight 15. 'Garibaldis'.

NOTTINGHAM FOREST

1. Founded in 1865, why were Forest FC called 'Forest'?
2. Who did Forest beat in winning the 1978 League Cup?
3. Who was the club's first full-time manager, appointed in 1936?
4. Who did Forest pay £3.5 million to when signing Pierre van Hooijdonk in March 1997?
5. Which Dutchman replaced Peter Shilton in goal for Nottingham Forest?
6. Where do the club play their home games?
7. Where was former Rangers midfielder Jim Baxter signed from?
8. Who is the club's most capped player?
9. Which club was Eugene Bopp signed from?
10. Which two former Derby players did Brian Clough sign for the Championship-winning team?
11. Which club was Tony Woodcock transferred to?
12. Who has made the most league appearances for the club?
13. Who scored the winning goal for Forest in the 1979 European Cup final against Malmo?
14. Which manager guided the team to promotion when winning the 1997/98 First Division title?
15. How much did Liverpool pay Forest for Stan Collymore in June 1995?

NOTTS COUNTY

1. The oldest senior club in the world, when were Notts County formed?
2. What was the club's original name?
3. Who did Notts county sign from Chelsea in November 1947, for £20,000, a British transfer record?
4. When did the club win two successive play-off finals?
5. When did Notts County play Nottingham Forest in the first cross-city derby match to be played anywhere?
6. Who replaced John Barnwell as manager in 1989?
7. Who did County sign in March 1951 from Sheffield Wednesday, breaking the British transfer record for the second time?
8. When did Notts County appear in their only F.A. Cup final?
9. Which club paid £2.5 million for Craig Short in September 1992?
10. What colour shirts do the team wear?
11. Which Scottish international had a second spell with the club in the early eighties?
12. Why did Notts County drop Nottingham Forest from their fixture list in 1877?
13. Which manager won the Fourth Division title with the club in 1971?
14. Who is the club's most capped player?
15. Where do the club play their home games?

1. 1864 2. Notts FC 3. Tommy Lawton 4. 1990 and 1991 5. 22 March 1866 6. Neil Warnock 7. Jackie Sewell 8. 1894 9. Derby County 10. Black and white striped shirts 11. Don Masson 12. Because they thought Forest's players with their humble, artisan backgrounds were not worthy enough opponents 13. Jimmy Sirrel 14. Kevin Wilson, Northern Ireland 15. The County Ground.

NOTTS COUNTY

1. Which Notts County chairman went on to become League president?
2. Who was the Yugoslavian goalkeeper signed by Jimmy Sirrel?
3. When did the club celebrate its centenary?
4. Who is the club's record league goalscorer?
5. What 'first' happened to the club in 1893?
6. Which self-made millionaire rescued the club by becoming chairman in the mid-eighties?
7. When did Notts County become the first team to play 4,000 league games?
8. What is the club's nickname?
9. Who has made the most league appearances for the club?
10. Who did Notts County pay £685,000 to Sheffield Utd for in November 1991?
11. Who was the first player to score a hat-trick in the F.A. Cup final?
12. Only the second League club to achieve promotion by March, which manager won the Third Division title in 1998?
13. Who did County beat on 22 April 1950, to ensure promotion to the Second Division?
14. Which club did Jocky Scott previously manage?
15. Who did Tommy Lawton join as player-manager in 1952, after scoring 90 league goals for the club?

1. Jack Dunnett 2. Raddy Avaramovic 3. 1962. Although it was founded in 1864, the club had played on an 'ad hoc' basis for two years before 4. Les Bradd, 124 5. The first club to be relegated via a 'test match' or 'play-off' 6. Derek Pavis 7. 1998 8. 'The Magpies' 9. Albert Iremonger, 564 10. Tony Agana 11. Jimmy Logan 12. Sam Allardyce 13. Nottingham Forest 14. Dundee 15. Brentford.

OLDHAM ATHLETIC

1. Where was Oldham's first ground?
2. What season were Oldham Division Three Champions?
3. From which club did George Hardwick join as a player-manager in 1950?
4. How many appearances did Dennis Irwin make for Oldham?
5. In which year did Oldham play their first F.A. Cup match?
6. Which current London club chairman bought the club in 1965?
7. Who conceded six goals in the first leg of the 1990 League Cup semi-final?
8. Who beat Oldham in the 1990 League Cup final?
9. Under what name did the club form in 1895?
10. What year did the club lay a miniturf playing surface?
11. Who wore the number '3' shirt for every league match during the 1999/00 season?
12. When were Oldham relegated to the Fourth Division?
13. When was Andy Ritchie appointed manager?
14. Who beat Oldham in the 1st round of the 1999/00 Worthington Cup?
15. Which team beat Oldham in the 1913 F.A. Cup semi-final?

THE FOOTBALL FACT AND QUIZ BOOK

OLDHAM ATHLETIC

1. What is Oldham's nickname?
2. Which former midfielder was appointed manager in 1970?
3. Who was goalkeeper during the 1989/90 Cup runs?
4. How much did Aston Villa pay for Earl Barrett?
5. Who is Oldham's most capped player?
6. What are the club's first choice colours?
7. Who scored six goals in the 1989 League Cup defeat of Scarborough?
8. What is the Oldham fanzine called?
9. Who beat Oldham in the 1994 F.A. Cup semi-final replay?
10. Which former England striker succeeded Jimmy Frizzell as manager?
11. Where was defender Scott McNiven born?
12. Where was midfielder Lee Duxberry transferred from?
13. At which club did manager Andy Ritchie start his playing career?
14. What is Oldham's ground called?
15. Who was the chairman who resigned in 1999, after mentioning the idea of a merger between Oldham, Bury and Rochdale?

1. The Latics 2. Jimmy Frizzell 3. Jon Hallworth 4. £1.7 million 5. Gunnar Halle 6. All blue with red trim 7. Frankie Bunn 8. 'Beyond the Boundary' 9. Manchester Utd 10. Joe Royle 11. Leeds 12. Bradford City 13. Manchester Utd 14. Boundary Park 15. Ian Stott.

OXFORD UNITED

1. Under what name was the club formed in 1893?
2. Which team did Oxford beat in the 1986 League Cup final?
3. Which player holds the record number of league appearances for the club?
4. Which striker was transferred from Newport County to Oxford?
5. Who succeeded Bill Asprey as manager in 1980?
6. When did Oxford change their name from Headington United?
7. Where do the club play their home games?
8. The collapse of which team led to Oxford's admittance to the Football League?
9. Which year did Oxford reach the quarter-finals of the F.A. Cup?
10. Who had a controversial plan to merge Oxford with Reading?
11. How much did Leicester have to pay for Matt Elliott?
12. From 14th November 1987, how long did the team go without a win?
13. Who is the club's most capped player?
14. Which wing-half captained the club under Arthur Turner?
15. Who was appointed for his second spell as manager in February 2000?

1. Headington F.C. 2. Q.P.R. 3. John Shuker, 478 4. John Aldridge 5. Ian Greaves 6. 1960 7. The Manor Ground 8. Accrington Stanley 9. 1964 10. Robert Maxwell 11. £1.6 million 12. 27 games 13. Jim Magilton, N. Ireland 14. Ron Atkinson 15. Dennis Smith.

THE FOOTBALL FACT AND QUIZ BOOK

OXFORD UNITED

1. What is Oxford's nickname?

2. Who is President of Oxford?

3. Who did Oxford beat in the 2nd round of the 1999/00 Worthington Cup?

4. Who was bought in to replace John Aldridge?

5. What is the name of Oxford's proposed new ground?

6. What club was Dean Windass transferred from?

7. Who beat Oxford in the 1964 F.A. Cup quarter-final?

8. In which year did the team first win the Third Division title?

9. Who was Oxford's top scorer in 1984-85?

10. Which BBC football pundit became manager in 1988?

11. Who knocked Oxford out of the 1999/00 F.A. Cup in the 3rd round?

12. Who did Liverpool pay £825,000 for in 1987?

13. What nationality is goalkeeper Paul Lundin?

14. What is the capacity of the Manor Ground?

15. What does supporters' organisation FOUL stand for?

1. The U's 2. The Duke of Marlborough 3. Everton 4. Dean Saunders 5. Minchery Farm 6. Aberdeen 7. Preston North End 8. 1968 9. John Aldridge 10. Mark Lawrenson 11. Nottingham Forest 12. Ray Houghton 13. Swedish 14. 9650 15. Fighting for Oxford United's Life.

THE FOOTBALL FACT AND QUIZ BOOK

PETERBOROUGH UNITED

1. Which club was suspended by the FA and disbanded in 1933?
2. Formed the following year, which league did Peterborough Utd play in?
3. Starting in 1955/56, how many successive Midland League titles did they win?
4. Which former Peterborough Cathedral chorister and owner of Pizza Express is the club chairman?
5. Which former Newcastle Utd keeper took Peterborough to the 3rd round of the F.A. Cup for the first time in 1953/54?
6. Which former Arsenal keeper suceeded Fairbrother in 1954?
7. When did Peterborough join the Football League?
8. Where do the club play their home games?
9. Who did Peterborough replace in the League?
10. How many goals did Terry Bly score in the 1960/61 season?
11. What record number of goals did the team score in winning the Fourth Division title at the first attempt?
12. Why did the FA and League launch a joint inquiry into the club in 1967?
13. What did the 1967 inquiry discover?
14. Which First Division club did they beat in the 1964/65 F.A. Cup?
15. Who has been manager of the club since 1996?

1. Peterborough and Fletton FC 2. The Midland League 3. Five 4. Peter Boizot 5. Jack Fairbrother 6. George Swindin 7. 1960 8. London Road Ground 9. Gateshead 10. 52 11. 134 goals 12. Because of alleged financial impropriety 13. The club had offered illegal bonuses to players 14. Arsenal 15. Barry Fry.

THE FOOTBALL FACT AND QUIZ BOOK

PETERBOROUGH UNITED

1. How many points were Peterborough deducted after the 1967 inquiry, just enough to put them bottom of the Third Division table?
2. What is the club's nickname?
3. Which manager gained promotion from the Fourth Division in 1974?
4. Which club did Mark Lawrenson leave to become United manager in 1989?
5. Who is Peterborough's record signing?
6. Which of Barry Fry's previous clubs did Peterborough beat in the 1999/00 play-off semi-finals?
7. Where was Martin O'Connor signed from in July 1996?
8. Who did Peterborough beat 1-0 in the Third Division play-off final in 1999/00?
9. Who is the club's record league goalscorer?
10. What colour shirts did the club wear in 1937?
11. Who is the club's most capped player?
12. What is the record transfer fee received by the club?
13. Who was their record 9-1 league win against in September 1998?
14. Who has made the most league appearances for the club?
15. Where was Simon Davies transferred to in December 1999?

1. 19 2. 'The Posh' 3. Noel Cantwell 4. Oxford Utd 5. Martin O'Connor, £350,000 6. Barnet 7. Walsall 8. Darlington 9. Jim Hall, 122 10. Green 11. Tony Millington, Wales 12. £700,000 for Simon Davies 13. Barnet 14. Tommy Robson, 482 15. Tottenham Hotspur.

THE FOOTBALL FACT AND QUIZ BOOK

PLYMOUTH ARGYLE

1. What name did the club form as in 1886?

2. Who was manager in 1995?

3. What is the record transfer fee Plymouth have paid?

4. Who has made the most appearances for the club, with 350 games?

5. What is the capacity of Home Park?

6. What colour shirts do the team wear?

7. Which team beat Plymouth in the 1974 League Cup semi-final?

8. Who was manager of the club from 1910 to 1938?

9. From the 1921/22 season, what position did Argyle finish in the Third Division (South) for six successive years?

10. Which striker was sold to Ipswich in 1976?

11. What were Plymouth the first winners of in 1959?

12. Who paid £750,000 for Mickey Evans in March 1997?

13. What is the club's nickname?

14. Which team beat Plymouth in the 4th round of the 1999/00 F.A. Cup?

15. Who was Plymouth manager from 1978 to 1979?

1. Argyle Athletic Club 2. Steve McCall 3. £250,000 for Paul Dalton 4. Kevin Hodges 5. 19,630 6. Green shirts with white sleeves 7. Manchester City 8. Bob Jack 9. Runners-up 10. Paul Mariner 11. The newly unified Third Division 12. Southampton 13. The Pilgrims 14. Preston North End 15. Malcolm Allison.

PLYMOUTH ARGYLE

1. What year did Argyle play Watford in the F.A. Cup semi-finals?
2. Who is Plymouth's all-time top scorer?
3. Where was forward Martin Gritton born?
4. Who was manager when Plymouth won promotion through the play-offs in 1996?
5. Who was sold to Rotherham in 1985?
6. Who is the club chairman?
7. Where was Jason Rowbotham signed from?
8. Which former England goalkeeper was manager between 1992 and 1995?
9. In which park is the Home Park ground situated?
10. Which club captain followed Malcolm Allison to Manchester City?
11. When were Plymouth relegated to the lowest division of the league for the first time in their history?
12. What is Argyle's record F.A. Cup win?
13. When did Plymouth play their first league game?
14. Which was Ian Stonebridge's only previous club?
15. Which former manager went on to coach Canada in the 1986 World Cup?

PORT VALE

1. Under what name were the club elected to the league in 1892?

2. Who succeeded Jack Mudie as general manager in 1967?

3. What did Port Vale become the first champions of in the 1928/29 season?

4. What name should the club have registered after a shareholders meeting in 1935?

5. What is the capacity of Vale Park?

6. Who did Port Vale replace in the Football League in 1919?

7. Where did the club play their home games prior to 1950?

8. Which player was sold to Derby County in 1995?

9. What is Vale's record league victory?

10. When did Port Vale achieve their highest league position?

11. How many goals did Port Vale concede when winning the 1953/54 Third Division (North) title?

12. Who was sold to Leicester City in 1984 for £66,000?

13. Who is the club's record transfer signing?

14. When was John Rudge appointed club manager?

15. What trophy did the team win in 1993?

PORT VALE

1. What is the club's nickname?

2. Who did Port Vale play in the 1954 F.A. Cup semi-final?

3. Who did Vale beat in the LDV Vans Trophy final in April 2001?

4. Who did Port Vale lose 5-2 against in the 1996 Anglo-Italian Cup?

5. Why were the club expelled from the League in 1965?

6. How much did Vale pay Rhyl in 1984 for striker Andy Jones?

7. How much did Charlton Athletic pay for Andy Jones two years later?

8. Who is the club's most capped player?

9. Which former manager has made most league appearances for the club?

10. Which country was Ville Viljamen born in?

11. Where was Darren Beckford transferred from, to replace Andy Jones?

12. What is the record transfer fee received by the club?

13. What colours do the team play in?

14. Who is the team's record league goalscorer?

15. Who was appointed manager in 1999, after fifteen years of John Rudge?

1. 'The Valiants' 2. West Bromwich Albion 3. Brentford 4. Genoa 5. For making illegal bonus payments to players 6. £5,000 7. £350,000 8. Sammy Morgan, Northern Ireland 9. Roy Sproson, 761 10. Finland 11. Manchester City 12. £2 million from Wimbledon for Gareth Ainsworth 13. White shirts, black shorts, white socks 14. Wilf Kirkham 15. Brian Horton.

PORTSMOUTH

1. What year was the club founded, in the offices of Alderman J.E. Pink?

2. What colour shirts did the club wear in 1899?

3. When did the team win the Third Division (South) title?

4. Who is the club's record league goalscorer?

5. What is the record transfer fee received by the club?

6. Who put Portsmouth out of the 1999/00 F.A. Cup in the 3rd round?

7. Who made his 800th first-team appearance on 22nd September 1999?

8. When did the team win two successive League titles?

9. What is Portsmouth's ground called?

10. Who beat Portsmouth in the 1929 F.A. Cup final?

11. Which two players were signed from Gosport Borough in 1946?

12. How many caps did Jimmy Dickinson win for England?

13. Which manager took the club to the First Division in 1987?

14. Who beat Portsmouth on penalties in the 1992 F.A. Cup semi-finals?

15. Who succeeded John Mortimore as manager in 1974?

1. 1898 2. Salmon-pink shirts with claret collar and cuffs 3. 1923/24 4. Peter Harris, 194 5. £3.5 million for Lee Bradbury 6. Sunderland 7. Alan Knight 8. 1948/49 and 1949/50 9. Fratton Park 10. Bolton 11. Jimmy Scoular and Peter Harris 12. 48 13. Alan Ball 14. Liverpool 15. Ian St. John.

PORTSMOUTH

1. Who was sold to Tottenham after the 1992 F.A. Cup semi-final?
2. Which manager left the club in 1995 to manage Derby County?
3. Who did Portsmouth play in the 1934 F.A. Cup final?
4. What is the club nickname?
5. Who was sold to Aston Villa for £10,000, after the 1934 F.A. Cup final?
6. Who did Portsmouth beat when winning the F.A. Cup in 1939?
7. Which Serbian businessman is the club chairman?
8. Which manager suffered a heart attack after a match with Barnsley in March 1979?
9. Which former England manager was invited to help run the club in 1996?
10. Which country appointed Venables as their national coach?
11. How many goals did Guy Whittingham score in the 1992/93 season?
12. Which club was Lee Bradbury sold to in August 1997?
13. Who has made the most league appearances for the club?
14. Who was the club's leading goalscorer for the 1999/00 season?
15. How much did Portsmouth pay Tottenham Hotspur for Rory Allen in July 1999?

1. Darren Anderton 2. Jim Smith 3. Manchester City 4. 'Pompey' 5. Jimmy Allen 6. Wolves 7. Milan Mandaric 8. Jimmy Dickinson 9. Terry Venables 10. Australia 11. 42 12. Manchester City 13. Jimmy Dickinson, 764 14. Steve Claridge, 14 15. £1 million.

THE FOOTBALL FACT AND QUIZ BOOK

PRESTON NORTH END

1. Which former players are the two new stands named after?
2. How long have Preston played at Deepdale?
3. Which club, formed in 1863, do Preston have their origins in?
4. Who preceeded Harry Catterick as manger?
5. Which Preston keeper was Britain's first black professional footballer?
6. By what score did the team beat Hyde in the 1st round of the 1887 F.A. Cup?
7. What did the club install in 1986?
8. When did Preston become the first champions of the Football League?
9. Who beat Preston to the league title on goal average in 1953?
10. Which former Preston player became manager in 1961?
11. What is the record transfer fee received by the club?
12. Which Preston forward began his career with IA Akranes?
13. What club was Kevin Kilbane transferred to in June 1997?
14. When were the club relegated to the Third Division for the first time in their history?
15. What assemblage of football memorabilia will be housed in the Football Museum at Deepdale?

PRESTON NORTH END

1. What is the club nickname?
2. What was Tom Finney's occupation before signing with Preston?
3. Who is Preston's record signing?
4. Who did Preston lose to in the 1989 Third Division play-off semi-final?
5. Which 17-year-old scored both goals in the 3-2 defeat by West Ham Utd in the 1964 F.A. Cup final?
6. How many caps did Tom Finney win for England?
7. Who were the only two ever-presents in the 1999/00 league season?
8. What colours do the team play in?
9. Who is the record league goalscorer for the club?
10. Which club was midfielder Rob Edwards signed from?
11. Who has made the most league appearances for the club?
12. With which club was manager David Moyes an apprentice?
13. When were Preston relegated to Division Four for the first time?
14. Who was Preston's top scorer for the 1999/00 season?
15. Who beat Preston in the 5th round of the 1999/00 F.A. Cup?

1. 'The Lilywhites' 2. A plumber 3. Michael Appleton, £500,000 4. Port Vale 5. Howard Kendall 6. 76 7. Graham Alexander and Michael Jackson 8. White shirts, navy shorts, white socks 9. Tom Finney, 187 10. Bristol City 11. Alan Kelly, 447 12. Celtic 13. 1985 14. Jonathan Macken, 22 15. Everton.

QUEENS PARK RANGERS

1. Which two clubs combined to form Q.P.R.?

2. Who has made most league appearances for the side, with 519 games?

3. In which year were Q.P.R. First Division runners-up?

4. From which club was Terry Venables signed?

5. Who scored 13 goals in 7 consecutive League and F.A. Cup games during 1933/34?

6. What year were Q.P.R. runners-up in the F.A. Cup final?

7. Which player was signed from Fulham in 1965/66 for £15,000?

8. Who did Q.P.R. beat 6-0 on the last day of the 1998/99 season to ensure First Division status?

9. Who succeeded Ray Wilkins as manager in 1996?

10. Who beat Q.P.R. 3-0 in the 1985/86 League Cup final?

11. What is the club's record F.A. Cup win?

12. Who beat Q.P.R. in the quarter-finals of the UEFA Cup in 1976/77?

13. When did the club install an Omniturf plastic pitch?

14. How long was Tommy Docherty manager of the club in 1968?

15. What is the record transfer fee received by Q.P.R.?

1. Christchurch Rangers and St. Jude's Institute 2. Tony Ingham 3. 1975/76 4. Spurs 5. Jack Blackman 6. 1982 7. Rodney Marsh 8. Crystal Palace 9. Stewart Houston 10. Oxford Utd 11. 8-1 v Bristol Rovers 12. AEK Athens 13. 1981 14. 28 days 15. £6 million for Les Ferdinand.

QUEENS PARK RANGERS

1. Who beat Q.P.R. to the league title in 1975/76?
2. From which club was Chris Kiwomya signed?
3. In which country was striker Sammy Koejoe born?
4. Who were Q.P.R.'s opponents in the 1982 F.A. Cup final?
5. Which other club shares Loftus Road?
6. What colour shirts did Q.P.R. play in before the current blue and white hoops?
7. Who was manager Alec Stock's first signing?
8. Which club was David Seaman signed from?
9. Who only missed one league match in the 1999/00 season?
10. Which club was Les Ferdinand transferred to in 1995?
11. Who did Gordon Jago sign to replace Rodney Marsh?
12. When were the club relegated from the Premier League?
13. Who is Q.P.R.'s all-time top scorer?
14. What is the capacity of Loftus Road?
15. Which club did manager Dave Sexton leave for in 1977?

READING

1. Where were the club formed in 1871?
2. Who defeated Reading 18-0 in the 1st round of the F.A. Cup in 1894?
3. How much did Newcastle Utd pay for Shaka Hislop in August 1995?
4. Who did Reading lose to in the 1995/96 Division One play-off final?
5. Where did Reading play their home games prior to 1998?
6. Why were the team known as 'The Biscuitmen' until 1974?
7. Who did Reading play in the 1927 F.A. Cup semi-final?
8. Who was appointed manager in succession to Maurice Evans in 1984?
9. Who did Reading beat in the 1988 Simod Cup Final?
10. Which joint-record signing came from Brentford for £800,000 in August 1977?
11. What is the name of their new stadium, completed in 1998?
12. How many goals did Ron Blackman score in the 1951/52 season?
13. Which management pair replaced Mark McGhee in 1994?
14. Which club was Trevor Senior signed from?
15. What colour shirts do Reading wear?

READING

1. On what site did Reading build their new stadium in 1988?

2. What is the club's nickname?

3. What happened to the team in their centenary season of 1970/71?

4. What was Robert Maxwell's name for the proposed merger of Oxford Utd and Reading?

5. Where was striker Kerry Dixon signed from?

6. Which joint record signing came from Cambridge Utd in February 2000?

7. Which toupee-loving goalkeeper replaced Shaka Hislop?

8. Who is the team's most capped player?

9. Where did Reading sign Darren Caskey from?

10. Who is the club's record league goalscorer?

11. How long did keeper Steve Death go without conceeding a goal in 1979?

12. How much did Chelsea pay for Kerry Dixon?

13. Who has made the most league appearances for the club?

14. Who was the club's leading scorer in the 1999/00 season?

15. Who beat Reading in the 3rd round of the 1999/00 F.A. Cup?

ROCHDALE

1. When was the club formed?
2. Who was manager of the club from 1979 to 1980?
3. Who were Rochdale's opponents in the 1962 League Cup final?
4. How old was the youngest player to have played for the club?
5. Who was Rochdale's top scorer in the league during the 1999/00 season?
6. What is the record transfer fee received by Rochdale?
7. Who did Rochdale beat 2-1 to reach the 4th round of the F.A. Cup for the first time in their history in 1971?
8. Where do Rochdale play their home games?
9. Who did Rochdale finish behind when runners-up in Division 3 (North) in 1924?
10. What is the club's record league victory?
11. Who has made most league appearances for Rochdale?
12. Which former Manchester Utd player was manager from 1983 to 1984?
13. Against which club was Rochdale's record attendance?
14. Who knocked Rochdale out of the 1989/90 F.A. Cup in the 5th round?
15. What have the local council officially renamed the ground?

1. 1907 2. Bob Stokoe 3. Norwich 4. Zac Hughes, 16 years 105 days 5. Tony Ellis 6. £400,000 for Stephen Bywater 7. Coventry City 8. Spotland 9. Wolverhampton 10. 8-1 v Chesterfield, 1926 11. Graham Smith, 317 12. Jimmy Greenhoff 13. Notts County 14. Crystal Palace 15. The Denehurst Park Stadium.

ROCHDALE

1. What is the club nickname?

2. When did the club have to make their first application for re-election?

3. Which club was goalkeeper Keith Welch transferred to?

4. Who played in all 46 league games during the 1999/00 season?

5. Which club did Steve Parkin manage before joining the club?

6. What colour shirts do the club play in?

7. What is the record transfer fee paid by Rochdale?

8. Which former Leeds Utd player was manager from 1986 to 1988?

9. Who has scored the most league goals for the club?

10. Which club did Harry Catterick manage after leaving Rochdale in 1958?

11. Which London club was Stephen Bywater transferred to in 1998?

12. Which team did Rochdale beat 6-0 in the 2000/01 season?

13. Where did defender Mark Monington begin his playing career?

14. From which club was Clive Platt signed?

15. Who do Rochdale share their ground with?

1. 'The Dale' 2. 1931 3. Bristol City 4. Wayne Evans 5. Mansfield Town 6. Blue shirts with white trim 7. £100,000 for Clive Platt 8. Eddie Gray 9. Reg Jenkins, 119 10. Sheffield Wednesday 11. West Ham Utd 12. Carlisle United 13. Burnley 14. Walsall 15. Rochdale Hornets RLFC.

THE FOOTBALL FACT AND QUIZ BOOK

ROTHERHAM UNITED

1. Under what name was the club formed in 1877?
2. Who beat Rotherham in the 1998/99 Third Division play-offs?
3. Which ex-Derby County duo shared managerial duties between 1994-1996?
4. In 1907, what did Thornhill change their name to?
5. What is Rotherham's home ground called?
6. Where did midfielder Andy Turner start his playing career?
7. For who did Sheffield Wednesday pay £325,000?
8. Who was appointed manager in 1997?
9. In 1952, identical record crowds turned up to see Rotherham play which two teams?
10. Who is Rotherham's all-time leading goalscorer?
11. Who beat the club in the 1999/00 F.A. Cup 2nd round?
12. In 1954/55, Rotherham finished third in the Second Division, level on points with which two other clubs?
13. When Rotherham were runners-up in the 1999/00 Third Division campaign, who won the title?
14. Which two clubs joined in 1925 to form Rotherham Utd?
15. Which team was Rotherham's Shaun Goater transferred to?

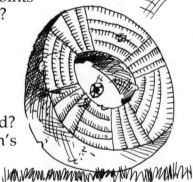

1. Thornhill United 2. Leyton Orient 3. Archie Gemmill and John McGovern 4. Rotherham County 5. Millmoor 6. Tottenham Hotspur 7. Matt Clarke 8. Ronnie Moore 9. Sheffield Utd and Sheffield Wednesday 10. Gladstone Guest, 130 11. Burnley 12. Birmingham and Luton 13. Swansea 14. Rotherham Town and Rotherham County 15. Bristol City.

ROTHERHAM UNITED

1. When did the team win the Third Division (North) Championship?
2. Who left Chelsea to manage Rotherham in 1967?
3. From which club did Leo Fortune-West join Rotherham?
4. Who was ever-present in goal for league games during the 1999/00 season?
5. Which first-ever final did the team reach in 1961?
6. Who did they beat in the first leg of the League Cup final?
7. Which scrap metal merchant became Chairman in 1987?
8. What is the club's nickname?
9. Which former Liverpool and England captain became player-manager in 1981?
10. What is the Rotherham fanzine called?
11. By what score did Rotherham beat Chelsea at Millmoor in the 1981/82 season?
12. How many goals did Leo Fortune-West score in the 1999/00 promotion season?
13. Who were the club's shirt sponsors in the 1999/00 season?
14. Which defender only made one appearance during the 1999/00 season?
15. Who did Rotherham beat in the 1996 Auto Windscreens Shield final?

1. 1951 2. Tommy Docherty 3. Brentford 4. Mike Pollitt 5. The League Cup 6. Aston Villa 7. Ken Booth 8. The Merry Millers 9. Emlyn Hughes 10. Moulin Rouge 11. 6-0 12. 17 13. One 2 One 14. David Artell 15. Shrewsbury Town.

THE FOOTBALL FACT AND QUIZ BOOK

SCUNTHORPE UNITED

1. What is the generally agreed year that Scunthorpe were formed?

2. Which team can Scunthorpe trace their roots back to, playing in the Old Show Ground in 1895?

3. What were the team called in 1910?

4. When was the '& Lindsey' dropped from the name?

5. When were Scunthorpe elected to the Football League?

6. Where did the team play before 1988?

7. What is the club's ground called?

8. Who did they play in their first league match?

9. What 'first' was the result of the East Stand at the Old Show Ground being burnt down by fire?

10. What colour shirts do Scunthorpe play in?

11. Which former England Youth international joined from Mansfield in September 1959?

12. Where was Thomas transferred to in January 1962, having already scored 31 goals in the season?

13. Which manager resigned after being relegated to the Third Division in 1964?

14. Which two strikers were responsible for Scunthorpe winning the Third Division (North) in 1958?

15. Which England manager started his career with the club?

1. 1910 2. Brumley Hall 3. Scunthorpe & Lindsey Utd 4. 1958 5. 1950 6. The Old Show Ground 7. Glanford Park 8. Shrewsbury Town 9. The first steel cantilevered stand in Britain 10. Claret and sky-blue 11. Barrie Thomas 12. Newcastle Utd 13. Dick Duckworth 14. Jack Haigh and Ron Waldock 15. Kevin Keegan.

SCUNTHORPE UNITED

1. What is the club nickname?
2. Which future England keeper started his career with the club in the sixties?
3. Which young apprentice made his first-team debut in December 1968?
4. Why did manager Ron Ashman change the team's claret and blue strip to all-red?
5. How did Liverpool manager Bill Shankly describe Keegan's transfer fee?
6. Which English cricketer made 11 appearances as a non-contract player for the club in the eighties?
7. Who did Scunthorpe play in the Division Three play-off final in 1992?
8. Where was record signing Steve Torpey transferred from in February 2000?
9. Where was striker Alex Calvo-Garcia born?
10. Which team paid £350,000 for Neil Cox in February 1991?
11. Who has made the most league appearances for the club?
12. How much did Liverpool pay for Kevin Keegan?
13. Who is Scunthorpe's record league goalscorer?
14. Who was the leading goalscorer in the 1999/00 season?
15. Which non-league club knocked Scunthorpe out of the 1999/00 F.A. Cup in the 1st round?

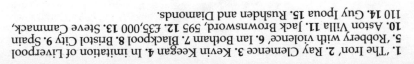

1. 'The Iron' 2. Ray Clemence 3. Kevin Keegan 4. In imitation of Liverpool 5. 'Robbery with violence' 6. Ian Botham 7. Blackpool 8. Bristol City 9. Spain 10. Aston Villa 11. Jack Brownsword, 595 12. £35,000 13. Steve Cammack, 110 14. Guy Ipoua 15. Rushden and Diamonds.

SHEFFIELD UNITED

1. How was the club formed in 1889?
2. Who did they finish runners-up to in their first year in the Second Division in 1892?
3. Who did United play in the 1992/93 F.A. Cup semi-final?
4. Where was Frenchman Laurent D'Jaffo signed from?
5. Which former pit-man was signed from Derby County?
6. Where did loan signing Carl Serrant come from for the 2000/01 season?
7. What is the club's nickname?
8. Who was Brian Deane sold to in July 1993?
9. Which manager won promotion with the team in 1982 and 1984?
10. When was the only time Sheffield United have won the League championship?
11. Who was the 22 stone goalkeeper who played for the club at the end of the 19th century?
12. Who is the club's most capped player?
13. Buying the freehold to Bramall Lane from the Duke of Norfolk in 1897 for £10,000, when did United repay the loan?
14. How many unbeaten games did Trevor Hockey and Tony Currie help the club achieve between March and October 1971?
15. Who scored over 100 league goals for the club before retiring in 1957?

1. Sheffield Wednesday stopped using Bramall Lane for important fixtures, so the ground's management resolved to keep football there by forming their own team 2. Small Heath 3. Sheffield Wednesday 4. Stockport County 5. Jimmy Hagan 6. Newcastle Utd 7. 'The Blades' 8. Leeds Utd 9. Ian Porterfield 10. 1897/98 11. Bill 'Fatty' Foulkes 12. Billy Gillespie, N. Ireland 13. 1947 14. 22 15. Jimmy Hagan.

THE FOOTBALL FACT AND QUIZ BOOK

SHEFFIELD UNITED

1. Which non-league team beat United in the 1901 F.A. Cup final?
2. Which centre-forward was bought from Sunderland for £325?
3. What colour shirts do the team play in?
4. Who succeeded Reg Freeman as manager in 1955?
5. When were Sheffield United relegated to the Fourth Division for the first time, after missing a penalty in the last minute of the last game that would have kept them up?
6. Which manager introduced Alan Birchenall and Mick Jones into the side?
7. When was the last county cricket match played at Bramall Lane?
8. Which club was Patrick Suffo transferred from?
9. Who has made the most league appearances for the club?
10. Who did the club beat in the 'Khaki Cup Final' in 1915, the crowd being mainly made up of soldiers?
11. Who beat the club in the last minute of the 1996/97 Division One play-off final?
12. Where was Don Hutchison signed from in January 1996?
13. Who is the club's Belarussian striker?
14. Which Sheffield-born manager replaced Adrian Heath as manager in 1999?
15. Who is the club's record league goalscorer?

1. Tottenham Hotspur 2. Alf Common 3. Red and white stripes 4. Joe Mercer 5. 1981 6. Johnny Harris 7. 7 August 1973 8. Nantes 9. Joe Shaw, 629 10. Chelsea 11. Crystal Palace 12. West Ham Utd 13. Peter Katchuro 14. Neil Warnock 15. Harry Johnson, 205.

SHEFFIELD WEDNESDAY

1. When did members of the Sheffield Wednesday Cricket Club form the club?

2. What name did they first play under?

3. Who led the team back to the First Division in 1984?

4. Which country does Gilles de Bilde play for?

5. Where was midfielder Wim Jonk signed from?

6. What is the club's nickname?

7. Who did Wednesday play in both the FA Cup and League Cup finals in 1993?

8. Which manager won back-to-back League Championships in 1929 and 1930?

9. What are the club colours?

10. Which three Wednesday players were involved in a betting scandal in 1964?

11. How many goals did Derek Dooley score in the 1951/52 season?

12. Who is the club's most capped player?

13. Who was appointed manager in 1977?

14. Who was Niclas Alexandersson sold to in summer 2000 for £2.3 million?

15. Who did Wednesday pay £4.7 million to in signing Paolo di Canio in August 1997?

1. 1867 2. The Wednesday FC 3. Howard Wilkinson 4. Belgium 5. PSV Eindhoven 6. 'The Owls' 7. Arsenal 8. Robert Brown 9. Blue and white striped shirts, black shorts and socks 10. Tony Kay, Peter Swan and 'Bronco' Layne 11. 46 12. Nigel Worthington, Northern Ireland 13. Jack Charlton 14. Everton 15. Celtic.

THE FOOTBALL FACT AND QUIZ BOOK

SHEFFIELD WEDNESDAY

1. Which manager arrived from Rochdale in 1958 and left for Everton in 1961?
2. Which Italian club was Des Walker transferred from?
3. Who scored both goals for Wednesday in their first F.A. Cup final victory against Wolves in 1896?
4. What was the score of the Boxing day match with Sheffield United in 1979?
5. Who is the club's record goalscorer?
6. Where was Paul Warhurst transferred to in September 1993?
7. Why did the Owlerton Ground change its name to Hillsborough in 1912?
8. Where did Harry Catterick transfer Albert Quixall to in 1958?
9. Who did Ron Atkinson sign John Sheridan from in 1989?
10. Who beat the club 8-0 in September 1999?
11. Who has made the most league appearances for the club?
12. Who was transferred to Brescia on a free transfer in 2000?
13. Who was club captain for the League Cup win over Manchester Utd in 1991?
14. Who was appointed manager after Ron Atkinson left to manage Aston Villa in 1991?
15. Which two Italian strikers played for Wednesday in the 1998/99 season?

SHREWSBURY TOWN

1. When did Shrewsbury join the Football League?
2. What cup did Town win for the first time in 1891?
3. Which Shrewsbury player holds the League record for goals scored?
4. What are the club's colours?
5. How much did Crewe pay for Dave Walton in 1997?
6. Who beat Shrewsbury in the 1982 F.A. Cup 6th round?
7. How much did Mark Blake cost when signed from Southampton in August 1990?
8. Why did Shrewsbury have nine rejections from trying to join the Football League?
9. Why did the club have a net attached to a long pole as part of the club equipment?
10. Which Shrewsbury striker became player-manager in 1984?
11. Who beat Town in the 1996 Auto Windscreens Trophy final?
12. Which Leicester City striker joined Town as player-manager in 1958?
13. What position did Shrewsbury finish in the Fourth Division when winning promotion in 1958/59?
14. Where do Shrewsbury play their home games?

1. 1950 2. The Welsh Cup 3. Arthur Rowley, 434 4. Amber and blue striped shirts, blue shorts, blue socks with amber trim 5. £500,000 6. Leicester City 7. £100,000 8. On the (unofficial) grounds that Shrewsbury was too isolated 9. To rescue over-hit passes and miscued clearances from the River Severn close-by 10. Chic Bates 11. Rotherham Utd 12. Arthur 'Gunner' Rowley 13. Fourth 14. Gay Meadow 15. 1985.

THE FOOTBALL FACT AND QUIZ BOOK

SHREWSBURY TOWN

1. Which school's old boys formed a club called Shrewsbury Town in 1876?
2. Which league did the club play in before and after World War I?
3. The current Shrewsbury Town being formed in 1886, what name do Shrewsbury School old boys now play under?
4. Who was manager when Shrewsbury were relegated to Division Four in 1974?
5. Which 'John Bond assistant' took the club to the Third Division title in 1992/93
6. Which 40-year old played for Shrewsbury in 1991?
7. What are the club's two nicknames?
8. Which manager took the club into the top half of the league for the first time when winning the Third Division title in 1979?
9. Which two players have won the most caps at Shrewsbury?
10. To which club did Shrewsbury pay £100,000 for John Dungworth?
11. Which central defender has made the most league appearances for the club?
12. Who did Shrewsbury beat on the last day of the 1999/00 season to stay in the Football League?
13. Which club did Gordon Turner go to manage in 1984?
14. Which player, in his third spell at the club, only missed two league games in the 1999/00 season?
15. When was the only time the club has reached the League Cup semi-finals?

1. Shrewsbury School 2. The Birmingham League 3. Old Salopians 4. Alan Durban 5. Fred Davies 6. Asa Hartford 7. 'Town' and 'Blues' 8. Graham Taylor 9. Jimmy McLaughlin and Bernard McNally, both N. Ireland 10. Aldershot 11. Colin Griffin, 406 12. Exeter City 13. Aston Villa 14. Mickey Brown 15. 1961.

SOUTHAMPTON

1. Which club did most of the team's founders come from?
2. Who scored the winning goal in the 1976 F.A. Cup final against Manchester Utd?
3. Who did Southampton finish runners-up to in Division One in 1983/84?
4. Which former Hampshire Cricket Club ground did the team play at in 1886?
5. Who did Glenn Hoddle sign on a free transfer from Tennis Borussia Berlin in 2000?
6. Whose members founded the club in 1885?
7. What colours do the team play in?
8. Who did Southampton sign at the end of the 1980/81 season?
9. Who is the club's record league scorer?
10. What are the names of the three Wallace brothers that played for the club in the eighties?
11. Why did an underground brook flood the pitch in World War II?
12. Whose ground did Southampton have a brief enforced residence at after World War II?
13. Who did Southampton finish runners-up to when winning promotion to the First Division in 1966?
14. Which local fish merchant and Southampton fan ploughed £10,000 into buying The Dell for the club in 1898?
15. What is the club's nickname?

1. Deanery FC 2. Bobby Stokes 3. Liverpool 4. The Antelope Ground 5. Uwe Rosler 6. St. Mary's Church YMCA 7. Red and white striped shirts, black shorts and socks 8. Kevin Keegan 9. Mick Channon, 185 10. Danny, Rod and Ray 11. After Nazi bombers blew an 18 foot crater in the pitch 12. Portsmouth's 13. Manchester City 14. George Thomas 15. 'The Saints'.

SOUTHAMPTON

1. Who did Glenn Hoddle leave to manage in April 2001?
2. Who has made the most league appearances for the club?
3. What were Southampton the first winners of in 1921?
4. Where was Matt Le Tissier born?
5. Who was appointed manager in 1953, a position he held for 18 years?
6. What country does Marian Pahars play international football for?
7. Which two Southampton players have devised their own internet-based fantasy football game?
8. When did the club reach their first F.A. Cup final?
9. When did they win the newly rationalised Third Division?
10. Who scored 39 goals in the 1959/60 promotion season?
11. Where did Welsh striker Ron Davies join the club from?
12. Who succeeded Ted Bates as manager in 1973?
13. Who did Southampton pay £2 million to Sheffield Wednesday for in October 1997?
14. Where did Lawrie McMenemy sign centre-half Mel Blyth from?
15. Where did Southampton play home games from 1898 to 2001?

1. Spurs 2. Terry Paine, 713 3. The newly-formed Third Division (South) 4. Guernsey 5. Ted Bates 6. Latvia 7. John Beresford and David Hughes 8. 1900 9. 1960 10. Derek Reeves 11. Norwich City 12. Lawrie McMenemy 13. David Hirst 14. Crystal Palace 15. The Dell.

THE FOOTBALL FACT AND QUIZ BOOK

SOUTHEND UNITED

1. When were Southend Utd founded?
2. Who was the club's first secretary-manager in 1906?
3. After their pitch had been turned into allotments during World War I, where did Southend play their home games?
4. Who did Southend play their first league game against?
5. Which former Chelsea player was appointed General Manager in 1988?
6. Which Southend player was sold to Tottenham in 1989?
7. Where do Southend play their home games?
8. Which England player did Dave Webb succeed as manager?
9. When did Southend play in Division One for the first time in their history?
10. Although only manager at the club for a few months, who signed Stan Collymore to the club?
11. How much did Southend pay Crystal Palace for Stan Collymore in November 1992?
12. What colour shirts do Southend play in?
13. Which two former managers were involved in legal action with the club over compensation claims?
14. Who is the club's record league goalscorer?
15. Where was striker Yemi Abiodun born?

THE FOOTBALL FACT AND QUIZ BOOK

 # SOUTHEND UNITED

1. What is Southend's record Cup victory, a score they have recorded three times?

2. When were Southend relegated to the Fourth Division for the first time?

3. Which club chairman was banned by the league because of share dealings with other clubs?

4. What is the club nickname?

5. What is the furthest the club has got in the League Cup?

6. Who was Stan Collymore sold to in June 1993?

7. What is the record attendance at Roots Hall?

8. What was the original Roots Hall?

9. Who has played the most league games for the club?

10. Who was the club's leading scorer in the 1999/00 season?

11. How many different clubs has keeper Mark Prudhoe played for?

12. What is the record transfer fee received by the club?

13. Who knocked the club out of the 1999/00 Worthington Cup in the 1st round?

14. Who is Southend's most capped player?

15. Which former York City boss was appointed manager in March 1999?

1. 10-1 2. 1966 3. Anton Johnson 4. 'The Shrimpers' 5. Never got past the 3rd round 6. Nottingham Forest 7. 31,090 v Liverpool, F.A. Cup 3rd round, 1979 8. An 18th century house in Prittlewell 9. Sandy Anderson, 452 10. Martin Carruthers, 19 11. Seventeen 12. £3.57 million (for Stan Collymore) 13. Oxford Utd 14. George Mackenzie, Eire 15. Alan Little.

STOCKPORT COUNTY

1. Who founded the club in 1893?

2. What was the team called in 1893?

3. In 1906, the team finished 10th in the Second Division, when did they surpass this?

4. Appointed manager in 1989, where was Danny Bergara born?

5. Who beat Stockport in the 1990 Division Four play-off semi-finals?

6. Where was midfielder Kent Bergersen born?

7. Who were the only two ever-presents in the 1999/00 league campaign?

8. What is the record transfer fee received by the club?

9. What is Stockport's home ground called?

10. Who beat the club in the 1992 Autoglass Trophy final?

11. Where was striker Brett Angell transferred to in 1990?

12. Who succeeded Bergara as manager in 1995?

13. What is the record transfer fee paid by the club?

14. Who is Stockport's record league goalscorer?

15. What are the club's colours?

1. Members of the Wycliffe Congregational Chapel 2. Heaton Norris Rovers 3. 1998 4. Uruguay 5. Chesterfield 6. Oslo 7. Mike Flynn and Kevin Cooper 8. £1.6 million for Alan Armstrong 9. Edgeley Park 10. Stoke City 11. Southend Utd 12. Dave Jones 13. £800,000 for Ian Moore 14. Jack Connor, 132 15. Blue shirts with a vertical white stripe down the middle, blue shorts, white socks.

THE FOOTBALL FACT AND QUIZ BOOK

STOCKPORT COUNTY

1. What is the club's nickname?
2. Which England keeper was sold to Everton in 1925?
3. After Stockport was moved into the new area of Greater Manchester in 1974, what name did the board discuss changing to?
4. Who took over as chairman and saved the club from liquidation in 1998?
5. Which Premiership team did Dave Jones leave Stockport to manage in 1997?
6. Where was goalkeeper Carlo Nash signed from?
7. When did Stockport win promotion to Division One?
8. When did the club reach the League Cup semi-finals?
9. Who beat Stockport in that semi-final?
10. Which club was Ian Moore signed from in July 1998?
11. Where was Alun Armstrong transferred to in February 1998?
12. Who is the club's most capped player?
13. Which 'hole-in-the-heart' player was appointed manager in 1987?
14. What punishment was inflicted on Stockport for fielding an ineligible player in 1926/27?
15. Who has made the most league appearances for the club?

1. 'Hatters' 2. Harry Hardy 3. Manchester South FC 4. Brendan Elwood 5. Southampton 6. Crystal Palace 7. 1996/97 8. 1997 9. Middlesbrough 10. Nottingham Forest 11. Middlesbrough 12. Martin Nash, Canada 13. Asa Hartford 14. They were docked two points 15. Andy Thorpe, 489.

STOKE CITY

1. What name were Stoke formed as in 1868?

2. Who was signed from Leicester City after winning the World Cup with England in 1966?

3. Which country was the consortium that took over the club in 1999/00 from?

4. Which manager won promotion to the First Division in 1979?

5. Who replaced the club in the Football League after Stoke had finished bottom in both years since its formation?

6. When did Stoke win the Second Division title for the first time?

7. Where did Stoke play prior to 1977?

8. What is the team's best finish in the Football League?

9. Who succeeded Tom Mather as manager in 1935?

10. Where was Stanley Matthews born?

11. What colour shirts do the team play in?

12. Which future club manager was transferred from Arsenal in the sixties?

13. Who beat Stoke in both the 1971 and 1972 F.A. Cup semi-finals?

14. Who is the club's most capped player?

15. Where have the club played their home games since 1997?

1. Stoke Ramblers 2. Gordon Banks 3. Iceland 4. Alan Durban 5. Sunderland 6. 1932/33 7. The Victoria Ground 8. Fourth in Division One in 1935/36 and 1946/47 9. Bob McGrory 10. Hanley 11. Red and white striped shirts 12. George Eastham 13. Arsenal 14. Gordon Banks, England 15. The Britannia Stadium.

STOKE CITY

1. Which opposition gave Stoke their record crowd of 51,380 in 1937?

2. How much did Stoke receive from QPR for Mike Sheron in July 1997?

3. Who has made the most league appearances for the club?

4. What is the club's nickname?

5. To which team was Stanley Matthews sold for £10,500, at the age of 32?

6. Which manager re-signed Stanley Matthews for £2,500 at the age of 46?

7. Who scored the goals in the 1972 League Cup final victory over Chelsea?

8. Which club was Dennis Viollet signed from?

9. Who beat Stoke in the 1996 Division One play-off semi-final?

10. Who is the club's record league goalscorer?

11. Which club was Brnynjar Gunnarsson signed from in December 1999?

12. Why was Gordon Banks forced to retire from top-class football in 1972?

13. Where was Graham Kavanagh signed from?

14. Who beat the side in the 1999/00 Division Two play-off semi-finals?

15. How many games did Stoke win when relegated from the First Division in 1984/85?

1. Arsenal 2. £2.75 million 3. Eric Skeels, 506 4. 'The Potters' 5. Blackpool 6. Tony Waddington 7. Terry Conroy and George Eastham 8. Manchester Utd 9. Leicester City 10. Freddie Steele, 142 11. Orgryte 12. After a head-on car crash caused him to lose the sight of one eye 13. Middlesbrough 14. Gillingham 15. Three.

SUNDERLAND

1. Who scored the winning goal in the 1973 F.A. Cup final against Leeds Utd?
2. What name did the team play under when formed in 1879?
3. What rival club did player Jimmy Allen start, in protest at the number of Scotsmen being imported to the club?
4. Whose transfer to Middlesbrough was the first to break the £1,000 barrier?
5. Who has scored the most league goals for the club?
6. How many times have Sunderland been League Champions?
7. Who was the team's goalkeeper for the 1973 F.A. Cup final?
8. How many goals did Kevin Phillips score as the Premiership's leading marksman in the 1999/00 season?
9. Who beat Sunderland in the 1989/90 Division One play-off final, but were demoted due to making illegal payments, Sunderland going up in their place?
10. When did the club move to the Stadium of Light?
11. Who was signed for a record £20,000 fee from Newcastle after World War II?
12. Where was striker Raich Carter born?
13. Who did Sunderland beat 3-1 in their first F.A. Cup final in 1937?
14. Who sustained a career-ending injury at Roker Park in 1962, after scoring 53 goals in 58 games for the club?
15. How many games did Sunderland lose when winning the First Division title in 1998/99?

1. Ian Porterfield 2. Sunderland and District Teachers' Association FC 3. Sunderland Albion 4. Alf Common 5. Charlie Buchan, 209 6. Six 7. Jim Montgomery 8. 30 9. Swindon Town 10. July 1997 11. Len Shackleton 12. Hendon 13. Preston North End 14. Brian Clough 15. Three.

SUNDERLAND

1. Who was top scorer for all three of the Championship winning sides in 1892, 1893 and 1895?
2. When were Sunderland relegated for the first time in their history?
3. Where was defender Stanislav Varga signed from for £650,000?
4. Which manager signed inside-forward Charles Buchan?
5. How many goals did Raich Carter and Bobby Gurney score in the Championship-winning side of 1936?
6. What Cup did Sunderland win in 1969?
7. Who has made the most league appearances for the club?
8. Who was transferred from Valencia in July 1999 for £3.5 million?
9. Which 19-year-old was signed for £3.5 million from Argentinos Juniors in 2000?
10. Where did Sunderland play prior to 1997?
11. Where was Don Hutchison signed from in 2000?
12. Who beat the team in a penalty shoot-out after a 4-4 draw in a Division One play-off semi-final in 1997/98?
13. Who was appointed manager in March 1995?
14. Who is the club's most capped player?
15. Who was Michael Bridges transferred to in July 1999 for £5.5 million?

1. Bobby Campbell 2. 1958 3. SK Slovan Bratislava 4. Bob Kyle 5. 31 each 6. The FA Youth Cup 7. Jim Montgomery, 537 8. Stefan Schwarz 9. Julio Arca 10. Roker Park 11. Everton 12. Charlton Athletic 13. Peter Reid 14. Charlie Hurley, Republic of Ireland 15. Leeds Utd.

SWANSEA CITY

1. Where do Swansea play their home games?

2. What name were the club founded as in 1912?

3. Who was Swansea's first Southern League match at the Vetch Field against in 1912?

4. What cup did they win at their first attempt?

5. Who beat Swansea in the 1926 F.A. Cup semi-finals?

6. Which brothers played for the team in the fifties?

7. Which Welshman joined the club as player-manager in March 1978?

8. What did Swansea win three months after Toshack's appointment?

9. What is the record transfer fee received by the club?

10. When were the team promoted to the First Division?

11. Which cup have Swansea appeared in on seven occasions?

12. How many Swansea players were in the Welsh team that played Ireland in 1981?

13. What position did they finish in the First Division in 1981/82?

14. When did Swansea win the Third Division (South) title?

15. Where is the new stadium that chairman Steve Hamer may move the club to?

SWANSEA CITY

1. When did the club change its name from Swansea Town to Swansea City?

2. What brought about the change of name?

3. What are the club colours?

4. Which two Anfield colleagues did John Toshack sign?

5. Who has made the most league appearances for the club?

6. Who resigned as manager in October 1983, only to be re-appointed in December that year?

7. When was Swansea City officially wound-up?

8. Who did the team play in the 1964 F.A. Cup semi-finals?

9. Which two Yugoslavs played for Swansea in the old First Division?

10. What club did Toshack leave to manage in 1984?

11. Which new chairman rescued the club in 1986?

12. Who beat Swansea 8-0 in the European Cup-Winners' Cup in 1992?

13. Who did the club beat in the 1994 Autoglass Trophy?

14. Replaced by Jan Molby in 1996, how long did P.E. teacher Kevin Cullis last as manager?

15. What is the club's nickname?

1. 1970 2. Swansea attained city status 3. All white, with black and maroon trim 4. Ray Kennedy and Colin Irwin 5. Wilfred Milne, 585 6. John Toshack 7. December 1985 8. Preston North End 9. Dzemal Hadziabdic and Ante Rajkovic 10. Sporting Lisbon 11. Doug Sharpe 12. Monaco 13. Huddersfield Town 14. Seven days 15. 'The Swans'.

SWINDON TOWN

1. Under what name was the club formed in 1881?
2. Who was their first manager, who held the post for 31 years?
3. Which country does striker Danny Invincible play for?
4. Who did the club pay a record fee of £800,000 for in August 1994?
5. Which club did Spartans join with to form Swindon Town?
6. What is the team's home ground called?
7. Who did Swindon beat 3-1 in the 1969 League Cup final?
8. Which team was Kevin Horlock transferred to in January 1997?
9. When were Swindon Division Four Champions?
10. Because of the alleged irregular payments in 1990, who was promoted instead of Swindon from the play-off finals?
11. Which former champion jockey is a board member of Swindon?
12. What unwanted Premiership record do Swindon hold?
13. What year did Swindon reach their first F.A. Cup final?
14. What was Guiliano Grazioli's previous club?
15. Who became manager in the 2000/01 season after Colin Todd's departure?

1. Spartans 2. Sam Allen 3. Australia 4. Joey Beauchamp 5. St. Mark's Young Men's Friendly Society 6. The County Ground 7. Arsenal 8. Manchester City 9. 1986 10. Sunderland 11. Willie Carson 12. Most goals conceded in a season (100) 13. 1910/11 14. Peterborough Utd 15. Andy King.

SWINDON TOWN

1. What is the record transfer fee received by Swindon?
2. Who became manager in 1984?
3. What new points record did the team set in 1986?
4. What year did Swindon win the Anglo-Italian Cup?
5. Who has made the most league appearances for the club?
6. Who beat Swindon in the 1999/00 Worthington Cup 1st round?
7. What was Mark Robinson's former club?
8. Who scored the first goal in the 1969 League Cup final win?
9. Who was Don Rogers transferred to?
10. Who succeeded Lou Macari as manager in 1989?
11. Who made his only appearance of the 1999/00 season as a substitute in the final game?
12. Who was manager for the 1993 play-off final?
13. Which club did Ardiles leave Swindon to become manager of?
14. Who did Swindon beat in the 1993 play-off final?
15. On which team did manager Bert Head base Swindon's kit

TORQUAY UNITED

1. What is the club nickname?
2. What was the merger between United and Ellacombe F.C. in 1910 called?
3. In 1992, after learning from pyschologists of the effects that different colours can have on behaviour, what colour did they paint the visitors' dressing-room?
4. What year did the club form?
5. What is United's record league victory?
6. What was significant about a Torquay home game in February 1992?
7. Who merged with Torquay Town in 1921 to become Torquay United?
8. What colour stripes are on the team shirts?
9. Which team did Torquay replace in the Third Division (South)?
10. Who did Torquay play in the first-ever league match in 1927?
11. Which former Tottenham favourite became manager in 1987?
12. What is the record transfer fee Torquay have received?
13. Who beat Torquay in the 1989 Sherpa Van Trophy Final?
14. Where was forward Jean-Pierre Simb born?
15. Why did Torquay remain in the league in 1996 after finishing bottom?

1. The Gulls 2. Torquay Town 3. Pink 4. 1899 5. 9-0 v Swindon Town, 1952 6. It was the first league game in modern times that there were no uniformed police on duty 7. Babbacombe 8. Yellow and white 9. Aberdare Athletic 10. Exeter City 11. Cyril Knowles 12. £500,000 for Rodney Jack 13. Bolton 14. Paris 15. Because Conference winners Stevenage Borough's ground was not up to league standard.

TORQUAY UNITED

1. What is the name of United's ground?
2. Who did United lose out to on goal average so missing promotion in 1957?
3. How much did Manchester Utd pay for Lee Sharpe in 1988?
4. Who was Torquay's top scorer in 1999/00?
5. Which former player taught the game to Prince Charles at Cheam?
6. What is the most Torquay have paid in the transfer market?
7. What non-league club was Eifion Williams signed from?
8. What is the record attendance at Plainmoor?
9. Where was Wes Saunders signed from?
10. Who is the club's leading all-time goalscorer?
11. Who was Rodney Jack transferred to in July 1998?
12. What is the name of the club fanzine?
13. Who became manager for a second spell in 1981?
14. What is the capacity of Plainmoor?
15. Who is the club's most capped player?

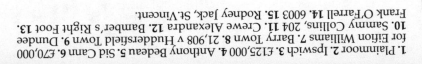

1. Plainmoor 2. Ipswich 3. £125,000 4. Anthony Bedeau 5. Sid Cann 6. £70,000 for Eifion Williams 7. Barry Town 8. 21,908 v Huddersfield Town 9. Dundee 10. Sammy Collins, 204 11. Crewe Alexandra 12. Bamber's Right Foot 13. Frank O'Farrell 14. 6003 15. Rodney Jack, St.Vincent.

TOTTENHAM HOTSPUR

1. Where was the Hotspur Football Club formed from in 1882?
2. What was the club named after?
3. Which former Spurs centre-half who had coached in Hungary, replaced Joe Hulme as manager in 1949?
4. Which club was Jimmy Greaves signed from?
5. Who did Spurs beat 5-1 in the 1963 European Cup-winners' Cup final, becoming the first British team to win a European trophy?
6. What did manager Keith Burkinshaw say when he resigned due to Irving Scholar and Paul Bobroft floating the club on the Stock Exchange?
7. Who did George Graham succeed as manger in October 1998?
8. Who has made the most league appearances for the club?
9. What style of play did Arthur Rowe introduce to the club?
10. Who was captain of Spurs when Bill Nicholson was appointed manager in 1958?
11. Which European club did Spurs sell Chris Waddle to?
12. Who did Spurs beat in the 1999 League Cup final?
13. Who is the club's record league goalscorer?
14. What position did Alf Ramsay play for Tottenham?
15. Which former player and supporters' favourite was appointed manager in 2001?

1. Members of the Hotspur Cricket Club 2. Harry Hotspur, member of the Northumberland family, which owned the land where they played cricket 3. Arthur Rowe 4. AC Milan 5. Atletico Madrid 6. 'There used to be a football club in there' 7. Christian Gross 8. Steve Perryman, 655 9. 'Push and run' 10. Danny Blanchflower 11. Marseilles 12. Leicester City 13. Jimmy Greaves, 220 14. Full-back 15. Glenn Hoddle.

TOTTENHAM HOTSPUR

1. Which founder member of the Football League played Spurs to inaugurate White Hart Lane?
2. Who scored the goals in the victory over Wolves in the 1972 UEFA Cup final?
3. Who is the club's most capped player?
4. When did Spurs win the League Championship for the first time?
5. Who scored four goals for Tottenham in the record 9-0 demolition of Bristol Rovers in 1977?
6. When did Bill Nicholson's 'Super Spurs' become the first team to achieve the 'double' in the 20th century?
7. Who paid £5.5 million for Paul Gascoigne in May 1992?
8. What tradition was started by the Lady Mayoress after Spurs won the 1901 FA Cup?
9. When did Alan Sugar become club chairman?
10. Where was Gary Lineker signed from in 1989, for £1.2 million?
11. Where did Les Ferdinand begin his playing career?
12. Who did Spurs pay £11 million to for Sergei Rebrov in May 2000?
13. Which country does Steffen Iversen play international football for?
14. Who did Spurs beat in the first FA Cup final replay at Wembley in 1981?
15. Which two members of Argentina's 1978 World Cup-winning side did Keith Burkinshaw sign?

1. Notts County 2. Martin Chivers and Alan Mullery 3. Pat Jennings, N. Ireland 4. 1951 5. Colin Lee 6. 1960/61 7. Lazio 8. Draping the team's colours round the trophy 9. 1991 10. Barcelona 11. QPR 12. Dynamo Kiev 13. Norway 14. Manchester City 15. Ossie Ardiles and Ricky Villa.

THE FOOTBALL FACT AND QUIZ BOOK

TRANMERE ROVERS

1. What name did the club play under when formed in 1884?

2. What is the club's nickname?

3. Who succeeded Ronnie Moore as manager in 1987?

4. What is the title of John Aldridge's autobiography?

5. Who was the youngest player to appear for the club, aged 16 years 355 days?

6. Who did Everton pay £3.3 million for in September 1998?

7. How many goals has John Aldridge scored for the club?

8. Which club was Tom 'Pongo' Waring sold to in 1928 for £4,700?

9. When did Tranmere have to apply for re-election?

10. Which American took over the club in 1985?

11. What colour shirts do Tranmere wear?

12. Which three clubs were in front of Tranmere when they won promotion from Division Four in 1967?

13. How many goals did Tranmere's Robert 'Bunny' Bell score in the 13-4 victory over Oldham in 1935?

14. Which former Liverpool defender was appointed manager in 1972?

15. Who is Tranmere's 'long throw' expert?

1. Belmont FC 2. 'The Rovers' 3. John King 4. 'My Story' 5. Dixie Dean 6. Steve Simonsen 7. 131 8. Aston Villa 9. 1981 10. Bruce Osterman 11. White with royal blue bands on the sleeves 12. Stockport, Southport and Barrow 13. Nine 14. Ron Yeats 15. Dave Challinor.

TRANMERE ROVERS

1. Losing 3-0 at half-time, which Premier team did Tranmere score four second-half goals against in the F.A. Cup in 2001?
2. When did Tranmere win their first promotion, winning the Third Division (North) Championship?
3. How many consecutive appearances did Harold Bell make for the club, a league record?
4. Which Tranmere manager changed the club's blue strip, proclaiming 'Liverpool are red, Everton are blue, now Tranmere are all-white'?
5. What trophy did the team win in 1990?
6. Where do Tranmere play their home games?
7. How much did Tranmere pay Aston Villa for Shaun Teale in August 1995?
8. Which club did John Aldridge join Tranmere from?
9. Who did Tranmere play in the 1999/00 League Cup final?
10. Who is the club's most capped player?
11. How many consecutive Division One play-off semi-final appearances have the team made?
12. Where did Tranmere sign striker Stuart Barlow from?
13. Who is the club's record league goalscorer?
14. Who was red-carded in the 1999/00 Worthington Cup final?
15. Who was the club's top-scorer in the 1999/00 season?

WALSALL

1. What name were the club founded as in 1888?
2. Which chairman announced his intention to merge the club with Birmingham City?
3. Who scored 40 goals in the 1933/34 season and the same the following year?
4. Who succeeded Kenny Hibbitt as manager in 1994?
5. Who scored over 20 goals in five successive seasons for the club in the early seventies?
6. At which club did striker Andy Rammell begin his career?
7. What colour shirts do the club play in?
8. Who scored five goals against Walsall in the 1999/00 Worthington Cup?
9. When did Ray Graydon succeed Jan Sorenson as manager?
10. Which Bermudan forward was transferred to Coventry?
11. Which Scottish club did Ray Graydon sell Roger Boli to?
12. Who did Walsall finish runners-up to, in the Second Division in 1998/99?
13. Who has made the most league appearances for the club?
14. Where was defender Gino Padula born?
15. Where did midfielder Ian Brightwell start his league career?

1. Walsall Town Swifts 2. Ken Wheldon 3. Gilbert Alsop 4. Chris Nicholl 5. Alan Buckley 6. Manchester Utd 7. Red shirts with black shoulder panels 8. Sunderland 9. May 1998 10. Kyle Lightbourne 11. Dundee Utd 12. Fulham 13. Colin Harrison, 467 14. Buenos Aires 15. Manchester City.

WALSALL

1. What is the name of Walsall's ground?
2. Which manager won promotion to the Second Division in 1988?
3. Where did Walsall play prior to the Bescot Stadium?
4. Which two players are the club's top league goalscorers?
5. Why did Falkirk play a friendly at the club in December 1957?
6. What is the club's nickname?
7. Which Herbert Chapman side did Walsall beat in the 1937 F.A. Cup?
8. How much did West Ham Utd pay for David Kelly in July 1988?
9. Which striker was sold to Northampton Town in summer 2000?
10. Who did Walsall buy from Birmingham City in June 1979 for £175,000?
11. Which chairman went bankrupt because of the stock-market crash on Black Monday?
12. Who is the club's most capped player?
13. Who beat the club 2-0 on the last day of the 1999/00 season to condemn them to relegation to the Second division?
14. Who beat Walsall in the 3rd round of the 1999/00 F.A. Cup?
15. Which country did non-league signing Charlie Ntamark play for?

1. The Bescot Stadium 2. Tommy Coakley 3. Fellows Park 4. Tony Richards and Colin Taylor, 184 5. To celebrate the official opening of the Fellows Park floodlights 6. 'The Saddlers' 7. Arsenal 8. £600,000 9. Jamie Forrester 10. Alan Buckley 11. Terry Ramsden 12. Mick Kearns, Republic of Ireland 13. Ipswich Town 14. Gillingham 15. Cameroon.

WATFORD

1. Who is Watford's piano-playing chairman?
2. When was Graham Taylor's first appointment as Watford manager?
3. Which two players have won the most international caps at the club?
4. What colour shirts do the team play in?
5. Who did Graham Taylor leave to manage in 1987?
6. Where does the club play its home games?
7. Who did Watford lose to in the 1984 F.A. Cup final?
8. Who paid £2.3 million for Paul Furlong in May 1994?
9. Who did Watford beat in the 1998/99 Division One play-off final?
10. When were Watford promoted to the top flight for the first time in their history?
11. Discovered playing parks football, who was sold to Liverpool in 1984?
12. Which manager changed the team colours to gold, instead of the 'unlucky' turquoise shirts?
13. Which Italian club paid £1 million for Luther Blissett in 1983?
14. Who did Watford finish second in the league to in 1982/83?
15. Which manager announced his retirement at the end of the 2000/01 season?

1. Sir Elton John 2. 1977 3. John Barnes, England and Kenny Jackett, Wales 4. Gold shirts with red and black piping 5. Aston Villa 6. Vicarage Road 7. Everton 8. Chelsea 9. Bolton Wanderers 10. 1982 11. John Barnes 12. Ron Burgess 13. AC Milan 14. Liverpool 15. Graham Taylor.

WATFORD

1. Who has made the most league appearances for the club?
2. Which two players scored 72 goals between them in 1960/61?
3. What is the club nickname?
4. Which European competition did the team play in during the 1983/84 season?
5. Which brewery bought Vicarage Road and leased it back to the club in 1920?
6. When did Watford win the Third Division title?
7. Who was goalkeeper for the 1969 promotion-winning side?
8. Which two Tottenham players joined Watford in summer 2000?
9. What year did the team form as Watford Rovers?
10. Who did Watford appoint in May 2001 as successor to Graham Taylor?
11. Who is the club's record league goalscorer?
12. What did Graham Taylor win in his first two seasons at the club?
13. Where did Dutchman Nordin Wooter begin his playing career?
14. To which club did Watford pay £1.5 million for Heidar Helguson in July 2000?
15. Who beat Watford 5-1 in the 1969/70 F.A. Cup semi-final?

1. Luther Blissett, 415 2. Dennis Uphill and Cliff Holton 3. 'The Hornets' 4. UEFA Cup 5. Benskins 6. 1969 7. Pat Jennings 8. Allan Nielsen and Espen Baardsen 9. 1881 10. Gianluca Vialli 11. Luther Blissett, 148 12. Two successive promotions 13. Ajax 14. Lillestrøm 15. Chelsea.

WEST BROMWICH ALBION

1. Why did workers of Salters Spring Works in West Bromwich send someone shopping to Wednesbury in 1878?
2. What was the name of the newly formed football club?
3. Which player was signed from Toulouse for £400,000 in summer 2000?
4. Who did West Bromwich beat 2-0 on the final day of the 1999/00 season to stay in Division One?
5. Who was manager when the club were relegated to the Third Division for the first time in their history in 1991?
6. Which Argentinian was appointed manager in 1992?
7. Who scored both goals for the club in the 1931 F.A. Cup final win over Birmingham City?
8. What colour shirts do the team play in?
9. Who has scored the most league goals for the club?
10. Where did midfielder Richard Sneekes begin his playing career?
11. Where have the team played their home games since 1900?
12. Which West Bromwich Albion striker became manager for the second time in 1981?
13. Which two players followed Ron Atkinson to Manchester Utd in 1981?
14. When did West Bromwich first win the Division Two title?
15. Who scored the winning goal in the 1968 F.A. Cup final against Everton?

1. Because they wanted to form a football club, but didn't have a football 2. West Bromwich Strollers 3. Derek McInnes 4. The champions, Charlton Athletic 5. Bobby Gould 6. Ossie Ardiles 7. Billy Richardson 8. Navy blue and white stripes 9. Tony Brown, 218 10. Ajax 11. The Hawthorns 12. Ronnie Allen 13. Bryan Robson and Remi Moses 14. 1901/02 15. Jeff Astle.

WEST BROMWICH ALBION

1. When did the team change their name to West Bromwich Albion?
2. How much did West Bromwich pay Preston for Kevin Kilbane in June 1997?
3. Who has made the most league appearances for the club?
4. Which Aston Villa president invited West Bromwich Albion to become founder members of the Football League?
5. What are the club's two nicknames?
6. What trophy did the team win in 1966, the first year they entered it?
7. Who did Ron Atkinson succeed as manager in 1987?
8. Who did West Bromwich play in their first F.A. Cup final?
9. Which club paid £4.3 million for Enzo Maresca in July 2000?
10. When was the only time West Bromwich have won the League Championship?
11. Which manager signed Bob Taylor from Bristol City?
12. Which non-league club beat the team 4-1 in the 1991 F.A. Cup 3rd round?
13. Who was the club's top scorer for the 1999/00 season?
14. How much was striker Jason Roberts signed for?
15. Who is the club's most capped player?

1. 1879 2. £1.25 million 3. Tony Brown, 574 4. William McGregor 5. 'Baggies' and 'Throstles' 6. The League Cup 7. Doug Saunders 8. Blackburn Rovers 9. Juventus 10. Bobby Gould 11. Woking 12. Woking 13. Lee Hughes 14. £2 million 15. Stuart Williams, Wales.

WEST HAM UNITED

1. Why were the team named Thames Ironworks FC in 1895?

2. Situated in the grounds of Upton Park, what is the official name of the club's ground?

3. When did West Ham reach their first cup final, the first to be played at Wembley?

4. Who did Bobby Moore succeed as captain of England?

5. Who did West Ham play in their first game on foreign soil in the 1964/65 Cup-Winners' Cup?

6. Which club did West Ham sign Frank McAvennie from?

7. Who succeeded Ted Fenton as manager in 1961?

8. How much did the club pay Lens for Marc-Vivien Foe in January 1999?

9. Which family has had a presence in the board-room since 1900?

10. Who scored both goals in the 1975 F.A. Cup final win against Fulham?

11. When did West Ham first win the Second Division title?

12. Who did West Ham beat in the 1964 F.A. Cup final?

13. Who is the club's most capped player?

14. Where did players Malcolm Allison, John Bond, Noel Cantwell and others gather to discuss tactics with salt cellars and vinegar bottles?

15. Who is the club's record league goalscorer?

1. After the biggest shipyard in London's East End docks, the Thames Ironworks 2. Boleyn Ground 3. 1923 4. Jimmy Armfield 5. Ghent 6. Celtic 7. Ron Greenwood 8. £4.2 million 9. The Cearns family 10. Alan Taylor 11. 1958 12. Preston North End, 3-2 13. Bobby Moore, England 14. Cassetari's Café 15. Vic Watson, 298.

THE FOOTBALL FACT AND QUIZ BOOK

WEST HAM UNITED

1. Who resigned as manager in May 2001?
2. What is the club's nickname?
3. Which West Ham player's first scouting report said that he could hold his own as a player, but was never going to set the world on fire?
4. What colour shirts do West Ham wear?
5. How much did the club receive from Wimbledon for John Hartson in July 1999?
6. Who ended a 30-year spell as manager when relegated to the Second Division in 1932?
7. Who scored both goals in the 1964/65 Cup-winners' Cup final against TSV Munich 1860?
8. Which First Division club did West Ham, then in the Second, beat in the 1980 F.A. Cup final?
9. Where did West Ham finish in the First Division in 1986, their highest ever position?
10. Who has made the most league appearances for the club?
11. Who was the club's leading goalscorer in the 1999/00 season?
12. Where was defender Steve Potts born?
13. Which former assistant manager and midfield player are father and son?
14. How many times have West Ham been runners-up in the League Cup?
15. Which was the last Italian club Paolo Di Canio played for before coming to Britain?

1. Harry Redknapp 2. 'The Hammers' 3. Bobby Moore 4. Claret with blue sleeves 5. £7.5 million 6. Syd King 7. Alan Sealey 8. Arsenal 9. Third 10. Billy Bonds, 663 11. Paolo Di Canio 12. Hartford, USA 13. Frank Lampard Senior and Frank Lampard Junior 14. Twice, 1966, 1981 15. AC Milan.

WIGAN ATHLETIC

1. What year was Wigan Athletic formed?

2. Which team's demise prompted the formation of Wigan Athletic?

3. What trophy did Wigan win in 1985?

4. Which manager left the club in 2001?

5. How many times have Wigan won the Northern Premier League?

6. Who is Wigan's multi-millionaire chairman?

7. When did Wigan win promotion from the Fourth Division?

8. Who has scored the most league goals for the club?

9. Where were players Jorg Smeets and Arjan De Zeeuw born?

10. Who is Wigan's record signing?

11. Which club was Simon Haworth signed from?

12. What are the club's colours?

13. What is the name of Wigan's ground, named after the chairman's company?

14. Who was top scorer for the 1999/00 season?

15. Which former league manager did John Benson appoint as chief scout?

1. 1932 2. Wigan Borough 3. Freight Rover Trophy 4. Bruce Rioch 5. Three times 6. Dave Whelan 7. 1981/82 8. David Lowe, 66 9. Holland 10. Simon Haworth 11. Coventry City 12. Blue shirts with white side panels, blue shorts and socks 13. JJB stadium 14. Stuart Barlow, 18 15. John Bond.

WIGAN ATHLETIC

1. What is the club's nickname?
2. Before moving to the JJB stadium, where did Wigan play their home games?
3. When did Wigan gain League status?
4. Who did Wigan replace in the Football League?
5. Who did they play their first game in the Football League against?
6. Which league club did Wigan obtain a free set of floodlights from?
7. Who is the club's most capped player?
8. Who do Wigan share their stadium with?
9. What year were Wigan Division Three champions?
10. Who was manager when Wigan were promoted to the League?
11. Which two Wigan players started their careers with Celtic?
12. Who was the only player to score a hat-trick for the club in the 1999/00 season?
13. What is Wigan's record victory?
14. Who took over as manager in April 2001 after Bruce Rioch's departure?
15. Who has made the most league appearances for the club?

1. 'The Latics' 2. Springfield Park 3. 1978 4. Southport 5. Hereford Utd (0-0) 6. Bristol City 7. Roy Carroll, Northern Ireland 8. Wigan Warriors Rugby League team 9. 1996/97 10. Ian McNeill 11. Brian McLaughlin and Stuart Balmer 12. Stuart Barlow 13. 7-1 (v Scarborough) 14. Steve Bruce 15. Kevin Langley, 317.

THE FOOTBALL FACT AND QUIZ BOOK

WIMBLEDON

1. What were the club known as when founded in 1889?

2. When did Wimbledon join the Football League?

3. Who did they replace in the Fourth Division?

4. Who did chairman Ron Noades appoint as manager halfway through the first season?

5. Who did they play their first league match against on 20 August 1977?

6. Where did they sign John Fashanu from in 1986?

7. Who beat Wimbledon on the last day of the 1999/00 season, condemning them to relegation?

8. Where have Wimbledon played home games since 1991?

9. Which manager signed Vinnie Jones in November 1987?

10. Who scored the winning goal in the 1988 F.A. Cup Final against Liverpool?

11. Whose penalty was saved by keeper Dave Beasant in that final?

12. Who has made most league appearances for the club?

13. Who did chairman Sam Hamman sell his share in the club to in 1999/00?

14. How long did Wimbledon play in the top Division?

15. What is the club nickname?

1. Wimbledon Old Centrals 2. June 1977 3. Workington Town 4. Dario Gradi 5. Halifax Town 6. Millwall 7. Southampton 8. Selhurst Park 9. Bobby Gould 10. Lawrie Sanchez 11. John Aldridge 12. Alan Cork, 430 13. A Norwegian shipping and trading company 14. Fourteen years 15. 'The Dons'.

THE FOOTBALL FACT AND QUIZ BOOK

WIMBLEDON

1. What unofficial nickname do the team have?

2. Why did Egil Olsen replace Joe Kinnear as manager in 1999?

3. Who is the club's record goalscorer?

4. What did Dave Bassett do to the clothes of new arrivals when he was manager?

5. Which club was Vinnie Jones signed from?

6. Who was transferred to Grasshoppers of Zurich in August 1999?

7. Where did Wimbledon play home games prior to 1991?

8. Which north-east club was Carl Cort sold to in July 2000?

9. What is Wimbledon's record transfer signing?

10. When was Dennis Wise transferred to Chelsea?

11. Who did Wimbledon sign from Benfica in 2000?

12. Where was Marcus Gayle signed from?

13. What is the record transfer fee received by Wimbledon?

14. Where did Hartson play before signing for the club in January 1999?

15. Who is the club's most capped player?

1. 'The Crazy Gang'. 2. After Joe Kinnear suffered a heart attack 3. Alan Cork 4. Cut them up, on the basis that if they could deal with that, they could face walking out at Old Trafford in front of 50,000 5. Wealdstone 6. Efan Ekoku 7. Plough Lane 8. Newcastle Utd 9. £7.5 million for John Hartson 10. 1990 11. Michael Thomas 12. Brentford 13. £7 million for Carl Cort 14. West Ham Utd 15. Kenny Cunningham, Republic of Ireland.

THE FOOTBALL FACT AND QUIZ BOOK

WOLVERHAMPTON WANDERERS

1. Which two clubs joined forces to form the club in 1877?

2. What is the club's nickname?

3. Who replaced Ronnie Allen as manager in 1968?

4. Who has made the most league appearances for the club?

5. What colours do the club play in?

6. Who did the club sell Robbie Keane to in 1999?

7. Which multi-millionaire bought the club from the Gallagher family in 1990?

8. When did Wolves start playing at the Molineux Grounds?

9. Which club paid £2 million for Neil Emblen in August 1997?

10. Which non-league team beat Wolves in the F.A. Cup in November 1986?

11. Which right-half who played in the 1908 F.A. Cup final was studying to be ordained as a priest?

12. Who succeeded Ted Vizard as manager in 1948?

13. When did the club win its first F.A. Cup final?

14. Who beat Wolves in the 1986/87 Division Four play-off final?

15. When did Wolves win the League Championship for the first time?

1. St. Luke's FC and Blakenhall Wanderers Cricket Club 2. 'Wolves' 3. Bill McGarry 4. Derek Parkin, 501 5. Old gold shirts, black shorts, gold socks 6. Coventry City 7. Jack Hayward 8. 1889 9. Crystal Palace 10. Chorley 11. Kenneth Hunt 12. Stan Cullis 13. 1893 14. Aldershot 15. 1953/54.

WOLVERHAMPTON WANDERERS

1. Who did Wolves pay Bristol City £3 million for in September 1999?
2. Who did Wolves beat in 1954 that had the press declaring them 'World Champions'?
3. Which Wanderers defender won 105 caps for England?
4. How many goals did Steve Bull score in all competitions in 1987/88?
5. Who scored the winning goal against Everton in the 1893 F.A. Cup final?
6. Who was captain of the side that finished runners-up to Arsenal in 1937/38?
7. When did the club go into voluntary liquidation?
8. Which Italian team did Wolves beat en route to the all-English UEFA Cup final in 1971/72?
9. Who was appointed manager in 1927?
10. Whose all-time scoring record did Steve Bull break in 1992?
11. Which brothers took over the club in 1982?
12. Which club was Kevin Muscat signed from?
13. When was the team relegated to the Fourth Division for the first time?
14. What trophy did the team win in 1971?
15. Where was Derek Dougan born?

1. Ade Akinbiyi 2. Honved 3. Billy Wright 4. 52 5. Harry Allen 6. Stan Cullis 7. 1982 8. Juventus 9. Major Frank Buckley 10. John Richards' 11. The Bhatti brothers 12. Crystal Palace 13. 1986 14. The Texaco Cup 15. Ulster.

WREXHAM

1. Who was the club formed by in 1872?
2. What were the club known as in 1884?
3. Which prolific striker became manager in 1985?
4. Where did the players change their kit in the early days?
5. Who did Wrexham beat in the 1999/00 F.A. Cup 3rd Round?
6. Who did Wrexham beat in the 1992 F.A. Cup?
7. What is the name of Wrexham's ground?
8. How many times have Wrexham won the Welsh Cup?
9. Which current midfielder has a famous manager father?
10. What is the record transfer fee received by Wrexham?
11. How many clubs has keeper Kevin Dearden played for?
12. What are the club colours?
13. Who is the club's all-time leading goalscorer?
14. Where was Bryan Hughes transferred to in March 1977?
15. Which sporting event was largely instrumental in rebuilding the Racecourse Ground?

TO THE CHANGING ROOMS

1. Wrexham Cricket Club 2. Wrexham Olympic 3. Dixie McNeil 4. The Turf Hotel 5. Middlesbrough 6. Arsenal 7. The Racecourse Ground 8. 23 9. Darren Ferguson (Sir Alex Ferguson) 10. £800,000 for Bryan Hughes 11. 14 12. Red shirts, white shorts 13. Tom Bamford 14. Birmingham City 15. The 1999 Rugby World Cup.

WREXHAM

1. When were Wrexham crowned Third Division Champions?
2. Which London club was Joey Jones transferred to?
3. How many seasons did Wrexham play in the European Cup-Winners Cup?
4. Which year did Wrexham finish bottom of the Football League?
5. On how many occasions have Wrexham reached the F.A. Cup 6th round?
6. Who was appointed manager in November 1989?
7. What is the record transfer fee paid by Wrexham?
8. How many times have Wrexham won the FAW Premier Cup?
9. What is the team's nickname?
10. Starting from 25 September 1999, what was the team's longest sequence without a league win?
11. Where was Joey Jones transferred from in October 1978?
12. Who has made the most appearances for the team?
13. Who beat Wrexham in the 1st round of the 1999/00 Worthington Cup?
14. Which position in Division Two did Wrexham finish in 2000?
15. Who is Wrexham's most capped player?

1. 1978 2. Chelsea 3. Eight 4. 1991 5. 3 times 6. Brian Flynn 7. £210,000 for Joey Jones 8. Twice 9. The Robins 10. 16 games 11. Liverpool 12. Arfon Griffiths, 592 13. Preston 14. 11th 15. Joey Jones (Wales).

THE FOOTBALL FACT AND QUIZ BOOK

WYCOMBE WANDERERS

1. What is the name of Wycombe's ground?
2. In which year did Wycombe first win the F.A. Trophy?
3. Who was appointed manager in 1990?
4. Which player has made most league appearances for the club?
5. What is Wycombe's record league victory?
6. Who did Wycombe beat 8-7 on penalties in the F.A. Cup 5th round in February 2001?
7. In which year did Wycombe win the GM Vauxhall Conference?
8. For who did manager Lawrie Sanchez score the F.A. Cup winning goal in 1988?
9. Who did Wycombe beat on the last day of the 1998/99 season to avoid relegation?
10. To which club was Keith Scott sold?
11. What is the nickname of Wycombe?
12. Where did goalkeeper Martin Taylor begin his career?
13. Who was appointed the first manager of the club in 1969?
14. Who knocked Wycombe out of the 1999/00 Worthington Cup?
15. To which club did Wycombe sell Mickey Bell?

WYCOMBE WANDERERS

1. When did Wycombe win admission to the Football League?
2. Who did Wycombe beat in the 1st round of the 1999/00 F.A. Cup?
3. To which club was Mark Stallard transferred?
4. Which club won the 1991/92 Conference on goal difference from Wycombe?
5. What is the highest transfer fee paid by Wycombe?
6. How were Wycombe teams selected prior to the appointment of a manager in 1969?
7. What colour quartered shirts do Wycombe wear?
8. What position did Wycombe finish in their first season in Division Three?
9. What was the result of Wycombe's first match in the Football League in 1993 against Colchester?
10. Which team did manager John Gregory leave to manage in February 1998?
11. Which visiting team produced a record attendance of 9,007 in the 1994/95 F.A. Cup?
12. Who did Wycombe beat in the 1991 F.A. Trophy final?
13. What league were Wycombe playing in during 1985?
14. Who is the club's highest league goal scorer?
15. Who did Wycombe beat in the 1993 F.A. Trophy?

YORK CITY

1. What is the club nickname?
2. What is the record transfer fee received by York City?
3. Who did York beat 5-3 on penalties to win the 1993 Third Division play-off final?
4. Where was Ted MacDougall transferred to in 1969?
5. Who was appointed manager in February 2000?
6. Who was beaten 3-0 at home by York in a 1995 League Cup tie?
7. From which club was Steve Agnew signed?
8. Where did 1999/00 top scorer Barry Conlon join the club from?
9. Which non-league team beat York in the 1st round of the 1999/00 F.A. Cup?
10. Who scored six goals in York's 7-1 win over Stockton in the 1928 F.A. Cup?
11. Who took over as caretaker manager in 1999 after the departure of Alan Little?
12. Who did York beat 1-0 in the 4th round of the F.A. Cup in 1985?
13. What addition to the club shirts did manager Tom Johnston make in 1974?
14. When York were elected to the league in 1929, who did they replace?
15. In which season were York Fourth Division Champions?

1. The Minstermen 2. £1 million for Jonathan Greening 3. Crewe 4. Bournemouth 5. Terry Dolan 6. Manchester Utd 7. Sunderland 8. Southend Utd 9. Hereford Utd 10. Jimmy Cowie 11. Neil Thompson 12. Arsenal 13. The addition of a white Y running down the front 14. Ashington 15. 1983/84.

YORK CITY

1. What are the York City colours?

2. Where did York City play before moving to Bootham Crescent?

3. In which year did York reach the semi-finals of the F.A. Cup?

4. What appears on the Club crest?

5. Where was striker Keith Walwyn born?

6. Who is York City's most capped player?

7. For how much was Richard Cresswell sold on transfer deadline day in 1999?

8. Who was the David Longhurst stand named after?

9. What was Bootham Crescent used for prior to its acquisition in 1932?

10. Who replaced John Ward as manager in 1993?

11. Which club beat York in the 1st round of the 1999/00 Worthington Cup?

12. Why did the board order the team to play in brown and cream striped shirts in 1930?

13. Who beat York City in the 1955 F.A. Cup semi-final?

14. What was the aggregate score in the 1996 League Cup victory over Everton?

15. Who succeeded Dennis Smith as manager in 1987?

1. Red shirts, navy shorts, red stockings 2. Fulfordgate 3. 1995 4. Bootham Bar (one of the City's medieval gates) flanked by two lions rampant 5. Jamaica 6. Peter Scott (N.Ireland) 7. £1 million 8. The York striker who collapsed and died on the pitch in 1990 9. Former Yorkshire County Cricket ground 10. Alan Little 11. Wigan Athletic 12. To try and increase support from workers in the local chocolate factory 13. Newcastle 14. 4-3 15. Bobby Saxton.

PLAYING THE GAMES

(football anagrams)

THE FOOTBALL FACT AND QUIZ BOOK

Can you name the Premier and Nationwide clubs from the anagrams below?

1. MOTH LAW PROVEN
2. WANT A NEW SOS
3. TRY BOIL TICS
4. HER HOT RAM
5. SPARE CLAY TALC
6. TEN FOOT HAMSTRING
7. C SLICED FLAME
8. PHANTOMS OUT
9. CAN THE HELM
10. BE WORMY DRAW SCENE
11. FRED THE SLICE
12. ROBE THE GROUP
13. A LOST ANVIL
14. DUD LIFER SHED
15. SPUN THE ROC

1. Wolverhampton 2. Swansea Town 3. Bristol City 4. Rotherham 5. Crystal Palace 6. Nottingham Forest 7. Macclesfield 8. Southampton 9. Cheltenham 10. Wycombe Wanderers 11. Chesterfield 12. Peterborough 13. Aston Villa 14. Huddersfield 15. Scunthorpe.

THE FOOTBALL FACT AND QUIZ BOOK

Can you name the Premier and Nationwide teams from the anagrams below?

1. SWINDON T FLAME

2. CARD HOLE

3. LONG D TRAIN

4. BOTH GLAD TO BE VAIN ON RHINO

5. BRING U DICED MEAT

6. RAVEL TOP

7. BORN BRAVER SULK C

8. DONT SHORTEN R PEN

9. LACTIC THREAT ON HL

10. CELERY SITE TIC

11. PORKY COTT COUNTS

12. REX AND ACE ARWEL

13. BLOWER TANNED ROS

14. SHUT ME IN A CENTRE D

15. H SHUT PATENT MOTOR

THE FOOTBALL FACT AND QUIZ BOOK

Can you name the Scottish clubs from the anagrams and clues below? (Anagrams in capital letters)

1. I STEAL STRING
2. DUE TUNE DINED
3. I HEN BRAIN
4. Red suit
5. DON'T CHEW ABE
6. But Dad's poorly
7. Fruity cake
8. SIFT A FEE
9. Biographer of Princess Diana
10. O SURE SHUT MINE
11. Sounds like British money
12. UM FRIEND LEN
13. LYNDA BECK
14. DARE HE PET
15. He almost met Stanley

THE FOOTBALL FACT AND QUIZ BOOK

Can you name the clubs in the Nationwide Conference and Dr Marten's Premier League from the clues below? (Anagrams are in capital letters)

1. Bad news, monarch
2. Did Robin's men wear this shade?
3. Not the northern harbour
4. The glovers' town
5. Sounds like the lads aren't hungry
6. "I'm the one with the glasses"
7. Bluebirds fly over the cliffs here
8. Monarch's girl-friend
9. GRAB OUR COSH
10. SO TON BED UNIT
11. TEACH HELI FIRST
12. FRED D SHONE
13. LO ICE VAN TOKENS FIT
14. Weight at end for wet weather
15. Spa town but no shower

Can you name the Premiership strikers from the anagrams below?

1. GIDDY HEN MASTER H
2. THEY DIG WORK
3. MU CRATES STRAW
4. ON CLEAR DEW
5. COOL PIANO DAI
6. IE BREAK BONE
7. VICE AIR PARK IT
8. A HOT SUE RANG
9. BORROW BELIEF
10. VALID ASSURES L
11. RAE HE LEARNS
12. ME SHEIK ELEY
13. RUIN JOES WIL
14. NO PURE ALMS
15. SING G GARY

1. Teddy Sheringham 2. Dwight Yorke 3. Marcus Stewart 4. Andrew Cole 5. Paolo Di Canio 6. Robbie Keane 7. Patrick Vieira 8. Shaun Goater 9. Robbie Fowler 10. Darius Vassell 11. Alan Shearer 12. Emile Heskey 13. Junior Lewis 14. Paul Merson 15. Ryan Giggs.

THE FOOTBALL FACT AND QUIZ BOOK

Can you name these leading goal-scorers from the anagrams below?

1. HEE I AM CLOWN
2. BRUISE MO A LOT
3. THORNY POET
4. AND FRES LINED
5. CARE SINGER CHER
6. I BAT SAME JETT
7. OUR KEEN AFC TRIED
8. UGH SHE EEL
9. HA SO I SAUL
10. YEARLY BRASH
11. L RAIN SHIRE
12. COME UNITE RAJ
13. THREE PEN ROT
14. ROB BOMB AYZA
15. WREATH ROBES RAN

Can you name the leading goal-scorers from the anagrams below?

1. PIP LIKES NIL TV
2. US JOE ALLEN
3. JAMS AT NETT
4. SLY GRUNT HN
5. DUCE BERRY
6. RAM BLUER TINT
7. MORE STRIFE JERA
8. JOE FARMED IN EE
9. GRATE ELI JOO
10. RINK NEEDS HOVEN
11. SOH ENDURING JOVE
12. ROBERT HUG WODEN
13. VETERAN EG RISK
14. MARKET CHISEL TIC
15. WORST CAN TED

THE FOOTBALL FACT AND QUIZ BOOK

Can you name the managers from the anagrams below?

1. OGRE AMUSES SEN
2. NUL FAXES OGRE
3. CLING MAN SPAKE
4. JAPE WELL LU
5. STARS IN V FORCE
6. FERRYING CARS
7. YEAR PLOTTER
8. GEE RUGBY LORE
9. DAI DAY LOVER
10. HARDY PN PARKER
11. I RULE REG HAROLD
12. ROGER A HAM EGG
13. EE NEW RANGERS
14. JOY OR EEL
15. STARCH ON DRAGON

1. Graeme Souness 2. Alex Ferguson 3. Nigel Spackman 4. Paul Jewell 5. Trevor Francis 6. Gerry Francis 7. Peter Taylor 8. George Burley 9. David O'Leary 10. Harry Redknapp 11. Gerard Houllier 12. George Graham 13. Arsène Wenger 14. Joe Royle 15. Gordon Strachan.

THE FOOTBALL FACT AND QUIZ BOOK

Can you name the Premier and Nationwide clubs from the clues below?

1. You're sent here in silence
2. Toffee or mint
3. Famous horse race
4. Pensioners live here
5. Home of the Beatles
6. The gap's here
7. World tennis tournament
8. These animals hunt in packs
9. Her Majesty's green keepers?
10. One of the three Rs
11. Army glasshouse town
12. The light blues
13. The dark blues
14. It has a crooked spire
15. A curly one

TOP SCORERS

Who were the leading marksmen for the 1999/00 season?

Who were the league's top-scorers at each club?

1. Manchester Utd?

2. Arsenal?

3. Leeds Utd?

4. Liverpool?

5. Chelsea?

6. Aston Villa?

7. Sunderland?

8. Leicester City?

9. West Ham Utd?

10. Tottenham Hotspur?

11. Newcastle Utd?

12. Middlesborough?

13. Everton?

14. Coventry City?

15. Southampton?

1. Dwight Yorke 2. Thierry Henry 3. Michael Bridges 4. Michael Owen 5. Tore Andre Flo/Gustavo Poyet 6. Dion Dublin 7. Kevin Phillips 8. Tony Cottee 9. Paolo Di Canio 10. Chris Armstrong 11. Alan Shearer 12. Hamilton Ricard 13. Kevin Campbell 14. Robbie Keane 15. Marian Pahars.

1. Derby County?

2. Bradford City?

3. Wimbledon?

4. Sheffield Wednesday?

5. Watford?

6. Charlton Athletic?

7. Manchester City?

8. Ipswich Town?

9. Barnsley?

10. Birmingham City?

11. Bolton Wanderers?

12. Wolverhampton Wanderers?

13. Huddersfield Town?

14. Fulham?

15. Queen's Park Rangers?

1. Rory Delap 2. Dean Windass 3. Carl Cort/John Hartson 4. Gilles De Bilde 5. Heidar Helguson 6. Andy Hunt 7. Shaun Goater 8. David Johnson 9. Craig Hignett 10. Paul Furlong 11. Eidur Gudjohnsen 12. Ade Akinbiyi 13. Clyde Wijnhard 14. Lee Clark 15. Chris Kiwomya.

1. Blackburn Rovers?

2. Norwich City?

3. Tranmere Rovers?

4. Nottingham Forest?

5. Crystal Palace?

6. Sheffield Utd?

7. Stockport County?

8. Portsmouth?

9. Crewe Alexandra?

10. Grimsby Town?

11. West Bromwich Albion?

12. Walsall?

13. Port Vale?

14. Swindon?

15. Preston North End?

1. Burnley?

2. Gillingham?

3. Wigan Athletic?

4. Millwall?

5. Stoke City?

6. Bristol Rovers?

7. Notts County?

8. Bristol City?

9. Reading?

10. Wrexham?

11. Wycombe Wanderers?

12. Luton Town?

13. Oldham Athletic?

14. Bury?

15. Bournemouth?

1. Andy Payton 2. R. Taylor 3. Stuart Barlow 4. Neil Harris 5. Peter Thorne 6. Jamie Cureton/Jason Roberts 7. Mark Stallard 8. Tony Thorpe 9. Darren Caskey 10. Karl Connolly 11. Sean Devine 12. Liam George 13. Mark Allott 14. Andy Preece 15. Mark Stein.

THE FOOTBALL FACT AND QUIZ BOOK

1. Brentford?

2. Colchester Utd?

3. Cambridge Utd?

4. Oxford Utd?

5. Cardiff City?

6. Blackpool?

7. Scunthorpe Utd?

8. Chesterfield?

9. Swansea City?

10. Rotherham Utd?

11. Northampton Town?

12. Darlington?

13. Peterborough Utd?

14. Barnet?

15. Hartlepool Utd?

THE FOOTBALL FACT AND QUIZ BOOK

1. Cheltenham Town?

2. Torquay Utd?

3. Rochdale?

4. Brighton and Hove Albion?

5. Plymouth Argyle?

6. Mansfield Town?

7. Hull City?

8. Lincoln City?

9. Southend Utd?

10. Mansfield Town?

11. Halifax Town?

12. Leyton Orient?

13. York City?

14. Exeter City?

15. Shrewsbury Town?

1. Neil Grayson 2. Anthony Bedeau 3. Tony Ellis 4. Darren Freeman 5. Paul McGregor 6. Richard Barker 7. John Eyre 8. Lee Thorpe 9. Martin Carruthers 10. Chris Greenacre 11. Robbie Painter 12. Iyseden Christie 13. Barry Conlon 14. G. Alexander 15. Lee Steele.

THE
RULES

THE FOOTBALL FACT AND QUIZ BOOK

1. Can a referee caution or send off a player before the match has started?

2. After a match has been stopped, must the referee blow his whistle to signal the start of play?

3. Just as a referee is about to begin a match he notices a player on the pitch who is under suspension. Must he refuse to let him play?

4. What should be the colour of assistant referees' flags?

5. What is the maximum length of a football pitch?

6. What is the minimum length of a football pitch?

7. What is the maximum width of a football pitch?

8. What is the minimum width of a football pitch?

9. What shape should the pitch always be?

10. How far is the penalty spot from the goal-line?

11. What is the diameter of the centre circle?

12. What is the minimum height of a corner flag above the ground?

13. What is the minimum width of a touch-line?

14. What is the maximum width of a touch-line?

15. What are the dimensions of the goals?

1. Yes 2. No 3. No 4. A bright colour, such as red or yellow 5. 130 yards 6. 100 yards 7. 100 yards 8. 50 yards 9. Rectangular (the length must always exceed the width) 10. 12 yards 11. 20 yards 12. 5 feet 13. 5 inches 14. 5 inches 15. 8 yards width by 8 feet high.

THE FOOTBALL FACT AND QUIZ BOOK

1. In a football match, are goal nets compulsory?
2. What is the weight of a football at the start of play?
3. What should be the pressure of a football at the start of play?
4. What is the maximum number of substitutes allowed in a competitive game?
5. Can a referee finish the second half of a game early because of fading light?
6. How long is the halftime interval in the English League?
7. When is the only occasion that time is 'extended' in a match?
8. In which direction does the ball have to go at a kick-off?
9. How many players are allowed to be involved when the referee re-starts play with a dropped ball?
10. What should happen if the ball rebounds into play from a flag post on the halfway line?
11. Can a goal be scored direct from a kick-off?
12. What is the result of an offside decision?
13. Can a player be adjudged offside from a goal-kick?
14. What action should a referee take if a player does not deliberately handle the ball but gain an advantage from the kindly bounce?
15. How should the game be re-started if the referee stops the game to caution a player for entering the field without permission?

1. No 2. 14-16 oz 3. 0.6 - 1.1 atmospheres or 8.5 - 15.6 lbs/sq.in 4. Three 5. No, the law says that a game should be of two equal periods 6. 15 minutes 7. So that the taking of a penalty kick can be completed 8. Forwards 9. As many as want to be. The law does not stipulate a number 10. A throw-in, as the flag at the halfway line must be at least a yard from the touch line 11. Yes 12. An indirect free kick to the defending side from the place where the opponent was standing when adjudged offside 13. No 14. No action 15. An indirect free kick to the player's opponents from where the ball was when the offence occurred.

THE FOOTBALL FACT AND QUIZ BOOK

1. Can a referee take action if a player commits an act of misconduct during the half-time interval?
2. For how long should the referee keep his arm vertical at the taking of an indirect free kick?
3. Can a free kick be passed backwards?
4. What should the referee do if a free kick is taken when the ball is not stationary?
5. How far must the defenders be from the ball if the other side has a free kick?
6. If a player takes a free kick and it rebounds off the referee, can the player play it for a second time?
7. Which one penal offence is not committed against an opponent?
8. Must the ball be played forwards at a penalty kick?
9. Which team takes the first kick at a penalty shoot-out to decide a drawn game?
10. Where must all the players be in a penalty shoot-out, apart from the two goalkeepers and the player taking the kick?
11. What decision does the referee give if a player taking a throw-in advances 6 yards further up the field before throwing the ball in?
12. What happens if the ball fails to enter the field of play at a throw-in?
13. Can a goalkeeper take a throw-in?
14. On what occasions can the ball pass into the goal and a goal-kick be awarded?
15. Can a goal be scored direct from a corner kick?

1. Yes 2. Until theball goes out of play or is touched by another player 3. Yes 4. Stop play, and re-take the free kick 5. 10 yards 6. No, the referee is considered as part of the field of play 7. Deliberate handball 8. Yes 9. The team that won the toss 10. Inside the centre circle 11. A foul throw. The throw-in is awarded to the other side 12. The throw is re-taken 13. Yes 14. When it goes into the goal direct from an indirect free kick 15. Yes.

ALL-TIME GREATS

OSVALDO ARDILES

1. With which club did he turn professional in 1969?
2. What year was Ardiles appointed manager of Swindon Town?
3. Who did Ardiles join on a free transfer in summer 1988?
4. Where was Ardiles born in 1952?
5. For how much was Ardiles sold to Spurs in 1978?
6. Which Argentinian team-mate joined Ardiles at Spurs in July 1978?
7. In his second spell at Spurs in 1983, why was Ardiles out of the game for 10 months?
8. What was the score when he won the UEFA Cup with Spurs in 1984 against Anderlecht?
9. What position in Group C did Argentina finish when Ardiles was playing in his second World Cup finals?
10. Who did Spurs beat in the 1981 F.A. Cup final replay, thus realising Ardiles' ambition?
11. Where did Ardiles go after being sacked as manager of Spurs?
12. Who did Spurs lose to for the first time ever in an F.A. Cup final in 1987?
13. Why did Ardiles return to Argentina in 1982?
14. With Ardiles playing in midfield, who did Argentina beat in the 1978 World Cup final?
15. Who did Ardiles succeed as manager of Spurs in 1993?

ROBERTO BAGGIO

1. For which club did Baggio make his league debut at 15?
2. Where was Baggio born in 1967?
3. Where was he transferred to in 1985?
4. When did Baggio make his international debut?
5. In which year did Baggio miss a penalty in the World Cup Final?
6. What did Baggio become only the third player in Italian football history to achieve in 1996?
7. What caused three days of fans' protests, needing the intervention of riot police, in 1990?
8. How much was Baggio sold to Juventus for, creating a new world record transfer fee?
9. What year was he voted FIFA World Footballer of the Year?
10. What is Baggio's nickname?
11. Why was Baggio substituted in a 1991 match against Fiorentina?
12. What second award did Baggio win in 1993?
13. Who did Juventus beat in the 1993 UEFA Cup final, Baggio scoring two goals?
14. How many goals did Baggio score in the 1994 World Cup finals?
15. In his fifth season at Fiorentina, how many goals did he score in 32 league games?

1. Vicenza 2. Caldogno 3. Fiorentina 4. 1988 5. 1994 6. To win the championship with different clubs in successive seasons 7. Baggio's transfer to Juventus 8. £8 million 9. 1993 10. The golden ponytail 11. He refused to take a penalty against his former club 12. European Footballer of the Year 13. Borussia Dortmund 14. 5 15. 17.

THE FOOTBALL FACT AND QUIZ BOOK

GORDON BANKS

1. Where was Gordon Banks born in 1937?

2. How many England caps has Banks won?

3. What year was he awarded the MBE for services to football?

4. What was Banks' first professional club?

5. Where was Banks transferred to in 1959?

6. Who were Banks and Leicester runners-up to in the 1961 F.A. Cup?

7. When did Gordon make his England debut at Wembley?

8. Which team was his England debut against?

9. Who did Leicester beat 4-3 on aggregate in the 1964 League Cup final?

10. In the 1966 World Cup semi-final, what did Eusebio end?

11. Where was he transferred in 1967, for a British goalkeeping record fee of £65,000?

12. Who played in goal in the 1970 World Cup quarter-final defeat against West Germany, due to Banks' illness?

13. What two awards did Gordon Banks win in 1972?

14. Who did Stoke beat in the 1972 League Cup final?

15. What did Banks lose after a serious car crash in 1972?

1. Sheffield 2. 73 3. 1970 4. Chesterfield 5. Leicester City 6. Tottenham Hotspurs' double-winning side 7. 1963 8. Scotland 9. Stoke City 10. Banks' record of seven consecutive clean sheets 11. Stoke City 12. Peter Bonetti 13. Footballer of the Year award and Sports Personality of the Year 14. Chelsea 15. The sight of one eye.

FRANCESCO 'FRANCO' BARESI

1. Where was Baresi born in 1960?
2. Who did he attend trials at Internazionale with in 1974?
3. Who did he join in 1974, a week after Inter had rejected him for being too frail?
4. How old was Baresi when he made his league debut in 1978?
5. What position was he playing when AC Milan won the Italian championship in 1979?
6. From what was Baresi found to be suffering from in 1980?
7. When were AC Milan relegated to the second division following a betting scandal?
8. Which national coach and twice AC Milan coach has Baresi served under?
9. How many times has Francesco been a national championship winner with AC Milan?
10. Although a member of the 1982 World Cup-winning squad, he didn't make his debut until later in the year against who?
11. Who did AC Milan beat 4-0 in the 1989 European Champions' Cup Final?
12. What colour shirts do AC Milan wear?
13. After winning two successive European Cup titles in 1989 and 1990, why were the team banned from the competition in 1991?
14. Why was Baresi not playing in the 4-0 Champions Cup final thrashing of Barcelona?
15. On his retirement, how many years had he played for Milan, his only club?

1. Travagliato 2. His elder brother 3. AC Milan 4. 18 5. Sweeper 6. A blood disorder 7. 1980 8. Arrigo Sacchi 9. 5 10. Romania 11. Steaua Bucharest 12. Red and black stripes 13. For refusing to take the field after a floodlight failure at Marseille 14. He was suspended 15. 20.

FRANZ BECKENBAUER

1. Where was Beckenbauer born in 1945?
2. Beckenbauer joined the Bayern Munich youth section in 1959 after playing for which schoolboy team?
3. What job did he give up in 1962 to sign full-time with Bayern?
4. Who was Beckenbauer's coach when he made his debut in a 4-0 win against St. Pauli, Hamburg?
5. When did he make his international debut in a 2-1 win over Sweden?
6. What was the score when he captained Bayern Munich to victory over Rangers in the 1967 European Cup-Winners' Cup?
7. What award did Franz win in 1972?
8. Who did West Germany beat when he was captain in the 1972 European Championship final?
9. Which two cups did Beckenbauer win when captain in 1974?
10. Who did West Germany beat in the 1974 World Cup final?
11. How many international caps has Beckenbauer won for his country?
12. Where was Beckenbauer transferred to in 1976?
13. What 'first' did Beckenbauer achieve in 1990?
14. Which French club did he coach in 1993?
15. When was Beckenbauer elected Bayern Munich club president?

1. Munich 2. FC 1906 Munich 3. Trainee insurance salesman 4. Tschik Cajkovski 5. 1965 6. 1-0 7. European Footballer of the Year 8. Soviet Union 9. European Cup and World Cup 10. Holland 11. 103 12. New York Cosmos 13. The first man to captain and then manage a World Cup-winning team 14. Olympique Marseille 15. 1995.

DENNIS BERGKAMP

1. After which of his father's favourite footballers was Bergkamp called Dennis?
2. How old was he when promoted to the Ajax first team in 1984?
3. Who was manager of Ajax when they won the 1987 European Cup-Winners' Cup?
4. When did Bergkamp make his international debut?
5. How many championships did Bergkamp win while at Ajax?
6. Bergkamp was the Dutch league's top scorer for how many successive years?
7. How many goals did Dennis score for Ajax?
8. Who did he replace in the Internazionale team when transferred there in 1993?
9. For how much was he transferred to Arsenal from Inter in 1995?
10. Who did Bergkamp score a hat-trick against in his first season at Arsenal?
11. In which tournament did he become Holland's highest goal-scorer?
12. Which country did Dennis score against to earn him the 1998 World Cup Goal of the Tournament award?
13. What is Bergkamps's great phobia?
14. When did Bergkamp win the top three goals in the BBC's Match of the Day 'Goal of the Month' competition?
15. What year was Bergkamp voted both World and PFA Footballer of the Year?

1. Denis Law 2. 17 3. Johan Cruyff 4. 1990 5. One 6. Three 7. 103 8. Jurgen Klinsmann 9. £7.5 million 10. Southampton 11. 1998 World Cup 12. Argentina 13. Fear of flying 14. September 1997 15. 1998.

GEORGE BEST

1. When was George Best born?
2. How old was Best when joining Manchester Utd as an amateur in 1961?
3. Who discovered Best in the back-streets of Belfast?
4. Who did Northern Ireland beat 3-2 when Best made his international debut?
5. How many league titles did George Best win with Manchester Utd?
6. Who nicknamed him 'El Beatle' in 1966?
7. How many goals did Best score in United's 4-1 victory over Benfica in the European Champions Cup final?
8. How many goals did George score in his 466 game Manchester Utd career?
9. What two awards was Best voted the winner of in 1968?
10. On his debut for Fulham in 1976, how soon in the game did he score?
11. How many caps had Best won when playing against Holland in his last international in 1978?
12. How many goals did Best score in the 1970 F.A. Cup 5th round 8-2 win against Northampton Town?
13. Which Scottish club did Best play for after leaving Fulham?
14. With which club did George Best finish his career?
15. Finish this quote by George Best; "I spent a lot of money on birds, booze and gambling - the rest _____ ".

1. 22 May 1946 2. 15 3. Assistant manager, Jimmy Murphy 4. Wales 5. Two 6. The Portugese, after Benfica had been beaten 5-1 in the Champions' Cup 7. 2 8. 178 9. Footballer of the Year and European Footballer of the Year 10. 71 seconds 11. 37 12. 6 13. Hibernian 14. Tampa Bay Rowdies 15. I just frittered away.

DANNY BLANCHFLOWER

1. What Irish side did Blanchflower join in 1945?

2. Which club did Blanchflower leave when transferred to Aston Villa in 1951?

3. Where was Danny Blanchflower born?

4. How much did Tottenham pay for his services in 1954?

5. What was the name of Blanchflower's brother who was badly injured in Manchester Utd's Munich air crash?

6. What feat did Spurs achieve with Blanchflower as captain in 1961?

7. What was special about the N.Ireland v England international on the 27th of November 1957, when Blanchflower captained the Irish?

8. What award did Blanchflower win in 1958?

9. What year did he captain Spurs to victory in the 3-1 F.A. Cup win against Burnley?

10. When did he win his second Footballer of the Year award?

11. Who did Spurs beat when becoming the first British side to win a European club trophy in 1963?

12. What was the score in the above mentioned final?

13. What caused Danny Blanchflower to retire from the game in June 1964?

14. What year did he become manager of Chelsea?

15. How many caps did Blanchflower win for N.Ireland?

1. Glentoran 2. Barnsley 3. Belfast, 1926 4. £30,000 5. Jackie Blanchflower 6. First team to win the league and cup double in the 20th century 7. First ever win over England at Wembley 8. Footballer of the Year award 9. 1962 10. 1961 11. Atlético Madrid 12. 5-1 13. A knee injury 14. 1978 15. 63.

BILLY BREMNER

1. Where was Billy Bremner born in 1942?
2. At what age did he make his Leeds Utd debut?
3. Who was Bremner's team-mate that would later become his manager?
4. Who did Bremner win his first international cap against in a 0-0 draw at Hampden Park?
5. Despite Bremner scoring, who defeated Leeds 2-1 in the 1965 F.A. Cup Final?
6. How many international caps did Bremner win in his career?
7. What domestic trophy was won with a 1-0 defeat of Arsenal in 1968?
8. Who did Leeds beat in winning the 1968 Inter-Cities Fairs Cup?
9. When did Leeds win their first-ever championship?
10. What year did Bremner win the Footballer of the Year award?
11. Who was sent off along with Bremner in the 1974 F.A.Charity Shield match for fighting?
12. How many goals did Bremner score in his 587 league appearances for Leeds?
13. Which club did Bremner join after leaving Leeds?
14. When did Bremner return to Leeds as manager?
15. Commemorated by a statue at Elland Road, what year was Bremner's untimely death?

HAT BOX –
No 54

ERIC CANTONA

1. Which French club did he make his league debut for in 1983?
2. Where was Cantona born?
3. Who did Cantona make his international debut against in 1987?
4. Which club did Eric join in 1988 for a transfer fee of £2 million?
5. For which team was he playing when winning the French Cup in 1990?
6. Why was he given a year-long ban from the French national team in 1990?
7. Which English club did Cantona have a trial with in 1992?
8. Who did Cantona join in 1992 for £900,000?
9. How much did Manchester Utd pay for his services at the end of 1992?
10. What was Cantona instrumental in winning for Manchester Utd in 1993?
11. What award did Eric win in 1996?
12. At whose ground did he make his 'scissors-kick' attack on a spectator in 1995?
13. What historic 'double' did he achieve as captain in 1996?
14. How old was Cantona when he retired?
15. In which film did Cantona play a French ambassador?

1. Auxerre 2. Paris 3. West Germany 4. Marseille 5. Montpelier 6. For insulting the manager, Henri Michel 7. Sheffield Wed 8. Leeds Utd 9. £1.2 million 10. The League Championship 11. Footballer of the Year 12. Crystal Palace 13. Winning Manchester Utd's second league and cup double win 14. 31 15. Elizabeth.

SIR BOBBY CHARLTON

1. How many caps has Charlton won playing for England?
2. Where was he born in 1937?
3. What year did he sign as a professional for Manchester Utd, becoming one of the 'Busby Babes'?
4. In 1963, Charlton won his first F.A. Cup winners medal, despite playing in his third final. Who were the opponents?
5. Still a record, how many goals has Bobby scored for England?
6. Against which team did Charlton score the first goal of the 1966 World Cup finals?
7. What award did Charlton win in 1966?
8. Who did Manchester Utd beat, with Charlton as captain, in the 1968 European Champions Cup final?
9. How many goals did Charlton score in the 4-1 win against Benfica?
10. Who was the only other player in that cup-winning team to have survived the Munich air disaster with Charlton?
11. What relation of Sir Bobby presents weather reports on BBC television?
12. When did Charlton win the European Footballer of the Year award?
13. How many goals did Bobby score for Manchester Utd in his 606 league appearances?
14. What club did Charlton move to as player-manager in 1972?
15. What year did Bobby Charlton receive his knighthood?

1. 106 2. Ashington, County Durham 3. 1954 4. Leicester City 5. 49 6. Mexico 1966 7. Footballer of the Year 8. Benfica 9. 2 10. Bill Foulkes 11. His daughter 12. 1966 13. 198 14. Preston N.E. 15. 1994.

THE FOOTBALL FACT AND QUIZ BOOK

JOHAN CRUYFF

1. Where was Johan Cruyff born?
2. How old was Cruyff when his mother enrolled him into the Ajax youth section?
3. On the recommendation of which English coach did he sign his first Ajax contract at 15?
4. Who did he score against when making his international debut?
5. Starting in 1971, how many successive European Cups did Cruyff win?
6. Who was he sold to in 1973, for a then world record transfer fee of £922,000?
7. What was the name given to the Dutch style of play in the 1974 World Cup finals?
8. Who did Holland, captained by Cruyff, lose to in the 1974 World Cup final?
9. What is Cruyff's son called, who previously played for Manchester Utd?
10. Which two American clubs has Johan played for?
11. What did Cruyff win in 1974 for the third time, the first player to achieve such a distinction?
12. When did Cruyff return to Ajax as technical director?
13. In what cup did he guide Ajax to victory, during 1987?
14. While manager at Barcelona, who did his team beat to win their first European Cup final?
15. How many consecutive league championships did Cruyff win as Barcelona coach?

1. Amsterdam, 1947 2. 12 3. Vic Buckingham 4. Hungary 5. Three 6. Barcelona 7. 'Total Football' 8. West Germany 9. Jordi 10. Los Angeles Aztecs, Washington Diplomats 11. European Footballer of the Year 12. 1984 13. European Cup-winners' Cup 14. Sampdoria 15. 4.

KENNY DALGLISH

1. In which city was Kenny born?
2. What did Celtic win in the year Dalglish joined them?
3. How many caps has Dalglish won while playing for his country - a Scottish record?
4. Who did Kenny replace when transferred to Liverpool in 1977?
5. How many league goals did Dalglish score for Celtic?
6. Who were Liverpool's opponents in the 1978 Europeans Champions Cup final when Dalglish scored the winning goal?
7. Who did Kenny succeed when appointed player-manager of Liverpool in 1985?
8. What piece of history was made by Dalglish in 1986?
9. With 30 goals to his credit in Scottish internationals, who does he share this record with?
10. How many league goals did Dalglish score during his league career?
11. After resigning from Liverpool in 1990, where did he become manager in 1991?
12. When did Dalglish win the Premiership title with Blackburn?
13. Who did Dalglish succeed as manager of Newcastle?
14. What position did Dalglish's Newcastle side finish in the Premiership in 1997?
15. Which former Anfield colleague did Dalglish appoint at Celtic in 1999?

1. Glasgow 2. The European Champions Cup 3. 102 4. Kevin Keegan 5. 112 6. Club Bruges 7. Joe Fagan 8. The only player-manager to win the league and cup double 9. Denis Law 10. 118 11. Blackburn Rovers 12. 1995 13. Kevin Keegan 14. Runners-up 15. John Barnes.

THE FOOTBALL FACT AND QUIZ BOOK

BILLY 'DIXIE' DEAN

1. Where was Dean born in January 1907?

2. Which club did he first sign professional terms for?

3. What did 'Dixie' break in a road accident in 1924?

4. Which club did Dean join in 1925, staying with them for 13 years?

5. How many goals did Dean score for England in his first five internationals?

6. In 1928, how many goals did he score from 39 league matches?

7. How many goals did Dean score in other competitions during his record 1928 season?

8. How many appearances did 'Dixie' make for England?

9. What was significant about the 3-0 victory in the 1933 F.A. Cup final against Manchester City?

10. What English club was he transferred to in 1938, before moving to Ireland?

11. Which Irish club did he help to the final of the Irish Cup?

12. How many hat-tricks did Dean score in his career?

13. From what profession did he retire in 1964?

14. When was 'Dixie' awarded a belated testimonial match by Everton?

15. At which football ground did 'Dixie' Dean die?

1. Birkenhead, Cheshire 2. Tranmere Rovers 3. His skull 4. Everton 5. 60 7. 22 8. 16 (18 goals) 9. First time numbered shirts were worn in the F.A. Cup final 10. Notts County 11. Sligo Rovers 12. 34 13. Licensee 14. 1964 15. He collapsed at Goodison Park while watching Everton play Liverpool.

DIDIER DESCHAMPS

1. For which club did Deschamps make his league debut in 1986?
2. Who did he make his debut for France against in 1989?
3. With which club did he win the 1990 French league championship?
4. Appearing in his first European Champions Cup final in 1991, who did Marseille lose to on penalties?
5. Deschamps was captain of the Marseille side which beat AC Milan 1-0 in the 1993 European Champions Cup final. Why were the team stripped of the title?
6. Which Italian club was Deschamps transferred to in July 1994?
7. What year did Deschamps help Juventus win the Italian league and cup double?
8. Who did Juventus lose to in the 1995 UEFA Cup final?
9. Who did France lose to in the Euro 96 semi-final?
10. Who did Juventus beat when Deschamps won his first European Champions Cup winners medal in 1996?
11. Who did Deschamps and Juventus lose to in the 1997 Champions Cup final?
12. As captain of France for the 1998 World Cup finals, what position did his team finish?
13. Where was he transferred to in 1999 from Juventus?
14. What cup did Deschamps help Chelsea win in 2000?
15. Who put Deschamps and Chelsea out of the 2000/01 F.A. Cup?

1. Nantes 2. Yugoslavia 3. Red Star Belgrade 4. Marseille 5. Because of allegations of corruption involving the club president Bernard Tapie 6. Juventus 7. 1995 8. Parma 9. Czech Republic 10. Ajax 11. Borussia Dortmund 12. Winners 13. Chelsea 14. The F.A. Cup 15. Arsenal.

ALFREDO DI STEFANO

1. Where was Di Stefano born in 1926?
2. At age 14, for which youth team did he score a hat-trick in 20 minutes?
3. Which of his father's old clubs did he join in 1942 after a row with the Los Cardales coach?
4. Against which Buenos Aires rivals did Di Stefano make his debut for River Plate?
5. Where was he transferred to on loan in 1944?
6. Who did he succeed at centre-forward on his return to River Plate in 1946?
7. What was the nickname given to the River Plate attack in 1946?
8. What year did Di Stefano win the South American Championship with Argentina?
9. During the 1949 Argentine players' strike, where did Di Stefano play?
10. Which Spanish side did he join in 1953?
11. How many successive European Cup victories did Di Stefano win at Real Madrid?
12. How many caps did he win for Spain, Argentina and Colombia?
13. How many goals did he score in the 7-3 victory over Eintracht Frankfurt in the 1960 European Cup final?
14. What happened to Di Stefano while on tour with Real Madrid in Venezuela in 1963?
15. What club did he coach on his return to Argentina in 1968?

1. Barracas 2. Los Cardales 3. River Plate 4. San Lorenzo 5. Huracan 6. Adolfo Pederrera 7. La Maquina (the Machine) 8. 1947 9. In Colombia, for Millionarios of Bogota 10. Real Madrid 11. 5 12. 31,7,3 13. A hat-trick 14. He was kidnapped 15. Boca Juniors.

THE FOOTBALL FACT AND QUIZ BOOK

EUSEBIO

1. What is Eusebio's full name?

2. Where was Eusebio born in 1942?

3. What youth team did he join at the age of 10?

4. Who did Eusebio join when he arrived in Lisbon?

5. How many league games had Eusebio played before making his international debut against England?

6. How many times did Eusebio win the Portugese league with Benfica?

7. Who did Benfica beat in the 1962 European Cup final, Eusebio scoring two goals?

8. When was Eusebio voted European Footballer of the Year?

9. How many caps did he win playing for Portugal?

10. What nickname was Eusebio given after the 1966 World Cup?

11. How many times did Eusebio win the Portugese Cup with Benfica?

12. How many league goals did he score in 294 matches?

13. Which North American club did he join in 1974?

14. Which stadium has a statue of Eusebio at it's entrance?

15. What was the 1992 film about Eusebio's life called?

SIR TOM FINNEY

1. Where was Sir Tom Finney born in 1922?
2. In 1938, he signed for his local, and only, senior club. Who was it?
3. With who did he serve in North Africa in 1942?
4. Despite playing for Preston in the 1941 F.A.Cup final, when did he make his league debut for the club?
5. How many England caps did Tom Finney win?
6. While playing for England in 1950, which team inflicted a humiliating 1-0 defeat?
7. When was Finney first voted English Footballer of the Year?
8. Who did Finney and Preston lose out to in the 1953 League Championship on goal average?
9. What was Finney's trade before signing with Preston?
10. Who did the Preston side, captained by Finney, lose the 1954 F.A.Cup final to?
11. Who broke Tom Finney's English record of 30 international goals?
12. How many goals did Finney score in his 433 league games for Preston?
13. When was Finney elected president of Preston North End?
14. When was Tom Finney awarded his knighthood in the New Year Honours List?
15. What did Preston, with Finney as president, win in April 2000?

1. Preston 2. Preston North End 3. British Eighth Army 4. 1946 5. 76 6. U.S.A. 7. 1954 8. Arsenal 9. Plumber 10. West Bromwich Albion, 3-2 11. Bobby Charlton 12. 187 13. 1975 14. 1998 15. The Second Division Championship.

PAUL GASGOIGNE

1. Where was Gascoigne born in 1967?
2. Who did he make his debut for in 1985, a month before he turned professional?
3. How much was he transferred to Tottenham for in July 1988?
4. Who did he make his full England debut against in August 1988?
5. Why did Gascoigne leave the 1990 World Cup semi-final against Germany in tears?
6. What BBC award did he win in 1990?
7. Which club did he join in 1992 for £5.5 million?
8. In the 1991 F.A.Cup final, who did Gascoigne make a rash challenge on, causing himself to be stretchered off?
9. How many games did he play in three seasons at Lazio, because of a broken leg?
10. In a famous sporting photograph, who was seen holding Gascoigne by his privates?
11. What did Gascoigne win in his first season at Rangers in 1996?
12. Which manager signed Gascoigne from Rangers and moved him to the north-east?
13. Which Gascoigne 'goal celebration' was judged to be inappropriately sectarian?
14. In which country was Gascoigne voted Footballer of the Year in 1996?
15. For which Premier League club did Gascoigne sign in 2000?

1. Gateshead 2. Newcastle Utd 3. £2 million 4. Denmark 5. He was booked, and would not have been able to play in the final if England had won the semi 6. The BBC's Sports Personality of the Year award 7. Lazio 8. Gary Charles, Nottingham Forest 9. 42 10. Vinnie Jones 11. Championship Medal 12. Bryan Robson 13. Pretending to play the flute (in a Rangers - Celtic derby game) 14. Scotland 15. Everton.

THE FOOTBALL FACT AND QUIZ BOOK

JIMMY GREAVES

1. Where was Jimmy Greaves born in 1940?
2. For which London club did he make his debut for in 1957?
3. How many league appearances had Greaves made for Chelsea when he reached 100 league goals?
4. Who did he make his England debut against in 1959?
5. Who was Greaves transferred to in June 1961 for £80,000?
6. When he transferred back to Tottenham in December 1961, why was the fee £99,999?
7. How many goals did Greaves score in the 5-1 win over Atletico Madrid in the 1963 European Cup-Winners' Cup?
8. Who did Spurs beat in the first all-London F.A.Cup final in 1967?
9. In the 1967 final, besides Jimmy Greaves, who was the only survivor of the 1961/62 F.A.Cup triumph?
10. How many caps did Greaves win playing for England?
11. Where was he transferred in 1970?
12. In that 1970 transfer, as part of the £200,000 deal, who went to Tottenham?
13. How many goals did Greaves score in his international career?
14. How many goals, all in the top division, had Greaves scored when he retired at 31 in 1971?
15. With which ex-Anfield star did Greaves form a television soccer pundit duo in the seventies and eighties?

1. London 2. Chelsea 3. 133 4. Peru 5. Milan 6. So Greaves would not be saddled with the label of being the first £100,000 footballer 7. 2 8. Chelsea 9. Dave Mackay 10. 45 11. West Ham United 12. Martin Peters 13. 44 14. 357 15. Ian St.John.

THE FOOTBALL FACT AND QUIZ BOOK

RUUD GULLIT

1. In which country was Ruud Gullit born?
2. Who was the Welsh coach who signed him for Haarlem in 1978?
3. What position did he play when he joined Feyenoord in 1980?
4. How many international caps has Gullit won playing for Holland?
5. Where did Gullit move to from PSV Eindhoven in 1987 for a then world record £5.5 million fee?
6. What did Gullit win for the first time in 1987?
7. How many goals did Gullit score when captaining Holland in the 1988 European Championship final against the Soviet Union?
8. Who did Milan beat 4-0 in the 1998 European Champions Cup final, Gullit scoring twice?
9. Who did Milan beat in the same competition the following year?
10. Which club did Gullit join in 1993?
11. Who was Chelsea manager when Gullit joined the London club in 1995?
12. Why was Gullit appointed player-manager of Chelsea in 1996?
13. What did Gullit become in the 1997 F.A.Cup?
14. Who replaced Gullit when he was sacked by Chelsea in 1998?
15. How did Gullit describe his style of football when replacing Kenny Dalglish as manager of Newcastle in 1999/00?

1. Surinam 2. Barry Hughes 3. Sweeper 4. 65 5. A.C. Milan 6. World Footballer of the Year award 7. One 8. Steaua Bucharest 9. Benfica 10. Sampdoria 11. Glenn Hoddle 12. Glenn Hoddle had left to become manager of England 13. The first continental coach to win an English cup 14. Gianluca Vialli 15. 'Sexy football'.

GHEORGE HAGI

1. Where was Hagi born in 1965?
2. How old was Hagi when he made his debut in the Romanian youth team?
3. Where was he playing after being transferred by FC Constanta at 17?
4. Who did Hagi make his full international debut against?
5. How many games did Romania win in the 1984 European Championship finals in France?
6. Against which country did Hagi contribute one goal towards a 5-1 victory on 4th of September 1999?
7. How many goals did Hagi score for Steaua Bucharest in 1985/86, including six in one match?
8. Why was no transfer fee involved when Hagi was "stolen" by Steaua Bucharest in 1986?
9. Who beat Romania in a penalty shoot-out in the 1990 World Cup finals?
10. Where was Hagi sold to in 1990?
11. Where was he transferred to in Italy in 1992, the team already having two other Romanian players and a Romanian coach?
12. Who was the Romanian coach at Brescia?
13. Where was Hagi transferred to after returning from the 1994 World Cup finals?
14. Who was the manager of Barcelona, who was so unimpressed with Hagi, he transferred him to Galatasaray in 1996?
15. In what final was he sent off, but still finished on the winning side in 2000?

1. Constanta 2. 15 3. Sportul Studentesc of Bucharest 4. Norway 5. None 6. Slovakia 7. 31 8. It was approved by the ruling Ceaucescu family, who were Steaua supporters and directors 9. Republic of Ireland 10. Real Madrid 11. Brescia 12. Mircea Lucescu 13. Barcelona 14. Johan Cruyff 15. The UEFA Cup final which Galatasaray won on penalties.

THE FOOTBALL FACT AND QUIZ BOOK

GLENN HODDLE

1. Which former Spurs player is credited with spotting Hoddle while playing a junior cup final?
2. Who did Hoddle score against on his international debut in 1979?
3. Who were the two teams that Hoddle won F.A.Cup winners medals against in 1981 and 1982?
4. How many appearances did he make for Spurs?
5. Which manager took Hoddle to Monaco for £750,000?
6. Who did Hoddle replace as manager of Swindon in 1991?
7. Who did Hoddle's Swindon team beat in the 1993 play-off finals?
8. Which Hoddle brother has played for Barnet?
9. Which club defeated Hoddle's Chelsea in the 1994/95 Cup-Winners Cup semi-final?
10. From which country did Hoddle sign goalkeeper Dmitri Kharin for Chelsea?
11. How many caps did Hoddle win for England?
12. What was the name of Hoddle's controversial faith healer?
13. Which trophy did Hoddle win in 1997 as English manager?
14. Which striker did Glenn Hoddle transfer to Chelsea for £1.25 million?
15. After returning to management with Southampton in 2000, who did he sell to Everton, one month after taking over?

SIR GEOFF HURST

1. Where was Geoff Hurst born in 1941?

2. When did Hurst sign for West Ham?

3. Originally a wing-half, which manager converted Hurst to a striker?

4. How many goals did Hurst score in 410 league games?

5. Who did West Ham beat 3-2 in the 1964 F.A.Cup final?

6. What was the score when West Ham beat TSV 1860 Munich in the 1965 European Cup-winners Cup final?

7. When did Geoff Hurst make his senior debut for England?

8. Who was Hurst a replacement for in the 1966 World Cup finals?

9. How many goals did Hurst score in the 1966 World Cup final?

10. Where was Geoff Hurst transferred to in 1972?

11. How many appearances did Hurst make for England?

12. What was the last club Hurst played for?

13. Who did Geoff Hurst manage in 1975?

14. How many goals did Geoff Hurst score for England?

15. When did Geoff Hurst receive his knighthood?

1. Ashton, Lancashire 2. 1959 3. Ron Greenwood 4. 180 5. Preston N.E. 6. 2-0 7. 1966 8. Jimmy Greaves, who injured himself against France 9. 3 10. Stoke City 11. 49 12. West Bromwich Albion 13. Chelsea 14. 24 15. 1998.

JAIRZINHO

1. What is Jairzinho's full name?

2. Where was he born in 1944?

3. Who did he sign professional terms with at 15?

4. What did Jairzinho win at the 1963 Pan American Games?

5. When did Jairzinho win his first cap for Brazil?

6. Why did Jairzinho make history in the 1970 World Cup finals?

7. How many goals did Jairzinho score in the 1970 World Cup finals?

8. To where was he transferred in 1972?

9. How many goals did Jairzinho score for Brazil?

10. How many times did he play for Brazil?

11. Where in South America did Jairzinho return to play in 1976?

12. What final did they reach in 1976?

13. Who did Cruzeiro lose to in the 1976 World Club Cup final?

14. What talented youngster did Jairzinho discover in 1991?

15. Which former club was he appointed coach at in 1991?

1. Jair Ventura Filho 2. Rio de Janeiro 3. Botafogo 4. A gold medal 5. 1964 6. He scored in every round 7. 7 goals 8. Marseille 9. 37 10. 87 11. Cruzeiro of Belo Horizonte 12. The South American Club Cup (the Copa Libertadores) 13. Bayern Munich 14. Ronaldo 15. Cruzeiro.

PAT JENNINGS

1. Who did Jennings make his debut in goal for in 1961?

2. Where was Pat Jennings born in 1945?

3. Which English club did he move to in 1963, playing 48 matches for them?

4. Who was he transferred to Tottenham as successor to in 1964?

5. What rare occurrence happened in the 1967 Charity Shield against Manchester Utd?

6. What cup winners medal did Jennings win in 1971 and 1973?

7. Which English club did Spurs beat when winning the 1972 UEFA Cup?

8. When was Jennings released by Tottenham after playing 472 league games in 12 years?

9. Who paid £40,000 for his services in 1977?

10. What did he win on his 41st birthday in the World Cup finals against Brazil?

11. How long did Jennings play for Arsenal?

12. Who did Arsenal beat 3-2 in the 1979 F.A.Cup final?

13. Which two teams played in his testimonial match in 1985?

14. What did he return to football as in 1993?

15. When was Jennings voted Footballer of the Year?

1. Newry 2. County Down, N.Ireland 3. Watford 4. Bill Brown 5. He scored a goal with a clearance straight from hand 6. The League Cup 7. Wolves 8. 1977 9. Arsenal 10. His 119th cap 11. 237 games over 7 years 12. Manchester Utd 13. Spurs and Arsenal 14. Goalkeeping coach with Tottenham 15. 1973.

THE FOOTBALL FACT AND QUIZ BOOK

JIMMY JOHNSTONE

1. Where was Johnstone born in 1944?
2. Who did he make his international debut against in 1964?
3. What phobia did Johnstone share with Dennis Bergkamp?
4. How many medals did Johnstone win in his career at Celtic?
5. Who was Johnstone's manager at Celtic?
6. What did Celtic become the first British club to achieve in 1967?
7. What nickname did they earn by beating Inter 2-1 in the 1967 final?
8. What other three trophies were won during 1967?
9. How many caps did Johnstone win for Scotland?
10. How many consecutive league championships had Celtic won in 1975?
11. Which English club did Celtic beat 3-1 in the 1970 European Cup semi-finals?
12. How many goals did Johnstone score for his country?
13. Who did Celtic lose the 1970 European Cup final to?
14. Who did Celtic play when reaching their eighth consecutive League Cup final in 1972?
15. Against which country did Johnstone make his final international appearance?

1. Glasgow 2. Wales 3. Fear of flying 4. 16 5. Jock Stein 6. Win the European Champions Cup 7. 'The Lisbon Lions' 8. The Scottish League, the League Cup and Scottish F.A.Cup 9. 23 10. 9 11. Leeds Utd 12. 4 13. Feyenoord 14. Partick Thistle 15. Spain.

KEVIN KEEGAN

1. Who did Keegan turn professional with in 1968?
2. How much was he transferred to Liverpool for in 1971?
3. Where was Keegan born in 1951?
4. When did Kevin win the first of his three league championships with Liverpool?
5. Who did Liverpool beat in the 1976 UEFA Cup final?
6. Who were Liverpool's opponents when they won their first European Champions Cup in 1977?
7. Where was Keegan transferred to immediately after the 1977 final?
8. How much did Hamburg pay for Keegan?
9. What award did Keegan win in 1978 and 1979?
10. What year did he win the German championship with Hamburg?
11. Which club did Keegan play for when he returned to England in 1980?
12. How many international caps did Keegan win for England?
13. Having already been a player at Newcastle, when did he become their manager?
14. Where was Keegan appointed Director of Football in 1997?
15. Who did Keegan succeed as England manager in 1999?

MARIO KEMPES

1. In which town was Kempes born?
2. Which home-town club did he turn professional with?
3. Where was Kempes transferred to in 1970?
4. When did Kempes make his international debut for Argentina?
5. Which Spanish club bought Kempes in 1976?
6. In 1978 he was the only foreign-based player recalled to the World Cup squad by which coach?
7. How many goals did Kempes score when top-scoring in the 1978 World Cup finals?
8. How many goals did Kempes score in the 1978 World Cup final?
9. What was the only European club trophy Kempes won?
10. When did Kempes win the South American Player of the Year award?
11. Where did Kempes play when returning to Argentina in 1981?
12. How many goals did Kempes score in his international career?
13. What was his nickname?
14. Who did Argentina beat 3-1 in the 1978 World Cup final?
15. How many internationals did Kempes play for Argentina?

JURGEN KLINSMANN

1. Where was Klinsmann born in 1964?
2. Where did he move to from TB Gingen in 1972?
3. Which club was he second-highest scorer for with 15 goals in 1984?
4. When did Klinsmann make his debut for Germany at under-21 level?
5. What did Klinsmann become only the eleventh player in Bundesliga history to do in 1986?
6. Who did Germany play when he made his full international debut in 1987?
7. In 1988, how many goals did he score in becoming the Bundesliga's top scorer?
8. What colour medal did he win in the German team which played at the Seoul Olympic Games?
9. Who did Stuttgart lose to in the 1989 UEFA Cup final?
10. Playing for Internazionale in 1990, how many goals did he score in his first season in Serie A?
11. From which team was Klinsmann transferred when he arrived at Tottenham in 1994?
12. What 'lucky' number did Klinsmann insist on wearing on his shirt at Spurs?
13. Where did he win his long-awaited league title in 1997?
14. Who did Klinsmann play for before returning to Spurs in 1997 to help them avoid relegation?
15. How many goals did Klinsmann score in the 6-2 thrashing of Wimbledon?

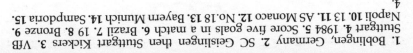

1. Boblingen, Germany 2. SC Geislingen then Stuttgart Kickers 3. VFB Stuttgart 4. 1984 5. Score five goals in a match 6. Brazil 7. 19 8. Bronze 9. Napoli 10. 13 11. AS Monaco 12. No.18 13. Bayern Munich 14. Sampdoria 15. 4.

MICHAEL LAUDRUP

1. Where was Laudrup born in 1964?

2. Which club did he join aged 14?

3. Who did Laudrup make his league debut for aged 17?

4. When was Laudrup voted Footballer of the Year?

5. When did he make his international debut against Norway?

6. Which Italian club was Laudrup transferred to in 1984?

7. Who did Juventus loan him to in 1984?

8. He was recalled by Juventus in 1985 as replacement for which player?

9. Which cup did Juventus win in 1985, with Laudrup scoring one goal, beating Argentinos Juniors?

10. How many successive league championships did he win at Barcelona from 1991?

11. Why did Laudrup miss the 1992 Danish European Championship win?

12. What did he win with Real Madrid in 1995?

13. What is the name of Michael's younger brother?

14. Where did Laudrup go to play in 1996?

15. What was Laudrup's position with the Danish national team in 2000?

1. Copenhagen 2. The youth section at Brøndby 3. KB Copenhagen 4. 1982 5. On his 18th birthday 6. Juventus 7. Lazio 8. Zbigniew Boniek 9. World Club Cup 10. 4 11. Because of a disagreement with coach Richard Moller Nielson over tactics and team selection 12. Their first league championship for 5 years 13. Brian 14. Vissel Kobe in Japan 15. Assistant coach to Morton Olsen.

DENIS LAW

1. Where was Denis born in 1940?
2. Which club did he join as a teenager in 1955?
3. Who was manager of Huddersfield when Law joined them?
4. Who was Law sold to in 1960 for a then British record £55,000?
5. Which Italian club did he join in 1961 for £100,000, then a world record?
6. Who bought Denis Law back to Manchester Utd, raising the world record transfer fee later the same year?
7. How many caps did Denis Law win for Scotland?
8. What record does he hold with Kenny Dalglish?
9. How many games did Denis Law play in his league career?
10. What was significant about his last league game in 1974?
11. How many goals did Denis Law score in the 3-1 victory over Leicester in the 1963 F.A. Cup final?
12. When did Law win the European Footballer of the Year award?
13. When did he win his first league championship medal for Manchester Utd?
14. Why did he miss the European Cup triumph in 1968 against Benfica?
15. Who did Denis Law play his last international against in his only World Cup finals appearance?

1. Aberdeen 2. Huddersfield Town 3. Bill Shankly 4. Manchester C 5. Torino
6. Matt Busby 7. 55 8. They've both scored 30 goals for Scotland 9. 452 10.
He scored the winner for Manchester City that relegated Manchester Utd
to the Second Division 11. One 12. 1964 13. 1965 14. He had knee trouble
15. Zaire.

TOMMY LAWTON

1. Where was Lawton born in 1919?
2. Who did he join as an amateur after scoring 570 goals in three seasons as a schoolboy?
3. Who did he make his debut against, four days after his 17th birthday?
4. What did he become the youngest player in the league to do on his senior debut?
5. Who did Everton want him to replace when paying £6,500, a record for a teenager in 1937?
6. How many goals did Lawton score when he was top scorer in the First Division in 1938?
7. What year did he help Everton win the Championship, scoring 34 goals?
8. What London club was Lawton sold to in 1946?
9. Who was he sold to in 1948 for a Third Division (South) record fee?
10. How many international caps did Lawton win for England?
11. Who did he become player-manager for in 1951?
12. When he retired in 1955, how many goals had he scored in 390 league games?
13. How many times was Lawton booked in his career?
14. Which non-league team did he join as player-manager in 1956?
15. How many goals did Lawton score during his England career?

1. Bolton, England 2. Burnley 3. Spurs 4. Score a hat-trick 5. 'Dixie' Dean 6. 28 7. 1939 8. Chelsea 9. Notts County 10. 23 11. Brentford 12. 231 13. Never 14. Kettering 15. 22.

THE FOOTBALL FACT AND QUIZ BOOK

GARY LINEKER

1. In which year was Lineker born?
2. Unsure that he would make the grade as a professional footballer, where did he carry on working?
3. How many League games has Lineker played?
4. How much did Leicester sell him to Everton for in 1985?
5. What year did he win the Golden Boot award in the World Cup finals?
6. How many goals did Lineker score for Barcelona in the 4-0 win over Real Madrid in 1987?
7. Who did Barcelona beat in the 1989 Cup-winners' Cup final?
8. How many international goals has Lineker scored?
9. Who was manager of Tottenham when Lineker was top-scorer in 1990?
10. What is Lineker's patriotic middle name?
11. Who was Leicester City manager when Lineker made his League debut in 1979?
12. What have Walkers called a flavour of crisps in Gary's honour?
13. Which university awarded Lineker an honorary Master of Arts degree in 1991?
14. What Japanese club did Lineker join in 1994?
15. Who saved Lineker's penalty in the 1991 F.A. Cup final?

1. 1960 2. At the family fruit 'n' veg stall in town 3. 430 4. £1.1 million 5. 1986 6. All four 7. Sampdoria 8. 48 9. Terry Venables 10. Winston 11. Frank McLintock 12. Salt and Lineker 13. Leicester 14. Nagoya Grampas Eight 15. Mark Crossley (Nottingham Forest).

BILLY MCNEILL

1. What year did McNeill make the first of over 600 appearances for Celtic?
2. Where was he born in 1940?
3. What was the score when he won his first cap in 1961 against England?
4. How many caps did McNeill win in his Scotland career?
5. What cup did he help Celtic win in 1965 after an eleven year gap?
6. What double did McNeill achieve in 1966 with Celtic?
7. In 1967, he captained Celtic to victory in every competition they played in. What four trophies did they win?
8. What year did he make his last international appearance for Scotland?
9. How many successive League championships did McNeill win with Celtic?
10. What award did he win in 1965?
11. Which English club did he become manager of in 1983?
12. Who did Celtic beat in winning the 1967 European Cup?
13. In 1986, which English club did he leave Manchester City to manage?
14. How long did McNeill stay as manager of Aston Villa?
15. After two spells as manager of Celtic, what is McNeill's current profession?

1. 1959 2. Blantyre, Scotland 3. England won 9-3 4. 29 5. The Scottish Cup 6. The League Cup and the League Championship 7. The Scottish Cup, League Cup, League Championship and the European Cup 8. 1972 9. Nine 10. Scotland's Footballer of the Year 11. Manchester City 12. Inter-Milan 13. Aston Villa 14. 8 months 15. Pub management.

THE FOOTBALL FACT AND QUIZ BOOK

DIEGO MARADONA

1. Where was Maradona born in 1960?

2. Who did he make his league debut for, aged 15?

3. How old was Maradona when he made his international debut?

4. How much was he sold to Boca Juniors for in 1980, a record for a teenager?

5. Who was Maradona transferred to for £3 million, another world record, in 1982?

6. Which Bilbao defender put Maradona out of the game for four months after a reckless tackle?

7. In 1984, he was sold for a third world record of £5 million to which Italian club?

8. In which match was the 'Hand of God' incident?

9. What did Napoli win for the first time in their history in 1987?

10. What is Maradona's only European final victory?

11. Who defeated Maradona's Argentinian side in the 1990 World Cup Final?

12. How long was he banned for in 1991 for failing a drugs test?

13. Where did Maradona make his 'comeback' in 1992?

14. During which tournament was he banned for a second time after another positive drugs test?

15. Which club has he attempted two comebacks with?

1. Lanus, Buenos Aires 2. Argentinos Juniors 3. 16 4. £1. 1 million 5. Barcelona 6. Andoni Goicochea 7. Napoli 8. 1986 World Cup quarter-final against England 9. The Italian League title 10. 1988 UEFA Cup Final victory against Stuttgart 11. West Germany 12. 15 months 13. Sevilla in Spain 14. The 1994 World Cup 15. Boca Juniors.

SIR STANLEY MATTHEWS

1. Where was Matthews born in 1915?

2. Who did he turn professional with, and play his first league game for, when only 17?

3. Who were the opponents when Matthews made his 1935 international debut in a 4-0 win?

4. How much was Stanley sold to Blackpool for in 1946?

5. What was the score in the victory over Italy in Turin, in which Matthews played a key role in 1948?

6. Which award was he the first winner of in 1948?

7. Who were Blackpool's opponents in the 1953 F.A. Cup Final ?

8. What is this final affectionately scored?

9. What was the final score in the "Matthews Final"?

10. Which inaugural award did he win in 1956?

11. How many caps did Matthews win in his England playing career?

12. Who was he transferred to in 1961 for £2,800, aged 46?

13. What record did he make in a 1965 league match against Fulham?

14. What year was he awarded a knighthood for his services to soccer?

15. What year did Matthews die, aged 85?

JOE MERCER

1. Where was Mercer born in 1914?

2. Who did Mercer sign for when only 16?

3. In what capacity did Mercer serve during World War II?

4. Where was he transferred to in 1946?

5. As captain of Arsenal, what did Mercer win in 1948?

6. With which manager did Mercer win the 1950 F.A. Cup?

7. What did Mercer win in 1950?

8. Why did his career end in 1954, when he was 40?

9. Which club did Mercer become manager of in 1955?

10. Which midlands club did he help to promotion and the League Cup in 1958

11. Who was coach at Manchester City when Joe was made manager?

12. What year did Manchester City win the Championship?

13. What European trophy did Mercer's Manchester City win in 1970

14. How many games did Joe Mercer have as England's caretaker manager in 1974?

15. What feat did Mercer achieve when winning the 1969 F.A. Cup?

1. Ellesmere Port, Cheshire 2. Everton 3. Physical training instructor 4. Arsenal 5. The Championship 6. Tom Whittaker 7. Footballer of the Year 8. A broken leg 9. Sheffield Utd 10. Aston Villa 11. Malcolm Allison 12. 1968 13. The Cup-winners' Cup 14. 7 15. He won the double 'double', as both player and manager.

BOBBY MOORE

1. Where was Bobby Moore born in 1941?

2. How many matches did Moore play for West Ham - a club record?

3. How many international caps did he win playing for England?

4. Who did he lead West Ham to victory against in the 1965 European Cup-winners' Cup?

5. Who did Bobby Moore receive the World Cup trophy from in 1966?

6. Why was Moore arrested in Colombia during the 1970 World Cup?

7. When did Moore win his last cap for England?

8. How many goals did he score in his international career?

9. Who were the opponents when Bobby won his 100th cap?

10. Where was he transferred to in 1974?

11. Who beat Fulham in Moore's final appearance at Wembley?

12. Which two American clubs did he play for?

13. What was his total number of appearances in his career, for two clubs and his country?

14. Where did he have a two year-spell as manager?

15. How old was Bobby Moore when he died?

1. Barking, England 2. 642 3. 108 4. Munich 1860 5. The Queen 6. Falsely accused of stealing a bracelet 7. 1973 8. 2 9. Scotland 10. Fulham 11. West Ham Utd, his old club 12. San Antonio Thunder and Seattle Sounders 13. 900 14. Southend 15. 53.

STAN MORTENSEN

1. Where was Stan born in 1921?

2. What was his position in the RAF in 1940?

3. Who did he make his full international debut against in 1947?

4. How many goals did he score on his debut?

5. Who did his Blackpool side lose to in the 1948 F.A. Cup?

6. In which tournament did he represent England in 1950?

7. Which two countries did England lose 1-0 to in those finals?

8. Who were Blackpool's opponents in the 1951 F.A. Cup final?

9. Despite Mortensen's hat-trick, what is the 1953 F.A. Cup final nicknamed?

10. How many goals did Mortensen score in his England career?

11. Who did England play in Mortensen's 25th and last international?

12. How many goals did he score in his league career with Blackpool?

13. What did Mortensen become the first to do in 1953?

14. When did Mortensen become manager of Blackpool?

15. What year was he made a Freeman of Blackpool?

1. South Shields 2. A wireless operator 3. Portugal 4. Four 5. Manchester Utd 6. England's first ever World Cup finals 7. USA and Spain 8. Newcastle 9. The 'Matthews Final' 10. 23 11. Hungary (England lost 6-3) 12. 197 13. Score a hat-trick in a Wembley final 14. 1967 15. 1989.

GERD MULLER

1. Where was Muller born in 1945?
2. Where was he playing before being transferred to Bayern Munich in 1964?
3. How many goals, a record, did Muller score in his Bundesliga career?
4. What was the first trophy Muller won with Bayern Munich in 1966?
5. Who did he make his international debut against in a 1966 2-0 win?
6. How many goals did he score in his international career?
7. Who were Bayern's opponents when they won the European Cup-winners' Cup in 1967?
8. What award did Muller win in 1967 and again in 1969?
9. How many times was Muller top scorer in the Bundesliga?
10. When did Muller win the first of his five league championships with Bayern?
11. How many goals did he score when top-scorer in the 1970 World Cup finals in Mexico?
12. Who did West Germany beat in the 1974 World Cup Final, with Muller scoring the winner in his home stadium?
13. Who did Bayern beat to win the World Club Cup in 1976?
14. Which club did he play for in America?
15. How many internationals did Muller play for West Germany?

1. Zinsen, Bavaria 2. TSV Nordlingen 3. 365 4. The West German Cup 5. Turkey 6. 68 7. Glasgow Rangers 8. Footballer of the Year 9. Seven times 10. 1969 11. Ten 12. Holland 13. Cruzeiro of Brazil 14. Fort Lauderdale 15. 62.

JOHANN NEESKENS

1. With which club did Neeskens start his playing career?

2. Where was he born in 1951?

3. Who did he help Ajax defeat in the European Champions Cup in 1971?

4. In which cup final did Ajax beat Internazionale 2-0 in 1972?

5. How old was Neeskens when winning his third successive European Champions Cup in 1973?

6. Who did they beat in the 1973 final?

7. Who was his coach in the Dutch national side in the 1974 World Cup finals?

8. What was the style of football Holland were encouraged to play?

9. What place in history did Neeskens earn in 1974?

10. Where did Ajax transfer Neeskens to in 1975?

11. How many trophies did he win in Spain?

12. Who beat Holland in the 1978 World Cup final?

13. What did he help Barcelona win in 1979?

14. Who did Barcelona beat in the 1979 final?

15. Where did Neeskens try an ill-fated comeback?

1. Haarlem 2. Heemstede, Holland 3. Panathinaikos 4. European Champions Cup 5. 22 6. Juventus, 1-0 7. Rinus Michels 8. 'Total Football' 9. The first person to score a penalty in the World Cup final 10. Barcelona 11. One 12. Argentina, 3-1 13. European Cup-winners' Cup 14. Fortuna Dusseldorf 15. Switzerland.

GUNTER NETZER

1. Who were Netzer's only senior German club, which he joined in 1961?

2. Who was the Borussian coach at that time?

3. How many caps did Netzer win for West Germany?

4. When did he win his first championship medal with Borussia?

5. When did Borussia next win the championship?

6. Who did Netzer replace in midfield in the 1972 European Nations Championship?

7. With which player did Netzer forge an inspired creative partnership in those championships?

8. What did Netzer win with Borussia in 1973?

9. What individual award did he win in 1973?

10. What shock result did West Germany suffer in qualifying for the 1974 World Cup?

11. Which Spanish club was he transferred to in 1974?

12. Which two successive years did Real Madrid win the Spanish league title?

13. Who did he join in 1977?

14. What club was he appointed general manager of in 1978?

15. Which English club beat Hamburg in the 1980 European Champions Cup final?

1. Borussia Monchengladbach 2. Hennes Weisweiler 3. 37 4. 1970 5. 1971 6. Wolfgang Overath 7. Franz Beckenbauer 8. The West German Cup 9. Footballer of the Year 10. A 1-0 defeat by East Germany 11. Real Madrid 12. 1975 and 1976 13. Grasshoppers in Switzerland 14. Hamburg 15. Nottingham Forest.

PELE

1. What is Pele's full name?
2. Where was he born in 1940?
3. Which club, where his father was coach, did he begin playing with in 1950?
4. For who did he make his league debut, at age 15?
5. At 16, who did he score against on his international debut?
6. What did Pele become in 1958?
7. In the 1958 finals, how many goals did Pele score in the 5-2 victory over France?
8. Although Brazil won the 1962 World Cup, Pele missed the final because of an injury in the first round. Who were the opponents?
9. Who did Santos beat in the 1962 World Club Cup final, Pele scoring a hat-trick in the second leg?
10. How many goals did Pele score in the 1963 World Club Cup final in the two legs against Milan?
11. After Pele opened the scoring in the 1970 World Cup final against Italy, what was the final score?
12. How many goals did Pele score in his career total of 1363 matches?
13. Despite retiring in 1974, who did he play two seasons for in America?
14. What award for outstanding service to the worldwide game was he presented with in 1982?
15. When was Pele appointed Brazil's Minister for Sport?

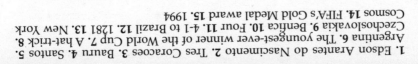

1. Edson Arantes do Nascimento 2. Tres Coracoes 3. Bauru 4. Santos 5. Argentina 6. The youngest-ever winner of the World Cup 7. A hat-trick 8. Czechoslovakia 9. Benfica 10. Four 11. 4-1 to Brazil 12. 1281 13. New York Cosmos 14. FIFA's Gold Medal award 15. 1994

MICHEL PLATINI

1. Where was Platini born in 1955?
2. In which competition did he make his international debut?
3. Who did he join after being transferred from AS Joeuf?
4. Who did he move to after appearing in the 1978 World Cup finals?
5. What position did France finish in the 1982 World Cup?
6. Who was he sold to after the 1982 World Cup?
7. For how many seasons was he the Italian league's top scorer?
8. What has Platini been the only player to win three years running?
9. Who did Platini captain France to victory against in the 1984 European Championship?
10. How many goals did Platini score as top scorer in the 1984 European Championship?
11. Who did he score the penalty against, which brought Juventus their first European Champions Cup in 1985
12. Why did he retire from football in 1987?
13. How many goals did Platini score in his 648 matches?
14. In which year was he persuaded back into football as France's national manager?
15. When the official proposal that the new World Cup stadium in Paris should be named after him, Platini turned it down. What was it called instead?

FERENC PUSKAS

1. In which year was Puskas born in Budapest?
2. Who did he make his debut for in 1943, his father's old club?
3. Who did he make his international debut against, aged 18, in 1945?
4. How many goals did Puskas score in his 84 internationals?
5. Who were the entire playing staff at Kispest transferred to in 1948?
6. Top scoring with 50 goals in the league in 1948, what was his nickname?
7. Who did Puskas captain Hungary to victory against in the 1952 Olympic Games in Helsinki?
8. What was the score when Hungary beat England at Wembley in 1953?
9. Despite captaining Hungary for the 1954 World Cup Final, and scoring a goal, who inflicted their first defeat for four years?
10. Who signed him for Real Madrid in 1958?
11. How many goals did Puskas score in 39 european games for Real Madrid?
12. How many goals did he score in Real Madrid's 7-3 victory over Eintracht Frankfurt in the European Cup final in 1960?
13. Which country did he play for in the 1962 World Cup finals in Chile?
14. Who did he coach to the European Cup final in 1971?
15. For which tournament was he appointed caretaker-manager of Hungary?

1. 2 April 1927 2. Kispest 3. Austria 4. 83 5. The new army club, Honved 6. 'The Galloping Major' 7. Yugoslavia 8. 6-3 9. West Germany 10. His old manager at Honved, Emil Oestreicher 11. 35 12. Four 13. Spain 14. Panathinaikos 15. 1994 World Cup Qualifiers.

BRYAN ROBSON

1. Where was Robson born in 1957?
2. Which club did he join after playing amateur football in 1975?
3. How many caps did Robson win for England?
4. How much did Ron Atkinson pay when transferring Robson to Manchester Utd, then the British record fee?
5. How many F.A. Cup winning appearances did Robson make as captain of Manchester Utd?
6. What did he do as England captain in the 1984 international against Turkey, something not seen for 75 years?
7. What injury did he suffer in the 1986 World Cup finals?
8. Who did Manchester Utd beat in the 1991 European Cup-winners' Cup?
9. How many times did Robson captain England?
10. Despite only making five appearances in the season, what did Manchester Utd win in 1993, for the first time in 25 years?
11. When was Robson appointed player-manager of Middlesbrough?
12. What did Robson win in 1995?
13. Despite relegation, what two finals did Middlesbrough reach in 1987, losing both?
14. When were Middlesbrough promoted back to the Premiership?
15. Which former England manager joined Robson on the Middlesbrough coaching staff in 2001?

1. Chester-le-Street 2. West Bromwich Albion 3. 90 4. £1.5 million 5. Three 6. Scored a hat-trick 7. Dislocated a shoulder 8. Barcelona 9. 65 10. The Championship 11. 1994 12. Promotion to the Premiership as champions of the new First Division 13. The League Cup and F.A. Cup 14. 1998 15. Terry Venables.

ROMARIO

1. What is Romario's full name?
2. Where was he born in 1966?
3. What was Romario's first club?
4. Who did he impress so much by scoring four goals against them in one match, that they signed him?
5. How many goals did he topscore with in the 1988 Seoul Olympics?
6. How many goals did he score in 123 matches at Vasco da Gama?
7. Where was he transferred to in 1989?
8. Why did he only play 65 minutes in the World Cup finals in Italy?
9. Which national manager was so incensed by Romario's outbursts he banned him from the Brazilian squad for the 1994 qualifying games?
10. Why was Romario sidelined for most of 1991?
11. After falling out with team-mates, and complaining about the weather at PSV, where was he transferred to in 1993 for £3 million?
12. What did Romario do in the match against Uruguay that would decide who qualified for U.S.A. 1994?
13. How many goals did Romario score in the 1994 World Cup finals?
14. Who did he return to Brazil to play with?
15. In which tournament did he score the winning goal against England in 1997?

1. Romario Da Souza Faria 2. Rio de Janeiro 3. Olario Juniors 4. Vasco da Gama 5. Seven 6. 73 7. PSV Eindhoven 8. For criticising team selection policies 9. Carlos Alberto Parreira 10. A broken leg 11. Barcelona 12. He scored both goals in a 2-0 win for Brazil 13. 5 14. Flamengo 15. Le Tournoi.

THE FOOTBALL FACT AND QUIZ BOOK

RONALDO

1. What is Ronaldo's full name?
2. Where was he born in 1976?
3. Which junior club did Ronaldo score 8 goals in 12 matches for?
4. Which former Brazilian international spotted Ronaldo in 1989?
5. Who did he transfer to in 1990, scoring 36 goals in 54 matches?
6. Which Brazilian giants rejected him in 1993?
7. Who did Ronaldo join in 1993, scoring 58 goals in 60 matches?
8. What South American rivals did he make his international debut against in 1994?
9. Which european club did he join in 1994, and score 35 goals for in his first season?
10. Who defeated Brazil on penalties when Ronaldo played in the 1995 Copa America?
11. What two awards did Ronaldo win in 1996?
12. How much did he cost Barcelona in 1996, having scored 55 goals for PSV in 56 matches?
13. Who did Barcelona beat in the 1997 European Cup-winners' Cup, Ronaldo scoring the winning goal?
14. Who did he move to in June 1997, for a record £19.5 million, having scored 47 goals for Barcelona in 49 games?
15. How many goals did Ronaldo score for Brazil in the 1998 World Cup finals?

1. Ronaldo Luiz Nazario da Lima 2. Belo Horizonte, Brazil 3. Social Ramos 4. Jairzinho 5. Sao Cristovao 6. Flamengo 7. Cruzeiro 8. Argentina 9. PSV Eindhoven 10. Uruguay 11. The Dutch Cup and World Footballer of the Year 12. £13 million 13. Paris Saint-Germain 14. Internazionale 15. 4.

THE FOOTBALL FACT AND QUIZ BOOK

PAOLO ROSSI

1. Where was Rossi born in 1956?
2. How many goals did he score in 48 internationals for Italy?
3. Why did Juventus give Rossi away to Como on a free transfer in 1975?
4. Which Serie B side did he sign for in 1976, gaining promotion with 21 goals in 36 games?
5. Who did he score against in the 1978 World Cup finals?
6. How much did Perugia pay to sign Rossi from relegation-bound Vincenza in 1979, then a world record?
7. Why was Rossi suspended in 1980 for two years?
8. Where was he sold in 1981, halfway through his suspension?
9. Only three matches out of his ban, who did he score a hat-trick against in the World Cup quarter-finals?
10. How many goals did Rossi score in the 3-1 World Cup final win over West Germany?
11. What two awards did Rossi win in 1982?
12. What did Rossi help Juventus win in the 2-1 defeat of Porto in 1984?
13. When Juventus won the European Champions Cup in 1985, where was the match played?
14. Who did Juventus beat on penalties in the 1985 World Club Cup?
15. Why did Rossi retire at 29?

1. Prato, Italy 2. 20 3. After operations on both his knees 4. Lanerossi Vicenza 5. France, Hungary and Austria 6. £3.5 million 7. After being convicted of alleged involvement in a betting and bribes scandal 8. Juventus 9. Brazil 10. One 11. European Footballer of the Year and World Footballer of the Year 12. European Cup-winners' Cup 13. Heysel Stadium, Brussels 14. Argentinos Juniors 15. Recurring knee trouble.

KARL-HEINZ RUMMENIGGE

1. Where was Rummenigge born in 1955?
2. What was his occupation when Bayern Munich paid £4,500 for him?
3. Who did Bayern beat when he won his only Champions Cup winners medal in 1976?
4. Who did Rummenigge help Bayern to beat in the 1976 World Club Cup?
5. Who did he make his international debut against in 1976?
6. How many goals did Rummenigge score in his international career?
7. In the 6-0 win over Mexico in the 1978 World Cup finals, how many did Karl-Heinz score?
8. Who did West Germany beat in their 1980 European Championship victory?
9. What award did Rummenigge win in 1980 and 1981?
10. As the captain of West Germany in the 1982 World Cup finals, who were his team runners-up to?
11. Where did Bayern sell Rummenigge in 1984 for £2 million?
12. Who were West Germany beaten by in the 1986 World Cup fiinals?
13. Where was he transferred to from Inter in 1987?
14. What did he do after his retirement from football in 1989?
15. How many international caps did he win for West Germany?

1. Lippstadt 2. Bank Clerk 3. St. Étienne 4. Cruzeiro of Brazil 5. Wales 6. 45 7. 2 8. Belgium 9. European Footballer of the Year 10. Italy 11. Internazionale 12. Argentina 13. Servette Geneva in Switzerland 14. Television commentator 15.

THE FOOTBALL FACT AND QUIZ BOOK

IAN RUSH

1. When was Ian Rush born in Flint, Wales?
2. Which club did he make his debut for at 17?
3. How much did Liverpool pay for his services in 1980, while still only 19?
4. How many caps did Rush win playing for Wales?
5. What years did Rush win successive League Cups with Liverpool?
6. How many goals did Ian score in all games during the 1984 season?
7. When did Liverpool and Rush win three successive league championships?
8. Who did Liverpool beat in the 1984 European Champions Cup?
9. Who did Rush score twice against in winning his first F.A. Cup final?
10. What match was the first in 140 games that Liverpool had lost after a Rush goal?
11. How much did Juventus pay for Rush in 1987?
12. When did Rush win his fifth Championship medal?
13. How many goals had Rush scored in F.A. Cup finals after having beaten Sunderland in 1992?
14. What five scoring records did Rush hold when his Liverpool career ended in 1996?
15. Which ex-colleague did he join up with when transferred to Newcastle in 1997?

1. 20 October 1961 2. Chester 3. £300,000 4. 73 5. 1982-1984 6. 48 7. 1982-1984 8. AS Roma 9. Everton 10. The 1987 League Cup Final defeat by Arsenal 11. £3.2 million 12. 1990 13. Five 14. Highest scorer in the club's history, top scorer in the F.A. Cup competition, top scorer in F.A. Cup finals this century, joint top scorer in the League Cup, top scorer for Wales 15. Kenny Dalglish.

PETER SCHMEICHEL

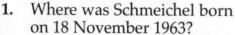

1. Where was Schmeichel born on 18 November 1963?
2. Which local club did he join in 1975?
3. Who did he join in 1984, the same year he made his U-21 debut?
4. When was Schmeichel transferred to Brondby?
5. What was the score in his first international against Greece?
6. What did Schmeichel help Brondby win in 1988?
7. What cup did Brondby and Schmeichel win in 1989?
8. How much did Manchester Utd pay for him in 1991?
9. What position did Schmeichel and Denmark finish in the 1992 European Championships, having only entered at the last minute because Yugoslavia were banned due to political unrest at home?
10. What did Schmeichel and Manchester Utd become the first to win in 1993?
11. In 1994, what did Manchester Utd become only the fourth club this century to achieve?
12. What two runners-up medals did Schmeichel receive in 1995?
13. What did Manchester Utd become the first team in English soccer to achieve in 1996?
14. What 'treble' did he help Manchester Utd win in 1999?
15. What did Schmeichel win in his first season at Sporting Lisbon?

1. Gladsaxe, Denmark 2. Gladsaxe Hero 3. Hvidovre 4. 1987 5. A 5-0 win 6. The Danish Championship 7. The Danish Cup 8. £500,000 9. Winners 10. The new Premiership title 11. The Championship and Cup double 12. F.A. Cup and Premiership 13. The double 'double' 14. F.A. Cup, European Cup and Premiership 15. The Portuguese League Championship.

DAVID SEAMAN

1. Where was Seaman born on 19 September 1963?
2. Who did Seaman join for £4,000 after serving his apprenticeship at Leeds?
3. Where was he transferred to in 1984 for £100,000?
4. What was the club he played for after his £225,000 move from Birmingham?
5. What score did Seaman mark his debut for England with against Saudi Arabia in 1988?
6. What goalkeeping record did Seaman break in 1990?
7. How many clean sheets did Seaman keep when helping Arsenal win the 1991 Championship?
8. Who did Arsenal beat in both the F.A. Cup and League Cup in 1993?
9. Which Italian club did Arsenal beat in the final of the 1994 European Cup-winners' Cup?
10. Which former Tottenham player, then at Real Zaragoza, lobbed Seaman from the halfway line,to prevent Arsenal winning the European Cup-winners' Cup for the second year running?
11. Who did England secure a vital 0-0 draw with when Seaman won his 38th cap?
12. Which former Arsenal goalkeeper was the best man at Seaman's wedding?
13. What is Seaman's nickname?
14. In what year did Seaman help Arsenal to their second 'double'?
15. What change to his appearance did Seaman make at the beginning of the 2000/01 season?

1. Rotherham 2. Peterborough Utd 3. Birmingham City 4. Q.P.R 5. 1-1 6. Transferred to Arsenal for £1.3 million - a then record for a goalkeeper 7. 29 (in his first 50 matches) 8. Sheffield Wednesday 9. Parma 10. Nayim 11. Italy, which secured Englands place in the 1998 World Cup finals 12. Bob Wilson 13. 'H' 14. 1998 15. He grew a ponytail.

UWE SEELER

1. Where was Seeler born in 1936?
2. Which of his father's old clubs did he join at the age of 15?
3. Why did Seeler make his international debut as a substitute against France when aged 17?
4. How many goals did Seeler score in his 72 internationals?
5. Who did he play in the 1958 World Cup semi-finals when West Germany lost 1-0?
6. Who did he win his only German league Championship with in 1960?
7. What 'first' did Seeler receive in 1960?
8. Who beat Hamburg in the 1961 European Champions Cup semi-final?
9. What did Seeler win with Hamburg in 1963?
10. How many goals did he score when he was the top-scorer in the first-ever unified Bundesliga Championship in 1964?
11. Who was Seeler's opposing captain in the 1966 World Cup Final?
12. What distinction does Seeler share with Pele?
13. Which match in the 1970 World Cup finals was Seeler's last for West Germany?
14. When retiring in 1971, how many clubs had he played for, apart from Hamburg?
15. What post did Seeler take up on his return to Hamburg in 1996?

1. Hamburg 2. Hamburg 3. Because the West German squad was badly hit by illness 4. 43 5. Sweden 6. Hamburg 7. The first German Footballer of the Year award 8. Barcelona 9. The German Cup 10. 30 11. Bobby Moore 12. The only men to have scored in four World Cups 13. The third-place match against Uruguay 14. None 15. Club President.

THE FOOTBALL FACT AND QUIZ BOOK

ALAN SHEARER

1. Where was Alan Shearer born in 1970?
2. What team did he join in 1986?
3. What did Shearer do on his full debut against Arsenal, aged 17?
4. How many goals did Shearer score in his 11 Under-21 games?
5. Who did Shearer score a brilliant goal against on his senior international debut in 1992?
6. Who paid Southampton £3.3 million, then a British record, for Shearer in 1992?
7. How many goals did Shearer score in 40 matches in the 1993/94 season?
8. In 1995, what did Shearer's goals help Blackburn win for the first time since 1914?
9. When was Shearer voted Player of the Year?
10. What landmark did Shearer reach in 1996?
11. How many goals did he score as the top scorer in the 1996 European Championships?
12. For how much was he sold to Newcastle, almost double the existing British transfer record at the time?
13. How many goals in all competitions did Shearer score for Newcastle in 1998/99?
14. Before Shearer's goal in the 1-0 defeat of Germany during Euro 2000, when was the last time England had beaten the Germans?
15. Who did Shearer play his last international match against in Euro 2000?

PETER SHILTON

1. Where was Peter Shilton born in 1949?
2. How old was he when he made his Football League debut for Leicester?
3. Who were Shilton's opponents in his only F.A. Cup final appearance in 1969?
4. Who did he make his England debut against?
5. Who did Shilton join for three seasons in 1974?
6. Who was the manager of the club Shilton signed for in 1977?
7. What trophy did he help Nottingham Forest win in 1979 and 1980?
8. How many World Cup matches has Shilton appeared in?
9. How many goals did Shilton and England concede when remaining unbeaten in the 1982 World Cup?
10. Who did he join when transferred by Forest in 1982?
11. Who scored a controversial goal against Shilton in the 1986 World Cup?
12. How many international caps, an English record, does Shilton hold?
13. During those games, how many goals did Shilton concede?
14. Who did Shilton play his 1000th league match for?
15. How old was Shilton when he played his 1000th game?

1. Leicester 2. 16 3. Manchester City 4. East Germany 5. Stoke City 6. Brian Clough 7. European Champions Cup 8. 17 9. One goal 10. Southampton 11. Maradona ('Hand of God') 12. 125 13. 80 14. Leyton Orient 15. 47.

THE FOOTBALL FACT AND QUIZ BOOK

GRAEME SOUNESS

1. Where was Souness born in 1953?
2. Who did he join as an apprentice in 1969?
3. How many appearances did he make for Spurs?
4. Who did Souness join in 1973 for £32,000?
5. Who did Souness make his Scottish debut against in 1974?
6. Transferred to Liverpool in 1978, how many appearances did Souness make for the team?
7. How many European Cups did Souness win with Liverpool?
8. Which Italian club was he transferred to in 1984?
9. Which club did Souness become the player-manager at in April 1986?
10. Why did Mo Johnston cause controversy when Souness signed him in 1990?
11. What medical treatment had Souness had before his Liverpool team beat Sunderland in the 1992 F.A. Cup?
12. What Turkish side did Souness manage in 1995?
13. After managing Southampton, then moving to Torino, which Portugese side did Souness join in 1997?
14. Which English Division One team was he appointed manager at in 2000?
15. How many caps did Souness win for Scotland?

MARCO VAN BASTEN

1. Where was Van Basten born in 1964?
2. Which club signed him in 1980?
3. How many goals did he score in the 1985/86 season with Ajax, winning the Golden Boot for the top league marksman in Europe?
4. Who did Van Basten captain Ajax to victory over in the 1987 European Cup-winners' Cup final?
5. How much was Van Basten sold to Milan for in 1987?
6. Which fellow Dutchman partnered Van Basten in attack when Milan won their first league title in nine years in 1988?
7. Who did Holland beat in the 1988 European Championship final, Van Basten scoring with a volley?
8. When was he voted the European Footballer of the Year for a second time?
9. Who did Van Basten score against in the 1989 European Champions final?
10. Who did Holland lose to in the second round phase of the 1990 World Cup?
11. When was Van Basten voted both the World and European Footballer of the Year?
12. Why was he advised to cut short his playing career in 1992?
13. How many appearances did Van Basten make for his country?
14. Who did Van Basten play his last match against in the 1993 European Champions Cup final, Milan losing 1-0?
15. How many international goals did Van Basten score?

1. Utrecht 2. Ajax 3. 37 4. Lokomotiv Leipzig 5. £1.5 million 6. Ruud Gullit 7. Soviet Union 8. 1989 9. Steaua Bucharest 10. West Germany 11. 1992 12. After a string of serious ankle injuries 13. 58 14. Marseille 15. 24.

GIANLUCA VIALLI

1. Where was Vialli born in 1964?
2. His first club, who did he make 105 appearances for?
3. Where was Vialli transferred to in 1984?
4. Who did Vialli make his international debut against in 1985?
5. When did he win a third Italian Cup winners' medal?
6. How many goals did Vialli score in the defeat of Anderlecht in the 1990 European Cup-winners'Cup final?
7. How many times did Vialli win the Italian league title with Sampdoria?
8. How many appearances did he make for Italy?
9. How many goals had Vialli scored for Sampdoria before his move to Juventus in 1992?
10. Who did Juventus beat 6-1 on aggregate in the UEFA Cup final in 1993?
11. How much did Vialli leave Juventus for, when moving to Chelsea?
12. Who did Chelsea beat in the 1997 F.A. Cup final?
13. Who did Vialli replace as the manager of Chelsea?
14. Who did Vialli's Chelsea beat in the 1998 European Cup-winners' Cup final?
15. Who was Gianluca's successor as the Chelsea coach in 2000?

1. Cremona, Italy 2. Cremonese 3. Sampdoria 4. Poland 5. 1989 6. Two 7. Once (1991) 8. 59 9. 85 10. Borussia Dortmund 11. Nothing, it was a free transfer 12. Middlesbrough 13. Ruud Gullit 14. Stuttgart 15. Claudio Ranieri.

BILLY WRIGHT

1. Where was Billy Wright born in 1924?

2. What was his only professional club?

3. Who signed Wright for Wolves?

4. Who did he make his England debut against in 1946?

5. In Wright's 105 matches for England, how many times was he captain?

6. Who did he captain Wolves to victory against in the 1949 F.A. Cup final?

7. How many World Cup finals did Wright play in?

8. What did Wright win in 1952?

9. What 'first' did he captain Wolves to in 1954?

10. Which Wolves manager left Wright out of a pre-season friendly in 1959, influencing Wright's decision to retire?

11. How many league games did Wright play for Wolves

12. What honour was Wright awarded in 1959?

13. Who did he move into management with in 1962?

14. After leaving Arsenal in 1966, what profession did he take up?

15. When was Wright made a director at Wolves?

1. Shropshire 2. Wolverhampton Wanderers 3. Major Buckley 4. Northern Ireland 5. 90 6. Leicester City 7. 3 (1950, 1954, 1958) 8. Footballer of the Year award 9. Their first League Championship title 10. Stan Cullis 11. 490 12. The CBE, for services to football 13. Arsenal 14. A match analyst and executive with independent television in the Midlands 15. 1990.

THE FOOTBALL FACT AND QUIZ BOOK

LEV YASHIN

1. Where was Yashin born in 1929?
2. What team did he join in 1946, as an ice-hockey goaltender?
3. When did Yashin win his first team debut for Moscow Dynamo?
4. Who did he succeed as Dynamo's first choice keeper in 1953?
5. Who did the Soviet Union beat 3-2 on Yashin's international debut?
6. What did Yashin win with the Soviet team in the 1956 Olympics?
7. Who did the Soviet Union beat in the inaugural European Nations Championships in 1960?
8. How many Russian League titles did Yashin win with Moscow Dynamo?
9. What did Yashin become the first goalkeeper to win in 1963?
10. Who did he play for in a match against England at Wembley, to mark the century of the Football Association?
11. How many caps did Yashin win in his international career?
12. What did the Soviet government award him in 1968?
13. Why did Pele, Eusebio, Bobby Charlton and Franz Beckenbauer fly to Moscow in 1971?
14. Where was he appointed manager the day after his farewell match, as a reward for services rendered?
15. What did he die of in 1990?

ZICO

1. What is Zico's proper name?
2. Where was Zico born in 1953?
3. Who did he sign for in 1968?
4. Why did Flamengo prescribe special diets and training?
5. How many goals did Zico score on his international debut in 1975 against Uruguay?
6. How many goals did he score in his international career?
7. When did he win his first South American Footballer of the Year award?
8. Who did he help Flamengo beat in the South American Club Cup final in 1981?
9. Which English club lost 3-0 to Flamengo in the 1981 World Club Cup final in Tokyo?
10. How many international caps did Zico win for Brazil?
11. Which Italian club was Zico transferred to in 1982?
12. Where did Udinese transfer him in 1985?
13. In the 1986 World Cup finals, when did he miss a spot-kick in a penalty shoot-out?
14. What government position did he take in 1992 after retiring from playing?
15. Who did he come out of retirement to play for in 1993?

1. Artur Antunes Coimbra 2. Rio de Janeiro 3. Flamengo 4. Because he was considered too lightweight 5. One 6. 66 7. 1977 8. Cobrelon 9. Liverpool 10. 88 11. Udinese 12. Back to Flamengo 13. The quarter-finals against France 14. Brazil's Sports Minister 15. Kashima Antlers in the J-League in Japan.

DINO ZOFF

1. Where was Zoff born in 1942?
2. Who did Zoff join after graduating through Udinese and Mantova?
3. When did he make his debut for Italy against Bulgaria?
4. Who did Italy beat when Zoff kept goal in their first European Championship win in 1968?
5. Where was Zoff transferred to in 1972?
6. How many Italian league titles did Zoff win with Juventus?
7. What world record did Zoff set in 1974?
8. Where did Italy and Zoff finish in the 1978 World Cup?
9. Who did Zoff captain Italy to World Cup victory against in 1982?
10. Which pre-war Juventus keeper had also captained his country to victory in the World Cup?
11. How many internationals did Zoff play for Italy - a record?
12. How many appearances did he make in his Italian league career?
13. As Juventus coach, which Italian club did Zoff win the 1990 UEFA Cup against?
14. Which club did Zoff join after leaving Juventus?
15. Who succeeded Zoff as the coach of the national team after his resignation following the Euro 2000 defeat?

EUROPEAN FOOTBALL

AUSTRIA

1. Who were the Austrian league champions in 1999/00?
2. Which Jewish bank clerk is regarded as the father of Austrian football?
3. Who were Vienna's first two football clubs founded by?
4. By what score did Austria beat Switzerland in the 1954 World Cup?
5. What is Austria's national stadium called?
6. In which park is the stadium situated?
7. Which son of Graz, and Hollywood star, helped fund the stadium now named after him in Graz?
8. Who did Austria play in the first international match to be played in continental Europe in 1902?
9. What was the nickname of Matthias Sindelar, the Austrian centre-forward in the thirties?
10. Who did Austria beat in a group match in the 1978 World Cup?
11. What are the colours of FK Austria?
12. Which country did Austria propose to host Euro 2004 with?
13. Under what name were FK Austria formed?
14. Who beat Juventus 7-0 in the 1958/59 European Cup?
15. Who beat Austria 9-0 in a Euro 2000 qualifier in March 1999?

1. Tirol Innsbruck 2. Hugo Meisl 3. English workers 4. 7-5 5. The Ernst Happel-stadion 6. Prater Park 7. Arnold Schwarzenegger 8. Hungary 9. 'Man of Paper' 10. West Germany, 3-2 11. Violet shirts, white shorts 12. Hungary 13. Vienna Cricket and Football Club 14. Wiener Sport-Club 15. Spain.

THE FOOTBALL FACT AND QUIZ BOOK

AUSTRIA

1. What group of workers founded SK Rapid in 1898?

2. International sweeper Bruno Pezzey was captain of which club?

3. At which club did Johann Krankl start his career?

4. Who were First Vienna formed by?

5. Which English coach practised in Vienna in 1912?

6. What cup final did SK Rapid reach in 1985?

7. Who did Admira merge with in 1971?

8. How many teams are in the max. Bundesliga?

9. Who won the Austrian title in 1998/99?

10. Who were the first provincial team to win the Austrian league in 1965?

11. How many times have SK Rapid won the Austrian League?

12. Who won the 2000 Austrian Cup on penalties for only the second time in their history?

13. Which former Leeds Utd player was signed in 2000 by FK Austria?

14. In which year were Austria runners-up in the Olympic football competition?

15. Who beat Austria 1-0 to win the first-ever international?

1. Workers from a hat factory 2. Wacker Innsbruck 3. rapid Vienna 4. English gardeners on Baron Rothschild's estate 5. Jimmy Hogan 6. European Cup-winners' Cup 7. Wacker Wien 8. Ten 9. Sturm Graz 10. Linzer ASK 11. 30 12. Grazer AK 13. Martin Hiden 14. 1936 15. Faroe Islands.

THE FOOTBALL FACT AND QUIZ BOOK

BELGIUM

1. What is the nickname of the Belgian national side?
2. Who won the 1999/00 Belgian Cup?
3. Who took a contractural dispute to the European Court of Justice in 1995?
4. Who was appointed as the national coach for Euro 2000?
5. Which two teams play at the Jan Breydel Stadium in Bruges?
6. What is Belgium's best achievement in a major tournament?
7. Which English coach took charge of both Anderlecht and the national team after WWII?
8. Who did Belgium co-host Euro 2000 with?
9. Belgium were the prime movers behind the setting up of which organisation?
10. What happened to Standard Liege after winning the 1982 Championship?
11. Which club dominated Belgian football before WWII?
12. Which club dominated Belgian football after WWII?
13. When was the Heysel Stadium tragedy?
14. Which Anderlecht player was arguably the greatest Belgian player of all time?
15. When taking part in the first World Cup in Uruguay 1930, what happened to Bernhard Voorhoof, Belgium's star forward on the journey?

1. The Red Devils 2. Racing Genk 3. Jean-Marc Bosman 4. Robert Waseige 5. Club Bruges and Cercle Bruges 6. Fourth place in the 1986 World Cup 7. Bill Gormlie 8. Holland 9. FIFA 10. They were involved in a bribery scandal 11. Union Saint Gilloise 12. Anderlecht 13. 1985 14. Paul van Himst 15. The journey to Montevideo by boat took ten days - he drank so much beer on board he put on eight kilos in weight.

BELGIUM

1. Who beat Belgium in the 1980 European Championship final in Italy?
2. Who won the Cup-winners' Cup final in 1982?
3. What is the name of the stadium that was built to replace Heysel?
4. What is the nickname of Anderlecht?
5. Which club was Bosman in dispute with in 1995?
6. Who was Belgium's Goalkeeper of the Tournament in the 1994 World Cup?
7. A mix of four old clubs, what is the full name of RWDM?
8. By what score did Club Bruges beat rivals Cercle Bruges in 1990/91?
9. What colour stripes are on Cercle Bruges' shirts?
10. Who beat Ajax in the European Cup-winners' Cup final of 1988?
11. Who did Enzo Schifo play for?
12. Which Austrian legend became coach at Club Bruge in 1974?
13. Who plays at Stade Joseph Marien, bordered by the forest of Parc Duden on one side and an old club bar on the other?
14. Which Dutch club did RWDM sign an accord with in spring 1999?
15. After a 20 match unbeaten home run, who did Anderlecht lose 4-1 at home to, in a Champions League match in February 2001?

BOSNIA

1. When did the Croat and Moslem leagues merge to form united league and cup competitions in Bosnia?
2. Who were the last of the regions' sides to play in Europe before Yugoslavia fell apart?
3. Who are the two 'big' clubs in Sarajevo?
4. How many of FK Sarajevo's squad were killed in the city's three year siege?
5. Where does Bosnian midfielder Hasan Salihamidzic play?
6. Who did Bosnia beat 3-0 at the Kosevo Stadium in August 1997?
7. During the siege of Sarajevo between 1992 and 1995, who did football players arrange matches against?
8. What colours do FK Sarajevo play in?
9. What colours do Zeljeznicar play in?
10. Who were the Bulgarian league champions in 1999/00?
11. Where did Bulgaria finish in the 1994 World Cup?
12. Who is the assistant coach of the national team?
13. Which Bulgarian side won nine titles in a row in the Fifties?
14. What colour medal did Bulgaria win at the 1968 Olympic Games?
15. In which two competitions was Stoichkov top scorer in 1988/89?

1. 2000/01 2. Velez Mostar 3. FK Sarajevo and Zeljeznicar 4. Nine 5. Bayern Munich 6. Denmark 7. Teams of UN 'peacekeepers' 8. Claret shirts, claret shorts 9. Azure and white shirts, azure shorts 10. Levski Sofia 11. Fourth 12. Hristo Stoichkov 13. CSKA 14. Silver 15. Bulgarian league and Cup-winners' Cup.

BULGARIA

1. Who did Bulgaria beat in the quarter-finals of the 1994 World Cup?

2. How many matches did Bulgaria win in the 1998 World Cup finals?

3. What was CSKA formed as by post-war Communist restructuring?

4. Where was Stoichkov transferred to in 1989?

5. When were Levski formed?

6. Who did Levski merge with to form Levski-Spartak?

7. Which former national coach was appointed to Levski in the 1999/00 season?

8. What colours do CSKA play in?

9. What name were CSKA forced to play under, after fighting with the Levski team in the 1985 Cup final?

10. What name were Levski forced to play under, after their part in the brawl?

11. How many times have CSKA knocked the holders out of the European Cup?

12. Who are the oldest Bulgarian club in existence?

13. What did Slavia achieve in 1996?

14. Where do Lokomotiv play?

15. What is Lokomotiv's nickname?

1. West Germany 2. None 3. The sports club of the Bulgarian army 4. Barcelona 5. 1914 6. Spartak Sofia 7. Dimitar Dimitrov 8. All red with white trim 9. Sredets 10. Vitosha 11. 3 12. Slavia 13. The league and cup double 14. Sofia 15. The Railwaymen.

THE FOOTBALL FACT AND QUIZ BOOK

CROATIA

1. What position did Croatia achieve in the 1998 World Cup?
2. Who did Croatia beat 3-1 in their opening 1998 World Cup finals match?
3. Which two London clubs has Davor Suker played for?
4. What did coach Ciro Blazevic take to wearing in the 1998 World Cup finals?
5. Who denied Croatia a place in Euro 2000 with a 2-2 draw?
6. What did Davor Suker win during the 1998 World Cup?
7. What name did Croatia Zagreb revert to in 2000 after eight years?
8. What have Dinamo Zagreb won for the last five seasons?
9. Who was appointed as coach for the 1999/00 season by Dinamo Zagreb?
10. How many trophies have NK Zagreb won?
11. What are club Hrvatski Dragovoljac known as?
12. What are Dinamo Zagreb's vociferous ultra group called?
13. Which former Southampton player returned to coach Hajduk Split in the nineties?
14. Where does the 'Hajduk' in Hajduk Split come from?
15. What colours do NK Split play in?

1. Third 2. Jamaica 3. Arsenal and West Ham 4. A lucky French policeman's kepi (cap) 5. Yugoslavia 6. The Golden Boot as top scorer 7. Dinamo Zagreb 8. The Croatian league Championship 9. Osvaldo Ardiles 10. None 11. The Croatian Volunteers 12. Bad Blue Boys 13. Ivan Katalinic 14. Hajduk was the name given to ferocious Dalmatian bandits at the time of the Ottoman empire 15. Blue shirts, white shorts.

THE FOOTBALL FACT AND QUIZ BOOK

CZECH REPUBLIC

1. What is the name of the Czech Republic's national football stadium?
2. Who beat the Czech side in the European Under-21 Championship final in 2000?
3. Which Czech club got to the second group phase of the Champions' League in 1999/00?
4. Who was the Czech coach when they reached the Euro 96 final?
5. Who did Karel Poborsky sign for after Euro 96?
6. Which Italian club did Pavel Nedvel help win the title in 1999/00?
7. What year did Czechoslovakia reach the World Cup final?
8. Who was the Czech coach for the Euro 2000 finals?
9. Which two Prague clubs won every league title bar one up to World War II?
10. What was the name of the Czech army side?
11. What colours do Slavia Prague play in?
12. Who has won the League Championship for the last four seasons?
13. What is the nickname of Bohemians, the animal in question appearing on the club badge?
14. What did Dukla Prague change their name to in summer 2000, also the name of the team's sponsor?
15. What English group wrote the song 'All I want for Christmas is a Dukla Prague away kit'?

1. The Strahov 2. Italy 3. Sparta Prague 4. Duran Uhrin 5. Manchester Utd 6. Lazio 7. 1962 8. Jozef Chovanec 9. Slavia and Sparta 10. Dukla Prague 11. Red and white halved shirts, white shorts 12. Sparta Prague 13. The Kangaroos 14. Marila Pribram 15. Half-man, half-biscuit.

DENMARK

1. Which two players scored for Denmark when winning the 1992 European Championships?
2. Who did they beat in the 1992 European Championship final?
3. Which coach replaced Bo Johansson to take charge of the national team after Euro 2000?
4. How many goals did Denmark score in Euro 2000?
5. Who won the Danish title in the 1999/00 season?
6. One of the oldest clubs in Europe, when were Kobenhavns Boldklub founded?
7. By what score did Denmark beat France in the opening match of the 1908 Olympic Games?
8. Still an international record, how many goals did Sophus Nielsen score in that game?
9. Which London club did Nils Middleboe play for between 1913 and 1921?
10. When did the Danish F.A. allow professionals into the national side?
11. Who did Allan Simonsen play for after Borussia Monchengladbach and Barcelona?
12. Which Danish player has appeared for Lazio, Juventus, Barcelona and Real Madrid?
13. Who did Denmark lose 3-2 to in the 1998 World Cup quarter-finals?
14. What are the Danish team's colours?
15. Who is the national team's most famous goalkeeper?

DENMARK

1. What was the outcome of the merger between KB and B1903 in 1991?
2. How many clubs play in the Danish Superliga?
3. What colours do Brondby play in?
4. Which club bought Parken, the national stadium?
5. Traditionally composed solely of students and professors from Copenhagen University, what club have the initials AB?
6. What year did AB win their first ever Danish Cup?
7. Which three members of the same family have worn the 'number 10' shirt for Brondby?
8. Who bought 100% of the shares in Hvidovre Fodbord A/S in December 1999?
9. What colours do Lyngby play in?
10. Not related, which two Anderson's played for Bristol City in the 98/99 season?
11. Which Danish club plays on an island?
12. Why do Fremad Armager play their home games on a sunday morning?
13. What colour shirts do BK Frem play in?
14. How many times have B93 won the Danish Cup?
15. Where was Lyngby's Carsten Fredgard transferred to in 1999?

1. F.C. Kobenhaven 2. 12 3. Yellow shorts, blue shorts 4. F.C. Kobenhaven 5. Akademisk Boldklub 6. 1999 7. Michael Laudrup, Brian Laudrup and their father, Finn Laudrup 8. Peter Schmeichel 9. Blue shirts, white shorts 10. Bo Anderson and Soren Anderson 11. Fremad Armager 12. Because their ground has no floodlights 13. Red and Blue 14. Once (1982) 15. Sunderland.

THE FOOTBALL FACT AND QUIZ BOOK

FINLAND

1. What do the initials HJK stand for?

2. What was HJK's founding president Fredrik Wathen's claim to fame?

3. When was the last time the national side got to the finals of a major competition?

4. Who did Litmanen replace when transferred to Ajax in 1993?

5. Which Brazilian forward helped HJK win the title in 1997?

6. Who were the sponsors of FinnPa?

7. Which two Finnish internationals play at Liverpool?

8. When was the first time the Suomen Cup was contested?

9. Which Scottish club does Mixu Paatelainen play for?

10. What colours do HJK play in?

11. What did Pallo-Kerho-35 (PK 35) change their name to in 1999?

12. Who did TPS Turku beat in 1987, away from home?

13. What is the Toolon Jakapalllostadion better known as?

14. Why are a quarter of the covered seats in the national stadium nice and warm?

15. Which English club does goalkeeper Teuvo Moilanen play for?

1. Helsingin Jalkapalloklubi 2. He was a former world champion speed skater 3. 1912 Olympics 4. Dennis Bergkamp 5. Rafael 6. FinnAir airlines 7. Sammy Hyypia and Jari Litmanen 8. 1955 9. Hibernian 10. Blue and white striped shirts, blue shorts 11. FC Jokerit 12. Internazionale, at the San Siro 13. Finnair Stadium 14. They are sauna-heated seats 15. Preston North End.

FRANCE

1. How many countries before France have won the European Championships while world champions?
2. Who did France beat in the 1998 World Cup final?
3. Which Frenchman co-founded FIFA in 1904?
4. Which French club played in the first-ever European Cup final in 1956?
5. Still a tournament record, who scored 13 goals in the 1958 World Cup finals?
6. Which Frenchman, FIFA's president for 30 years, was behind the introduction of the World Cup?
7. How many times were St. Etienne French champions between 1967 and 1976?
8. Which was Michel Platini's first and home-town team?
9. Bound by a law of 1901, what were French clubs not allowed to do until the mid-eighties?
10. Who became the first French team to win the European Cup in 1993?
11. Who was the successor to Michel Platini as French coach?
12. Who was red-carded in the 1998 World Cup semi-final against Croatia?
13. Who scored the winning 'golden goal' in the Euro 2000 final?
14. What team consisting of all shopkeepers got to the French Cup final in 1999/00?
15. Which team did David Trezeguet help to win the title in 2000?

1. None 2. Italy 3. Robert Guérin 4. Reims 5. Just Fontaine 6. Jules Rimet 7. Seven times 8. AS Nancy-Lorraine 9. Make a profit or pay high transfer fees 10. Olympique Marseille 11. Gerard Houllier 12. Laurent Blanc 13. David Trezeguet 14. Calais 15. AS Monaco.

THE FOOTBALL FACT AND QUIZ BOOK

FRANCE

1. How many teams are in the French First Division?

2. Which TV company saved Paris Saint-Germain from oblivion in 1991?

3. Which French player scored the only goal in the 1996 F.A. Cup final?

4. Which two clubs merged to form Paris Saint-Germain?

5. Where do PSG play their home games?

6. What colours do PSG play in?

7. Who did PSG sell to Newcastle after Luis Fernandez returned as coach in 1994?

8. Which Nigerian did PSG pay £10 million for in 1998, a new French record?

9. Who formed Red Star 93 in 1897?

10. Where did Red Star 93 play home games before moving to Stade de Marville?

11. Stade Colombes, Racing Club's ground, provided the backdrop to the football action in which film?

12. Who kept goal for France in the 1998 World Cup final?

13. What is the nickname of RC Lens?

14. Which Cameroon international played in midfield for Lens in the early nineties?

15. Which two former Nantes team-mates, who first met when they were at training school, now play for Chelsea?

THE FOOTBALL FACT AND QUIZ BOOK

FRANCE

1. What colour shirts do Nantes wear?
2. Which five clubs merged to form Football Club Nantes?
3. Which old boy was coach of Olympique Lyonnais in 1995?
4. Which record French signing from Barcelona was top scorer for Olympic Lyonnais in 1999/00?
5. Who were League Champions in 1999?
6. What colours do Girondins de Bordeaux play in?
7. Why did Girondins president Alain Afflelou change the shirts from Marine blue to claret red in the nineties?
8. Who did Girondins transfer Sylvain Wiltord to in 2000?
9. What did AS Monaco win for the second time in 2000?
10. Which Nancy coach was appointed at AS Monaco in 1987/88?
11. Which Monaco striker was sold to Juventus after Euro 2000?
12. What did Olympique Marseille win in 1993?
13. Who was the Marseille president who served two years in jail on corruption charges?
14. Which Republic of Ireland player was top-scorer at Marseille in 1996?
15. Trailing leagues behind their more famous neighbours Marseille, what colour shirts do SC Endoume wear?

1. Yellow and green stripes 2. Saint-Pierre, Mellenet, Loire, ASO Nantes, Stade Nantes 3. Jean Tigana 4. Sonny Anderson 5. Girondins de Bordeaux 6. Marine blue with white chevron 7. To try and attract support from the region's wealthy wine regions 8. Arsenal 9. The French Championship 10. Arsene Wenger 11. David Trezeguet 12. The European Cup 13. Bernard Tapie 14. Tony Cascarino 15. Red.

GERMANY

1. When was the Bundesliga formed?
2. What did West Germany win for the first time in 1954, on their debut in the competition?
3. Who beat West Germany in the 1966 World Cup final?
4. Who did West Germany beat in the 1970 World Cup quarter-final?
5. Who did West Germany beat 2-1 in the 1974 World Cup final?
6. How many of the semi-finalists in the 1980 UEFA Cup were from West Germany?
7. Who did West Germany lose to in the 1986 World Cup final?
8. One from each side, which two players were sent off in the Holland /West Germany match in the 1990 World Cup finals?
9. Who did West Germany beat in a penalty shootout in the 1990 World Cup semi-final?
10. Who beat Germany 2-0 in the Euro '92 final?
11. Who scored the 'golden goal' that beat the Czechs in the Euro '96 final?
12. Who defeated the Germans 3-0 in the 1998 World Cup quarter-final?
13. Which coach, appointed in 1999, started the Euro 2000 qualifying tournament with a 1-0 defeat by Turkey?
14. How many games did Germany win in their Euro 2000 finals group?
15. What is the name of the longest-established (and most respected) football magazine in Germany, founded in 1920?

GERMANY

1. What happened in a match between Munich 1860 and Bayern Munich in 1999/00?

2. When were FC Bayern Munchen formed?

3. During which three successive years did Bayern win the European Cup?

4. Who did Bayern defeat to win the first national championships in 1932?

5. What was the club's first european honour, beating Rangers, in 1967

6. What colours do Bayern play in?

7. How long was Bayern's unbeaten home record which started in 1970?

8. How many championships did Bayern win between 1985 and 1991?

9. Who scored two goals in stoppage time to defeat Bayern in the 1998/99 Champions' League final?

10. Where do TSV 1860 Munchen play their home games?

11. Which local brewery logo appears on the 1860 shirts?

12. When was the only occasion that Munich 1860 were league champions?

13. Who scored two goals for West Ham Utd when they beat 1860 in the 1965 Cup-winners' Cup final?

14. What is the full name of SpVgg Unterhaching?

15. Founded in 1925, when were 'Haching' promoted to the Bundesliga to join the other two Munich clubs?

1. 1860 beat Bayern in a competitive match for the first time in 21 years 2. 1900 3. 1974, 1975, 1976 4. Eintracht Frankfurt 5. Cup-winners' Cup 6. Red with black trim 7. 4 years and 73 games 8. Five 9. Manchester Utd 10. Olympiastadion 11. The lion of Lowenbrau 12. 1966 13. Alan Sealey 14. Spielvereinigung Unterhaching 15. 1999/00.

GERMANY

1. Which team won the first ever Bundesliga title?
2. Which two teams merged to form I.FC Cologne in 1948?
3. Which German international, with 81 caps, played his entire career with Cologne?
4. What did Cologne achieve in 1978?
5. What Nottingham Forest player signed for Cologne in 1980?
6. What happened to the club for the first time in their history in 1988?
7. How many seasons have Fortuna Cologne spent in the top division of the Bundesliga?
8. Which Fortuna coach was sacked in 1999/00, while giving his half-time team talk?
9. Which former Austrian striker took over as coach from Schumacher?
10. Which club was formed from a large chemical plant's sports club in 1904?
11. Which former national team coach was appointed to Leverkausen in 1985?
12. Who was Leverkusen coach in 1996, taking the club their first Champions' League appearance?
13. What was the result of the first inter-city match between Berlin and Hamburg in 1896?
14. Who were the army side of East Berlin?
15. Who were Dynamo Dresden and Carl Zeiss Jena formed by?

1. I.FC Cologne 2. Kolner Ballspiel-Club and Sulz 07 3. Wolfgang Overath 4. The League and Cup double 5. Tony Woodcock 6. They were relegated 7. One 8. Schumacher 9. Hans Krankl 10. Bayer Leverkusen 11. Erich Ribbeck 12. Christoph Daum 13. Berlin won 13-0 14. ASK Vorwarts Berlin 15. Factory workers.

GERMANY

1. Which media company are the backers to Hertha BSC Berlin?
2. What colours do Hertha play in?
3. Which former Bayern Munich coach is now at Hertha?
4. What competition did Hertha qualify to play for in 2000/01?
5. Who did Hertha beat 2-0 to win promotion in 1996/97, watched by 75,000 spectators?
6. Which former Manchester City player currently plays for Tennis Borussia Berlin?
7. What colours do Te-Be play in?
8. When was the only time I.FC Union Berlin won the East German Cup?
9. From which club were Dynamo Berlin formed, as an offshoot, in 1954?
10. Who were playing in the 1972 Cup-winners' Cup semi-final, billed as 'The Stasi against the KGB'?
11. What is the nickname of Kaiserslautern?
12. Who is the Betzenberg Stadium now re-named after?
13. Who did Kaiserslautern beat 3-2 on the final day of the season to win the 1997/98 title?
14. Which French player was signed by Kaiserslautern to bolster their midfield in 1999/00?
15. Where do Borussia Dortmund play their home games?

1. UFA 2. Blue and white striped shirts, blue shorts 3. Robert Schwan 4. The UEFA Cup 5. 1.FC Kaiserslautern 6. Uwe Rosler 7. Violet 8. 1968 9. Dynamo Dresden 10. Dynamo Berlin and Dynamo Moscow 11. The Red Devils (die Roten Teufel) 12. Kaiserslautern's most famous player, Fritz Walter, a local boy, who went on to manage a PoW football team in the Ukraine, and then went on to lift the World Cup for West Germany 13. Bayern Munich 14. Youri Djorkaeff 15. The Westfalen Stadium.

GERMANY

1. What is unusual about Borussia Dortmund's yellow shirts?
2. What did Dortmund win in 1997?
3. Which English club did Dortmund beat in the 1965/66 European Cup-winners' Cup final?
4. What is the full name of BVB Dortmund?
5. Who did Dortmund beat in the 1997 European Cup final?
6. Which former Dortmund and European Player of the Year has been groomed to take over as coach in 2000/01?
7. Which Ruhr-based team was essentially a miner's team in 1924?
8. Who did Schalke 04 beat in the final of the 1996/97 UEFA Cup at the San Siro?
9. Which record signing cured Schalke 04's goal drought in 1999/00?
10. Who was Germany's first dedicated football club, founded in 1887?
11. How many times have Hamburg SV been relegated from the top division of the Bundesliga?
12. Which Kop favourite did Hamburg sign in 1978?
13. Which English club was Tony Yeboah signed to in 1997/98?
14. Who would you support if you were wearing a brown and white scarf?
15. St. Pauli fans pride themselves on their anti-racist stance - what is the slogan on their badges, posters and T-shirts?

GREECE

1. Which three clubs have won every Greek league title bar four, since World War II?
2. When did Greece appear in the World Cup finals for the first time?
3. What colours do Panathinaikos play in?
4. What were Panathinaikos called, when formed by English gentlemen at the turn of the century?
5. What were AEK Athens formed as in 1924 by Greek refugees who had fled Constantinople?
6. What colours do AEK play in?
7. Where do Panathinaikos and Olympiakos play their home games?
8. After beating Ajax, Porto and Croatia Zagreb, who did Olympiakos lose to in the 1998/99 Champions' League?
9. Founded in 1917, Athinaikos are one of Athens' oldest clubs. How many times have they won the league title?
10. While their own Neopolis ground is being overhauled, where are Ionikos Nikea playing their home games?
11. Which former Liverpool midfielder was hired as coach by Panionios in 1998?
12. After Panionios lost 4-1 at home to OFI Crete, what action did their fans take?
13. Who won the first Greek title in 1928?
14. The biggest league club outside Athens, what is the nickname of PAOK?
15. Regularly banned from Europe, why were PAOK given a five-match home ban?

1. Panathinaikos, AEK Athens, Olympiakos 2. 1994 3. All green with white trim 4. Panhellenic 5. Athletiki Enosis Konstantinopoulos 6. All black with yellow trim 7. The Olympic Stadium (Stadio OAKA 'Spiros Louis') 8. Juventus 9. Never 10. Olympiakos' old ground at Karniskakis 11. Ronnie Whelan 12. They set fire to the cars of their captain and star player 13. Aris Salonika 14. The Black Devils 15. After a pitch invasion.

HOLLAND

1. Who was the Dutch coach for Euro 2000?
2. Who were the first Dutch team to be founded in 1879?
3. When the Dutch proposed an international football association in 1902, what did it become two years later?
4. When was professional football officially sanctioned in Holland?
5. Who won Holland's first European Cup in 1970?
6. Which club won the European Cup for the next three successive years?
7. Who did Holland play in the 1974 World Cup final?
8. Which two brothers played in the 1978 World Cup finals in Argentina?
9. In the 1988 European Championship, who did Holland beat in the final?
10. Who was Holland's captain in the 1974 World Cup final?
11. Why was there dissent in the squad for Euro '96?
12. Which player, sent home from Euro '96, rewarded Hiddink with a star performance in the 1998 World Cup?
13. Who scored a hat-trick in the 6-1 demolition of Yugoslavia in the Euro 2000 quarter-finals?
14. How many teams are in the Dutch Eredivisie (Premier) League?
15. On what day is the Dutch Cup final always played?

1. Frank Rijkaard 2. Haarlemse Football Club 3. FIFA 4. 1956 5. Feyenoord 6. Ajax 7. West Germany 8. Willy and Rene van de Kerkhof 9. Soviet Union 10. Johan Cruyff 11. Because several of the Ajax contingent were openly at war with coach Guus Hiddink 12. Edgar Davids 13. Patrick Kluivert 14. 18 15. Ascension Day.

HOLLAND

1. What is Ajax's new stadium, opened in 1996, called?
2. Which team, now no more, won the first Dutch title in 1898?
3. Where is Ajax's famed soccer academy situated?
4. Where did Ajax's Johan Cruyff follow coach Rinus Michels in 1973?
5. What colour shirts do Feyenoord wear?
6. How many times have Ajax won the European Cup?
7. What city do Feyenoord play in?
8. What is Holland's oldest stadium?
9. Who plays at The Castle?
10. Which club acts as a feeder club for Feyenoord?
11. PSV are the richest club in Holland, and have a stadium to match. Who are Eindhoven's backers?
12. How many goals did Romario score in his five seasons at PSV Eindhoven?
13. Which team was formed by Vitesse Cricket Club in 1892, and was still run along amateur lines up to 1985?
14. What is unique about Vitesse Arnhem's ground, the Gelre Dome?
15. Which ex-Nottingham Forest striker scored 25 goals for PSV in 1999/00?

1. The Amsterdam Arena 2. RAP Amsterdam 3. In an area known as 'de Toekomst' ('The Future) 4. Barcelona 5. Red and white halved shirts 6. Four times 7. Rotterdam 8. The Castle ('het Kasteel') 9. Sparta Rotterdam 10. Excelsior 11. Phillips 12. 100 13. Vitesse Arnhem 14. It has a pitch that can be rolled away in four hours 15. Pierre van Hooijdonk.

THE FOOTBALL FACT AND QUIZ BOOK

HUNGARY

1. Who did Hungary play in the first full international in continental Europe in 1902?
2. At the end of World War I, which former Bolton player arrived in Budapest to coach MTK?
3. Who did Hungary beat 3-1 in the 1966 World Cup finals?
4. Who scored a hat-trick in the 6-3 defeat of England at Wembley, 1953?
5. What prompted several key players and most of the Hungary Youth team not to stay in Hungary in 1956?
6. What colour shirts do Ferencvaros play in?
7. Who are the only Hungarian club to have won a European trophy?
8. A shortened version of it's German name, Franzstadt, what is the club known as?
9. Allegedly the richest man in Hungary, who has been able to buy success for MTK, as boss of Fotex Holding?
10. What did MTK win in 1997?
11. Who did Ujpesti sweeper and Hungarian international Vilmos Seebok join in 1998?
12. What was Ujpesti TE's name during the Communist era?
13. What name were Kispest AC made to play under during Communism?
14. Ferenc Puskas learnt his football at Kispest, but which other member of the fifties 'Golden Team' is the Kispet-Honved Stadium named after?
15. Traditionally the team of the iron workers, what colours do Vasas play in?

1. Austria 2. Jimmy Hogan 3. Brazil 4. Nander Hidegkuti 5. The 1956 Hungarian uprising and subsequent invasion by Soviet troops 6. Green and white striped shirts 7. Ferencvaros, Fairs Cup, 1965 8. Fradi 9. Gabor Varszegi 10. The league and cup double 11. Bristol City 12. Ujpesti Dozsa 13. Honved 14. Jozsef Bozsik, captain, and holder of 100 caps for his country 15. All red with blue trim.

THE REPUBLIC OF IRELAND

1. Which former English international coached the national side to the 1990 and 1994 World Cup finals?
2. Who succeeded Jack Charlton as manager of the national side?
3. International matches are currently being played at Lansdowne Road. Where is the new all-purpose, all-seated arena to be built?
4. Why did Derry withdraw from the Northern Ireland League in 1972?
5. In Italia '90, who scored the penalty that beat Romania in the second round?
6. What colours do Shamrock Rovers play in?
7. What was the nickname of Shamrock Rovers during the fifties, taken from their player-coach?
8. Which former Leeds Utd star became manager of Shamrock Rovers in 1977?
9. Who are the oldest club in the Republic?
10. What is the name of Bohemian's ground, where they have played since 1901, and where internationals were played up to 1971?
11. What did Shelbourne achieve in 1999/00?
12. Which family-run club won the 1996, 1998 and 1999 league titles?
13. Which team won the Irish cup in 1999 in the third replay, but were also relegated from the Premier Division in the same season?
14. Which team has earnt itself a place in the 2000/01 Intertoto Cup as a result of finishing fourth in the league?
15. Who is the most famous player to be produced by Home Farm Fingal, the former nursery club for Everton?

ITALY

1. What is the nickname for the Italian game?
2. What is the name given to groups of fans that produce most of the noise and colour at Italian games?
3. Why do Juventus wear black and white striped shirts?
4. When did Vittorio Pozzo organise the formation of a national league in Italy?
5. When did Italy host the first World Cup to be staged in Europe?
6. Which entire team perished in the Superga air disaster in 1949?
7. Who beat Italy in the 1966 World Cup at Ayresome Park?
8. How many times did Juventus win the title between 1972 and 1986?
9. Who did Italy beat to win their third World Cup in 1982?
10. In 1987, who won the title, the first time it had been won by a team from the south?
11. Which bankrupt club did Silvio Berlusconi buy in 1986?
12. Which Milan coach took on the national side in 1994?
13. Who beat Barcelona 4-0 in the 1994 European Cup final?
14. When were Italian clubs forced to form themselves into limited companies from informal associations, by changes in Italian law?
15. What is the nickname of the national side?

THE FOOTBALL FACT AND QUIZ BOOK

ITALY

1. Who took on the job of national coach after the 1998 World Cup?
2. Which Italian goalkeeper saved three penalties in the Euro 2000 semi-final against Holland?
3. Who took over as national coach after Zoff's resignation due to criticisms of the team in Euro 2000?
4. How many teams are in the Italian Serie A?
5. What does winning the title give sides the right to wear?
6. What does a gold star above the club badge on a shirt signify?
7. Who are the only club to have two gold stars above their badge?
8. Which two clubs share the San Siro?
9. The precursor of Milan FC (later AC), what did Englishman Alfred Edwards found in 1899?
10. What was the result of a breakaway Italian and Swiss faction of the club in 1908?
11. In 1989, which Dutch trio bought AC Milan their first European title for 20 years?
12. In 1989, which German trio brought Inter their first Italian title for 10 years?
13. Which great Italian footballer was the San Siro re-named after, in 1979, after his death?
14. What colour shirts do AC Milan play in?
15. Which tyre magnate and Milan FC founder member, put his money behind the building of the San Siro in 1926?

1. Dino Zoff 2. Francesco Toldo 3. Giovanni Trapattoni 4. 18 5. 'Lo Scudetto', the green, white and red shield on their shirts for the whole of the following season 6. The club has been crowned champions ten times 7. Juventus 8. AC Milan and Internazionale 9. Milan Cricket and Football Club 10. Internazionale Milano 11. Gullit, van Basten and Rijkaard 12. Klinsmann, Matthaus and Brehme 13. Giuseppe Meazza 14. Red and Black stripes 15. Piero Pirelli.

THE FOOTBALL FACT AND QUIZ BOOK

ITALY

1. How many titles did Gianni Rivera win with AC Milan?

2. Which two future national coaches played together alongside Rivera?

3. Who did AC Milan beat 5-0 in the 1989 European Cup semi-final?

4. In 1991, why didn't AC Milan defend the European Cup they'd won in 1990?

5. Named after a football chant, what was the name of Berlusconi's political party?

6. Which Ukranian striker joined AC Milan in 1999/00?

7. How many times have Internazionale been relegated?

8. What did the Fascist Party change the name of Internazionale to in the thirties?

9. What colours do Inter play in?

10. After taking over as president of Inter in 1955, which coach did Angelo Moratti hire to resurrect the team?

11. Who did Inter sign for a world record fee in 1997?

12. What colours do Fiorentina play in?

13. What Italian city claims Fiorentina as their own?

14. Which two clubs merged to form Fiorentina?

15. When did Fiorentina win their only European title, beating Rangers in the final?

1. Ten 2. Cesare Maldini and Giovanni Trappatoni 3. Real Madrid 4. They were banned from Europe for a season, having refused to take the field after a floodlight failure in Marseille 5. Forza Italia 6. Andriy Shevchenko 7. Never 8. Ambrosiana-Inter 9. Blue and black striped shirts, black shorts 10. Helenio Herrera 11. Ronaldo 12. All lilac with red and white trim 13. Florence 14. Libertas and Club Sportivo 15. The European Cup-winners' Cup in 1961.

ITALY

1. Which Argentinian player, nicknamed 'The Bat', did Fiorentina sign in 1994?
2. What were Parma founded as in 1913, to celebrate the centenary of a composer's birth?
3. Who did Parma lose to in the 1976 Anglo-Italian Cup?
4. Where did Parma sell Argentine Hernan Crespo in 2000?
5. What is the club president's company and club sponsor that appears on the Parma team shirts?
6. Which two Turin clubs currently share the Stadio delle Alpi?
7. Who has been financing Juventus since 1923?
8. What unique place in Italian football do Internazionale Torino hold, who later merged to form Torino with FC Torino?
9. With 25 title wins, who is Italy's most successful team?
10. What is the nickname of Juventus?
11. Which Welsh striker joined Juventus from Leeds Utd, and helped them win three titles in four years?
12. Which Juventus player was the top scorer in Italy for three years between 1984 and 1986?
13. Which former Irish and Arsenal player scored the late penalty, in his last match for Juventus in 1982, which gave the club two stars for their twentieth title?
14. What colours do Torino play in?
15. Who did Torino lose to in their only European final, the 1992 UEFA Cup?

1. Gabriel Battistuta 2. Verdi FC 3. Scarborough 4. Lazio 5. Parmalat 6. Juventus and Torino 7. The Agnelli family, owners of Fiat 8. They were Italy's first football club 9. Juventus 10. La Vecchia Signora' (The Old Lady) 11. John Charles 12. Michel Platini 13. Liam Brady 14. Claret shirts, white shorts 15. Ajax.

ITALY

1. Which club celebrated their 90th anniversary in 1999?

2. Who did Bologna sign for a bargain £1.7 million in 1997/98?

3. What is the nickname of Bologna?

4. What team was formed by the merger of Andrea Doria and Sampierdarenese?

5. What colours do Genoa play in?

6. Which team won six out of the first seven Italian Championships?

7. How many times have Genoa won the Italian Cup?

8. What colour shirts do Sampdoria play in?

9. Which future Chelsea player-manager did Sampdoria sign from Cremenose in 1984?

10. Which English international did Vialli form a strike partnership with at Sampdoria?

11. Which future English coach was appointed as the Sampdoria coach in the early nineties?

12. How much did Lazio pay to buy Hernan Crespo from Parma?

13. Which two clubs share the Stadio Olimpico?

14. Which club did Mussolini support?

15. What colours do Roma play in?

1. Bologna 2. Roberto Baggio 3. Il rossoblu (The red and blues) 4. Sampdoria 5. Red and blue halved shirts, blue shorts 6. Genoa 7. Once, in 1937 8. Blue shirts with white, red and black hoops 9. Gianluca Vialli 10. Trevor Francis 11. Sven Goran Eriksson 12. £35 million 13. Lazio and Roma 14. Lazio 15. All burgundy with yellow trim.

THE FOOTBALL FACT AND QUIZ BOOK

ITALY

1. In March 2001, how much did Roma agree to pay Bari for teenage striker Antonio Cassano?
2. How many times have Roma won the Italian Championship?
3. How much did Roma pay for Gabriel Batistuta?
4. Which national flag inspired the choice of club colours at Lazio?
5. Where did 1973/74 Serie A top-scorer Giorgio Chinaglia join Lazio from?
6. What happpened to young Lazio midfielder Luciano Re Cecconi when he pretended to rob a jeweller's store?
7. Which Geordie favourite arrived at Lazio in 1992?
8. Who did Lazio beat in the last ever Cup-winners' Cup final in 1999?
9. What year did Lazio win the league and cup double?
10. How many season ticket holders does Napoli have?
11. Where did Napoli sign Maradona from?
12. What did Naples win for the first time in sixty years in 1987?
13. What drug did Maradona test positive for in 1991?
14. Which current Chelsea favourite did Napoli sign to replace Maradona?
15. What are the two satellite channels that show Pay-per-view in Italy?

THE FOOTBALL FACT AND QUIZ BOOK

NORWAY

1. Who were the 1999/00 Norwegian League Champions?
2. Nicknamed 'Drillo', who was installed as national coach in 1990?
3. What is Norway's Premier Division called?
4. When did Norway appear in their first World Cup finals?
5. What city do Rosenborg play in?
6. Who scored the goal in Euro 2000 that defeated Spain?
7. What did Norway win in 1995?
8. Which Norwegian striker plays his football at Old Trafford?
9. Who are the Polish Communist's army side?
10. What colours do Polonia play in?
11. Which club did former Celtic and Bristol City star Dariusz Dziekanowski play for?
12. Which Polish keeper, described as a 'clown' by Brian Clough, denied England in a 1973 World Cup qualifying match?
13. Who did Zbigniew Boniek help to win two titles before being transferred to Juventus?
14. Who are the oldest club currently in the Polish top division?
15. What colour shirts do Cracovia play in?

1. Rosenborg 2. Egil Olsen 3. The Tippeliga 4. 1938 5. Trondheim 6. Steffen Iversen 7. The Women's World Cup 8. Ole Gunnar Solskjaer 9. Legia Warsaw 10. Red shorts, black shorts 11. Gwardia 12. Jan Tomaszewski 13. Widzew Lodz 14. Wisla 15. Red and white stripes

PORTUGAL

1. What are Portugal hosting in 2004?

2. What world record transfer fee was paid by Barcelona to Real Madrid for the Portugese star Luis Figo?

3. Who was Eusebio playing for when winning the European Cup in 1961 and 1962?

4. Where did Portugal finish in the 1966 World Cup?

5. Why were eleven of the Portugese squad suspended from the 1986 World Cup?

6. Who won the European Cup in 1987?

7. What did the Portugese Under-20 side win in 1989 and 1991?

8. Who scored all the goals in the 3-0 win over Germany in Euro 2000?

9. Which Everton player gave away the penalty that put France into the Euro 2000 final?

10. Where do Benfica play home games?

11. What is Benfica's nickname?

12. How many times did Benfica win the title between 1963 and 1977?

13. Which three English players did Graeme Souness sign for Benfica in 1999?

14. To which of their rivals did Benfica sell Joao Pinto?

15. What colours do Sporting Clube of Lisbon play in?

1. The European Championship 2. £37.4 million 3. Benfica 4. Third 5. Because they were demanding extra appearance money 6. Porto 7. The World Youth Cup 8. Sergio Conceicao 9. Abel Xavier 10. Estadio da Luz (Stadium of Light) 11. The Eagles 12. 12 times 13. Dean Saunders, Michael Thomas and Mark Pembridge 14. Sporting 15. Green and white hooped shirts, black shorts.

PORTUGAL

1. What did Sporting win in 2000?

2. Who was Sporting manager the last time they won the title in 1982?

3. Who did Bobby Robson go to manage, when sacked by the Sporting president in 1993?

4. Which Danish international joined Sporting in the summer of 1999?

5. Who are the only club outside of Benfica, Sporting and Porto to have won the Portugese championship?

6. Which Brazilian have Belenenses appointed as their coach for the 2000/01 season?

7. What is the nickname of FC Porto?

8. Before Sporting this year, how many successive titles had Porto won?

9. Which player, still at the club, signed for Porto as a 15-year old apprentice in 1971?

10. Who did Porto beat when winning the 1987 European Cup?

11. Which Porto player, now at Galatasaray, was the country's top scorer for the last four years?

12. What colours do Boavista play in?

13. What will Boavista play in for the first time in 2000/01?

14. Which Sporting player have Salgueiros had on loan for the past year?

15. What colours do Salgueiros play in?

1. The League title 2. Malcolm Allison 3. Porto 4. Peter Schmeichel 5. Os Belenenses (in 1946) 6. Marinho Peres 7. The Dragons 8. Five 9. Fernando Gomes 10. Bayern Munich 11. Brazilian Mario Jardel 12. Black and white chessboard shirts, black shorts 13. The Champions' League 14. Hungarian Miki Feher 15. Red shirts, white shorts.

THE FOOTBALL FACT AND QUIZ BOOK

ROMANIA

1. What were the four major teams in Bucharest between the wars?
2. After Communist restructuring of football, which club became the army side?
3. Who picked the players for the national team, when they entered the 1930 World Cup?
4. Who did Romania beat 3-1 in their opening game in the 1994 World Cup?
5. Who did the team then beat in the second round of the same tournament?
6. Who scored the winning goal in the 2-1 win over England in the 1998 World Cup?
7. What did the entire Romanian team do after qualifying for the second round in France 1998?
8. For which competition did Gheorghe Hagi come out of retirement for?
9. How did Hagi end his international career in Euro 2000?
10. What did Steaua Bucharest become the first East European team to win in 1986?
11. If Steaua were the team of the army, who were the team of the interior ministry and the police?
12. What did Dinamo win in 2000?
13. Who did Dinamo sell to Internazionale in January 2000?
14. How many times have Rapid Bucharest won the league title?
15. What colours do FC National play in?

THE FOOTBALL FACT AND QUIZ BOOK

RUSSIA

1. Who introduced football to the Russians in 1887?
2. Who were represented by Moscow Dynamo and CSKA?
3. Who did the Soviet Union beat in the first ever European Championship in Paris?
4. What colour kit was goalkeeper Lev Yashin always dressed in?
5. Who was President Khrushchev's favourite club?
6. After the break-up of the Soviet Union, what banner did a Russian team compete under in Euro '92?
7. Taken from their founders' favourite team, Blackburn Rovers, what colours do Moscow Dynamo play in?
8. How many league titles have Spartak Moscow won in the last eight years?
9. Which Brazilian club did Marcao and Alesandre join Spartak from in 2000?
10. What are Torpedo Luzhniki named after?
11. Named after Eduard Streltsov, Torpedo's most famous player, what is known as a 'Streltsov'?
12. Run by the Red Army since 1923, what were CSKA originally known as?
13. What colours do CSKA play in?
14. Which of the Moscow grounds played host for most of the filming for the Coca-Cola 'Eat, Drink, Sleep Football' TV commercial?
15. Which British club beat Lokomotiv Moscow 7-1 on aggregate in the 1999 UEFA Cup?

1. English mill-owners 2. The KGB (Dynamo) and the Red Army (CSKA) 3. Yugoslavia 4. Black 5. Dynamo Kiev 6. 'Commonwealth of Independent States' 7. All blue with white trim 8. Seven 9. Fluminense 10. Torpedo was the first soviet-built production car 11. A back-heel pass 12. The Society of Ski Sport Enthusiasts 13. Red shirts, blue shorts 14. Lokomotiv Stadium 15. Leeds Utd.

SLOVAKIA

1. Which Slovak international was tragically killed in a driving accident in June 2000?
2. How many clubs play in the Slovak top division, the Superliga?
3. Which team plays in the Slovak national colours of blue and white?
4. What were Bratislava first known as?
5. Which British club bought the Bratislava defender Varga for £1 million?
6. What colours do Inter Bratislava play in?
7. What did Inter win in 2000?
8. Who are Slovakia's first professional football club, founded in 1892?
9. Which Slovenian, having played for VfB Stuttgart and Sampdoria, came back to manage the national team for Euro 2000?
10. Who did Slovenia beat to qualify for Euro 2000?
11. Who scored three goals for Slovenia in Euro 2000?
12. What colours do NK Maribor play in?
13. Which competition were NK Maribor the first Slovene team to play in?
14. Who won the Slovenia Cup in 2000?
15. What is the name of Olimpija Ljubljana's main group of fans?

SPAIN

1. Which two Spanish teams played each other in the 1999/00 Champions' League final?
2. In 2000, who became only the fourteenth team since the war, apart from Real Madrid and Barcelona, to win the Spanish title?
3. What was the original name of the Bernabeu Stadium?
4. What is the nickname of Real Madrid striker Emilie Butrageno?
5. Which Barcelona player returned as their coach fourteen years later, winning the title both times?
6. Who beat Spain 3-2 in their first game in the 1998 World Cup?
7. Who scored four goals in a Euro 2000 qualifier against Austria which Spain won 9-0?
8. Who beat Spain in the 1984 European Championship?
9. In the 1998 World Cup, and 3-2 down to Yugoslavia with 90 minutes played, who scored the two goals that gave them a 4-3 win?
10. What, in a tradition borrowed from bullfighting, is waved to express satisfaction after a stunning goal has been scored?
11. How many teams are in the Spanish first division?
12. What was written on a banner displayed by Barcelona fans while Dutch coach Louis van Gaal was in charge?
13. Who was the Spanish coach for the 1998 World Cup finals?
14. Who replaced Clemente after Spain lost 3-2 in a Euro 2000 qualifying game?
15. When was La Copa del Rey, initiated by King Alfonso XIII first played for?

1. Real Madrid and Valencia 2. Deportivo La Coruna 3. The Chamartin 4. The Vulture (El Buitre) 5. Johan Cruyff 6. Nigeria 7. Raul 8. France 9. Mendieta and Alfonso 10. White handkerchiefs 11. 20 12. 'No more tulips' (after a lot of Dutch players had been signed by the club) 13. Javier Clemente 14. Jose Camacho 15. 1902.

THE FOOTBALL FACT AND QUIZ BOOK

SPAIN

1. Which former Liverpool striker is the presenter of a Spanish TV football highlights programme?
2. Which Spanish club won the European Cup for a record eighth time in 2000?
3. Who were relegated from the Spanish First Division for the first time since WWII in 2000?
4. Which Spanish club did General Franco support?
5. What colours do Real Madrid play in?
6. When did Real Atletico last win the Spanish title?
7. Who did former Real Madrid president Don Santiago Bernabeu and his brother Marcel play for as teenagers?
8. Who were 'la quinta del Buitre' (the Vulture Squad), that helped win five straight titles for Real Madrid in the eighties?
9. Which Welshman, in his second spell as manager at Real Madrid, signed Steve McManaman?
10. How much did Real Madrid pay Arsenal for Nicolas Anelka?
11. Who is president at Atletico Madrid, despite having faced and survived charges of corruption and nepotism, and punch-ups on live television?
12. Which former Real Atletico coach scored a goal that kept Luton in the old first division, famously prompting manager David Pleat to run across the Maine Road pitch to hug him?
13. Who did Atletico lose to in the 1996/97 Champions' League quarter-final?
14. Who is Spain's only female football club president, in charge at Rayo Vallecano, Madrid's third club?
15. What colours do Rayo Vallecano play in?

SPAIN

1. Which two Seville football teams were relegated in 1999/00?
2. Who are the oldest Spanish club still in operation?
3. After merging with Sevilla Balompie, and making King Alfonso XIII the honorary president, what did Betis call itself?
4. What does the mosaic at the entrance to the Sevilla FC ground incorporate?
5. Why did Sevilla FC lose half it's team two years after being founded in 1905?
6. Who did Sevilla's Argentinian coach bring to the club in 1992 to try and help cure a cocaine addiction?
7. Which Croatian scored more than 60 goals in four seasons with Sevilla?
8. What colour shirts do Real Betis play in?
9. Who did Real Betis sell Croatian Robert Jarni to in 1998/99?
10. Who did Real Mallorca lose the 1998 Spanish Cup final to in a penalty shoot-out?
11. Where did Real Mallorca buy the striker Dani from?
12. Where do FC Barcelona play their home games?
13. Which club were formed by the Swiss national Hans Gamper, who placed a classified advert, desperately seeking 'foot-vall'?
14. What colour shirts do Barcelona play in, taken from the colours of Gamper's native Swiss canton of Ticino?
15. Which club was formed by local students, in mockery of Barcelona's Swiss connections?

1. Sevilla FC and Real Betis 2. Recreativo Huelva, first founded in 1889 3. Real Betis Balompie 4. Badges from all the teams that have played there 5. After a dispute about hiring a local factory worker at the club, so half the team left in protest and started Betis 6. Diego Maradona 7. Davor Suker 8. Green and white striped shirts 9. Real Madrid 10. Barcelona 11. Real Madrid 12. The Nou Camp 13. Barcelona 14. Blue and grenadine stripes 15. Espanol (now Espanyol).

SPAIN

1. Who is Barcelona member No. 108,000?
2. Which three Brazilian 'R's' have played for Barcelona?
3. Which Catalan defender returned from injury to help Barcelona to the 1998/99 title?
4. What 'double' did Espanyol celebrate in 2000?
5. Which club have won more Spanish Cups than anyone else?
6. Why do Athletic Bilbao play in red and white striped shirts?
7. What is Athletic Bilbao's San Mames stadium nicknamed?
8. Which English coach at Athletic Bilbao rejected the penthouse apartment offered him in favour of a more spartan one overlooking the training ground?
9. Which team were founded by the merger of the Fortuna and Sporting club in Galicia's Celta?
10. In the 1999/00 UEFA Cup, after beating Benfica 7-0, who did Celta Vigo beat 4-0 in the fourth round?
11. Which two Lopez's left Valencia in 2000?
12. Which Brazilian, after arriving at Valencia, said that 'the night is my friend'?
13. Who did Valencia play in the quarter-finals of the 2000/01 Champions' League?
14. What colours do UD Levante, Valencia's second club, play in?
15. What is Spain's award for the top goalscorer, El Pichichi, named after?

THE FOOTBALL FACT AND QUIZ BOOK

SWEDEN

1. Which club bought the entire front line of the Swedish Olympic side in 1949?

2. What were the players concerned, Gunnar Gren, Gunnar Nordahl and Nils Liedholm, known as?

3. What year did Sweden play in the World Cup final?

4. Who did Malmo FF play in the European Cup final in 1979?

5. What is the name of the Swedish domestic league?

6. Who were the first Swedish club to win a European trophy in 1982?

7. Who won the Swedish title in 1999/00?

8. What colour shirts do AIK Stockholm play in?

9. Which UEFA president was chairman of AIK for 16 years?

10. Which team plays at the Olympiastadion in Stockholm?

11. Despite never having won the league title or cup, which team is the most popular in Stockholm?

12. Who coached IFK Gothenburg from being a part-time team to winning the UEFA Cup?

13. How many consecutive titles did IFK win in the nineties?

14. When did Orgryte IS win the Swedish title, their first since 1928?

15. What colour shirts do Goteborg Atlet & Idrottsalskap (GAIS) play in?

1. AC Milan 2. The Gre-no-li, (using parts from each surname) 3. 1958 4. Nottingham Forest 5. The Allsvenskan 6. IFK Gothenburg (UEFA Cup) 7. Helsingborg 8. Black and yellow 9. Lennart Johansson 10. Djurgardens IF 11. Hammarby IF 12. Sven Goran Eriksson 13. Four 14. 1985 15. Green and black striped shirts.

THE FOOTBALL FACT AND QUIZ BOOK

SWITZERLAND

1. Which two international football bodies are based in Switzerland?
2. Who played the first organised games of football in continental Europe in the 1850s?
3. Despite being the oldest club in Switzerland, formed in 1879, who won the league title in 1999/00?
4. Which three Swiss teams have won over fifty Swiss titles between them?
5. Which Englishman, and former Bristol City manager, took over from Uli Stielike as coach of the national team in 1991?
6. Which Swiss side had Roy Hodgson previously been in charge of?
7. Who did Switzerland beat 4-1 in the USA '94 World Cup?
8. Which former Tottenham coach is now in charge of F.C. Basle?

9. Who have 25 league titles and 18 cup wins to their credit?
10. Where did Grasshoppers play their Champions' League fixtures against Ajax and Real Madrid?
11. What colours do Grasshoppers play in?
12. Who won the league title in 1997?
13. Which club were formed from the merger of FC Turicum, FC Excelsior and FC Viktoria in 1896?
14. What Scottish team did FC Zurich beat 5-3 on aggregate in the 1999/00 UEFA Cup?
15. Who did Servette sell to Monaco, and then, due to a sell-on clause, on to Barcelona?

1. FIFA and UEFA 2. Teams of English and Swiss students 3. FC St. Gallen 4. Zurich's Grasshoppers, Servette of Geneva and Young Boys of Berne 5. Roy Hodgson 6. Xamax Neuchatel 7. Romania 8. Christian Gross 9. Grasshoppers of Zurich 10. The Hardturm Stadium 11. Blue and white halved shirts, white shorts 12. F.C. Sion 13. FC Zurich 14. Celtic 15. Sonny Anderson.

TURKEY

1. Who were the first Turkish side to win a European trophy?
2. How far did the national team get in Euro 2000?
3. Which Turkish coach at Galatasaray left to coach at Fiorentina?
4. When were Trabzonspor founded?
5. When did they win their first league title?
6. Which two Ankara sides have only managed three cup wins between them?
7. Which former Liverpool player coached Besiktas to three titles before leaving for Japan?
8. Which stadium, Besiktas' home ground, did Pele describe as 'one of the most beautiful football grounds in the world'?
9. Which current Spurs player did Gordon Milne bring to Besiktas to improve their strike-rate?
10. Which Welshman coached Besiktas to their first Champions' League appearance?
11. What colour shirts do Fenerbahce play in?
12. Who is the 'Bernard Tapie' of Turkish football?
13. Who did Fenerbahce beat 2-1 in an exhibition game in 1923?
14. Who did Fenerbahce beat in their first Champions' League appearance in 1996?
15. Who did Fenerbahce sell to Paris Saint-Germain in the 1997/98 season?

1. Galatasaray (beat Arsenal in the 2000 UEFA Cup) 2. The quarter-finals 3. Fatih Terim 4. 1967 5. 1976 6. MKE Ankaragucu and Genclerbirligi 7. Gordon Milne 8. The Inonu Stadi 9. Les Ferdinand 10. John Toshack 11. Yellow and blue striped shirts 12. Fenerbahce president Ali Sen 13. A British Army XI 14. Manchester Utd 15. Jay-Jay Okocha.

TURKEY

1. Beside the UEFA Cup, what else did Galatasaray win in 2000?
2. What colours do Galatasaray play in?
3. Why is the Galatasaray nickname 'Cim Bom Bom'?
4. In the seventies, how many league and cup goals did Metin Oktay score for Galatasaray?
5. Whose nickname is 'The Bull of the Bosphorus'?
6. Which Romanian was signed to provide midfield support to Sukur?
7. Who did Galatasaray sign from Porto for £20 million?
8. Which two Istanbul clubs were relegated in 1996/97 and have not yet returned to the top flight?

THE UKRAINE

1. Which former player, coach and national coach remoulded modern Ukranian football?
2. Who have been the Ukranian league champions since 1993?
3. Who did Dynamo lose to in the 1998/99 Champions' League semi-final?
4. Where did Dynamo sign Serhiy Rebrov from in 1996?
5. What colour shirts do Dynamo Kiev play in?
6. What did Dynamo suffer in July 2000?
7. What colours do the former Army team CSCA Kiev play in?

THE FOOTBALL FACT AND QUIZ BOOK

THE
FACTS

FACTS CONTENTS

A CENTURY OF FOOTBALL

THE FOOTBALL FACT AND QUIZ BOOK

PRE 1900

YEAR	FIRST DIVISION CHAMPIONS	RUNNERS-UP
1888/89	Preston North End	Aston Villa
1890	Preston North End	Everton
1891	Everton	Preston North End
1892	Sunderland	Preston North End
1893	Sunderland	Preston North End
1894	Aston Villa	Sunderland
1895	Sunderland	Everton
1896	Aston Villa	Derby County
1897	Aston Villa	Sheffield Utd
1898	Sheffield Utd	Sunderland
1899	Aston Villa	Liverpool

YEAR	SECOND DIVISION CHAMPIONS	RUNNERS-UP
1893	Small Heath	Sheffield Utd
1894	Liverpool	Small Heath
1895	Bury	Notts County
1896	Liverpool	Manchester City
1897	Notts County	Newton Heath
1898	Burnley	Newcastle Utd
1899	Manchester City	Glossop NE

F.A. CUP WINNERS

1872	Wanderers	1886	Blackburn Rovers
1873	Wanderers	1887	Aston Villa
1874	Oxford University	1888	West Bromwich Albion
1875	Royal Engineers	1889	Preston North End
1876	Wanderers	1890	Blackburn Rovers
1877	Wanderers	1891	Blackburn Rovers
1878	Wanderers	1892	West Bromwich Albion
1879	Old Etonians	1893	Wolverhampton W
1880	Clapham Rovers	1894	Notts County
1881	Old Carthusians	1895	Aston Villa
1882	Old Etonians	1896	The Wednesday
1883	Blackburn Olympic	1897	Aston Villa
1884	Blackburn Rovers	1898	Nottingham Forest
1885	Blackburn Rovers	1899	Sheffield Utd

1900

ENGLISH AND SCOTTISH FOOTBALL

Champions: Aston Villa
Runners-up: Sheffield Utd
Division 2: The Wednesday
Runners-up: Bolton Wanderers
Division 3 (S): n/a
Runners-up: n/a
Division 3 (N): n/a
Runners-up: n/a
FA Cup winners: Bury
League Cup winners: n/a
Scottish Champions: Rangers
Runners-up: Celtic
Scottish Cup: Celtic
Scottish League Cup: n/a

EUROPEAN LEAGUE CHAMPIONS

Austria: n/a
Ireland: Belfast Celtic
Belgium: Racing Club Brussels
Italy: Genoa 1893
Bulgaria: n/a
Norway: n/a
Czechoslovakia: Slavia Prague
Poland: n/a
Denmark: Akademisk BK/B93
Portugal: n/a
Finland: n/a
Romania: n/a
France: n/a
Russia: n/a
Germany: n/a
Spain: n/a
Greece: n/a
Sweden: AIK Stockholm
Holland: HVV (Den Haag)
Switzerland: Grasshopper Club
Hungary: n/a
Turkey: n/a

ENGLAND INTERNATIONALS

17 Mar   Ireland 0   England 2
26 Mar   Wales 1   England 1
7 Apr   Scotland 4   England 1

1901

ENGLISH AND SCOTTISH FOOTBALL

Champions: Liverpool   Runners-up: Sunderland
Division 2: Grimsby Town   Runners-up: Small Heath
Division 3 (S): n/a   Runners-up: n/a
Division 3 (N): n/a   Runners-up: n/a
FA Cup winners: Tottenham Hotspur   League Cup winners: n/a
Scottish Champions: Rangers   Runners-up: Celtic
Scottish Cup: Hearts   Scottish League Cup: n/a

EUROPEAN LEAGUE CHAMPIONS

Austria: n/a   Ireland: Distillery
Belgium: Racing Club Brussels   Italy: AC Milan
Bulgaria: n/a   Norway: n/a
Czechoslovakia: Slavia Prague   Poland: n/a
Denmark: B 93   Portugal: n/a
Finland: n/a   Romania: n/a
France: n/a   Russia: n/a
Germany: n/a   Spain: n/a
Greece: n/a   Sweden: AIK Stockholm
Holland: HVV (Den Haag)   Switzerland: Grasshopper Club
Hungary: BTC   Turkey: n/a

ENGLAND INTERNATIONALS

9 Mar   England 3 Ireland 0
18 Mar   England 6 Wales 0

1902

ENGLISH AND SCOTTISH FOOTBALL

Champions: Sunderland — Runners-up: Everton
Division 2: West Bromwich Albion — Runners-up: Middlesborough
Division 3 (S): n/a — Runners-up: n/a
Division 3 (N): n/a — Runners-up: n/a
FA Cup winners: Sheffield Utd — League Cup winners: n/a
Scottish Champions: Rangers — Runners-up: Celtic
Scottish Cup: Hibernian — Scottish League Cup: n/a

EUROPEAN LEAGUE CHAMPIONS

Austria: n/a
Belgium: Racing Club Brussels
Bulgaria: n/a
Czechoslovakia: CAFC Vinohrady
Denmark: BK Frem
Finland: n/a
France: n/a
Germany: n/a
Greece: n/a
Holland: HVV (Den Haag)
Hungary: BTC

Ireland: Linfield
Italy: Genoa 1893
Norway: n/a
Poland: n/a
Portugal: n/a
Romania: n/a
Russia: n/a
Spain: n/a
Sweden: Orgryte IS
Switzerland: FC Zurich
Turkey: n/a

ENGLAND INTERNATIONALS

3 Mar	Wales 0 England 0
22 Mar	Ireland 0 England 1
3 May	England 2 Scotland 2

1903

ENGLISH AND SCOTTISH FOOTBALL

Champions: The Wednesday   Runners-up: Aston Villa
Division 2: Manchester City   Runners-up: Small Heath
Division 3 (S): n/a   Runners-up: n/a
Division 3 (N): n/a   Runners-up: n/a
FA Cup winners: Bury   League Cup winners: n/a
Scottish Champions: Hibernian   Runners-up: Dundee
Scottish Cup: Rangers   Scottish League Cup: n/a

EUROPEAN LEAGUE CHAMPIONS

Austria: n/a   Ireland: Distillery
Belgium: Racing Club Brussels   Italy: Genoa 1893
Bulgaria: n/a   Norway: n/a
Czechoslovakia: n/a   Poland: n/a
Denmark: KB 1876   Portugal: n/a
Finland: n/a   Romania: n/a
France: n/a   Russia: n/a
Germany: VfB Leipzig   Spain: n/a
Greece: n/a   Sweden: Gothenburg IF
Holland: HVV (Den Haag)   Switzerland: BSC Young Boys
Hungary: Ferencvaros   Turkey: n/a

ENGLAND INTERNATIONALS

14 Feb   England 4   Ireland 0
2 Mar   England 2   Wales 1
4 Apr   England 1 Scotland 2

1904

ENGLISH AND SCOTTISH FOOTBALL

Champions: The Wednesday   Runners-up: Manchester City
Division 2: Preston North End   Runners-up: Woolwich Arsenal
Division 3 (S): n/a   Runners-up: n/a
Division 3 (N): n/a   Runners-up: n/a
FA Cup winners: Manchester City   League Cup winners: n/a
Scottish Champions: Third Lanark   Runners-up: Heart of Midlothian
Scottish Cup: Celtic   Scottish League Cup: n/a

EUROPEAN LEAGUE CHAMPIONS

Austria: n/a   Ireland: Linfield
Belgium: Union Saint-Gilloise   Italy: Genoa 1893
Bulgaria: n/a   Norway: n/a
Czechoslovakia: n/a   Poland: n/a
Denmark: BK Frem   Portugal: n/a
Finland: n/a   Romania: n/a
France: n/a   Russia: n/a
Germany: n/a   Spain: n/a
Greece: n/a   Sweden: Orgryte IS
Holland: HBS (Den Haag)   Switzerland: FC St Gallen
Hungary: MTK   Turkey: n/a

ENGLAND INTERNATIONALS

29 Feb   Wales 2   England 2
12 Mar   Ireland 1   England 3
9 Apr   Scotland 0   England 1

1905

ENGLISH AND SCOTTISH FOOTBALL

Champions: Newcastle Utd
Division 2: Liverpool
Division 3 (S): n/a
Division 3 (N): n/a
FA Cup winners: Aston Villa
Scottish Champions: Celtic
Scottish Cup: Third Lanark

Runners-up: Everton
Runners-up: Bolton Wanderers
Runners-up: n/a
Runners-up: n/a
League Cup winners: n/a
Runners-up: Rangers
Scottish League Cup: n/a

EUROPEAN LEAGUE CHAMPIONS

Austria: n/a
Belgium: Union Saint-Gilloise
Bulgaria: n/a
Czechoslovakia: n/a
Denmark: n/a
Finland: n/a
France: n/a
Germany: Union 92 Berlin
Greece: n/a
Holland: HVV (Den Haag)
Hungary: Ferencvaros

Ireland: Glentoran
Italy: Juventus
Norway: n/a
Poland: n/a
Portugal: n/a
Romania: n/a
Russia: n/a
Spain: n/a
Sweden: Orgryte IS
Switzerland: Grasshopper Club
Turkey: n/a

ENGLAND INTERNATIONALS

25 Feb	England 1 Ireland 1
27 Mar	England 3 Wales 1
1 Apr	England 1 Scotland 0

THE FOOTBALL FACT AND QUIZ BOOK

1906

ENGLISH AND SCOTTISH FOOTBALL

Champions: Liverpool
Division 2: Bristol City
Division 3 (S): n/a
Division 3 (N): n/a
FA Cup winners: Everton
Scottish Champions: Celtic
Scottish Cup: Heart of Midlothian

Runners-up: Preston North End
Runners-up: Manchester Utd
Runners-up: n/a
Runners-up: n/a
League Cup winners: n/a
Runners-up: Heart of Midlothian
Scottish League Cup: n/a

EUROPEAN LEAGUE CHAMPIONS

Austria: n/a
Belgium: Union Saint-Gilloise
Bulgaria: n/a
Czechoslovakia: n/a
Denmark: B 93
Finland: n/a
France: n/a
Germany: VfB Leipzig
Greece: Ethnikos GS (Athens)
Holland: HBS (Den Haag)
Hungary: n/a

Ireland: Cliftonville
Italy: AC Milan
Norway: n/a
Poland: n/a
Portugal: n/a
Romania: n/a
Russia: n/a
Spain: n/a
Sweden: Orgryte IS
Switzerland: FC Winterthur
Turkey: n/a

ENGLAND INTERNATIONALS

17 Feb   Ireland 0   England 5
19 Mar   Wales 0   England 1
7 Apr   Scotland 2   England 1

1907

ENGLISH AND SCOTTISH FOOTBALL

Champions: Newcastle Utd   Runners-up: Bristol City
Division 2: Nottingham Forest   Runners-up: Chelsea
Division 3 (S): n/a   Runners-up: n/a
Division 3 (N): n/a   Runners-up: n/a
FA Cup winners: The Wednesday   League Cup winners: n/a
Scottish Champions: Celtic   Runners-up: Dundee
Scottish Cup: Celtic   Scottish League Cup: n/a

EUROPEAN LEAGUE CHAMPIONS

Austria: n/a   Ireland: Linfield
Belgium: Union Saint-Gilloise   Italy: AC Milan
Bulgaria: n/a   Norway: n/a
Czechoslovakia: n/a   Poland: n/a
Denmark: KB 1876 / B 93   Portugal: n/a
Finland: n/a   Romania: n/a
France: n/a   Russia: n/a
Germany: Freiburger   Spain: n/a
Greece: Ethnikos GS (Athens)   Sweden: Orgryte IS
Holland: HVV (Den Haag)   Switzerland: Servette
Hungary: Ferencvaros   Turkey: n/a

ENGLAND INTERNATIONALS

16 Feb   England 1 Ireland 0
18 Mar   England 1 Wales 1
6 Apr   England 1 Scotland 1

1908

ENGLISH AND SCOTTISH FOOTBALL

Champions: Manchester Utd — Runners-up: Aston Villa
Division 2: Bradford City — Runners-up: Leicester Fosse
Division 3 (S): n/a — Runners-up: n/a
Division 3 (N): n/a — Runners-up: n/a
FA Cup winners: Wolverhampton W — League Cup winners: n/a
Charity Shield: Manchester Utd
Scottish Champions: Celtic — Runners-up: Falkirk
Scottish Cup: Celtic — Scottish League Cup: n/a

EUROPEAN LEAGUE CHAMPIONS

Austria: n/a
Belgium: Racing Club Brussels
Bulgaria: n/a
Czechoslovakia: n/a
Denmark: B 93
Finland: Unitas Helsinki
France: n/a
Germany: Viktoria 89 Berlin
Greece: Gudi (Athens)
Holland: Quick (Den Haag)
Hungary: MTK

Ireland: Linfield
Italy: Pro Vercelli
Norway: n/a
Poland: n/a
Portugal: n/a
Romania: n/a
Russia: n/a
Spain: n/a
Sweden: IFK Gothenburg
Switzerland: FC Winterthur
Turkey: n/a

ENGLAND INTERNATIONALS

15 Feb	Ireland 1 England 3
16 Mar	Wales 1 England 7
4 Apr	Scotland 1 England 1
6 Jun	Austria 1 England 6
8 Jun	Austria 1 England 11
10 Jun	Hungary 0 England 7
13 Jun	Bohemia 0 England 4

1909

ENGLISH AND SCOTTISH FOOTBALL

Champions: Newcastle Utd   Runners-up: Everton
Division 2: Bolton Wanderers   Runners-up: Tottenham Hotspur
Division 3 (S): n/a   Runners-up: n/a
Division 3 (N): n/a   Runners-up: n/a
FA Cup winners: Manchester Utd   League Cup winners: n/a
Charity Shield: Newcastle Utd
Scottish Champions: Celtic   Runners-up: Dundee
Scottish Cup: Withheld due to riot   Scottish League Cup: n/a

EUROPEAN LEAGUE CHAMPIONS

Austria: n/a
Belgium: Union Saint-Gilloise
Bulgaria: n/a
Czechoslovakia: Starometsky Olympia
Denmark: B 93
Finland: PUS Helsinki
France: n/a
Germany: Phonix Karlsruhe
Greece: Piraikos Sindesmos (Pireus)
Holland: Sparta
Hungary: Ferencvaros

Ireland: Linfield
Italy: Pro Vercelli
Norway: n/a
Poland: n/a
Portugal: n/a
Romania: n/a
Russia: n/a
Spain: n/a
Sweden: Orgryte IS
Switzerland: BSC Young Boys
Turkey: n/a

ENGLAND INTERNATIONALS

13 Feb	England 4	Ireland 0
15 Mar	England 2	Wales 0
3 Apr	England 2	Scotland 0
29 May	Hungary 2	England 4
31 May	Hungary 2	England 8
1 Jun	Austria 1	England 8

1910

ENGLISH AND SCOTTISH FOOTBALL

Champions: Aston Villa   Runners-up: Liverpool
Division 2: Manchester City   Runners-up: Oldham Athletic
Division 3 (S): n/a   Runners-up: n/a
Division 3 (N): n/a   Runners-up: n/a
FA Cup winners: Newcastle Utd   League Cup winners: n/a
Charity Shield: Brighton
Scottish Champions: Celtic   Runners-up: Falkirk
Scottish Cup: Dundee   Scottish League Cup: n/a

EUROPEAN LEAGUE CHAMPIONS

Austria: n/a   Ireland: Cliftonville
Belgium: Union Saint Gilloise   Italy: Internazionale
Bulgaria: n/a   Norway: n/a
Czechoslovakia: n/a   Poland: n/a
Denmark: KB 1876   Portugal: n/a
Finland: AIFK Turku   Romania: Olympia Bucharest
France: n/a   Russia: n/a
Germany: Karlsruher FV   Spain: n/a
Greece: Gudi (Athens)   Sweden: IFK Gothenburg
Holland: HVV (Den Haag)   Switzerland: BSC Young Boys
Hungary: Ferencvaros   Turkey: n/a

ENGLAND INTERNATIONALS

12 Feb   Ireland 1   England 1
14 Mar   Wales 0   England 1
2 Apr   Scotland 2   England 0

THE FOOTBALL FACT AND QUIZ BOOK

1911

ENGLISH AND SCOTTISH FOOTBALL

Champions: Manchester Utd   Runners-up: Aston Villa
Division 2: West Bromwich Albion   Runners-up: Bolton Wanderers
Division 3 (S): n/a   Runners-up: n/a
Division 3 (N): n/a   Runners-up: n/a
FA Cup winners: Bradford City   League Cup winners: n/a
Charity Shield: Manchester Utd
Scottish Champions: Rangers   Runners-up: Aberdeen
Scottish Cup: Celtic   Scottish League Cup: n/a

EUROPEAN LEAGUE CHAMPIONS

Austria: n/a   Ireland: Linfield
Belgium: Cercle Bruges   Italy: Pro Vercelli
Bulgaria: n/a   Norway: n/a
Czechoslovakia: n/a   Poland: n/a
Denmark: KB 1876   Portugal: n/a
Finland: HJK Helsinki   Romania: Olympia Bucharest
France: n/a   Russia: n/a
Germany: Viktoria 89 Berlin   Spain: n/a
Greece: Panelinos Podosferikos Omilos Sweden: AIK Stockholm
Holland: Sparta   Switzerland: BSC Young Boys
Hungary: Ferencvaros   Turkey: n/a

ENGLAND INTERNATIONALS

11 Feb   England 2   Ireland 1
13 Mar   England 3   Wales 0
1 Apr   England 1   Scotland 1

THE FOOTBALL FACT AND QUIZ BOOK

1912

ENGLISH AND SCOTTISH FOOTBALL

Champions: Blackburn Rovers

Runners-up: Everton

Division 2: Derby County

Runners-up: Chelsea

Division 3 (S): n/a

Runners-up: n/a

Division 3 (N): n/a

Runners-up: n/a

FA Cup winners: Barnsley

League Cup winners: n/a

Charity Shield: Blackburn Rovers

Scottish Champions: Rangers

Runners-up: Celtic

Scottish Cup: Celtic

Scottish League Cup: n/a

EUROPEAN LEAGUE CHAMPIONS

Austria: Rapid Vienna

Belgium: Daring CB

Bulgaria: n/a

Czechoslovakia: Sparta Prague

Denmark: Osterbros BK

Finland: HJK Helsinki

France: n/a

Germany: Holstein Kiel

Greece: Gudi (Athens)

Holland: Sparta

Hungary: Ferencvaros

Ireland: Glentoran

Italy: Pro Vercelli

Norway: n/a

Poland: n/a

Portugal: n/a

Romania: United FC Ploiesti

Russia: n/a

Spain: n/a

Sweden: Djurgardens IF

Switzerland: FC Aarau

Turkey: n/a

ENGLAND INTERNATIONALS

10 Feb	Ireland 1	England 6
11 Mar	Wales 0	England 2
23 Mar	Scotland 1	England 1

1913

ENGLISH AND SCOTTISH FOOTBALL

Champions: Sunderland
Runners-up: Aston Villa
Division 2: Preston North End
Runners-up: Burnley
Division 3 (S): n/a
Runners-up: n/a
Division 3 (N): n/a
Runners-up: n/a
FA Cup winners: Aston Villa
League Cup winners: n/a
Charity Shield: Professionals
Scottish Champions: Rangers
Runners-up: Celtic
Scottish Cup: Falkirk
Scottish League Cup: n/a

EUROPEAN LEAGUE CHAMPIONS

Austria: Rapid Vienna
Ireland: Glentoran
Belgium: Union Saint-Gilloise
Italy: Pro Vercelli
Bulgaria: n/a
Norway: n/a
Czechoslovakia: Slavia Prague
Poland: n/a
Denmark: Kopenhavns Boldklub
Portugal: n/a
Finland: KIF Helsinki
Romania: Colentina Bucharest
France: n/a
Russia: n/a
Germany: VfB Leipzig
Spain: n/a
Greece: n/a
Sweden: Orgryte IS
Holland: Sparta
Switzerland: Montriond Lausanne
Hungary: Ferencvaros
Turkey: n/a

ENGLAND INTERNATIONALS

15 Feb	Ireland 2	England 1
17 Mar	England 4	Wales 3
5 Apr	England 1	Scotland 0

1914

ENGLISH AND SCOTTISH FOOTBALL

Champions: Blackburn Rovers
Division 2: Notts County
Division 3 (S): n/a
Division 3 (N): n/a
FA Cup winners: Burnley
Charity Shield: n/a
Scottish Champions: Celtic
Scottish Cup: Celtic

Runners-up: Aston Villa
Runners-up: Bradford Park Avenue
Runners-up: n/a
Runners-up: n/a
League Cup winners: n/a

Runners-up: Rangers
Scottish League Cup: n/a

EUROPEAN LEAGUE CHAMPIONS

Austria: WAF
Belgium: Daring CB
Bulgaria: n/a
Czechoslovakia: n/a
Denmark: Kopenhavns Boldklub
Finland: n/a
France: n/a
Germany: SpVgg Furth
Greece: n/a
Holland: HVV (Den Haag)
Hungary: MTK

Ireland: Linfield
Italy: Casale
Norway: n/a
Poland: n/a
Portugal: n/a
Romania: Colentina Bucharest
Russia: n/a
Spain: n/a
Sweden: Aik Stockholm
Switzerland: FC Aarau
Turkey: n/a

ENGLAND INTERNATIONALS

14 Feb   England 0   Ireland 3
16 Mar   Wales 0   England 2
4 Apr   Scotland 3   England 1

1915

ENGLISH AND SCOTTISH FOOTBALL

Champions: Everton
Runners-up: Oldham Athletic

Division 2: Derby County
Runners-up: Preston North End

Division 3 (S): n/a
Runners-up: n/a

Division 3 (N): n/a
Runners-up: n/a

FA Cup winners: Sheffield Utd
League Cup winners: n/a

Charity Shield: n/a

Scottish Champions: Celtic
Runners-up: Heart of Midlothian

Scottish Cup: n/a
Scottish League Cup: n/a

EUROPEAN LEAGUE CHAMPIONS

Austria: WAC
Ireland: Belfast Celtic

Belgium: n/a
Italy: Genoa 1893

Bulgaria: n/a
Norway: n/a

Czechoslovakia: Slavia Prague
Poland: n/a

Denmark: n/a
Portugal: n/a

Finland: KIF Helsinki
Romania: Romania-Americana Buch't

France: n/a
Russia: n/a

Germany: n/a
Spain: n/a

Greece: n/a
Sweden: Djurgardens IF

Holland: Sparta
Switzerland: Bruhl St Gallen

Hungary: n/a
Turkey: n/a

N.B.:- From 1916-1919 there was little in the way of competitive football due to the First World War.

1920

ENGLISH AND SCOTTISH FOOTBALL

Champions: West Bromwich Albion   Runners-up: Burnley
Division 2: Tottenham Hotspur   Runners-up: Huddersfield Town
Division 3 (S): n/a   Runners-up: n/a
Division 3 (N): n/a   Runners-up: n/a
FA Cup winners: Aston Villa   League Cup winners: n/a
Charity Shield: West Bromwich Albion
Scottish Champions: Rangers   Runners-up: Celtic
Scottish Cup: Kilmarnock   Scottish League Cup: n/a

EUROPEAN LEAGUE CHAMPIONS

Austria: Rapid Vienna   Ireland: Belfast Celtic
Belgium: Club Bruges   Italy: Internazionale
Bulgaria: n/a   Norway: n/a
Czechoslovakia: Sparta Prague   Poland: n/a
Denmark: B 93   Portugal: n/a
Finland: AIFK Turku   Romania: Venus Bucharest
France: n/a   Russia: n/a
Germany: IFC Nuremburg   Spain: n/a
Greece: n/a   Sweden: Djurgardens IF
Holland: Be Quick (Groningen)   Switzerland: BSC Young Boys
Hungary: MTK   Turkey: n/a

ENGLAND INTERNATIONALS

15 Mar   England 1   Wales 2
10 Apr   England 5   Scotland 4
23 Oct   England 2   Ireland 0

1921

ENGLISH AND SCOTTISH FOOTBALL

Champions: Burnley	Runners-up: Manchester City
Division 2: Birmingham City	Runners-up: Cardiff City
Division 3 (S): Crystal Palace	Runners-up: Southampton
Division 3 (N): n/a	Runners-up: n/a
FA Cup winners: Tottenham Hotspur	League Cup winners: n/a
Charity Shield: Tottenham Hotspur	
Scottish Champions: Rangers	Runners-up: Celtic
Scottish Cup: Partick Thistle	Scottish League Cup: n/a

EUROPEAN LEAGUE CHAMPIONS

Austria: Rapid Vienna	Ireland: Glentoran
Belgium: Daring CB	Italy: Pro Vercelli
Bulgaria: n/a	Norway: n/a
Czechoslovakia: Sparta Prague	Poland: Cracovia Krakow
Denmark: Akademisk Boldclub	Portugal: n/a
Finland: HPS Helsinki	Romania: Venus Bucharest
France: n/a	Russia: n/a
Germany: IFC Nuremburg	Spain: n/a
Greece: n/a	Sweden: IFK Eskilstunn
Holland: NAC (Breda)	Switzerland: Grasshopper Club
Hungary: MTK	Turkey: n/a

ENGLAND INTERNATIONALS

14 Mar	Wales 0	England 0
9 Apr	Scotland 3	England 0
21 May	Belgium 0	England 2
22 Oct	Ireland 1	England 1

1922

ENGLISH AND SCOTTISH FOOTBALL

Champions: Liverpool   Runners-up: Tottenham Hotspur
Division 2: Nottingham Forest   Runners-up: Stoke City
Division 3 (S): Southampton   Runners-up: Plymouth Argyle
Division 3 (N): Stockport County   Runners-up: Darlington
FA Cup winners: Huddersfield Town   League Cup winners: n/a
Charity Shield: Huddersfield Town
Scottish Champions: Celtic   Runners-up: Rangers
Scottish Cup: Morton   Scottish League Cup: n/a

EUROPEAN LEAGUE CHAMPIONS

Austria: Wiener Sport-Club   Ireland: Linfield
Belgium: Beerschot   Italy: Pro Vercelli
Bulgaria: n/a   Norway: n/a
Czechoslovakia: Sparta Prague   Poland: Pogon Lwow
Denmark: Kopenhavns Boldklub   Portugal: Porto
Finland: HPS Helsinki   Romania: Chinezul Timisoara
France: n/a   Russia: n/a
Germany: n/a   Spain: n/a
Greece: POPA (Athens)   Sweden: GAIS
Holland: Go Ahead (Deventer)   Switzerland: Servette
Hungary: MTK   Turkey: n/a

ENGLAND INTERNATIONALS

13 Mar	England 1	Wales 0
8 Apr	England 0	Scotland 1
21 Oct	England 2	Ireland 0

1923

ENGLISH AND SCOTTISH FOOTBALL

Champions: Liverpool Runners-up: Sunderland
Division 2: Notts County Runners-up: West Ham United
Division 3 (S): Bristol City Runners-up: Plymouth Argyle
Division 3 (N): Nelson Runners-up: Bradford Park Avenue
FA Cup winners: Bolton Wanderers League Cup winners: n/a
Charity Shield: Professionals
Scottish Champions: Rangers Runners-up: Airdrieonians
Scottish Cup: Celtic Scottish League Cup: n/a

EUROPEAN LEAGUE CHAMPIONS

Austria: Rapid Vienna Ireland: Linfield
Belgium: Union Saint-Gilloise Italy: Genoa 1893
Bulgaria: n/a Norway: n/a
Czechoslovakia: Sparta Prague Poland: Pogon Lwow
Denmark: BK Frem Portugal: Sporting Lisbon
Finland: HJK Helsinki Romania: Chiezul Timisoara
France: n/a Russia: n/a
Germany: Hamburg Spain: n/a
Greece: Panathinaikos Sweden: Aik Stockholm
Holland: RCH (Heemstede) Switzerland: n/a
Hungary: MTK Turkey: n/a

ENGLAND INTERNATIONALS

5 Mar	Wales 2	England 2
19 Mar	England 6	Belgium 0
14 Apr	Scotland 2	England 2
10 May	France 1	England 4
21 May	Sweden 2	England 4
24 May	Sweden 1	England 3
20 Oct	Ireland 2	England 1
1 Nov	Belgium 2	England 2

THE FOOTBALL FACT AND QUIZ BOOK

1924

ENGLISH AND SCOTTISH FOOTBALL

Champions: Huddersfield Town   Runners-up: Cardiff City
Division 2: Leeds Utd   Runners-up: Bury
Division 3 (S): Portsmouth   Runners-up: Plymouth Argyle
Division 3 (N): Wolverhampton W   Runners-up: Rochdale
FA Cup winners: Newcastle Utd   League Cup winners: n/a
Charity Shield: Professionals
Scottish Champions: Rangers   Runners-up: Airdrieonians
Scottish Cup: Airdrieonians   Scottish League Cup: n/a

EUROPEAN LEAGUE CHAMPIONS

Austria: Amateure (FK Austria)   Ireland: Queen's Island
Belgium: Beerschot   Italy: Genoa 1893
Bulgaria: n/a   Norway: n/a
Czechoslovakia: Slavia Prague   Poland: n/a
Denmark: B 1903   Portugal: Olhanense
Finland: AIFK Turku   Romania: Chinezul Timisoara
France: n/a   Russia: n/a
Germany: IFC Nuremburg   Spain: n/a
Greece: Apollon   Sweden: Fassberg
Holland: Feyenoord   Switzerland: FC Zurich
Hungary: MTK   Turkey: n/a

ENGLAND INTERNATIONALS

3 Mar	England 1	Wales 2
12 Apr	England 1	Scotland 1
17 May	France 1	England 3
22 Oct	England 3	Ireland 1
8 Dec	England 4	Belgium 0

1925

ENGLISH AND SCOTTISH FOOTBALL

Champions: Huddersfield Town

Runners-up: West Bromwich Albion

Division 2: Leicester City

Runners-up: Manchester Utd

Division 3 (S): Swansea Town

Runners-up: Plymouth Argyle

Division 3 (N): Darlington

Runners-up: Nelson

FA Cup winners: Sheffield Utd

League Cup winners: n/a

Charity Shield: Amateurs

Scottish Champions: Rangers

Runners-up: Airdrieonians

Scottish Cup: Celtic

Scottish League Cup: n/a

EUROPEAN LEAGUE CHAMPIONS

Austria: Hakoah

Belgium: Beerschot

Bulgaria: Vladislov Varna

Czechoslovakia: Slavia Prague

Denmark: Kopenhavns Boldklub

Finland: HJK Helsinki

France: n/a

Germany: IFC Nuremburg

Greece: Panathinaikos

Holland: HBS (Den Haag)

Hungary: MTK

Ireland: Glentoran

Italy: Bologna

Norway: n/a

Poland: Pogon Lwow

Portugal: Porto

Romania: Chinezul Timisoara

Russia: n/a

Spain: n/a

Sweden: Brynas

Switzerland: Servette

Turkey: n/a

ENGLAND INTERNATIONALS

28 Feb	Wales 1	England 2
4 Apr	Scotland 2	England 0
21 May	France 2	England 3
24 Oct	Ireland 0	England 0

1926

ENGLISH AND SCOTTISH FOOTBALL

Champions: Huddersfield Town   Runners-up: Arsenal
Division 2: Sheffield Wednesday   Runners-up: Derby County
Division 3 (S): Reading   Runners-up: Plymouth Argyle
Division 3 (N): Grimsby Town   Runners-up: Bradford Park Avenue
FA Cup winners: Bolton Wanderers   League Cup winners: n/a
Charity Shield: Amateurs
Scottish Champions: Celtic   Runners-up: Airdrieonians
Scottish Cup: St Mirren   Scottish League Cup: n/a

EUROPEAN LEAGUE CHAMPIONS

Austria: Amateure (FK Austria)   Ireland: Belfast Celtic
Belgium: Beerschot   Italy: Juventus
Bulgaria: Vladislov Varna   Norway: n/a
Czechoslovakia: Sparta Prague   Poland: Pogon Lwow
Denmark: B 1903   Portugal: Maritimo
Finland: HPS Helsinki   Romania: Chinezul Timisoara
France: n/a   Russia: n/a
Germany: SpVgg Furth   Spain: n/a
Greece: n/a   Sweden: Orgryte IS
Holland: SC Enschede   Switzerland: Servette
Hungary: Ferencvaros   Turkey: n/a

ENGLAND INTERNATIONALS

1 Mar	England 1	Wales 3
17 Apr	England 0	Scotland 1
24 Apr	Belgium 3	England 5
20 Oct	England 3	Ireland 3

1927

ENGLISH AND SCOTTISH FOOTBALL

Champions: Newcastle Utd
Runners-up: Huddersfield Town
Division 2: Middlesborough
Runners-up: Portsmouth
Division 3 (S): Bristol City
Runners-up: Plymouth Argyle
Division 3 (N): Stoke City
Runners-up: Rochdale
FA Cup winners: Cardiff City
League Cup winners: n/a
Charity Shield: Cardiff City
Scottish Champions: Rangers
Runners-up: Motherwell
Scottish Cup: Celtic
Scottish League Cup: n/a

EUROPEAN LEAGUE CHAMPIONS

Austria: Admira
Ireland: Belfast Celtic
Belgium: Cercle Bruges
Italy: Torino
Bulgaria: n/a
Norway: n/a
Czechoslovakia: Sparta Prague
Poland: Wisla Krakow
Denmark: B 93
Portugal: 'Os Belenenses'
Finland: HPS Helsinki
Romania: Chinezul Timisoara
France: n/a
Russia: n/a
Germany: IFC Nuremburg
Spain: n/a
Greece: Panathinaikos
Sweden: GAIS
Holland: Heracles
Switzerland: Grasshopper Club
Hungary: Ferencvaros
Turkey: n/a

ENGLAND INTERNATIONALS

12 Feb	Wales 3 England 3
24 Apr	Scotland 1 England 2
11 May	Belgium 1 England 9
21 May	Luxembourg 2 England 5
26 May	France 0 England 6
22 Oct	Ireland 2 England 0
28 Nov	England 1 Wales 2

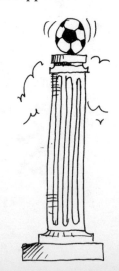

1928

ENGLISH AND SCOTTISH FOOTBALL

Champions: Everton   Runners-up: Huddersfield Town
Division 2: Manchester City   Runners-up: Leeds Utd
Division 3 (S): Millwall   Runners-up: Nottingham Forest
Division 3 (N): Bradford Park Avenue   Runners-up: Lincoln City
FA Cup winners: Blackburn Rovers   League Cup winners: n/a
Charity Shield: Everton
Scottish Champions: Rangers   Runners-up: Celtic
Scottish Cup: Rangers   Scottish League Cup: n/a

EUROPEAN LEAGUE CHAMPIONS

Austria: Admira   Ireland: Belfast Celtic
Belgium: Beerschot   Italy: Torino
Bulgaria: Slavia Sofia   Norway: n/a
Czechoslovakia: Viktoria Zizhov   Poland: Wisla Krakow
Denmark: No winners   Portugal: Carcavelinhos
Finland: TPS Turku   Romania: Coltea Brasov
France: n/a   Russia: n/a
Germany: Hamburg   Spain: n/a
Greece: Aris   Sweden: Orgryte IS
Holland: Feyenoord   Switzerland: Grasshopper Club
Hungary: Ferencvaros   Turkey: n/a

ENGLAND INTERNATIONALS

31 Mar   England 1   Scotland 5
17 May   France 1   England 5
19 May   Belgium 1   England 3
22 Oct   England 2   Ireland 1
17 Nov   Wales 2   England 3

THE FOOTBALL FACT AND QUIZ BOOK

1929

ENGLISH AND SCOTTISH FOOTBALL

Champions: Sheffield Wednesday   Runners-up: Leicester City
Division 2: Middlesborough   Runners-up: Grimsby Town
Division 3 (S): Charlton Athletic   Runners-up: Crystal Palace
Division 3 (N): Bradford City   Runners-up: Stockport County
FA Cup winners: Bolton Wanderers   League Cup winners: n/a
Charity Shield: Professionals
Scottish Champions: Rangers   Runners-up: Celtic
Scottish Cup: Kilmarnock   Scottish League Cup: n/a

EUROPEAN LEAGUE CHAMPIONS

Austria: Rapid Vienna   Ireland: Belfast Celtic
Belgium: Antwerp   Italy: Bologna
Bulgaria: Botev Plovdiv   Norway: n/a
Czechoslovakia: Slavia Prague   Poland: Warta Poznan
Denmark: B 93   Portugal: 'Os Belenenses'
Finland: HPS Helsinki   Romania: Venus Bucharest
France: n/a   Russia: n/a
Germany: SpVgg Furth   Spain: Barcelona
Greece: n/a   Sweden: Helsingborgs
Holland: PSV Eindhoven   Switzerland: BSC Young Boys
Hungary: MTK   Turkey: n/a

ENGLAND INTERNATIONALS

13 Apr   Scotland 1   England 0
9 May   France 1   England 4
11 May   Belgium 1   England 5
15 May   Spain 4   England 3
19 Oct   Ireland 0   England 3
20 Nov   England 6   Wales 0

THE FOOTBALL FACT AND QUIZ BOOK

1930

ENGLISH AND SCOTTISH FOOTBALL

Champions: Sheffield Wednesday   Runners-up: Derby County
Division 2: Blackpool   Runners-up: Chelsea
Division 3 (S): Plymouth Argyle   Runners-up: Brentford
Division 3 (N): Port Vale   Runners-up: Stockport County
FA Cup winners: Arsenal   League Cup winners: n/a
Charity Shield: Arsenal
Scottish Champions: Rangers   Runners-up: Motherwell
Scottish Cup: Rangers   Scottish League Cup: n/a

EUROPEAN LEAGUE CHAMPIONS

Austria: Rapid Vienna   Ireland: Linfield
Belgium: Cercle Bruges   Italy: Internazionale
Bulgaria: Slavia Sofia   Norway: n/a
Czechoslovakia: Slavia Prague   Poland: Cracovia Krakow
Denmark: B 93   Portugal: Benfica
Finland: HIFK Helsinki   Romania: Juventus Bucharest
France: n/a   Russia: n/a
Germany: Hertha BSC Berlin   Spain: Athletic Bilbao
Greece: Panathinaikos   Sweden: Helsingborgs
Holland: Go Ahead (Deventer)   Switzerland: Servette
Hungary: Ujpest   Turkey: n/a

ENGLAND INTERNATIONALS

5 Apr	England 5	Scotland 2
10 May	Germany 3	England 3
14 May	Austria 0	England 0
20 Oct	England 5	Ireland 1
22 Nov	Wales 0	England 4

INTERNATIONAL CUP WINNERS

World Cup: Uruguay

THE FOOTBALL FACT AND QUIZ BOOK

1931

ENGLISH AND SCOTTISH FOOTBALL

Champions: Arsenal   Runners-up: Aston Villa
Division 2: Everton   Runners-up: West Bromwich Albion
Division 3 (S): Notts County   Runners-up: Crystal Palace
Division 3 (N): Chesterfield   Runners-up: Lincoln City
FA Cup winners: West Bromwich Albion League Cup winners: n/a
Charity Shield: Arsenal
Scottish Champions: Rangers   Runners-up: Celtic
Scottish Cup: Celtic   Scottish League Cup: n/a

EUROPEAN LEAGUE CHAMPIONS

Austria: First Vienna   Ireland: Glentoran
Belgium: Antwerp   Italy: Juventus
Bulgaria: AC23 Sofia   Norway: n/a
Czechoslovakia: Slavia Prague   Poland: Garbarnia Krakow
Denmark: BK Frem   Portugal: Benfica
Finland: HIFK Helsinki   Romania: UDR
France: n/a   Russia: n/a
Germany: Hertha BSC Berlin   Spain: Athletic Bilbao
Greece: Olympiakos   Sweden: GAIS
Holland: Ajax   Switzerland: Grasshopper Club
Hungary: Ujpest   Turkey: n/a

ENGLAND INTERNATIONALS

28 Mar   Scotland 2   England 0
14 May   France 5   England 2
16 May   Belgium 1   England 4
17 Oct   Ireland 2   England 6
18 Nov   England 3   Wales 1
9 Dec   England 7   Spain 1

1932

ENGLISH AND SCOTTISH FOOTBALL

Champions: Everton   Runners-up: Arsenal
Division 2: Wolverhampton Wanderers   Runners-up: Leeds Utd
Division 3 (S): Fulham   Runners-up: Reading
Division 3 (N): Lincoln City   Runners-up: Gateshead
FA Cup winners: Newcastle Utd   League Cup winners: n/a
Charity Shield: Everton
Scottish Champions: Motherwell   Runners-up: Rangers
Scottish Cup: Rangers   Scottish League Cup: n/a

EUROPEAN LEAGUE CHAMPIONS

Austria: Admira
Belgium: Lierse SK
Bulgaria: Shipchenski Sokol Varna
Czechoslovakia: Sparta Prague
Denmark: Kopenhavns Boldklub
Finland: HPS Helsinki
France: n/a
Germany: Bayern Munich
Greece: Aris
Holland: Ajax
Hungary: Ferencvaros

Ireland: Linfield
Italy: Juventus
Norway: n/a
Poland: Cracovia Krakow
Portugal: Porto
Romania: Venus Bucharest
Russia: n/a
Spain: Real Madrid
Sweden: AIK Stockholm
Switzerland: Lausanne-Sports
Turkey: n/a

ENGLAND INTERNATIONALS

9 Apr	England 3 Scotland 0
17 Oct	England 1 Ireland 0
16 Nov	Wales 0 England 0
7 Dec	England 4 Austria 3

1933

ENGLISH AND SCOTTISH FOOTBALL

Champions: Arsenal
Division 2: Stoke City
Division 3 (S): Brentford
Division 3 (N): Hull City
FA Cup winners: Everton
Charity Shield: Arsenal
Scottish Champions: Rangers
Scottish Cup: Celtic

Runners-up: Aston Villa
Runners-up: Tottenham Hotspur
Runners-up: Exeter City
Runners-up: Wrexham
League Cup winners: n/a

Runners-up: Motherwell
Scottish League Cup: n/a

EUROPEAN LEAGUE CHAMPIONS

Austria: First Vienna
Belgium: Union Saint-Gilloise
Bulgaria: Levski Sofia
Czechoslovakia: Slavia Prague
Denmark: BK Frem
Finland: HIFK Helsinki
France: Olympique Lillois
Germany: Fortuna Dusseldorf
Greece: Olympiakos
Holland: Go Ahead (Deventer)
Hungary: Ujpest

Ireland: Belfast Celtic
Italy: Juventus
Norway: n/a
Poland: Ruch Chorzow
Portugal: 'Os Belenenses'
Romania: Ripensia Timisoara
Russia: n/a
Spain: Real Madrid
Sweden: Helsingborg
Switzerland: Servette
Turkey: n/a

ENGLAND INTERNATIONALS

1 Apr	Scotland 2 England 1
13 May	Italy 1 England 1
20 May	Switzerland 0 England 4
14 Oct	Ireland 0 England 3
15 Nov	England 1 Wales 2
6 Dec	England 4 France 1

1934

ENGLISH AND SCOTTISH FOOTBALL

Champions: Arsenal   Runners-up: Huddersfield Town
Division 2: Grimsby Town   Runners-up: Preston North End
Division 3 (S): Norwich City   Runners-up: Coventry City
Division 3 (N): Barnsley   Runners-up: Chesterfield
FA Cup winners: Manchester City   League Cup winners: n/a
Charity Shield: Arsenal
Scottish Champions: Rangers   Runners-up: Motherwell
Scottish Cup: Rangers   Scottish League Cup: n/a

EUROPEAN LEAGUE CHAMPIONS

Austria: Admira   Ireland: Linfield
Belgium: Union Saint-Gilloise   Italy: Juventus
Bulgaria: Vladislav Varna   Norway: n/a
Czechoslovakia: Slavia Prague   Poland: Ruch Chorzow
Denmark: B 93   Portugal: Sporting Lisbon
Finland: HPS Helsinki   Romania: Venus Bucharest
France: Sete   Russia: n/a
Germany: Schalke 04   Spain: Athletic Bilbao
Greece: Olympiakos   Sweden: Helsingborgs
Holland: Ajax   Switzerland: Servette
Hungary: Ferencvaros   Turkey: n/a

ENGLAND INTERNATIONALS

14 Apr   England 3   Scotland 0
10 May   Hungary 2   England 1
16 May   Czechoslovakia 2   England 1
29 Sep   Wales 0   England 4
14 Nov   England 3   Italy 2

INTERNATIONAL CUP WINNERS

World Cup: Italy

1935

ENGLISH AND SCOTTISH FOOTBALL

Champions: Arsenal   Runners-up: Sunderland
Division 2: Brentford   Runners-up: Bolton Wanderers
Division 3 (S): Charlton Athletic   Runners-up: Reading
Division 3 (N): Doncaster Rovers   Runners-up: Halifax Town
FA Cup winners: Sheffield Wednesday   League Cup winners: n/a
Charity Shield: Sheffield Wednesday
Scottish Champions: Rangers   Runners-up: Celtic
Scottish Cup: Rangers   Scottish League Cup: n/a

EUROPEAN LEAGUE CHAMPIONS

Austria: Rapid Vienna   Ireland: Linfield
Belgium: Union Saint-Gilloise   Italy: Juventus
Bulgaria: Sportclub Sofia   Norway: n/a
Czechoslovakia: Slavia Prague   Poland: Ruch Chorzow
Denmark: B 93   Portugal: Benfica
Finland: HPS Helsinki   Romania: Ripensia Timisoara
France: Sochaux-Montbeliard   Russia: n/a
Germany: Schalke 04   Spain: Real Betis
Greece: n/a   Sweden: IFK Gothenburg
Holland: PSV Eindhoven   Switzerland: Lausanne-Sports
Hungary: Ujpest   Turkey: n/a

ENGLAND INTERNATIONALS

6 Feb	England 2	Ireland 1
6 Apr	Scotland 2	England 0
18 May	Holland 0	England 1
19 Oct	Ireland 1	England 3
4 Dec	England 3	Germany 0

1936

ENGLISH AND SCOTTISH FOOTBALL

Champions: Sunderland
Division 2: Manchester Utd
Division 3 (S): Coventry City
Division 3 (N): Chesterfield
FA Cup winners: Arsenal
Charity Shield: Sunderland
Scottish Champions: Celtic
Scottish Cup: Rangers

Runners-up: Derby County
Runners-up: Charlton Athletic
Runners-up: Luton Town
Runners-up: Chester
League Cup winners: n/a

Runners-up: Rangers
Scottish League Cup: n/a

EUROPEAN LEAGUE CHAMPIONS

Austria: Admira
Belgium: Daring Cb
Bulgaria: Slavia Sofia
Czechoslovakia: Sparta Prague
Denmark: BK Frem
Finland: HJK Helsinki
France: RC Paris
Germany: IFC Nuremburg
Greece: Olympiakos
Holland: Feyenoord
Hungary: MTK

Ireland: Belfast Celtic
Italy: Bologna
Norway: n/a
Poland: Ruch Chorzow
Portugal: Sporting Lisbon
Romania: Ripensia Timisoara
Russia: Spartak Moscow
Spain: Athletic Bilbao
Sweden: IF Elfsborg
Switzerland: Lausanne-Sports
Turkey: n/a

ENGLAND INTERNATIONALS

5 Feb	England 1	Wales 2
4 Apr	England 1	Scotland 1
6 May	Austria 2	England 1
9 May	Belgium 3	England 2
17 Oct	Wales 2	England 1
18 Nov	England 3	Ireland 1

ENGLISH AND SCOTTISH FOOTBALL

Champions: Manchester City   Runners-up: Charlton Athletic
Division 2: Leicester City   Runners-up: Blackpool
Division 3 (S): Luton Town   Runners-up: Notts County
Division 3 (N): Stockport County   Runners-up: Lincoln City
FA Cup winners: Sunderland   League Cup winners: n/a
Charity Shield: Manchester City
Scottish Champions: Rangers   Runners-up: Aberdeen
Scottish Cup: Celtic   Scottish League Cup: n/a

EUROPEAN LEAGUE CHAMPIONS

Austria: Admira   Ireland: Belfast Celtic
Belgium: Daring CB   Italy: Bologna
Bulgaria: Levski Sofia   Norway: n/a
Czechoslovakia: Slavia Prague   Poland: Cracovia Krakow
Denmark: Akademisk Boldklub   Portugal: Porto
Finland: HIFK Helsinki   Romania: Venus Bucharest
France: Olympique Marseille   Russia: Dynamo Moscow
Germany: Schalke 04   Spain: n/a
Greece: Olympiakos   Sweden: AIK Stockholm
Holland: Ajax   Switzerland: Grasshopper Club
Hungary: MTK   Turkey: n/a

ENGLAND INTERNATIONALS

17 Apr   Scotland 3   England 1
14 May   Norway 0   England 6
17 May   Sweden 0   England 4
20 May   Finland 0   England 8
23 Oct   Ireland 1   England 5
17 Nov   England 2   Wales 1
1 Dec   England 5   Czechoslovakia 4

1938

ENGLISH AND SCOTTISH FOOTBALL

Champions: Arsenal
Division 2: Aston Villa
Division 3 (S): Millwall
Division 3 (N): Tranmere Rovers
FA Cup winners: Preston North End
Charity Shield: Arsenal
Scottish Champions: Celtic
Scottish Cup: East Fife

Runners-up: Wolverhampton W
Runners-up: Manchester Utd
Runners-up: Bristol City
Runners-up: Doncaster Rovers
League Cup winners: n/a

Runners-up: Hearts
Scottish League Cup: n/a

EUROPEAN LEAGUE CHAMPIONS

Austria: Rapid Vienna
Belgium: Beerschot
Bulgaria: Ticha Varna
Czechoslovakia: Sparta Prague
Denmark: B 1903
Finland: HJK Helsinki
France: Sochaux-Montbeliard
Germany: Hannoverscher SV 96
Greece: Olympiakos
Holland: Feyenoord
Hungary: Ferencvaros

Ireland: Belfast Celtic
Italy: Internazionale
Norway: Frederikstad
Poland: Ruch Chorzow
Portugal: Sporting Lisbon
Romania: Ripensia Timisoara
Russia: Spartak Moscow
Spain: n/a
Sweden: IF Sleipner
Switzerland: FC Lugano
Turkey: n/a

ENGLAND INTERNATIONALS

9 Apr	England 0	Scotland 1
14 May	Germany 3	England 6
21 May	Switzerland 2	England 1
26 May	France 2	England 4
22 Oct	Wales 4	England 2
26 Oct	England 3	FIFA 0
9 Nov	England 4	Newcastle 0
16 Nov	England 7	Ireland 0

INTERNATIONAL CUP WINNERS

World Cup: Italy

1939

ENGLISH AND SCOTTISH FOOTBALL

Champions: Everton   Runners-up: Wolverhampton W
Division 2: Blackburn Rovers   Runners-up: Sheffield Utd
Division 3 (S): Newport County   Runners-up: Crystal Palace
Division 3 (N): Barnsley   Runners-up: Doncaster Rovers
FA Cup winners: Portsmouth   League Cup winners: n/a
Charity Shield: n/a
Scottish Champions: Rangers   Runners-up: Celtic
Scottish Cup: Clyde   Scottish League Cup: n/a

EUROPEAN LEAGUE CHAMPIONS

Austria: Admira   Ireland: Belfast Celtic
Belgium: Beerschot   Italy: Bologna
Bulgaria: Slavia Sofia   Norway: Frederikstad
Czechoslovakia: Sparta Prague   Poland: n/a
Denmark: B 93   Portugal: Porto
Finland: TPS Turku   Romania: Venus Bucharest
France: FC Sete   Russia: Spartak Moscow
Germany: Schalke 04   Spain: n/a
Greece: AEK   Sweden: IF Elfsborg
Holland: Ajax   Switzerland: Grasshopper Club
Hungary: Ujpest   Turkey: n/a

ENGLAND INTERNATIONALS

15 Apr   Scotland 1   England 2
13 May   Italy 2   England 2
18 May   Yugoslavia 2   England 1
24 May   Romania 0   England 2

1947

ENGLISH AND SCOTTISH FOOTBALL

Champions: Liverpool   Runners-up: Manchester Utd
Division 2: Manchester City   Runners-up: Burnley
Division 3 (S): Cardiff City   Runners-up: Queen's Park Rangers
Division 3 (N): Doncaster Rovers   Runners-up: Rotherham Utd
FA Cup winners: Charlton Athletic   League Cup winners: n/a
Charity Shield: n/a
Scottish Champions: Rangers   Runners-up: Hibernian
Scottish Cup: Aberdeen   Scottish League Cup: n/a

EUROPEAN LEAGUE CHAMPIONS

Austria: Wacker   Ireland: n/a
Belgium: Anderlecht   Italy: Torino
Bulgaria: Levski Sofia   Norway: n/a
Czechoslovakia: Slavia Prague   Poland: Warta Poznan
Denmark: Akademisk Boldklub   Portugal: Sporting Lisbon
Finland: HIFK Helsinki   Romania: UT Arad
France: Roubaix-Tourcoing   Russia: CSKA Moscow
Germany: n/a   Spain: Valencia
Greece: Olympiakos   Sweden: IFK Norrkoping
Holland: Ajax   Switzerland: FC Biel-Bienne
Hungary: Ujpest   Turkey: n/a

ENGLAND INTERNATIONALS

12 Apr	England 1 Scotland 1
3 May	England 3 France 0
18 May	Switzerland 1 England 0
27 May	Portugal 0 England 10
21 Sep	Belgium 2 England 5
18 Oct	Wales 0 England 3
5 Nov	England 2 N. Ireland 2
19 Nov	England 4 Sweden 2

1948

ENGLISH AND SCOTTISH FOOTBALL

Champions: Arsenal	Runners-up: Manchester Utd
Division 2: Birmingham City	Runners-up: Newcastle Utd
Division 3 (S): Queen's Park Rangers	Runners-up: Bournemouth
Division 3 (N): Lincoln City	Runners-up: Rotherham Utd
FA Cup winners: Manchester Utd	League Cup winners: n/a
Charity Shield: Arsenal	
Scottish Champions: Hibernian	Runners-up: Rangers
Scottish Cup: Rangers	Scottish League Cup: East Fife

EUROPEAN LEAGUE CHAMPIONS

Austria: Rapid Vienna	Ireland: Belfast Celtic
Belgium: FC Mechelen	Italy: Torino
Bulgaria: CSKA Sofia	Norway: Freidig Trondheim
Czechoslovakia: Slavia Prague	Poland: Cracovia Krakow
Denmark: Kopenhavns Boldklub	Portugal: Sporting Lisbon
Finland: VPS Vaasa	Romania: UT Arad
France: Olympique Marseille	Russia: CSKA Moscow
Germany: IFC Nuremburg	Spain: Barcelona
Greece: Olympiakos	Sweden: IFK Norrkoping
Holland: BVV (Den Bosch)	Switzerland: AC Bellinzona
Hungary: Csepel	Turkey: n/a

ENGLAND INTERNATIONALS

10 Apr	Scotland 0 England 2
16 May	Italy 0 England 4
26 Sep	Denmark 0 England 0
9 Oct	N. Ireland 2 England 6
10 Nov	England 1 Wales 0
1 Dec	England 6 Switzerland 0

THE FOOTBALL FACT AND QUIZ BOOK

1949

ENGLISH AND SCOTTISH FOOTBALL

Champions: Portsmouth   Runners-up: Manchester Utd
Division 2: Fulham   Runners-up: West Bromwich Albion
Division 3 (S): Swansea Town   Runners-up: Reading
Division 3 (N): Hull City   Runners-up: Rotherham Utd
FA Cup winners: Wolverhampton W   League Cup winners: n/a
Charity Shield: Portsmouth
Scottish Champions: Rangers   Runners-up: Dundee
Scottish Cup: Rangers   Scottish League Cup: Rangers

EUROPEAN LEAGUE CHAMPIONS

Austria: FK Austria
Belgium: Anderlecht
Bulgaria: Levski Sofia
Czechoslovakia: NV Bratislava
Denmark: Kopenhavn Boldklub
Finland: TPS Turku
France: Stade de Reims
Germany: VfR Mannheim
Greece: Panathinaikos
Holland: SVV (Schiedam)
Hungary: Ferencvaros
Ireland: Linfield
Italy: Torino
Norway: Frederikstad
Poland: Wisla Krakow
Portugal: Sporting Lisbon
Romania: Progresul
Russia: Dynamo Moscow
Spain: Barcelona
Sweden: Malmo
Switzerland: FC Lugano
Turkey: n/a

ENGLAND INTERNATIONALS

9 Apr	England 1	Scotland 3
13 May	Sweden 3	England 1
18 May	Norway 1	England 4
22 May	France 1	England 3
21 Sep	England 0	Rep. of Ireland 2
15 Oct	Wales 1	England 4
16 Nov	England 9	N. Ireland 2
30 Nov	England 2	Italy 0

1950

ENGLISH AND SCOTTISH FOOTBALL

Champions: Portsmouth   Runners-up: Wolverhampton W
Division 2: Tottenham Hotspur   Runners-up: Sheffield Wednesday
Division 3 (S): Notts County   Runners-up: Northampton Town
Division 3 (N): Doncaster Rovers   Runners-up: Gateshead
FA Cup winners: Arsenal   League Cup winners: n/a
Charity Shield: World Cup Team
Scottish Champions: Rangers   Runners-up: Hibernian
Scottish Cup: Rangers   Scottish League Cup: East Fife

EUROPEAN LEAGUE CHAMPIONS

Austria: FK Austria   Ireland: Linfield
Belgium: Anderlecht   Italy: Juventus
Bulgaria: Levski Sofia   Norway: Fram
Czechoslovakia: NV Bratislava   Poland: Wisla Krakow
Denmark: Kopenhavn Boldklub   Portugal: Benfica
Finland: Ilves-Kissat   Romania: UT Arad
France: Girondins de Bordeaux   Russia: CSKA Moscow
Germany: VfB Stuttgart   Spain: Atletico Madrid
Greece: n/a   Sweden: Malmo
Holland: Limburgia   Switzerland: Servette
Hungary: Honved   Turkey: n/a

ENGLAND INTERNATIONALS

15 Apr Scotland 0   England 1   2 Jul   Spain 1   England 0
14 May Portugal 3   England 5   7 Oct   N. Ireland 1   England 4
18 May Belgium 1   England 4   15 Nov England 4   Wales 2
15 Jun Chile 0   England 2   22 Nov England 2   Yugoslavia 2
29 Jun USA 1   England 0

INTERNATIONAL CUP WINNERS

World Cup: Uruguay

1951

ENGLISH AND SCOTTISH FOOTBALL

Champions: Tottenham Hotspur — Runners-up: Manchester Utd
Division 2: Preston North End — Runners-up: Manchester City
Division 3 (S): Nottingham Forest — Runners-up: Norwich City
Division 3 (N): Rotherham — Runners-up: Mansfield Town
FA Cup winners: Newcastle Utd — League Cup winners: n/a
Charity Shield: Tottenham Hotspur
Scottish Champions: Hibernian — Runners-up: Rangers
Scottish Cup: Celtic — Scottish League Cup: Motherwell

EUROPEAN LEAGUE CHAMPIONS

Austria: Rapid Vienna
Belgium: Anderlecht
Bulgaria: CSKA Sofia
Czechoslovakia: NV Bratislava
Denmark: Akademisk Boldklub
Finland: KTP Kotka
France: OGC Nice
Germany: IFC Kaiserslautern
Greece: Olympiakos
Holland: PSV Eindhoven
Hungary: MTK
Ireland: Glentoran
Italy: AC Milan
Norway: Frederikstad
Poland: Ruch Chorzow
Portugal: Sporting Lisbon
Romania: CCA
Russia: CSKA Moscow
Spain: Atletico Madrid
Sweden: Malmo
Switzerland: Lausanne-Sports
Turkey: n/a

ENGLAND INTERNATIONALS

14 Apr	England 2	Scotland 3
9 May	England 2	Argentina 1
19 May	England 5	Portugal 2
3 Oct	England 2	France 2
20 Oct	Wales 1	England 1
14 Nov	England 2	N. Ireland 0
28 Nov	England 2	Austria 2

1952

ENGLISH AND SCOTTISH FOOTBALL

Champions: Manchester Utd
Runners-up: Tottenham Hotspur
Division 2: Sheffield Wednesday
Runners-up: Cardiff City
Division 3 (S): Plymouth Argyle
Runners-up: Reading
Division 3 (N): Lincoln City
Runners-up: Grimsby Town
FA Cup winners: Newcastle Utd
League Cup winners: n/a
Charity Shield: Manchester Utd
Scottish Champions: Hibernian
Runners-up: Rangers
Scottish Cup: Motherwell
Scottish League Cup: Dundee

EUROPEAN LEAGUE CHAMPIONS

Austria: Rapid Vienna
Ireland: Glenavon
Belgium: FC Liege
Italy: Juventus
Bulgaria: CSKA Sofia
Norway: Frederikstad
Czechoslovakia: Sparta Prague
Poland: Ruch Chorzow
Denmark: Akademisk Boldklub
Portugal: Sporting Lisbon
Finland: KTP Kotka
Romania: CCA
France: OGC Nice
Russia: Spartak Moscow
Germany: VfB Stuttgart
Spain: Barcelona
Greece: n/a
Sweden: IFK Norrkoping
Holland: Willem II
Switzerland: Grasshopper Club
Hungary: Honved
Turkey: n/a

ENGLAND INTERNATIONALS

5 Apr   Scotland 1   England 2
18 May   Italy 1   England 1
25 May   Austria 2   England 3
28 May   Switzerland 0   England 3
4 Oct   N. Ireland 2   England 2
12 Nov   England 5   Wales 2
26 Nov   England 5   Belgium 0

THE FOOTBALL FACT AND QUIZ BOOK

1953

ENGLISH AND SCOTTISH FOOTBALL

Champions: Arsenal   Runners-up: Preston North End
Division 2: Sheffield Utd   Runners-up: Huddersfield Town
Division 3 (S): Bristol Rovers   Runners-up: Millwall
Division 3 (N): Oldham Athletic   Runners-up: Port Vale
FA Cup winners: Blackpool   League Cup winners: n/a
Charity Shield: Arsenal
Scottish Champions: Rangers   Runners-up: Hibernian
Scottish Cup: Rangers   Scottish League Cup: Dundee

EUROPEAN LEAGUE CHAMPIONS

Austria: FK Austria   Ireland: Glentoran
Belgium: FC Liege   Italy: Internazionale
Bulgaria: Levski Sofia   Norway: Larvik Turn
Czechoslovakia: Dukla Prague   Poland: Ruch Chorzow
Denmark: Kopenhavn Boldklub   Portugal: Sporting Lisbon
Finland: VIFK Vassa   Romania: CCA
France: Stade de Reims   Russia: Spartak Moscow
Germany: IFC Kaiserslautern   Spain: Barcelona
Greece: Panathinaikos   Sweden: Malmo
Holland: RCH (Heemstede)   Switzerland: FC Basel
Hungary: Voros Lobogo   Turkey: n/a

ENGLAND INTERNATIONALS

18 Apr	England 2	Scotland 2
24 May	Chile 1	England 2
31 May	Uruguay 2	England 1
8 Jun	USA 3	England 6
10 Oct	Wales 1	England 4
21 Oct	England 4	Rest of Europe 4
11 Nov	England 3	N. Ireland 1
25 Nov	England 3	Hungary 6

1954

ENGLISH AND SCOTTISH FOOTBALL

Champions: Wolverhampton W   Runners-up: West Bromwich Albion
Division 2: Leicester City   Runners-up: Everton
Division 3 (S): Ipswich Town   Runners-up: Brighton
Division 3 (N): Port Vale   Runners-up: Barnsley
FA Cup winners: West Bromwich Albion League Cup winners: n/a
Charity Shield: Wolverhampton W
Scottish Champions: Celtic   Runners-up: Heart of Midlothian
Scottish Cup: Celtic   Scottish League Cup: East Fife

EUROPEAN LEAGUE CHAMPIONS

Austria: Rapid Vienna   Ireland: Linfield
Belgium: Anderlecht   Italy: Internazionale
Bulgaria: CSKA Sofia   Norway: Frederikstad
Czechoslovakia: Sparta Prague   Poland: Polonia Bytom
Denmark: Koge BK   Portugal: Sporting Lisbon
Finland: Pyrkiva Turku   Romania: UT Arad
France: Lille OSC   Russia: Dynamo Moscow
Germany: Hannoverscher SV 96   Spain: Real Madrid
Greece: Olympiakos   Sweden: GAIS
Holland: Eindhoven   Switzerland: La Chaux-de-Fonds
Hungary: Honved   Turkey: n/a

ENGLAND INTERNATIONALS

3 Apr   Scotland 2   England 4   26 Jun Uruguay 4   England 2
16 May Yugoslavia 1   England 0   2 Oct   N. Ireland 0   England 2
23 May Hungary 7   England 1   10 Nov England 3   Wales 2
17 Jun Belgium 4   England 4   1 Dec   England 3   W. Germany 1
20 Jun Switzerland 0   England 2

INTERNATIONAL CUP WINNERS

World Cup: West Germany

THE FOOTBALL FACT AND QUIZ BOOK

1955

ENGLISH AND SCOTTISH FOOTBALL

Champions: Chelsea   Runners-up: Wolverhampton W
Division 2: Birmingham City Runners-up: Luton Town
Division 3 (S): Bristol City Runners-up: Leyton Orient
Division 3 (N): Barnsley   Runners-up: Accrington Stanley
FA Cup winners: Newcastle Utd League Cup winners: n/a
Charity Shield: Chelsea
Scottish Champions: Aberdeen   Runners-up: Celtic
Scottish Cup: Clyde   Scottish League Cup: Hearts

EUROPEAN LEAGUE CHAMPIONS

Austria: First Vienna   Ireland: Linfield
Belgium: Anderlecht   Italy: AC Milan
Bulgaria: CSKA Sofia   Norway: Larvik Turn
Czechoslovakia: Slovan Bratislava Poland: Legia Warsaw
Denmark: AGF   Portugal: Benfica
Finland: KIF Helsinki   Romania: Dynamo Bucharest
France: Stade de Reims   Russia: Dynamo Moscow
Germany: SC Rot-Weiss Essen   Spain: Real Madrid
Greece: Olympiakos   Sweden: Djurgardens IF
Holland: Willem II   Switzerland: La Chaux-de-Fonds
Hungary: Honved   Turkey: n/a

ENGLAND INTERNATIONALS

2 Apr	Scotland 2 England 7
15 May	France 1 England 0
18 May	Spain 1 England 1
22 May	Portugal 3 England 1
2 Oct	Denmark 1 England 5
22 Oct	Wales 1 England 1
2 Nov	England 3 N. Ireland 0
30 Nov	England 4 Spain 1

1956

ENGLISH AND SCOTTISH FOOTBALL

Champions: Manchester Utd   Runners-up: Blackpool
Division 2: Sheffield Wednesday   Runners-up: Leeds Utd
Division 3 (S): Leyton Orient   Runners-up: Brighton
Division 3 (N): Grimsby Town   Runners-up: Derby County
FA Cup winners: Manchester City   League Cup winners: n/a
Charity Shield: Manchester Utd
Scottish Champions: Rangers   Runners-up: Aberdeen
Scottish Cup: Heart of Midlothian   Scottish League Cup: Aberdeen

EUROPEAN LEAGUE CHAMPIONS

Austria: Rapid Vienna   Ireland: Linfield
Belgium: Anderlecht   Italy: Fiorentina
Bulgaria: CSKA Sofia   Norway: Larvik Turn
Czechoslovakia: Dukla Prague   Poland: Legia Warsaw
Denmark: AGF   Portugal: Porto
Finland: KuPS Kuopio   Romania: CCA
France: OGC Nice   Russia: Spartak Moscow
Germany: Borussia Dortmund   Spain: Athletic Bilbao
Greece: Olympiakos   Sweden: IFK Norrkoping
Holland: Rapid JC (Heerlen)   Switzerland: Grasshopper Club
Hungary: n/a   Turkey: n/a

ENGLAND INTERNATIONALS

14 Apr Scotland 1 England 1   6 Oct N. Ireland 1 England 1
9 May England 4 Brazil 2   14 Nov England 3 Wales 1
16 May Sweden 0 England 0   28 Nov England 3 Yugoslavia 0
20 May Finland 1 England 5   5 Dec England 5 Denmark 2
26 May W. Germany 1 England 3

INTERNATIONAL CUP WINNERS

European Cup: Real Madrid

THE FOOTBALL FACT AND QUIZ BOOK

1957

ENGLISH AND SCOTTISH FOOTBALL

Champions: Manchester Utd
Runners-up: Tottenham Hotspur
Division 2: Leicester City
Runners-up: Nottingham Forest
Division 3 (S): Ipswich Town
Runners-up: Torquay Utd
Division 3 (N): Derby County
Runners-up: Hartlepool Utd
FA Cup winners: Aston Villa
League Cup winners: n/a
Charity Shield: Manchester Utd
Scottish Champions: Rangers
Runners-up: Hearts
Scottish Cup: Falkirk
Scottish League Cup: Celtic

EUROPEAN LEAGUE CHAMPIONS

Austria: Rapid Vienna
Ireland: Glentoran
Belgium: Antwerp
Italy: AC Milan
Bulgaria: CSKA Sofia
Norway: Frederikstad
Czechoslovakia: n/a
Poland: Gornik Zabrze
Denmark: AGF
Portugal: Benfica
Finland: HPS Helsinki
Romania: n/a
France: Saint-Etienne
Russia: Dynamo Moscow
Germany: Borussia Dortmund
Spain: Real Madrid
Greece: Olympiakos
Sweden: IFK Norrkoping
Holland: Ajax
Switzerland: BSC Young Boys
Hungary: Vasas
Turkey: n/a

ENGLAND INTERNATIONALS

6 Apr   England 2   Scotland 1
8 May   England 5   Rep. of Ireland 1
15 May Denmark 1   England 4
19 May Rep. of Ireland 1   England 1
19 Oct Wales 0   England 4
6 Nov   England 2   N. Ireland 3
27 Nov England 4   France 0

INTERNATIONAL CUP WINNERS

European Cup: Real Madrid

1958

ENGLISH AND SCOTTISH FOOTBALL

Champions: Wolverhampton W   Runners-up: Preston North End
Division 2: West Ham Utd   Runners-up: Blackburn Rovers
Division 3 (S): Brighton   Runners-up: Brentford
Division 3 (N): Scunthorpe Utd   Runners-up: Accrington Stanley
FA Cup winners: Bolton Wanderers   League Cup winners: n/a
Charity Shield: Bolton Wanderers
Scottish Champions: Hearts   Runners-up: Rangers
Scottish Cup: Clyde   Scottish League Cup: Celtic

EUROPEAN LEAGUE CHAMPIONS

Austria: Wiener Sport-Club   Ireland: Ards
Belgium: Standard Liege   Italy: Juventus
Bulgaria: CSKA Sofia   Norway: Viking Stavanger
Czechoslovakia: Dukla Prague   Poland: LKS Lodz
Denmark: Vejle BK   Portugal: Sporting Lisbon
Finland: KuPS Kuopio   Romania: Petrolul Ploiesti
France: Stade de Reims   Russia: Spartak Moscow
Germany: Schalke 04   Spain: Real Madrid
Greece: Olympiakos   Sweden: IFK Gothenburg
Holland: DOS (Utrecht)   Switzerland: BSC Young Boys
Hungary: MTK   Turkey: n/a

ENGLAND INTERNATIONALS

19 Apr Scotland 0   England 4   22 Oct England 5   USSR 0
7 May   England 2   Portugal 1   26 Nov England 2   Wales 2
11 May Yugoslavia 5   England 0
18 May USSR 1   England 1
8 June USSR 2   England 2
11 Jun Brazil 0   England 0
15 Jun Austria 2   England 2
17 Jun USSR 1   England 0
4 Nov   N. Ireland 3   England 3

INTERNATIONAL CUP WINNERS

European Cup: Real Madrid
European Cup-Winners' Cup: Barcelona
World Cup: Brazil

1959

ENGLISH AND SCOTTISH FOOTBALL

Champions: Wolverhampton W   Runners-up: Manchester Utd
Division 2: Sheffield Wednesday   Runners-up: Fulham
Division 3 : Plymouth Argyle   Runners-up: Hull City
Division 4 : Port Vale   Runners-up: Coventry City
FA Cup winners: Nottingham Forest   League Cup winners: n/a
Charity Shield: Wolverhampton W
Scottish Champions: Rangers   Runners-up: Hearts
Scottish Cup: St. Mirren   Scottish League Cup: Hearts

EUROPEAN LEAGUE CHAMPIONS

Austria: Wiener Sport-Club   Ireland: Linfield
Belgium: Anderlecht   Italy: AC Milan
Bulgaria: CSKA Sofia   Norway: Lillestrom
Czechoslovakia: Cervena Bratislava Poland: Gornik Zabrze
Denmark: B 1909   Portugal: Porto
Finland: HIFK Helsinki   Romania: Petrolul Ploiesti
France: OGC Nice   Russia: Dynamo Moscow
Germany: Eintracht Frankfurt   Spain: Barcelona
Greece: Olympiakos   Sweden: Djurgardens
Holland: Sparta   Switzerland: BSC Young Boys
Hungary: Csepel   Turkey: n/a

ENGLAND INTERNATIONALS

11 Apr England 1 Scotland 0   28 May USA 1   England 8
6 May   England 2 Italy 2   17 Oct Wales 1   England 1
13 May Brazil 2   England 0   28 Oct England 2 Sweden 3
17 May Peru 4   England 1   18 Nov England 2 N. Ireland 1
24 May Mexico 2   England 1

INTERNATIONAL CUP WINNERS

European Cup: Real Madrid

1960

ENGLISH AND SCOTTISH FOOTBALL

Champions: Burnley	Runners-up: Wolverhampton W
Division 2: Aston Villa	Runners-up: Cardiff City
Division 3: Southampton	Runners-up: Norwich City
Division 4: Walsall	Runners-up: Notts County
FA Cup winners: Wolverhampton W	League Cup winners: n/a
Charity Shield: Burnley	
Scottish Champions: Hearts	Runners-up: Kilmarnock
Scottish Cup: Rangers	Scottish League Cup: Hearts

EUROPEAN LEAGUE CHAMPIONS

Austria: Rapid Vienna
Belgium: Lierse SK
Bulgaria: CSKA Sofia
Czechoslovakia: Spartak Hradec Kralove
Denmark: AGF
Finland: Haka Valkeakoski
France: Stade de Reims
Germany: Hamburg SV
Greece: Panathinaikos
Holland: Ajax
Hungary: Ujpesti Dozsa

Ireland: Glenavon
Italy: Juventus
Norway: Frederickstad
Poland: Ruch Chorzow
Portugal: Benfica
Romania: CCA
Russia: Torpedo Moscow
Spain: Barcelona
Sweden: IFK Norrkoping
Switzerland: BSC Young Boys
Turkey: Besiktas

ENGLAND INTERNATIONALS

19 Apr Scotland 1 England 1	8 Oct N. Ireland 2 England 5
11 May England 3 Yugoslavia 3	19 Oct Luxembourg 0 England 9
15 May Spain 3 England 0	26 Oct England 4 Spain 2
22 May Hungary 2 England 0	23 Nov England 5 Wales 1

INTERNATIONAL CUP WINNERS

European Cup: Real Madrid
European Championship: USSR

Fairs Cup: Barcelona

THE FOOTBALL FACT AND QUIZ BOOK

1961

ENGLISH AND SCOTTISH FOOTBALL

Champions: Tottenham Hotspur   Runners-up: Sheffield Wednesday
Division 2: Ipswich Town   Runners-up: Sheffield Utd
Division 3: Bury   Runners-up: Walsall
Division 4: Peterborough Utd   Runners-up: Crystal Palace
FA Cup winners: Tottenham Hotspur   League Cup winners: Aston Villa
Charity Shield: Tottenham Hotspur
Scottish Champions: Rangers   Runners-up: Kilmarnock
Scottish Cup: Rangers   Scottish League Cup: Rangers

EUROPEAN LEAGUE CHAMPIONS

Austria: FK Austria   Ireland: Linfield
Belgium: Standard Liege   Italy: Juventus
Bulgaria: CSKA Sofia   Norway: Frederikstad
Czechoslovakia: Dukla Prague   Poland: Gornik Zabrze
Denmark: Esbjerg fB   Portugal: Benfica
Finland: HIFK Helsinki   Romania: CCA
France: AS Monaco   Russia: Dynamo Moscow
Germany: IFC Nuremburg   Spain: Real Madrid
Greece: Panathinaikos   Sweden: IF Elfsborg
Holland: Feyenoord   Switzerland: Servette
Hungary: Vasas   Turkey: Fenerbahce

ENGLAND INTERNATIONALS

15 Apr England 9 Scotland 3   28 Sep England 4 Luxembourg 1
10 May England 8 Mexico 0   14 Oct Wales 1 England 1
21 May Portugal 1 England 1   25 Oct England 2 Portugal 0
24 May Italy 2 England 3   22 Nov England 1 N. Ireland 1
27 May Austria 3 England 1

INTERNATIONAL CUP WINNERS

European Cup: Benfica   Fairs Cup: Roma
European Cup-Winners' Cup: Fiorentina

1962

ENGLISH AND SCOTTISH FOOTBALL

Champions: Ipswich Town   Runners-up: Burnley
Division 2: Liverpool   Runners-up: Leyton Orient
Division 3: Portsmouth   Runners-up: Grimsby Town
Division 4: Millwall   Runners-up: Colchester Utd
FA Cup winners: Tottenham Hotspur   League Cup winners: Norwich City
Charity Shield: Tottenham Hotspur
Scottish Champions: Dundee   Runners-up: Rangers
Scottish Cup: Rangers   Scottish League Cup: Rangers

EUROPEAN LEAGUE CHAMPIONS

Austria: FK Austria   Ireland: Linfield
Belgium: Anderlecht   Italy: AC Milan
Bulgaria: CSKA Sofia   Norway: Brann (Bergen)
Czechoslovakia: Dukla Prague Poland: Polonia Bytom
Denmark: Esbjerg fB   Portugal: Sporting Lisbon
Finland: Haka Valkeakoski   Romania: Dynamo Bucharest
France: Stade de Reims   Russia: Spartak Moscow
Germany: IFC Koln   Spain: Real Madrid
Greece: Panathinaikos   Sweden: IFK Norrkoping
Holland: Feyenoord   Switzerland: Servette
Hungary: Vasas   Turkey: Galatasaray

ENGLAND INTERNATIONALS

4 Apr   England 3   Austria 1   7 Jun   Bulgaria 0   England 0
14 Apr Scotland 2 England 0   10 Jun Brazil 3   England 1
9 May   England 3   Switzerland 1 3 Oct   England 1   France 1
20 May Peru 0   England 4   20 Oct N. Ireland 1 England 3
31 May Hungary 2   England 1   21 Nov England 4   Wales 0
2 Jun   Argentina 1 England 3

INTERNATIONAL CUP WINNERS

European Cup: Benfica   Fairs Cup: Valencia
European Cup-Winners' Cup: Atletico Madrid
World Cup: Brazil

1963

ENGLISH AND SCOTTISH FOOTBALL

Champions: Everton — Runners-up: Tottenham Hotspur
Division 2: Stoke City — Runners-up: Chelsea
Division 3: Northampton Town — Runners-up: Swindon Town
Division 4: Brentford — Runners-up: Oldham Athletic
FA Cup winners: Manchester Utd — League Cup winners: Birmingham City
Charity Shield: Everton
Scottish Champions: Rangers — Runners-up: Kilmarnock
Scottish Cup: Rangers — Scottish League Cup: Hearts

EUROPEAN LEAGUE CHAMPIONS

Austria: FK Austria — Ireland: Distillery
Belgium: Standard Liege — Italy: Internazionale
Bulgaria: Spartak Plovdiv — Norway: Brann (Bergen)
Czechoslovakia: Dukla Prague — Poland: Gornik Zabrze
Denmark: Esbjerg fB — Portugal: Benfica
Finland: Reipas Lahti — Romania: Dynamo Bucharest
France: AS Monaco — Russia: Dynamo Moscow
Germany: Borussia Dortmund — Spain: Real Madrid
Greece: AEK — Sweden: IFK Norrkoping
Holland: PSV Eindhoven — Switzerland: FC Zurich
Hungary: Gyori ETO — Turkey: Galatasaray

ENGLAND INTERNATIONALS

27 Feb   France 2   England 5 — 5 Jun   Switzerland 1   England 8
6 Apr   England 1   Scotland 2 — 12 Oct   Wales 0   England 4
8 May   England 1   Brazil 1 — 23 Oct   England 2   Rest of the World 1
20 May   Czechoslovakia 2   England 4 — 20 Nov   England 8   N. Ireland 3
2 Jun   E. Germany 1   England 2

INTERNATIONAL CUP WINNERS

European Cup: AC Milan — Fairs Cup: Valencia
European Cup-Winners' Cup: Spurs

1964

ENGLISH AND SCOTTISH FOOTBALL

Champions: Liverpool
Division 2: Leeds Utd
Division 3: Coventry City
Division 4: Gillingham
FA Cup winners: West Ham Utd
Charity Shield: Liverpool
Scottish Champions: Rangers
Scottish Cup: Rangers

Runners-up: Manchester Utd
Runners-up: Sunderland
Runners-up: Crystal Palace
Runners-up: Carlisle Utd
League Cup winners: Leicester City

Runners-up: Kilmarnock
Scottish League Cup: Rangers

EUROPEAN LEAGUE CHAMPIONS

Austria: Rapid Vienna
Belgium: Anderlecht
Bulgaria: Lokomotiv Sofia
Czechoslovakia: Dukla Prague
Denmark: B 1909
Finland: HJK Helsinki
France: Saint-Etienne
Germany: IFC Koln
Greece: Panathinaikos
Holland: DWS (Amsterdam)
Hungary: Ferencvaros

Ireland: Glentoran
Italy: Bologna
Norway: SOFK Lyn (Oslo)
Poland: Gornik Zabrze
Portugal: Benfica
Romania: Dynamo Bucharest
Russia: Dynamo Tbilisi
Spain: Real Madrid
Sweden: Djurgardens IF
Switzerland: La Chaux-de-Fonds
Turkey: Fenerbahce

ENGLAND INTERNATIONALS

11 Apr   Scotland 1   England 0
6 May   England 2   Uruguay 1
17 May   Portugal 3   England 4
24 May   Rep. of Ireland 1   England 3
27 May   USA 0   England 10
30 May   Brazil 5   England 1
4 Jun   Portugal 1   England 1
6 Jun   Argentina 1   England 0
3 Oct   N. Ireland 3   England 4
21 Oct   England 2   Belgium 2
18 Nov   England 2   Wales 1

9 Dec   Holland 1   England 1

INTERNATIONAL CUP WINNERS

European Cup: Internazionale
Fairs Cup: Zaragoza
European Cup-Winners' Cup: Sporting Lisbon
European Championship: Spain

1965

ENGLISH AND SCOTTISH FOOTBALL

Champions: Manchester Utd — Runners-up: Leeds Utd
Division 2: Newcastle Utd — Runners-up: Northampton Town
Division 3: Carlisle Utd — Runners-up: Bristol City
Division 4: Brighton — Runners-up: Millwall
FA Cup winners: Liverpool — League Cup winners: Chelsea
Charity Shield: Manchester Utd
Scottish Champions: Kilmarnock — Runners-up: Hearts
Scottish Cup: Celtic — Scottish League Cup: Rangers

EUROPEAN LEAGUE CHAMPIONS

Austria: LASK
Belgium: Anderlecht
Bulgaria: Levski Sofia
Czechoslovakia: Sparta Prague
Denmark: Esbjerg fB
Finland: Haka Valkeakoski
France: Nantes
Germany: Werder Bremen
Greece: Panathinaikos
Holland: Feyenoord
Hungary: Vasas
Ireland: Derry City
Italy: Internazionale
Norway: Valerengens
Poland: Gornik Zabrze
Portugal: Benfica
Romania: Dynamo Bucharest
Russia: Torpedo Moscow
Spain: Real Madrid
Sweden: Malmo
Switzerland: Lausanne Sports
Turkey: Fenerbahce

ENGLAND INTERNATIONALS

10 Apr England 2 Scotland 2
5 May England 1 Hungary 0
9 May Yugoslavia 1 England 1
12 May W. Germany 0 England 1
16 May Sweden 1 England 2
2 Oct Wales 0 England 0
20 Oct England 2 Austria 3
10 Nov England 2 N. Ireland 1
8 Dec Spain 0 England 2

INTERNATIONAL CUP WINNERS

European Cup: Internazionale — Fairs Cup: Ferencvaros
European Cup-Winners' Cup: West Ham Utd

THE FOOTBALL FACT AND QUIZ BOOK

1966

ENGLISH AND SCOTTISH FOOTBALL

Champions: Liverpool   Runners-up: Leeds Utd
Division 2: Manchester City   Runners-up: Southampton
Division 3: Hull City   Runners-up: Millwall
Division 4: Doncaster Rovers   Runners-up: Darlington
FA Cup winners: Everton   League Cup winners: WBA
Charity Shield: Liverpool
Scottish Champions: Celtic   Runners-up: Rangers
Scottish Cup: Rangers   Scottish League Cup: Celtic

EUROPEAN LEAGUE CHAMPIONS

Austria: Admira   Ireland: Linfield
Belgium: Anderlecht   Italy: Internazionale
Bulgaria: CSKA Sofia   Norway: Skeid
Czechoslovakia: Dukla Prague   Poland: Gornik Zabrze
Denmark: Hvidovre IF   Portugal: Sporting Lisbon
Finland: KuPS Kuopio   Romania: Petrolul Ploiesti
France: Nantes   Russia: Dynamo Kiev
Germany: 1860 Munich   Spain: Atletico Madrid
Greece: Olympiakos   Sweden: Djurgardens IF
Holland: Ajax   Switzerland: FC Zurich
Hungary: Vasas   Turkey: Besiktas

ENGLAND INTERNATIONALS

5 Jan	England 1	Poland 1	16 Jul	England 2	Mexico 0
23 Feb	England 1	W. Germany 0	20 Jul	England 2	France 0
2 Apr	Scotland 3	England 4	23 Jul	England 1	Argentina 0
4 May	England 2	Yugoslavia 0	26 Jul	England 2	Portugal 1
26 Jun	Finland 0	England 3	30 Jul	England 4	W. Germany 2
29 Jun	Norway 1	England 6	22 Oct	N. Ireland 0	England 2
3 Jul	Denmark 0	England 2	2 Nov	England 0	Czechoslovakia 0
5 Jul	Poland 0	England 1	16 Nov	England 5	Wales 1
11 Jul	England 0	Uruguay 0			

INTERNATIONAL CUP WINNERS

European Cup: Real Madrid   Fairs Cup: Barcelona
European Cup-Winners' Cup: Borussia Dortmund
World Cup: England

1967

ENGLISH AND SCOTTISH FOOTBALL

Champions: Manchester Utd — Runners-up: Nottingham Forest
Division 2: Coventry City — Runners-up: Wolverhampton W
Division 3: Queen's Park Rangers — Runners-up: Middlesborough
Division 4: Stockport County — Runners-up: Southport
FA Cup winners: Tottenham Hotspur — League Cup winners: QPR
Charity Shield: Manchester Utd
Scottish Champions: Celtic — Runners-up: Rangers
Scottish Cup: Celtic — Scottish League Cup: Celtic

EUROPEAN LEAGUE CHAMPIONS

Austria: Rapid Vienna — Ireland: Glentoran
Belgium: Anderlecht — Italy: Juventus
Bulgaria: Botev Plovdiv — Norway: Rosenborg
Czechoslovakia: Sparta Prague — Poland: Gornik Zabrze
Denmark: Akademisk Boldklub — Portugal: Benfica
Finland: Reipas Lahti — Romania: Rapid Bucharest
France: Saint-Etienne — Russia: Dynamo Kiev
Germany: Braunschweiger TSV Eintracht — Spain: Real Madrid
Greece: Olympiakos — Sweden: Malmo
Holland: Ajax — Switzerland: FC Basel
Hungary: Ferencvaros — Turkey: Besiktas

ENGLAND INTERNATIONALS

15 Apr England 2   Scotland 3 — 21 Oct Wales 0   England 3
24 May England 2   Spain 0 — 22 Nov England 2   N. Ireland 0
27 May Austria 0   England 1 — 6 Dec England 2   USSR 2

INTERNATIONAL CUP WINNERS

European Cup: Celtic — Fairs Cup: Dynamo Zagreb
European Cup-Winners' Cup: Bayern Munich

1968

ENGLISH AND SCOTTISH FOOTBALL

Champions: Manchester City   Runners-up: Manchester Utd
Division 2: Ipswich Town   Runners-up: QPR
Division 3: Oxford Utd   Runners-up: Bury
Division 4: Luton Town   Runners-up: Barnsley
FA Cup winners: WBA   League Cup winners: Leeds Utd
Charity Shield: Manchester City
Scottish Champions: Celtic   Runners-up: Rangers
Scottish Cup: Dunfermline Athletic   Scottish League Cup: Celtic

EUROPEAN LEAGUE CHAMPIONS

Austria: Rapid Vienna   Ireland: Glentoran
Belgium: Anderlecht   Italy: AC Milan
Bulgaria: Levski Sofia   Norway: SOFK Lyn (Oslo)
Czechoslovakia: Spartak Trnava   Poland: Ruch Chorzow
Denmark: Kopenhavns Boldklub   Portugal: Benfica
Finland: TPS Turku   Romania: Steaua Bucharest
France: Saint-Etienne   Russia: Dynamo Kiev
Germany: IFC Nuremburg   Spain: Real Madrid
Greece: AEK   Sweden: Osters
Holland: Ajax   Switzerland: FC Zurich
Hungary: Ferencvaros   Turkey: Fenerbahce

ENGLAND INTERNATIONALS

24 Feb Scotland 1   England 1   5 Jun   Yugoslavia 1 England 0
3 Apr   England 1   Spain 0   8 Jun   USSR 0   England 2
8 May   Spain 1   England 2   6 Nov   Romania 0   England 0
22 May England 3   Sweden 1   11 Dec   England 1   Bulgaria 1
1 Jun   W. Germany 1   England 0

INTERNATIONAL CUP WINNERS

European Cup: Manchester Utd   Fairs Cup: Leeds Utd
European Cup-Winners' Cup: AC Milan
European Championship: Italy

1969

ENGLISH AND SCOTTISH FOOTBALL

Champions: Leeds Utd

Runners-up: Liverpool

Division 2: Derby County

Runners-up: Crystal Palace

Division 3: Watford

Runners-up: Swindon Town

Division 4: Doncaster Rovers

Runners-up: Halifax Town

FA Cup winners: Manchester City

League Cup winners: Swindon Town

Charity Shield: Leeds Utd

Scottish Champions: Celtic

Runners-up: Rangers

Scottish Cup: Celtic

Scottish League Cup: Celtic

EUROPEAN LEAGUE CHAMPIONS

Austria: FK Austria

Belgium: Standard Liege

Bulgaria: CSKA Sofia

Czechoslovakia: Spartak Trnava

Denmark: B 1903

Finland: KPV Kokkola

France: Saint-Etienne

Germany: Bayern Munich

Greece: Panathinaikos

Holland: Feyenoord

Hungary: Ujpesti Dozsa

Ireland: Linfield

Italy: Fiorentina

Norway: Rosenborg

Poland: Legia Warsaw

Portugal: Benfica

Romania: UT Arad

Russia: Spartak Moscow

Spain: Real Madrid

Sweden: IFK Gothenburg

Switzerland: FC Basel

Turkey: Galatasaray

ENGLAND INTERNATIONALS

15 Jan   England 1   Romania 1

12 Mar   England 5   France 0

3 May   N. Ireland 1   England 3

7 May   England 2   Wales 1

10 May   England 4   Scotland 1

1 Jun   Mexico 0   England 0

8 Jun   Uruguay 1   England 2

12 Jun   Brazil 2   England 1

5 Nov   Holland 0   England 1

10 Dec   England 1   Portugal 0

INTERNATIONAL CUP WINNERS

European Cup: AC Milan

Fairs Cup: Newcastle Utd

European Cup-Winners' Cup: Slovan Bratislava

THE FOOTBALL FACT AND QUIZ BOOK

ENGLISH AND SCOTTISH FOOTBALL

Champions: Everton   Runners-up: Leeds Utd
Division 2: Huddersfield Town   Runners-up: Blackpool
Division 3: Leyton Orient   Runners-up: Luton Town
Division 4: Chesterfield   Runners-up: Wrexham
FA Cup winners: Chelsea   League Cup winners: Manchester City
Charity Shield: Everton
Scottish Champions: Celtic   Runners-up: Rangers
Scottish Cup: Aberdeen   Scottish League Cup: Celtic

EUROPEAN LEAGUE CHAMPIONS

Austria: FK Austria   Ireland: Glentoran
Belgium: Standard Liege   Italy: Cagliari
Bulgaria: Levski Sofia   Norway: Stromsgodset
Czechoslovakia: Slovan Bratislava   Poland: Legia Warsaw
Denmark: B 1903   Portugal: Sporting Lisbon
Finland: Reipas Lahti   Romania: UT Arad
France: Saint-Etienne   Russia: CSKA Moscow
Germany: Borussia Monchengladbach Spain: Atletico Madrid
Greece: Panathinaikos   Sweden: Malmo
Holland: Ajax   Switzerland: FC Basel
Hungary: Ujpesti Dozsa   Turkey: Fenerbahce

ENGLAND INTERNATIONALS

14 Jan   England 0   Holland 0   24 May Ecuador 0   England 2
25 Feb   Belgium 1   England 3   2 Jun   Romania 0 England 1
18 Apr   Wales 1   England 1   7 Jun   Brazil 1   England 0
21 Apr   England 3   N. Ireland 1   11 Jun   Czechoslovakia 0 England 1
25 Apr   Scotland 0   England 0   14 Jun   W. Germany 3   England 2
20 May   Colombia 0   England 4   25 Nov England 3   E. Germany 1

INTERNATIONAL CUP WINNERS

European Cup: Feyenoord   Fairs Cup: Arsenal
European Cup-Winners' Cup: Manchester City
World Cup: Brazil

1971

ENGLISH AND SCOTTISH FOOTBALL

Champions: Arsenal   Runners-up: Leeds Utd
Division 2: Leicester City   Runners-up: Sheffield Utd
Division 3: Preston North End   Runners-up: Fulham
Division 4: Notts County   Runners-up: Bournemouth
FA Cup winners: Arsenal   League Cup winners: Spurs
Charity Shield: Leicester City
Scottish Champions: Celtic   Runners-up: Aberdeen
Scottish Cup: Celtic   Scottish League Cup: Rangers

EUROPEAN LEAGUE CHAMPIONS

Austria: Wacker Innsbruck   Ireland: Linfield
Belgium: Standard Liege   Italy: Internazionale
Bulgaria: CSKA Sofia   Norway: Rosenborg
Czechoslovakia: Spartak Trnava   Poland: Gornik Zabrze
Denmark: Vejle BK   Portugal: Benfica
Finland: TPS Turku   Romania: Dynamo Bucharest
France: Olympique Marseille   Russia: Dynamo Kiev
Germany: Borussia Monchengladbach   Spain: Valencia
Greece: AEK   Sweden: Malmo
Holland: Feyenoord   Switzerland: Grasshopper Club
Hungary: Ujpesti Dozsa   Turkey: Galatasaray

ENGLAND INTERNATIONALS

3 Feb   Malta 0   England 1
21 Apr   England 4   Greece 0
12 May   England 5   Malta 0
15 May   N. Ireland 0   England 1
19 May   England 0   Wales 0
22 May   England 3   Scotland 1
13 Oct   Switzerland 2   England 3
10 Nov   England 1   Switzerland 1
1 Dec   Greece 0   England 2

INTERNATIONAL CUP WINNERS

European Cup: Ajax   Fairs Cup: Leeds Utd
European Cup-Winners' Cup: Chelsea

1972

ENGLISH AND SCOTTISH FOOTBALL

Champions: Derby County

Runners-up: Leeds Utd

Division 2: Norwich City

Runners-up: Birmingham City

Division 3: Aston Villa

Runners-up: Brighton

Division 4: Grimsby Town

Runners-up: Southend Utd

FA Cup winners: Leeds Utd

League Cup winners: Stoke City

Charity Shield: Manchester City

Scottish Champions: Celtic

Runners-up: Aberdeen

Scottish Cup: Celtic

Scottish League Cup: Partick Thistle

EUROPEAN LEAGUE CHAMPIONS

Austria: Wacker Innsbruck

Belgium: Anderlecht

Bulgaria: CSKA Sofia

Czechoslovakia: Spartak Trnava

Denmark: Vejle BK

Finland: TPS Turku

France: Olympique Marseille

Germany: Bayern Munich

Greece: Panathinaikos

Holland: Ajax

Hungary: Ujpesti Dozsa

Ireland: Glentoran

Italy: Juventus

Norway: Viking (Stavanger)

Poland: Gornik Zabrze

Portugal: Benfica

Romania: Arges Pitesti

Russia: Zarya Voroshilovgrad

Spain: Real Madrid

Sweden: Atvidabergs

Switzerland: FC Basel

Turkey: Galatasaray

ENGLAND INTERNATIONALS

29 Apr England 1 W. Germany 3

13 May W. Germany 0 England 0

20 May Wales 0 England 3

23 May England 0 N. Ireland 1

27 May Scotland 0 England 1

11 Oct England 1 Yugoslavia 1

5 Nov Wales 0 England 1

INTERNATIONAL CUP WINNERS

European Cup: Ajax

European Cup-Winners' Cup: Rangers

European Championship: W. Germany

UEFA Cup: Tottenham Hotspur

1973

ENGLISH AND SCOTTISH FOOTBALL

Champions: Liverpool
Division 2: Burnley
Division 3: Bolton Wanderers
Division 4: Southport
FA Cup winners: Sunderland
Charity Shield: Burnley
Scottish Champions: Celtic
Scottish Cup: Rangers

Runners-up: Arsenal
Runners-up: QPR
Runners-up: Notts County
Runners-up: Hereford Utd
League Cup winners: Spurs

Runners-up: Rangers
Scottish League Cup: Hibernian

EUROPEAN LEAGUE CHAMPIONS

Austria: Wacker Innsbruck
Belgium: Club Bruges
Bulgaria: CSKA Sofia
Czechoslovakia: Spartak Trnava
Denmark: Hvidovre IF
Finland: HJK Helsinki
France: Nantes
Germany: Bayern Munich
Greece: Olympiakos
Holland: Ajax
Hungary: Ujpesti Dozsa

Ireland: Crusaders
Italy: Juventus
Norway: Viking Stavanger
Poland: Stal Mielec
Portugal: Benfica
Romania: Dynamo Bucharest
Russia: Ararat Erevan
Spain: Atletico Madrid
Sweden: Atvidabergs
Switzerland: FC Basel
Turkey: Galatasaray

ENGLAND INTERNATIONALS

24 Jan	England 1	Wales 1	
14 Feb	Scotland 0	England 5	
12 May	England 2	N. Ireland 1	
15 May	England 3	Wales 0	
19 May	England 1	Scotland 0	
27 May	Czechoslovakia 1	England 1	

6 Jun	Poland 2	England 0	
10 Jun	USSR 1	England 2	
14 Jun	Italy 2	England 0	
26 Sep	England 7	Austria 0	
17 Oct	England 1	Poland 1	
14 Nov	England 0	Italy 1	

INTERNATIONAL CUP WINNERS

European Cup: Ajax
European Cup-Winners' Cup: AC Milan

UEFA Cup: Liverpool

THE FOOTBALL FACT AND QUIZ BOOK

1974

ENGLISH AND SCOTTISH FOOTBALL

Champions: Leeds Utd — Runners-up: Liverpool
Division 2: Middlesborough — Runners-up: Luton Town
Division 3: Oldham Athletic — Runners-up: Bristol Rovers
Division 4: Peterborough Utd — Runners-up: Gillingham
FA Cup winners: Liverpool — League Cup winners: Wolves
Charity Shield: Liverpool
Scottish Champions: Celtic — Runners-up: Hibernian
Scottish Cup: Celtic — Scottish League Cup: Dundee

EUROPEAN LEAGUE CHAMPIONS

Austria: Voest Linz
Belgium: Anderlecht
Bulgaria: Levski Sofia
Czechoslovakia: Slovan Bratislava
Denmark: Kopenhavns Boldklub
Finland: KuPS Kuopio
France: Saint-Etienne
Germany: Bayern Munich
Greece: Olympiakos
Holland: Feyenoord
Hungary: Ujpesti Dozsa
Ireland: Coleraine
Italy: Lazio
Norway: Viking (Stavanger)
Poland: Ruch Chorzow
Portugal: Sporting Lisbon
Romania: Universitatea Craiova
Russia: Dynamo Kiev
Spain: Barcelona
Sweden: Malmo
Switzerland: FC Zurich
Turkey: Fenerbahce

ENGLAND INTERNATIONALS

3 Apr	Portugal 0	England 0		29 May	E. Germany 1	England 1
11 May	Wales 0	England 2		1 Jun	Bulgaria 0	England 1
15 May	England 1	N. Ireland 0		5 Jun	Yugoslavia 2	England 2
18 May	Scotland 2	England 0		30 Oct	England 3	Czechoslovakia 0
22 May	England 2	Argentina 2		20 Nov	England 0	Portugal 0

INTERNATIONAL CUP WINNERS

European Cup: Bayern Munich — UEFA Cup: Feyenoord
European Cup-Winners' Cup: Magdeburg
World Cup: West Germany

THE FOOTBALL FACT AND QUIZ BOOK

1974

ENGLISH AND SCOTTISH FOOTBALL

Champions: Derby County

Runners-up: Liverpool

Division 2: Manchester Utd

Runners-up: Aston Villa

Division 3: Blackburn Rovers

Runners-up: Plymouth Argyle

Division 4: Mansfield Town

Runners-up: Shrewsbury Town

FA Cup winners: West Ham United

League Cup winners: Aston Villa

Charity Shield: Derby County

Scottish Champions: Rangers

Runners-up: Hibernian

Scottish Cup: Celtic

Scottish League Cup: Celtic

EUROPEAN LEAGUE CHAMPIONS

Austria: Wacker Innsbruck

Belgium: Racing White Daring Molenbeek

Bulgaria: CSKA Sofia

Czechoslovakia: Slovan Bratislava

Denmark: Koge BK

Finland: TPS Turku

France: Saint-Etienne

Germany: Borussia Monchengladbach

Greece: Olympiakos

Holland: PSV Eindhoven

Hungary: Ujpesti Dozsa

Ireland: Linfield

Italy: Juventus

Norway: Viking (Stavanger)

Poland: Ruch Chorzow

Portugal: Benfica

Romania: Dynamo Bucharest

Russia: Dynamo Kiev

Spain: Real Madrid

Sweden: Malmo

Switzerland: FC Zurich

Turkey: Fenerbahce

ENGLAND INTERNATIONALS

12 Mar England 2   W. Germany 0

16 Apr England 5   Cyprus 0

11 May Cyprus 0   England 1

17 May N. Ireland 0   England 0

21 May England 2   Wales 2

24 May England 5   Scotland 1

3 Sep   Switzerland 1   England 2

30 Oct Czechoslovakia 2 England 1

19 Nov Portugal 1   England 1

INTERNATIONAL CUP WINNERS

European Cup: Bayern Munich

UEFA Cup: Borussia Monchengladbach

European Cup-Winners' Cup: Dynamo Kiev

THE FOOTBALL FACT AND QUIZ BOOK

1976

ENGLISH AND SCOTTISH FOOTBALL

Champions: Liverpool	Runners-up: QPR
Division 2: Sunderland	Runners-up: Bristol City
Division 3: Hereford Utd	Runners-up: Cardiff City
Division 4: Lincoln City	Runners-up: Northampton Town
FA Cup winners: Southampton	League Cup winners: Manchester City
Charity Shield: Liverpool	
Scottish Champions: Rangers	Runners-up: Celtic
Scottish Cup: Rangers	Scottish League Cup: Rangers

EUROPEAN LEAGUE CHAMPIONS

Austria: FK Austria	Ireland: Crusaders
Belgium: Club Bruges	Italy: Torino
Bulgaria: CSKA Sofia	Norway: Lillestrom
Czechoslovakia: Banik Ostrava	Poland: Stal Mielec
Denmark: B 1903	Portugal: Benfica
Finland: KuPS Kuopio	Romania: Steaua Bucharest
France: Saint-Etienne	Russia: Torpedo Moscow
Germany: Borussia Monchengladbach	Spain: Real Madrid
Greece: PAOK	Sweden: Halmstad
Holland: PSV Eindhoven	Switzerland: FC Zurich
Hungary: Ferencvaros	Turkey: Trabzonspor

ENGLAND INTERNATIONALS

24 Mar Wales 1 England 2	13 Jun Finland 1 England 4
8 May Wales 0 England 1	8 Sep England 1 Rep. of Ireland 1
11 May England 4 N. Ireland 0	13 Oct England 2 Finland 1
15 May Scotland 2 England 1	17 Nov Italy 2 England 0
23 May Brazil 1 England 0	

INTERNATIONAL CUP WINNERS

European Cup: Bayern Munich	UEFA Cup: Liverpool
European Cup-Winners' Cup: Anderlecht	
European Championship: Czechoslovakia	

1977

ENGLISH AND SCOTTISH FOOTBALL

Champions: Liverpool — Runners-up: Manchester City
Division 2: Wolverhampton W — Runners-up: Chelsea
Division 3: Mansfield Town — Runners-up: Brighton
Division 4: Cambridge Utd — Runners-up: Exeter City
FA Cup winners: Manchester Utd — League Cup winners: Aston Villa
Charity Shield: Liverpool
Scottish Champions: Celtic — Runners-up: Rangers
Scottish Cup: Celtic — Scottish League Cup: Aberdeen

EUROPEAN LEAGUE CHAMPIONS

Austria: Wacker Innsbruck — Ireland: Glentoran
Belgium: Club Bruges — Italy: Juventus
Bulgaria: Levski Sofia — Norway: Lillestrom
Czechoslovakia: Dukla Prague — Poland: Slask Wroclaw
Denmark: OB — Portugal: Benfica
Finland: Haka Valkeakoski — Romania: Dynamo Bucharest
France: Nantes — Russia: Dynamo Kiev
Germany: Borussia Monchengladbach — Spain: Atletico Madrid
Greece: Panathinaikos — Sweden: Malmo
Holland: Ajax — Switzerland: FC Basel
Hungary: Vasas — Turkey: Trabzonspor

ENGLAND INTERNATIONALS

9 Feb   England 0   Holland 2
30 Mar England 5   Luxembourg 0
28 May N. Ireland 1   England 2
31 May England 0   Wales 1
4 Jun   England 1   Scotland 2
8 Jun   Brazil 0   England 0

12 Jun Argentina 1   England 1
15 Jun Uruguay 0   England 0
7 Sep   England 0   Switzerland 0
12 Oct Luxembourg 0   England 2
16 Nov England 2   Italy 0

INTERNATIONAL CUP WINNERS

European Cup: Liverpool — UEFA Cup: Juventus
European Cup-Winners' Cup: Hamburg

THE FOOTBALL FACT AND QUIZ BOOK

1978

ENGLISH AND SCOTTISH FOOTBALL

Champions: Nottingham Forest   Runners-up: Liverpool
Division 2: Bolton Wanderers   Runners-up: Southampton
Division 3: Wrexham   Runners-up: Cambridge Utd
Division 4: Watford   Runners-up: Southend Utd
FA Cup winners: Ipswich Town   League Cup winners: Nottingham Forest
Charity Shield: Nottingham Forest
Scottish Champions: Rangers   Runners-up: Aberdeen
Scottish Cup: Rangers   Scottish League Cup: Rangers

EUROPEAN LEAGUE CHAMPIONS

Austria: FK Austria   Ireland: Linfield
Belgium: Club Bruges   Italy: Juventus
Bulgaria: Lokomotiv Sofia   Norway: IK Start
Czechoslovakia: Zbrojovka Brno   Poland: Wisla Krakow
Denmark: Vejle fB   Portugal: Porto
Finland: HJK Helsinki   Romania: Steaua Bucharest
France: AS Monaco   Russia: Dynamo Torpedo
Germany: IFC Koln   Spain: Real Madrid
Greece: AEK   Sweden: Osters
Holland: PSV Eindhoven   Switzerland: Grasshopper Club
Hungary: Ujpesti Dozsa   Turkey: Fenerbahce

ENGLAND INTERNATIONALS

22 Feb W. Germany 2   England 1   24 May England 4   Hungary 1
19 Apr England 1   Brazil 1   20 Sep Denmark 3   England 4
13 May Wales 1   England 3   25 Oct Rep. of Ireland 1 England 1
16 May England 1   N. Ireland 0   29 Nov England 1 Czechoslovakia 0
20 May Scotland 0   England 1

INTERNATIONAL CUP WINNERS

European Cup: Liverpool   UEFA Cup: PSV Eindhoven
European Cup-Winners' Cup: Anderlecht
World Cup: Argentina

1979

ENGLISH AND SCOTTISH FOOTBALL

Champions: Liverpool   Runners-up: Nottingham Forest
Division 2: Crystal Palace   Runners-up: Brighton
Division 3: Shrewsbury Town   Runners-up: Watford
Division 4: Reading   Runners-up: Grimsby Town
FA Cup winners: Arsenal   League Cup winners: Nottingham Forest
Charity Shield: Liverpool
Scottish Champions: Celtic   Runners-up: Rangers
Scottish Cup: Rangers   Scottish League Cup: Rangers

EUROPEAN LEAGUE CHAMPIONS

Austria: FK Austria   Ireland: Linfield
Belgium: SK Beveren   Italy: AC Milan
Bulgaria: Levski Sofia   Norway: Viking (Stavanger)
Czechoslovakia: Dukla Prague   Poland: Ruch Chorzow
Denmark: Esbjerg fB   Portugal: Porto
Finland: OPS Oulu   Romania: Arges Pitesti
France: RC Strasbourg   Russia: Spartak Moscow
Germany: Hamburg SV   Spain: Real Madrid
Greece: AEK   Sweden: Halmstad
Holland: Ajax   Switzerland: Servette
Hungary: Ujpesti Dozsa   Turkey: Trabzonspor

ENGLAND INTERNATIONALS

7 Feb   England 4   N. Ireland 0   10 Jun   Sweden 0   England 0
19 May N. Ireland 0   England 2   13 Jun   Austria 4   England 3
23 May England 0   Wales 0   12 Sep   England 1   Denmark 0
26 May England 3   Scotland 1   17 Oct   N. Ireland 1   England 5
6 Jun   Bulgaria 0   England 3   22 Nov   England 2   Bulgaria 0

INTERNATIONAL CUP WINNERS

European Cup: Nottingham Forest
UEFA Cup: Borussia Monchengladbach
European Cup-Winners' Cup: Barcelona

ENGLISH AND SCOTTISH FOOTBALL

Champions: Liverpool — Runners-up: Manchester Utd
Division 2: Leicester City — Runners-up: Sunderland
Division 3: Grimsby Town — Runners-up: Blackburn Rovers
Division 4: Huddersfield Town — Runners-up: Walsall
FA Cup winners: West Ham Utd — League Cup winners: Wolves
Charity Shield: Liverpool
Scottish Champions: Aberdeen — Runners-up: Celtic
Scottish Cup: Celtic — Scottish League Cup: Dundee Utd

EUROPEAN LEAGUE CHAMPIONS

Austria: FK Austria — Ireland: Linfield
Belgium: Club Bruges — Italy: Internazionale
Bulgaria: CSKA Sofia — Norway: IK Start
Czechoslovakia: Banik Ostrava — Poland: Szombierki Bytom
Denmark: Kopenhavns Boldklub — Portugal: Sporting Lisbon
Finland: OPS Oulu — Romania: Universitatea Craiova
France: Nantes — Russia: Dynamo Kiev
Germany: Bayern Munich — Spain: Real Madrid
Greece: Olympiakos — Sweden: Osters
Holland: Ajax — Switzerland: FC Basel
Hungary: Honved — Turkey: Trabzonspor

ENGLAND INTERNATIONALS

6 Feb   England 2 Rep. of Ireland 0 — 12 Jun Belgium 1   England 1
26 Mar Spain 0   England 2 — 15 Jun Italy 1   England 0
13 May England 3   Argentina 1 — 18 Jun Spain 1   England 2
17 May Wales 4   England 1 — 10 Sep England 4   Norway 0
20 May England 1   N. Ireland 1 — 15 Oct Romania 2   England 1
24 May Scotland 0   England 2 — 19 Nov England 2   Switzerland 1
31 May Australia 1   England 2

INTERNATIONAL CUP WINNERS

European Cup: Nottingham Forest — UEFA Cup: Eintracht Frankfurt
European Cup-Winners' Cup: Valencia
European Championship: W. Germany

THE FOOTBALL FACT AND QUIZ BOOK

1981

ENGLISH AND SCOTTISH FOOTBALL

Champions: Aston Villa — Runners-up: Ipswich Town
Division 2: West Ham United — Runners-up: Notts County
Division 3: Rotherham Utd — Runners-up: Barnsley
Division 4: Southend Utd — Runners-up: Lincoln City
FA Cup winners: Tottenham Hotspur — League Cup winners: Liverpool
Charity Shield: Aston Villa
Scottish Champions: Celtic — Runners-up: Aberdeen
Scottish Cup: Rangers — Scottish League Cup: Dundee Utd

EUROPEAN LEAGUE CHAMPIONS

Austria: FK Austria
Belgium: Anderlecht
Bulgaria: CSKA Sofia
Czechoslovakia: Banik Ostrava
Denmark: Hvidovre IF
Finland: HJK Helsinki
France: Saint-Etienne
Germany: Bayern Munich
Greece: Olympiakos
Holland: AZ '67 (Alkmaar)
Hungary: Ferencvaros
Ireland: Glentoran
Italy: Juventus
Norway: Valerengens
Poland: Widzew Lodz
Portugal: Benfica
Romania: Universitatea Craiova
Russia: Dynamo Kiev
Spain: Real Sociedad
Sweden: Osters
Switzerland: FC Zurich
Turkey: Trabzonspor

ENGLAND INTERNATIONALS

25 Mar England 1 Spain 2
29 Apr England 0 Romania 0
12 May England 0 Brazil 1
20 May England 0 Wales 0
23 May England 0 Scotland 1
30 May Switzerland 2 England 1
6 Jun Hungary 1 England 3
9 Sep Norway 2 England 1
18 Nov England 1 Hungary 0

INTERNATIONAL CUP WINNERS

European Cup: Liverpool — UEFA Cup: Ipswich Town
European Cup-Winners' Cup: Dynamo Tbilisi

1982

ENGLISH AND SCOTTISH FOOTBALL

Champions: Liverpool   Runners-up: Ipswich Town
Division 2: Luton Town   Runners-up: Watford
Division 3: Burnley   Runners-up: Carlisle Utd
Division 4: Sheffield Utd   Runners-up: Bradford City
FA Cup winners: Tottenham Hotspur League Cup winners: Liverpool
Charity Shield: Liverpool
Scottish Champions: Celtic   Runners-up: Aberdeen
Scottish Cup: Aberdeen   Scottish League Cup: Rangers

EUROPEAN LEAGUE CHAMPIONS

Austria: Rapid Vienna   Ireland: Linfield
Belgium: Standard Liege   Italy: Juventus
Bulgaria: CSKA Sofia   Norway: Viking
Czechoslovakia: Dukla Prague   Poland: Widzew Lodz
Denmark: OB   Portugal: Sporting Lisbon
Finland: Kuusysi Lahti   Romania: Dynamo Bucharest
France: AS Monaco   Russia: Dynamo Minsk
Germany: Hamburg SV   Spain: Real Sociedad
Greece: Olympiakos   Sweden: IFK Gothenburg
Holland: Ajax   Switzerland: Grasshopper Club
Hungary: Raba ETO Gyor   Turkey: Besiktas

ENGLAND INTERNATIONALS

23 Feb England 4   N. Ireland 0   25 Jun Kuwait 0   England 1
25 May England 2   Holland 0   29 Jun W. Germany 0   England 0
29 May Scotland 0   England 1   5 Jul   Spain 0   England 0
2 Jun   Iceland 1   England 1   22 Sep Denmark 2   England 2
3 Jun   Finland 1   England 4   13 Oct England 1   W. Germany 2
16 Jun France 1   England 3   17 Nov Greece 0   England 3
20 Jun Czechoslovakia 0 England 2   15 Dec England 9   Luxembourg 0

INTERNATIONAL CUP WINNERS

European Cup: Aston Villa
UEFA Cup: IFK Gothenburg
European Cup-Winners' Cup: Barcelona
World Cup: Italy

THE FOOTBALL FACT AND QUIZ BOOK

1983

ENGLISH AND SCOTTISH FOOTBALL

Champions: Liverpool

Runners-up: Watford

Division 2: Queen's Park Rangers

Runners-up: Wolverhampton W

Division 3: Portsmouth

Runners-up: Cardiff City

Division 4: Wimbledon

Runners-up: Hull City

FA Cup winners: Manchester Utd

League Cup winners: Liverpool

Charity Shield: Manchester Utd

Scottish Champions: Dundee Utd

Runners-up: Celtic

Scottish Cup: Aberdeen

Scottish League Cup: Celtic

EUROPEAN LEAGUE CHAMPIONS

Austria: Rapid Vienna

Ireland: Linfield

Belgium: Standard Liege

Italy: AS Roma

Bulgaria: CSKA Sofia

Norway: Valerengens

Czechoslovakia: Bohemians

Poland: Lech Poznan

Denmark: Lyngby BK

Portugal: Benfica

Finland: Ilves-Kissat

Romania: Dynamo Bucharest

France: Nantes

Russia: Dnepr Dnepropetrovsk

Germany: Hamburg SV

Spain: Athletic Bilbao

Greece: Olympiakos

Sweden: AIK Stockholm

Holland: Ajax

Switzerland: Grasshopper Club

Hungary: Raba ETO Gyor

Turkey: Fenerbahce

ENGLAND INTERNATIONALS

23 Feb England 2 Wales 1

15 Jun Australia 0 England 1

30 Mar England 0 Greece 0

19 Jun Australia 1 England 1

27 Apr England 2 Hungary 0

21 Sep England 0 Denmark 1

28 May N. Ireland 0 England 0

12 Oct Hungary 0 England 3

1 Jun England 2 Scotland 0

16 Nov Luxembourg 0 England 4

12 Jun Australia 0 England 0

INTERNATIONAL CUP WINNERS

European Cup: Hamburg SV

UEFA Cup: Anderlecht

European Cup-Winners' Cup: Aberdeen

ENGLISH AND SCOTTISH FOOTBALL

Champions: Liverpool   Runners-up: Southampton
Division 2: Chelsea   Runners-up: Sheffield Wednesday
Division 3: Oxford Utd   Runners-up: Wimbledon
Division 4: York City   Runners-up: Doncaster Rovers
FA Cup winners: Everton   League Cup winners: Liverpool
Charity Shield: Everton
Scottish Champions: Aberdeen   Runners-up: Celtic
Scottish Cup: Aberdeen   Scottish League Cup: Rangers

EUROPEAN LEAGUE CHAMPIONS

Austria: FK Austria   Ireland: Linfield
Belgium: SK Beveren   Italy: Juventus
Bulgaria: Levski Sofia   Norway: Valerengens
Czechoslovakia: Sparta Prague   Poland: Lech Poznan
Denmark: Vejle BK   Portugal: Benfica
Finland: Kuusysi Lahti   Romania: Dynamo Bucharest
France: Girondins de Bordeaux   Russia: Zenit Leningrad
Germany: VfB Stuttgart   Spain: Athletic Bilbao
Greece: Panathinaikos   Sweden: IFK Gothenburg
Holland: Feyenoord   Switzerland: Grasshoppers Club
Hungary: Honved   Turkey: Trabzonspor

ENGLAND INTERNATIONALS

29 Feb France 2 England 0   13 Jun Uruguay 2 England 0
4 Apr England 1 N. Ireland 0   17 Jun Chile 0 England 0
2 May Wales 1 England 0   12 Sep England 1 E. Germany 0
26 May Scotland 1 England 1   17 Oct England 5 Finland 0
2 Jun England 0 USSR 2   14 Nov Turkey 0 England 8
10 Jun Brazil 0 England 2

INTERNATIONAL CUP WINNERS

European Cup: Liverpool   UEFA Cup: Tottenham Hotspur
European Cup-Winners' Cup: Juventus
European Championship: France

THE FOOTBALL FACT AND QUIZ BOOK

1985

ENGLISH AND SCOTTISH FOOTBALL

Champions: Everton

Runners-up: Liverpool

Division 2: Oxford Utd

Runners-up: Birmingham City

Division 3: Bradford City

Runners-up: Millwall

Division 4: Chesterfield

Runners-up: Blackpool

FA Cup winners: Manchester Utd

League Cup winners: Norwich City

Charity Shield: Everton

Scottish Champions: Aberdeen

Runners-up: Celtic

Scottish Cup: Celtic

Scottish League Cup: Rangers

EUROPEAN LEAGUE CHAMPIONS

Austria: FK Austria

Belgium: Anderlecht

Bulgaria: Levski Sofia

Czechoslovakia: Sparta Prague

Denmark: Bronby IF

Finland: HJK Helsinki

France: Girondins de Bordeaux

Germany: Bayern Munich

Greece: PAOK

Holland: Ajax

Hungary: Honved

Ireland: Linfield

Italy: Verona

Norway: Rosenborg

Poland: Gornik Zabrze

Portugal: Porto

Romania: Steaua Bucharest

Russia: Dynamo Kiev

Spain: Barcelona

Sweden: Malmo

Switzerland: Servette

Turkey: Fenerbahce

ENGLAND INTERNATIONALS

27 Feb N. Ireland 0   England 1

26 Mar England 2 Rep. of Ireland 1

1 May Romania 0   England 0

22 May Finland 1   England 1

25 May Scotland 1   England 0

6 Jun   Italy 2   England 1

9 Jun   Mexico 1   England 0

12 Jun W. Germany 0   England 3

16 Jun USA 0   England 5

11 Sep England 1   Romania 1

16 Oct England 5   Turkey 0

13 Nov England 0   N. Ireland 0

INTERNATIONAL CUP WINNERS

European Cup: Juventus

European Cup-Winners' Cup: Everton

UEFA Cup: Real Madrid

1986

ENGLISH AND SCOTTISH FOOTBALL

Champions: Liverpool | Runners-up: Everton
Division 2: Norwich City | Runners-up: Charlton Athletic
Division 3: Reading | Runners-up: Plymouth Argyle
Division 4: Swindon Town | Runners-up: Chester City
FA Cup winners: Liverpool | League Cup winners: Oxford Utd
Charity Shield: Everton
Scottish Champions: Celtic | Runners-up: Hearts
Scottish Cup: Aberdeen | Scottish League Cup: Aberdeen

EUROPEAN LEAGUE CHAMPIONS

Austria: FK Austria | Ireland: Linfield
Belgium: Anderlecht | Italy: Juventus
Bulgaria: Beroe Staroe Zagora | Norway: Lillestrom
Czechoslovakia: TJ Vitkovice | Poland: Gornik Zabrze
Denmark: AGF | Portugal: Porto
Finland: Kuusysi Lahti | Romania: Steaua Bucharest
France: Paris Saint Germain | Russia: Dynamo Kiev
Germany: Bayern Munich | Spain: Real Madrid
Greece: Panathinaikos | Sweden: Malmo
Holland: PSV Eindhoven | Switzerland: BSC Young Boys
Hungary: Honved | Turkey: Besiktas

ENGLAND INTERNATIONALS

29 Jan Egypt 0 England 4 | 6 Jun Morocco 0 England 0
26 Feb Israel 1 England 2 | 11 Jun Poland 0 England 3
26 Mar USSR 0 England 1 | 18 Jun Paraguay 0 England 3
23 Apr England 2 Scotland 1 | 22 Jun Argentina 2 England 1
17 May Mexico 0 England 3 | 10 Sep Sweden 1 England 0
24 May Canada 0 England 1 | 15 Oct England 3 N. Ireland 0
3 Jun Portugal 1 England 0 | 12 Nov England 2 Yugoslavia 0

INTERNATIONAL CUP WINNERS

European Cup: Steaua Bucharest UEFA Cup: Real Madrid
European Cup-Winners' Cup: Dynamo Kiev
World Cup: Argentina

THE FOOTBALL FACT AND QUIZ BOOK

1987

ENGLISH AND SCOTTISH FOOTBALL

Champions: Everton
Runners-up: Liverpool
Division 2: Derby County
Runners-up: Portsmouth
Division 3: Bournemouth
Runners-up: Middlesborough
Division 4: Northampton Town
Runners-up: Preston North End
FA Cup winners: Coventry City
League Cup winners: Arsenal
Charity Shield: Everton
Scottish Champions: Rangers
Runners-up: Celtic
Scottish Cup: St. Mirren
Scottish League Cup: Rangers

EUROPEAN LEAGUE CHAMPIONS

Austria: Rapid Vienna
Ireland: Linfield
Belgium: Anderlecht
Italy: Napoli
Bulgaria: CSKA Sofia
Norway: Moss
Czechoslovakia: Sparta Prague
Poland: Gornik Zabrze
Denmark: Brondby IF
Portugal: Benfica
Finland: HJK Helsinki
Romania: Steaua Bucharest
France: Girondins de Bordeaux
Russia: Spartak Moscow
Germany: Bayern Munich
Spain: Real Madrid
Greece: Olympiakos
Sweden: Malmo
Holland: PSV Eindhoven
Switzerland: Neuchatel-Xamax
Hungary: MTK-VM
Turkey: Galatasaray

ENGLAND INTERNATIONALS

10 Feb Spain 2 England 4
23 May Scotland 0 England 0
1 Apr N. Ireland 0 England 2
9 Sep W. Germany 3 England 1
29 Apr Turkey 0 England 0
14 Oct England 8 Turkey 0
19 May England 1 Brazil 1
11 Nov Yugoslavia 1 England 4

INTERNATIONAL CUP WINNERS

European Cup: Porto
UEFA Cup: IFK Gothenburg
European Cup-Winners' Cup: Ajax

1988

ENGLISH AND SCOTTISH FOOTBALL

Champions: Liverpool — Runners-up: Manchester Utd
Division 2: Millwall — Runners-up: Aston Villa
Division 3: Sunderland — Runners-up: Brighton
Division 4: Wolverhampton W — Runners-up: Cardiff City
FA Cup winners: Wimbledon — League Cup winners: Luton Town
Charity Shield: Liverpool
Scottish Champions: Celtic — Runners-up: Hearts
Scottish Cup: Celtic — Scottish League Cup: Rangers

EUROPEAN LEAGUE CHAMPIONS

Austria: Rapid Vienna
Belgium: Club Bruges
Bulgaria: Levski Sofia
Czechoslovakia: Sparta Prague
Denmark: Brondby IF
Finland: HJK Helsinki
France: AS Monaco
Germany: Werder Bremen
Greece: Larissa
Holland: PSV Eindhoven
Hungary: Honved
Ireland: Glentoran
Italy: AC Milan
Norway: Rosenborg
Poland: Gornik Zabrze
Portugal: Porto
Romania: Steaua Bucharest
Russia: Dnepr Dnepropetrovsk
Spain: Real Madrid
Sweden: Malmo
Switzerland: Neuchatel-Xamax
Turkey: Galatasaray

ENGLAND INTERNATIONALS

17 Feb Israel 0   England 0
23 Mar England 2   Holland 2
27 Apr Hungary 0   England 0
21 May England 1   Scotland 0
24 May England 1   Colombia 1
28 May Switzerland 0   England 1
12 Jun Rep. of Ireland 1 England 0
15 Jun Holland 3   England 1
18 Jun USSR 3   England 1
14 Sep England 1   Denmark 0
19 Oct England 0   Sweden 0
16 Nov Saudi Arabia 1   England 1

INTERNATIONAL CUP WINNERS

European Cup: PSV Eindhoven — UEFA Cup: Bayer Leverkusen
European Cup-Winners' Cup: Mechelen
European Championship: Holland

THE FOOTBALL FACT AND QUIZ BOOK

1989

ENGLISH AND SCOTTISH FOOTBALL

Champions: Arsenal

Runners-up: Liverpool

Division 2: Chelsea

Runners-up: Manchester City

Division 3: Wolverhampton W

Runners-up: Sheffield Utd

Division 4: Rotherham Utd

Runners-up: Tranmere Rovers

FA Cup winners: Liverpool

League Cup winners: Nottingham Forest

Charity Shield: Liverpool

Scottish Champions: Rangers

Runners-up: Aberdeen

Scottish Cup: Celtic

Scottish League Cup: Rangers

EUROPEAN LEAGUE CHAMPIONS

Austria: FC Tirol Innsbruck

Belgium: KV Mechelen

Bulgaria: CSKA Sofia

Czechoslovakia: Sparta Prague

Denmark: OB

Finland: Kuusysi Lahti

France: Olympique Marseille

Germany: Bayern Munich

Greece: AEK

Holland: PSV Eindhoven

Hungary: Honved

Ireland: Linfield

Italy: Internazionale

Norway: Lillestrom

Poland: Ruch Chorzow

Portugal: Benfica

Romania: Steaua Bucharest

Russia: Spartak Moscow

Spain: Real Madrid

Sweden: Malmo

Switzerland: FC Lucerne

Turkey: Fenerbahce

ENGLAND INTERNATIONALS

8 Feb   Greece 1   England 2

8 Mar   Albania 0   England 2

26 Apr   England 5   Albania 0

23 May   England 0   Chile 0

27 May   Scotland 0   England 2

3 Jun   England 3   Poland 0

7 Jun   Denmark 1   England 1

6 Sep   Sweden 0   England 0

11 Oct   Poland 0   England 0

15 Nov   England 0   Italy 0

13 Dec   England 2   Yugoslavia 1

INTERNATIONAL CUP WINNERS

European Cup: AC Milan

UEFA Cup: Napoli

European Cup-Winners' Cup: Barcelona

ENGLISH AND SCOTTISH FOOTBALL

Champions: Liverpool
Division 2: Leeds Utd
Division 3: Bristol Rovers
Division 4: Exeter City
FA Cup winners: Manchester Utd
Charity Shield: Liverpool
Scottish Champions: Rangers
Scottish Cup: Aberdeen

Runners-up: Aston Villa
Runners-up: Sheffield Utd
Runners-up: Bristol City
Runners-up: Grimsby Town
League Cup winners: Nottingham Forest

Runners-up: Aberdeen
Scottish League Cup: Aberdeen

EUROPEAN LEAGUE CHAMPIONS

Austria: FC Tirol Innsbruck
Belgium: Club Bruges
Bulgaria: CSKA Sofia
Czechoslovakia: Sparta Prague
Denmark: Brondby IF
Finland: HJK Helsinki
France: Olympique Marseille
Germany: Bayern Munich
Greece: Panathinaikos
Holland: Ajax
Hungary: Ujpesti Dozsa

Ireland: Portadown
Italy: Napoli
Norway: Rosenborg
Poland: Lech Poznan
Portugal: Porto
Romania: Dynamo Bucharest
Russia: Dynamo Kiev
Spain: Real Madrid
Sweden: IFK Gothenburg
Switzerland: Grasshopper Club
Turkey: Besiktas

ENGLAND INTERNATIONALS

28 Mar England 1 Brazil 0
25 Apr England 4 Czechoslovakia 2
15 May England 1 Denmark 0
22 May England 1 Uruguay 2
2 Jun Tunisia 1 England 1
11 Jun Rep. of Ireland 1 England 1
16 Jun Holland 0 England 0
21 Jun Egypt 0 England 1

27 Jun Belgium 0 England 1
1 Jul Cameroon 2 England 3
4 Jul W. Germany 1 England 1
7 Jul Italy 2 England 1
12 Sep England 1 Hungary 0
17 Oct England 2 Poland 0
14 Nov Rep. of Ireland 1 England 1

INTERNATIONAL CUP WINNERS

European Cup: AC Milan
European Cup-Winners' Cup: Sampdoria
World Cup: W. Germany

UEFA Cup: Juventus

THE FOOTBALL FACT AND QUIZ BOOK

1991

ENGLISH AND SCOTTISH FOOTBALL

Champions: Arsenal   Runners-up: Liverpool
Division 2: Oldham Athletic   Runners-up: West Ham Utd
Division 3: Cambridge Utd   Runners-up: Southend Utd
Division 4: Darlington   Runners-up: Stockport County
FA Cup winners: Tottenham Hotspur   League Cup winners: Sheffield Wed.
Charity Shield: Arsenal
Scottish Champions: Rangers   Runners-up: Aberdeen
Scottish Cup: Motherwell   Scottish League Cup: Rangers

EUROPEAN LEAGUE CHAMPIONS

Austria: FK Austria   Ireland: Portadown
Belgium: Anderlecht   Italy: Sampdoria
Bulgaria: Etar Veliko Tarnovo   Norway: Viking
Czechoslovakia: Sparta Prague   Poland: Zaglebie Lubin
Denmark: Brondby IF   Portugal: Benfica
Finland: Kuusysi Lahti   Romania: Universitatea Craiova
France: Olympique Marseille   Russia: CSKA Moscow
Germany: IFC Kaiserslautern   Spain: Barcelona
Greece: Panathinaikos   Sweden: IFK Gothenburg
Holland: PSV Eindhoven   Switzerland: Grasshopper Club
Hungary: Honved   Turkey: Besiktas

ENGLAND INTERNATIONALS

6 Feb   England 2   Cameroon 0   3 Jun   New Zealand 0   England 1
27 Mar   England 1   Rep. of Ireland 1   8 Jun   New Zealand 0   England 2
1 May   Turkey 0   England 1   12 Jun   Malaysia 2   England 4
21 May   England 3   USSR 1   11 Sep   England 0   Germany 1
25 May   England 2   Argentina 2   16 Oct   England 1   Turkey 0
1 Jun   Australia 0   England 1   13 Nov   Poland 1   England 1

INTERNATIONAL CUP WINNERS

European Cup: Red Star Belgrade   UEFA Cup: Internazionale
European Cup-Winners' Cup: Manchester Utd

1992

ENGLISH AND SCOTTISH FOOTBALL

Champions: Leeds Utd   Runners-up: Manchester Utd
Division 2: Ipswich Town   Runners-up: Middlesborough
Division 3: Brentford   Runners-up: Birmingham City
Division 4: Burnley   Runners-up: Rotherham Utd
FA Cup winners: Liverpool   League Cup winners: Manchester Utd
Charity Shield: Leeds Utd
Scottish Champions: Rangers   Runners-up: Hearts
Scottish Cup: Rangers   Scottish League Cup: Hibernian

EUROPEAN LEAGUE CHAMPIONS

Austria: FK Austria   Ireland: Glentoran
Belgium: Club Bruges   Italy: AC Milan
Bulgaria: CSKA Sofia   Norway: Rosenborg
Czechoslovakia: Slovan Bratislava   Poland: Lech Poznan
Denmark: Lyngby BK   Portugal: Porto
Finland: HJK Helsinki   Romania: Dynamo Bucharest
France: Olympique Marseille   Russia: Spartak Moscow
Germany: VfB Stuttgart   Spain: Barcelona
Greece: AEK   Sweden: AIK Stockholm
Holland: PSV Eindhoven   Switzerland: FC Sion
Hungary: Ferencvaros   Turkey: Besiktas

ENGLAND INTERNATIONALS

19 Feb England 2   France 0   11 Jun Denmark 0   England 0
25 Mar Czechoslovakia 2 England 2   14 Jun France 0   England 0
29 Apr CIS 2   England 2   17 Jun Sweden 2   England 1
12 May Hungary 0   England 1   9 Sep   Spain 1   England 0
17 May England 1   Brazil 1   14 Oct England 1   Norway 1
3 Jun   Finland 1   England 2   18 Nov England 4   Turkey 0

INTERNATIONAL CUP WINNERS

European Cup: Barcelona   UEFA Cup: Ajax
European Cup-Winners' Cup: Werder Bremen
European Championship: Denmark

1993

ENGLISH AND SCOTTISH FOOTBALL

Premier: Manchester Utd
Division 1: Newcastle Utd
Division 2: Stoke City
Division 3: Cardiff City
FA Cup winners: Arsenal
Charity Shield: Manchester Utd
Scottish Champions: Rangers
Scottish Cup: Rangers

Runners-up: Aston Villa
Runners-up: West Ham Utd
Runners-up: Bolton Wanderers
Runners-up: Wrexham
League Cup winners: Arsenal

Runners-up: Aberdeen
Scottish League Cup: Rangers

EUROPEAN LEAGUE CHAMPIONS

Austria: FK Austria
Belgium: Anderlecht
Bulgaria: Levski Sofia
Czechoslovakia: Sparta Prague
Denmark: FC Kobenhavn
Finland: Jazz Pori
France: Olympique Marseille
Germany: SV Werder Bremen
Greece: AEK
Holland: Feyenoord
Hungary: Kispest-Honved

Ireland: Linfield
Italy: AC Milan
Norway: Rosenborg
Poland: Lech Poznan
Portugal: Porto
Romania: Steaua Bucharest
Russia: Spartak Moscow
Spain: Barcelona
Sweden: IFK Gothenburg
Switzerland: FC Aarau
Turkey: Galatasaray

ENGLAND INTERNATIONALS

17 Feb England 6   San Marino 0
31 Mar Turkey 0   England 2
28 Apr England 2   Holland 2
29 May Poland 1   England 1
2 Jun   Norway 2   England 0
9 Jun   USA 2   England 0
13 Jun Brazil 1   England 1
19 Jun Germany 2   England 1
8 Sep   England 3   Poland 0
13 Oct Holland 2   England 0
17 Nov San Marino 1   England 7

INTERNATIONAL CUP WINNERS

European Cup: Marseille
European Cup-Winners' Cup: Parma

UEFA Cup: Juventus

1994

ENGLISH AND SCOTTISH FOOTBALL

Premier: Manchester Utd   Runners-up: Blackburn Rovers
Division 1: Crystal Palace   Runners-up: Nottingham Forest
Division 2: Reading   Runners-up: Port Vale
Division 3: Shrewsbury Town   Runners-up: Chester City
FA Cup winners: Manchester Utd   League Cup winners: Aston Villa
Charity Shield: Manchester Utd
Scottish Champions: Rangers   Runners-up: Aberdeen
Scottish Cup: Dundee Utd   Scottish League Cup: Rangers

EUROPEAN LEAGUE CHAMPIONS

Austria: Austria Salzburg   Ireland: Linfield
Belgium: Anderlecht   Italy: AC Milan
Bulgaria: Levski Sofia   Norway: Rosenborg
Czechoslovakia: Sparta Prague   Poland: Legia Warsaw
Denmark: Silkeborg IF   Portugal: Benfica
Finland: TPV Tampere   Romania: Steaua Bucharest
France: Paris Saint-Germain   Russia: Spartak Moscow
Germany: Bayern Munich   Spain: Barcelona
Greece: AEK   Sweden: IFK Gothenburg
Holland: Ajax   Switzerland: Servette
Hungary: Vac-Samsung   Turkey: Galatasaray

ENGLAND INTERNATIONALS

9 Mar   England 1   Denmark 0   7 Sep   England 2   USA 0
17 May England 5   Greece 0   16 Nov England 1   Nigeria 0
22 May England 0   Norway 0

INTERNATIONAL CUP WINNERS

European Cup: AC Milan   UEFA Cup: Internazionale
European Cup-Winners' Cup: Arsenal
World Cup: Brazil

1995

ENGLISH AND SCOTTISH FOOTBALL

Premier: Blackburn Rovers

Runners-up: Manchester Utd

Division 1: Middlesborough

Runners-up: Reading

Division 2: Birmingham City

Runners-up: Brentford

Division 3: Carlisle Utd

Runners-up: Walsall

FA Cup winners: Everton

League Cup winners: Liverpool

Charity Shield: Everton

Scottish Champions: Rangers

Runners-up: Motherwell

Scottish Cup: Celtic

Scottish League Cup: Raith Rovers

EUROPEAN LEAGUE CHAMPIONS

Austria: Austria Salzburg

Belgium: Anderlecht

Bulgaria: Levski Sofia

Czechoslovakia: Sparta Prague

Denmark: AaB Aalborg

Finland: Haka Valkeakoski

France: Nantes

Germany: Borussia Dortmund

Greece: Panathinaikos

Holland: Ajax

Hungary: Ferencvaros

Ireland: Crusaders

Italy: Juventus

Norway: Rosenborg

Poland: Legia Warsaw

Portugal: Porto

Romania: Steaua Bucharest

Russia: n/a

Spain: Real Madrid

Sweden: IFK Gothenburg

Switzerland: Grasshopper Club

Turkey: Besiktas

ENGLAND INTERNATIONALS

29 Mar England 0 Uruguay 0

3 Jun England 2 Japan 1

8 Jun England 3 Sweden 3

11 Jun England 1 Brazil 3

6 Sep England 0 Colombia 0

11 Oct Norway 0 England 0

15 Nov England 3 Switzerland 1

12 Dec England 1 Portugal 1

INTERNATIONAL CUP WINNERS

European Cup: Ajax

European Cup-Winners' Cup: Zaragoza

UEFA Cup: Parma

1996

ENGLISH AND SCOTTISH FOOTBALL

Premier: Manchester Utd   Runners-up: Newcastle Utd
Division 1: Sunderland   Runners-up: Derby County
Division 2: Swindon Town   Runners-up: Oxford Utd
Division 3: Preston North End   Runners-up: Gillingham
FA Cup winners: Manchester Utd   League Cup winners: Aston Villa
Charity Shield: Manchester Utd
Scottish Champions: Rangers   Runners-up: Celtic
Scottish Cup: Rangers   Scottish League Cup: Aberdeen

EUROPEAN LEAGUE CHAMPIONS

Austria: Rapid Vienna   Ireland: Portadown
Belgium: Club Bruges   Italy: AC Milan
Bulgaria: Slavia Sofia   Norway: Rosenborg
Czechoslovakia: Slavia Prague   Poland: Widzew Lodz
Denmark: Brondby IF   Portugal: Porto
Finland: Jazz Pori   Romania: Steaua Bucharest
France: AJ Auxerre   Russia: Spartak Moscow
Germany: Borussia Dortmund   Spain: Atletico Madrid
Greece: Panathinaikos   Sweden: IFK Gothenburg
Holland: Ajax   Switzerland: Grasshopper Club
Hungary: Ferencvaros   Turkey: Fenerbahce

ENGLAND INTERNATIONALS

27 Mar   England 1   Bulgaria 0   18 Jun   England 4   Holland 1
24 Apr   England 0   Croatia 0   22 Jun   England 0   Spain 0
18 May   England 3   Hungary 0   26 Jun   England 1   Germany 1
23 May   China 0   England 3   1 Sep   Moldova 0   England 3
8 Jun   England 1   Switzerland 1   9 Oct   England 2   Poland 1
15 Jun   England 2   Scotland 0   9 Nov   Georgia 0   England 2

INTERNATIONAL CUP WINNERS

European Cup: Juventus   UEFA Cup: Bayern Munich
European Cup-Winners' Cup: Paris Saint-Germain
European Championship: Germany

THE FOOTBALL FACT AND QUIZ BOOK

ENGLISH AND SCOTTISH FOOTBALL

Premier: Manchester Utd Runners-up: Newcastle Utd
Division 1: Bolton Wanderers Runners-up: Barnsley
Division 2: Bury Runners-up: Stockport
Division 3: Wigan Athletic Runners-up: Fulham
FA Cup winners: Chelsea League Cup winners: Leicester City
Charity Shield: Manchester Utd
Scottish Champions: Rangers Runners-up: Celtic
Scottish Cup: Kilmarnock Scottish League Cup: Rangers

EUROPEAN LEAGUE CHAMPIONS

Austria: Austria Salzburg Ireland: Crusaders
Belgium: Lierse SK Italy: Juventus
Bulgaria: CSKA Sofia Norway: Rosenborg
Czechoslovakia: Sparta Prague Poland: Widzew Lodz
Denmark: Brondby IF Portugal: Porto
Finland: HJK Helsinki Romania: Steaua Bucharest
France: AS Monaco Russia: Spartak Moscow
Germany: Bayern Munich Spain: Real Madrid
Greece: Olympiakos Sweden: Halmstad
Holland: PSV Eindhoven Switzerland: FC Sion
Hungary: MTK Turkey: Galatasaray

ENGLAND INTERNATIONALS

12 Feb England 0 Italy 1 7 Jun France 0 England 1
29 Mar England 2 Mexico 0 10 Jun Brazil 1 England 0
30 Apr England 2 Georgia 0 10 Sep England 4 Moldova 0
24 May England 2 South Africa 1 11 Oct Italy 0 England 0
31 May Poland 0 England 2 15 Nov England 2 Cameroon 0
4 Jun Italy 0 England 2

INTERNATIONAL CUP WINNERS

European Cup: Borussia Dortmund UEFA Cup: Schalke 04
European Cup-Winners' Cup: Barcelona

1998

ENGLISH AND SCOTTISH FOOTBALL

Premier: Arsenal   Runners-up: Manchester Utd
Division 1: Nottingham Forest   Runners-up: Middlesborough
Division 2: Watford   Runners-up: Bristol City
Division 3: Notts County   Runners-up: Macclesfield Town
FA Cup winners: Arsenal   League Cup winners: Chelsea
Charity Shield: Arsenal
Scottish Champions: Celtic   Runners-up: Rangers
Scottish Cup: Heart of Midlothian   Scottish League Cup: Celtic

EUROPEAN LEAGUE CHAMPIONS

Austria: Sturm Graz   Ireland: Cliftonville
Belgium: Club Bruges   Italy: Juventus
Bulgaria: Litex Lovetch   Norway: Rosenborg
Czechoslovakia: Sparta Prague   Poland: LKS-Ptak Lodz
Denmark: Brondby IF   Portugal: Porto
Finland: Haka Valkeakoski   Romania: Steaua Bucharest
France: Racing Club Lens   Russia: Spartak Moscow
Germany: IFC Kaiserslautern   Spain: Barcelona
Greece: Olympiakos   Sweden: AIK Stockholm
Holland: Ajax   Switzerland: Grasshopper Club
Hungary: Ujpesti TE   Turkey: Galatasaray

ENGLAND INTERNATIONALS

11 Feb England 0   Chile 2
25 Mar Switzerland 1   England 1
22 Apr England 3   Portugal 0
23 May England 0   Saudi Arabia 0
27 May Morocco 0   England 2
29 May Belgium 0   England 0
15 Jun Tunisia 0   England 2
22 Jun Romania 2   England 1
26 Jun Colombia 0   England 2
30 Jun Argentina 2   England 2

INTERNATIONAL CUP WINNERS

European Cup: Real Madrid   UEFA Cup: Internazionale
European Cup-Winners' Cup: Chelsea
World Cup: France

THE FOOTBALL FACT AND QUIZ BOOK

1999

ENGLISH AND SCOTTISH FOOTBALL

Premier: Manchester Utd — Runners-up: Arsenal
Division 1: Sunderland — Runners-up: Bradford City
Division 2: Fulham — Runners-up: Walsall
Division 3: Brentford — Runners-up: Cambridge Utd
FA Cup winners: Manchester Utd — League Cup winners: Spurs
Charity Shield: Arsenal
Scottish Champions: Rangers — Runners-up: Celtic
Scottish Cup: Rangers — Scottish League Cup: Rangers

EUROPEAN LEAGUE CHAMPIONS

Austria: Sturm Graz
Belgium: Racing Genk
Bulgaria: Liex Lovetch
Czechoslovakia: Sparta Prague
Denmark: AaB Aalborg
Finland: Haka Valkeakoski
France: Girondins de Bordeaux
Germany: Bayern Munich
Greece: Olympiakos
Holland: Feyenoord
Hungary: MTK
Ireland: Glentoran
Italy: AC Milan
Norway: Rosenborg
Poland: Wisla Krakow
Portugal: Porto
Romania: Rapid Bucharest
Russia: Spartak Moscow
Spain: Barcelona
Sweden: Helsingborg
Switzerland: Servette
Turkey: Galatasaray

ENGLAND INTERNATIONALS

10 Feb England 0 France 2
27 Mar England 3 Poland 1
28 Apr Hungary 1 England 1
5 Jun England 0 Sweden 0
9 Jun Bulgaria 1 England 1
4 Sep England 6 Luxembourg 0
8 Sep Poland 0 England 0
10 Oct England 2 Belgium 1
13 Nov Scotland 0 England 2
17 Nov England 0 Scotland 1

INTERNATIONAL CUP WINNERS

European Cup: Manchester Utd — UEFA Cup: Parma
European Cup-Winners' Cup: Lazio

ENGLISH AND SCOTTISH FOOTBALL

Premier: Manchester Utd   Runners-up: Arsenal
Division 1: Charlton Athletic   Runners-up: Manchester City
Division 2: Preston North End   Runners-up: Burnley
Division 3: Swansea City   Runners-up: Rotherham Utd
FA Cup winners: Chelsea   League Cup winners: Leicester City
Charity Shield: Chelsea
Scottish Champions: Rangers   Runners-up: Celtic
Scottish Cup: Rangers   Scottish League Cup: Celtic

EUROPEAN LEAGUE CHAMPIONS

Austria: FC Tirol Innsbruck   Ireland: Linfield
Belgium: Anderlecht   Italy: Lazio
Bulgaria: Levski Sofia   Norway: Rosenborg
Czechoslovakia: Sparta Prague   Poland: Polonia Warsaw
Denmark: Herfolge BK   Portugal: Sporting Lisbon
Finland: Haka Valkeakoski   Romania: Dynamo Bucharest
France: AS Monaco   Russia: Spartak Moscow
Germany: Bayern Munich   Spain: Deportivo La Coruna
Greece: Olympiakos   Sweden: Halmstad
Holland: PSV Eindhoven   Switzerland: FC St. Gallen
Hungary: Dunaferr FC   Turkey: Galatasaray

ENGLAND INTERNATIONALS

23 Feb England 0 Argentina 0   12 Jun Portugal 3 England 2
27 May England 1 Brazil 1   17 Jun Germany 0   England 1
31 May England 2 Ukraine 0   20 Jun Romania 3   England 2
3 Jun   Malta 1   England 2   7 Oct   England 0   Germany 1

INTERNATIONAL CUP WINNERS

European Cup: Real Madrid   UEFA Cup: Galatasaray
European Championship: France

WORLD GAZETTEER

AFGHANISTAN

The Football Federation of the National Olympic Committee was founded in 1933 and affiliated to FIFA in 1948. Afghanistan was a founder member of the Asian Football Confederation in 1954. It played in the 1948 Olympic Games tournament. Afghanistan has never entered the World Cup.

F.I.F.A. RANKINGS:

December 1998: N/A   January 1999: N/A   December 1999: N/A
January 2000: N/A   December 2000: N/A   May 2001: N/A

ALBANIA

The Fédération Albanaise de Football was founded in 1930 and affiliated to FIFA in 1932. Albania affiliated to UEFA in 1954. It first entered the Olympic Games tournament in 1964 and the World Cup in 1966. Albania first entered the European Championships in 1964. It has never entered the Women's World Cup or European Championship for Women.

F.I.F.A. RANKINGS:

December 1998: 106   January 1999: 91   December 1999: 83
January 2000: 83   December 2000: 72   May 2001: 79

ALGERIA

The Fédération Algérienne de Football was formed in 1962 and affiliated to FIFA in 1963. Algeria affiliated to the Confédération Africaine de Football in 1964. It reached the quarter-finals of the 1980 Olympic Games tournament and first entered the African Cup of Nations in 1969. It has yet to enter the Women's World Cup.

F.I.F.A. RANKINGS:

December 1998: 71   January 1999: 77   December 1999: 86
January 2000: 86   December 2000: 82   May 2001: 83

AMERICAN SAMOA

American Samoa is an associate member of the Oceania Football Confederation. It first entered the Women's World Cup in 1998 but did not make the finals in 1999.

F.I.F.A. RANKINGS:

December 1998: 193   January 1999: 195   December 1999: 198
January 2000: 198   December 2000: 203   May 2001: 201

THE FOOTBALL FACT AND QUIZ BOOK

ANDORRA

The Federacio Andorrana de Futbol was founded in 1994 and affiliated to FIFA and UEFA in 1996. Andorra's first international tournament entry was in the 2000 European Championships.

F.I.F.A. RANKINGS:

December 1998: 171   January 1999: 165   December 1999: 145
January 2000: 146   December 2000: 145   May 2001: 143

ANGOLA

The Fédération Angolaise de Football was founded in 1979 and affiliated to FIFA and the Confédération Africaine de Football in 1980. Angola first entered the Olympic Games tournament in 1984 and the World Cup in 1986. Angola played in the qualifiers for the 1995 Women's World Cup and first entered the African Cup of Nations in 1982.

F.I.F.A. RANKINGS:

December 1998: 50   January 1999: 59   December 1999: 52
January 2000: 53   December 2000: 55   May 2001: 52

ANGUILLA

The Anguilla Football Association affiliated to FIFA and the Confederacion Norte-Centroamerican y del Caribe de Futbol in 1996.

F.I.F.A. RANKINGS:

December 1998: 197   January 1999: 198   December 1999: 202
January 2000: 202   December 2000: 196   May 2001: 194

ANTIGUA AND BARBUDA

The Antigua Football Association was founded in 1928 and affiliated to FIFA in 1970. It affiliated to the Confederacion Norte-Centroamerican y del Caribe de Futbol in 1980. Antigua first entered the World Cup in 1974 but has not progressed beyond the qualifying tournament in this or the Olympic Games.

F.I.F.A. RANKINGS:

December 1998: 137   January 1999: 148   December 1999: 147
January 2000: 149   December 2000: 143   May 2001: 151

ARGENTINA

The Asociacion del Futbol Argentino was formed in 1893 and joined FIFA in 1912. Argentina was a founder member of the Confederacion Sudamericana de Futbol in 1916. Argentina were silver medal winners at the 1928 Olympic Games tournament, and entered the first World Cup in 1930. Argentina first entered the Women's World Cup in 1995.

F.I.F.A. RANKINGS:

December 1998: 5   January 1999: 6   December 1999: 6
January 2000: 6   December 2000: 3   May 2001: 3

ARMENIA

The Football Federation of Armenia was originally founded in 1934. The association was reformed in 1992 when the country affiliated to both FIFA and UEFA. Armenia first entered the World Cup in 1998 and the European Championship in 1996. It has not yet entered the Women's World Cup.

F.I.F.A. RANKINGS:

December 1998: 100   January 1999: 89   December 1999: 85
January 2000: 85   December 2000: 90   May 2001: 95

ARUBA

The Arubaanse Voetbal Bond was formed in 1932 and joined FIFA and the Confederacion Norte-Centroamerican y del Caribe de Futbol in 1988. Aruba has not qualified for the Olympic Games finals tournament and first entered the World Cup in 1998.

F.I.F.A. RANKINGS:

December 1998: 180   January 1999: 182   December 1999: 191
January 2000: 191   December 2000: 184   May 2001: 184

AUSTRALIA

The Football Association, Soccer Australia, was founded in 1882. Australia affiliated to FIFA in 1963 and the Oceania Football Confederation in 1966. Australia reached the semi-final of the 1992 Olympic Games tournament and qualified for the finals tournament of the 1995 Women's World Cup. Australia first entered the World Cup in 1966.

F.I.F.A. RANKINGS:

December 1998: 39   January 1999: 50   December 1999: 89
January 2000: 89   December 2000: 72   May 2001: 68

THE FOOTBALL FACT AND QUIZ BOOK

AUSTRIA

The Österreichischer Fussball-Bund was founded in 1904 and affiliated to FIFA in 1905. Austria became affiliated to UEFA in 1954. Austria first entered the World Cup in 1934, won the silver medal in the 1936 Olympic Games and reached the quarter-finals of the 1960 European Championships.

F.I.F.A. RANKINGS:

December 1998: 22   January 1999: 18   December 1999: 28
January 2000: 29   December 2000: 44   May 2001: 34

AZERBAIJAN

The Association of Football Federations of Azerbaijan was founded in 1991. Azerbaijan joined FIFA and UEFA in 1994. It first entered the World Cup in 1998 and the European Championships in 1996. It has not entered the Women's World Cup.

F.I.F.A. RANKINGS:

December 1998: 99   January 1999: 101   December 1999: 97
January 2000: 97   December 2000: 115   May 2001: 117

BAHAMAS

The Bahamas Football Association was formed in 1967 and affiliated to FIFA in 1968. It affiliated to the Confederacion Norte-Centroamerican y del Caribe de Futbol in 1981. The Bahamas first entered the World Cup in 1998 but has yet to enter the Women's World Cup.

F.I.F.A. RANKINGS:

December 1998: n/a   January 1999: n/a   December 1999: 189
January 2000: 189   December 2000: 178   May 2001: 182

BAHRAIN

The Bahrain Football Association was formed in 1951 and affiliated to FIFA in 1966. Bahrain affiliated to the Asian Confederation in 1970. Bahrain lost in the qualifiers of the 1992 Olympic Games tournament, and first entered the World Cup in 1978.

F.I.F.A. RANKINGS:

December 1998: 119   January 1999: 117   December 1999: 136
January 2000: 136   December 2000: 138   May 2001: 118

BANGLADESH

The Bangladesh Football Federation was formed in 1972 and affiliated to
FIFA and the Asian Confederation in 1974. It entered the Olympic Games
tournament in 1992 and first entered the World Cup in 1986. Bangladesh
first entered the Asian Cup of Nations in 1980.

F.I.F.A. RANKINGS:

December 1998: 157   January 1999: 155   December 1999: 130
January 2000: 131   December 2000: 151   May 2001: 145

BARBADOS

The Barbados Football Association was founded in 1910. Barbados affiliated
to FIFA and the Confederacion Norte-Centroamerican y del Caribe de Futbol
in 1968. It first entered the World Cup in 1978. Barbados has yet to enter the
Women's World Cup.

F.I.F.A. RANKINGS:

December 1998: 121   January 1999: 120   December 1999: 113
January 2000: 113   December 2000: 104   May 2001: 103

BELARUS

The Belarus Football Association was formed in 1992 and affiliated to FIFA
the same year. It affiliated to UEFA in 1993. Belarus first entered the World
Cup in 1998 and the European Championship in 1996. It entered the
Women's World Cup in 1999.

F.I.F.A. RANKINGS:

December 1998: 104   January 1999: 93   December 1999: 95
January 2000: 96   December 2000: 95   May 2001: 88

BELGIUM

The Union Royale Belge des Sociétés de Football Association was formed in
1895. It was a founder member of FIFA in 1904 and of UEFA in 1954.
Belgium first entered the Olympic Games tournament in 1920, winning the
trophy. It first entered the World Cup in 1930 and the European
Championships in 1964. Belgium's first appearance in the European
Championships for Women was in 1984, but it has never qualified for the
finals tournament of the Women's World Cup.

F.I.F.A. RANKINGS:

December 1998: 35   January 1999: 21   December 1999: 33
January 2000: 33   December 2000: 27   May 2001: 30

BELIZE

The Belize National Football Association was formed in 1980 and affiliated to both FIFA and the Confederacion Norte-Centroamerican y del Caribe de Futbol in 1986. Belize first entered the World Cup in 1998. It has never qualified for the Olympic Games finals tournament.

F.I.F.A. RANKINGS:

December 1998: 186   January 1999: 185   December 1999: 190
January 2000: 190   December 2000: 186   May 2001: 187

BENIN

The Fédération Béninoise de Football was formed in 1968. Benin affiliated to FIFA and the Confédération Africaine de Football in 1969. Benin first entered the Olympic Games tournament in 1964 and the World Cup in 1974. Benin first entered the African Cup of Nations in 1972 and has yet to enter the Women's World Cup.

F.I.F.A. RANKINGS:

December 1998: 127   January 1999: 129   December 1999: 140
January 2000: 141   December 2000: 148   May 2001: 154

BERMUDA

The Bermuda Football Association was formed in 1928 and affiliated to FIFA in 1962. It affiliated to the Confederacion Norte-Centroamerican y del Caribe de Futbol in 1966. Bermuda first entered the World Cup in 1970 but has yet to enter the Women's World Cup.

F.I.F.A. RANKINGS:

December 1998: 185   January 1999: 180   December 1999: 163
January 2000: 163   December 2000: 153   May 2001: 158

BOLIVIA

The Federacion Boliviana de Futbol was founded in 1925. Bolivia affiliated to FIFA and the Confederacion Sudamericana de Futbol in 1926. Bolivia finished last in their qualifying group for the 1992 Olympic Games and last in their qualifying tournament for the 1995 Women's World Cup. Bolivia played in the first World Cup finals in 1930.

F.I.F.A. RANKINGS:

December 1998: 61   January 1999: 56   December 1999: 61
January 2000: 61   December 2000: 65   May 2001: 75

BOSNIA-HERZEGOVINA

The Bosnia and Herzegovina Football Federation was founded in 1992, and affiliated to FIFA and UEFA in 1996. Bosnia-Herzegovina first entered the European Championship in 2000 and the World Cup in 1998. It entered the Women's World Cup in 1999.

F.I.F.A. RANKINGS:

December 1998: 96   January 1999: 97   December 1999: 75
January 2000: 75   December 2000: 78   May 2001: 72

BOTSWANA

The Botswana Football Association was formed in 1970 and affiliated to FIFA and the Confédération Africaine de Football in 1976. Botswana has not yet entered the Women's World Cup and lost in the 1992 qualifying tournament for the Olympic Games in the preliminary round. It first entered both the World Cup and the African Cup of Nations in 1994.

F.I.F.A. RANKINGS:

December 1998: 155   January 1999: 157   December 1999: 165
January 2000: 165   December 2000: 150   May 2001: 152

BRAZIL

The Confederação Brasileira de Futebol was founded in 1980. Football had previously been administered by the Confederação Brasileira de Desportos. Brazil affiliated to FIFA in 1923 and was a founder member of the Confederacion Sudamericana de Futbol in 1916. Brazil were silver medal winners at the 1984 Olympic Games tournament and first entered the World Cup in 1930. Brazil first entered the Copa America in 1916 and qualified for the Women's World Cup finals tournament in 1991 and 1995.

F.I.F.A. RANKINGS:

December 1998: 1   January 1999: 1   December 1999: 1
January 2000: 1   December 2000: 1   May 2001: 2

BRITISH VIRGIN ISLANDS

The British Virgin Islands Football Association affiliated to FIFA and the Confederacion Norte-Centroamerican y del Caribe de Futbol in 1996.

F.I.F.A. RANKINGS:

December 1998: 187   January 1999: 187   December 1999: 161
January 2000: 161   December 2000: 172   May 2001: 163

BRUNEI DARUSSALAM

The Football Association of Brunei Darussalam was formed in 1959 and affiliated to FIFA in 1969. It affiliated to the Asian Confederation in 1970. Brunei entered the 1986 World Cup but has not entered the Women's World Cup. It entered the Asian Cup of Nations in 1976.

F.I.F.A. RANKINGS:

December 1998: 183   January 1999: 184   December 1999: 185
January 2000: 185   December 2000: 193   May 2001: 190

BULGARIA

The Bulgarski Futbolen Soius was formed in 1923 and affiliated to FIFA in 1924. Bulgaria was a founder member of UEFA in 1954. It has never entered the Women's World Cup and has never got past the first-round stage of the European Championship for Women. Bulgaria entered the World Cup in 1934 and the European Championships in 1960. Bulgaria were runners-up in the 1968 Olympic Games tournament.

F.I.F.A. RANKINGS:

December 1998: 49   January 1999: 30   December 1999: 37
January 2000: 37   December 2000: 53   May 2001: 43

BURKINA FASO

The Fédération Burkinabe de Foot-Ball was formed in 1960. Burkina Faso affiliated to FIFA and the Confédération Africaine de Football in 1964. It entered the 1976 Olympic Games tournament and the World Cup in 1978. Burkina Faso first entered the African Cup of Nations in 1968 but has yet to enter the Women's World Cup.

F.I.F.A. RANKINGS:

December 1998: 75   January 1999: 84   December 1999: 71
January 2000: 74   December 2000: 69   May 2001: 74

BURUNDI

The Fédération de Football du Burundi was formed in 1948. Burundi affiliated both to FIFA and to the Confédération Africaine de Football in 1972. Burundi first entered the Olympic Games tournament in 1996 and the World Cup in 1994. Burundi has yet to enter the Women's World Cup. It entered the African Cup of Nations for the first time in 1976.

F.I.F.A. RANKINGS:

December 1998: 141   January 1999: 138   December 1999: 133
January 2000: 133   December 2000: 126   May 2001: 132

CAMBODIA

The Fédération Khmère de Football Association formed in 1933 and affiliated to FIFA in 1953. It affiliated to the Asian Football Confederation in 1957. Cambodia first entered the World Cup in 1998 but has not entered the Women's World Cup.

F.I.F.A. RANKINGS:

December 1998: 162   January 1999: 171   December 1999: 168
January 2000: 168   December 2000: 169   May 2001: 169

CAMEROON

The Fédération Camerounaise de Football formed in 1960 and affiliated to FIFA in 1962. It affiliated to the Confédération Africaine de Football in 1963. Cameroon entered the first Women's World Cup tournament in 1991 and first entered the World Cup in 1970. It first entered the African Cup of Nations in 1968.

F.I.F.A. RANKINGS:

December 1998: 41   January 1999: 42   December 1999: 58
January 2000: 57   December 2000: 39   May 2001: 37

CANADA

The Canadian Soccer Association (formerly the Dominion of Canada Football Association) formed in 1912 and affiliated to FIFA the same year. It affiliated to the Confederacion Norte-Centroamerican y del Caribe de Futbol in 1978. Canada took part in the 1976 Olympic Games tournament as hosts and first entered the World Cup in 1958. Canada entered the first Women's World Cup tournament in 1991.

F.I.F.A. RANKINGS:

December 1998: 101   January 1999: 90   December 1999: 81
January 2000: 80   December 2000: 63   May 2001: 71

THE FOOTBALL FACT AND QUIZ BOOK

CAPE VERDE ISLANDS

The Federação Cabo-Veriana de Futebol was formed in 1982 and became affiliated to FIFA and the Confédération Africaine de Football in 1986. It first entered the African Cup of Nations in 1994.

F.I.F.A. RANKINGS:

December 1998: 167   January 1999: 169   December 1999: 177
January 2000: 177   December 2000: 156   May 2001: 159

CAYMAN ISLANDS

The Cayman Islands Football Association formed in 1966 and became affiliated to FIFA and the Confederacion Norte-Centroamerican y del Caribe de Futbol in 1992. The Cayman Islands first entered the World Cup in 1998 but have not entered the Women's World Cup or qualified for the Olympic Games tournament.

F.I.F.A. RANKINGS:

December 1998: 153   January 1999: 157   December 1999: 147
January 2000: 149   December 2000: 159   May 2001: 160

CENTRAL AFRICAN REPUBLIC

The Fédération Centrafricaine de Football Amateur formed in 1937 and affiliated to FIFA in 1963. It affiliated to the Confédération Africaine de Football in 1965. The Central African Republic first entered the African Cup of Nations in 1974.

F.I.F.A. RANKINGS:

December 1998: 191   January 1999: 194   December 1999: 175
January 2000: 175   December 2000: 176   May 2001: 179

CHAD

The Chad Football Association formed in 1962 and affiliated to FIFA and the Confédération Africaine de Football in 1988. Chad first entered the African Cup of Nations in 1992.

F.I.F.A. RANKINGS:

December 1998: 178   January 1999: 181   December 1999: 166
January 2000: 166   December 2000: 163   May 2001: 170

CHILE

The Federacion de Futbol de Chile formed in 1895 and affiliated to FIFA in 1912. Chile was a founder member of the Confederacion Sudamericana de Futbol in 1916, and first entered the Olympic Games tournament in 1928 and the World Cup in 1930. Chile entered the Women's World Cup in 1991 and the first Copa America tournament in 1910.

F.I.F.A. RANKINGS:

December 1998: 16   January 1999: 20   December 1999: 23
January 2000: 23   December 2000: 19   May 2001: 32

CHINA PR

The Football Association of the People's Republic of China formed in 1924 and affiliated to FIFA in 1931. It joined the Asian Football Confederation in 1974. China PR qualified for the 1936 Olympic Games tournament and first entered the World Cup in 1982. China PR first entered the Asian Cup of Nations in 1976 and hosted the first Women's World Cup tournament in 1991.

F.I.F.A. RANKINGS:

December 1998: 37   January 1999: 52   December 1999: 88
January 2000: 88   December 2000: 74   May 2001: 63

CHINESE TAIPEI

The Chinese Taipei Football Association was formed in 1936 and affiliated to FIFA in 1954. It was a founder member of the Asian Football Confederation in 1954. Chinese Taipei played in the 1960 Olympic Games finals tournament and reached the quarter-finals of the 1991 Women's World Cup. Chinese Taipei first entered the World Cup in 1958 and Asian Cup of Nations in 1956.

F.I.F.A. RANKINGS:

December 1998: 169   January 1999: 163   December 1999: 174
January 2000: 174   December 2000: 162   May 2001: 167

COLOMBIA

The Federacion Colombiana de Futbol was formed in 1971, replacing earlier federations. Colombia affiliated to FIFA in 1936 and to the Confederacion Sudamericana de Futbol in 1940. Colombia qualified for the Olympic Games finals tournament for the first time in 1968. It entered the Women's World Cup for the first time in 1999 and the World Cup for the first time in 1958. It first entered the Copa America in 1945.

F.I.F.A. RANKINGS:

December 1998: 34   January 1999: 27   December 1999: 25
January 2000: 24   December 2000: 15   May 2001: 16

THE FOOTBALL FACT AND QUIZ BOOK

CONGO

The Fédération Congolaise de Football formed in 1962 and affiliated to FIFA the same year. It affiliated to the Confédération Africaine de Football in 1966. The Congo first entered the African Cup of Nations in 1968, and the World Cup in 1974.

F.I.F.A. RANKINGS:

December 1998: 112   January 1999: 105   December 1999: 94
January 2000: 94   December 2000: 86   May 2001: 90

CONGO DR

The Fédération Congolaise de Football-Association formed in 1919 and affiliated to FIFA in 1962. It joined the Confédération Africaine de Football in 1963. Congo DR first entered the Olympic Games tournament in 1976 and the African Cup of Nations in 1965, as Congo-Kinshasa. It first entered the World Cup in 1974 as Zaïre, and the Women's World Cup in 1999.

F.I.F.A. RANKINGS:

December 1998: 62   January 1999: 51   December 1999: 59
January 2000: 59   December 2000: 69   May 2001: 77

COOK ISLANDS

The Cook Islands Football Association formed in 1971 and affiliated to FIFA and the Oceania Football Confederation in 1994. It first entered the World Cup in 1998 but has entered neither the Olympic Games tournament nor the Women's World Cup.

F.I.F.A. RANKINGS:

December 1998: 173   January 1999: 175   December 1999: 182
January 2000: 182   December 2000: 170   May 2001: 174

COSTA RICA

The Federacion Costarricense de Futbol formed in 1921 and affiliated to FIFA the same year. It joined the Confederacion Norte-Centroamerican y del Caribe de Futbol in 1962. Costa Rica qualified for the Olympic Games finals tournament in 1980 and entered the Women's World Cup in 1991. Costa Rica first entered the World Cup in 1958.

F.I.F.A. RANKINGS:

December 1998: 67   January 1999: 69   December 1999: 64
January 2000: 64   December 2000: 60   May 2001: 54

CÔTE D'IVOIRE

The Fédération Ivoirienne de Football formed in 1960. It also became affiliated to FIFA and the Confédération Africaine de Football in 1960. Côte D'Ivoire first entered the World Cup in 1974.

F.I.F.A. RANKINGS:

December 1998: 44   January 1999: 40   December 1999: 53
January 2000: 49   December 2000: 51   May 2001: 41

CROATIA

The Croatian Football Federation was formed in 1912 and again in 1991. It affiliated to FIFA and UEFA in 1992. Croatia first entered the Women's World Cup in 1995 and the European Championship for Women the same year. Croatia first entered the European Championship in 1996 and the World Cup in 1998.

F.I.F.A. RANKINGS:

December 1998: 4   January 1999: 3   December 1999: 9
January 2000: 9   December 2000: 18   May 2001: 19

CUBA

The Associacion de Futbol de Cuba formed in 1924 and affiliated to FIFA in 1931. It affiliated to the Confederacion Norte-Centroamerican y del Caribe de Futbol in 1961. Cuba qualified for the Olympic Games finals tournament in 1976. It first entered the World Cup in 1934.

F.I.F.A. RANKINGS:

December 1998: 107   January 1999: 109   December 1999: 77
January 2000: 77   December 2000: 77   May 2001: 81

CYPRUS

The Cyprus Football Association was formed in 1934 and affiliated to FIFA in 1948. Cyprus was a founder member of UEFA in 1954. It has never qualified for the finals tournament of the Olympic Games and has yet to enter the Women's World Cup. It first entered the World Cup in 1962 and the European Championships in 1968.

F.I.F.A. RANKINGS:

December 1998: 78   January 1999: 64   December 1999: 63
January 2000: 62   December 2000: 62   May 2001: 65

CZECH REPUBLIC

The Football Association of the Czech Republic was originally formed in 1901 and reformed in 1990. The Czech Republic affiliated to FIFA originally in 1907 and again in 1994, and affiliated to UEFA in 1993. It first entered the European Championship in 1996 and the World Cup in 1998. It first entered the European Championship for Women in 1995 and has not qualified for the finals of the Women's World Cup.

F.I.F.A. RANKINGS:

December 1998: 8   January 1999: 7   December 1999: 2
January 2000: 2   December 2000: 4   May 2001: 7

DENMARK

The Danish Football Association was formed in 1889. It was a founder member of FIFA in 1904 and of UEFA in 1954. Denmark were runners-up in the 1908 Olympic Games tournament. Denmark first entered the World Cup in 1958 and won the 1992 European Championship. They played in the first women's Olympic Games tournament in 1996 and first entered the European Championships for Women in 1984, and the Women's World Cup in 1991.

F.I.F.A. RANKINGS:

December 1998: 19   January 1999: 15   December 1999: 11
January 2000: 11   December 2000: 22   May 2001: 20

DJIBOUTI

The Fédération Djiboutienne de Football formed in 1977 and affiliated to FIFA and the Confédération Africaine de Football in 1994.

F.I.F.A. RANKINGS:

December 1998: 191   January 1999: 190   December 1999: 195
January 2000: 195   December 2000: 189   May 2001: 191

DOMINICA

The Dominica Football Association formed in 1970 and affiliated to FIFA and the Confederacion Norte-Centroamerican y del Caribe de Futbol in 1994. Dominica first entered the World Cup in 1998.

F.I.F.A. RANKINGS:

December 1998: 133   January 1999: 144   December 1999: 149
January 2000: 148   December 2000: 152   May 2001: 157

DOMINICAN REPUBLIC

The Federacion Dominicana de Futbol formed in 1953 and affiliated to FIFA in 1958. It affiliated to the Confederacion Norte-Centroamerican y del Caribe de Futbol in 1964. The Dominican Republic first entered the World Cup in 1978.

F.I.F.A. RANKINGS:

December 1998: 152   January 1999: 154   December 1999: 155
January 2000: 155   December 2000: 157   May 2001: 162

ECUADOR

The Federacion Ecuatoriana de Futbol was founded in 1957 (previously known as Federacion Deportiva Guayaquil). It affiliated to FIFA in 1926 and the Confederacion Sudamericana de Futbol in 1930. Ecuador first entered the Women's World Cup in 1995 and the World Cup in 1962. Ecuador first entered the Copa America in 1939.

F.I.F.A. RANKINGS:

December 1998: 63 January 1999: 61   December 1999: 65
January 2000: 65   December 2000: 53   May 2001: 45

EGYPT

The Egyptian Football Association formed in 1921 and affiliated to FIFA in 1923. It became a founder member of the Confédération Africaine de Football in 1957. Egypt first entered the Women's World Cup in 1999 and was the first African team to play in the World Cup finals, in 1934. Egypt entered the first African Cup of Nations tournament in 1957.

F.I.F.A. RANKINGS:

December 1998: 28   January 1999: 32   December 1999: 38
January 2000: 38   December 2000: 33   May 2001: 35

EL SALVADOR

The Federacion Salvadorena de Futbol was founded in 1935 and affiliated to FIFA in 1938. It affiliated to the Confederacion Norte-Centroamerican y del Caribe de Futbol in 1962. El Salvador qualified for the Olympic Games finals tournament in 1968, and first entered the World Cup in 1970, qualifying for the finals tournament.

F.I.F.A. RANKINGS:

December 1998: 92   January 1999: 85   December 1999: 95
January 2000: 94   December 2000: 83   May 2001: 93

ENGLAND

The Football Association was founded in 1863. England affiliated to FIFA in 1905 and was a founder member of UEFA in 1954. England won the 1908 Olympic Games tournament, and first entered the World Cup in 1950 and the European Championships in 1964. England first qualified for the finals tournament in the Women's World Cup in 1995 and first entered the European Championship for Women in 1984.

F.I.F.A. RANKINGS:

December 1998: 9   January 1999: 11
December 1999: 12   January 2000: 12
December 2000: 17   May 2001: 14

EQUATORIAL GUINEA

The Federacion Equatoguineana de Futbol formed in 1976 and affiliated to both FIFA and the Confédération Africaine de Football in 1986. It first entered the African Cup of Nations in 1982.

F.I.F.A. RANKINGS:

December 1998: 195   January 1999: 190   December 1999: 188
January 2000: 188   December 2000: 187   May 2001: 188

ERITREA

The Eritrean Football Association formed in 1992 and affiliated to FIFA in 1998. It affiliated to the Confédération Africaine de Football in 1994. Eritrea first entered the African Cup of Nations in 1998.

F.I.F.A. RANKINGS:

December 1998: 189   January 1999: 189   December 1999: 168
January 2000: 168   December 2000: 158   May 2001: 166

ESTONIA

The Estonian Football Association formed in 1921 and reformed in 1989. It affiliated to FIFA in 1923 and reaffiliated in 1992. It also affiliated to UEFA in 1992. It first entered the Olympic Games tournament in 1924 and the World Cup in 1934. Estonia first entered the European Championships in 1996 and the Women's World Cup in 1999. It first entered the European Championships for Women in 1998.

F.I.F.A. RANKINGS:

December 1998: 90   January 1999: 92   December 1999: 70
January 2000: 69   December 2000: 67   May 2001: 65

ETHIOPIA

The Ethiopian Football Federation formed in 1943 and affiliated to FIFA in 1953. It was a founder member of the Confédération Africaine de Football in 1957. Ethiopia first entered the Olympic Games tournament in 1956 and the World Cup in 1962.

F.I.F.A. RANKINGS:

December 1998: 145   January 1999: 136   December 1999: 142
January 2000: 143   December 2000: 133   May 2001: 140

FAEROE ISLANDS

The Faeroe Islands Football Association formed in 1979 and affiliated to both FIFA and UEFA in 1988. It has never entered the Olympic Games tournament or the Women's World Cup. It first entered the World Cup in 1994 and the European Championships in 1992.

F.I.F.A. RANKINGS:

December 1998: 125   January 1999: 110   December 1999: 112
January 2000: 112   December 2000: 117   May 2001: 123

FIJI

The Fiji Football Association formed in 1938 and affiliated to both FIFA and the Oceania Football Confederation in 1963. Fiji first entered the World Cup in 1982.

F.I.F.A. RANKINGS:

December 1998: 124   January 1999: 122   December 1999: 135
January 2000: 135   December 2000: 141   May 2001: 122

THE FOOTBALL FACT AND QUIZ BOOK

FINLAND

The Finland Football Association formed in 1907. It affiliated to FIFA in 1908 and was a founder member of UEFA in 1954. It first entered the Olympic Games tournament in 1912 and the World Cup in 1938. Finland first entered the European Championships in 1968. It first entered the European Championships for Women in 1984 and has yet to qualify for the Women's World Cup.

F.I.F.A. RANKINGS:

December 1998: 55   January 1999: 53   December 1999: 56
January 2000: 56   December 2000: 59   May 2001: 57

FRANCE

The Fédération Française de Football was formed in 1919. France was a founder member of UEFA in 1954 and of FIFA in 1904. France played in the first Olympic Games tournament in 1908 and first entered the World Cup in 1930, and the European Championship in 1960. It entered the Women's World Cup in 1991 and the European Championship for Women in 1982.

F.I.F.A. RANKINGS:

December 1998: 2   January 1999: 2   December 1999: 3
January 2000: 3   December 2000: 2   May 2001: 1

FYR MACEDONIA

The Football Association of the Former Yugoslav Republic of Macedonia formed in 1908 and affiliated to FIFA and UEFA in 1994. FYR Macedonia first entered the World Cup in 1998.

F.I.F.A. RANKINGS:

December 1998: 59   January 1999: 58   December 1999: 68

GABON

The Fédération Gabonese de Football formed in 1962. It affiliated to FIFA in 1963 and the Confédération Africaine de Football in 1967. Gabon first entered the Olympic Games tournament in 1968, and the World Cup in 1990. It first entered the African Cup of Nations in 1972.

F.I.F.A. RANKINGS:

December 1998: 82   January 1999: 83   December 1999: 74
January 2000: 72   December 2000: 89   May 2001: 99

GAMBIA

The Gambia Football Association formed in 1952. It affiliated to FIFA in 1966 and the Confédération Africaine de Football in 1962. The Gambia first entered the Olympic Games in 1976, and the World Cup in 1982. The Gambia first entered the African Cup of Nations in 1976.

F.I.F.A. RANKINGS:

December 1998: 135   January 1999: 139   December 1999: 151
January 2000: 152   December 2000: 154   May 2001: 160

GEORGIA

The Georgian Football Federation was formed in 1991. It affiliated to FIFA in 1992 and UEFA in 1993. Georgia first entered the Women's World Cup in 1999 and the European Championship for Women in 1998. Georgia first entered the World Cup in 1998 and the European Championship in 1996.

F.I.F.A. RANKINGS:

December 1998: 52   January 1999: 53   December 1999: 66
January 2000: 66   December 2000: 66   May 2001: 72

GERMANY

Deutscher Fussball-Bund was formed in 1900. It was a founder member of FIFA in 1904. West Germany rejoined FIFA in 1950 and joined UEFA as a founder member in 1954. East Germany joined FIFA in 1950 and was assimilated into the unified German Association in 1990. Germany first entered the Olympic games in 1912, the World Cup in 1934 and the European Championship in 1968. Germany first entered the Women's World Cup in 1991 and the European Championship for Women in 1984.

F.I.F.A. RANKINGS:

December 1998: 3   January 1999: 5   December 1999: 5
January 2000: 5   December 2000: 11   May 2001: 9

GHANA

The Ghana Football Association was formed in 1957. It affiliated to FIFA and the Confédération Africaine de Football in 1958. It first qualified for the Olympic Games finals tournament in 1964. Ghana first entered the World Cup in 1962. It first entered the Women's World Cup in 1991.

F.I.F.A. RANKINGS:

December 1998: 48 January 1999: 41 December 1999: 48
January 2000: 50 December 2000: 57 May 2001: 61

GREECE

The Hellenic Football Association Federation was formed in 1926. It affiliated to FIFA in 1927 and was a founder member of UEFA in 1954. Greece first entered the Olympic Games in 1920. It has never qualified for the Women's World Cup. Greece first entered the World Cup in 1934 and the European Championships in 1960. It first entered the European Championship for Women in 1993.

F.I.F.A. RANKINGS:

December 1998: 53 January 1999: 46 December 1999: 34
January 2000: 34 December 2000: 42 May 2001: 48

GRENADA

The Grenada Football Association was formed in 1924. It affiliated to FIFA in 1976 and the Confederacion Norte-Centroamerican y del Caribe de Futbol in 1969. Grenada has never qualified for the Olympic Games finals tournament. It first entered the World Cup in 1982.

F.I.F.A. RANKINGS:

December 1998: 117 January 1999: 124 December 1999: 121
January 2000: 122 December 2000: 143 May 2001: 133

GUAM

The Guam Soccer Association was formed in 1975. It affiliated to FIFA and the Asian Football Confederation in 1996. It first entered the Women's World Cup in 1999 and the Asian Cup of Nations in 1996.

F.I.F.A. RANKINGS:

December 1998: 197 January 1999: 197 December 1999: 200
January 2000: 200 December 2000: 199 May 2001: 199

GUATEMALA

The Federacion Nacional de Futbol de Guatemala was formed in 1926. It affiliated to FIFA in 1946 and the Confederacion Norte-Centroamerican y del Caribe de Futbol in 1961. Guatemala reached the quarter-finals of the Olympic Games in 1968 and first entered the Women's World Cup in 1999. Guatemala first entered the World Cup in 1958 and entered the first CONCACAF tournament in 1963.

F.I.F.A. RANKINGS:

December 1998: 73   January 1999: 76   December 1999: 73
January 2000: 73   December 2000: 56   May 2001: 59

GUINEA

The Federacion Guinéenne de Football was formed in 1959. It affiliated to FIFA in 1961 and the Confédération Africaine de Football in 1962. Guinea qualified for the Olympic Games finals tournament in 1968 and first entered the World Cup in 1974. It first entered the Women's World Cup in 1991 and the African Cup of Nations in 1968.

F.I.F.A. RANKINGS:

December 1998: 79   January 1999: 71   December 1999: 91
January 2000: 91   December 2000: 79   May 2001: 85

GUINEA-BISSAU

The Federação de Futebol da Guiné-Bissau was formed in 1974. It affiliated to FIFA and the Confédération Africaine de Football in 1986. Guinea-Bissau first entered the World Cup in 1998. It first entered the African Cup of Nations in 1994.

F.I.F.A. RANKINGS:

December 1998: 165   January 1999: 162   December 1999: 173
January 2000: 173   December 2000: 177   May 2001: 180

GUYANA

The Guyana Football Association was formed in 1902. It became affiliated to FIFA in 1968 and the Confederacion Norte-Centroamerican y del Caribe de Futbol in 1969. Guyana first entered the World Cup in 1978.

F.I.F.A. RANKINGS:

December 1998: 161   January 1999: 165   December 1999: 171
January 2000: 171   December 2000: 183   May 2001: 175

THE FOOTBALL FACT AND QUIZ BOOK

HAITI

The Fédération Haïtienne de Football was formed in 1904. It affiliated to FIFA in 1933 and the Confederacion Norte-Centroamerican y del Caribe de Futbol in 1957. Haiti first entered the World Cup in 1934 and the Women's World Cup in 1991. It has never qualified for the Olympic Games finals tournament.

F.I.F.A. RANKINGS:

December 1998: 109   January 1999: 119   December 1999: 99
January 2000: 99   December 2000: 83   May 2001: 88

HONDURAS

The Federacion Nacional Autonoma de Futbol de Honduras was formed in 1935. It affiliated to FIFA in 1946 and the Confederacion Norte-Centroamerican y del Caribe de Futbol in 1961. Honduras first entered the World Cup in 1962 and has never qualified for the Olympic Games finals tournament. Honduras entered the first CONCACAF Championship tournament in 1963.

F.I.F.A. RANKINGS:

December 1998: 91   January 1999: 77   December 1999: 69
January 2000: 71   December 2000: 46   May 2001: 48

HONG KONG

The Hong Kong Football Association was formed in 1914 and affiliated to FIFA in 1954. Hong Kong was a founder member of the Asian Football Confederation in 1954. Hong Kong has never qualified for the Olympic Games finals tournament and first entered the World Cup in 1974. Hong Kong first entered the Asian Cup of Nations in 1956 and first entered the first Women's World Cup tournament in 1991.

F.I.F.A. RANKINGS:

December 1998: 136   January 1999: 131   December 1999: 122
January 2000: 119   December 2000: 123   May 2001: 128

HUNGARY

The Hungarian Football Federation was formed in 1901 and affiliated to FIFA in 1906. It was a founder member of UEFA in 1954. Hungary first entered the Olympic Games tournament in 1912 and the World Cup in 1934. Hungary first entered the European Championship in 1960, and the Women's World Cup in 1991.

F.I.F.A. RANKINGS:

December 1998: 46   January 1999: 45   December 1999: 45
January 2000: 46   December 2000: 47   May 2001: 53

ICELAND

The Football Association of Iceland was formed in 1929 and affiliated to FIFA in 1947. Iceland was a founder member of UEFA in 1954. Iceland has never qualified for a finals tournament of the Olympic Games. It first entered the World Cup in 1958 and the European Championships in 1964. It first entered the Women's World Cup in 1995.

F.I.F.A. RANKINGS:

December 1998: 64   January 1999: 60   December 1999: 43
January 2000: 43   December 2000: 50   May 2001: 55

INDIA

The All India Football Federation was formed in 1937 and affiliated to FIFA in 1948. India was a founder member of the Asian Football Confederation in 1954. India first played in an Olympic Games finals tournament in 1948 and first entered the World Cup in 1986. India first entered the Asian Cup of Nations in 1960 and first entered the Women's World Cup tournament in 1999.

F.I.F.A. RANKINGS:

December 1998: 110   January 1999: 116   December 1999: 106
January 2000: 106   December 2000: 122   May 2001: 116

INDONESIA

The All Indonesia Football Federation was formed in 1930 and affiliated to FIFA in 1952. Indonesia was a founder member of the Asian Football Confederation in 1954. Indonesia played in an Olympic Games finals tournament in 1956 and first entered the World Cup in 1938. Indonesia first entered the Asian Cup of Nations in 1968 and first entered the Women's World Cup tournament in 1999, but withdrew before the qualifying tournament.

F.I.F.A. RANKINGS:

December 1998: 87   January 1999: 108   December 1999: 89
January 2000: 89   December 2000: 97   May 2001: 84

IRAN

The IR Iran Football Federation was formed in 1920 and affiliated to FIFA in 1945. Iran affiliated to the Asian Football Confederation in 1958. Iran first qualified for an Olympic Games finals tournament in 1964 and first entered the World Cup in 1974. Iran first entered the Asian Cup of Nations in 1960.

F.I.F.A. RANKINGS:

December 1998: 27   January 1999: 46   December 1999: 48
January 2000: 43   December 2000: 36   May 2001: 41

IRAQ

The Iraqi Football Association was formed in 1948 and affiliated to FIFA in 1950. Iraq affiliated to the Asian Football Confederation in 1971. Iraq first qualified for an Olympic Games finals tournament in 1980, reaching the quarter-finals. It first qualified for the World Cup finals tournament in 1986.

F.I.F.A. RANKINGS:

December 1998: 93   January 1999: 99   December 1999: 77
January 2000: 78   December 2000: 79   May 2001: 68

IRELAND (THE REPUBLIC OF)

The Football Association of Ireland was formed in 1921 and affiliated to FIFA in 1923. Ireland was a founder member of UEFA in 1954. Ireland first entered the Olympic Games in 1924, reaching the quarter-finals and the World Cup in 1934. It first entered the European Championship in 1960. Ireland entered the first European Championship for Women in 1984.

F.I.F.A. RANKINGS:

December 1998: 56   January 1999: 44   December 1999: 35
January 2000: 35   December 2000: 31   May 2001: 27

ISRAEL

The Israel Football Association was formed in 1948 and affiliated to FIFA the same year. It became affiliated to UEFA in 1992. It first entered the World Cup in 1934 as Palestine and the European Championships in 1996. Israel first entered the Women's World Cup in 1999 and the European Championship for Women in 1997.

F.I.F.A. RANKINGS:

December 1998: 43   January 1999: 38   December 1999: 26
January 2000: 26   December 2000: 41   May 2001: 47

ITALY

The Federazione Italiana Giuoco Calcio was formed in 1888 and affiliated to FIFA in 1905. Italy was a founder member of UEFA in 1954. Italy first entered the Olympic Games in 1912 and the World Cup in 1934. It first entered the European Championship in 1964. Italy entered the first European Championship for Women and the 1991 World Cup for Women.

F.I.F.A. RANKINGS:
December 1998: 7   January 1999: 3   December 1999: 14
January 2000: 14   December 2000: 4   May 2001: 4

JAMAICA

The Jamaica Football Confederation was formed in 1910. It affiliated to FIFA in 1962 and the Confederacion Norte-Centroamerican y del Caribe de Futbol in 1963. Jamaica first entered the World Cup in 1966 and has never qualified for the Olympic Games finals tournament. Jamaica entered the first CONCACAF Championship tournament in 1963. Jamaica entered the first Women's World Cup tournament in 1991.

F.I.F.A. RANKINGS:
December 1998: 33   January 1999: 39   December 1999: 41
January 2000: 41   December 2000: 48   May 2001: 46

JAPAN

The Football Association of Japan was formed in 1921 and affiliated to FIFA in 1929. Japan was a founder member of the Asian Football Confederation in 1954. Japan first entered the Olympic Games tournament in 1936 and reached the quarter-finals. Japan first entered the World Cup in 1954. Japan first entered the Asian Cup of Nations in 1968.

F.I.F.A. RANKINGS:
December 1998: 20   January 1999: 33   December 1999: 57
January 2000: 58   December 2000: 38   May 2001: 44

JORDAN

The Jordan Football Association was formed in 1949 and affiliated to FIFA in 1958. Jordan affiliated to the Asian Football Confederation in 1970. Jordan has never qualified for an Olympic Games finals tournament. Jordan first entered the World Cup in 1986. Jordan first entered the Asian Cup of Nations in 1984.

F.I.F.A. RANKINGS:
December 1998: 126   January 1999: 130   December 1999: 115

KAZAKHSTAN

The Football Association of the Republic of Kazakhstan was formed in 1914 and affiliated to FIFA and the Asian Football Confederation in 1994. Kazakhstan first entered the Olympic Games in 1996. Kazakhstan first entered the World Cup in 1998. Kazakhstan first entered the Asian Cup of Nations in 1996 and the Women's World Cup in 1999.

F.I.F.A. RANKINGS:
December 1998: 102   January 1999: 112   December 1999: 123
January 2000: 123   December 2000: 120   May 2001: 106

KENYA

The Kenya Football Confederation was formed in 1932. It affiliated to FIFA in 1960 and the Confédération Africaine de Football in 1968. It first entered the Olympic Games in 1964. Kenya first entered the World Cup in 1974. It first entered the Women's World Cup in 1999. It first entered the African Cup of Nations in 1968.

F.I.F.A. RANKINGS:
December 1998: 93   January 1999: 96   December 1999: 103
January 2000: 103   December 2000: 107   May 2001: 104

KOREA DPR

The Football Association of the Democratic People's Republic of Korea was formed in 1945 and affiliated to FIFA in 1958. It affiliated to the Asian Football Confederation in 1974. Korea DPR qualified for the finals tournament of the Olympic Games in 1976. Korea DPR first entered the World Cup in 1966, reaching the quarter-finals. Korea DPR first entered the Asian Cup of Nations in 1972 and qualified for the finals tournament of the Women's World Cup in 1999.

F.I.F.A. RANKINGS:
December 1998: 158   January 1999: 156   December 1999: 172
January 2000: 172   December 2000: 142   May 2001: 147

KOREA REPUBLIC (SOUTH KOREA)

The Korea Football Association was formed in 1928 and affiliated to FIFA in 1948. It was a founder member of the Asian Football Confederation in 1954. Korea Republic first qualified for the finals tournament of the Olympic Games in 1948. Korea Republic first entered the World Cup in 1954, when it qualified for the finals tournament. Korea Republic first entered the Asian Cup of Nations in 1956, winning the trophy. It entered the Women's World Cup in 1991.

F.I.F.A. RANKINGS:
December 1998:17   January 1999: 34   December 1999: 51
January 2000: 52   December 2000: 40   May 2001: 39

KUWAIT

The Kuwait Football Association was formed in 1952 and affiliated to FIFA in 1962. It affiliated to the Asian Football Confederation in 1964. Kuwait reached the quarter-finals of the Olympic Games in 1980. Kuwait first entered the World Cup in 1974, reaching the finals in 1982. Kuwait first entered the Asian Cup of Nations in 1972 but has not entered the Women's World Cup.

F.I.F.A. RANKINGS:

December 1998: 24   January 1999: 49   December 1999: 82
January 2000: 82   December 2000: 74   May 2001: 70

KYRGYZSTAN

The Football Confederation of the Kyrgyz Republic was formed in 1992 and is affiliated to FIFA and the Asian Football Confederation. Kyrgyzstan has never qualified for the Olympic Games finals tournament. Kyrgyzstan first entered the World Cup in 1998. Kyrgyzstan first entered the Asian Cup of Nations in 1996 but has yet to enter the Women's World Cup.

F.I.F.A. RANKINGS:

December 1998: 151   January 1999: 150   December 1999: 159
January 2000: 159   December 2000: 174   May 2001: 164

LAOS

The Fédération Lao de Football was formed in 1951 and affiliated to FIFA in 1952. It affiliated to the Asian Football Confederation in 1968. Laos has never entered the Olympic Games nor the Women's World Cup.

F.I.F.A. RANKINGS:

December 1998: 144   January 1999: 151   December 1999: 156
January 2000: 156   December 2000: 165   May 2001: 171

LATVIA

The Latvian Football Confederation was formed in 1921. It became affiliated to FIFA in 1922 and reaffiliated in 1991. Latvia joined UEFA in 1992. It first entered the Olympic Games tournament in 1924 and the World Cup in 1938. Latvia first entered the European Championships in 1996, the Women's World Cup in 1995 and the European Championship for Women in 1995.

F.I.F.A. RANKINGS:

December 1998: 77   January 1999: 66   December 1999: 62
January 2000: 62   December 2000: 92   May 2001: 96

THE FOOTBALL FACT AND QUIZ BOOK

LEBANON

The Fédération Libanaise de Football-Association formed in 1933 and affiliated to FIFA in 1935. It affiliated to the Asian Football Confederation in 1964. Lebanon has never qualified for the finals tournament of the Olympic Games. Lebanon first entered the World Cup in 1994 and the Asian Cup of Nations in 1980, but has not entered the Women's World Cup.

F.I.F.A. RANKINGS:

December 1998: 85   January 1999: 102   December 1999: 111
January 2000: 111   December 2000: 110   May 2001: 111

LESOTHO

The Lesotho Football Association formed in 1932. It affiliated to FIFA in 1962 and the Confédération Africaine de Football in 1964. It first entered the Olympic Games tournament in 1980. Lesotho first entered the World Cup in 1974, and the Women's World Cup in 1999. It first entered the African Cup of Nations in 1974.

F.I.F.A. RANKINGS:

December 1998: 140   January 1999: 149   December 1999: 154
January 2000: 154   December 2000: 136   May 2001: 134

LIBERIA

The Liberia Football Association formed in 1936. It affiliated to FIFA and the Confédération Africaine de Football in 1962. Liberia first entered the Olympic Games tournament in 1964, and the World Cup in 1982. It has not entered the Women's World Cup. Liberia first entered the African Cup of Nations in 1968.

F.I.F.A. RANKINGS:

December 1998: 108   January 1999: 103   December 1999: 105
January 2000: 105   December 2000: 95   May 2001: 78

LIBYA

The Libyan Arab Football Confederation formed in 1962. It affiliated to FIFA in 1963 and the Confédération Africaine de Football in 1965. It first entered the Olympic Games tournament in 1968. Libya first entered the World Cup in 1970, but has not entered the Women's World Cup. It first entered the African Cup of Nations in 1968.

F.I.F.A. RANKINGS:

December 1998: 147   January 1999: 159   December 1999: 130
January 2000: 123   December 2000: 116   May 2001: 113

LIECHTENSTEIN

The Liechtenstein Fussball-Verband formed in 1934. It became affiliated to FIFA and UEFA in 1974. It has yet to enter the Women's World Cup or European Championship for Women. It first entered the European Championship in 1996 and the World Cup in 1998.

F.I.F.A. RANKINGS:

December 1998: 159   January 1999: 135   December 1999: 125
January 2000: 126   December 2000: 147   May 2001: 143

LITHUANIA

The Lithuanian Football Confederation formed in 1922. It was originally affiliated to FIFA in 1923 then reaffiliated in 1992. It also affiliated to UEFA in 1992. Lithunania first entered the World Cup in 1934 and the European Championship in 1996. It first entered the 1995 Women's World Cup.

F.I.F.A. RANKINGS:

December 1998: 54   January 1999: 48   December 1999: 50
January 2000: 51   December 2000: 85   May 2001: 92

LUXEMBOURG

The Fédération Luxembourgeoise de Football was formed in 1908. It was a founder member of UEFA in 1954 and affiliated to FIFA in 1908. Luxembourg first played in the Olympic Games finals tournament in 1920 and first entered the World Cup in 1934. Luxembourg first entered the European Championship in 1964. It has yet to enter the Women's World Cup and the European Championship for Women.

F.I.F.A. RANKINGS:

December 1998: 143   January 1999: 127   December 1999: 123
January 2000: 123   December 2000: 138   May 2001: 142

MACAO

The Associação de Futebol de Macau was formed in 1939 and affiliated to FIFA and the Asian Football Confederation in 1976. Macao has never qualified for the Olympic Games finals tournament. It has never entered the Women's World Cup. Macao entered the World Cup for the first time in 1982 and the Asian Cup of Nations in 1980.

F.I.F.A. RANKINGS:

December 1998: 174   January 1999: 168   December 1999: 176
January 2000: 176   December 2000: 179   May 2001: 181

MADAGASCAR

The Fédération Malagasy de Football formed in 1961. It affiliated to FIFA in 1962 and the Confédération Africaine de Football in 1963. Madagascar first entered the Olympic Games tournament in 1968. It first entered the World Cup in 1982 and Women's World Cup in 1999. It first entered the African Cup of Nations in 1972.

F.I.F.A. RANKINGS:

December 1998: 150   January 1999: 145   December 1999: 134
January 2000: 134   December 2000: 114   May 2001: 119

MALAWI

The Football Association of Malawi formed in 1966. It affiliated to FIFA in 1967 and the Confédération Africaine de Football in 1968. Malawi first entered the Olympic Games tournament in 1972. It first entered the World Cup in 1978 but has yet to enter the Women's World Cup. It first entered the African Cup of Nations in 1976.

F.I.F.A. RANKINGS:

December 1998: 89   January 1999: 98   December 1999: 114
January 2000: 114   December 2000: 113   May 2001: 119

MALAYSIA

The Football Association of Malaysia was formed in 1933 and affiliated to FIFA in 1956. It was a founder member of the Asian Football Confederation in 1954. Malaysia qualified for the Olympic Games finals tournament in 1972. It entered the 1991 Women's World Cup. Malaysia entered the World Cup for the first time in 1974 and the Asian Cup of Nations in 1956.

F.I.F.A. RANKINGS:

December 1998: 113   January 1999: 113   December 1999: 117
January 2000: 117   December 2000: 107   May 2001: 108

MALDIVES

The Football Association of Maldives formed in 1982 and affiliated to FIFA in 1986. It affiliated to the Asian Football Confederation in 1983. The Maldives entered the World Cup for the first time in 1998 and the Asian Cup of Nations in 1996.

F.I.F.A. RANKINGS:

December 1998: 166   January 1999: 165   December 1999: 143
January 2000: 144   December 2000: 154   May 2001: 147

MALI

The Fédération Malienne de Foot-Ball formed in 1960. It affiliated to FIFA in 1962 and to the Confédération Africaine de Football in 1963. Mali has never qualified for the Olympic Games finals tournament. It was runner-up in the African Cup of Nations in 1972.

F.I.F.A. RANKINGS:

December 1998: 70   January 1999: 79   December 1999: 71
January 2000: 70   December 2000: 98   May 2001: 105

MALTA

The Malta Football Association formed in 1900. It affiliated to FIFA in 1959 and to UEFA in 1960. It first entered the World Cup in 1974 and the European Championship in 1964. Malta first entered the Olympic Games tournament in 1960 but has not yet entered the Women's World Cup.

F.I.F.A. RANKINGS:

December 1998: 130   January 1999: 123   December 1999: 116
January 2000: 116   December 2000: 119   May 2001: 130

MAURITANIA

The Fédération de Foot-Ball de la République de Mauritainie formed in 1961. It affiliated to FIFA in 1964 and to the Confédération Africaine de Football in 1968. Mauritania first entered both the Olympic Games qualifying tournament and the African Cup of Nations in 1980. Mauritania first entered the World Cup in 1978.

F.I.F.A. RANKINGS:

December 1998: 142   January 1999: 147   December 1999: 160
January 2000: 160   December 2000: 161   May 2001: 168

MAURITIUS

The Mauritius Football Association formed in 1952. It affiliated to FIFA in 1962 and to the Confédération Africaine de Football in 1963. Mauritius first entered the Olympic Games tournament in 1976. It first entered the World Cup in 1974, but has yet to enter the Women's World Cup. It qualified for the finals tournament of the African Cup of Nations in 1974.

F.I.F.A. RANKINGS:

December 1998: 148   January 1999: 139   December 1999: 118
January 2000: 118   December 2000: 118   May 2001: 121

MEXICO

The Federacion Mexicana de Futbol formed in 1927 and affiliated to FIFA in 1929. Mexico was a founder member of the Confederacion Norte-Centroamerican y del Caribe de Futbol in 1961. Mexico first entered the World Cup in 1930 and were placed fourth in the 1968 Olympic Games tournament. Mexico first entered the Women's World Cup in 1991.

F.I.F.A. RANKINGS:

December 1998: 10   January 1999: 12   December 1999: 10
January 2000: 10   December 2000: 12   May 2001: 13

MOLDOVA

The Moldavian Football Association formed in 1991. It affiliated to FIFA and to UEFA in 1994. It first entered the World Cup in 1998 and the European Championship in 1996. Moldova has not yet entered the Women's World Cup.

F.I.F.A. RANKINGS:

December 1998: 116   January 1999: 107   December 1999: 93
January 2000: 93   December 2000: 94   May 2001: 102

MONGOLIA

The Football Federation of the Mongolian People's Republic affiliated to FIFA in 1998 and is also affiliated to the Asian Football Confederation.

F.I.F.A. RANKINGS:

December 1998: 196   January 1999: 195   December 1999: 198
January 2000: 198   December 2000: 196   May 2001: 186

MONTSERRAT

The Montserrat Football Association affiliated to FIFA and to the Confederacion Norte-Centroamerican y del Caribe de Futbol in 1996.

F.I.F.A. RANKINGS:

December 1998: n/a   January 1999: n/a   December 1999: 200
January 2000: 200   December 2000: 202   May 2001: 203

MOROCCO

The Fédération Royale Marocaine de Football formed in 1955 and affiliated to FIFA in 1956. Morocco affiliated to the Confédération Africaine de Football in 1966. Morocco first qualified for the Olympic Games finals tournament in 1964, and first entered the African Cup of Nations in 1970. Morocco first entered the World Cup in 1962 but has yet to enter the Women's World Cup.

F.I.F.A. RANKINGS:

December 1998: 13   January 1999: 19   December 1999: 24
January 2000: 25   December 2000: 28   May 2001: 26

MOZAMBIQUE

The Federacao Mocambicana de Futebol formed in 1975 and affiliated to FIFA and the Confédération Africaine de Football in 1978. Mozambique first entered the Olympic Games tournament in 1984. It first qualified for the finals tournament of the African Cup of Nations in 1986. Mozambique first entered the World Cup in 1982 and first entered the Women's World Cup in 1999.

F.I.F.A. RANKINGS:

December 1998: 80   January 1999: 87   December 1999: 71
January 2000: 74   December 2000: 112   May 2001: 115

MYANMAR

The Myanmar Football Confederation was formed in 1947 and affiliated to FIFA in 1957. It affiliated to the Asian Football Confederation in 1958. Myanmar qualified for the Olympic Games finals tournament in 1972 and were runners-up in the Asian Cup of Nations in 1968.

F.I.F.A. RANKINGS:

December 1998: 115   January 1999: 118   December 1999: 126
January 2000: 127   December 2000: 124   May 2001: 135

NAMIBIA

The Namibia Football Association formed in 1989 and affiliated to FIFA in 1992. Namibia affiliated to the Confédération Africaine de Football in 1990. Namibia first entered both the Olympic Games tournament and the African Cup of Nations in 1996. Namibia first entered the World Cup in 1994 and first entered the Women's World Cup in 1999.

F.I.F.A. RANKINGS:
December 1998: 69   January 1999: 81   December 1999: 80
January 2000: 81   December 2000: 87   May 2001: 87

NEPAL

The All-Nepal Football Association formed in 1951 and affiliated to FIFA in 1970. It affiliated to the Asian Football Confederation in 1971. Nepal has never qualified for the Olympic Games finals tournament and has never entered the Women's World Cup. Nepal first entered the World Cup in 1986 and first entered the Asian Cup of Nations in 1984.

F.I.F.A. RANKINGS:
December 1998:176   January 1999: 164   December 1999: 157
January 2000: 157   December 2000: 166   May 2001: 156

NETHERLANDS

The Koninklijke Nederlandsche Voetbalbond formed in 1889. The Netherlands became affiliated to FIFA in 1904, one of its founder members, and was also a founder member of UEFA in 1954. The Netherlands were placed third in the 1908 Olympic Games tournament. They first qualified for the World Cup finals in 1934 and for the European Championship finals tournament in 1980. The Netherlands first entered the Women's World Cup in 1991 and entered the first European Championship for Women.

F.I.F.A. RANKINGS:
December 1998: 11   January 1999: 8   December 1999: 19
January 2000: 19   December 2000: 8   May 2001: 8

NETHERLANDS ANTILLES

The NederlandsAntiliaanse Voetbal Unie formed in 1921 and affiliated to FIFA in 1932. Netherlands Antilles was a founder member of the Confederacion Norte-Centroamerican y del Caribe de Futbol in 1961. Netherlands Antilles reached the second round of the qualifying tournament for the World Cup in 1962.

F.I.F.A. RANKINGS:
December 1998: 156   January 1999: 161   December 1999: 167
January 2000: 167   December 2000: 175   May 2001: 178

NEW ZEALAND

The Football Association, Soccer New Zealand, was founded in 1891 and affiliated to FIFA in 1948. New Zealand affiliated to the Oceania Football Confederation in 1966. New Zealand has never qualified for the finals of the Olympic Games tournament. New Zealand first entered the Women's World Cup in 1991, having entered the World Cup in 1970.

F.I.F.A. RANKINGS:

December 1998: 103   January 1999: 100   December 1999: 100
January 2000: 100   December 2000: 90   May 2001: 97

NICARAGUA

The Federacion Nicaragüense de Futbol formed in 1931 and affiliated to FIFA in 1950. Nicaragua affiliated to the Confederacion Norte-Centroamerican y del Caribe de Futbol in 1968. Nicaragua entered the World Cup for the first time in 1994 but has yet to enter the Women's World Cup.

F.I.F.A. RANKINGS:

December 1998: 188   January 1999: 186   December 1999: 193
January 2000: 193   December 2000: 191   May 2001: 193

NIGER

The Fédération Nigerienne de Football formed in 1967 and affiliated to FIFA and the Confédération Africaine de Football the same year. Niger first entered the Olympic Games competition in 1968 but has not qualified for the finals tournament. It first entered the African Cup of Nations in 1970. Niger first entered the World Cup in 1978 but has yet to enter the Women's World Cup.

F.I.F.A. RANKINGS:

December 1998: 154   January 1999: 142   December 1999: 163
January 2000: 163   December 2000: 182   May 2001: 184

NIGERIA

The Nigeria Football Association formed in 1945 and affiliated to FIFA and the Confédération Africaine de Football in 1958. Nigeria won the Olympic Games title in 1996. It first won the African Cup of Nations in 1980. Nigeria reached the second round of the World Cup in 1994 and 1998, and entered the first Women's World Cup in 1991.

F.I.F.A. RANKINGS:

December 1998: 65   January 1999: 57   December 1999: 76
January 2000: 76   December 2000: 52   May 2001: 50

NORTHERN IRELAND

The Irish Football Association was formed in 1880 and affiliated to FIFA in 1911. Northern Ireland was a founder member of UEFA in 1954. Northern Ireland first entered the World Cup in 1950, and the European Championship in 1964. Northern Ireland entered the first European Championship for Women in 1984.

F.I.F.A. RANKINGS:
December 1998: 86   January 1999: 67   December 1999: 84
January 2000: 83   December 2000: 93   May 2001: 101

NORWAY

The Norges Fotballforbund formed in 1902 and affiliated to FIFA in 1908. Norway was a founder member of UEFA in 1954. Norway won a bronze at the 1936 Olympic Games tournament, and first entered the World Cup in 1938. It reached the first round of the 1960 and 1964 European Championships. Norway hosted the 1987 European Championship for Women and competed in the first Women's World Cup in 1991.

F.I.F.A. RANKINGS:
December 1998: 14   January 1999: 13   December 1999: 7
January 2000: 7   December 2000: 14   May 2001: 17

OMAN

The Oman Football Association formed in 1978 and affiliated to FIFA in 1980. It affiliated to the Asian Football Confederation in 1979. Oman has never qualified for the Olympic Games finals tournament and has never entered the Women's World Cup. Oman first entered the World Cup in 1990.

F.I.F.A. RANKINGS:
December 1998: 58   January 1999: 85   December 1999: 92
January 2000: 92   December 2000: 106   May 2001: 94

PAKISTAN

The Pakistan Football Association formed in 1948 and affiliated to FIFA the same year. It affiliated to the Asian Football Confederation in 1960. Pakistan has never entered the Women's World Cup, but first entered the World Cup in 1990 and the Asian Cup of Nations in 1960.

F.I.F.A. RANKINGS:
December 1998: 168   January 1999: 176   December 1999: 179
January 2000: 179   December 2000: 190   May 2001: 192

PALESTINE

The Palestine Football Association affiliated to FIFA and to the Asian Football Confederation in 1998. Palestine first entered the Asian Cup of Nations in 2000.

F.I.F.A. RANKINGS:

December 1998: 184   January 1999: 188   December 1999: 170
January 2000: 170   December 2000: 171   May 2001: 149

PANAMA

The Federacion Panamena de Futbol formed in 1937 and affiliated to FIFA in 1938. Panama was a founder member of the Confederacion Norte-Centroamerican y del Caribe de Futbol in 1961. Panama first entered the World Cup in 1994 and reached the qualifying tournament second round at the 1992 Olympic Games.

F.I.F.A. RANKINGS:

December 1998: 131   January 1999: 133   December 1999: 138
January 2000: 138   December 2000: 121   May 2001: 124

PAPUA NEW GUINEA

The Papua New Guinea Football (Soccer) Association was founded in 1962 and affiliated to FIFA and the Oceania Football Confederation in 1963. Papua New Guinea reached the first round of the qualifying tournament of the 1992 Olympic Games. Papua New Guinea first entered the Women's World Cup in 1991, and the World Cup in 1998.

F.I.F.A. RANKINGS:

December 1998: 172   January 1999: 174   December 1999: 183
January 2000: 183   December 2000: 192   May 2001: 195

PARAGUAY

The Liga Paraguaya de Futbol was formed in 1906 and affiliated to FIFA and the Confederacion Sudamericana de Futbol in 1921. Paraguay were quarter-finalists at the 1992 Olympic Games tournament and entered the first World Cup in 1930. Paraguay first entered the Women's World Cup in 1999.

F.I.F.A. RANKINGS:

December 1998: 25   January 1999: 22   December 1999: 17
January 2000: 17   December 2000: 9   May 2001: 10

PERU

The Federacion Peruana de Futbol was formed in 1922 and affiliated to FIFA in 1944. Peru affiliated to the Confederacion Sudamericana de Futbol in 1926. Peru reached the quarter-finals of the 1970 World Cup, and first entered the Women's World Cup in 1999.

F.I.F.A. RANKINGS:
December 1998: 72   January 1999: 62   December 1999: 42
January 2000: 42   December 2000: 45   May 2001: 51

PHILIPPINES

The Philippine Football Confederation formed in 1907 and affiliated to FIFA in 1928. It affiliated to the Asian Football Confederation in 1954. The Philippines have never qualified for the finals tournament of the Olympic Games and first entered the Women's World Cup in 1999 but failed to qualify for the finals tournament. The Philippines first entered the World Cup in 1998 and the Asian Cup of Nations in 1956.

F.I.F.A. RANKINGS:
December 1998: 175   January 1999: 177   December 1999: 181
January 2000: 181   December 2000: 179   May 2001: 177

POLAND

The Fédération Polonaise de Football was formed in 1919. It was a founder member of UEFA in 1954 and affiliated to FIFA in 1923. Poland won the 1972 Olympic Games tournament and first entered the World Cup in 1934. Poland first entered the Women's World Cup in 1991 but failed to qualify for the finals tournament. Poland first entered the European Championship for Women in 1991 but again failed to qualify for the finals tournament.

F.I.F.A. RANKINGS:
December 1998: 31   January 1999: 29   December 1999: 32
January 2000: 32   December 2000: 43   May 2001: 23

PORTUGAL

The Federação Portuguesa de Futebol was founded in 1914. It was affiliated to FIFA in 1923 and a founder member of UEFA in 1954. Portugal first entered the Olympic Games tournament in 1928 and first entered the World Cup in 1934. Portugal first entered the Women's World Cup in 1995 but failed to qualify for the finals tournament. Portugal first entered the European Championship in 1960 and the European Championship for Women in 1995.

F.I.F.A. RANKINGS:
December 1998: 36   January 1999: 17   December 1999: 15
January 2000: 15   December 2000: 6   May 2001: 5

PUERTO RICO

The Federaccion Puertorriqueña de Futbol formed in 1940 and affiliated to FIFA and the Confederacion Norte-Centroamerican y del Caribe de Futbol in 1960. Puerto Rico first entered the World Cup in 1974 and the Women's World Cup in 1999.

F.I.F.A. RANKINGS:
December 1998: 182   January 1999: 178   December 1999: 186
January 2000: 186   December 2000: 195   May 2001: 197

QATAR

The Qatar Football Association formed in 1960 and affiliated to FIFA in 1970. It affiliated to the Asian Football Confederation in 1972. Qatar first qualified for the finals tournament of the Olympic Games in 1984 and first entered the World Cup in 1978. It first entered the Asian Cup of Nations in 1976.

F.I.F.A. RANKINGS:
December 1998: 60   January 1999: 73   December 1999: 107
January 2000: 107   December 2000: 102   May 2001: 85

ROMANIA

The Fédération Roumaine de Football formed in 1909. It was affiliated to FIFA in 1930 and a founder member of UEFA in 1954. Romania first entered the Olympic Games tournament in 1924 and first entered the World Cup in 1930. Romania first entered the Women's World Cup in 1995 but failed to qualify for the finals tournament. Romania first entered the European Championship in 1960 and the European Championship for Women in 1993.

F.I.F.A. RANKINGS:
December 1998: 12   January 1999: 10   December 1999: 8
January 2000: 8   December 2000: 13   May 2001: 12

RUSSIA

The Football Union of Russia formed in 1912 and was affiliated to FIFA in the same year. It was a founder member of UEFA in 1954. Russia first entered the Olympic Games tournament in 1912 and first entered the World Cup as an independent state in 1998. Russia first entered the European Championship as an independent state in 1996. Russia first entered the Women's World Cup in 1995 and qualified for the finals tournament in 1999. Russia first entered the European Championship for Women in 1995, reaching the quarter-final stage.

F.I.F.A. RANKINGS:
December 1998: 40   January 1999: 30   December 1999: 18
January 2000: 18   December 2000: 21   May 2001: 18

RWANDA

The Fédération Rwandaise de Football Amateur formed in 1972 and affiliated to FIFA and the Confédération Africaine de Football in 1976. Rwanda first entered the Olympic Games competition in 1988 but has not qualified for the finals tournament. It first entered the African Cup of Nations in 1982. Rwanda first entered the World Cup in 1998.

F.I.F.A. RANKINGS:

December 1998: 170   January 1999: 173   December 1999: 145
January 2000: 146   December 2000: 128   May 2001: 136

ST. KITTS & NEVIS

The St. Kitts-Nevis Amateur Football Association formed in 1932 and affiliated to FIFA and to the Confederacion Norte-Centroamerican y del Caribe de Futbol in 1992. St. Kitts & Nevis first entered the World Cup in 1998.

F.I.F.A. RANKINGS:

December 1998: 132   January 1999: 137   December 1999: 137
January 2000: 137   December 2000: 145   May 2001: 150

ST. LUCIA

The St. Lucia Football Association formed in 1979 and affiliated to FIFA and to the Confederacion Norte-Centroamerican y del Caribe de Futbol in 1988. St. Lucia first entered the World Cup in 1998. It has never qualified for the finals tournament of the Olympic Games.

F.I.F.A. RANKINGS:

December 1998: 139   January 1999: 142   December 1999: 151
January 2000: 138   December 2000: 135   May 2001: 127

ST. VINCENT/GRENADINES

The St. Vincent and the Grenadines Football Confederation formed in 1979 and affiliated to FIFA and the Confederacion Norte-Centroamerican y del Caribe de Futbol in 1988. St. Vincent and the Grenadines reached the qualifying tournament second round of the 1998 World Cup.

F.I.F.A. RANKINGS:

December 1998: 138   January 1999: 132   December 1999: 141
January 2000: 142   December 2000: 127   May 2001: 126

SAMOA

The Samoa Football (Soccer) Association was founded in 1968 and affiliated to FIFA and the Oceania Football Confederation in 1986. Samoa did not qualify for the 1999 Women's World Cup finals tournament and first entered the World Cup in 1998.

F.I.F.A. RANKINGS:

December 1998: 164   January 1999: 172   December 1999: 179
January 2000: 179   December 2000: 173   May 2001: 172

SAN MARINO

The Federazione Sammarinese Giuoco Calcio was formed in 1831 and affiliated to FIFA and UEFA in 1988. San Marino first entered the Olympic Games tournament in 1992 and the World Cup in 1994. It first entered the European Championship in 1992.

F.I.F.A. RANKINGS:

December 1998: 179   January 1999: 153   December 1999: 149
January 2000: 151   December 2000: 168   May 2001: 165

SAO TOMÉ E PRINCIPE

The Federação Santomense de Futebol formed in 1975 and affiliated to FIFA and the Confédération Africaine de Football in 1986.

F.I.F.A. RANKINGS:

December 1998: 194   January 1999: 192   December 1999: 187
January 2000: 187   December 2000: 181   May 2001: 183

SAUDI ARABIA

The Saudi Arabian Football Confederation formed in 1959 and affiliated to FIFA in the same year. It affiliated to the Asian Football Confederation in 1972. Saudi Arabia first qualified for the finals tournament of the Olympic Games in 1984 and first entered the World Cup in 1978. It first won the Asian Cup of Nations in 1984.

F.I.F.A. RANKINGS:

December 1998: 30   January 1999: 36   December 1999: 38
January 2000: 39   December 2000: 36   May 2001: 28

SCOTLAND

The Scottish Football Association was founded in 1873. Scotland affiliated to FIFA in 1910 and was a founder member of UEFA in 1954. Scotland first entered the World Cup in 1950 and the European Championships in 1968. Scotland has never qualified for the finals tournament of the Women's World Cup and first entered the European Championship for Women in 1984.

F.I.F.A. RANKINGS:

December 1998: 38   January 1999: 26   December 1999: 20
January 2000: 20   December 2000: 25   May 2001: 24

SENEGAL

The Fédération Sénégalaise de Football formed in 1960 and affiliated to FIFA in 1962. It affiliated to the Confédération Africaine de Football in 1963. Senegal first entered the Olympic Games in 1972 but has not qualified for the finals tournament. It first entered the African Cup of Nations in 1965. Senegal first entered the World Cup in 1970.

F.I.F.A. RANKINGS:

December 1998: 95   January 1999: 88   December 1999: 79
January 2000: 79   December 2000: 88   May 2001: 76

SEYCHELLES

The Seychelles Football Confederation formed in 1979 and affiliated to FIFA and the Confédération Africaine de Football in 1986. The Seychelles first entered the African Cup of Nations in 1990.

F.I.F.A. RANKINGS:

December 1998: 181   January 1999: 183
December 1999: 192
January 2000: 192   December 2000: 188
May 2001: 189

SIERRA LEONE

The Sierra Leone Football Association formed in 1923 and affiliated to FIFA and the Confédération Africaine de Football in 1967. Sierra Leone first entered the Olympic Games competition in 1980 but has not qualified for the finals tournament. It first qualified for the finals tournament of the African Cup of Nations in 1994. Sierra Leone first entered the World Cup in 1974.

F.I.F.A. RANKINGS:
December 1998: 111   January 1999: 104   December 1999: 120
January 2000: 121   December 2000: 129   May 2001: 131

SINGAPORE

The Football Association of Singapore formed in 1892 and affiliated to FIFA in 1952. It was a founder member of the Asian Football Confederation in 1954. Singapore has never qualified for the finals tournament of the Olympic Games. It first entered the World Cup in 1978. It first entered the Asian Cup of Nations in 1960, and also entered the Women's World Cup in 1991.

F.I.F.A. RANKINGS:
December 1998: 81   January 1999: 94   December 1999: 104
January 2000: 104   December 2000: 101   May 2001: 107

SLOVAKIA

The Slovak Football Association was founded in 1993. Slovakia affiliated to FIFA in 1994 and to UEFA in 1993. Slovakia first entered the World Cup in 1998 and the European Championships in 1996. Slovakia first entered the Women's World Cup in 1995 but has never qualified for the finals tournament. It first entered the European Championship for Women in 1996.

F.I.F.A. RANKINGS:
December 1998: 32   January 1999: 24   December 1999: 21
January 2000: 21   December 2000: 24   May 2001: 25

SLOVENIA

The Football Association of Slovenia was founded in 1920. Slovenia affiliated to FIFA in 1992 and to UEFA in 1993. Slovenia first entered the World Cup in 1998 and the European Championships in 1996. Slovenia first entered the Women's World Cup in 1995 but has never qualified for the finals tournament. It first entered the European Championship for Women in 1995 but lost all six matches.

F.I.F.A. RANKINGS:
December 1998: 88   January 1999: 80   December 1999: 40
January 2000: 40   December 2000: 35   May 2001: 38

SOLOMON ISLANDS

Solomon Islands Football Confederation was founded in 1978 and affiliated to FIFA and the Oceania Football Confederation in 1988. Solomon Islands first entered the World Cup in 1994.

F.I.F.A. RANKINGS:

December 1998: 128   January 1999: 134   December 1999: 144
January 2000: 145   December 2000: 130   May 2001: 138

SOMALIA

Somali Football Confederation formed in 1951 and affiliated to FIFA in 1960. Somalia affiliated to the Confédération Africaine de Football in 1968. Somalia first entered the Olympic Games in 1992. It first entered the African Cup of Nations in 1974. Somalia first entered the World Cup in 1982.

F.I.F.A. RANKINGS:

December 1998: 190   January 1999: 193   December 1999: 197
January 2000: 197   December 2000: 194   May 2001: 196

SOUTH AFRICA

South African Football Association formed in 1892 and affiliated to FIFA in 1910. South Africa affiliated to the Confédération Africaine de Football in 1957. South Africa first entered the Olympic Games in 1962. It first competed in the African Cup of Nations in 1994. South Africa first entered the World Cup in 1994 and the Women's World Cup in 1995.

F.I.F.A. RANKINGS:

December 1998: 26   January 1999: 24   December 1999: 30
January 2000: 30   December 2000: 20   May 2001: 22

SPAIN

Real Federacion Espanyola de Futbol formed in 1913. Spain affiliated to FIFA in 1904 and was a founder member of UEFA in 1954. Spain first entered the World Cup in 1934 and won the European Championships in 1964. Spain has never qualified for the finals tournament of the Women's World Cup and first entered the European Championship for Women in 1987.

F.I.F.A. RANKINGS:

December 1998: 15   January 1999: 9   December 1999: 4
January 2000: 4   December 2000: 7   May 2001: 6

SRI LANKA

Football Confederation of Sri Lanka formed in 1939 and affiliated to FIFA in 1950. It affiliated to the Asian Football Confederation in 1958. Sri Lanka first entered the World Cup in 1994. It first entered the Asian Cup of Nations in 1980, and has yet to enter the Women's World Cup.

F.I.F.A. RANKINGS:

December 1998: 134   January 1999: 141   December 1999: 153
January 2000: 153   December 2000: 149   May 2001: 155

SUDAN

Sudan Football Association formed in 1936 and affiliated to FIFA in 1948. Sudan was a founder member of the Confédération Africaine de Football in 1957. Sudan were placed third in the African Cup of Nations in 1957. Sudan first entered the World Cup in 1958 but has yet to enter the Women's World Cup.

F.I.F.A. RANKINGS:

December 1998: 114   January 1999: 114   December 1999: 132
January 2000: 132   December 2000: 132   May 2001: 125

SURINAM

Surinaamse Voetbal Bond formed in 1920 and affiliated to FIFA in 1929. Surinam was a founder member of the Confederacion Norte-Centroamerican y del Caribe de Futbol in 1961. Surinam first entered the World Cup in 1962.

F.I.F.A. RANKINGS:

December 1998: 160   January 1999: 159   December 1999: 162
January 2000: 162   December 2000: 164   May 2001: 153

SWAZILAND

National Football Association of Swaziland formed in 1968 and affiliated to FIFA and the Confédération Africaine de Football in 1976. Swaziland first entered the African Cup of Nations in 1986. Swaziland first entered the World Cup in 1994 but has yet to enter the Women's World Cup.

F.I.F.A. RANKINGS:

December 1998: 149   January 1999: 152   December 1999: 127
January 2000: 128   December 2000: 137   May 2001: 129

SWEDEN

Svenska Fotbollförbundet formed in 1904. Sweden was a founder member of FIFA in 1904 and of UEFA in 1954. Sweden first entered the World Cup in 1934 and the European Championships in 1968. Sweden hosted the Women's World Cup in 1995. It first entered the European Championship for Women in 1984, winning the competition. Sweden won the 1948 Olympic Games tournament.

F.I.F.A. RANKINGS:
December 1998: 18   January 1999: 14   December 1999: 16
January 2000: 16   December 2000: 22   May 2001: 21

SWITZERLAND

Schweizerischer Fussball-Verband was founded in 1895. Switzerland was a founder member of FIFA in 1904 and was a founder member of UEFA in 1954. Switzerland first entered the World Cup in 1934 and the European Championships in 1964. Switzerland has never qualified for the finals tournament of the Women's World Cup and first entered the European Championship for Women in 1984. Switzerland were runners-up in the 1924 Olympic Games tournament.

F.I.F.A. RANKINGS:
December 1998: 83   January 1999: 65   December 1999: 47
January 2000: 48   December 2000: 57   May 2001: 58

SYRIA

Syrian Football Confederation formed in 1936 and affiliated to FIFA in 1937 and the Asian Football Confederation in 1970. Syria first entered the World Cup in 1950. It first entered the Asian Cup of Nations in 1980, and has yet to enter the Women's World Cup.

F.I.F.A. RANKINGS:
December 1998: 84   January 1999: 95   December 1999: 109
January 2000: 109   December 2000: 100   May 2001: 91

TAHITI

Fédération Tahitienne de Football was founded in 1989 and affiliated to FIFA and the Oceania Football Confederation in 1990. Tahiti first entered the World Cup in 1994 and the Women's World Cup in 1999.

F.I.F.A. RANKINGS:
December 1998: 123   January 1999: 128   December 1999: 139
January 2000: 140   December 2000: 131   May 2001: 137

TAJIKISTAN

Tajikistan Football Confederation formed in 1991 and affiliated to FIFA and the Asian Football Confederation in 1994. Tajikistan first entered the World Cup in 1998. It first entered the Asian Cup of Nations in 1996, and has yet to enter the Women's World Cup. Tajikistan has never qualified for the finals tournament of the Olympic Games.

F.I.F.A. RANKINGS:

December 1998: 120   January 1999: 125   December 1999: 119
January 2000: 120   December 2000: 134   May 2001: 139

TANZANIA

Football Association of Tanzania formed in 1930 and affiliated to FIFA in 1964 and the Confédération Africaine de Football in 1960. Tanzania first entered the African Cup of Nations in 1968. Tanzania first entered the World Cup in 1974 but has yet to enter the Women's World Cup. Tanzania first entered the Olympic Games in 1968.

F.I.F.A. RANKINGS:

December 1998: 118   January 1999: 115   December 1999: 127
January 2000: 128   December 2000: 140   May 2001: 146

THAILAND

Football Association of Thailand formed in 1916 and affiliated to FIFA in 1925 and the Asian Football Confederation in 1957. Thailand first entered the World Cup in 1974. It won third place at the Asian Cup of Nations in 1972, and entered the Women's World Cup in 1991.

F.I.F.A. RANKINGS:

December 1998: 45   January 1999: 69   December 1999: 60
January 2000: 60   December 2000: 61   May 2001: 62

TOGO

Fédération Togolaise de Football formed in 1960 and affiliated to FIFA in 1962 and the Confédération Africaine de Football in 1963. Togo first entered the African Cup of Nations in 1968. Togo first entered the World Cup in 1974 but has yet to qualify for the Women's World Cup. Togo first entered the Olympic Games in 1972.

F.I.F.A. RANKINGS:

December 1998: 68   January 1999: 72   December 1999: 87
January 2000: 87   December 2000: 81   May 2001: 80

TONGA

Tonga Football Association was founded in 1965 and affiliated to FIFA and the Oceania Football Confederation in 1994. Tonga first entered the World Cup in 1998 but has yet to enter the Women's World Cup.

F.I.F.A. RANKINGS:

December 1998: 163   January 1999: 170   December 1999: 177
January 2000: 177   December 2000: 185   May 2001: 176

TRINIDAD & TOBAGO

Trinidad and Tobago Football Association formed in 1908 and affiliated to FIFA in 1963. Trinidad and Tobago affiliated to the Confederacion Norte-Centroamerican y del Caribe de Futbol in 1964. Trinidad and Tobago first entered the World Cup in 1964, and the Women's World Cup in 1991. It has never qualified for the finals tournament of the Olympic Games.

F.I.F.A. RANKINGS:

December 1998: 51   January 1999: 68   December 1999: 43
January 2000: 43   December 2000: 29   May 2001: 35

TUNISIA

Fédération Tunisienne de Football formed in 1956 and affiliated to FIFA and the Confédération Africaine de Football in 1960. Tunisia first entered the African Cup of Nations in 1962. Tunisia first entered the World Cup in 1962 but has yet to enter the Women's World Cup. Tunisia first entered the Olympic Games in 1960.

F.I.F.A. RANKINGS:

December 1998: 21   January 1999: 28   December 1999: 31
January 2000: 28   December 2000: 26   May 2001: 31

TURKEY

Türkiye Futbol Federasyonu was founded in 1923 and affiliated to FIFA in the same year. Turkey affiliated to UEFA in 1962. It first entered the Olympic Games tournament in 1924 and the World Cup in 1950. Turkey first entered the European Championships in 1960. It has never entered the Women's World Cup or European Championship for Women.

F.I.F.A. RANKINGS:

December 1998: 57   January 1999: 42   December 1999: 29
January 2000: 30   December 2000: 30   May 2001: 29

TURKMENISTAN

Turkmenistan Football Confederation formed in 1992 and affiliated to FIFA and the Asian Football Confederation in 1994. Turkmenistan first entered the World Cup in 1998. It first entered the Asian Cup of Nations in 1996, and has yet to enter the Women's World Cup. Turkmenistan has never qualified for the finals tournament of the Olympic Games.

F.I.F.A. RANKINGS:

December 1998: 122   January 1999: 121   December 1999: 129
January 2000: 130   December 2000: 125   May 2001: 114

TURKS AND CAICOS ISLANDS

Football Association of Turks and Caicos affiliated to FIFA in 1998 and to the Confederacion Norte-Centroamerican y del Caribe de Futbol in 1998 as a full member.

F.I.F.A. RANKINGS:

December 1998: n/a   January 1999: n/a   December 1999: 196
January 2000: 196   December 2000: 200   May 2001: 200

UGANDA

Confederation of Uganda Football Associations formed in 1924 and affiliated to FIFA and the Confédération Africaine de Football in 1959. Uganda first entered the African Cup of Nations in 1962. Uganda first entered the World Cup in 1978 but has yet to enter the Women's World Cup. It first entered the Olympic Games in 1964 but has never qualified for the finals tournament.

F.I.F.A. RANKINGS:

December 1998: 105   January 1999: 105   December 1999: 108
January 2000: 108   December 2000: 102   May 2001: 108

UKRAINE

Football Confederation of Ukraine formed in 1991 and affiliated to FIFA in 1992. Ukraine affiliated to UEFA in 1993. It first entered the World Cup in 1998. Ukraine first entered the European Championships in 1996. It first entered the Women's World Cup in 1995 and the European Championship for Women the same year.

F.I.F.A. RANKINGS:

December 1998: 47   January 1999: 34   December 1999: 26
January 2000: 26   December 2000: 34   May 2001: 40

UNITED ARAB EMIRATES

United Arab Emirates Football Association formed in 1971 and affiliated to FIFA in 1972 and the Asian Football Confederation in 1974. United Arab Emirates first entered the World Cup in 1986. It first entered the Asian Cup of Nations in 1980 but has yet to enter the Women's World Cup. United Arab Emirates has never qualified for the finals tournament of the Olympic Games.

F.I.F.A. RANKINGS:

December 1998: 42   January 1999: 55   December 1999: 53

January 2000: 54   December 2000: 64
May 2001: 64

UNITED STATES

American Football Association formed in 1884 and was replaced in 1913 by the United States Soccer Confederation. It affiliated to FIFA in 1913. United States affiliated to the Confederacion Norte-Centroamerican y del Caribe de Futbol in 1961. United States first entered the World Cup in 1930 and the Women's World Cup in 1991, which it won. It hosted the 1904 Olympic Games where football was a demonstration sport.

F.I.F.A. RANKINGS:

December 1998: 23   January 1999: 23   December 1999: 22
January 2000: 22   December 2000: 16   May 2001: 15

URUGUAY

Asociacion Uruguaya de Futbol was formed in 1900 and affiliated to FIFA in 1923. Uruguay affiliated to the Confederacion Sudamericana de Futbol in 1916. Uruguay were winners at the 1924 Olympic Games and hosted and won the initial World Cup in 1930. Uruguay first entered the Women's World Cup in 1999. It entered the first Copa America in 1910.

F.I.F.A. RANKINGS:

December 1998: 76   January 1999: 63   December 1999: 45
January 2000: 46   December 2000: 32   May 2001: 33

US VIRGIN ISLANDS

Football Association is an associate member of the Confederacion Norte-Centroamerican y del Caribe de Futbol.

F.I.F.A. RANKINGS:

December 1998: n/a   January 1999: n/a   December 1999: 194
January 2000: 194   December 2000: 198   May 2001: 198

UZBEKISTAN

Uzbekistan Football Confederation formed in 1946 and affiliated to FIFA and the Asian Football Confederation in 1994. Uzbekistan first entered the World Cup in 1998. It first entered the Asian Cup of Nations in 1996, and first entered the Women's World Cup in 1999. Uzbekistan has never qualified for the finals tournament of the Olympic Games.

F.I.F.A. RANKINGS:

December 1998: 66   January 1999: 82   December 1999: 55
January 2000: 55   December 2000: 71   May 2001: 60

VANUATU

Vanuatu Football Confederation was founded in 1934 and affiliated to FIFA and the Oceania Football Confederation in 1988. Vanuatu first entered the World Cup in 1994 but has yet to enter the Women's World Cup or Olympic Games tournament.

F.I.F.A. RANKINGS:

December 1998: 177   January 1999: 179   December 1999: 184
January 2000: 184   December 2000: 167   May 2001: 173

VENEZUELA

Federacion Venezolana de Futbol was formed in 1926 and affiliated to FIFA and the Confederacion Sudamericana de Futbol in 1952. Venezuela has never qualified for the finals tournament of the Olympic Games and first entered the World Cup in 1966. Venezuela first entered the Women's World Cup in 1991.

F.I.F.A. RANKINGS:

December 1998: 129   January 1999: 126   December 1999: 110
January 2000: 110   December 2000: 111   May 2001: 112

THE FOOTBALL FACT AND QUIZ BOOK

VIETNAM SR

Vietnam Football Confederation formed in 1962 and affiliated to FIFA in 1964. It affiliated to the Asian Football Confederation in 1954 as South Vietnam. Vietnam first entered the World Cup in 1974 as South Vietnam, and as the unified country in 1994. It has yet to enter the Women's World Cup.

F.I.F.A. RANKINGS:

December 1998: 98   January 1999: 111   December 1999: 102
January 2000: 102   December 2000: 99   May 2001: 98

WALES

The Football Association of Wales was founded in 1876 and affiliated to FIFA in 1910. Wales was a founder member of UEFA in 1954. It first entered the World Cup in 1950. Wales first entered the European Championships in 1964. It has never qualified for the finals tournament of the Women's World Cup. Wales first entered the European Championship for Women 1995.

F.I.F.A. RANKINGS:

December 1998: 97   January 1999: 74   December 1999: 98
January 2000: 98   December 2000: 109   May 2001: 110

YEMEN

Yemen Football Association formed in 1962 and affiliated to FIFA and the Asian Football Confederation in 1980. Yemen first entered the World Cup in 1994. It first entered the Asian Cup of Nations in 1994 but has yet to enter the Women's World Cup. Yemen first entered the Olympic Games in 1992.

F.I.F.A. RANKINGS:

December 1998: 146   January 1999: 146   December 1999: 158
January 2000: 158   December 2000: 160   May 2001: 141

YUGOSLAVIA

Yugoslav Football Association was founded in 1919 and affiliated to FIFA in the same year. Yugoslavia was a founder member of UEFA in 1954. It first entered the Olympic Games tournament in 1920 and the World Cup in 1930. Yugoslavia first entered the European Championships in 1960. It has never qualified for the Women's World Cup.

F.I.F.A. RANKINGS:

December 1998: 6   January 1999: 16   December 1999: 13
January 2000: 13   December 2000: 9   May 2001: 11

ZAMBIA

Football Association of Zambia formed in 1929 and affiliated to FIFA and the Confédération Africaine de Football in 1964. Zambia first entered the African Cup of Nations in 1970. Zambia first entered the World Cup in 1970 and the Women's World Cup in 1991. It first qualified for the Olympic Games finals tournament in 1980 and reached the quarter-finals in 1988.

F.I.F.A. RANKINGS:

December 1998: 29   January 1999: 37   December 1999: 36
January 2000: 36   December 2000: 48   May 2001: 56

ZIMBABWE

Zimbabwe Football Association formed in 1965 and affiliated to FIFA in 1965. It affiliated to the Confédération Africaine de Football in 1980. Zimbabwe first entered the African Cup of Nations in 1982. Zimbabwe first entered the World Cup in 1970 as Rhodesia and the Women's World Cup in 1991.

F.I.F.A. RANKINGS:

December 1998: 74   January 1999: 75   December 1999: 67
January 2000: 67   December 2000: 68   May 2001: 65

BRITISH RECORDS

THE ENGLISH PREMIER LEAGUE

Highest Home Win
Manchester Utd 9   Ipswich 0   4 Mar 1995

Highest Away Win
Nottingham Forest 1   Manchester Utd 8   6 Feb 1999

Most League Goals Scored in a Season
97 goals in 38 games   Manchester Utd   1999/00

Most League Goals Conceded in a Season
100 goals in 42 games   Swindon Town   1993/94

Least League Goals Scored in a Season
28 goals in 38 games   Leeds United   1996/97

Least League Goals Conceded in a Season
17 goals in 38 games   Arsenal   1998/99

Most League Victories in a Season
28 wins in 38 games   Manchester Utd   1999/00

Least League Victories in a Season
5 wins in 42 games   Swindon Town   1993/94

THE ENGLISH PREMIER LEAGUE

Most League Defeats in a Season

29 defeats in 42 games   Swindon Town   1994/95

Least League Defeats in a Season

3 defeats in 38 games   Manchester Utd   1999/00
3 defeats in 38 games   Manchester Utd   1998/99
3 defeats in 38 games   Chelsea   1998/99

Most League Games Drawn in a Season

18 draws in 42 games   Manchester City   1993/94
18 draws in 42 games   Sheffield Utd   1993/94
18 draws in 42 games   Southampton   1994/95

Most League Goals Scored by One Player in a Season

Andy Cole scored 34 goals in 40 games for Newcastle Utd in the 1993/94 season.

Alan Shearer scored 34 goals in 42 games for Blackburn Rovers in the 1994/95 season.

Most Goals Scored by One Player in One Match

Andy Cole scored 5 goals for Manchester Utd against Ipswich on 4 March 1995.

Alan Shearer scored 5 goals for Newcastle Utd against Sheffield Wednesday on 19 September 1999.

DIVISION 1

Highest Home Wins

West Bromwich Albion 12   Darwen 0   4 Apr 1892

Nottingham Forest 12   Leicester Fosse 0   21 Apr 1909

Highest Away Wins

Newcastle 1   Sunderland 9   5 Dec 1908

Cardiff 1   Wolverhampton W 9   3 Sept 1955

Most League Goals Scored in a Season

128 goals in 42 games   Aston Villa   1930/31

Most League Goals Conceded in a Season

125 goals in 42 games   Blackpool   1930/31

Least League Goals Scored in a Season

24 goals in 42 games   Stoke City   1984/85

Least League Goals Conceded in a Season

16 goals in 42 games   Liverpool   1978/79

Most League Victories in a Season

31 wins in 42 games   Tottenham Hotspur 1960/61

Least League Victories in a Season

3 wins in 22 games   Stoke City   1889/90

3 wins in 38 games   Woolwich Arsenal   1912/13

3 wins in 42 games   Stoke City   1984/85

DIVISION 1

Most League Defeats in a Season

31 defeats in 42 games   Stoke City   1984/85

Least League Defeats in a Season

0 defeats in 22 games   Preston North End 1888/89
1 defeat in 38 games   Arsenal   1990/91
2 defeats in 40 games   Liverpool   1987/88
2 defeats in 42 games   Leeds Utd   1968/69

Most League Games Drawn in a Season

23 draws in 42 games   Norwich City   1978/79

Most League Goals Scored by One Player in a Season

Dixie Dean scored 60 goals in 39 games for Everton in the 1927/28 season.

Most Goals Scored by One Player in One Match

Ted Drake scored 7 goals for Arsenal against Aston Villa on 14 December 1935.

James Ross scored 7 goals for Preston North End against Stoke City on 6 October 1888.

DIVISION 2

Highest Home Win

Newcastle Utd 13   Newport County 0   5 Oct 1946

Highest Away Win

Burslem PV 0   Sheffield Utd 10   10 Dec 1892

Most League Goals Scored in a Season

122 goals in 42 games   Middlesbrough   1926/27

Most League Goals Conceded in a Season

141 goals in 34 games   Darwen   1898/89

Least League Goals Scored in a Season

24 goals in 42 games   Watford   1971/72
30 goals in 46 games   Leyton Orient   1994/95

Least League Goals Conceded in a Season

23 goals in 42 games   Manchester Utd   1924/25
34 goals in 46 games   West Ham Utd   1990/91

Most League Victories in a Season

32 wins in 42 games   Tottenham Hotspur 1919/20

DIVISION 2

Least League Victories in a Season

1 win in 34 games	Loughborough Tn.	1899/00
4 wins in 42 games	Cambridge Utd	1983/84

Most League Defeats in a Season

31 defeats in 42 games	Tranmere Rovers	1984/85
33 defeats in 46 games	Chester City	1992/93

Least League Defeats in a Season

0 defeats in 28 games	Liverpool	1893/94
2 defeats in 30 games	Burnley	1897/98
2 defeats in 38 games	Bristol City	1905/06
3 defeats in 42 games	Leeds Utd	1963/64
5 defeats in 46 games	Chelsea	1966/67

Most League Goals Scored by One Player in a Season

George Camsell scored 59 goals in 37 games for Middlesbrough in the 1926/27 season.

Most Goals Scored by One Player in One Match

Tommy Briggs scored 7 goals for Blackburn Rovers against Bristol Rovers on 5 February 1955.

Neville Coleman scored 7 goals for Stoke City against Lincoln City on 23 February 1957.

DIVISION 3

Highest Home Win
Gillingham 10   Chesterfield 0   5 Sept 1987

Highest Away Win
Halifax 0   Fulham 8   16 Sept 1969

Most League Goals Scored in a Season
111 goals in 46 games   QPR   1961/62

Most League Goals Conceded in a Season
123 goals in 46 games   Accrington Stanley 1959/60

Least League Goals Scored in a Season
27 goals in 46 games   Stockport County   1969/70

Least League Goals Conceded in a Season
20 goals in 46 games   Gillingham   1995/96

Most League Victories in a Season
32 wins in 46 games   Aston Villa   1971/72

Least League Victories in a Season
2 wins in 46 games   Rochdale   1973/74

Most League Defeats in a Season
34 defeats in 46 games   Doncaster Rovers   1997/98

Least League Defeats in a Season
5 defeats in 46 games   QPR   1966/67
5 defeats in 46 games   Bristol Rovers   1989/90
5 defeats in 46 games   Notts County   1997/98

DIVISION 3

Most League Games Drawn in a Season

| 23 draws in 46 games | Cardiff City | 1997/98 |
| 23 draws in 46 games | Hartlepool Utd | 1997/98 |

Most League Goals Scored by One Player in a Season
Derek Reeves scored 39 goals in 46 games for Southampton in the 1959/60 season.

Most Goals Scored by One Player in One Match
Steve Earle scored 5 goals for Fulham against Halifax Town on 16 September 1969.

Barry Thomas scored 5 goals for Scunthorpe Utd against Luton Town on 24 April 1965.

Keith East scored 5 goals for Swindon Town against Mansfield Town on 20 November 1965

Alf Wood scored 5 goals for Shrewsbury Town against Blackburn Rovers on 2 October 1971.

Tony Caldwell scored 5 goals for Bolton Wanderers against Walsall on 10 September 1983.

Andy Jones scored 5 goals for Port Vale against Newport County on 4 May 1987.

Steve Wilkinson scored 5 goals for Mansfield Town against Birmingham City on 3 April 1990.

DIVISION 3 (SOUTH)

Highest Home Win
Luton Town 12   Bristol Rovers 0   13 Apr 1936

Highest Away Win
Northampton Town 0   Walsall 8   2 Feb 1947

Most League Goals Scored in a Season
127 goals in 42 games   Millwall   1927/28

Most League Goals Conceded in a Season
135 goals in 42 games   Merthyr T   1929/30

Least League Goals Scored in a Season
33 goals in 46 games   Crystal Palace   1950/51

Least League Goals Conceded in a Season
21 goals in 42 games   Southampton   1921/22

Most League Victories in a Season
30 wins in 42 games   Millwall   1927/28
30 wins in 42 games   Plymouth Argyle   1929/30
30 wins in 42 games   Cardiff City   1946/47
30 wins in 46 games   Nottingham Forest   1950/51
30 wins in 46 games   Bristol City   1954/55

Least League Victories in a Season
6 wins in 42 games   Merthyr T   1929/30
6 wins in 42 games   QPR   1925/26

DIVISION 3 (SOUTH)

Most League Defeats in a Season

29 defeats in 42 games	Merthyr T	1924/25
29 defeats in 46 games	Walsall	1952/53
29 defeats in 46 games	Walsall	1953/54

Least League Defeats in a Season

4 defeats in 42 games	Southampton	1921/22
4 defeats in 42 games	Plymouth Argyle	1929/30

Most League Goals Scored by One Player in a Season

Joe Payne scored 55 goals in 39 games for Luton Town in the 1936/37 season.

Most Goals Scored by One Player in One Match

Joe Payne scored 10 goals for Luton Town against Bristol Rovers on 13 April 1936.

DIVISION 3 (NORTH)

Highest Home Win

Stockport County 13   Halifax 0   6 Jan 1934

Highest Away Win

Accrington Stanley 0   Barnsley 9   3 Feb 1934

Most League Goals Scored in a Season

Bradford City   128 goals in 42 games   1928/29

Most League Goals Conceded in a Season

136 goals in 42 games   Nelson   1927/28

Least League Goals Scored in a Season

32 goals in 42 games   Crewe Alexandra   1923/24

Least League Goals Conceded in a Season

21 goals in 46 games   Port Vale   1953/54

Most League Victories in a Season

33 wins in 42 games   Doncaster Rovers   1946/47

Least League Victories in a Season

4 wins in 40 games   Rochdale   1931/32

DIVISION 3 (NORTH)

Most League Defeats in a Season

33 defeats in 40 games	Rochdale	1931/32

Least League Defeats in a Season

3 defeats in 46 games	Port Vale	1953/54
3 defeats in 42 games	Doncaster Rovers	1946/47
3 defeats in 42 games	Wolverhampton W	1975/76

Most League Goals Scored by One Player in a Season

Ted Harston scored 55 goals in 41 games for Mansfield Town in the 1936/37 season.

Most Goals Scored by One Player in One Match

Bunny Bell scored 9 goals for Tranmere Rovers against Oldham Athletic on 26 December 1935.

Oldest Player

52-year-old Neil McBain played for New Brighton against Hartlepool United on 15 March 1947.

DIVISION 4

Highest Home Win

Oldham Athletic 11   Southport 0   26 Dec 1962

Highest Away Win

Crewe Alexandra 1 Rotherham Utd 8   8 Sept 1973

Most League Goals Scored in a Season

134 goals in 46 games   Peterborough Utd   1960/61

Most League Goals Conceded in a Season

109 goals in 46 games   Hartlepool Utd   1959/60

Least League Goals Scored in a Season

29 goals in 46 games   Crewe Alexandra   1981/82

Least League Goals Conceded in a Season

25 goals in 46 games   Lincoln City   1980/81

Most League Victories in a Season

32 wins in 46 games   Lincoln City   1975/76
32 wins in 46 games   Swindon Town   1985/86

DIVISION 4

Least League Victories in a Season

3 wins in 46 games   Southport   1976/77

Most League Defeats in a Season

33 defeats in 46 games   Newport County   1987/88

Least League Defeats in a Season

4 defeats in 46 games   Lincoln City   1975/76

4 defeats in 46 games   Sheffield Utd   1981/82

4 defeats in 46 games   Bournemouth   1981/82

Most League Games Drawn in a Season

23 draws in 46 games   Exeter City   1986/87

Most League Goals Scored by One Player in a Season

Terry Bly scored 52 goals in 46 games for Peterborough in the 1960/61 season.

Most Goals Scored by One Player in One Match

Bert Lister scored 6 goals for Oldham Athletic against Southport on 26 December 1962.

THE SCOTTISH PREMIER DIVISION

Highest Home Win

Aberdeen 8   Motherwell 0   26 Mar 1979

Highest Away Win

Hamilton Academical 0   Celtic 8   5 Nov 1988

Most League Goals Scored in a Season

101 goals in 44 games	Rangers	1991/92
96 goals in 36 games	Rangers	1999/00

Most League Goals Conceded in a Season

100 goals in 36 games	Morton	1984/85
100 goals in 44 games	Morton	1987/88

Least League Goals Scored in a Season

19 goals in 36 games	Hamilton A	1988/89
22 goals in 44 games	Dunfermline Ath	1991/92

Least League Goals Conceded in a Season

19 goals in 36 games	Rangers	1989/90
23 goals in 44 games	Rangers	1986/87
23 goals in 44 games	Celtic	1987/88

THE SCOTTISH PREMIER DIVISION

Most League Victories in a Season

27 wins in 36 games	Rangers	1995/96
27 wins in 36 games	Aberdeen	1984/85
33 wins in 44 games	Rangers	1991/92
33 wins in 44 games	Rangers	1992/93

Least League Victories in a Season

3 wins in 36 games	St Johnstone	1975/76
3 wins in 36 games	Kilmarnock	1982/83
3 wins in 44 games	Morton	1987/88

Most League Defeats in a Season

29 defeats in 36 games	Morton	1984/85

Least League Defeats in a Season

3 defeats in 36 games	Rangers	1995/96
3 defeats in 44 games	Celtic	1987/88

Most League Games Drawn in a Season

21 draws in 44 games	Aberdeen	1993/94

Most Goals Scored by One Player in One Match

Paul Sturrock scored 5 goals for Dundee Utd against Morton on 17 November 1984.

SCOTTISH DIVISION 1 (OLD)

Highest Home Win

Celtic 11   Dundee 0   26 Oct 1895

Highest Away Win

Airdrieonians 1   Hibernian 11   24 Oct 1950

Most League Goals Scored in a Season

132 goals in 34 games   Hearts   1957/58

Most League Goals Conceded in a Season

137 goals in 38 games   Leith Athletic   1931/32

Least League Goals Scored in a Season

30 goals in 44 games   Brechin City   1993/94

20 goals in 34 games   Ayr Utd   1966/67

Least League Goals Conceded in a Season

14 goals in 38 games   Celtic   1913/14

Most League Victories in a Season

35 wins in 42 games   Rangers   1920/21

Least League Victories in a Season

0 wins in 22 games   Vale of Leven   1891/92

SCOTTISH DIVISION 1 (OLD)

Most League Defeats in a Season

31 defeats in 42 games   St Mirren   1920/21

Least League Defeats in a Season

0 defeats in 18 games   Rangers   1898/99

1 defeat in 42 games   Rangers   1920/21

Most League Goals Scored by One Player in a Season

William McFadyen scored 52 goals in 34 games for Motherwell in the 1931/32 season.

Most Goals Scored by One Player in One Match

Jimmy McGrory scored 8 goals for Celtic against Dunfermline Athletic on 14 September 1928.

SCOTTISH DIVISION 2 (OLD)

Highest Home Win
Airdrieonians 15   Dundee Wanderers 1   1 Dec 1894

Highest Away Win
Alloa Athletic 0   Dundee 10   8 Mar 1947

Most League Goals Scored in a Season
142 goals in 34 games   Raith Rovers   1937/38

Most League Goals Conceded in a Season
146 goals in 38 games   Edinburgh City   1931/32

Least League Goals Scored in a Season
20 goals in 38 games   Lochgelly Utd   1923/24

Least League Goals Conceded in a Season
20 goals in 38 games   Morton   1966/67

Most League Victories in a Season
33 wins in 38 games   Morton   1966/67

Least League Victories in a Season
1 win in 22 games   East Stirlingshire   1905/06
1 win in 38 games   Forfar Athletic   1974/75

SCOTTISH DIVISION 2 (OLD)

Most League Defeats in a Season

30 defeats in 36 games	Brechin City	1962/63
30 defeats in 38 games	Lochgelly	1923/24

Least League Defeats in a Season

1 defeat in 36 games	Clyde	1956/57
1 defeat in 36 games	Morton	1962/63
1 defeat in 36 games	St Mirren	1967/68

Most League Goals Scored by One Player in a Season
Jim Smith scored 66 goals in 38 games for Ayr Utd in the 1927/28 season.

Most Goals Scored by One Player in One Match
Owen McNally scored 8 goals for Arthurlie against Armadale on 1 October 1927.

Jim Dyet scored 8 goals for King's Park against Forfar Athletic on 2 January 1930.

John Calder scored 8 goals for Morton against Raith Rovers on 18 April 1936.

Norman Hayward scored 8 goals for Raith Rovers against Brechin City on 20 August 1937.

SCOTTISH DIVISION 1 (NEW)

Most League Goals Scored in a Season

93 goals in 44 games   Dunfermline Ath   1993/94

92 goals in 39 games   Motherwell   1981/82

Most League Goals Conceded in a Season

99 goals in 39 games   Queen of the South   1988/89

109 goals in 44 games   Cowdenbeath   1992/93

Least League Goals Scored in a Season

18 goals in 39 games   Stirling Albion   1980/81

23 goals in 36 games   Dumbarton   1995/96

Least League Goals Conceded in a Season

23 goals in 36 games   St Johnstone   1996/97

24 goals in 39 games   Hibernian   1980/81

32 goals in 44 games   Falkirk   1993/94

Most League Victories in a Season

28 wins in 36 games   Hibernian   1998/99

Least League Victories in a Season

2 wins in 39 games   Queen of the South   1988/89

3 wins in 44 games   Cowdenbeath   1992/93

SCOTTISH DIVISION 1 (NEW)

Most League Defeats in a Season

29 defeats in 39 games	Queen of the South	1988/89
31 defeats in 36 games	Dumbarton	1995/96
34 defeats in 44 games	Cowdenbeath	1992/93

Least League Defeats in a Season

2 defeats in 26 games	Partick Thistle	1975/76
2 defeats in 39 games	St. Mirren	1976/77
4 defeats in 44 games	Raith Rovers	1992/93
4 defeats in 44 games	Falkirk	1993/94

Most League Games Drawn in a Season

21 draws in 44 games	East Fife	1986/87

SCOTTISH DIVISION 2 (NEW)

Most League Goals Scored in a Season
95 goals in 39 games   Ayr Utd   1987/88

Most League Goals Conceded in a Season
89 goals in 39 games   Meadowbank Th   1977/78

Least League Goals Scored in a Season
22 goals in 36 games   Brechin City   1994/95

Least League Goals Conceded in a Season
24 goals in 39 games   St Johnstone   1987/88
24 goals in 39 games   Stirling Albion   1990/91

Most League Victories in a Season
27 wins in 39 games   Forfar Athletic   1983/84
27 wins in 39 games   Ayr Utd   1987/88

Least League Victories in a Season
4 wins in 26 games   Forfar Athletic   1975/76
4 wins in 39 games   Stranraer   1987/88

Most League Defeats in a Season
29 defeats in 39 games   Berwick Rangers   1987/88

Least League Defeats in a Season
1 defeat in 26 games   Raith Rovers   1975/76
3 defeats in 26 games   Clydebank   1975/76
3 defeats in 39 games   Forfar Athletic   1983/84
3 defeats in 39 games   Raith Rovers   1986/87
3 defeats in 36 games   Livingston   1998/99

SCOTTISH DIVISION 3 (NEW)

Most League Goals Scored in a Season
78 goals in 36 games   Alloa   1997/98

Most League Goals Conceded in a Season
82 goals in 36 games   Albion Rovers   1994/95

Least League Goals Scored in a Season
26 goals in 36 games   Alloa   1995/96

Least League Goals Conceded in a Season
21 goals in 36 games   Brechin City   1995/96

Most League Victories in a Season
25 wins in 36 games   Forfar Athletic   1994/95

Least League Victories in a Season
5 wins in 36 games   Albion Rovers   1994/95

Most League Defeats in a Season
28 defeats in 36 games   Albion Rovers   1994/95

Least League Defeats in a Season
6 defeats in 36 games   Forfar Athletic   1994/95
6 defeats in 36 games   Inverness Town   1996/97

KICKING THEMSELVES IN THE MOUTH

THE FOOTBALL FACT AND QUIZ BOOK

Scunthorpe manager Brian Laws on Carlisle after they had three men sent off and their manager Ian Atkins ordered from the dugout:

"I almost had in my mind the thought they were deliberately trying to go down to seven men to try and get the game abandoned. But that probably reflects their club, their manager and their chairman - chaotic, hectic and indisciplined."

Brian Clough on whether Martin O'Neill could become as good as he was:

"No, that's being ridiculous!"

Peterborough boss Barry Fry after seeing his side lose against Wrexham:

"I spent a lot of time explaining to my defence what Wrexham striker Lee Trundle likes to do, but they obviously ignored me because he had a few practice shots before he finally grabbed the winner."

Hector Cuper, who is sick and tired of rumours about him moving to Barcelona, and also about his private life:

"Everything is rumours. I cannot continue to deny them. If tomorrow somebody says I am gay, everybody will think I am gay."

Chelsea's Danish winger Jesper Gronkjaer, who would love to see Jan Koller arrive at Stamford Bridge:

"I have met him a few times. One time with the national team and once with Anderlecht. He is a big player with even bigger feet."

Kilmarnock's Govan-born defender Martin Baker wasn't happy about his manager omitting him from the starting line-up against Celtic in the CIS Insurance Cup Final:

"At 2.10pm I wanted to punch him, but then I thought 'What is the point?'".

Andy Kilner, the Stockport County boss who returned home to find out that one of his players, Kevin Cooper, had left the club for Wimbledon:

"I think he's completed his move. Nobody's told me from here that it's happened but the lad left a message on my answerphone."

Oxford manager David Kemp defending one of his young players:

"Saying that Chris Hackett is going to elbow somebody is like accusing the Pope of murder."

Brian Clough on whether Terry Venables would stay at Middlesbrough at the end of the 2000-01 season:

"He says that he's going to go at the end of the season but he's a butterfly who has been known on the odd occasion to change his mind. Terry can be a bit like one of those fickle women, when he says no it's a definite maybe - probably."

Sir Alex Ferguson on Fabien Barthez:

"I know about Fabien's smoking. I was even aware of that before he joined us. He must think I don't know about it, but he's mistaken. In England, it's a rare thing to see a player smoking, but, all in all, I prefer that to an alcoholic."

Bayern Munich manager Ottmar Hitzfeld on his team's Champions' League visit to Moscow:

"Whatever a cross-country skier can do, a player from Bayern Munich can do with a laugh on his face. We are taking warm underwear, liver protectors, gloves, woolly hats and Vaseline. That's enough!"

Coventry City's John Hartson on his gambling habit:

"It got to the point where I owed one bookie £65,000, another £40,000 and a third £25,000. To be honest, I don't know how much I've lost over the years - I haven't got a clue. Thankfully my debts never got to what I would call crazy money - like £500,000. But the bookies would have let me get into that much debt because of the money I was earning."

West Ham defender Christian Dailly on the last few minutes of a West Ham v Manchester Utd FA Cup match:

"There's Cole, Yorke, Sheringham and Solskjaer swarming all over us, plus Giggs and Keane. We are trying to make sure they are all marked when one of the lads shouts out 'Who's picking up the keeper in midfield?'"

Following Birmingham's 4-1 win over Ipswich Town to reach the Worthington Cup Final, Martin Grainger exclaimed:

"I have never been kissed by so many men in my life!"

Samuel Cabellero was all set for a move to Serie A, when Verona president Giambattista Pastorello pulled the plug on the deal, citing backlash from racist fans as the reason they didn't secure his signature:
"We are all equal in the eyes of God, and anyway people must know that coloured people are the best equipped at sport."

German international Sebastian Deisler on the problems of fame and attracting women:
"I surely have become more suspicious. Several people think that I have become arrogant now but I'm well aware of my present situation. If I get to know women I always ask myself if they are interested in me as a person or the famous football player."

Chelsea chairman Ken Bates on the Minister for Sport Kate Hoey, after she ranked 11th in a poll of Top Women in Sport:
"In 11th place on the list was our Minister for Sport Kate Hoey - I would hate to meet the girl who came 12th on a dark night."

Bradford City manager Jim Jefferies on Arsenal youngster Isiah Rankin:
"Rankin couldn't finish a bowl of cornflakes!"

Scunthorpe boss Brian Laws on the decision to call off an FA Cup match against Burnley:
"I've seen harder pitches in August. The referee said he called it off because of what might happen. If he's got that kind of foresight I want him to pick my lottery numbers."

West Ham boss Harry Redknapp deciding not to pursue the Greek striker Zizis Vryas from Perugia:
"That's the boy from the kebab shop - and he can't get off on Saturdays!"

Middlesbrough's Christian Karembeu on his one problem with English life:
"The only thing that bothers me is the way people seem to be against the French beef at the moment!"

Newcastle manager Bobby Robson after Nolberto Solano was dismissed for handling the ball on the line:
"I'd like to smash the ball at the referee and see if he can get out of the way."

Exeter manager Noel Blake about on-loan player Carl Hutchings:
"I don't ever want to set eyes on him again. He's walked out on the football club, and as far as I'm concerned, it's good riddance. I wouldn't give him the time of day - that's how I feel about it. He was like a tortoise in training. He wasn't walking, never mind running. People like him are robbing the profession because all he was interested in was picking up his wages."

Liverpool keeper Sander Westerveld on the conditions during a Boxing Day match at Middlesbrough:
"The pitch at the Riverside had a lot of ice on it. My feet and gloves were soaking and it was unbelievably cold. It doesn't seem that Middlesbrough have undersoil heating, which is a pity, because on occasions you'd see the ball with ice stuck to it."

Tranmere defender Dave Challinor on how he broke his leg:
"It wasn't the kick that was responsible for the injury, it was the way he landed on top of me and twisted my leg that made it snap. The slippery conditions probably had something to do with it too."

Leeds Utd chairman Peter Risdale on reports linking his club to making an offer for Liverpool's Robbie Fowler:
"There's more chance of us signing Father Christmas than Robbie Fowler."

Dennis Bergkamp on how some football terms get a little confused in translation:
"My goals in Holland were known as 'stiffies', which means something quite different in England of course."

Gary Blumberg, Lucas Radebe's agent, getting confused about the meaning of 'a one club man':
"Lucas has always been a one club person. He proved that in South Africa with Kaizer Chiefs and he's only ever played for Leeds Utd in England."

Blackpool manager Steve McMahon about his relationship with chairman Karl Oyston and the club finances:
"I can't even get a plate of sandwiches for the manager's room after the game let alone sign a player. It is absolutely frightening."

Tottenham's David Pleat on Sergei Rebrov:
"Sergei is a very talented player waiting to explode."

66

Former Tottenham chairman Alan Sugar about Chelsea:
"It's like looking at a winelist when you look at their team sheet."

Stuart Pearce on Paolo Di Canio:
"Paolo can be a geezer, but he can also be a fruitcake."

Ron Atkinson on Panathinaikos defender Rene Henriksen after being outpaced by Manchester Utd's Teddy Sheringham:
"I tell you something though - he's deceptive. He must be lightning slow."

Rangers Bert Konterman expresses his footballing beliefs:
"Sometimes you think the devil is playing games with your squad to stop you getting the ball in the net."

Fabien Barthez on his footballing celebrations:
"I will always remember the way that I got plastered after the Euro final. That will go down in history."

Bayern Munich General Manager Uli Hoeness:
"I'm here to talk about sausages not Christophe Daum."

Italian coach Giovanni Trapattoni suggesting that Paolo Di Canio is a little down the pecking order for a place in the Italy side:
"It would take a bubonic plague for Di Canio to get into the side."

Former Middlesbrough star Mikkel Beck on how rumours can get to people:
"One team-mate would not get undressed in the changing-room because he thought I was gay. I can take a lot of things, but these rumours got to me."

Arsene Wenger on how his players deal with the cold:
"I must admit that they are not happy...but we will give them some vodka before the game!"

Former Southampton player Patrik Colleter on saying farewells:
"Sadly I didn't have a chance to say goodbye to Glenn Hoddle. In a way it's better or I would have told him exactly what I think about him."

Rangers manager Dick Advocaat on two-faced journalists:
"The players are behind me, but it is a different story as far as the media are concerned. One week you are seen as king, the next week as a pastry chef!"

99

THE FOOTBALL FACT AND QUIZ BOOK

Tottenham defender Ben Thatcher, speaking before his red card in a game against Sunderland:
"I've worked on my discipline all season, and have only had two bookings. Hopefully I'll keep my nose clean again on Saturday."

Real Oviedo coach Radomir Antic about signing Stan Collymore:
"I think the club will conclude a financial deal with Collymore, but his lawyers have asked for a little more time to study some of the details. He could be the best signing ever made by Oviedo."

Stan Collymore before his expected debut for Real Oviedo:
"I'm coming to Oviedo to improve as a footballer; - physically, I'm ready."

Oviedo coach Raddy Antic on why Collymore was left out of the squad that travelled to Real Zaragoza:
"Stan has been left out of the squad because he has a long way to go to get in shape."

Stan Collymore on his reasons for leaving the game:
"To explore interests outside football."

Stuart Pearce talking about Alan Shearer's physique:
"I told him that he's so fat it was very difficult to get the ball with this big fat backside in your face."

Middlesbrough's Hamilton Ricard on trying to get a full game out of Bryan Robson:
"We play, we lose. Hamil come off, Hamil no score. I am not happy here."

Newcastle's Bobby Robson on his transfer philosophy:
"I did not want to sign Clarence Acuna, but he is such a good player he forced me to do so."

Jose Luis Chilavert on his animosity towards Martin Palermo:
"I never greet a person who dresses up as a woman."

Jose Luis Chilavert responding to criticisms from Maradona:
"Even the number one drug addict of Argentina talks about me from Cuba, that means I am a very important person."

Jose Luis Chilavert on the world's paparazzi:
"Journalists are racist and discriminate against me because of my success in my career."

Luton's Ricky Hill on new signing Rocky Baptiste:
"People have likened him to Kanu, he's got nice feet, nice technique. He's slim and deceptively tall!"

Roy Hodgson on hearing that he was 10-1 for the England manager's job:
"If my odds come down to evens though, I might put a bet on myself."

Colin Hutchinson after hearing rumours of interest in Marcel Desailly:
"Marcel is very happy at Chelsea, he recently signed a new deal and we have had no contact whatsoever from PSG and if we did they would get a two word answer."

Paul Jewell, when at Sheffield Wednesday, following rumours of Gerald Sibon's walk-out:
"He didn't storm out of the ground - he's not that quick."

Terry Butcher about playing with Tony Adams:
"There was certainly a few tigers caged and a few doors slammed."

Claus Jorgenson after hearing of interest in him from Aston Villa:
"I saw something in one of the Sunday newspapers, and although it is probably just a rumour, I have cut it out and will keep it."

Marcello Lippi's uncannily prophetic post-match comment:
"If I was Inter's president, I would fire the coach and I would take all the players and kick them up the arse."

Paul Jewell on youth policy:
"I'm putting out the Grange Hill XI, we're thinking of applying for an early kick-off so they won't miss their bedtimes."

Sir Alex Ferguson's views on retirement:
"I want to stay active - I don't want to sit in a chair with a pipe and slippers because then you just fade away."

THE FOOTBALL FACT AND QUIZ BOOK

Walsall keeper Jimmy Walker discussing team-mate Brett Angell:
"Believe me, if whingeing was an Olympic sport he would be heading for
Sydney next week with a real chance of striking gold."

Rudi Voller on Michael Owen:
"He is a better striker than I ever was, that's for sure."

Rotherham manager Ronnie Moore was surprised by Leo Fortune-West's
loyalty to his club:
"It's unusual for footballers to do that because sometimes you think they
would sell their own mother for a tenner."

Mark Bosnich on his treatment by Sir Alex Ferguson:
"I'd rather die on my feet than live on my
knees."

Ken Bates' on his continuing feud with Villa
boss John Gregory:
"John is a very well balanced individual, he
has a chip on both shoulders."

Newcastle's Nikos Dabizas on his hobbies:
"I go to the cinema. I don't always
understand what's going on but I laugh
along with the rest of the audience
anyway."

Steve Claridge on the appointment of new
Palace manager Alan Smith:
"I can't understand why they've given the job to Smith. He certainly wasn't
the best or most knowledgeable manager I've ever played for - and I could say
a lot more!"

Jean-Luis Triaud, Bordeaux chairman, suggesting his side could do better:
"If, with such a squad, we are not able to beat Troyes at home, we might just
have to play handball or rugby."

Sir Alex Ferguson v Ken Bates:
"Ken Bates is always going to use a platform to get himself into the
newspapers."

Ken Bates v Sir Alex Ferguson:
"I think he was trying desperately to scrape up even more sales for his
flagging autobiography, I took it as a compliment."

Paul Gascoigne on not drinking:
"I no longer drink, at most I will have a glass of wine. I want to play until I am 38 and I think Everton can win the title."

Swedish international Mats Gren on trying to win damages after being sacked from Grasshoppers Zurich:
"The club can't escape the contract which is signed with figures and everything."

Sir Alex Ferguson v Ken Bates again:
"Has any chairman since Mao had more faith in his own opinions than Ken has?"

Gary Megson on the players' dress-code at WBA:
"If you take your wife to a nice hotel it can cost you £80 to eat. So the last thing you want is someone sat behind you mouthing off wearing a baseball cap and flip-flops."

Erik Mykland showing not a very keen sense of direction:
"I am not sure where we are. All I know is that we are four hours from Munich."

Ken Bates, less than pleased with the exploits of Jody Morris on holiday:
"Jody Morris claimed he wasn't involved in porn videos, he was only in Cyprus for the boozing. That's alright then!"

Florentino Perez, before being appointed president of Real Madrid:
"If I am appointed Real president and Luis Figo does not sign for this club - then I pledge to you that I will refund every season ticket holder's money."

Luis Figo suggesting that Perez may soon be paying refunds:
"I have made an irrevocable decision: I will not be a Real Madrid player whoever wins the elections. If any of the fans have felt upset or disappointed about what has happened, I would like them to forgive me, but they should only believe what I say. I am sure that the whole affair will be just an anecdote in the career of Luis Figo as a Barcelona player."

Swansea boss John Collins hoping that Mark Stein's drive to Swansea was not a waste of time:
"He certainly hasn't come all this way just to look at the beach."

"

An England fan:
"I am not a racist - I just hate Turks."

Hagi, after he and his team-mates dyed their hair yellow:
"To beat them we must be more intelligent and more cunning, if we win we will shave our heads like Ronaldo."

Preston manager David Moyes showing his true colours over the transfer of Iain Anderson:
"He is actually worried that he will not get the chance to join the club if this drags on any longer, but at £700,000 I feel that he is probably over-priced, not because he is not worth it, but because I am a Scotsman and I always like a bargain."

Tommy Soderberg on the pressures of being a national coach in Scandinavia:
"When it goes bad, people are disappointed and want to cut our heads off. I believe the pressure is worse in other countries."

Ladies from a Dutch Red Light area, commenting on why football is not good for business:
"It's enormously quiet during the matches. After that customers begin to drift in, but then we have to close."

More ladies from a Dutch Red Light area, with their verdict about the English fans:
"We are seeing many people wearing the shirts of their country, but the English are either a pain in the backside or too drunk to perform."

Erik Mykland on unusual Norwegian training routines:
"We love each other...on and off the pitch."

The Spanish press criticise Arsenal's England keeper, David Seaman:
"A piece of meat with eyes."

George Best, with a not-too-serious comment on David Beckham:
"He can't head the ball, tackle or kick with his left foot and doesn't score enough goals."

"

THE FOOTBALL FACT AND QUIZ BOOK

Mark Lawrenson, remembering his time as a Liverpool player:
"I'm going to sue Alan Hansen as he used to make me head all the balls. If I get Alzheimer's in 10 years, I'm going to take civil action against him."

Max Clifford, Fulham's new PR consultant, on his relationship with chairman Mohammed Al-Fayed:
"My job will be to try to make sure he scores more goals than own-goals."

John Gregory on trying to remember his team:
"I looked at my subs bench sometimes and there were just babies sitting there. Most of the people outside of Birmingham wouldn't know their names - and some in Birmingham for that matter."

Wimbledon manager Egil Olsen explaining Ben Thatcher's use of the elbow on Sunderland's Nicky Summerbee:
"He was running with his arms out and it's impossible to put them down and that was the contact."

Watford's Graham Taylor on why he wouldn't sign players for the sake of it:
"You can spend £2 million and find the player cannot trap the ball."

Arsene Wenger after the penalty shoot-out which cost Arsenal the UEFA Cup:
"We practise penalties and it was frustrating that the two we missed hit the post and bar."

Burnley's Ronnie Jepson on trying to break into coaching:
"It's a question of getting on the roundabout of who you know and I won't kiss anyone's arse to get there."

Tony Cottee getting sentimental:
"I can remember back in 1983 looking at 2000 and thinking it would be lovely to be playing then."

Leeds Utd boss David O'Leary after his players had got involved in a brawl with Tottenham players:
"It's not my fault if Tottenham players can't stand on their feet. Bowyer's tackle was fair, unfortunately he didn't get the ball."

66

Sasa Curcic, ex-Palace and Bolton:
"I would not sign for another club, not even if I was offered £10 million. However, it would be different if they were to offer me 15 different women from all around the world instead. I can't achieve an orgasm looking at a team-mate, but it would be a totally different matter with Cindy Crawford."

Derby boss Jim Smith on Georgi Kinkladze:
"Georgi does things you will never see any other player do better, but if I'm honest he can be a bit of a luxury."

Bobby Robson before taking his team out for a F.A. Cup semi-final:
"Wembley is a cathedral and it is for unique matches."

Roy Keane on 'questioning' the referee after 'Boro were awarded a penalty:
"What happened was unfortunate... although if he (referee Andy D'Urso) had stood still I don't think we would have been chasing him, but he kept running and we kept chasing."

Sheffield Wednesday striker Gilles de Bilde with his thoughts on English football:
"English players love to compensate their lack of ideas with three important qualities; they are powerful, run for everything and fight for every centimetre."

Jimmy Armfield on Sir Stanley Matthews:
"He was the first great superstar. With only newspapers and radio and TV just starting, everybody knew Stanley Matthews."

Dzemal Hadziabdic, Qatar coach and ex-Swansea player:
"If I was Mark Hughes and my best players didn't turn up, they wouldn't play again."

Graeme Souness on inevitable team selections and transfer errors:
"You're trapped inside a coconut shy. Every time you duck, someone else is ready to let fly at you."

Harry Redknapp on Di Canio after a 5-4 win:
"What a footballer, the man is a genius."

99

THE FOOTBALL FACT AND QUIZ BOOK

Cowdenbeath's Craig Levein on a particularly bruising encounter with East Fife:
"I don't think six ice packs were enough for our dressing room."

Ray Parlour, showing sympathy for newcomer Oleg Luzhny:
"I would hate to be stuck in the middle of Ukraine without being able to speak the language."

Sami Hyypia, in awe of Liverpool's history:
"When I bring friends over for a visit, I take them to the museum at the club. The winning tradition at Liverpool is clear."

Peter Reid, after Sunderland had gone 13 matches without a win:
"300 fans would probably have 300 different opinions, so I'd have to sign 300 players to satisfy them."

Ian St John on advice from Bill Shankly:
"At first he told us to wear boxing gloves in bed on Friday nights, then later he would tell us to send the wife to her mother."

Tim Flowers on the future of football in this country:
""They (the star players) only want to go to two places, London or Manchester Utd."

Sheffield Wednesday's Pavel Srnicek on the stresses of a relegation battle:
"You have to be diplomatic, but sometimes in training we kick each other because we don't like our team-mates."

Frank Worthington on why he made so few appearances for England:
"Down to one man, Don Revie. He preferred the workhorse type of player."

Bryan Robson about Middlesbrough's new training complex:
"We have a one-sided window looking over the players' gym from our physio room. It means we can keep an eye on them - and they don't know if we are there or not."

Everton's Kevin Campbell on manager Walter Smith:
"He can be as quiet as a mouse or he can go absolutely ballistic."

THE FOOTBALL FACT AND QUIZ BOOK

Kevin Keegan on seeing that the bookies were offering 8 to 1 on England to win Euro 2000:
"I reckon we are worth a bet for Euro 2000 along with nations like France and Holland."

Peter Osgood, ex-Chelsea and England player, not showing any surprise at England's performance in Euro 2000:
"Outplayed by Portugal, outplayed by Romania, and we only beat the Germans because they are a worse team than we are."

Glenn Hoddle on beating Germany 1-0:
"It wasn't brilliant football, but it was effective."

Eusebio, after England went 2-0 up against Portugal:
"Portugal controlled the game even when they were losing."

Marcel Desailly on life in the Premiership after five years in Serie A:
"When you go to Derby four days after playing in Milan, you still have a picture of the San Siro in your head and it can be a shock."

Bobby Robson trying to lift morale at Newcastle:
"Under Gullit the best players were on the bench... we have to face the fact he did nothing for this club."

Ron Atkinson after seeing Barthez kick a clearance into the stands:
"He might be the first player to kick the ball out of Old Trafford."

David Beckham on the problems celebrities have when eating out:
"In the Ivy they don't let anyone ask for autographs. I know this because Michael Jordan was in there one night and I wasn't able to get his signature."

Kevin Keegan after Romania's late winner against England:
"They outplayed and outpassed us, and probably deserved the result."

Alan Shearer on getting booked in his last international for a blatant dive:
"That was in desperation. I was wanting to do something for my country."

Martin Keown on England's Euro 2000 campaign:
"We were inept tactically and exposed against teams we could have beaten."

Spanish daily newspaper 'Marca' after Spain's 4-3 victory over Yugoslavia:
"Long live the mother who gave birth to you."

Celtic's Kenny Dalglish after losing the Scottish Championship by 21 points:
"I've been sacked and I don't know why."

England fan Scott Vessey, who thinks that Phil Neville should have suffered the same fate for giving away the penalty against Romania as that given to the hooligans at Euro 2000:
"Phil Neville should have his passport confiscated and not be allowed to leave the country."

Portugal's Paulo Sousa on England's Euro 2000 performance:
"I was even laughing on the bench when I saw their defenders heading back towards their own penalty area rather than trying to tackle Figo or Rui Costa."

Dion Dublin, TV pundit, after the Yugoslavia v Spain game where Hierro had not been playing:
"Hierro has been magnificent for the Spaniards tonight."

Liam Brady showing no surprise about England's current lack of technique and talent:
"I would say that 85 percent of the teams we play at youth level kick the ball long and by-pass midfield. They play for territory."

Belgium's coach Robert Waseige demonstrating his vast coaching skills:
"We have to improve in two key areas: defence and attack."

Dutch porn actresses on their own kind of riot control:
"We set out to kiss people in order to calm them down. We made a point of kissing those who looked most like hooligans."

Hull City's Theo Whitmore on a possible move to Scotland:
"People have told me about Aberdeen, but even if they are interested I don't want to go. It's cold enough here!"

West Ham's former boss Harry Redknapp on the fuel crisis:
"I haven't a care in the world about anything. I have a full tank of petrol, my wife has stocked up with extra cans of baked beans in case there is a crisis and I know we will finish in the top half of the table."

Paulo di Canio on being Italian:
"I wagged my finger at him because I'm Italian. They shouldn't take that away from me. Lots of English people drink too much but I don't try to stop them doing that."

Barcelona defender Michael Reizeger sharing his views on how to win matches:
"We will have to provoke Keane in some way: perhaps holding his shirt or walking into him after he passes the ball. Players are also known to whisper comments about another player's mother or the size of parts of his body. I don't like that side of the game very much but if it helps us to win then it's worthwhile."

Swedish doctor Magnus Forsblad on Ronald Nilsson:
"There is no danger - he got a brainshaking, but he will join us today. After being under observation it appears that the damage was just on the outside and not to the brain."

Jose Camacho, Spanish coach, on referees:
"I thought the referee had a bad game. He didn't meet the criteria that we have seen in other matches and I'm not sure he has the class to referee at this level."

Huddersfield Town chairman Ian Ayre on a surplus of players:
"No disrespect to the lads here but there are seven or eight of them that we are trying to get off the wage-bill. We cannot even give them away at the moment!"

Ex-Nottingham Forest manager Brian Clough:
"I'm as bad a judge of strikers as Walter Winterbottom - he only gave me two caps."

Argentine Ossie Ardiles, who has been working on some new coaching methods:
"Maybe I dream too much - I would rather play with a goalkeeper and ten front players."

THE FOOTBALL FACT AND QUIZ BOOK

"

Aston Villa's John Gregory:
"Strikers win matches, defenders win championships."

Rangers centre-back Scott Wilson on his team's performance this year:
"I can't put my finger on why we have not been doing well -
apart from playing rubbish."

Celtic manager Martin O'Neill on an injury crisis at the club:
"If they declare themselves fit on the bus they'll play."

Portsmouth chairman Milan Mandaric on hearing that Portsmouth had announced a £3 million loss for the year:
"The potential of Portsmouth FC was going to take longer to realise than was first indicated during negotiations to purchase the club."

Rudi Voller, German coach, suggesting that foreign referees should be tried in the Bundesliga:
"I have the impression that our Bundesliga referees do not behave in domestic matches the way they do in international games."
This was backed up by Franz Beckenbauer after the Borussia Dortmund v Bayern Munich match, where there were three red cards and twelve yellow cards shown.

Sunderland's Peter Reid on referees:
"I don't want to start a witch-hunt, but I do think referees need to be accountable. At the moment, they aren't required to explain their decisions and players, managers and fans are all being left in the dark. If I'm not doing my job properly, I get sacked."

Chelsea's Gianluca Vialli's prophetic comment after Chelsea won the 2000 FA Cup final:
"I'm bloody tired, I need a long rest."

Takis Gonias, captain of Greek club Panionios, calling for a month-long strike in protest at refereeing standards, after a match with PAS Ioannina finished with two sendings-off, nine yellow cards, three penalties and a disallowed goal:
"This theatre of the absurd has to stop."

"

"

Paul Ince on the relegation challenge at Middlesbrough:
"It's another challenge. It's not a challenge that I would have liked - I'd rather have had the challenge of getting into Europe - but it's another challenge and it's a challenge that I relish. It's a challenge and I'm up for the challenge."

Frank Leboeuf reflects on the bad press he has had over the years:
"There are a lot of unintelligent people who still believe we are in the Napoleon times and that the English and the French still hate each other."

Scotland captain Colin Hendry on elbowing San Marino's Nicola Albani in the throat:
"Between the sub and the captain, they were trying to get at me. It was two against one. I was just trying to shrug them off and I didn't know where their guy was. You're asking me if I have any regrets. I don't regret challenging players. You have to fight your corner."

Patrick Nally on producing 'Manchester United - The Musical':
"It is a marvellous, emotional tale and will appeal to more than just football fans."

Arsene Wenger has a joke at the Aston Villa manager's expense:
"Does John Gregory want a holiday? My chairman gives me what I want. I give him what he wants."

John Gregory on the trials and tribulations of working with his chairman Doug Ellis:
"He's stuck in a time-warp... We're dragging him, kicking and screaming, into the millennium."

Bradford's Jim Jefferies on the stresses of being manager after losing 3-0 at Chelsea:
"To say the job I took on is difficult is an understatement."

Harry Redknapp on the West Ham players' reaction to Paolo Di Canio's sporting catch of the day at Goodison Park:
"The rest of the lads have beaten him up in the dressing-room and I'm not sure whether he's fit enough to travel home."

"

THE FOOTBALL FACT AND QUIZ BOOK

"

Charlton manager Alan Curbishley after a defeat at West Ham:
"I took my team back to my old club today, and we were so bad, I wished I'd played myself."

Tottenham midfielder Oyvind Leonhardsen after a defeat at Ipswich:
"We didn't show much character today."

Ken Bates denying that there is a language barrier at Chelsea:
"Let's forget all this rubbish about him not speaking English. The manager of Fulham doesn't speak English, or doesn't want to, but he doesn't get anything like as much stick."

Peter Reid on the one that got away:
"I'm delighted to have taken seven points from three games over Christmas, but if we had not shown Arsenal so much respect in the first half it could have been even better."

Coventry boss Gordon Strachan on the Premiership debut of referee Matt Messias:
"When I'm playing golf and I'm 67 years old I'll turn round to my mate and say: 'In the year 2000 I saw an unforgettable performance.'"

Glenn Hoddle finding his London roots hard to forget, even while at Southampton:
"We haven't given silly goals away this season but today three turned up, a bit like London buses."

Derby boss Jim Smith on his team's performance after beating Coventry:
"Everybody was rubbish."

Bobby Robson looking on the bright side after beating Bradford City:
"We've gone up to seventh - so we're not quite a club in crisis."

Walter Smith bemoaning Everton's long injury list:
"We have nine players out now and there are not that many clubs that could handle that and still compete."

Terry Venables on working with Middlesbrough:
"There is no magic here. It is just a lot of people working very hard behind the scenes."

"

THE FOOTBALL FACT AND QUIZ BOOK

Ipswich coach Tony Mowbray on his recipe for Premiership success:
"It's all about putting your feet in the water and testing the temperature."

Sir Alex Ferguson replying to Arsene Wenger's suggestion that teams are intimidated by Manchester Utd:
"Arsene says many things."

Ex-Manchester City boss Joe Royle after a defeat by Charlton:
"Some of our players weren't readily looking for the ball."

Arsene Wenger after drawing with Chelsea:
"It is more of a concern who could beat us for the second automatic place in the Champions' League rather than if we can catch United."

Harry Redknapp looks on the bright side about the game:
"Players' wages have gone through the roof since Grobbelaar was first in the dock, and there is no way they would be tempted now."

Paul Merson bemoans Aston Villa's goalscoring problems:
"I watched Arsenal score six against Leicester and thought 'We won't score six in the whole of January'."

Sunderland's Peter Reid, disagreeing with the referee after losing a match against Manchester Utd:
"It's difficult to comment on these things because you're not allowed to, but I've had Mr. Poll once or twice and I haven't been able to comment once or twice, and I'm finding it really difficult not to."

Bradford's Jim Jefferies on playing without Collymore and Carbone:
"We made certain decisions which people found strange, and I think everybody's now seeing the benefits of that."

Bobby Robson describes his team's win over Coventry:
"It was a little bit of a ding-dong without much music, I guess."

Chelsea boss Claudio Ranieri on his new approach to the press:
"I have decided not to speak now if we have won or drawn and will send a players' representative to speak instead because the results are to their merit. I will continue to speak after matches, however, when we have lost."

66

Terry Venables on Hamilton Ricard's broken nose:
"The lad's nose was all over the place and he was angry."

Gordon Strachan on crowd trouble at Maine Road:
"Do I look like a steward? Have I got a yellow coat on?"

Gordon Strachan after a poor showing at Leeds:
"The whole thing was an embarrassment to ourselves and an embarrassment to
the club and that includes myself, the squad, the coaching staff and even the
players who were not playing - if they're not good enough to get picked for that
they really must be embarrassed."

Joe Royle after his Manchester City side beat Coventry in the FA Cup:
"It is the first time this season we've got a result we didn't deserve."

**Everton vice-chairman Bill Kenwright on the club's
injury list:**
"Someone must have put a witch's curse on us."

**Peter Taylor, after his Leicester players Robbie
Savage and Gerry Taggart had a first-half
disagreement:**
"They apologised to each other at half-time and then kissed
and cuddled in the usual manner afterwards."

David O'Leary on Lee Bowyer's workrate:
"I'm glad I'm not paying him by the mile."

**West Ham's Joe Cole on winning the man-of-the-match
award against Coventry:**
"The champagne doesn't mean anything when you don't
get the three points."

**Sir Alex Ferguson on Arsenal's chances of the title after being humiliated at
Old Trafford:**
"I think the goal difference is 20 or 30 or something and there's a 16-point
difference, so that makes it difficult for Arsenal."

John Gregory on the settling-in problems of Juan Pablo Angel at Villa:
"He's desperately short of confidence and I took him off more for his own good
than anything else."

99

THE FOOTBALL FACT AND QUIZ BOOK

66

Bobby Robson on thinking about cancelling his players' mid-season break:
"I don't particularly want to go to La Manga. We were going for a bit of sun - but I tell you now we will be training like mad."

Terry Venables on the current state of play at Middlesbrough:
"People might say that draws are boring every week but I'm very happy."

Chelsea's Colin Hutchinson on new signing Jesper Gronkjaer:
"The good thing is that when he is 100 per cent, from what we've seen already, he's going to be a little bit tasty."

Sir Alex Ferguson after the demolition of Arsenal:
"I don't think it was our best performance of the season, although it was our best result."

Joe Royle after his Manchester City side won at Newcastle:
"I think we're too good to go down."

Everton's Walter Smith's new method of preparing for games:
"Our full concentration must be on getting three points in whatever game we play in."

Tottenham's David Buchler on the sacking of George Graham:
"I am not prepared to have someone who is not a team player and who is not looking after the club's interests."

Sven Goran Eriksson:
"I am from Sweden, I can't help that."

Everton's American striker Joe-Max Moore on relaxing:
"It may sound strange, but I enjoy studying companies and I'm really into stocks and shares; I'm always on my laptop looking up investments on the internet."

Wycombe manager Lawrie Sanchez after signing his new striker, Essendoh, from the internet:
"We didn't even know him last Tuesday, and I don't think he knows the names of half of his team-mates."

99

Bobby Robson on David Beckham:
"Beckham is probably England's best player, but as a captain? They probably gave it to him last time because he's a great player but that's not necessarily the ticket for captaincy."

Bobby Robson on his own future:
"I didn't pay any attention to the stories about me leaving because I knew it was rubbish. I'm not intending to move. I've got a 12-month roll-on contract."

Bobby Robson on Kieron Dyer:
"We court-martialled Kieron. We told him he had to respect women and we advised him not to take alcohol. I think he's learnt his lesson. It was like a car crash for him. If you crash you don't half drive more carefully afterwards."

Bobby Robson on David Ginola:
"David Ginola never tracks back, but, as a manager, you'd say to yourself 'I'll compensate for that because he's going to get 15 crosses in. From them we might score three goals'."

Villa keeper David James is still trying to shake off the 'Calamity James' tag given to him while at Liverpool:
"My lows always seem to be lower than anyone else's. I acquired that Calamity James nickname and it seems like it's impossible to get rid of it. If I went abroad I wouldn't be Calamity James and that's crossed my mind more than once, I will admit."

Derby County's Jim Smith on an embarrassment of foreign players:
"It was not intentional to over-stock ourselves with non-league players. We thought Asanovic would leave sooner than he did.

Arsene Wenger on the title race:
"We are out of the Premiership race because it is played in England and not dreamland."

Derby captain Craig Burley expressing an opinion of the game:
"The crowd were right to boo and I would have booed as well."

Republic of Ireland manager Mick McCarthy, on rumours and speculations:
"I am glad my name is being linked with Celtic rather than Division Three jobs."

THE FOOTBALL FACT AND QUIZ BOOK

"

Sunderland's Peter Reid on a new training routine:
"After those 45 minutes, people might wonder if I know what I am doing. It was that bad. It was like Billy Smart's Circus!"

Roma coach Fabio Capello, after his captain had been sent off for questioning the referee's decision:
"Who else but the captain can argue over a decision with the referee?"

Paul Jewell, on hearing rumours that he was being linked with Lionel Perez:
"There's more chance of me signing Lionel Blair."

Fiorentina president, Vittorio Cecchi Gori:
"Nobody will leave Florence, if the boat sinks, all will sink!"

John Carew, on hearing of a possible transfer to Valencia:
"It is my dream place. The town is very nice, and I have watched the team a lot on TV. And their stadium rocks!"

Rosenborg official on John Carew:
"John Carew is as fast as a rocket and he shoots like an animal."

Juan Sebastian Veron:
"In such an important match, maybe we could've put the first team on the field."

Kevin Keegan, talking about Argentina:
"They're the second best team in the world - and there's no higher praise than that."

A Vitesse Arnhem spokesman, playing the percentages:
"The club agrees with the suspension, but only because van Hooijdonk is injured at the moment, otherwise the club would have appealed to the commission."

Chris Kamara, sharing his great football knowledge on Sky Sports:
"They only count when they go in the goal."

"

THE FOOTBALL FACT AND QUIZ BOOK

"

Emmanuel Petit displaying his culinary knowledge:
"When you are forced to eat porridge every day, you get sick of it."

Arsene Wenger, showing that his culinary tastes are a little more refined:
"When you get used to caviar, it's difficult to come back to sausages."

Bordeaux manager Elie Baup before their Champions' League match with Manchester Utd:
"Everyone talks about the football in Manchester and only the wine in Bordeaux. You never speak of football in Bordeaux, but then you never hear of wine in Manchester."

Bobby Robson on a Kieron Dyer goal:
"He twisted and turned, he ran like a little rabbit and then he scored."

Strasbourg coach Claude Le Roy after a shock defeat by Calais:
"In one word it is bloody stupidity."

Manchester United youngster Bojan Djordjic on women:
"The English women are okay but I prefer one Swedish girl to 22 English."

A newspaper's view on new Milan signing Jose Mari:
"The Spanish player, until now, has just proved skilful at missing the goal."

Harry Redknapp on the future:
"Let's face it, I'll get the sack one day because everyone gets the elbow in football."

Villa's Benito Carbone taking his enthusiasm for the club a little too far:
"I am ready to break my legs for this club."

Gianluca Vialli looking forward to Chelsea's forthcoming Champions' League games:
"Now we face Cassius Clay, Mike Tyson and George Foreman."

Bobby Robson, again:
"After the season we have had this is an extra bit of cream to our bottle of milk. And we are very thirsty."

"

THE FOOTBALL FACT AND QUIZ BOOK

Liverpool's keeper Sander Westerveld on the never-ending 'dodgy keeper' joke:
"If someone two metres away from me drops their glass of beer on the floor, as was the case on Saturday night, you can bet that a wise guy has asked if it was me."

Leeds manager David O'Leary on being realistic:
"It does not take a rocket scientist to work it out, we all know who the best team in the country is and it's not us."

Gerard Houllier on the value of Steven Gerrard:
"Inter would have to offer Recoba, Zanetti and Vieri plus money."

Tromso chairman Gunnar Wilhelmsson on the subject of selling their star player:
"Rune Bratseh and myself have agreed that we are not in agreement."

Birmingham's Martin Grainger, showing a deep concern for his fellow Midlands players:
"There will be someone nastier about who will probably get him (Wolves' Kevin Muscat) off the ball one day."

Stefan Schwarz on realising his injury against Austria was more serious than he first thought:
"I first looked at my left heel and then touched my right to compare. I noticed the right was much thinner, that there was a hole and then I knew it was off. It felt like 11 Austrians were stamping on me."

Jose Maria Quevedo, the Seville captain, on Spanish referees:
"The referee who disallowed two 'perfectly good' goals has beheaded us. Referees are laughing at us - we should withdraw from the league."

Sergi puts everything in perspective:
"It is not true, but if it were true then I would say the same, that it's not true."

Marcello Lippi on facing criticisism:
"Did you see the movie 'Rocky' with Sylvester Stallone? Well, I am the same, everyone could hit me with criticism but I will never fall on the ground."

Arsene Wenger on his Euro stars:
"Suker has paid the price for the way Thierry Henry has exploded this season."

The Real Betis manager on Brazilians:
"Denilson cannot keep on playing here with his head located in Italy."

The French Kilmarnock star Christophe Cocard on Scotland:
"Here they see things in a different way. The only important thing is that you put in some hard work. Frank Sauzee is a true star in Scotland."

Paolo Maldini and his first lesson in diplomacy:
"People should realise that the Premiership isn't just Manchester United - it is also about the other teams who are certainly not beautiful to watch."

Lars Bohinen on his sense of humour transplant:
"I played for 70 minutes in Mark Crossley's testimonial. I was booed the whole time. The man who started all this, Frank Clark, was there and he found it all very amusing. I didn't."

Arsenal's Fredrik Ljungberg on getting interesting new injuries:
"I have to overcome the mental barrier. Sometimes I lost balls due to wondering if all was okay. I wanted to take a real test and it felt fine."

Reading assistant manager Martin Allen, who whilst on a scouting mission to Norway ended up in Sweden, after flying to Kirstenstad instead of Kristensand:
"I was stranded in the middle of nowhere with no money in the smallest airport I'd ever seen. It looked like it was built by IKEA."

Gabriel Batistuta on arriving at his new club, Roma:
"I want to underline I'm not joining AS Roma to be the king there. I'm just another player! But I have to admit as well, it's difficult to imagine myself with another number other than nine...besides there is the chance Montella won't play in AS Roma any more in a couple of months, who knows!"

Vincenzo Montella deciding that possession is nine tenths of the law:
"I want to keep the number nine shirt - it is mine. I really don't think that Batistuta can decide my future - only Roma can make that decision. I cannot guarantee to the fans that I will be playing in Rome next year."

66

Vincenzo Montella deciding it is better to have worn the number nine shirt and lost, than never to have worn the number nine shirt at all:
"I didn't want to get into an argument with Batistuta - I respect him a great deal. This is a lot of fuss about a shirt!"

Italian captain Paolo Maldini speaks for the rest of Italy:
"With just ten days left until the European Championship and all that is being talked about is the Roma number nine shirt! Frankly, everybody is sick of it!"

Fabien Barthez after his arrival at Manchester Utd, ensuring he'd be first choice keeper:
"You can say it is a dream and my head has been buzzing for some hours with a lot of things. It is the greatest club in the world, without any doubt."

Kilmarnock fans singing to the Rangers keeper after he'd been diagnosed with mild schizophrenia:
"Two Andy Gorams, there's only two Andy Gorams... "

Peterborough manager Chris Turner's stirring pep-talk before the 1992 League Cup semi-final:
"I've told the players we need to win so that I can have some cash to buy new ones."

NY Cosmos executive, commenting on Franz Beckenbauer's positioning on the field:
"Tell the Kraut to get his ass up front. We don't pay a million for a guy to hang around in defence."

George Best on being George Best:
"I spent a lot of money on booze, birds and fast cars. The rest I just squandered."

Bryan Robson while at Manchester Utd:
"If we played like that every week we wouldn't be so inconsistent.'

Partick Thistle manager John Lambie on being told that a concussed striker did not know who he was:
"That's great, tell him he's Pele, and get him back on."

99

THE FOOTBALL FACT AND QUIZ BOOK

"

Andy Gray demonstrating his vast medical knowledge:
"I was saying the other day, how often the most vulnerable area for goalies is between their legs."

Sky Sport's Richard Keys: "Well Roy, do you think that you'll have to finish above Manchester United to win the league?"
Roy Evans: "You have to finish above everyone to win the league Richard."

Terry Venables on Capital Gold explaining his home's layout:
"If you can't stand the heat in the dressing-room, get out of the kitchen."

Radio 5 Live:
"It's now 1-1, an exact reversal of the score on Saturday."

Newcastle Utd fan on Radio 5 Live:
"Football today, it's like a game of chess. It's all about money."

Alan Ball, proving that having a high-pitched voice in no way affects the brain-cells:
"I'm not a believer in luck ...but I do believe you need it."

Trevor Brooking and his impeccable memory:
"Merseyside derbies usually last 90 minutes and I'm sure today's won't be any different."

Tom Ferrie:
"Dumbarton player Steve McCahill has limped off with a badly cut forehead."

Dave Bassett showing great optimism and great pessimism:
"And I honestly believe we can go all the way to Wembley ... unless somebody knocks us out."

Peter Jones:
"And Arsenal now have plenty of time to dictate the last few seconds."

Jimmy Hill showing why he was such a good TV pundit:
"What makes this game so delightful is that when both teams get the ball they are attacking their opponents' goal."

"

Brian Moore, nice and straightforward:
"Newcastle, of course, unbeaten in their last five wins."

David Ackfield:
"Strangely, in slow motion replay, the ball seemed to hang in the air for even longer."

Gerry Francis, showing a fine command of modern media:
"What I said to them at half-time would be unprintable on the radio."

New York Post, 1993:
"John Harkes going to Sheffield, Wednesday."

Derek Johnstone, BBC TV Scotland:
"He's one of those footballers whose brains are in his head."

Barry Davies:
"The crowd think that Todd handled the ball... they must've seen something that nobody else did."

Arrigo Sacchi, Italian coach, wondering if he's in the right sport:
"You don't have to have been a horse to be a jockey."

Sunderland v Leicester, Radio 5 Live, a match with not a lot to recommend it:
"The score is Sunderland nil, Leicester nil, the temperature is nil and the entertainment value is not much above nil."

Ian Wright, never at a loss for words:
"The referee was booking everyone. I thought he was filling in his lottery numbers."

Tommy Docherty, another one seldom without a quip:
"I've always said there's a place for the press, but they haven't dug it yet."

David 'Calamity' James on shopping:
"It's not a nice feeling when you're in a supermarket shopping, and the checkout girl is thinking 'dodgy keeper.'"

THE FOOTBALL FACT AND QUIZ BOOK

Stuart Hall, Radio 5 Live:
"What will you do when you leave football, Jack - will you stay in football?"

Ray Wilkins, speaking on BBC 1, on whether to shoot or kick:
"Unfortunately, we keep kicking ourselves in the foot."

Alan Sugar, also demonstrating great medical knowledge:
"I've got a gut feeling in my stomach."

Chris Jones, Evening Standard:
"The new West Stand casts a giant shadow over the entire pitch, even on a sunny day."

Ron Atkinson:
"I would not say he (David Ginola) is the best left winger in the Premiership, but there are none better."

Dave Bassett, speaking on Sky Sports:
An inch or two either side of the post and that would have been a goal."

Peter Withe, speaking on Radio 5 Live:
"Both sides have scored a couple of goals, and both sides have conceded a couple of goals."

Bruce Rioch, on ITV:
"What's it like being in Bethlehem, the place where Christmas began? I suppose it's like seeing Ian Wright at Arsenal..."

John Motson, BBC, the sheepskin commentator:
"And I suppose they (Spurs) are nearer to being out of the FA Cup now than at any other time since the first half of this season, when they weren't ever in it anyway."

Paul Gascoigne, on seeing into the future but not into the fog on the Tyne:
"I never make predictions, and I never will."

Jimmy Hill, doing a little weather forecasting:
"And there's Ray Clemence looking as cool as ever out in the cold."

"

Brian Moore, also in on the weather predictions:
"...and the news from Guadalajara where the temperature is 96 degrees, is that Falcao is warming up."

Terry Venables on Terry Venables on Terry Venables on ...
"If history is going to repeat itself I think we can expect the same thing again."

Mike Ingham, informing us all that cannibalism is alive and well and living in South America:
"The Uruguayans are losing no time in making a meal around the referee."

Ron Atkinson again:
"I think that was a moment of cool panic there."

Yet more Ron Atkinson:
"Beckenbauer really has gambled all his eggs."

Derek Rae on an unusual anatomical arrangement:
"Celtic manager David Hay still has a fresh pair of legs up his sleeve."

Derek Rae, using his:
"It's headed away by John Clark, using his head."

Mike Ingham on the magic of the cup:
"Tottenham are trying tonight to become the first London team to win this cup. The last team to do so was the 1973 Spurs side."

Bobby Robson, on speed trials:
"He's very fast and if he gets a yard ahead of himself nobody will catch him."

John Motson:
"The game is balanced in Arsenal's favour."

Dave Bassett's strange philosophy:
"You have to miss them to score sometimes."

John Hollins, on the difference between two pieces of paper:
"A contract on a piece of paper, saying you want to leave, is like a piece of paper saying you want to leave."

THE FOOTBALL FACT AND QUIZ BOOK

Alan Green:
"It was that game that put the Everton ship back on the road."

Kevin Keegan, another one with a strange idea of anatomy:
"Bobby Robson must be thinking of throwing some fresh legs on."

Richard Park:
"Celtic were at one time nine points ahead, but somewhere along the road, their ship went off the rails."

Trevor Brooking, showing great mathematical prowess:
"That's football, Mike, Northern Ireland have had several chances and haven't scored but England have had no chances and scored twice."

Sports roundup:
"... and so they have not been able to improve their 100% record."

John Lyall, not sure whether to take up Geology or Meteorology:
"In terms of the Richter Scale this defeat was a force eight gale."

Ron Greenwood:
"In comparison, there's no comparison."

Ron Atkinson:
"I would also think that the action replay showed it to be worse than it actually was."

Malcolm McDonald, proving if you head a ball enough times ...
"Mirandinha will have more shots this afternoon than both sides put together."

John Greig:
"Football's not like an electric light. You can't just flick the switch and change from quick to slow."

Terry Venables:
"Certain people are for me and certain people are pro me."

THE FOOTBALL FACT AND QUIZ BOOK

Ron Atkinson, sitting on the fence:
"I'm going to make a prediction - it could go either way."

Ian Darke:
"And with 4 minutes gone, the score is already 0-0."

Mick Lyons:
"If there weren't such a thing as football, we'd all be frustrated footballers."

Stuart Pearce:
"I can see the carrot at the end of the tunnel."

Kevin Keegan, engaging mouth before brain:
"They compare Steve McManaman to Steve Heighway and he's nothing like him, but I can see why - it's because he's a bit different."

Ron Greenwood:
"Glenn Hoddle hasn't been the Hoddle we know. Neither has Bryan Robson."

Denis Law:
"There's no way Ryan Giggs is another George Best. He's another Ryan Giggs."

Norman Whiteside:
"The only thing I have in common with George Best is that we come from the same place, play for the same club and were discovered by the same man."

Ron Atkinson:
"I never comment on referees and I'm not going to break the habit of a lifetime for that prat."

Kevin Keegan:
"I don't think there is anybody bigger or smaller than Maradona."

Glenn Hoddle:
"The minute's silence was immaculate, I have never heard a minute's silence like that."

Jimmy Hill: "Don't sit on the fence Terry, what chance do you think Germany has got of getting through?"
Terry Venables: "I think it's fifty-fifty."

Ian Darke:
"Never go for a 50-50 ball unless you're 80-20 sure of winning it."

Lord Denning QC:
"What I don't understand is how a Frenchman can be playing for Manchester United. He's not even from England."

Des Lynam talking about referee Jamal Al-Sharif who went card crazy in the 1994 Bulgaria v Mexico game:
"A film called Passport to Terror will follow and I think this referee will be in it."

Bulgarian Hristo Stoichkov after his team won the above game:
"God is a Bulgarian."

Hristo Stoichkov after defeat against Italy in the next game:
"God is still a Bulgarian, but the referee was French."

Alan Rothenberg, 1994 World Cup chairman:
"There were three countries in the world that would have caused us problems, so we're very pleased they won't be coming; Iran, Iraq and England."

Mark Crossley:
"If I played for Scotland my grandma would be the proudest woman in the country - if she wasn't dead."

Roy Hodgson:
"The England manager has a choice of Gascoigne, Platt, Beardsley and Ince. Any of those would be in the Swiss side. I've got to pick between Sforza, Sforza and Sforza. I usually pick Sforza."

Bertie Vogts when German coach:
"If people saw me walking on the water you can be sure someone would say: 'Look at that Bertie Vogts, he can't even swim.'"